THE GENESIS OF
GERMAN
CONSERVATISM

KLAUS EPSTEIN

THE GENESIS OF GERMAN CONSERVATISM

PRINCETON, NEW JERSEY

PRINCETON UNIVERSITY PRESS

1966

For William Henry, David Frederick,
and Catherine Ann

PREFACE

THE VOLUME here presented traces the history of German Conservatism from its origins around 1770 to the collapse of the Holy Roman Empire in 1806. At times it inevitably becomes a general history of Germany during this period, partly because Conservatism cannot be treated properly as a specialized phenomenon, partly because the book is intended for the general reader interested in modern history as much as for colleagues in the field of German history. It is based primarily upon contemporary books and pamphlets, though the author has also drawn heavily upon the abundant secondary literature. The book is not a work of research in the sense of presenting facts previously unknown; it is intended, rather, to be a work of synthesis which weaves together miscellaneous materials—many of them familiar, all of them drawn from printed sources—into a fresh picture of a long-controversial period of German history.

The attempt has been made to analyze German Conservatism not just as an intellectual movement, but also to correlate it with political and social forces. While the political history of Germany in the late eighteenth century has long been well explored, its social and economic history is, unfortunately, still largely a virgin field of research. This must excuse, in part at least, the fact that the connections between social and intellectual history are frequently not so explicitly drawn in this volume as one would wish; an additional explanation lies in the spontaneous, amorphous character of Conservative thought and action prior to the existence of organized Conservative political parties (which emerged only after our period). The materials presented suffice, however, to substantiate the point that German Conservative thought and action was from its beginning closely connected with particular political and economic interest groups.

Much effort has been made to identify specific Conservative ideas as they arose in connection with specific controversies. It has appeared best to examine the argument of a single thinker, or a single pamphlet, in detail instead of piling up a wearisome number of references to authors and pamphlets which largely repeat one another. Quotations have been used liberally both to document individual points and to convey the flavor of particular arguments. An attempt has been made to analyze not only the *genesis* of Conservative ideas, but their *percolation* through journals, reading clubs, and secret societies. The reader must avoid, however, exaggerated expectations concerning what he can learn about public opinion in the eighteenth century—an age in which public opinion surveys were still unknown and to which statistical methods can be applied only in small measure.

The attempt has been made, in the Introduction, to place German Conservatism in the general modern framework of a "Conservative response" to a "Progressive challenge." The question of terminology has presented considerable difficulty. Suffice it to say at this point that the term Progressive is used broadly to cover all political groups which seek to change the *status quo* in the name of their "forward-looking" conception of what constitutes a "good society." The term Conservative is used broadly to describe the several varieties of Conservative response to the Progressive challenge distinguished in the Introduction: Defenders of the *Status Quo*, Reactionaries, and Reform Conservatives. The precise type referred to will be clear from the particular context.

A work like this cannot hope (and perhaps should not seek) to avoid value judgments. No historian can be indifferent to, or impartial about, the conflict between Progressive and Conservative forces which is the distinctive hallmark of the modern world. The author has striven to understand every position covered in this volume, but he does not wish to conceal that his sympathies lie more with the Reform Conservative position outlined in the Introduction than with any of the others. It is up to the reader to judge to what extent this "ideological bias" has adversely affected the presentation of the subject matter.

Brown University   Klaus Epstein
Providence, R.I.
June 1, 1966

ACKNOWLEDGMENTS

It is a pleasure to acknowledge the help I have received from many people in the completion of this book. The following friends and colleagues kindly read and commented upon individual chapters: Carl Bridenbaugh, William Church, Immanuel Geiss, Stephen Graubard, Walther Hubatsch, Shirley Robin Letwyn, Peter Magrath, Heinz Matthes, Eberhard Pikart, Donald Rohr, Detler Schuman, Stephan Skalweit, and Margaret Anderson Yarvin. My father helped me at every stage as a never-failing source of bibliographical information.

I began this book in Germany in 1959-60 with fellowship support from the Social Science Research Council and the Howard Foundation; a fellowship from the American Council of Learned Societies permitted me to continue my researches in Germany in 1962-63. The Brown University Research Fund provided a grant for the typing of the final draft. My typist, Mrs. Winifred Barton, did a superb job in deciphering a very difficult manuscript. My editors at the Princeton University Press made many valuable improvements in the text.

Finally, my wife shared the labors of this book over the last seven years, and performed prodigies in turning my illegible scrawl into a typed manuscript.

CONTENTS

THE GENESIS OF
GERMAN
CONSERVATISM

ABBREVIATIONS
USED IN FOOTNOTES

ADB	*Allgemeine Deutsche Biographie*
AHR	*American Historical Review*
DVSLG	*Deutsche-Vierteljahresschrift für Literaturgeschichte*
ESS	*Encyclopedia of the Social Sciences*
FBPG	*Forschungen zur brandenburgischen und preussischen Geschichte*
Hist-Polit. Blätter	*Historisch-Politische Blätter*
HZ	*Historische Zeitschrift*
NDB	*Neue Deutsche Biographie*

INTRODUCTION

A *Preliminary Definition*

CONSERVATIVE individuals, in the broad sense of opponents to religious, socioeconomic, and political change, have existed since the beginning of recorded history; yet it is a truism of modern scholarship that a Conservative movement appeared in Europe only toward the end of the eighteenth century. What explains the emergence of such a movement at that particular time? The answer must be sought in the dynamism introduced into Europe by the intellectual movement known as the Enlightenment, the cumulative impact of commercial capitalism, and the rise of a bourgeois class dissatisfied with traditional patterns of government. These three broad tendencies—whose interconnection is apparent today and was widely suspected by contemporaries—made for an acceleration of change, and a broad awareness of change, which was bound to provoke a strong Conservative reaction.

A brief delineation of the new dynamic forces will serve to define the problem confronting Conservatives at the end of the eighteenth century. The *Weltanschauung* of the Enlightenment constituted in its essence the triumph of this-worldly, materialist, and hedonist values over the otherworldliness, spiritualism, and asceticism of traditional Christianity. The principles and practices of the Enlightenment—however transcended in spirit and repudiated in detail by subsequent intellectual and political currents—drastically and irreversibly transformed man's picture of himself and the world. To live for the next world rather than this became an eccentric aberration from the generally recognized norm; to repudiate material values, the outlook of the saint and the crank; now happiness became the universally recognized desideratum of a "good society." Happiness was, moreover, not only desirable but attainable if only economic and political affairs were arranged by "enlightened" rulers with intelligence and good will.

The development of capitalism heralded the end of the predominantly rural stage of European history. Earlier society had been structured with a legally privileged landowning nobility standing at the apex. The forward thrust of capitalism was accompanied by the development of a dynamic, wealthy, and increasingly self-conscious *bourgeoisie*, resentful of aristocratic privilege; it demanded social mobility and "equality before the law," two goals incompatible with any hierarchic society. Economic advances made under capitalism— first in the form of the "domestic system," later in the early stages of the Industrial Revolution—led to the emergence of the vision, and to

3

a lesser extent the reality, of a society in which all men could be liberated, for the first time in history, from the scourges of poverty and social degradation. The full achievement of these goals required the destruction of legal privileges and the active encouragement of capitalist enterprise by sympathetic governments.

This work was begun toward the middle of the eighteenth century by several "enlightened monarchs" in the name of Reason of State; for the intelligent pursuit of power—the main preoccupation of eighteenth-century statecraft—required a prosperous and contented population. It became clear, however, that a complete orientation of governmental policy toward the general welfare, and more specifically the full achievement of legal equality, could not ultimately be left to monarchs who were, after all, by their nature part and parcel of the world of inequality; nor could they be expected—laudable examples to the contrary notwithstanding—to identify completely their dynastic interest with the general welfare. These considerations suggested the necessity of replacing the traditional monarchical-authoritarian state (what Germans call the *Obrigkeitsstaat*) by self-government (preferably of a popular character). The participation of the people in the work of government was bound, incidentally, to give a tremendous impetus to the sentiment of nationality, since the nation appeared as the "natural unit" of political self-consciousness at the end of the eighteenth century. Nationalism, though not immune to Conservative appropriation, was originally Progressive in inspiration; and it proved an additional dynamic element in the history of Europe as it discredited both supranational units (such as the Holy Roman Empire) and parochial territorial states (embracing but part of a nation, as was the case with that empire's component states).

The challenge confronting Conservatives was not confined to these impersonal forces working to create a secular, egalitarian, and self-governing society; it was compounded by the emergence of a group of men who devoted themselves, with zeal and determination, to the repudiation of the *status quo* and the reconstruction of society in accordance with the principles of the Enlightenment. Many labels can be attached to these men: "Radicals," because they wanted to strike at the roots of the existing society; "Progressives," because they worked for a better society in accordance with their conception of progress; or "Party of Movement," because they believed that they were cooperating with the forward march of history. The terms Radical, Progressive, and Party of Movement will be used interchangeably in this volume for men who aimed systematically at repudiating the *status quo* in the

4

name of a new pattern of society; it must be clearly understood that they name a genus which includes numerous species differing widely from one another. Among these species are *Liberals*, concerned primarily with civil liberty, legal equality, and laissez-faire; *Democrats*, concerned primarily with popular sovereignty; and *Socialists*, concerned with social equality and economic planning. In our context these species may be considered successive radicalizations of a single Party of Movement appearing in rough chronological sequence. Strong Liberal demands began to be voiced in Germany after about 1770; a significant Democratic movement arose only around 1790 without, however, crowding Liberalism off the stage; while Socialism, championed by isolated voices before the end of the eighteenth century, did not become an important movement until 1848.

The *raison d'être* of Conservatism as an articulate movement is conscious opposition to the deliberate efforts of the Party of Movement to transform society in a secular, egalitarian, and self-governing direction. The purpose of this volume is to trace the history of German Conservatism from the moment—around 1770—when the challenge of German Radicalism had become sufficiently strong to provoke a significant Conservative response. It may be noted that the Conservatism here described and analyzed is a specific historical phenomenon during the specific historical period starting about 1770; its essence is resistance —or, in some cases, accommodation—to the specific challenge of German Radicalism.

The definition of Conservatism given here differs from other definitions employed by various authors which are either too broad or too unhistorical to serve our purposes. The definition of Conservatism as any defense of the *status quo*, irrespective of the substantive nature of the *status quo*, is too broad to be useful; under it, all ruling groups which seek to preserve their power—and what ruling group does not? —would be Conservative, including successful revolutionaries (for example, Robespierre and Stalin).[1] At the opposite extreme from this functional definition of Conservatism stand various substantive definitions of Conservatism in terms of an unchanging ideology expressing certain absolute values, valid (though, of course, not attained) everywhere and at all times. A recent critic of Conservatism has described the key values of this ideology to be harmony and tranquillity, two

---

[1] See Robert Michels, "Conservatism," *ESS*, iv (1931), 230, for the uselessness of a general definition like "the tendency to maintain the *status quo*," and consequent plea for a "philosophical use and meaning" which "implies a particular *Weltanschauung*." Michels fails to develop the intermediate, specifically historical definition used in this book.

qualities possible only where friction is avoided by the curbing of individual desire and the absence of conflicting interests. By this exalted standard it is clear that a Conservative society has never existed and never can exist, and that all Conservatives always fall short of their own professed principles (Q.E.D.).[2]

Many self-styled modern Conservatives—especially in the ranks of America's so-called "New Conservatives"—are highly arbitrary in identifying one specific historical form of Conservatism with Conservatism per se.[3] They tend to canonize the admittedly great figure of Edmund Burke and attach an absolute value to the principles of eighteenth-century England (or the pre-1789 regime generally) which he defended against the Jacobin challenge. These Conservatives make themselves ridiculous when they try to apply the principles of Burkean Conservatism to a contemporary America where its foundations (a landowning aristocracy, an established clergy, and an ancient monarchy) do not exist now, have existed only in a vestigial manner in earlier times, and are quite irrelevant to the solution of contemporary problems. Suffice it to say that the Conservatism described in this book does not claim any universal significance; it only describes—let it be repeated—the specific response of Conservatives to the specific challenge of the Party of Movement under the specific historical circumstances of Germany during the last third of the eighteenth century.

It is important to stress this specificity of German—or any other type of—Conservatism, for in this quality lies the major obstacle to the writing of any general history of European Conservatism. Ruggiero, the brilliant historian of European Liberalism, confronted a manageable task in writing his general history; for Liberalism was a general movement which aimed at creating a Liberal society, with relatively homogeneous characteristics, in every European country.[4] It possessed common intellectual roots (such as the Renaissance, certain aspects of the Reformation, Cartesianism, and the Enlightenment) and a common program.[5] Conservatism usually appears, on the contrary, as a

---

[2] A. Morton Auerbach, *The Conservative Illusion* (New York, 1959), passim, especially pp. 7ff. A definition which stresses the universal psychological roots of Conservatism—love of the familiar and fear of the unknown—is no more useful than Auerbach's universal ideology for the understanding of specific post-1770 European Conservatism.

[3] Russell Kirk is a prime offender in this respect. See, for example, his *The Conservative Mind: from Burke to Santayana* (Chicago, 1953).

[4] Guido de Ruggiero, *History of European Liberalism*. English translation by R. G. Collingwood (Oxford, 1927).

[5] Though it must not be forgotten, of course, that Liberalism knows national

specific defense of a concrete and ever-changing *status quo*, and is therefore as variegated as the conditions which it defends. Its thinkers —excepting the special case of Burke—rarely exercise much influence outside their own countries and times, whether one thinks of Coleridge in England, Maistre and Bonald in France, or Möser, Müller, and Haller in Germany. The future historian of European Conservatism will be required to immerse himself in the specific conditions of every European country in order to secure a realistic understanding of what diverse conditions different Conservatives wanted to *conserve*. In the light of these considerations it appeared overambitious and premature to deal with European Conservatism on a comparative scale at this time. The author has instead selected the more limited topic of German Conservatism during its formative stage; he hopes that it will prove significant not only in itself but also will serve as one of many preliminary studies for the general history of modern European Conservatism to be written in the future.

The Three Types of Conservatives

Three major types of Conservatives can be identified in the period following the emergence of self-conscious Conservatism around 1770. They are all confronted by the advance of modern forces outlined above: they all deplore that the institutions, conditions, and principles of the *ancien régime* are placed on the defensive. The three types, which will be labeled Defenders of the *Status Quo*, Reform Conservatives, and Reactionaries, constitute three different responses to this common challenge. Each is characterized by a distinct outlook and a special set of problems. The three will be initially characterized as "ideal types"; the reader must remember, however, that the real Conservatives dealt with in the various chapters of this book are frequently mixed breeds that do not conform to these stereotypes. Nevertheless, an analysis of these types has value in pointing up the difficulties and dilemmas encountered by Conservatism in its various forms.

The first type is the Defender of the *Status Quo*. He is fundamentally contented with the world, whereas the Reform Conservative is restless and the Reactionary, embittered. The *Status Quo* Conservative is satisfied with enjoying what he *has* rather than pursuing something he *wants*. He is usually ahistorical in his outlook—a tendency connected with his essentially static view of the world. He has no reason to quar-

---

variations. For Germany, see the important book by Leonard Krieger, *The German Idea of Freedom* (Boston, 1957).

rel with past historical development, since it has led to a society satisfactory to himself; but any future development is considered a departure from the eternal principles of "natural society" embodied in the
status quo. The Defender of the *Status Quo* is generally a member of
the upper classes, enjoys the external and internal advantages of high
social status, and sees positions of authority occupied by men like himself.[6] He tends to deify the existing social framework and to identify
it with the dictates of justice itself, and he naturally places a high value
upon order, authority, law, and established institutions. He refuses to
see that all these have an ephemeral element and must be adapted to
changing conditions in order to retain their vitality; and that they
benefit primarily the upper classes and cannot be expected to retain
the loyalty of the lower classes permanently.

The main difficulty confronting the *Status Quo* Conservative is the
fundamental hopelessness of his over-all goal—hopeless because of the
ever-changing nature of the *status quo* he seeks to defend. It is clear
that the preservation of the *status quo* is, in the long run, impossible;
the dynamic flow of modern history is no more tolerant of the present
than of the past. It relentlessly changes society and daily alters the task
of society's defenders. Conservatives are doomed to fight what is essentially a rear-guard action in which victories are at best successful holding operations. As the *status quo* changes, its defenders find themselves in the ridiculous position of justifying today what they had assailed only yesterday, because it has meanwhile prevailed despite their
best efforts to the contrary. Frequently the only way to escape this
position is to become a Reactionary, and this is one reason why the
dividing line between the two tends in practice to be fluid. The *Status
Quo* Conservative's theoretical position in the political spectrum is,
however, easy to define: unlike the Reformer, he does not want to adjust to modern needs; unlike the Reactionary, he recognizes the impossibility of moving backward; wishing things to remain as they are,
he is dragged along by history instead of voluntarily cooperating with
it.

Voluntary cooperation with history is the main characteristic of the
second type of Conservative, here called the Reform Conservative.
He has an understanding of the course of historical development and
sees the inevitability of certain changes, although he does not pretend
any enthusiasm for them. He is, however, impressed by their inevita-

---

[6] Though *Status Quo* Conservatism also appeals to certain sections of the
lower class with whom "the cake of custom" (Bagehot) is still unbroken and
deference to social superiors unimpaired.

bility (in the sense of being dictated by objective, irreversible causes) and sees in consequence only the following alternative: changes *will* occur either with the active cooperation of men like himself, who will spare whatever can still be preserved from the past, or by Radicals, who will frequently go much farther than necessary in destroying the *ancien régime* and will place no value whatsoever upon maintaining the maximum possible historical continuity. The lot of the Conservative Reformer is a hard one: champions of the Party of Movement accuse him of being half-hearted in the pursuit of the "good society"; other Conservatives suspect him of unchaining sleeping dogs, and if he comes from the upper classes he is hated with special bitterness as a "traitor to his class." He is frequently forced into an *ad hoc* alliance with the Radicals of his day, one in which it is not always clear who is using whom.

The Reform Conservative can (in theory, not always in practice) be clearly differentiated from the Radical reformer both by his methods and his ultimate aims. He prefers gradual reform, if possible within the existing constitutional framework, to violent and rapid change; he reforms only what is necessary when it becomes necessary, instead of seeking to implement a theoretically conceived blueprint *in toto*; and he seeks above all to maximize continuity in institutions and ideas. His cautious method is closely connected with his over-all conception of what constitutes a good society: he values the colorful variety of life as it has evolved historically, has reverence for the past even as he removes surviving anachronisms, and is free of the illusion that utopia can be achieved in a necessarily imperfect world. He has, in short, what Burke called "a tendency to preserve with an inclination to improve."

It may be added that the successful Reform Conservative usually receives from historians the acclaim denied to him by contemporaries. There is danger, however, in looking for Reform Conservatives in every modern historical situation as *dei ex machina* to solve the massive problem of adaptation to modernity without any violent break in continuity. It should be stressed, therefore, that Reform Conservatism is feasible only where two far from universally prevalent conditions exist: (1) an over-all structure of society capable of adapting to new needs without altering its fundamental structure; (2) the availability of constitutional processes allowing for piecemeal changes, whether through parliamentary institutions or a reforming absolutism. Great Britain is the classic country for meeting both conditions, and it is no accident that it possesses the most successful record of any European country of Conservative adaptation to new needs. The eighteenth-century parliamentary system, however encrusted with privilege, was not completely unresponsive to reform needs and did maintain a tradition of self-government; it was able to be democratized in the nineteenth century through a succession of reform bills. It is doubtful, on the other hand, whether the situation in France before the Great Revolution met either condition. The established structure of society was characterized by incompetent monarchical authority, intransigent aristocratic privilege, and intolerant clericalism. There is no warrant for the belief —advanced, for example, by Burke—that these basic evils could have been remedied by Conservative Reformers acting in a patient and reverential spirit; nor were adequate constitutional processes available for piecemeal reform. The theoretically absolute monarch lacked reforming vigor; the aristocratic Assembly of Notables proved Reactionary in its outlook; the revival of the long obsolete Estates-General meant revolution. In these facts must be sought what little mercy the French Revolution is able to find in Conservative eyes.

The third type of Conservative, the Reactionary, is, logically speaking, not a Conservative in the strict sense of the term, since he does not wish to conserve what now exists, but rather to restore an earlier condition which history has passed by. He does not believe—like the *Status Quo* Conservative—that the world is relatively static, nor does he wish it to be so; he knows all too well that it has changed, believes that recent changes have been for the worse, and wishes, therefore, to return to an earlier condition. He desires backward motion, and insists that history does not know any irreversible unilinear movement. Man is not the prisoner of history: he can shape his social, political, and cultural world as he wishes. Reactionaries are usually bitterly hostile toward existing society, and are logical in lacking reverence for historical development whose result has been a hated *status quo*. Their indiscriminate enmity toward the present is usually accompanied by a romantic transfiguration of some particular period of the past. Thus the Reactionaries of the period of the French Revolution glorified the *ancien régime* or, going back farther, the medieval *Ständestaat*; their picture of earlier social relations as patriarchal rather than exploitative did more credit to their romantic imagination than to their sense of historical accuracy.

The Reactionary mind is rather at a loss when it seeks to explain how a glorious past developed into the miserable present. Legitimate grievances of the lower classes cannot explain the change, because the golden past excludes such grievances by definition. The responsibility

10

cannot be ascribed to inevitable historical development, since this would lead to defeatist conclusions; the true Reactionary is, on the contrary, an incorrigible optimist in his belief in the possibility of restoring a vanished past. The Reactionary tends to ascribe all trouble to "damned agitators," that is, to demagogues who create imaginary grievances which they then exploit to serve their personal ambitions; the Reactionary mind is especially prone to fall victim to the "conspiracy theory" analyzed in Ch. 10. There is a perverse consistency in this Reactionary view: Reactionaries, who believe that they—a small elite standing above the masses—can turn back history, believe quite logically that a small group of agitators can push history forward. Reactionaries gain confidence in the attainability of their program from the belief that it is based, not upon their subjective will, but rather upon the objective "nature of things." They believe that man must return—under Reactionary guidance—to a "natural order" from which society has departed but temporarily due to ascertainable (and reversible) causes. What they cannot accept is the existence of "forward-moving," irrepressible historical forces, for to do so would lead to the recognition that the much hated "Radical agitators" are more the symptom than the cause of the modern situation which dooms the Reactionary program to quixotic futility.[7]

[7] The triple typology here used does not make provision for the "Revolutionary Conservative," a type that has played such an important role in twentieth-century German history (i.e., men like Moeller van den Bruck, Ernst Jünger, and Oswald Spengler). The omission is deliberate and inevitable in a work dealing with Conservatism in the years 1770-1806, for it reflects the fact that the challenges confronting Conservatism in the twentieth century are fundamentally different from those of the eighteenth. The Conservatism dealt with in this book was a defensive movement which sought to preserve the *ancien régime* characterized by the principles and practice of social hierarchy, political authoritarianism, and Christian culture. It fought modernity from an entrenched position of social, political, and ecclesiastical power—even the Reactionary usually belongs to a class which has been only partly dispossessed. Where he has been totally dispossessed—and when his vision of the good society has little objective resemblance to an earlier condition of society—the line of distinction between the Reactionary and the Revolutionary Conservative becomes fluid.

The Revolutionary Conservatives during the Weimar Republic were an offensive group dedicated to the overthrow—not the conservation—of the German political, social, and cultural *status quo*. That *status quo* was determined by the triumph—however temporary—of the "modern forces" of egalitarianism, democracy, and secularism in 1918—a belated triumph which had been preceded by more than a hundred years of unusually tenacious and successful Conservative defense of the survivals of the *ancien régime* (the beginnings of which are covered in this book). Many pre-1918 Conservative defenders of monarchy, Junker domination, and the "Christian state" became Reactionaries after 1918. They hankered after the "good old days" of imperial Germany, remaining true to their pre-1918 substantive convictions on society and politics; from being *Status*

11

The Recurring Core of Conservative Argument

Conservatives, though they tend to be better at governing than at arguing, are forced by the exigencies of modern political life to enter the arena of public controversy. They do so with heavy hearts, and their thinking is in fact a reluctant concession to the challenge of the Party of Movement. They know that Conservatism is a way of life, not a complex of arguments, and that it flourishes best, as unself-conscious Traditionalism, before it is compelled to justify itself as theory. As Conservative thinkers are compelled to make a virtue of a necessity they are usually best at defending specific challenged institutions, worst at developing a comprehensive theory of Conservatism.

Conservatives usually dislike abstraction and general argument, and they think system-building is a distinctive Radical vice. One can discover, nonetheless, a core of recurring Conservative argument

---

Quo Conservatives they became Reactionaries *pari passu* with the alteration of the German *status quo*.

The Revolutionary Conservatives were not Conservative in any of the three senses of our typology. They hated the *status quo*; they were not Reactionaries and in fact dissociated themselves from the Reactionary *Deutschnationale Volkspartei*, realizing that the pre-1918 world was irretrievably gone; and they were not Reform Conservatives because they wished to destroy the Weimar state rather than adapt it to new needs through a creative synthesis of the new and the old. They shared the Radical desire for a total reconstruction of society in accordance with theoretical blueprints, while differing, of course, in their substantive goals and the use of a vocabulary studded with Conservative phrases (used, however, with connotations divorced from their traditional meanings). Their Radicalism of intent alone suffices to put them outside the Conservative fold; their paradoxical role as Revolutionary Conservatives, a *contradictio in adjecto*, was only possible in a society where Conservatives could no longer act defensively from a position of established economic, political, or ecclesiastical power. It may be added that their positive goals were hopelessly fuzzy, and never had any chance of realization since Revolutionary Conservatism could not possibly become a mass movement or compete with Nazi demagoguery on equal terms. Its historic impact was completely destructive because Revolutionary Conservatism helped to tear down the Weimar state for the ultimate benefit of Nazism. On the phenomenon of the Conservative Revolutionary during the history of the Weimar Republic—one of the most thoroughly explored topics of recent German history—see the following excellent studies, all strong on the ideological and comparatively weak on the sociological side: Armin Mohler, *Die konservative Revolution in Deutschland* (Stuttgart, 1950); Klemens von Klemperer, *Germany's New Conservatism* (Princeton, 1957); Fritz Stern, *The Politics of Cultural Despair* (Berkeley, 1960); Otto Ernst Schüddekopf, *Linke Leute von Rechts* (Stuttgart, 1960); Kurt Sontheimer, *Anti-demokratisches Denken in der Weimarer Republik* (Munich, 1962); H. J. Schwierskott, *Moeller van den Bruck und der revolutionäre Nationalismus der Weimarer Republik* (Göttingen, 1962); and Hans Peter Schwarz, *Der konservative Anarchist. Politik und Zeitkritik Ernst Jüngers* (Freiburg, 1962).

which is quite independent of the defense of any particular *status quo*, and may be considered—when stated in systematic form—the general Conservative answer to the general challenge of modern Progressivism. This recurring core does not, however, constitute a set of substantive Conservative principles concerning the "best form of government" or the "best order of society"; it defines only a framework into which the most variegated Conservative defenses of the most variegated *status quos* can be fitted.

It may be added that even the greatest of Conservative thinkers have hesitated—because of their instinctive hostility to *all* system-making—to state the general Conservative case in a systematic manner; it must be extracted from the wealth of specific argumentation dealing with particular cases. Edmund Burke, to name only the most influential Conservative, has almost all the elements of the general Conservative case in his *Reflections on the Revolution in France*; but he embeds them somewhat inconspicuously within the rich framework of his colorful and highly specific defense of the eighteenth-century English constitution. It may nonetheless prove useful to outline this case as an "ideal type" to serve as background to the fragmentary voices presented in this volume; although it goes without saying that many German Conservatives did not subscribe—least of all explicitly—to all of the propositions outlined here.

Since Conservatism is primarily a defensive movement against the efforts of the Progressives to change the world, it naturally seeks to expose the weaknesses of its enemy. It is easy to state what Conservatism, in each of its three forms, is *against*. It is above all against rationalism and utopianism, since reason is the *method* and a secular utopia the *goal* of Progressivism. Conservatives insist that the systematic application of reason to political, economic, and religious problems usually leads to disastrous results. To tear down existing beliefs and institutions through acid criticism is easy; to find satisfactory and workable substitutes capable of attracting broad consent, difficult. Hence it appears far better to "make do" with the legacy of the past, however imperfect it may appear in the light of reason. Conservatives believe that this legacy incorporates—usually, not always—a "collective wisdom" far more trustworthy than the opinions of any individual thinker: this wisdom is enshrined in custom, tradition, and even sheer prejudice. Rationalist criticism is purely destructive, as it seeks to uproot these society-preserving factors though they are, fortunately, so deeply rooted in the instinctive needs of man as to be virtually indestructible. They are, furthermore, buttressed by established authority and consecrated by traditional religion, at least prior to the spread of democracy and secularism. The Conservative rejoices in the fact that religious faith, civic loyalty, and the emotional needs of man constitute a formidable barrier against rationalism, and he expects that the triumph of rationalism will never prove more than ephemeral.

Conservatives believe that the modern goal of establishing an earthly utopia—that is, a society characterized by universal happiness—is intrinsically unrealizable. It is unrealizable because the main handicap to establishing the millennium is not some easily overcome external social obstacle, such as monarchy, aristocracy, or clericalism, but rather the internal obstacle which exists in each individual as ineradicable original sin. Conservatives consider it a typically modern illusion that mankind can start life *de novo* by the mere wish to repudiate the past; indeed, they rarely resist a feeling of *Schadenfreude* that the noble ideals of the Party of Movement tend to break down in implementation after every apparent triumph. They point to what happened to the ideals of 1789 in the course of the French Revolution: liberty turned into the tyranny of the Committee of Public Safety; equality provided the legal framework for the exploitation of the lower classes by the *bourgeoisie*; fraternity led to militant nationalism and a quarter century of destructive war. Liberty is always in danger of degenerating into anarchy, which leads easily to tyranny; the egalitarian creed is defeated from the start by the inescapable fact that men differ from childhood in important respects for hereditary rather than environmental reasons; while fraternity usually expresses itself through participation in a parochial "in-group" marked by hostility toward supposedly less desirable outsiders.

Conservatives assert, moreover, that man's cumulative experience with rationalism teaches that its erosion of the traditional bases of civilized conduct—religion, habit, and reverence for established custom— has unintentionally unchained primitive human drives for wealth, power, and pleasure on a scale unparalleled in history. This unintentional unleashing of drives, when combined with the pursuit of intrinsically utopian goals, has made frustration and discontent the hallmark of the modern world. Even where modernity has achieved great things —as in the creation of higher living standards—the rise of expectations characteristic of the modern temper has increased faster still, the result being a net increase in dissatisfaction. The eternal facts of frustration and suffering, previously accepted as part of God's plan for maturing and regenerating man, are inexplicable to the impatient hedonism of modernity.

14

Conservatives question, furthermore, not only the attainability but also the desirability of the Radical vision of utopia. They see it as but the final culmination of that secularist hedonism which was the basic value of the Enlightenment. Secularism meant the repudiation of all transcendental religious conceptions, including the view that man possesses an immortal soul whose salvation in the Hereafter is at least as important as happiness in our brief earthly life. Many of the thinkers of the Enlightenment tended to view man as only a higher type of animal destined to seek and find happiness here and now; they tended to identify happiness too narrowly with material welfare and emancipation from "superstition" at the expense of "ideal" endeavors. The hidden recesses of personality remained a closed book to them. They tended to ignore certain uncomfortable facts—for example, that the attainment of material goals usually creates frustration rather than satisfaction, since material wants are almost infinitely extensible and our comparative position vis-à-vis that of our neighbors often affects us psychologically more than our absolute standard of living; that the jealousy and envy which accompanies status-seeking creates problems as great as those of poverty and exploitation; and that the stress upon pleasure rather than duty, egotistic self-interest rather than altruistic service, usually proves self-defeating in practice. The personal "enlightenment" achieved through education solves some problems only to create new ones: familiarity with other ways of life breeds discontent with one's own; the opening of opportunity probably creates at least as much frustration for the many who do not advance in the social scale as satisfaction to the few that do; while half-education leads to the vulgarization of culture and threatens that religious faith which is psychologically comforting, regardless of whether it be "true" or "false."

These, then, are the flaws which Conservatives denounce in the method and goals of the Party of Movement. But what are Conservatives *for*? The answer has been largely implied in the previous discussion but may now be stated systematically.

In its mode of thought—its epistemology—Conservatism rejects rationalism; although Conservatives do, of course, use their heads exactly as do men of other political persuasions, they warn against the excessive or exclusive use of speculative reason. They praise experience as a more reliable guide to truth than a priori conceptions, and assert that, at least when dealing with human affairs, cautious induction is preferable to the deductive reasoning beloved by too many Radicals. Above all, they insist upon the necessity of balancing the use of reason

15

by listening to the voice of natural emotion and supernatural faith, and they believe that the individual reasoner should humbly subordinate his personal opinions to the collective wisdom of the race as expressed in customs and traditions. The habit of deference to what exists and reverence for what has developed are deemed more valuable human qualities than intellectual skill at constructing syllogisms.

Conservatives differ from Radicals not only in their epistemology but in their view of what is most significant in the world. They tend to emphasize the importance of variety, whereas their opponents stress general norms; they proclaim the need for compromise in a pluralistic universe, whereas their opponents seek the triumph of "right reason" everywhere and at all times; and while willing to acquiesce (albeit reluctantly) in natural historical changes, they insist that the artificial human manipulation of history can only affect society for the worse.

Conservatives not only emphasize variety; they also love it. The spontaneous development of human society has led to a colorful richness which Conservatives find emotionally and aesthetically satisfying. They do not bother to rationalize this preference in terms of any metaphysical system, for they consider it to be simply "natural," i.e., in accordance with the "real" needs of "uncorrupted" human nature. Conservatives usually accuse Radicals of wishing to destroy existing variety—expressing what is old and familiar—by implementing the precepts of an abstract and uniform rationalism. The Conservative love of the customary is usually accompanied by a fear of the unknown—two of the taproots of what may be called the eternal appeal of Conservatism to at least part of every man.

The Conservative view of the world affirms in theory (not always in practice) the existence of a plurality of competing values. We have seen above how the Conservative epistemology rejects rationalism but accepts the use of reason when balanced by the equally valuable—but partially incompatible—dictates of emotion and faith. This outlook of "yes, but—provided that" is characteristic of Conservatism; it likes to criticize the Party of Movement for its frequent tendency to absolutize some single good, such as liberty, and to apply it ruthlessly and one-sidedly at the expense of other equally important values. Burke stated this point in a classic fashion when he replied to a French critic who accused him of being insufficiently enthusiastic about the progress of French liberty:

> I should suspend my congratulations on the new liberty of France, until I was informed how it had been combined with government,

with public force, with the discipline and obedience of armies, with the collection of an effective and well-distributed revenue, with morality and religion, with solidity and property, with peace and order, with civil and social manners. All these (in their way) are good things, too; and without them, liberty is not a benefit while it lasts, and is not likely to continue long.[8]

The Conservative affirmation of a plurality of values calls for an equilibrium between liberty and order, equality and hierarchy, individualism and collectivism, self-government and authority, cosmopolitanism and nationalism, material goods and ideal aspirations, pleasure and asceticism, reason and emotion, secularism and religion, dynamism and stability. It is true that the actual conduct of Conservatives (especially Reactionaries and Defenders of the *Status Quo*) is often motivated by a single-minded emphasis upon the latter of each of the above antinomies (order, hierarchy, collectivism, et cetera). This Conservative one-sidedness usually parallels and neutralizes equally one-sided exaggerations of Progressivism on behalf of liberty, equality, individualism, et cetera; the difference between these two "lapses" is, however, that Conservatives generally acknowledge the principle of pluralism, while Progressives too often deny any value to at least some of the above-mentioned elements. One can also say that the existence of Progressivism makes the disturbance of the intra-Conservative equilibrium of values necessary to serve the interests of the equilibrium of society as a whole. Hence moderate Conservatives (or moderate Progressives) often admit that Progressives and Conservatives are both essential for the best functioning of modern society—an insight which sometimes leads to the tolerance which we associate with civilized political conduct.

A constant danger confronting Conservatives is that they will too easily get angry at history; only Reform Conservatives are free of this danger. Yet even the latter tend to deplore the dynamism of the modern world, and more especially the velocity of its changes. They inevitably resent the Progressive habit of never taking the foot off the accelerator as mankind drives into the future. Conservatives—if the automobile analogy may be continued—keep their foot constantly on or near the brake; they attach the greatest importance to enforcing speed limits and safety regulations; they view the road ahead as bumpy and do not mind occasional road obstacles; above all, they see no reason

[8] *The Works of the Right Honorable Edmund Burke* (Boston, 1865), III, 241-42.

why the approaching *terra incognita* should necessarily be superior to the familiar landscape being left behind.

The Conservative function is one of avoiding unnecessary journeys and slowing the pace of those that are really necessary. It is the belief of Reform Conservatives, however, that this negative work must be accompanied by the positive work of adapting the old to the new. Old institutions are revitalized by eliminating anachronistic abuses, even as the life of a tree is prolonged by careful pruning and removing of dead limbs. The problem to be solved by the Reform Conservative is to differentiate between what is still viable and what is inevitably doomed to die. He must then select the proper method for strengthening the former while not hesitating to be ruthless in eliminating the latter. The precise method of action of the Reform Conservative will always depend upon time and circumstances, but certain general guidelines are nonetheless clear. The Reform Conservative will always seek to maximize continuity; when encountering a defective institution, he will try reform before consenting to its abolition; he will, if possible, pour new wine into old bottles rather than create completely new institutions to cope with new needs. His action will always aim at rearranging the elements of the existing structure of society instead of aiming at a total reconstruction *de novo*; his reform work will be done in sorrow rather than in anger, in a spirit of reluctant bowing to necessity rather than joyful triumph. He will view with reverence what was valuable in the past even though it must be eliminated for the sake of the future; and he will seek to maintain an over-all pattern of society where the old always overbalances the new. The "social engineering" done by Reform Conservatives is always of a strictly prophylactic character. They do only what is necessary, as it becomes necessary, and with a primary view to preventing worse things being done by the Party of Movement. They never forget that society ought to be considered primarily as a *given* whose fundamental structure is shaped by God, or history, or the essentially unchangeable nature of man—not by any deliberate manipulation following man's subjective will. The Reform Conservative emphatically repudiates any kind of subjective caprice as he goes about his reform work; he only does, humbly and reverently, what he believes is objectively necessary to adjust the old to the new in the inescapable stream of historical development.

The question arises, Is Reform Conservatism only a doctrine of adjustment to the inevitable? Is it only an attitude and a method which seeks to minimize the evils of modernity by maximizing continuity, and by preventing revolution through timely reform? As adjustments accumulate quantitatively, the entire quality of society changes despite the absence of any sharp break in continuity at any particular point. Thus England has been changed in the last two hundred years from an agrarian to an industrial, an oligarchic to a democratic, a religious to a secular society, without any political revolution—a smooth record of adjustment of which Englishmen have reason to be proud. Today's English Conservative champions and defends positions on liberty, local self-government, progressive income tax, et cetera, which would have done honor to any eighteenth-century Radical. Should the Conservative be considered, therefore, a mere opportunist who lacks any substantive principles which may not be compromised at any price? Or are there certain unchangeable Conservative substantive principles, or at least ways of looking at the world?

For the Catholic Conservative there is, in the religious field, the clear-cut case of revealed dogma: he obviously cannot compromise the slightest part of the infallible teachings of his Church (though the possibility of differences in emphasis to meet differences in situations allows Catholics, in practice, to act far more flexibly than the above statement would suggest). Are there in the fields of politics and economics any absolutely valid beliefs, institutions, or patterns of life which possess the same sacrosanctity as revealed dogma in religion? Many Conservatives have thought so at specific times with reference to specific institutions. In politics they have believed in the absolute value of monarchy or oligarchy or (some particular interpretation of) the American Constitution; in economics, in mercantilism, the free market, or some type of state socialism. Yet the very diversity of ideals which have evoked absolute loyalties indicates that all possessed but a relative, historical, and—philosophically speaking—ephemeral character. It follows that Conservatism per se cannot be committed to any specific form of political or economic organization, and that there is, therefore, in principle no limit to Conservative adjustment to modern political and economic forces.

One is tempted to say, somewhat paradoxically, that Conservatism is static in aim but dynamic in character, since it constantly adjusts to historical development; while Progressivism is dynamic in aim but often static in the character of its unchangeable goal. We have seen that Conservatism cannot be identified with any absolute allegiance to any particular social or political order (though individual Conservatives have, of course, such allegiances). One can, however, identify an underlying general Conservative conception of society which remains constant in the midst of the unending process of adjustment to historical change. This conception is based upon the belief that human nature has remained essentially the same, at least insofar as its fundamental needs and some of its essential qualities are concerned. These needs can be met, these qualities can be taken into account, only by a general framework of society as constant as human nature itself and hence dictated by God or, if God be not allowed, by Nature. Its constituent elements are defined by the following basic needs of human nature: Man requires society because he is, as Aristotle said, a social animal; the maintenance of society requires some kind of governmental authority which enforces law and order, and a degree of social differentiation (hierarchy) which guarantees the performance of all socially necessary tasks. The social needs of man seeking to live a good life are, however, so diverse that they require far more than just satisfactory political institutions. Man requires a family which fulfills biological needs (not to mention the needs of the young); property, to provide security and independence; and some local roots in his place of birth or neighborhood to avoid becoming an unhappy nomad. All these relationships can be maintained satisfactorily only where moral codes and customs establish a tradition with a certain degree of continuity. Since man is more than a customary animal, he also needs some measure of freedom and opportunity for personal development. He is, finally, a religious creature who will never cease to wonder from where he has come and to where he is going, and what the significance of his earthly life is. He needs, therefore, religion or some modern surrogate which performs most of the functions of traditional religion.

These dictates of Nature, as seen by Conservatives, are at once inflexible and flexible: inflexible in the sense of being necessary (or at least desirable) at all times and places; flexible as regards their substantive content. Authority can be embodied in many different kinds of institutions; law is not simply the embodiment of "natural justice" but the reflection of changing social circumstances; order is a relative thing in view of the sinfulness of human nature and man's irrepressible (though variable) desire for freedom. The elements of social hierarchy vary from one society to another, both in their content and the permissible degrees of social mobility. The structure of families has changed throughout history; the forms of property are as heterogeneous as societies and their laws; while neighborhood roots are infinitely variable both in their intensity and substance. Codes of morality, customs, and traditions and the extent of their continuity differ from place to place, as do specific religions. The important point is, however, that all these elements must be present in *some* form at all times if man is to lead a satisfactory life. Conservatives point an accusing finger at Progressives for ignoring this fundamental fact, as in their frequently intransigent hostility to authority, hierarchy, and traditional religion; and for likewise failing to understand that the value of all these elements is greatly enhanced if they are relatively stable, deeply rooted in the past, and comparatively noncontroversial in substance. They deplore the Radical habit of throwing everything into controversy, despising the legacy of the past, and delighting in the dynamism of the modern world.

Reform Conservatives, however willing to adapt themselves to the continuous needs of historical development, will always keep in mind the above-stated eternal needs of man in society; this will put some limitation to their adaption and opportunism (a word which need not have a negative connotation). The essential characteristics of Conservatism per se are adherence to this eternal framework, dislike of unnecessary social change, and a propensity to find satisfaction in the *status quo*. Conservatism as thus defined has existed throughout recorded history, but it has become self-conscious, argumentative, and explicit only since it has been forced, beginning with the late eighteenth century, to meet the challenge of an aggressive Progressivism operating within an ever more dynamic society.

It may be well to round out the picture by pointing out some of the characteristic vices of Conservatives: complacency, callousness, and shortsightedness. Defenders of the *Status Quo* emphatically, Reform Conservatives and Reactionaries to a lesser degree, feel very much "at ease in Zion." Their recruitment from the upper classes (with the corollary possession of wealth and power) make them too frequently indifferent to the condition of the less fortunate part of the human race; even Reform Conservatives tend to patronize the lower classes and to promote reforms more from prudence than genuine sympathy with human suffering. When defending the existing structure of society, Conservative theorists too often stress the beauty of its over-all configuration while ignoring the ugliness of many of its component parts. To give only one example: the Conservative sympathy for the principle of hierarchy expresses an aesthetic appreciation of its resulting colorful variety—an appreciation marked (like all aesthetic appreciation) by a detachment often incompatible with a sense of social responsibility. A society headed by landowning aristocrats will naturally have more color and variety than a "leveled" Jeffersonian democracy of small farmers; but the aesthetic beauty of the whole is marred—at least to observers not captives of Conservative phrases—by the monotony and squalor of life seen from the bottom of the pyramid. Conservatives like to assert that they are defending concrete society against Radical abstractions; but in fact their idealization of the Whole amounts to an aesthetic appreciation of a pure abstraction which becomes amoral when it ignores the very concrete sufferings of the poor. There is justice in Paine's response to Burke's lament on the fate of the French aristocracy: "He pities the plumage, but forgets the dying bird."

Callousness toward the sufferings beneath them is often accompanied—even among Reform Conservatives—by shortsightedness in the face of the problems ahead of them. Since the irresistible character of the modern forces which are transforming the world is either denied or their impact minimized, Conservatives have little incentive to analyze the long-range needs of society. Conservatism easily becomes a philosophy for doing tomorrow (or not at all) what should be done today. Thus Conservative reforms are rarely introduced in time, and more rarely still do they suffice to set a controversy even temporarily at rest. Complacency toward existing conditions—even worse, nostalgia toward the past—is poor equipment for coping with the problems of the dynamic world of the last two centuries. The Conservative penchant for belated stopgap measures bears a heavy share of responsibility for that chronic maladjustment between old institutions and new needs which is the source of much of the turbulence of modern history.

The Plan of This Book

It is time to turn from generalizations concerning Conservatism to the specific German Conservatism which forms the subject matter of this book. Our chronological limit spans from about 1770, when Conservatism first emerged as an articulate movement, to the dissolution of the Holy Roman Empire in 1806, which marked a milestone in the collapse of the German *ancien régime*. This period covers, literally speaking, the *Vorgeschichte* (preliminary history) of Conservatism in a party sense, since Conservative parties, like all organized parties, can develop only within the framework of parliamentary bodies; these began to exist in Germany only after our terminal date (in 1818) and at first only in South Germany. The absence of Conservative parties did not, however, preclude the emergence of traceable Conservative intellectual currents. The last third of the eighteenth century saw the appearance in Germany of Progressive critics who aimed at the deliberate overthrow of the entire *ancien régime*; their criticism naturally provoked specific defenses of the challenged political, economic, and religious *status quo*. The novelty and intensity of the Radical attack meant that age-old, inert traditionalism developed into an alert and self-conscious Conservatism. This Conservatism (like the Radical attack) was never a purely intellectual movement; it was inevitably associated with definite socioeconomic interest groups. A given Conservative (or Radical) statement, however general in its nature and seemingly disinterested in its motive, in fact usually served the material or spiritual interests of a particular class or group. An attempt will be made to show such connections wherever possible, but the connection was frequently unclear in the mind of contemporaries and is quite impossible to "prove" by the later historian. Frequently one cannot go beyond the statement that such and such opinions were expressed by such and such a writer in such and such a place; whom the writer spoke *for*, or whom he spoke *to*, can only be surmised.

Our analysis is partly organized around themes, partly around key figures, and follows a generally chronological pattern. Part One covers the twenty years (1770-90) prior to the outbreak of the French Revolution, and seeks to establish the general theme that Germany possessed a well-articulated Conservative movement before, and therefore independent of, that cataclysmic event in the history of modern Europe. The chapter immediately following this introduction characterizes the spirit, doctrine, and propagandist methods of the German Enlightenment; a discussion of the genesis of a self-conscious Conservatism and of the methods employed by it to combat its Radical enemies follows. Chapter 2 examines the secret societies of Masonry and Illuminism, which served as agencies for spreading Enlightenment, and the Rosicrucian Order, which pursued specifically Conservative objectives. Chapters 3 to 5 deal with particular controversies in the fields of religion, social policy, and politics. In each field the reader will see how a specific Progressive attack provoked a specific Conservative defense.

In the religious field both Catholics and Protestants were divided between champions of Orthodoxy and their "enlightened" critics, the latter being subdivided (though the division is often hard to make in practice and necessarily controversial in individual cases) between Radicals deeply hostile to traditional religion and Reform Conservatives who wished to strengthen religion by adapting it to the conditions of modern life. In the socioeconomic field all controversies may be viewed as aspects of the painful transition from the feudal-hierarchic world of the *ancien régime* to the beginnings of a capitalist-egal-

23

itarian pattern of society. There were specific controversies about still surviving aristocratic privileges, serfdom and the lot of the peasantry, the oligarchic character of handicraft guilds, and the emancipation of two considerable groups—women and Jews—from their traditional status of inferiority. In the political field there was much debate concerning the condition of such obviously anachronistic structures as the Holy Roman Empire, the ecclesiastical states, and the Imperial Free Cities. The only flourishing type of polity to be found in Germany, princely absolutism, stood in the crossfire of political controversy. It was praised by many Progressives (and some Reform Conservatives) as an instrument of modernity when it took the form of "enlightened absolutism"; it was criticized by other Progressives as an obstacle on the road to self-government and for its tendency toward arbitrariness. Defenders of the *Status Quo* saw it, on the other hand, as a bulwark against Radical demands "from below"; whereas Reactionaries hated it as the mortal enemy of the *Ständestaat* to which they wished to return.

Many of the Conservative positions described in Chapters 3 to 5 are expressed in a distinctly personal form in the writings of Justus Möser (1720-94), the "patriarch from Osnabrück" who stands at the beginning of Germany's Conservative tradition. He deserves extended treatment because of his historical position at the focal point where unreflective traditionalism turned into self-conscious Conservatism. The comprehensive character of his Conservatism—its biographical and environmental background, its philosophical premises, and their application to political, social, and religious issues—will be analyzed in Chapter 6.

Part Two covers the years from 1790 to 1806, beginning with the impact of the French Revolution upon Germany and ending with the collapse of both the Holy Roman Empire and the Prussian monarchy. Its first two chapters are devoted to an analysis of developments in Prussia and Austria, the two most important states in Germany—with special emphasis upon the problems and rulers of the 1790's. The next three chapters are devoted to the German response to the challenge of the French Revolution after 1789. A brief description of the general enthusiasm aroused throughout Germany by the storming of the Bastille leads to the discussion of the problem, Was there a revolutionary danger in Germany? with special attention given to the Saxon peasant revolt of 1790, the attitude of the Rhenish population toward the French conqueror, and the "Jacobin conspiracy" in Vienna in 1794. The "official" response to the revolution, as expressed in the pattern of repression of Radical voices, the encouragement of counterrevolutionary propaganda, and the conduct of the war against France is also investigated.

Chapter 10 analyzes the crystallization of the prevalent spirit of anti-Jacobin hysteria in the form of an elaborate "conspiracy theory" which explained the revolution as the work of Masons and Illuminati. This theory was international in its appeal, as shown by the influence of the French writer Barruel and the Scottish writer Robison. The main German spokesmen were the philosopher J. A. Starck, court preacher at Darmstadt; the journalist L. A. Hoffmann, editor of the *Wiener Zeitschrift*; and a group of Conservative writers who published the counterrevolutionary journal *Eudämonia* from 1795 to 1798.

The life and writings of A. W. Rehberg, one of the most distinguished German antirevolutionary publicists, is examined next. He was the leading figure of a so-called "Hannoverian school," whose outlook owed much to the special conditions of this Lower Saxon electorate. Rehberg was notable for his criticism of the theory and practice of the French revolutionaries, and his attempt to build up German immunity to the revolutionary contagion by a specific program of Reform Conservatism.

Chapters 12 and 13 analyze the Conservative response to the Napoleonic Revolution in Germany. They describe the cooperation between France and its German allies in the destruction of all the "rotten members" of the German constitution: the ecclesiastical states, the Imperial Knights, the Free Cities, and finally the Holy Roman Empire itself. French ascendancy in Central Europe reached its apogee with the collapse of the Prussian state after the battle of Jena. German Conservatism stood at a nadir in its fortunes in 1806; its revival in the following years and triumph during the Metternichean era will be reserved for treatment in a subsequent volume.

PART ONE

THE ORIGINS OF CONSERVATISM
(TO 1790)

CHAPTER 1

The Enlightenment, the Constellation of Social Forces, and the Rise of Conservatism

The Enlightenment

ITS SIGNIFICANCE IN EUROPEAN HISTORY

FRIENDS AND foes of the Enlightenment are in agreement on at least one point: it constitutes, for better or worse, a decisive turning point in European history, one which may be defined as the definitive break with the "medieval view of the world." Individuals and even small groups (for example, many Renaissance humanists), had completed this break long before the eighteenth century; but a break on a mass scale, possessing an irreversible character, was the distinctive new development characterizing the "age of Enlightenment."[1]

What were the key elements of the medieval *Weltanschauung* now being repudiated? They included—if a very rough and stereotyped sketch may be permitted—in the religious field, supernatural revelation and the preoccupation with salvation and the life to come; in psychology, belief in the sinful nature of man and the consequent need of supernatural grace to attain salvation; in science, a mysterious universe animated by the will of God and (insofar as God permitted) his foe, the Devil; in history, the conception of Providence which guided the world from a known beginning (described in the Book of Genesis) to a foreseeable and possibly imminent end (foretold in the Book of Revelation). Medieval man further believed—if unquestioned acceptance

---

[1] The character of this break is explored brilliantly in Bernhard Groethuysen, *Die Entstehung der bürgerlichen Welt-und Lebensanschauung in Frankreich* (2 vols., Halle, 1927-30); its long-range impact in Fritz Valjavec, *Geschichte der abendländischen Aufklärung* (Vienna and Munich, 1961). The thesis of Carl Becker in *The Heavenly City of the Eighteenth Century Philosophers* (New Haven, 1932)—that the Enlightenment was only a secularized version of the medieval world view, and therefore has more in common with medievalism than modernity—is a brilliant half-truth which does not do justice to the revolutionary character of Enlightenment thought. Becker rightly stresses that St. Thomas and Voltaire agreed upon such fundamentals as an orderly world created by God, a meaningful unilinear pattern of history, a fundamental anthropocentricity, a similar conception of natural law, and a belief in the value of striving to overcome evil and to win future bliss—all propositions which modern skepticism and relativism has thrown into doubt; but he does not emphasize sufficiently how different the specific content of their respective "closed system" actually was. On the entire question see the valuable symposium edited by Raymond O. Rockwood, *Carl Becker's Heavenly City Revisited* (Ithaca, 1958).

may be equated with belief—that the structure of society and the substance of law were essentially static and eternal. He accepted the king's authority without thinking about defining it precisely in either absolutist or constitutional terms (a polarity of concepts still unknown); he accepted a society dominated by a landowning aristocracy and a Church owning vast properties and exercising broad jurisdictions. It is of crucial importance to recognize that medieval people believed that the existing pattern of politics and economics constituted a permanent and natural order sanctioned by God; social change was neither desired nor expected nor, in most cases, even contemplated as a possibility. Man did not see himself as an autonomous creature destined to achieve, by his own unaided efforts, happiness in this world: his destiny was rather to serve God for that brief mortal life—a mere second of eternity—which constituted but the vestibule before the infinitely more important life to come.

The Enlightenment brought about a sharp break with all these views. The rise of rational or natural religion led to a de-emphasis or even abandonment of divine revelation; a new mood of secularist hedonism robbed the Hereafter first of its terror, then of its relevance; man now believed himself to be good, hence felt no need for any supernatural grace to achieve "salvation" (a concept easily watered down and soon neglected without being necessarily repudiated); science—the mechanical-mathematical science of Newton—provided an explanation of the universe from which God had retired after an initially necessary, but now very remote, act of creation; belief in the Devil was dismissed as the product of the diseased imagination of an earlier superstitious age, and so-called "miracles of nature" were viewed as promising areas for future scientific research. Man now began to see himself as the master of his political and economic life and believed he could manipulate both to serve the needs of his terrestrial happiness. The stranglehold of tradition—now seen for the first time as a hostile force—must be broken through a rationally conceived and deliberately implemented program of social planning. Traditional monarchy must either become "enlightened" or be superseded by self-government; a broadly conceived catalogue of the "rights of man" must be respected by the state; religious toleration must be established and clerical privilege broken; the hierarchic structure of society, with landowning aristocrats at the apex of the social pyramid, must yield to the principle of social equality; while the traditional collectivist regulation of the economy, oriented to the end of preserving a social pattern viewed as divinely created and therefore just, must give way to a laissez-faire system based upon the self-asserting energies of free men. History was no longer viewed as the unfolding of the providential will of God but rather, in Gibbon's famous phrase, as the record of the crimes and follies of mankind—a dark picture yet one relieved by the belief that progress, long moving at a snail's pace, had at last accelerated as the distinctive hallmark of the eighteenth century. The prevalent mood became one of optimism and even complacency. Life was already good for some and ultimately destined to be good for all; death was a regrettable fact about which it was unprofitable to brood. The task here and now was to maximize happiness through the spread of the principles of Enlightenment: rationalism, secularism, science, natural rights, equality, and laissez-faire.[2]

The Enlightenment challenged, in short, Europe's traditional religion, its traditional social organization, and its traditional system of government—and it did this with such ceaseless persistence as to throw every area of life into permanent crisis. It ended, presumably forever, the quasi-unanimous acceptance of the *status quo* which had characterized—at least outside the field of religion—the previous fifteen centuries of European history. The ensuing fact of unceasing ferment constitutes one of the greatest transformations in human affairs—certainly the greatest since Christianity, with its supernatural, ascetic, and unilinear view of the world, replaced the secular, hedonist, and cyclical outlook characteristic of Greco-Roman civilization. A passive acceptance of the world yielded to an activist desire to change it; the right of rebellion replaced the duty of resignation; the fanning of discontent became the recognized, and not necessarily disreputable, function of radical intellectuals.

It is important to note that the Enlightenment meant not only the proclamation of new theoretical principles but the attempt to implement them in practice. The principles of Enlightenment were very similar in every area of Europe within its reach, and may be summarized as follows: rational science, the key to human progress, must be advanced; there was no fear that it might lead to knowledge deleterious to man's welfare. Knowledge must not only be accumulated by the few; it must be spread among the many. There was a deep faith in the educability, and even perfectibility, of the masses. Obscurantism and bigotry must be combated because they were the primary obstacles

[2] The contrast between medievalism and the Enlightenment has been frequently stated, most succinctly perhaps in Ernst Troeltsch's famous article: "Aufklärung," *Realencyclopädie für protestantische Theologie und Kirche* (3rd edn., ed. A. Hauck, 1897), II, 225-41.

to progress; in practice this meant a vigorous anticlericalism. A further deadly enemy was any kind of prejudice, whether it made men prefer a particular religion, or nation, or class (usually their own) to another. It was necessary to replace revealed religion by natural religion, political parochialism by cosmopolitanism, and class privilege by the triumph of legal—and perhaps even actual—equality. In the field of economics it was necessary to remove all obstacles which stood in the way of the "natural system of liberty"; this meant the sweeping away of the time-honored principle of state regulation of economic activity.

In the political field the thinkers of the Enlightenment demanded that government should respect the natural "rights of man" and undertake a large catalogue of reforms. In practice this meant an active attack upon aristocratic and clerical privilege. There was, incidentally, no agreement among "enlightened" men on what kind of government was most likely to conduct this kind of attack most expeditiously. Some put their faith in "enlightened" despots like Frederick the Great or Joseph II; others favored the aristocratic-oligarchic parliamentary system practiced in England; still others despaired of these existing systems and placed their faith in the development of full democracy. This diversity of outlook was due to the fact that none of these three types of government offered any solid guarantee that rulers would act in accordance with the program of Enlightenment. An enlightened monarch might cease to be enlightened, or be succeeded by an obscurantist heir; an oligarchic parliament could easily degenerate into a stronghold of traditionalist privilege; a democratic polity could fall prey to either popular demagogy or tyranny of a majority. These considerations explain why most of the champions of Enlightenment spoke of political questions with less stridency, and much less unanimity, than about reforms in other areas of life.

PARTICULAR CHARACTERISTICS OF THE GERMAN ENLIGHTENMENT

Quite apart from the frequently stressed quantitative differences were the qualitative differences in the character of the Enlightenment as it spread through the various countries of Europe—differences which reflect differing economic, political, and cultural development of the various countries. A broad contrast must be drawn between the German *Aufklärung*—as it will henceforth be called in this book—and the Western (Anglo-French) type of Enlightenment; this contrast was due primarily to four major factors: the economic backwardness of Germany, resulting in a weak *bourgeoisie*; the overdevelopment of monarchical-authoritarian patterns of government, resulting in a stifling of civic consciousness; the high prestige enjoyed by universities, giving an academic flavor to all intellectual movements; and the long-standing national preoccupation with religious controversy.[3]

The securely established *bourgeoisie* of England and the aggressively advancing *bourgeoisie* of France provided a solid social base for the Western European Enlightenment. A poet like Alexander Pope, or a man of letters like Voltaire, could appeal to an identifiably bourgeois reading public which demanded to be entertained as well as instructed as it lived its busy life in which time for reading had to compete with more practical interests. The authors of the German *Aufklärung* wrote, on the contrary, for a motley reading public composed of university professors, progressive bureaucrats, marginal intellectuals, and a *bourgeoisie* which was half-embryonic and half-decadent—all groups which did not make the same demand for literary quality. (This is one reason why this literature is read today by the specialist only.)

The principles of the Enlightenment could appeal to men of affairs as well as men of business in Western Europe. England was a self-governing country; France aspired to become one. Literature in both countries was expected, and could afford to be, political, practical, and down-to-earth. Its themes were usually drawn from real life and were expected to exercise specific influence here and now. The writers of the German *Aufklärung* wrote, on the contrary, for a public which could scarcely envisage self-government as yet; social and political protest was vigorous but remained naïvely unpolitical, as is shown by the fact that it rarely looked for remedies more realistic than a prayer that God should bless Germany with better princes. The over-all constellation of political and social forces in Germany—which will be analyzed in detail shortly—discouraged the discussion of public affairs despite some notable individual polemicists like the Göttingen professor Schlözer and the Berlin bookseller Nicolai.

Schlözer was one of Germany's leading public figures though he was a university professor rather than an active statesman. His central role in the spread of political *Aufklärung* was symptomatic of the role played by academic figures in the German movement from its very beginning. Christian Thomasius (1655-1728), generally considered the founder of the *Aufklärung*, was the son of a Leipzig professor and himself a professor at Halle. Christian Wolff (1679-1754), the great popu-

---

[3] The distinctive character of the German *Aufklärung* was ably analyzed by Karl Biedermann, *Deutschland im 18. Jahrhundert* (Leipzig, 1858), Vol. ii, Sect. 1, 381-83. This distinctive character did not, of course, preclude important—indeed decisive—French influence. See, for example, H. A. Korff, *Voltaire im literarischen Deutschland des 18. Jahrhunderts* (2 vols., Heidelberg, 1917-18).

larizer of Leibnitz and very embodiment of the *Aufklärung* spirit, taught philosophy at Halle and Marburg. The theological *Aufklärung* was championed by a long line of professors of theology, most prominently Johann Semler (1725-91), who also taught at Halle. This marriage between enlightened thought and respectable university establishments was unique to Germany and stood in sharp contrast to the situation in Western Europe. Universities in England and France stood at one of their periodic nadirs of intellectual influence. The scientific impulse given by Newton to Cambridge was quickly exhausted; Oxford, long the "home of lost causes and impossible loyalties," was impervious to the intellectual currents of the Enlightenment; while the Sorbonne was equally the stronghold of the French Obscurantist party. How different was the position of Schlözer's Göttingen, founded in 1737 with the deliberate purpose of training statesmen, administrators, and lawyers, while by no means neglecting the classical and scientific disciplines. Though Göttingen was untypical for Germany, it was widely admired as the kind of university which most other universities wanted to become; it quickly outpaced Halle as a center of *Aufklärung*. Its graduates spread its modern ideals, absorbed from Schlözer and a band of other distinguished professors, throughout German-speaking lands. It goes without saying that this professorial *Aufklärung* was of a thoroughly moderate character, and that its votaries feared the loss of respectability and tended to despise the "mob." They were "academic" in the sense of being proud of their culture and appealing pretty exclusively to an educated audience. They were afraid of the radicalism implied by their premises and tended to become frightened of their own courage as they attacked the *status quo.*

The German *Aufklärung* was primarily preoccupied with religious questions—a fact not surprising in a country still economically and politically "backward" and perennially preoccupied with confessional controversies. The absorption in religious polemics was a clear indication of the comparative youth of the German *Aufklärung*. In England the deistical controversy had raged at the end of the seventeenth century, while Voltaire's preoccupation with *Ecrasez l'Infame* was more characteristic of the early French Enlightenment than the age of Rousseau and Condorcet. The greatest figures of the German *Aufklärung* of the 1770's—men like Lessing, Nicolai, and Mendelssohn—were all primarily concerned with religious controversy and relatively indifferent to political and social questions. Their preoccupation was shared by broad sections of the reading public, as is demonstrated by the unending stream of religious and antireligious tracts which poured from Germany's printing presses. Only in Germany could an "enlightened" author complain that many people believed that *Aufklärung* was limited to the purification of religion:

> Many people think *only* of religion when they hear of *Aufklärung*. No reasonable man will deny . . . that *Aufklärung* is of course of the greatest importance in the field of religion. . . . But it must not be confined to this field; indeed one cannot conceive a thorough religious *Aufklärung* without the prior triumph of *Aufklärung* in many other fields of human life. The term [*Aufklärung*] extends far beyond the comparatively narrow field of religion.[4]

Another popular author provided a correction of the one-sided view deplored above by the following simple yet comprehensive definition of *Aufklärung*: "It is, put simply, the effort of the human mind to examine not only the world of *ideas* but rather of *all things* which exercise any influence upon human affairs, in accordance with the pure teachings of reason, and with a view to promoting whatever is useful."[5]

THE METHOD OF ATTACK

How was *Aufklärung* actually spread throughout Germany? The answer is: partly through dedicated private individuals who edited journals, wrote books and pamphlets, ran progressive schools, founded reading clubs, and organized secret societies; partly through the work of rulers who made the promotion of *Aufklärung* their public responsibility.

A band of devoted editors lived a heroic life under the adverse conditions of a small and scattered reading public, governmental censorship, and intense competition. The day of the specialized journal which appealed to a specialized (and therefore relatively stable) audience had not yet come; most journals competed directly with others, and attempted to provide a balanced intellectual diet which in practice

---

[4] G. N. Fischer, "Was ist Aufklärung?" *Berlinisches Journal für Aufklärung*, I, (Berlin, 1788), 26-27.

[5] A. Riem, *Über Aufklärung. Ob sie dem Staate—der Religion—oder überhaupt gefährlich sey, und seyn könne. Ein Wort zur Beherzigung für Regenten, Staatsmänner und Priester. Erstes Fragment* (Berlin 1788), p. 35. This simple definition may be compared with the more famous definitions of Moses Mendelssohn, "Was heisst Aufklärung?" *Berliner Monatsschrift* (Sept. 1784) and of Immanuel Kant, "Beantwortung der Frage:Was ist Aufklärung" (1784). Reprinted in *Kant's gesammelte Schriften*, edited by the Prussian Academy of Science (Berlin, 1912), VIII, 35-42. The latter is analyzed by G. Beyerhaus in "Kants Programm der Aufklärung aus dem Jahre 1784," *Kantstudien*, XXVI (1921), 1ff.

was usually a confused miscellany. An editor was expected to place his personal imprint upon a journal, and there was a recurring (and potentially fatal) danger that he would do most of the writing himself. The leading "enlightened" journals were A. L. Schlözer's *Briefwechsel, meist historischen und politischen Inhalts* (1776-82) and its successor, the famous *Staatsanzeigen* (1783-93); Wilhelm Ludwig Wekhrlin's short-lived successive *Chronologen* (1779-81), *Das Graue Ungeheure* (1784-87), and *Hyperboreische Briefe* (1788-90); Christian Schubert's *Deutsche Chronik* (1774-77) and—following his ten years of arbitrary imprisonment—*Vaterlands-Chronik* (1787-91); the *Berliner Monatsschrift* of J. E. Biester and Friedrich Gedike; and Friedrich Nicolai's *Allgemeine Deutsche Bibliothek* (1765-1806), a journal composed exclusively of book reviews but which in fact aimed at commenting on all aspects of life by liberally reviewing *all* books on *all* subjects.[6]

These editors, speaking for all "enlightened" men in the country, demanded the establishment of absolute freedom of the press. This was not only a professional interest if they were to carry out their work under reasonably predictable conditions; it also expressed their genuine conviction that free and unfettered *Publizität* (roughly, discussion of all public issues) was the royal road to progress. It must be stressed that eighteenth-century German editors usually had an idealistic and responsible conception of their calling, which they pursued in a self-sacrificing spirit despite frequent governmental harassment and chronic conflict with cost-conscious publishers. They were sustained by their belief that they were serving humanity rather than themselves, and naturally demanded full freedom to serve humanity.[7]

[6] Some information on all these publications may be found in the first volume of the pedestrian work by Ludwig Salomon, *Geschichte des Deutschen Zeitungswesens von den ersten Anfängen bis zur Wiederaufrichtung des Deutschen Reiches* (3 vols., 2nd edn., Leipzig, 1906). Only one of them, the *Berliner Monatsschrift*, has been studied thoroughly by modern scholars. See Joseph Hay, *Staat, Volk und Weltbürgertum in der Berlinischen Monatsschrift von F. Gedike und J. E. Biester* (Berlin, 1913), originally a Breslau dissertation; A. Hass, *Johann Erich Biester* (Frankfurt, 1925). See also the older study by E. Meyen, "Die Berliner Monatsschrift von Gedike und Biester. Ein Beitrag zur Geschichte des deutschen Journalismus," *Literarhistorisches Taschenbuch* (ed. R. E. Prutz), v (1847), 151-222, written from a distinctly Radical point of view. Meyen deplores that the BM fell short of its own principles in its refusal to give unconditional support to the French Revolution, social equality, and atheism.

[7] Several examples of the demand for absolute press freedom are given by W. Wenck, *Deutschland vor hundert Jahren* (1887), Vol. i, Ch. 2: "Fortschritte der politischen Aufklärung. Mittel und Wege," esp. pp. 77-83. The actual degree of freedom naturally differed from state to state; the Prussian case has been exhaustively analyzed by F. Etzin, "Die Freiheit der öffentlichen Meinung unter der Regierung Friedrichs des Grossen," *FBPG*, xxiii (1920-21), 89-129, 293-326.

The influence of journals, books, and pamphlets was greatly enhanced by the development of reading clubs. The conscientious archivist Josef Hansen has assembled some interesting information about these clubs in his monumental source collection about Rhenish conditions during the revolutionary period.[8] The surviving membership lists of the reading club at Trier show that it was composed of priests, professors, bureaucrats, city council members (*Stadträte*), and guild officials (*Schöffen*).[9] The records of the Mainz club reveal that it subscribed to twenty-three "scholarly journals" (*Gelehrte Zeitungen*), twenty-four political newspapers and gazettes, and 41 other periodicals (including several in French and one each in English and Italian).[10] It may be noted that all the reading clubs in the Rhineland asked and received the approbation of their governments before opening their doors; the princes and bishops approached were eager to secure an "enlightened" reputation by encouraging culture. The charge soon to be leveled against the reading clubs by Conservatives—that they were a conspiratorial network dedicated to the destruction of German society—was prima facie ridiculous. That they sought, however, to spread *Aufklärung* they did not deny; it was, indeed, their proudest boast.

The spirit of *Aufklärung* promoted an educational revolution in Germany, beginning with the founding of the Progressive *Philanthropin* at Dessau in 1774 by Johann Bernhard Basedow (1723-90)—a revolution which provoked endless discussion in German periodicals. The purpose of the Progressive schools was to allow the spontaneous development of the rational and benevolent faculties inherent in children (which in practice meant abandonment of conventional religious instruction), postponement of traditional subjects until pupils felt subjectively "ready" for them, and a classroom atmosphere notable for playfulness and indiscipline. Basedow was in chronic financial straits, though he made up in sense of mission and skillful self-advertising what he lacked in business acumen. One of his frequent public appeals for donations called his *Philanthropin* "an entail for cosmopolitans dedicated to the purpose—which no false modesty should conceal—of improving all posterity; while those nations which originally

---

[8] Josef Hansen, *Quellen zur Geschichte des Rheinlandes im Zeitalter der französischen revolution* (4 vols., Bonn, 1931-38), I, 16-37. There is no reason to believe that Rhenish conditions were in any way untypical, at least so far as the smaller states were concerned.

[9] Ibid., 37.   [10] Ibid., 16-17.

founded, or at least imitated *Philanthropine* will become unfailingly both famous and happy."[11]

It is of course impossible to measure the impact made by the *Aufklärung* upon the mind and heart of Germany; but it is clear that no thinking—and few unthinking—Germans of the second half of the eighteenth century could escape its impact. All of the leading intellectual figures of the age—Kant, Wieland, Lessing, Herder, Goethe, Schiller— were molded by it to a significant degree even if they attempted to resist its embrace. The over-all weakness of the German *Aufklärung* is shown, however, by the fact that it never produced leaders of a caliber equal to those of Western Europe. One vainly looks in Germany for a polemicist with the rapier thrust of Voltaire, a historian with the range and ironic gifts of Gibbon, a social philosopher with the depth of Montesquieu, an economist creating the comprehensive system of an Adam Smith, or an essayist with the charm and power of Diderot. The German intellectual giants most marked by the *Aufklärung* spirit all strove consciously to transcend the movement: Kant's critical philosophy gave a deathblow to its naïve rationalism; Herder's historicism overthrew its unhistorical way of looking at the world; while Lessing, though often hailed as the leading voice of the German *Aufklärung*, was in fact preoccupied with the problem of transcending what he felt was the shallowness of "natural religion." The movement never found a truly great leader; but it possessed several representative leaders, of whom the bookseller Friedrich Nicolai (1733-1811) may serve as an example. He was the leading *Aufklärer* of Berlin, the city which by broad consensus was considered the most "enlightened" in all of Germany; his commanding position requires a brief description of his career.[12]

---

[11] Quoted by J. G. Schlosser in his anti-Basedow article: "Schreiben an Herrn Rathschreiber Iselin über die Philanthropinen," *Ephemeriden der Menschheit*, I (1776), 28. On J. B. Basedow, see two contemporary biographies that appeared just after his death: H. Rathmann, *Beiträge zur Lebensgeschichte Basedows* (Magdeburg, 1791) and J. C. Meyer, *Leben, Charakter und Schriften Basedows* (2 vols., Hamburg, 1791-92). On the level of rural villages the greatest educational progress was registered in Prussia, where a progressive landlord, Rochow of Rekahn, took the lead. He described his famous school in a letter solicited by Iselin, the editor, in "Schreiben über seine Erziehungsanstalten," *Ephemeriden der Menschheit*, II (1777), 74-84.

[12] The standard work on Nicolai is the family biography by L. F. G. von Göckingk, *Friedrich Nicolai's Leben und literarischer Nachlass* (Berlin, 1820); the most famous attack on him is by J. G. Fichte, *Friedrich Nicolai's Leben und sonderbare Meinungen; ein Beitrag zur litterargeschichte des vergangenen und zur pädagogik des angehenden Jahrhunderts* (A. W. Schlegel, ed., Tübingen, 1801); a conventional modern criticism is Jacob Minor, "Christoph Friedrich

Nicolai was a man of superior native intelligence and superabundant energy who had reluctantly abandoned a scholarly career in order to take over the parental publishing house after the unexpected death of an older brother. His business acumen brought him financial success, though money was never a primary object for Nicolai (the famous gibe of Goethe and Schiller to the contrary notwithstanding).[13] He was a prominent member of Berlin society and used his social contacts with Frederician ministers like Hertzberg (Foreign Affairs) and Zedlitz (Culture) to suggest many properly "enlightened" candidates for vacant positions in the governmental service. Nicolai belonged to every Berlin organization worth belonging to, including the honorific Academy and the influential *Mittwochsgesellschaft*. Lessing, Mendelssohn, and a host of other authors were his intimate friends. His influence upon his contemporaries was enhanced by what most historians have considered his major flaw of character—his enviable cocksureness. Nicolai was never paralyzed by internal doubt, never hesitant about entering literary battle, never troubled about adding new enemies to his numerous old ones. A story of his later years is revealing in this respect. A friend told him that the philosopher Fichte had called him an old dog, only to be surprised when Nicolai agreed with his critic: "Yes indeed, I *am* a barking dog; a dog who raises his warning voice whenever there is something out of order in German literature."[14] Nicolai felt very much at ease in his enlightened Zion, never doubting that he was in secure possession of the whole truth and that all his opponents were fools at best and knaves at worst.

It was in this spirit that Nicolai published the most influential German review of its day, the *Allgemeine Deutsche Bibliothek*. It appeared —268 volumes—from 1765 to 1806 and wielded in its best period— around 1785—something akin to a literary dictatorship over at least Protestant Germany. Though never selling more than 2,500 copies, it reached a broad public because every reading club was certain to subscribe to it. Some significant regional circulation figures reveal the

---

Nicolai," in "Lessings Jugendfreunde" (Berlin and Stuttgart, n.d. [ca. 1883]), pp. 277-323; the best modern "rehabilitation" is Karl Aner, *Der Aufklärer Friedrich Nicolai* (Giessen, 1912). His controversy with Goethe is covered in Martin Sommerfeld, *Friedrich Nicolai und der Sturm und Drang. Ein Beitrag zur Geschichte der deutschen Aufklärung* (Halle, 1921); that with Kant and Fichte in Walter Strauss, *Friedrich Nicolai und die kritische Philosophie; ein Beitrag zur Geschichte der Aufklärung* (Stuttgart, 1927).

[13] Cf. the following sarcastic remark from the *Xenien*: "Hast du auch wenig genug verdient um die Bildung der Deutschen, Fritz Nicolai, sehr viel hast du dabei doch verdient."

[14] Quoted in Aner, op.cit., p. 30.

role played by religious confession in the German magazine market of the late eighteenth century. The *ADB* had 184 subscribers in Hamburg, 60 in Nürnberg, and 40 in Zurich (all Protestant cities), but only 23 in Catholic Vienna (despite Nicolai's effort to flatter Gerhard van Swieten, the court physician of Maria Theresia, by printing his portrait as a frontispiece of one of the issues). The *ADB* had some 400 contributors in its long life, a roster which included practically every "enlightened" man of letters in Germany; it sought to review all publications in every field of knowledge in a nonspecialized manner intelligible to the general reader. Its reviews frequently determined the success or failure of a book—a fact of which Nicolai, who selected his reviewers personally, was complacently aware.[15]

Nicolai's fame and power did not rest exclusively upon the *ADB*. He was himself a prolific and gifted writer, and above all the possessor of an uncanny instinct concerning what the German reading public wanted at any specific time. His didactic novels lampooned with equal vigor intolerant orthodoxy, mystical pietism, romantic enthusiasm, and manipulative Rosicrucianism; his main phobia, open and veiled, was the Jesuits, whom he feared in a manner suggesting a pathological obsession. Other enemies included Goethe, whose *Werther* Nicolai denounced as an irresponsible incitement to suicide, and Kant, whose high-flying metaphysics struck him as insufficiently utilitarian. He showed the self-confidence of the self-educated man in tackling one formidable foe after another, and he succeeded for many years in having the predominant voice of German public opinion—so long as it remained "enlightened"—on his side.[16]

Nicolai's fanatical rationalism and intolerant championing of tolerance ceased to be fashionable after about 1790. His later years constitute a sad anticlimax to a great career. The intellectuals of the rising romantic movement—figures like Schlegel and Schleiermacher—viewed him as a ridiculous anachronism. The eclipse of the Frederician *Aufklärung* after the succession of Frederick William II placed Nicolai in an uncomfortable and unaccustomed defensive position. The Ob-

---

[15] Günther Ost, *Friedrich Nicolai's Allgemeine Deutsche Bibliothek* (Berlin, 1928) is a model analysis of the editorial policy, circulation, and business side of the *ADB*, which wisely avoids the herculean task of a "content analysis."

[16] His main polemical works, usually presented in the form of a novel, are: *Sebaldus Nothanker* (3 vols., 1773-76), ridiculing orthodoxy and pietism; *Freuden des jungen Werther* (1775), attacking Goethe; *Feyner Kleyner Almanach* (2 vols., 1778-89), poking fun at the romantic discovery of the *Volkslied*; *Leben und Meinungen des Sempronius Gundibert, eines deutschen Philosophen* (1798), an attack upon Kant and Fichte; and *Vertraute Briefe von Adelheid B. an ihre Freundin Julie S* (1799), ridiculing romanticism.

scurantist policies of Wöllner forced the migration of the *ADB* in 1793 from Berlin to the more tolerant atmosphere of Danish Kiel. The journal never recovered from this blow, though it should be noted that it had begun to lose ground (even before it was driven abroad) to the better-edited *Jenaische Allgemeine Literatur Zeitung*. Nicolai failed to understand the spirit of the new age dawning in the 1790's; he had the misfortune to live long enough to preside over the piecemeal decline and finally collapse of his journal. It is best to ignore this later period when assaying the historical role of this indefatigable man, and to remember him as the clarion voice of the most strident period of the German *Aufklärung* in the two decades from 1770 to 1790.

The private promotion of *Aufklärung* was supplemented by its public promotion by rulers such as Frederick the Great and Joseph II, figures who gave great prestige to "enlightened despotism." Many of their policies were also pursued by several lesser princes, of whom Karl Friedrich of Baden (1728-1811) is an example.[17]

Karl Friedrich became ruler of the small Southwest German principality of Baden-Durlach at the age of ten in 1738, but did not assume effective personal rule until 1746. His almost legendary reputation rests in some part upon his successful territorial aggrandizement; his brilliant matrimonial policies, which made various granddaughters respectively a tsarina of Russia, a queen of Sweden, an electress of Bavaria, a duchess of Württemberg, and a grand duchess of Hessen; and his able piloting of his duchy through the storms of the Napoleonic era. He was, in short, a master of dynastic statecraft as it was practiced in the eighteenth century, and never neglected foreign in favor of domestic policy; yet his main interest and greatest pride lay in ameliorat-

---

[17] His reign has been studied with unusual thoroughness. See Carl William F. L. von Drais, *Geschichte der Regierung und Bildung von Baden unter Karl Friedrich vor der Revolution* (2 vols., Karlsruhe, 1816-18), a very full near-contemporary chronicle; A. Kleinschmidt, *Karl Friedrich von Baden* (Heidelberg, 1878), still the best biography; Friedrich v. Weech, "Karl Friedrich, Grossherzog von Baden," *ADB*, xv (1882), 241-48, a superb summary; two valuable studies by Wolfgang Windelband, *Staat und katholische Kirche in der Markgrafschaft Baden zur Zeit Karl Friedrichs* (Tübingen, 1912) and *Badische Finanz-und Wirtschaftspolitik zur Zeit des Markgrafen Karl Friedrich* (Erfurt, 1916); Willy Andreas, *Geschichte der badischen Verwaltungsorganisation und Verfassung 1802-18. Der Aufbau des Staates im Zusammenhang der allgemeinen Politik* (Leipzig, 1913), a great work in administrative history which throws much light upon the pre-1802 period as well. The best discussion of the ideological roots of "enlightened absolutism" (not specifically related to Baden) is still Hans von Voltelini, "Die naturrechtlichen Lehren und die Reformen des 18. Jahrhunderts," *HZ*, cv (1910), 65-104, though the author goes to absurd pains to show that reforms in Germany went back to the natural-law doctrines of Pufendorf and Wolff rather than the Western European Enlightenment.

ing the condition of his subjects in accordance with the principles of the *Aufklärung*. Their influence can be traced in his educational, philanthropic, and religious policies.

Karl Friedrich established a special educational fund in 1749 to improve teachers' salaries and to fill the vast gaps which still existed in the Badenese system of popular education. Some sixty new schools were built in the forty years from 1750 to 1790 with the deliberate but as-yet utopian aim of abolishing illiteracy. A special seminar for training teachers was opened in 1768, and promising young teachers were sent to Basedow's *Philanthropin* at Dessau to observe the most progressive educational techniques. Karl Friedrich was especially proud of the *Gymnasium* of his capital city of Karlsruhe; he sometimes visited classes, personally participated in examining the pupils, and invited successful teachers to social gatherings at the palace. His court set a distinguished example of cultural and intellectual activity. The duke himself was deeply interested in political and economic theory, and even wrote an anonymous economic treatise which was republished as recently as 1908.[18] His duchess, the admirable Karoline Luise (1723-83), was a great art collector and a passionate botanist. Karlsruhe became a favorite visiting place for leading intellectual figures like Voltaire, Goethe, and Herder. Its cultural resources—court library, art gallery, and collection of natural specimens—were made readily accessible to the general public.

Karl Friedrich's philanthropic policies were characteristic of the humanitarian temper of the *Aufklärung* at its best. The use of torture was formally abolished in 1767. Conditions in the hitherto indescribably filthy prisons were substantially improved. A great advance in the treatment of lunatics was made by the humane measure of separating them from ordinary criminals. Karl Friedrich also took pity upon the sad plight of the widows of bureaucrats, who had hitherto often sunk from a comfortable prosperity to beggary after the death of their husbands; they henceforth received pensions upon a regular schedule. Karl Friedrich acted, it may be added, in the tradition of "enlightened absolutism" by not hesitating to employ authoritarian coercion to make his subjects happy, as when he introduced fire insurance upon a compulsory basis.

The same may be said of his economic policies, though he looked upon coercion as a purely transitional phenomenon while his subjects were still unprepared for full economic freedom. He himself took the

[18] *Abrégé des principes de l'économie politique* (1772), new edition edited by the German land reformer Damaschke (1908).

lead in founding experimental factories when his subjects showed no spontaneous desire to follow the progressive example of England; he justified protective tariffs by the "infant industries" argument. Agriculture remained, however, closest to his heart. The duke turned some of his own lands into experimental farms, and took a personal interest in the introduction of novel farming methods. He was deeply influenced by the economic doctrines of the Physiocrats, and was eager to put their theories into practice. After corresponding with Dupont de l'Eure and the elder Mirabeau (two leading Physiocrats), Karl Friedrich decreed the introduction of some key Physiocratic doctrines (the single tax upon land, free choice of profession, et cetera) in three small Badenese communities in 1769. Though the experiment did not prove an unqualified success, it did not discourage the duke from engaging in further reforms. Serfdom was formally abolished in 1783 upon Karl Friedrich's personal initiative, a measure which provoked an outpouring of loyalty from his grateful subjects—to which Karl Friedrich replied graciously that it was his pleasure to preside over "a free, opulent, moral and Christian people."[19]

It should be stressed that the duke was very much the enlightened despot in all these measures. He had no intention of transferring his princely powers to the people of Baden; his political reforms, which came only toward the end of his long reign, aimed exclusively at administrative rationalization and at no time contemplated any advance toward self-government. Karl Friedrich lived and died as a benevolent autocrat who believed that his personal rule was far more "enlightened" than any elected government was likely to be.

This was certainly borne out by the popular opposition offered to his exceptionally tolerant religious policy. Karl Friedrich himself was a rationalist Protestant before developing in middle age a pietist mystical streak under the influence of Lavater, a frequent visitor to his court. He was driven, however, by both principle and interest to seek good relations with his Catholic subjects. The court provided funds for the building of a Catholic school and church in the previously solidly Protestant residential city of Karlsruhe—an action which earned Karl Friedrich the gratitude of both the Vatican and Count Limburg-Styrum, bishop of nearby Speyer. The Protestant Church flourished during his reign under a new *Kirchenrathsinstruktion* which combined a latitudinarian tolerance in matters of dogma with insistence upon a necessary minimum of uniformity in ritual and catechetical instruction.

[19] Quoted by v. Weech in *ADB*, xv, 243.

In all these ways Karl Friedrich acted as a conspicuous champion of *Aufklärung*. His policies were truly impressive; yet the man was more impressive still. He combined a passionate zeal for the happiness of his subjects with restless practical energy and a profound grasp of the theories of the *Aufklärung*. His cosmopolitan culture and wide travel in England and Holland never made him feel superior to the parochial problems of his native Baden. Karl Friedrich showed that a high devotion to the interests of the state was not incompatible with deep concern for the individual welfare of each of its members. His long reign of sixty-five years gave time for his policies to mature and yield maximum results. These showed dramatically how much progress could be made on the *Aufklärung* road within the lifetime of a single enlightened ruler.

SOURCES OF ATTACK OTHER THAN THE AUFKLÄRUNG

The attack upon the German *status quo* during the second half of the eighteenth century was primarily conducted in the name of *Aufklärung*; but this was not the only source of attack. Certain other currents of thought, while critical of the *Aufklärung*, frequently shared its antipathies. Here one must consider, above all, the interrelated movements of the poetic *Sturm und Drang*, the pre-romantic cult of the common man, and the rise of German national feeling in opposition to upper-class "Gallomania."

The *Sturm und Drang* was the expression of the buoyant spirit of a young generation of poets which came of age in the 1770's. The struggle between generations has been especially acute throughout modern German history, whether one thinks of the *Sturm und Drang*, the *Burschenschaften* after 1815, the Young Germany of the 1830's, or the Wilhelminian *Jugendbewegung*. The common theme of all these youth movements has been a hostility to philistine complacency and "bourgeois" respectability; the common failing, an inability to cope with the real political and social problems confronting German society—a fact attested by the chronic escape into a romantic and essentially unpolitical idealism. The *Sturm und Drang* began as a literary protest against the narrow dictates of the Gottschedian school of criticism: it was a declaration of independence on the part of artists claiming the right to original creation unfettered by literary conventions. The movement quickly broadened into a protest against a society where convention appeared as a stifling force, as was undoubtedly the case with German middle-class life. It is idle to argue about whether the *Sturm und Drang* was a bourgeois force of liberation (as Marxists tend to assert), or an antibourgeois protest against bourgeois respectability (the more common view of literary historians). What is certain is that its champions rebelled against the German *status quo* as they pitted spontaneity against conventional rules, enthusiastic emotion against utilitarian reason, and the claims of individuality against stereotyped patterns of behavior. Every one of their values—spontaneity, enthusiasm, and individuality—was to characterize the Conservative thought of the future; yet it would be foolish to label the *Sturm und Drang* as intrinsically Conservative on that account. It expressed, rather, in an unusually sharp form the perennial protest of individualists against the conventional shackles which everywhere confine life; it constituted a protest against the existing social order in the name of freedom, not in the name of any competing scheme of social order. Its political purpose, insofar as it possessed a political purpose, was anarchical rather than radical in content; and it abhorred what it took to be the rationalism, utilitarianism, and philistinism of the *Aufklärung*.[20]

The authors of the *Sturm und Drang* discovered the common man as a literary hero and attractive social type. This was partly due to the attraction of opposites, partly an anticipation of the romantic view of the dysgenic character of civilization. The poets of the *Sturm und Drang* and their favorite literary creations—for example, Werther—were complicated characters psychologically, torn by internal doubt and conflict, and frequently oscillating between an euphoric feeling of joy and a gloomy mood of cosmic despair. They often proved incapable of maintaining that minimum of routine and steadiness in their personal lives which is essential for a useful human existence. It was easy for them to look with nostalgic envy upon the common man—and more especially the simple peasant—who was spared all the agonies of the "romantic hero" as he lived a healthy, tranquil, practical, God-fearing life in intimate contact with the beauties of nature. The rising school of preromanticism turned these nostalgic attitudes into a theory. The preromantics condemned all the so-called "progressive" forces which had created a society in which men were increasingly di-

[20] Space does not permit listing the numerous useful works about the *Sturm und Drang*. The best introduction is A. H. Korff, *Die Dichtung von Sturm und Drang im Zusammenhang der Geistesgeschichte* (Leipzig, 1928). The problem of the social basis of the literature of the period is discussed brilliantly (though, I believe, with needlessly subtle distinctions) by Fritz Brüggemann, "Der Kampf um die bürgerliche Welt und Lebensanschauung in der deutschen Literatur des 18. Jahrhunderts," *DVSLG*, III (1925), 94-127. A good English introduction is Ludwig Kahn, *Social Ideals in German Literature 1770-1830* (New York, 1930), Ch. 2. G. Stockmeyer, *Soziale Probleme im Drama des Sturm und Dranges* (Frankfurt, 1922) is an especially useful monograph.

vorced from nature, alienated from God, chained to an artificial urban environment, and divided in soul if they preserved a soul. The ensuing cult of the common (rural) people included an implicit, and increasingly explicit, critique of the belief in progress so dear to the *Aufklärung*—a critique voiced most powerfully by Jean Jacques Rousseau in his *Discourse on the Moral Effects of the Arts and Sciences* (1750), which was widely read in Germany.[21]

The cult of the common man, and the accompanying hostility to modernity, was sometimes accompanied by an ideological consecration of the rural *status quo*. Often, but not always; for a deep sympathy with the lower classes (and especially the peasantry) easily led to criticism of the various types of aristocratic exploitation practiced in the countryside. It would be absurd to depict Rousseau and his German disciples as Conservative thinkers because Conservative elements abounded in their thought. They were obviously motivated by a "Radical" hostility to injustice, a deep sympathy for the victims of exploitation, and an abiding hatred of the relics of feudalism. The romantic cult of the peasant was in practice often associated with the Radical criticism of anachronistic social conditions; romantic poet and rationalist reformer, however far apart in their ultimate vision of society, were frequently agreed in their criticism of the rural *status quo*.[22]

The rise of national sentiment was inevitably accompanied by a criticism of the German cultural situation. The upper classes of German society had been thoroughly Gallicized in the age of Louis XIV. At many courts, of which Prussia was the best-known example, only French was spoken: French literature, French tutors, French cooks, and even French mistresses were all at a premium in polished society throughout Germany. Where national sentiment existed it was widely considered a rather boorish form of provincialism. The protest against French ways in the name of German nationality began in literature, where French poetic forms stifled the creative impulses of the poets of the *Sturm und Drang*; but it easily entered the sphere of social and political criticism as well. The denunciation of the dissolute manners and morals of the Gallicized upper classes in the name of simple "German morality" was in substance not very different from the "enlight-

[21] The best introduction to Rousseau's influence upon German thought is still L. Levy-Bruhl, "L'influence de J. J. Rousseau en Allemagne," *Annales de l'école libre des sciences politiques*, II (1887), 325-58.

[22] A good example of the "discovery of the common people" leading to a criticism of the *status quo* (though not necessarily specific reform demands) is Friedrich Müller, *Idyllen* (ed., O. Heuer, 3 vols., Leipzig, 1914), esp. "Das Nuss-Kernen, eine pfälzische Idylle," in III, 59-152.

ened" criticism based upon the principles of equality. The criticism of monarchical absolutism as a French import, advanced in the name of the old tradition of German liberty, could win the approval of many *Aufklärers*. In both cases nationalism could be—though it was not necessarily—combined with adherence to the *Aufklärung* program of eliminating social privilege and advancing constitutional self-government.

The three literary currents mentioned contributed to the widespread criticism of the German *status quo* in the second half of the eighteenth century. Their alliance with the program of the *Aufklärung* was, however, strictly of an *ad hoc* character. They could be and were all incorporated into the new Conservatism when it came to maturity. Nationalism was to become the strongest asset of nineteenth-century Conservatism; cosmopolitanism and imitation of the "advanced" countries of Western Europe (especially France), the gravest embarrassment for German Radicalism. The exposure of the hollow character of the alleged "progressiveness" of modern society and the exaltation of the "unspoiled" character of rural life both became stocks in trade of German Conservatism. The sentiments of the *Sturm und Drang*—irrationalism, spontaneity, antiutilitarianism—proved central in the emergence of Conservatism. It will be desirable, however, before studying this emergence to examine briefly the social milieu in which German Conservatism first arose.

The Constellation of Social Forces

We have just examined the development of the German *Aufklärung* and its method of attack upon the *status quo*; the function of this section is to place this attack in the social framework of eighteenth-century Germany. Historical experience shows that the spread of religious, social, and political ideas is quite independent of their "truth" —even supposing there is such a thing as "truth" outside of the natural sciences. This spread depends, rather, upon the degree to which ideas express the interests (economic or psychological) of certain groups (or at least what they "subjectively" *believe* to be their interests, whether or not "objectively" verifiable). It will prove useful, therefore, to provide a brief analysis of what social groups were likely either to welcome or oppose enlightened ideas in this period. What groups were progressive? What groups were ambivalent? What groups were likely to be hostile to the new ideas? Among the (at least potentially) progressive groups must be reckoned entrepreneurs, the embryonic proletariat, and intellectuals; among ambivalent groups,

47

university professors, bureaucrats, professionals, and clergymen; among "Conservative" groups, princes and courtiers, aristocrats and officers, urban patricians and guild masters, and that broad mass of peasants with whom the "cake of custom" was still unbroken. It goes without saying that such a general categorization is subject to many individual exceptions, and fails to touch upon the crucial problem of the intensity (as contrasted with the substantive content) of political belief. A brief survey of the characteristics of these groups, even if clichés and stereotypes cannot be avoided, should help in understanding the spread of *Aufklärung* in Germany and the opposition which it provoked.[23]

PROGRESSIVE SOCIAL FORCES

The progressive forces in German life consisted potentially of the entrepreneurial class, the lower class of the towns, and, above all, the intelligentsia. There were, however, special reasons why none of these groups was able (or, in some cases, willing) to exercise much political influence—a fact absolutely crucial for the understanding of German affairs during this period.

The capitalistic entrepreneurs were without question the most dynamic class in German life; one must not, however, exaggerate either their economic importance or political drive. It must always be remembered that Germany remained an overwhelmingly agricultural country until the middle of the nineteenth century and that more than 85% of the population still lived in the countryside in 1770. The territorial divisions of Germany constituted a formidable handicap to the development of industry, while the prevalent mercantilist system gave little scope to individual enterprise, since the state exercised the key role in German economic life.

Over and above the low level of economic development there were further reasons why the entrepreneurs could exercise only an insignificant political influence. They were, to begin with, a most heterogeneous group, whether one looks at their social origins or the nature

[23] This entire section is based upon secondary sources rather than primary research, and aims only at providing a background survey. It owes much to the standard works on the eighteenth century by Karl Biedermann (Vol. I, 1854), C. T. Perthes (1945), K. T. Heigel (1899), and W. H. Bruford (1935); the modern economic histories of J. Kulischer (1928 2nd edn., 1958), F. Lütge (1952 2nd edn., 1960), H. Bechtel (1956), and H. Haussherr (1954 3rd edn., 1960); and, above all, the brilliant work of Rudolf Vierhaus, *Deutschland vor der französischen Revolution*, whose Ch. 2, "Das soziale Gefüge," supersedes all earlier treatments. I am grateful to Professor Vierhaus for letting me read his manuscript prior to its publication.

of their economic operations—two factors which prevented a sense of solidarity and common outlook. One can find among the "private entrepreneurs" successful merchants, aspiring guildsmen, reckless adventurers, enterprising Jews, and numerous descendants of Huguenot refugees. Many enterprises (especially in the field of mining) were owned by princes or individual nobles and therefore operated by civil servants or dependent agents, whose outlook was very different from that of private manufacturers. There were also great differences between those who administered the "putting out" system—coordinating the decentralized work of predominantly rural artisans—and those who established centrally located "factories," usually with privileges conferred by the state. Both groups had in common only a high degree of dependence upon mercantilistic governments which intervened constantly in such fields as labor regulation, tariffs, and the supply of raw materials—a condition which certainly militated against the development of an independent outlook. The entrepreneurs' interest in political questions was further diminished by their divorce from local roots, as the need to escape from annoying guild regulations forced the migration of industry from city to countryside; in the rare cases where political interest did exist, it lacked any opportunity for institutional expression; and the entrepreneurs were generally a rather poorly educated class with limited horizons. The complete absorption in their work limited their developing of nonprofessional interests, while contact with the intellectual world of the *Aufklärung* remained superficial. The habit of relying upon the powerful and predominantly benevolent state, and a deference toward the often highly trained bureaucrats with whom they came into official contact, made most entrepreneurs instinctively Conservative or (what was practically the same thing) completely unpolitical. Their dynamic economic function was quite compatible with an unbroken traditionalism in other spheres of life; hence the entrepreneurial class did not give much direct impetus to the cause of *Aufklärung*.

Some older capitalist groups proved somewhat more accessible to the new ideas. One may mention merchants with international connections, whose knowledge of foreign countries had broken their provincialism and made them aware of German backwardness compared to the "progressive West"; also banking circles, whose professional work required a modernity and flexibility of outlook. Both groups suffered, however, from the same dependence upon the mercantilistic state as the entrepreneurs; both included a considerable proportion of Jews as yet incapable of even contemplating an independent political role.

The same political impotence was characteristic of the incipient German proletariat which arose *pari passu* with the entrepreneurial class. It was so downtrodden as to be incapable of any political action going beyond a local riot. Widespread illiteracy, as well as the daily struggle for existence, precluded participation in *Aufklärung* ideas; indeed, traditionalist prejudices, especially of a confessional character, made urban mobs the easy instrument of obscurantist agitators. The social origins of this proletariat were at least as heterogeneous as those of the entrepreneurial class. When factories were first established, the state often provided the entrepreneurs with orphans and jailbirds as a labor supply; this would be supplemented by miserable artisans (especially those who could not become even journeymen), escaped or dispossessed serfs, beggars, and vagabonds. The "putting-out" system relied upon the full or part-time services of ruined guildsmen and redundant rural laborers. These unpromising social materials defied organization and could scarcely be led toward constructive political purposes. Their backbreaking economic work was crucial in building the Germany of the future; but they can nonetheless be practically disregarded when one analyzes the constellation of political forces in the last third of the eighteenth century.

In Germany, as in other underdeveloped societies, the main Radical group consisted of a numerous but rather amorphous intelligentsia—a class hard to define because it lacked any specific relationship to the forces of production (the usual criterion for defining classes). The German intelligentsia may be said to have included all those who possessed higher education but failed to win participation in a recognized, secure, and respectable profession (such as the bureaucracy, clergy, and university professorate). The intelligentsia in this sense included many transitional alongside its permanent members. The transitional group consisted of most students as well as a good many university graduates during the years spent waiting for respectable employment. The student body of German universities was divided into two groups which had relatively little in common: the sons of aristocrats and urban patricians, who usually concentrated upon legal studies and could rely upon family influence in finding jobs after (or even before) graduation; and the far larger group of the "academic proletariat" which concentrated upon theology or the liberal arts and faced a most uncertain future. The former group no doubt contained some individuals with a Radical outlook, a Radicalism often stimulated by the brief period of "privileged freedom" between the authoritarian family experienced in childhood and the well-defined social norms of adult life. This

50

Radicalism was, however, more often one of personal conduct (cheating artisans, seducing lower-class girls, intoning republican hymns of defiance to tyrants) than of deeply felt political conviction.

The Radicalism of the "academic proletariat" was of a sterner quality because it was rooted in a very different life experience. University study meant for the able and the ambitious an opportunity to climb a rung on the social ladder; but it was an opportunity accompanied by prolonged material sacrifice and personal humiliation as aristocratic students did little to conceal their contempt for their starving fellows. A widespread bitterness was enflamed by the knowledge that graduation would not bring the end of social travail; it was generally followed by years of private tutoring or degrading junior ecclesiastical employment, a period often blighted by nagging doubt whether one would ever "arrive" in a world where connection counted for more than personal merit. The intelligentsia here analyzed was naturally permeated by *Aufklärung* ideas which expressed its own discontent. Its private Radicalism of conviction was, however, usually restrained in public for fear of antagonizing the future bestowers of possible favors.[24]

The permanent members of the intelligentsia were university graduates who "failed to arrive" or deliberately embarked upon the precarious literary profession. Contemporaries estimated that there were between 3,000 and 6,000 professional authors in Germany around 1780 —a number which included a goodly proportion of journalists and pitiable hack writers. It was virtually impossible for even very distinguished authors to live from the sale of their writings: the reading public was numerically small, the market suffocated by excess supply, and a national copyright law unknown (and impossible to achieve in view of Germany's territorial divisions). This situation forced authors to seek jobs as court poets, librarians, or political secretaries, all positions dependent upon the favor of the mighty. Many strove to secure posts as bureaucrats or clergymen which would leave them enough leisure to continue writing; but most remained in a hopelessly insecure position as literary vagabonds. It was from this group that Germany

---

[24] An especially valuable study of the intelligentsia is Hans Gerth, *Die sozialgeschichtliche Lage der bürgerlichen Intelligenz um die Wende des 18. Jahrhunderts. Ein Beitrag zur Soziologie des deutschen Frühliberalismus* (Frankfurt, 1935). A critical contemporary account is Ernst Brandes, *Über den Einfluss und die Wirkung des Zeitgeistes auf die höheren Stände Deutschlands* (2 vols., Hannover, 1810), II, 193-250. (The section is entitled "Die Schriftsteller".) A useful contribution to the understanding of the hard lot of lower-class university graduates is Franz Neumann, *Der Hofmeister, ein Beitrag zur Geschichte der Erziehung im 18. Jahrhundert* (Halle, 1930).

51

was inundated by a flood of books, pamphlets, magazines, and fly sheets which propagated the cause of *Aufklärung*.

AMBIVALENT SOCIAL FORCES

Of far greater importance for the spread of *Aufklärung* than entrepreneurs, proletarians, and intelligentsia were significant portions of four groups whose prevailing outlook must be considered Conservative: university professors, bureaucrats, professionals, and clergymen. There were special reasons why individuals in these groups should be accessible to Progressive ideas. Their members were usually professionally concerned with books and ideas, and proud of constituting the intellectual vanguard of the nation; their contact with English and French literature often made them feel the backwardness of Germany and stimulated a desire to catch up. This intellectually motivated Progressivism was often reinforced by specific social circumstances. University professors were notable for their geographical and social mobility, two factors incompatible with traditionalism. There was, moreover, an intense competition among universities for the services of genuinely distinguished teachers; among the attractions offered was freedom from censorship and the opportunity to engage in state-financed foreign travel. The professorate remained predominantly a stuffy, pedantic, privileged, and hence thoroughly Conservative group; but many of its most distinguished members became champions of *Aufklärung*. The faculties of theology usually included several pronounced Liberals, and the faculties of law had at least a sprinkling of men whose attachment to natural law led to a criticism of the *status quo*. New chairs for political economy (*Kameralistik*) began to be established after 1770, and they were usually occupied by men who believed in the novel doctrine of laissez-faire rather than the old practice of mercantilism. Philosophy chairs were practically monopolized by followers of Christian Wolff until the proliferation of the Kantian school in the 1790's. Most Philosophical Faculties fell under the domination of the neohumanist school radiating from Heyne, the great Göttingen classicist, after about 1770. An "enlightened" tendency was promoted by the fact that the pre-Christian world of antiquity had much in common with the post-Christian world of the *Aufklärung*. It is certain that the vast majority of German students during the last third of the eighteenth century came into some contact with "enlightened ideas" in the course of their university studies.

This proved one reason why a considerable number of upper bureaucrats (all university-trained) had a remarkably enlightened outlook in this period; in fact, one must view the bureaucracy as the single most important Progressive force in Germany at the end of the eighteenth century. Aspiring bureaucrats usually entered the service (increasingly through competitive examination) after several years of university study; their motivation was as frequently an idealistic desire to serve mankind as a personal desire to make a career for themselves. Their employment (at least in such large monarchies as Prussia and Austria) pried them loose from any local roots as they were sent, as a matter of policy, to parts of the country far removed from their place of birth; while it was customary, especially for citizens of smaller states, to take service in states other than their own. It has often been noted that most of the Prussian reformers after 1806 were not Prussians by birth; Stein was a Free Knight from Nassau, Hardenberg a Hannoverian noble, Niebuhr the son of a German-Danish explorer. The reputation for *Aufklärung* possessed by Frederician Prussia attracted many able men to her service. Their self-respect required that they view themselves as servants of the law and the general welfare rather than instruments of the king's arbitrary whim: their "enlightened" emphasis upon the *Rechtsstaat* arose as frequently from personal pride as from attachment to law and justice. They were also concerned with winning a secure legal status for themselves as a group; the idea of tenure upon good behavior required a preliminary "enlightened" curtailment of arbitrary despotism. The very nature of bureaucracy—a trained group devoted to rational administration—tended to promote legal equality among its members. Promotion was, ideally at least, to be based upon individual achievement rather than aristocratic birth or royal favor. Another factor which led some bureaucrats to *Aufklärung* was their contact with practical affairs. Mercantilistic administrators sometimes saw the value of laissez-faire as they confronted the rigidities created by state paternalism; this was true of a man like Stein's collaborator, Theodor von Schön, whose contact with the grain-exporting Junkers of East Prussia made him a convert to the doctrines of free trade.

A tendency to Progressive views was, however, frequently counteracted by other considerations. The conception that bureaucrats were essentially servants of the community rather than the prince was still in its infancy, and in smaller territories (whether despotic or patriarchal) virtually unknown. The very excellence of many bureaucrats in terms of education and professional competence led easily to an arrogant attitude of superiority compatible with *good* government but utterly hostile to the idea of *self*-government. "Everything *for* the peo-

ple, nothing *by* the people" was the motto of many of the best bureaucrats: their very devotion to "enlightened" policies made them
hostile to any erosion of the authoritarian *Obrigkeitsstaat* through increased popular participation in public affairs. Were mobs led by
demagogues as "enlightened" as bureaucrats motivated by zeal for the
general welfare? A further element tending toward a Conservative outlook was the above-mentioned desire for a secure professional status;
it led to a hostility to despotism but also to a drive for exclusive (and
increasingly hereditary) status. This tendency was most evident in the
notorious *Schreiberkaste* of Württemberg, but it was not unknown
even in the "exemplary" Prussian bureaucracy. It betrayed that very
principle of "accessibility to talent" so largely responsible for what
excellence the bureaucracy possessed.[25]

To generalize about the political outlook of the professions is very
difficult. Doctors and lawyers were frequently in the enviable position of possessing a high social and economic position without the need
to work very hard; their leisure time frequently went into reading and
writing. Their autonomous intellectual interests frequently led them
to hold—and sometimes to advocate—"enlightened" opinions. Doctors tended to be proud of their scientific outlook with its emancipation from prescientific obscurantism; lawyers were often appalled by
the chaotic complexity of existing law and hence attracted to the simple conceptions of natural law, which offered a yardstick for cleaning
up the legal rubbish inherited from the past. These factors were frequently counteracted by the natural identification of doctors with their
patients and lawyers with their clients. It may be added that national
professional associations, with their encouragement of uniformity of
opinion (usually in a Conservative direction) were as yet unknown in
Germany, and that the political views of doctors and lawyers were
consequently a highly individual matter.

Great differences of outlook existed within the clergy, partly on the
confessional line separating Protestant and Catholic, but even more
on the social line separating bishops and superintendents from the
lower clergy. It is a commonplace that the Catholic parts of Germany

---

[25] The discussion of the bureaucracy owes much to the brilliant work of Hans
Gerth, op.cit., Ch. 2. I have also drawn upon the earlier treatments by K. Biedermann, *Deutschland*, Vol. I, Ch. 3 (Leipzig, 1854); S. Isaaksohn, *Geschichte des
preussischen Beamtentums* (2 vols., Leipzig, 1873-78); A. Lotz, *Geschichte des
deutschen Beamtentums* (Berlin, 1909); the important work of Hans Rosenberg,
Bureaucracy, Aristocracy, and Autocracy. The Prussian Experience 1660-1815
(Cambridge, 1958), which debunks many "Borussian legends"; and the thorough
articles by Walter Dorn, "The Prussian Bureaucracy in the Eighteenth Century,"
Political Science Quarterly, XLVI (1931).

were less "enlightened" than the Protestant lands and that this was obviously due to the hostility of the Catholic Church to the *Aufklärung*; but it should not be forgotten that in the 1780's several Catholic states were catching up fast at the very time when the *Aufklärung* was put on the defensive by Wöllner in its Prussian stronghold. The Catholic clergy of the eighteenth century was in fact a sharply divided body where a small, potentially "enlightened" group (mostly at the top of the hierarchy) confronted a large mass of pure traditionalists among monks and parish clergy. The upper group consisted of bishops, aristocratic canons, and abbots—men who differed from secular princes and aristocrats in little but their celibate status and the occasional conduct of ecclesiastical services. Their prevalent Conservatism was rooted in their participation in a privileged *status quo* they naturally wished to preserve. This did not preclude some bishops from acting, in their other role as territorial princes, exactly like secular "enlightened" despots in advancing religious toleration (!), rational economic policies, and the spread of education—in short, measures to promote the general welfare as the eighteenth century understood that term. A bishop like Dalberg, regent of Erfurt, sought and found the applause of his "enlightened" contemporaries rather than of Rome.

The lower Catholic clergy was very traditionalist in its background and convictions. It was recruited largely from the peasantry, a class deeply suspicious of modernity; entry into the clergy usually constituted a social rise for the individual and naturally involved gratitude to the Church which had made this possible. Celibacy precluded concern for the social rise of one's children—a consideration which made Protestant clergymen personally interested in a relaxation of social barriers. The education of the lower clergy was often so primitive as to exclude contact with modern ideas, while the unstimulating life of the parish discouraged intellectual interests and made enlarged horizons the exception rather than the rule. The same must be said about the vast army of monks and nuns, who additionally had reason to resent the incessant "enlightened" attack directed not only against the abuses (real or alleged) of their mode of life, but against their mode of life per se. Defense proved useless against secularist critics who denied the salvationist and other-worldly premises which provided the very *raison d'être* of monastic life.

Two groups in the lower Catholic clergy became champions of *Aufklärung*. Some clerics were influenced by their reading to succumb to the *Weltanschauung* prevalent among those who claimed the title of "educated"—a danger all the greater because decadent scholasticism, which continued to dominate the curriculum of Catholic seminaries, offered little effective defense against modernity. Such "enlightened" priests sought to reform their Church from the inside, only to find frequently that their desire to *reform* Catholicism proved the first stage in its *repudiation*. The second, more numerous group of "enlightened" priests were the so-called "Josephine clergy," priests who became "enlightened" more through external command than internal conviction. The Emperor Joseph, and the other Catholic princes who followed his example, wanted a clergy more conspicuous for secular usefulness than spiritual fervor. They valued priests as preachers of morality, educators, promoters of agricultural improvement, census takers, et cetera— all useful functions, no doubt, but not requiring for their performance a priesthood possessing the supernatural power to administer sacraments. The Josephine clergy became, at any rate, an indispensable instrument in the hands of secular rulers bent upon forwarding the cause of *Aufklärung*, but this type probably remained a minority even in Austria. The bulk of the upper as well as lower Catholic clergy must be reckoned natural supporters of some type of Conservatism. They frankly viewed *Aufklärung* as the work of the Devil bent upon destruction of God's holy Church, and used their still unchallenged position in the countryside to influence their parishioners (who scarcely needed influencing) in this sense.[26]

Most of the Protestant clergy found itself in the position of the Josephine priesthood—of being valued by the government more for its secular usefulness than for its traditional ecclesiastical function. The gap between the Protestant upper and lower clergy was not quite so great as in the Catholic Church. There were (with insignificant exceptions) no prince-bishops or aristocratic canons in Lutheran Germany, and the leading ecclesiastical positions were often accessible to talent even when unaccompanied by aristocratic birth. The lower clergy was recruited from a higher social base than its Catholic equivalents (with sons of pastors tending to predominate); it was certainly less closely attached to the peasantry with its traditionalist ways. The gap between superintendent and village pastors remained substantial, nonetheless. One must avoid any rosy view of the condition of the ordinary Protestant village pastor. The low level of theological examinations made entry into the clergy easy for anyone who had sat through

[26] An exceptionally balanced statement of the "condition of Catholic Germany" is to be found in the article by Max Braubach, "Die kirchliche Aufklärung im katholischen Deutschland im Spiegel des 'Journal von und für Deutschland' (1784-1792)," *Historisches Jahrbuch*, LIV (1934), 1-63, 178-220. See also Ch. 3.

the required number of university lectures, while the mode of life of the rural pastor led to intellectual atrophy. Appointment depended upon patronage, a system inviting grave abuse; it was not unknown for marriage to a lord's discarded mistress being made a condition for accepting a living. Salaries were low and often paid in devalued currency; families, large and providing for them a major distraction from more spiritual concerns. Pastors were expected to be "maids of all work," exactly as was the case with the Josephine priesthood. The undignified situation of many of the clergy made for a good deal of individual bitterness but led only rarely to the explicit advocacy of Radical political or social views. The Protestant lower clergy was certainly a harassed and dependent group, but it was not completely lacking in status; and there was always the hope that the next generation might do better.

The upper group of Protestant clergymen—superintendents, *Konsistorialräte*, court preachers, and *Hauptpastoren* of major churches—may be described as a contented part of the upper *bourgeoisie*, with whom they harmonized in outlook, mode of life, and family interest. Their children frequently became state officials or university professors, and they could mix on equal social terms with the best of the nonaristocratic world. There were few social contacts with aristocrats, from whom they were separated by lack of blue blood and cavalier manners; but this was more an annoyance than a bitterly felt grievance. The Conservative outlook of the upper clergy partly reflected their prestige and adequate pay, partly the strictly Conservative political doctrine traditionally associated with Lutheranism. The idea of absolute obedience to constituted authority was supplemented by affirmation of a hierarchic order of society where everybody pleased God by contentedly performing the duties of his appointed station. The upper clergy felt itself to be part of the established order; the nineteenth-century "alliance of throne and altar" already existed *in nascendo*. The quasi-hereditary character of the upper clergy also stimulated (when it did not cause) a guild attitude toward impertinent outsiders; indeed, the upper clergy showed a jealousy usually characteristic of entrenched oligarchies.

The social position of the upper clergy made any advocacy of social Radicalism unthinkable, though it did not preclude the advocacy of "advanced theological opinions." These proved frequently fully compatible with a Conservative (or even Reactionary) outlook on political and social questions. There were, however, several considerations which could drive clergymen, even of the highest rank, in the direction of *Aufklärung* ideas outside of the field of theology. They considered themselves (and frequently were) the intellectual cream of Germany, and educated men almost always show a tendency to gravitate toward "advanced ideas." They sought and found contact with professors, writers, and other champions of *Aufklärung,* whether in Masonic lodges, reading clubs, or literary societies. They found themselves valued (and therefore valued themselves) more for their worldly than their spiritual functions, and became increasingly secularized in their outlook. Secularism meant a far-reaching acceptance of the values of the *Aufklärung* and very emphatic repudiation of the obscurantism, fanaticism, et cetera, of the "barbarous" Middle Ages (and their alleged perpetuation in contemporary Catholicism). Pharisaism toward their less "enlightened" Catholic colleagues was matched by a complacent belief that "enlightened" Protestantism stood in the vanguard of the world's progress. This attitude was fully compatible with a sincere horror of every kind of Radicalism; the Protestant clergy believed that the pace of progress must be set by educated, moderate, sensible men like themselves. There can be little question that the elite of the Protestant clergy was in fact a predominantly Progressive force until it became frightened by the French Revolution.[27]

CONSERVATIVE SOCIAL FORCES

We have seen that the broad body of university professors, bureaucrats, professionals, and clergymen tended to be Conservative, but that influential members of these groups were frequently found on the Progressive side of controversies. In this they differ (though the distinction is, of course, not absolute) from the following groups which constituted a reliable core for German Conservatism: the princes and their

[27] There is no comprehensive work on the position of the Protestant clergy in eighteenth-century Germany. Important material is to be found in K. Aner, *Die Theologie der Lessingzeit* (Halle, 1929) and in two recent monographs: Rudolf von Thadden, *Die brandenburgisch-preussischen Hofprediger im 17. und 18. Jahrhundert. Ein Beitrag zur Geschichte der absolutistischen Staatsgesellschaft in Brandenburg-Preussen* (Berlin, 1959), especially valuable for the upper clergy; and M. Hasselhorn, *Der altwürttembergische Pfarrstand im 18. Jahrhundert* (Stuttgart, 1958), especially valuable for the lower clergy. A sharp contemporary denunciation of the liberal tendency of many clergymen can be found in Brandes, *Ueber den Einfluss und die Wirkungen des Zeitgeistes,* II, 178-93. The well-known fact that an unusual number of (usually "enlightened") intellectuals were the sons of pastors is explored by Lydia Rösch in *Der Einfluss des evangelischen Pfarrhauses auf die Literatur des 18. Jahrhunderts* (Tübingen, 1932). Two pedestrian studies with some valuable information about the eighteenth-century Protestant clergy are P. Drews, *Der evangelische Geistliche in der deutschen Vergangenheit* (Jena, 1905) and H. Werdermann, *Studien zur Geschichte des evangelischen Pfarrerstandes* (Leipzig, 1925).

court entourage (always excepting the few but important "enlightened despots"); the aristocracy and the officer corps of the numerous standing armies (usually recruited from the aristocracy); the patriciate of the cities; the guild masters threatened by new economic developments; and the broad mass of the peasantry whose unbroken traditionalism made them immune to the *Aufklärung* rather than actively hostile to it.

Germany was notable for its numerous princes surrounded by elaborate courts, the whole making for a Conservative vested interest for which it would be difficult to find a parallel elsewhere in Europe. The princes claimed their position either by divine right or by an absolutist interpretation of the social contract theory; in either case they were threatened by the doctrine of popular sovereignty and at least embarrassed by the "enlightened" doctrine that rulers exist for the benefit of the people rather than vice versa. The ideal of the *Rechtsstaat* (i.e., state where the government abided by existing law) curbed their absolutist caprice, while the "bourgeois virtues" preached by the champions of *Aufklärung* placed aristocratic court society on the defensive. Eighteenth-century courts were notable for their balls, theatricals, opera and hunting parties, expensive activities which tended to benefit only a small group of courtiers and were therefore vulnerable to "enlightened" criticism. Anyone who wanted to become somebody in Germany was drawn to the courts as the source of favors; there was a multiplication of unnecessary offices, especially at petty courts with their ridiculous desire to emulate Versailles. The main preoccupation of courtiers was the never-ending struggle against boredom: it was a real problem to make life not only gay but interesting for people notably devoid of any positive social function. The empty glitter of court life, and the exploitation of the masses upon which it rested, were threatened by the *Aufklärung* well before 1789; but the courts lost their self-assurance—an essential ingredient of their way of life—only when the French Revolution destroyed their model and prototype at Versailles.[28]

It should be remembered that the vested interests of a court were by no means limited to the immediate circle of courtiers. The economic welfare of most capital cities was dependent upon the prince and his entourage. Architects and painters lived off princely patronage,

[28] The outlook of court society can be conveniently studied in W. H. Bruford, *Germany in the 18th Century* (2nd edn., Cambridge, 1952), Pt. II, Ch. 2, "Courts and Courtiers." The fullest account is the antiquated and gossipy work by Eduard Vehse, *Geschichte der deutschen Höfe seit der Reformation* (48 vols. in 22, Hamburg, 1851-60).

luxury manufacturers ministered to the needs of courtiers, artisans derived self-esteem (quite apart from livelihood) from identification with their exalted clients. Every court employed directly hundreds or even thousands of domestic servants, stablemasters, gardeners, musicians, and other humble retainers who knew that their fortunes rose or fell with those of the prince. The residential cities were to a considerable extent parasitic bodies which battened on the country population: the inhabitants of these cities knew quite well that they benefited from the prevailing *Kleinstaaterei,* and had much to lose from social and political change.[29]

The highest court officials (as well as administrators) were invariably aristocrats—a fact which had great influence in shaping the outlook of the nobility as a whole. The *frondeur* spirit was either dying or dead as *Stände* bodies became obsolete and individual aristocrats became financially and socially dependent upon court favor. The reason for this dependence was partly economic, as many aristocratic estates had been ruined by war, mismanagement or multiplication of heirs (in the absence of primogeniture), and could be salvaged only by governmental favor, cheap credit, or a salary earned through court employment; it arose partly from the increased demands made by aristocrats who no longer viewed an isolated rural existence as acceptable. There was also a new solidarity of interest between princes and nobles as both were attacked by the *Aufklärung* for being idle, poorly educated, and immoral; both were anxious to flaunt the presumptuous *roture* by defiantly continuing a mode of life from which the *bourgeoisie* was excluded. Nobles increasingly accepted court employment which brought prestige, salary, and an opportunity to lend a helping hand to children and relatives. Princes were interested in raising the prestige of their court by making it the magnet for men of distinguished lineage.[30]

It is necessary to remember that the German aristocracy was a fantastically heterogeneous body which ranged in a sense from the princes themselves, who might be described as "aristocrats of the empire," to petty "territorial nobles" whose pattern of life did not differ signif-

[29] This has been demonstrated especially well in the case of Weimar. See H. Eberhardt, *Goethes Umwelt, Forschungen zur gesellschaftlichen Struktur Thüringens* (Weimar, 1951) and W. H. Bruford, *Society and Culture* (Cambridge, 1962).

[30] The Conservative outlook of the aristocracy can be studied *inter alia* in Hans Rosenberg, *Bureaucracy* (cited above in n. 25); A. Goodwin, "Prussia," *The European Nobility in the Eighteenth Century* (London, 1953), pp. 83-101; and the delightfully outspoken contemporary pamphlet, Hans Albert Freiherr von S., *Apologies des Adels* (Berlin, 1807), fully paraphrased in Ch. 13 of this study.

icantly from their prosperous peasant neighbors. For our purposes it is essential that there was no social dividing line between many a prince (defined technically by his "immediacy" to the emperor) and many a territorial noble who lacked this immediacy. Both were dedicated to a way of life which was threatened by the *Aufklärung*: but both could temporarily secure advantages for themselves by a policy of accommodation rather than resistance. The princes could strengthen their political position through "enlightened absolutism"; the nobles, their economic position through the application of laissez-faire principles to agriculture. Princes and nobles alike were torn between traditionalism and an "enlightened" view of their own self-interest (at least short-run self-interest). One must distinguish, however, between accommodation to the *Aufklärung* and acceptance of its basic principles: the latter could not be expected from either prince or noble, since it would constitute a form of suicide. A self-respecting prince *must* believe in his own hereditary right to rule, a right which only unconvincing fictions could square with the doctrine of natural law; a self-respecting noble *must* believe in his own superiority, however contradicted by the novel principle of equality. Both groups inevitably treated the *Aufklärung* with some suspicion before 1789 and outright hostility thereafter.

The officer class of Germany's numerous armies was almost exclusively drawn from the aristocracy and naturally shared the political values of its class of origin. For some aristocracies—most notable the Prussian Junkers—military employment was not so much a matter of choice as a foregone conclusion; the relationship to the king was characterized by an exalted ethic of duty far exceeding the ordinary loyalty expected from ordinary citizens. The "gentleman's agreement" of the seventeenth century, under which the Junkers served the state as officers and administrators, while continuing to dominate, by an implied *quid pro quo*, the serfs on their estates, was still intact and made any social changes highly suspect to the Junkers. Administrators drawn from the Junker class were sometimes infected by the "enlightened" outlook of their bourgeois colleagues; Junker officers were in little danger from this kind of contagion since officer positions remained practically an aristocratic monopoly. Their professional experience immunized them still further against "enlightened" ideas, since such ideas are obviously inapplicable to military affairs. An army is based upon discipline, not liberty; hierarchy, not equality; and it serves the interests of a particular state rather than the interests of humanity. Officers cannot be expected to be pacifists, humanitarians, or cosmopolitans, and they are bound to be somewhat skeptical of that "modern progress" which leads in their own professional sphere from simplicity to complexity and from chivalrous tournaments to scientific mass destruction.[31]

The "urban patriciate" was another group with a clearly defined Conservative outlook. Its composition differed from one Free Imperial City to another, but it may be defined as those families which monopolized governmental functions and lived not only *for* but *off* those public responsibilities. By this definition this group was relatively unimportant in "territorial cities" where governmental power was exercised (or at least supervised) by the agents of the absolutist prince. It constituted, however, the dominant oligarchy in the fifty odd Free Cities scattered through Southern, Western, and Northern Germany. The urban patriciate sometimes consisted of as few as twenty families, even in such a comparatively large city as Nürnberg; their members often displayed a pride and exclusiveness calculated to make any but the most arrogant aristocrat blush. These families voted each other into governmental office with an eye more upon perquisites than service; they got their cuts from public contracts bestowed upon the basis of influence rather than competitive efficiency; they leased urban properties to themselves at rates far below market value; and suppressed ruthlessly any challenge directed against their anachronistic position. The "charmed circle" involved in these malpractices—which could not stand the light of criticism—was understandably bitterly hostile to the *Aufklärung*. It knew that any alteration in the *status quo* was bound to affect its own interests adversely. Its intransigence did much, incidentally, to discredit the republican idea in Germany by identifying it with oligarchic corruption and jealousy.[32]

The urban patriciate sometimes—though not usually—included the class of masters standing at the top of the guild structure. These mas-

[31] The outlook of the officer class, as determined by its connection with the aristocracy, is brilliantly analyzed in the case of Prussia in a pioneering study by Otto Busch, *Militärsystem und Sozialleben im alten Preussen 1713-1807: Die Anfänge der sozialen Militärisierung der preussisch-deutschen Gesellschaft* (Berlin, 1962). See also Karl Demeter, *Das deutsche Offizierskorps in seinen historischsoziologischen Grundlagen* (Berlin, 1930; 2nd rev. edn., Frankfurt, 1962).

[32] Some characteristic examples of malpractice among the ruling oligarchies of several Free Cities will be discussed in Ch. 5. An excellent survey of the problem is to be found in Vierhaus, *Deutschland*, mss., pp. 84-102. Conditions in many "territorial cities" were not much better, even in Prussia. See J. Ziekursch, *Das Ergebniss der friderizianischen Städteverwaltung Steins. Am Beispiel der schlesischen Städte dargestellt* (Jena, 1908)—though Ziekursch probably portrayed conditions in too dark a light and wrongly assumed that Silesian malpractices were typical for the entire monarchy.

ters felt themselves threatened by the relatively old class of large-scale merchants and the new class of manufacturers; more generally by the dynamic features of the mercantilistic system (aiming at country-wide prosperity) and the novel principle of laissez-faire. Both were irrevocably destroying the municipal organization of economic life with which the guild had been so intimately associated. Guild production could not easily adjust to the condition of a larger market; the natural reaction of guildsmen was to cling all the more firmly to their privileged local markets. Methods of production remained frozen; the number of masters was kept stationary to assure a guaranteed market for guild products; while guild membership became increasingly hereditary or dependent upon journeymen marrying the daughters (or widows!) of masters. The resistance of journeymen to these oligarchic practices was ruthlessly crushed by guildsmen who controlled (or at least influenced) municipal governments. Their well-justified suspicion of economic change was often extended to political and cultural changes as well.[33]

The strongest bulwark of the existing structure of German society was found among the peasantry, though its outlook was marked by sheer traditionalism rather than any explicit Conservatism such as could be found with princes, aristocrats, officers, urban oligarchs, and guild masters. It requires some imagination in our traffic-ridden twentieth century to visualize the primitiveness of provincial life two hundred years ago. The ordinary peasant rarely traveled more than ten miles away from his place of birth unless he had the misfortune to be drafted into military service. It was a rare rural school which succeeded in breaking the illiteracy of its peasant pupils. Books and newspapers were virtually unknown outside the houses of the gentry, while the Sunday sermon was geared to peasant horizons. Living standards never departed far from a starvation level, while the prevalent pattern of economic exploitation was such as to make any hu-

[33] The condition and outlook of the guildsmen in the late eighteenth century can be conveniently studied in two old-fashioned works: Gustav Schmoller, "Das brandenburgisch-preussische Innungswesen von 1640-1800," *Umrisse und Untersuchungen zur Verfassungs-, Verwaltungs und Wirtschaftsgeschichte* (Leipzig, 1898), pp. 314-456; and K. von Rohrscheidt, *Vom Zunftzwange zur Gewerbefreiheit* (Berlin, 1898). Three modern works are Hugo Rachel, *Das Berliner Wirtschaftsleben im Zeitalter des Frühkapitalismus* (Berlin, 1931), a superb monograph; H. Kraft, "Die Entwicklung des Zunftwesens und die geistesgeschichtlichen Grundlagen der Gewerbefreiheit," *Zeitschrift für die gesamte Staatswissenschaft*, cvi (1950); and August Voigt, *Handwerk und Handel in der späteren Zunftzeit* (Stuttgart, 1929). The intellectual horizons of the artisans is explored in the pioneering, but rather inconclusive, work of Rudolf Stadelmann and Wolfram Fischer, *Die Bildungswelt des deutschen Handwerkers um 1800* (Berlin, 1955).

mane man shudder. These facts were true of the peasantry through-out Germany, whether serfs or formally free, though they were natural-ly aggravated in those areas (predominantly in Eastern Prussia) where outright serfdom continued to prevail. The important point to remem-ber is that the peasantry was still so primitive that it could scarcely as yet envisage a better life for itself. Its dominant attitude was one of acquiescence in the condition to which it had been called by God, an attitude consecrated by all the Christian religions. This did not pre-vent the occasional outbreak of ferocious violence directed against particular evils, such as the prohibition of game killing even when the lord's game was ruining the peasant's crop. It did, however, prevent the development of a generally Radical outlook aiming at over-all so-cial improvement under the stimulus of a vision of a better life. The tra-ditionalism of the peasantry would inevitably weaken in the future; but while it lasted—and it lasted another century at least—it made any general transformation of German society impossible. When peasant emancipation came during the Napoleonic period, it was usually a gift from above—prepared by Progressive administrators dominated by enlightened ideas—rather than a concession to a demand from below which could no longer be denied. Its terms proved as miserable as might be expected under such circumstances.[34]

It is clear from this brief survey of social forces that Germany was bound to experience a long delay between the first articulation and the eventual implementation of the ideas of the *Aufklärung*. They were originally an intellectual rather than a social force, and it is not surpris-ing that they had their greatest initial influence in the field of religion and education rather than politics and economics. They did, however, begin the crucial process—which constitutes, perhaps, the greatest dif-ference between the medieval and the modern world—of leaving no institution, no matter how old, venerable and holy, immune to criti-cism. They thereby compelled Conservatives to answer argument with counterargument, and to leave the sheltered world of an unquestioned traditionalism for the uncongenial condition of intellectual combat. They compelled, in short, the transition from traditionalism to Con-

[34] The best introduction to the world of the peasantry is Christian Garve, "Über den Charakter der Bauern und ihr Verhältniss gegen die Gutsherren und gegen die Regierung," *Vermischte Aufsätze* (2 vols., Breslau, 1796-1800), I, 1-228. Two valuable modern studies are J. von Jordan Rozwadowski, "Die Bauern des 18. Jahrhunderts und ihre Herren," *Conrads Jahrbücher für Nationalökonomie und Statistik*, 3rd ser., xx (1900), and Johannes Nichtweiss, *Das Bauernlegen in Mecklenburg* (East Berlin, 1954), valuable despite its Marxist outlook.

servatism—the traumatic experience which constitutes the beginning of Germany's articulate and self-conscious Conservative tradition.

The Rise of Conservatism

FROM TRADITIONALISM TO CONSERVATISM[35]

Conservative attitudes have existed throughout recorded history, in the sense that men have felt hostile to changes in their accustomed and cherished world. They are correlative with the fact of change itself, and are basically rooted in the human fear of the unknown and desire for a predictable environment. There have been many changes throughout history which have provoked not only a psychological uneasiness but an articulate expression of Conservative defense. The conspirators who assassinated Caesar believed themselves to be defending the old senatorial constitution against a new type of tyranny. The Saxon Widuking defended the gods of his fathers against the new religion of Charlemagne. The Dominican Inquisition defended Catholic Orthodoxy against the Albigensian heresy, and the Jesuits of the Counter Reformation defended the unity of Christendom against the rebellion of the Protestant Reformers. John Hampden defended, against the new claims of royal prerogative, the ancient right of Englishmen not to be taxed without their consent; at the same time the Prussian nobleman Kalckstein defended the traditional rights of the East Prussian *Stände* against the encroaching absolutism of the Great Elector.

All these cases—selected at random—are examples of defense of a specific *status quo* at a specific time against specific attack. What is significant in the eighteenth century—in Germany around 1770—is that Conservatism, while remaining in substance a defense of concrete institutions *ad hoc*, developed for the first time the *self-conscious* attitude of a distinctive *Weltanschauung*.

Brutus, Widuking, Hampden, et al., did not feel that they were de-

[35] For this entire section see Part I of the excellent article by Karl Mannheim, "Das konservative Denken. Soziologische Beiträge zum Werden des politisch-historischen Denkens in Deutschland," *Archiv für Sozialwissenschaft*, LVII (1927), 68-142, 470-95. The article is notable for expressing rather simple ideas in intolerably cumbersome professorial German. Two historically oriented studies of the same theme are Fritz Valjavec, *Die Entstehung der politischen Strömungen in Deutschland 1770-1815* (Munich, 1951), excellent in its theme that Conservatism arose in answer to the *Aufklärung* challenge well before 1789; and the same author's "Die Entstehung des europäischen Konservativismus," *Ostdeutsche Wissenschaft—Jahrbuch des ostdeutschen Kulturrates*, I (1954), 255-77, devoted primarily to the Latin countries but especially good in correlating the rise of Conservatism with the interests of certain challenged groups.

fending a social, political, and cultural order *in toto* against a general attack animated by the vision of a wholly new conception of what society should be. They felt, no doubt, that what they defended had an importance going beyond the immediate case, and that defeat might have far-reaching repercussions. From this feeling it was in theory only a small step toward an explicit Conservative *Weltanschauung*—a small though crucial step, and one which was not taken in Germany before Justus Möser. It was taken at that time as an inescapable response to the challenge of the *Aufklärung* with its general program of transforming every sector of life. The *Aufklärung* forced men with Conservative inclinations to abandon their unreflective Traditionalism—their instinctive and inarticulate acceptance of the *status quo*—in favor of an explicit and self-conscious defense of the *totality* of society. Even more, it forced Conservative men to criticize the practice of *Aufklärung* criticism per se, since the case-by-case reply to specific attacks upon specific institutions never yielded more than temporary defensive victories. It was the fate of Conservatism from its very beginning that, although it condemned criticism and argument, it was unable to avoid either. The emergence of Conservative thought and argument in fact contributed to that perennial battle of ideas which Conservatives find perhaps the most deplorable aspect of modernity.

It must be repeated that the tragic predicament of Conservatism is apparent from the hour of its birth. Conservatives value a society in which everyone accepts the established order without controversy, and where intellectual activity is either at a low level or devoted to the refinement of existing pattern of life rather than to criticism. They abhor and resent the critical habit—systematized during the *Aufklärung*—of questioning everything and never being contented with anything. They are forced, however, by the insuppressible new critical mood to defend traditional institutions—Churches, governments, and social structures—when and as they are attacked. They instinctively feel that the battle is already half lost because of the fact that they are compelled to fight it at all. They must argue, though they hate argument; defend, where unquestioned acceptance alone can give emotional satisfaction; persuade, where persuasion ought to be unnecessary and is unlikely to be effective. The terms of controversy are invariably set by the Party of Movement, and Conservatism is forever doomed to fight an essentially defensive battle. Its argumentative triumphs are at best Pyrrhic victories, for even a successfully defended institution is transformed into something very different from one which was never challenged sufficiently to necessitate defense. A militant virtue is only a poor substitute for the charms of innocence, and innocence once lost can never be regained. This is the fundamental meaning of the saying attributed to Talleyrand that "no one who has not lived before 1789 can ever know how good life can be." The necessity of developing an *explicit* Conservatism is for true Conservatives the infallible symptom that the golden age has vanished forever.

THE CRITIQUE OF THE CRITICISM OF THE AUFKLÄRUNG

It was natural for Conservatives to break out of their defensive ramparts and launch a vigorous counterattack against the spirit and methods of the *Aufklärer*. Their counterattack may be usefully analyzed under two headings: first, the criticism of the results of the *Aufklärung*, on the theory that a tree may be judged by its fruits; second, an attack upon the motives of the *Aufklärer*, and their alleged vices.

Conservatives asserted that the *Aufklärung* led, visibly and inevitably, to the triple evils of skepticism, immorality, and the undermining of all constituted authority. The rationalist approach to religion destroyed belief in the basic truths of traditional religion. These truths were not (in the Conservative view) contrary to reason, but they certainly did not rest upon reason alone, and the *Aufklärer* were fundamentally misguided when they declared reason the sole yardstick of credibility. The *Aufklärer* were in fact deeply hostile to miracle, mystery, and authority. The outlook which resulted from their repudiation of these three cardinal elements of historic Christianity might initially be a "natural" religion which retained the essence of Christianity (such as the Creator-God, the moral law, and immortality) while repudiating all of its so-called "historical accidents." This position, however, was neither logically compelling to intellectuals nor practically attractive to the broad mass of the people; it frequently proved a mere halfway house to outright skepticism and materialism.

The Swiss poet and scientist Albrecht von Haller (1708-77) was an early critic of skepticism. His argument is especially significant because it rested upon purely utilitarian grounds instead of appealing to religious dogma. Haller asserted that skepticism inevitably undermined belief in the foundations of morality by encouraging the emergence of a new type of man—one who devoted his life to the pursuit of sensuous pleasures unrestrained by the thought of an avenging God in the world to come. Such a man would recognize no moral restraints at all—an attitude leading to the following results in private life: the replacement of marriage by temporary liaisons; the neglect of children or even their exposure as a nuisance; the murder of elderly parents as their survival became an inconvenience; while friendship, because it usually required some sacrifice, would become virtually unknown. The public results would be equally disastrous: honor in commercial transactions would disappear; servants would cease to be loyal to their masters; oaths would become worthless; the fear of temporal punishment would become the only restraint upon crime, and even this would be diluted by the corruptibility of judges; while no prince could henceforth rely upon his administrative personnel, or even entrust his personal safety to his bodyguard. It was truly a situation where Hobbes' "war of all against all" would be an accurate description of man's condition.[36]

Haller provided the following portrait of the new skeptical man:

The skeptic who denies an avenging God, and an eternal life to come, restricts our happiness to the brief period of our terrestrial life, in duration, and to the enjoyment of sensual pleasure in substance. . . . He asserts that every man has a right to happiness and that he must find it where he may; and that a criminal deserves it as much as a saint. The pleasures of love—more especially the animal side of love—and the most refined tickling of our senses are considered man's highest good; they alone make us happy even if it is a happiness without honor and devoid of approval by our fellow-men. This happiness must never be restrained by that old pedant called VIRTUE. The very concept is a figment of the imagination, a mere invention of human contrivance, indeed an alien plant which does not grow up naturally in our hearts. The torments of an uneasy conscience, or that sense of guilt which relentlessly pursues us, must be dismissed as a mere prejudice incubated in us through parental blows administered during childhood; one must anesthetize conscience or at least so stuff its mouth that it will be forced to shut up. One must never think of God, and it has been proved that there is no Afterlife: there is, therefore, nothing to fear except the single creature that can still mar our happiness: the public hangman. Even philosophers, who otherwise fear nothing either above or below the earth, must watch out for him, but for him alone.

Haller then contrasted the moral anarchy produced by skepticism, and the ensuing "war of all against all," with a picture of the harmonious life of a traditionalist Christian:

[36] Albrecht von Haller (ed. and tr.), *Prüfung einer Sekte, die an allem zweifelt* (Göttingen, 1751), pp. 14-28.

Christian faith brings results exactly opposite to those produced by unbelief. Religion unites competing efforts and wills in the single center which is God. His law demands that we love Him above all else and our neighbor as ourselves. What infinite wisdom and what infinite power for good rests in this simple faith! Revelation teaches us that we are not destined for this world alone; that worldly goods should therefore be enjoyed only with reserve and that our hearts should never cling to them. We know that our sojourn in this world is but temporary, and that death will see us passing into a spiritual world from which fleshly pleasures are banished and all ambition loses its meaning. We are, indeed, by nature *lowly* creatures who require transfiguration by the grace of God before being worthy of entering into his presence and that of thousands of creatures with a nature far superior to ours [the angels].

In this present world we are all brothers charged with the obligation of doing unto others whatever we would do toward an infinitely rewarding God if He appeared in our midst in human disguise and required our help: a conception far more compelling than any ethical code promulgated by mere human rhetoric. From these few basic laws flow all civic virtues, and if they were obeyed the happiness of mankind would ensue spontaneously and inevitably.[37]

To balance his earlier portrait of the vices of the skeptic Haller devoted the rest of his essay to the virtues of the Christian. He contrasted the comfort of Christian family life with the disorder produced by temporary sexual liaisons; the Christian education of children with their neglect by parents absorbed in the pursuit of pleasure; the Christian satisfaction with every station in life, and the moral duty to perform the obligations of one's station, with the skeptic's pursuit of ambition and sensual gratification without bounds; the Christian observance of the moral law, enforced by consciousness of an omnipresent God, with the skeptic's license restrained only by fear of police detection; and the Christian conception of government, where obedience to duly constituted authority was a sacred duty, with the "war of all against all" inevitable in a society of skeptics.[38] Haller stated the classic Conservative contention that no civilized society can dispense with religious foundations; he added that these foundations could only be Christian so far as European society was concerned. The total disintegration of European civilization was still prevented by the residual influence exercised by Christianity. European society was depicted as

[37] Ibid., pp. 15-16, 29-30.   [38] Ibid., pp. 30-34.

living off the religious capital accumulated during the centuries preceding the *Aufklärung*. There could only be gloomy perspectives about what would happen if the replenishing of Europe's Christian capital were not soon begun.[39]

Other Conservative writers joined Haller in the contention that reason could never provide the basis for a morality adequate to meet society's needs. A prominent Bavarian Conservative, Karl von Eckartshausen (1752-1803), argued emphatically that traditional religion was the foundation of what morality still survived in Europe—and that morality could only be based upon religious custom and tradition, not the rational convictions of individual persons:

"Are you not aware," he asked the *Aufklärer* who never ceased to criticize traditional custom, "that the moral law loses much of its efficacy if it is not drummed into us during childhood—at a period long before our reason is in a position to judge all the misfortunes which vice inevitably brings upon man?"[40] Eckartshausen accused the *Aufklärer* of destroying the sense of shame: "The feeling of shame which we experience when we are justly punished is one of the most precious gifts which nature has bestowed upon us."[41] There was no substitute for the fear of divine punishment in buttressing morality, especially for materialists who tended to view earthly punishment through "the wheel or even more cruel tortures as no different in principle from a heavy attack of gout or colic."[42] These utilitarian reasons made it imperative for Europe to continue to cherish its Christian traditions, even apart from their dogmatic truth. Eckartshausen went so far as to insist that, if Christianity were by chance untrue—though he himself was a fervid believer—it would nonetheless require preservation since it

[39] Ibid., pp. 50ff.

[40] Karl von Eckartshausen, *Über Religion, Freydenkerey und Aufklärung. Eine Schrift zu den Schriften unsrer Zeiten, der Jugend geweiht* (Augsburg, 1789), p. 58. The author was a prominent official of the Bavarian archival administration. He had joined the *Illuminati* as a young man but became a fiery renegade in 1784; he thereafter propagated Conservative doctrines—mostly of a religious, mystical, and even cabalistic type—in an endless series of repetitive and homiletic writings. He was a close friend of Sailer, Jung-Stilling, and other prominent figures of the religious revival of the early nineteenth century; his influence can be traced in the work of many romantic figures (Baader, Schelling, Novalis, Hölderlin). It even extended into Russia, where Alexander I compared Eckartshausen's *Wolke über dem Heiligthum* (1802) to St. Augustine's *City of God*. Both Gogol and Goncharov acknowledged their indebtedness to him. See the brief biographical sketch by Hans Grassl and F. Merzbacher in *NDB*, IV (1959), 284-85; L. Kleeberg, "Studien zu Novalis," *Euphorion*, XXIII (1921), 603-39 (tracing his influence upon Novalis); and the unpublished Freiburg doctoral dissertation by D. Struss, *Carl von Eckartshausen* (1955).

[41] Eckartshausen, op.cit., p. 59.   [42] Ibid., p. 60.

constituted the only possible basis for European morality. He appealed to the *Aufklärer* to heed the example of Socrates, whom they often hailed as an early fellow spirit: Socrates had always carefully observed Athenian religious customs—which he did not pretend to respect upon religious grounds—since he understood that they were the only possible basis for Athenian morality.[43]

A further result of the *Aufklärung* was the destruction of all respect for constituted authority. No institution, however venerable, was immune to criticism; the *Aufklärer* not only turned destructive criticism into a personal habit, but also urged all men, however common or uneducated, to join them in this habit. A Lutheran clergyman of Pomerania named Daniel Joachim Köppen was one of many Conservative authors who defended the need for authority, secular and divine, on general grounds. He wrote in 1789—quite independently of the French Revolution—that no one had yet demonstrated that

> the common people, as they are now constituted or are ever likely to become, are capable of discovering for themselves the True and the Good. It is notorious that the common people—that is, the greater part of mankind: servants, day-laborers, proletarians, common artisans and many others whose formal status may be superior, but whose character is similarly primitive—are incapable of doing so, both on account of their biological stupidity and their external circumstances of life. They obviously require guidance from above. This fact will remain a fact so long as common people remain common people . . . ; so long as men are born brutish and ignorant—and this will remain the case until mankind disappears from the earth—and secure moral education only through instruction and leadership from some outside source . . . ; so long as the content of this education is not an indifferent matter but something which shapes the entire adult character of a people. All these considerations make it indispensable to have some supervision over the religious and moral principles which are imposed upon the common people from outside their ranks. And who is to exercise this necessary supervision? It is obviously the task of constituted authority.[44]

This elitist and authoritarian argument has been used time and again by Conservatives from the eighteenth century until our own age. Conservatives were not satisfied with pointing out the disastrous

[43] Ibid., pp. 63-67.
[44] D. J. Köppen, *Das Recht der Fürsten, die Religionslehrer auf ein feststehendes Symbol zu verpflichten* (Leipzig, 1789), pp. 30-31.

consequences wrought by the *Aufklärung* in destroying religion, morality, and authority; they also proceeded to argue *ad hominem* against the personal vices of the *Aufklärer*. It would be unfair to accuse Conservatives of being the first to stoop to personal attack, for Radical publicists chronically denounced their foes as a band of stupid, egotistic, obscurantist, callous, and unimaginative men. The Conservatives replied to this unflattering stereotype by denouncing the *Aufklärer* as a band of fanatical and ruthless zealots dedicated to purely negative criticism because they were unsuited to any constructive profession. They were also attacked as unbalanced personalities who lacked any sense of the importance of emotion, mystery, and tradition in human affairs, and were blind to the claims of national feeling.

Conservatives loved nothing better than to castigate the fanaticism and intolerance of the *Aufklärer*—attitudes all the more offensive because the *Aufklärer* claimed self-righteously that *they* sought to slay intolerance and fanaticism as distinctively *Conservative* vices. Eckartshausen devoted an entire public speech (April 5, 1785) to the *Literary Intolerance of Our Century*, exclaiming:

> O tolerance, tolerance, what a wonderful word! frequently exclaimed but seldom practiced in our "enlightened" century! The false philosophers of the *Aufklärung* shout imperiously: Think as we think! or else we will brand you as obscurantists in our writings and whip and scourge you through half the world. So shout the executioners of literature, and they do not hesitate to nail the honest man to the gallows of their journals.[45]

Eckartshausen went on to brand the superstitious fanaticism of the *Aufklärung* in the following rhetorical appeal to his enemies:

> Tell me, when was superstition as ridiculous as your philosophy? When has it shown such a hot-tempered zeal to win proselytes? When did superstition flood the world with so many ridiculous, contradictory raging pamphlets? When did it seek to prejudice the world against hostile sects with so many falsifications, dictionaries, verses and anecdotes?[46]

The pamphleteers of the *Aufklärung* were notorious in Eckartshausen's eyes for their bad temper, prejudice, vindictiveness, and penchant for character assassination.

[45] Karl von Eckartshausen, *Über die literarische Intoleranz unsers Jahrhunderts. Eine akademische Rede abgelesen in einer öffentlichen Versammlung . . . in München den 5. April 1785* (Augsburg, 1789), p. 114.
[46] Ibid., pp. 116-17.

There was much Conservative criticism directed against the ruthless methods employed by "enlightened despots"—more especially the Habsburg Emperor Joseph II—as they promoted the cause of *Aufklärung*. To give only one example: the Hannoverian Conservative writer Ernst Brandes wrote a sharp attack against the method of Joseph's ecclesiastical reforms. It should be noted that Brandes, as a Protestant, had no sympathy for monasticism, and fully recognized the fiscal needs of the Austrian state which made some suppression of monasteries inevitable. He protested, however, against the precipitate character of the emperor's actions, the needless cruelty directed against individual monks, the barbarous destruction of priceless art treasures, the utter want of reverence toward foundations often hundreds of years old, and the failure to prepare public opinion gradually for whatever steps were necessary. Brandes attacked the reforming emperor for his characteristic indifference to the feelings of others, so that even his most benevolent actions were resented as tyrannical, especially when they interfered with the customary life of the common people; examples were his suppression of superfluous holidays and his campaign against burial in unsanitary and uneconomical wooden coffins. Joseph was a typical *Aufklärer* in his arrogant belief that he knew best what was good for other people; that traditional society must be reconstructed in accordance with rationalist blueprints; that every opponent of reform was either stupid or vicious, and probably both; and that the whole program of *Aufklärung* must be implemented as quickly as possible regardless of any obstacles which stood in the way.[47]

Conservatives frequently denounced the pamphleteers of the *Aufklärung* as a group of unemployable hacks incapable of holding down respectable jobs. Eckartshausen drew the following unflattering picture of the publicists of the *Aufklärung* in the vigorous language characteristic of the polemics of the age:

> They are men devoid of true philosophy, filled with confused so-called "enlightened" concepts which they have sucked up in a thoroughly fuzzy manner, and regurgitate without prior digestion. They lack all knowledge of human nature, since their life has been confined to the study or at best the coffee-house. They are in fact so-called "men of genius" with holes in their pants (*meistentheils Genies in zerrissenen Hosen*); lackeys or members of secret societies; or self-styled wits (*Witzlinge*) who pour out their gall upon who-

[47] Ernst Brandes, *Betrachtungen über den Zeitgeist in Deutschland* (Hannover, 1808), pp. 98-104. Though written only in 1807 it faithfully reflects views already held by Brandes twenty years before.

ever lacks concepts as confused as their own. Their helpers and satellites, scattered through the length and breadth of Germany, include everywhere perennial malcontents and many conceited people who believe that they possess a monopoly of wisdom,—when in fact they are only eager to find a pot where they can place their (intellectual) excrement (*die dann froh sind, wenn sie einen Topf haben, wo sie ihren Unrath ausleeren können*). They believe that they possess the capacity to rule states while in fact they cannot even manage their private affairs and are up to their necks in debts they are unable to pay.[48]

Conservatives asserted that the *Aufklärer* were unbalanced men oblivious to many important sides of human life. Their cocksure rationalism easily led to an atrophy of the emotional faculties (*Gefühl*); on this point the early Conservatives agreed with the poets of the *Sturm und Drang* and such prophetic-mystical writers as Johann Georg Hamann (1730-1787), the "Magus of the North."[49] They asserted that the *Aufklärer* tended to forget the claims of passion, reverence, and sentiment as they viewed life in a spirit of narrowly philistine utilitarianism. Their rationalism tended, moreover, to make them dangerously "unhistorical" in their view of the world. They cared little for the individuality which characterized historical development; their preoccupation was rather to discover and apply general principles valid everywhere and at all times. The "historicist movement"—what Friedrich Meinecke called "one of the greatest intellectual revolutions achieved by the Western mind"[50]—inevitably became a powerful ally of Conservatism, though many of its founders and early champions, most notably Johann Gottfried Herder (1744-1803), personally sympathized with much of the program of the *Aufklärung*.[51]

---

[48] Eckartshausen, "Einige Worte über Journalisterey und Publizität," Appendix to *Über Religion und Aufklärung*, pp. 157-58.

[49] The literature on Johann Georg Hamann (1730-88) is endless. I have found most valuable Rudolf Unger, *Hamann und die Aufklärung, Studien zur Vorgeschichte des romantischen Geistes im 18. Jahrhundert* (2 vols., Jena, 1911); Jean Blum, *La vie et l'oeuvre de J. G. Hamann, le 'Mage du Nord'* (Paris, 1912); and Jakob Minor, *J. G. Hamann in seiner Bedeutung für die Sturm und Drang Periode* (Frankfurt, 1881). A useful English introduction to his thought is Ronald G. Smith, *J. G. Hamann: a Study in Christian existence: with Selections from his Writings* (New York, 1960).

[50] Friedrich Meinecke, *Die Entstehung des Historismus* (n.e. ed. Carl Hinrichs, Berlin, 1959), p. 1.

[51] The endless literature on Herder cannot be listed here. On the relationship of his Historicism to emerging Conservatism see especially F. Meinecke, op.cit., Ch. 9; Rudolf Stadelmann, *Der historische Sinn bei Herder* (Halle, 1928); Robert

Conservatives objected to the a priori faith of the *Aufklärer* that the universe—far from being either mysterious or opaque, as had long been thought—was in fact easily intelligible. Eckartshausen was one of many Conservative writers who not only stated, but positively reveled in, the belief that much of the world was ultimately incomprehensible. Only God could understand the mysterious universe which He had created. How could the finite intelligence of man possibly secure a full understanding of a universe whose infinity was obviously incongruous with it? God in His mercy wisely supplemented the inevitable defects of human understanding through Revelation, but even Revelation contained many mysterious elements. If it were otherwise, argued Eckartshausen, belief would become mere mechanical assent and cease to be a Christian virtue. A mature man must learn to live with mystery and like it; he must avoid the naïve error of the *Aufklärer* of believing that all useful and necessary truth was crystal-clear; for "doctrine may contain much that is unintelligible without on that account ceasing to be necessary and useful truth."[52]

The belief of the thinkers of the *Aufklärung* in human progress was primarily based upon their faith in the beneficial results of scientific knowledge, which included the enhancement of material welfare and human happiness. But what if knowledge in the really essential areas of life—religion, morality, et cetera—was in fact stationary because of the inapplicability of scientific method, and in practice even regressive because of the rise of skepticism? Brandes for one rejected the idea that genuine progress had actually taken place in recent centuries. There had, to be sure, been some advance in the standard of living; but this had only led to an increase in luxury, extravagance, and immorality. There had been some advance in literacy, but this only exposed uncritical minds to the disastrous doctrines of the *Aufklärung* and thereby led them into temptations which it would have been better to avoid. Real progress could only mean individual *moral* progress and a more profound grasp of Christian truth; there was, unhappily, not a shred of evidence that either had taken place. On the contrary, the rise of immorality and skepticism was all too evident. Only shallow philistines could believe that there had been cultural progress since the ancient Greeks. Did the *Aufklärung* produce a greater philosopher than Plato, a greater historian than Thucydides, a

---

Ergang, *Herder and the Foundations of German Nationalism* (New York, 1931); Heinz Stolpe, *Die Auffassung des jungen Herder vom Mittelalter; ein Beitrag zur Geschichte der Aufklärung* (Weimar, 1955).
[52] Eckartshausen, *Über Religion, Freiheit und Aufklärung*, pp. 78ff.

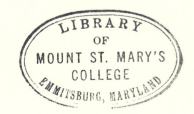

greater biographer than Plutarch, or a greater painter than Raphael? The worst aspect of the doctrine of progress was—in Brandes' eyes— that it provided men with a psychological surrogate for belief in personal immortality and thereby helped to undermine a Christian doctrine essential for personal morality and social stability. It also provided men with an utopian vision of the future in which everything appeared possible, and paralyzed Conservatives with an enervating fatalism arising from the belief that they were fighting an ultimately hopeless battle against an irresistible tide.[53]

A final charge delivered against the *Aufklärer* was that they were devoid of German national sentiment. Their ideas were universal in content and Western European in origin; these facts suggested the effectiveness of a nationalist counterattack. Should Germans not cherish German ideas and institutions which were the result of Germany's distinctive historical heritage? This theme played as yet a comparatively small role in the predominantly cosmopolitan eighteenth century; but it anticipated what was to prove the most influential Conservative argument in the nineteenth.[54]

Suffice it to say at this point that German Conservatism could rely not only sociologically upon the main forces of German society—as outlined in the previous section—but intellectually upon many of the most powerful currents of German cultural life. The cult of *Gefühl* of the *Sturm und Drang*, the prophetic mysticism of Hamann, the historicism of Herder, the discontent with civilization expressed by Brandes, and the rising German national sentiment—all these could be used by intellectual Conservatives in their assault upon *Aufklärer* and *Aufklärung*.

METHODS OF CONSERVATIVE DEFENSE

The public defense of German society of the 1770's and 1780's consisted primarily of the suppression of voices of Radical criticism—a task made difficult, as we shall see later, by the multiplicity of the German state system. There were, however, many attempts at censorship which were invariably justified by the argument that ordinary men were quite incapable of discussing public affairs in a mature manner. Even the Prussian government, generally known for its liberal attitudes, sometimes employed this argument in order to silence editors who had

[53] Ernst Brandes, *Betrachtungen über den Zeitgeist*, pp. 206-27; Brandes, *Über den Einfluss und die Wirkung des Zeitgeistes auf die höheren Stände Deutschlands* (Hannover, 1810), pp. 210-16.
[54] Justus Möser frequently used this argument. It will be examined in detail in Ch. 6.

caused offense. To give only one example: some articles in Gökingk's *Journal von und für Deutschland* had led to complaints by some of Prussia's neighboring states whose princes had been criticized. Two Prussian ministers, Count Finkenstein and Count Hertzberg (the latter, incidentally, known for his *Aufklärung* principles), thereupon sent a stiffly worded reprimand to the *Regierung* of Halberstadt (the district in which the *Journal* was published) on December 13, 1784:

A private individual does not possess the right to issue public judgments (let alone unfavorable judgments) upon the actions, procedures, laws, proclamations or decrees of sovereigns, their ministers, administrative boards, or courts of justice. This applies, of course, also to the publication and distribution of news privately received about such sovereigns, their courts, et cetera. It is obvious that a private individual, necessarily lacking intimate knowledge of the general context of affairs and the motives of public figures, is quite incapable of rendering a judgment concerning them which is worth hearing. . . .

The nation will neither be intellectually illuminated nor morally improved by being exposed to reckless discussion of its affairs; rather it will be corrupted. The incautious drive for *Aufklärung*, which characterizes the present age, degenerates all too easily into an impertinent license; it tramples upon whatever is sacred and venerable; it makes all established values contemptible in the eyes of the people, confuses its concepts, and promotes sedition, disobedience, license and rebelliousness without either educating or improving the nation.[55]

This general argument was frequently implemented by the call for the suppression of specific journals which had caused offense. Enraged Conservatives did not hesitate to recommend the employment of economic and other pressures upon those princes who refused to silence "seditious" editors. A much-discussed example involved Count August von Limburg-Styrum, the masterful bishop of Speyer, who had issued an exceedingly Conservative political catechism to his subjects. It was ridiculed by Schlözer in the *Staatsanzeigen* in a manner most offensive to the bishop. Schlözer wrote as a Hannoverian subject, which made the Hannoverian government responsible—at least in Styrum's view—for the opinions expressed. When a direct complaint to the Hannoverian government yielded no results, the bishop called upon the Regensburg Diet to punish Hannover; when the Diet refused to take

[55] Quoted in Eckartshausen, *Über Religion*, pp. 177-78.

77

any action, he called upon his fellow sovereigns to strike at Hannoverian interests by an organized boycott of Göttingen, Schlözer's university.[56] This farfetched proposal was, however, turned down by his fellow princes; the suggestion shows, however, how far Conservatives were willing to go in opposition to the *Aufklärung*. This was shown even better in the famous suppression of the *Illuminati* by the Bavarian government (discussed in the next chapter).

Conservatives frequently lamented the rise of *Publizität* and newspapers per se;[57] they were sometimes not far from the view that the invention of printing, so often hailed by the *Aufklärung* as a milestone and guarantee of human progress, was in fact the main source of mankind's modern troubles. A corollary of this view was to deplore the rise of that popular education which was beginning to make some small encroachments upon mass illiteracy. Did this not merely result in giving common men access to poisonous ideas and thereby making them discontented with their traditional lot in life? The *Popularphilosoph* Christian Garve, in a book dealing with agrarian conditions in his native Silesia, reported the view of the landlord class upon this problem in the following paraphrase:

> Our forefathers never had occasion to quarrel with their illiterate serfs: an illiteracy which did not prevent fields from being cultivated at least as well as they are today, and manners being unquestionably purer. Today many peasants can not only read and write, but they also begin to master arithmetic; some even start to read books. Does this make them better men? do their lives become less dissolute? have they become more obedient subjects, or better cultivators of the soil? On the contrary: is it not true that manners have visibly declined? and that lords experience far more difficulty in maintaining authority over their serfs than they did when the latter were still illiterate? If one investigates who have been the village troublemakers [Silesia experienced some minor peasant turbulence], who have been the misleaders of the people: one always finds that they come from the ranks of those who have attended school the longest, who are puffed up by their pretence to wisdom.... It is a general rule

[56] Limburg-Styrum, *Kurze Bemerkungen, wie sich gegen den Göttingischen Professor Schlözer zu benehmen sei* (Regensburg, 1784). It is easy to assemble a host of Conservative voices critical of the freedom of the press, as has been done by W. Wenck in his *Deutschland vor hundert Jahren* (2 vols., Leipzig, 1887-90), I, 92-99.

[57] See, for example, Brandes, *Betrachtungen über den Zeitgeist*, pp. 252-57, and Eckartshausen, "Einige Worte über Journalisterey und Publizität," in *Über Religion*, pp. 154ff.

today that the most honest peasant is invariably the stupidest and the most ignorant. The officer on the drill ground has exactly the same experience as the landlord on his estate: the most uncouth and ignorant peasant will invariably make the best soldier. He can be treated as if he were a machine, and when he is so treated one can rely upon him absolutely.[58]

Conservatives attacked with special venom the progressive education introduced by Basedow and his disciples. They asserted that the *Philanthropine* were corrupters of youth which produced men strong on *Aufklärung* but useless for any kind of constructive work in society. Basedow's ideal of training the *whole* man—instead of encouraging specialization—and of teaching children in a playful spirit only what they wanted to learn when they felt themselves ready for it aroused a mixture of hostility and ridicule. J. G. Schlosser (1739-99), a prominent Badenese official who wrote widely on political, economic, and educational topics, put the case for early specialization in the following terms:

> The vocations of men are in most cases so incompatible with the all-around development of their faculties [advocated by Basedow] that I would almost say that one cannot start early enough to encourage the atrophy of two-thirds of those faculties; for most men are destined for vocations where they cannot use them in later life. Why do you castrate oxen and colts when you prepare them for the yoke and the cart, yet wish to develop the totality of human powers in men similarly condemned to the yoke and the cart? They will jump the furrow if you give them the wrong preparation, or kick against the traces until they die.[59]

The function of education was, in Schlosser's view, *not* the production of versatile "all-around" men, but rather the preparation of men

[58] Christian Garve, "Über den Charakter der Bauern und ihr Verhältniss gegen die Regierung," *Vermischte Aufsätze* (2 vols., Breslau, 1796-1800), i, 203.

[59] Johann Georg Schlosser, "Zweytes Schreiben über die Philanthropinen," *Ephemeriden der Menschheit*, i (1776), 38-39. Schlosser's four letters were reprinted in his *Kleine Schriften* (Basel, 1779), i, 1-114. The two standard works on Schlosser are Alfred Nicolovius, *J. G. Schlosser's Leben und literarisches Wirken* (Bonn, 1844) and Eberhard Gothein, *J. G. Schlosser als badischer Beamter* (Heidelberg, 1899). A valuable modern "rediscovery" is Detlev W. Schumann, "Neuorientierung im 18. Jahrhundert," *Modern Language Quarterly*, ix (1948), 66-73; the same author reports on "Eine politische Zirkularkorrespondenz J. G. Schlossers und seiner oberrheinischen Freunde," *Goethe, Neue Folge des Jahrbuchs der Goethe Gesellschaft*, xxii (1960), 240-68. Schlosser's political views, an interesting medley of Conservative and "enlightened" views, can best be studied in his "Politische Fragmente," *Kleine Schriften* (Basel, 1780) ii, 224-60.

capable of performing useful—however humble—social functions un-spoiled by excessive expectations: "It is very simple to idealise the 'highest degree of perfection'; it is very difficult to define the appropriate degree of the good."[60] As an example of the danger of too much well-roundedness Schlosser condemned Basedow's penchant for athletics: what was the point of turning all children into athletes when most of them would be forced to live sedentary lives as adults? The greatest danger of all lay in the playful, joyful, diversified life of the *Philanthropine* (Basedow believed that children should change activities every half hour). This was the worst kind of preparation for real life: "Are the philanthropists not mistaken when they fail to accustom their charges early to steady work, especially continuous, prolonged, and strenuous mental work?"[61] Life required that allotted work be finished before a man started on recreation; Basedow taught his pupils, on the contrary, a hopeless confusion between work and recreation. An example was his teaching of foreign languages as a sort of game, instead of relying upon the traditional method of memorizing words. Schlosser was skeptical about the substantive results of the new method; and he was certain that the traditional method possessed "character building value" in encouraging industry, attention, and patience: "A man who spent his childhood in play must, on the other hand, remain a playing child all his life."[62]

Ernst Brandes criticized the principle of teaching children only what they could understand when and as they were ready for it. This principle ignored the fact that some important things were not a matter of understanding at all, but rather of sentiment and habit—for example, religion, which Basedow treated lightly because its principles obviously exceeded the comprehension of children. Basedow provoked Brandes' anger by his refusal to teach his charges any prayers before they were ten on the grounds that earlier prayers could only be a mumbling of ill-understood words.[63]

Eckartshausen passed the following final judgment upon the practices of the educational reformers à la Basedow:

[60] *Zweytes Schreiben*, p. 33. [61] Ibid., p. 40.
[62] Ibid., p. 50.
[63] Brandes, *Betrachtungen über den Zeitgeist*, pp. 44-50, 130-39. For a vitriolic attack upon the irreligious character of the Philanthropine see a pastoral letter read from all Lutheran pulpits in Hamburg on April 25, 1764, at the command of the Senate: *Pastoralschreiben an die Gemeinden Gottes in Hamburg, um dieselben vor der Gottesvergessenheit, Gottlosigkeit und Gotteslästerung dieser Zeiten väterlich zu warnen und treulich zu vermahnen.* The author was J. M. Goeze, whose famous controversy with Lessing will be examined in Ch. 3.

They are too impatient to wait for the autumn: they want to have blossoms and fruits at the same time. They claim to see the adult in the child, in fact they turn the adult into a perpetual child. They provide us with forced green plants from their hothouses, plants which carry the hotbed flavor (*Mistbettengeschmack*) for the rest of their life, and offend the gums of every healthy man. They expect our children to learn everything as a game—and produce young men who remain playboys all their lives and look down upon every serious and strenuous activity as mere barbarism.[64]

Although Conservatives often deplored the rise of popular education (especially progressive education), the spread of literacy, and the prevalence of *Publizität*, they reluctantly realized that all of these developments had an irreversible character. There was little to be gained by nostalgic regret for the past and sterile denunciation of the present: the task facing Conservatives was rather one of "getting the Conservative message across" in competition with the writings of *Aufklärung* authors. To this end Conservatives wrote and distributed in quantity a number of popular expositions of Conservative religious and political principles in the 1780's. For example, Jakob Friedrich Feddersen, a Lutheran *Domprediger* of Braunschweig, wrote a *Christian Book of Moral Instruction for Townspeople and Peasants*,[65] which was circulated in tens of thousands of copies upon the suggestion of King Christian VII of Denmark. Written in a simple style, it was replete with homely examples drawn from everyday life as it described the duties of a Christian man in marriage, in educating his children, in earning a livelihood, in church attendance, in political loyalty, et cetera. Feddersen urged his lower-class readers to abide by the traditional Christian virtues, and demonstrated that it was equally to their temporal and eternal advantage to do so. The same theme was developed—this time for political life only—by Bishop Styrum in his *Volkskatechismus* (1784), which will be paraphrased in detail in Ch. 5.

A series of Conservative journals began publication around 1780 in a deliberate attempt to break the power of the *Aufklärung* over the mind of the educated classes of Germany. They were at first exclusively of a religious-theological character. The Giessen theology professor H. Köster, a figure easily ridiculed by the *Aufklärer* because he had written a defense of the Devil's existence which quickly reached a

---

[64] Eckartshausen, Über die litterarische Intoleranz," pp. 128-29.
[65] J. F. Feddersen, *Christliches Sittenbuch für den Bürger und Landmann* (Hamburg and Kiel, 1783).

third edition,[66] sought to rally all the Protestant foes of the *Aufklärung* in his *Die neuesten Religionsbegebenheiten* (Giessen, 1777-96). The Mainz Jesuit Hermann Goldhagen (1718-94) attempted the same task for the Catholic part of Germany in his Mainzer *Religionsjournal* (1776-94);[67] Goldhagen was an especially virulent foe of Josephinism. He secured powerful support from a group of Augsburg Jesuits under the leadership of Joseph Anton Weissenbach (1734-1801), a prolific writer best known for his two-volume work on *Die Vorbothen des neuen Heidenthums* (*The Harbingers of the New Paganism*).[68] The Augsburg Jesuits published a vigorous review journal, *Kritik über gewisse Kritiker, Rezensenten und Broschürenmacher* (1787-96), which sought to refute every book and pamphlet produced by the writers of the German *Aufklärung*. The Jesuits also stressed the need to fight pamphlets not just with critical reviews but with counterpamphlets written in a popular style and distributed on a scale similar to that of the propaganda of the *Aufklärung*. They themselves wrote many pamphlets and reprinted numerous others, especially anti-Josephine tracts, in a series launched in 1783.[69]

Conservatives felt rather helpless in the face of the "enlightened absolutism" of men like Joseph II. They could not easily preach rebellion

[66] H. Köster, *Demütige Bitte um Bekehrung an die grossen Männer, welche keinen Teufel glauben* (3rd edn., Giessen, 1775). Köster's academic defense of Protestantism was paralleled on the popular level by a Hamburg journal edited by Pastor Christian Ziegra after 1758, *Freiwillige Beiträge zu den Hamburgen Nachrichten aus dem Reiche der Gelehrsamkeit*, popularly called *Die Schwarze Zeitung*. It denounced not only theological *Aufklärung* but the "frivolous and immoral poetry" of Wieland, Goethe, and Bürger. See G. R. Röpe, *J. M. Goeze* (Hamburg, 1860).

[67] See the competent (unpublished) Cologne doctoral dissertation by J. Hompesch, *Hermann Goldhagens Religionsjournal* (1923).

[68] J. A. Weissenbach, *Die Vorbothen des neuen Heidenthums und die Anstalten, die dazu vorgekehrt worden sind . . . zum Gebrauch derjenigen, denen daran liegt, die Welt zu kennen* (2 vols., n.p. [Basel], 1779). The book was originally published anonymously but the author soon became known.

[69] *Neueste Sammlung jener Schriften, die vor einigen Jahren her über verschiedene wichtigsten Gegenstände zum Steuer der Wahrheit im Druck erschienen sind* (Augsburg, 1783ff.). Followed in 1789 by *Gesammelte Schriften unserer Zeit zur Vertheidigung der Religion und Wahrheit*. The work of the Augsburg Jesuits is examined in the thorough and sympathetic study of Hildegard Mahler, *Das Geistesleben Augsburgs im 18. Jahrhundert im Spiegel der Augsburger Zeitschriften* (Augsburg, 1934), Ch. 11: "Die Augsburger Katholiken im Kampf mit dem Zeitgeist." Augsburg also became the center of the *Deutsche Gesellschaft zur Beförderung reiner Lehre und wahrer Gottseligkeit* (1777), the German equivalent of the *English Society for the Promotion of Christian Knowledge*. The founder, J. A. Urlsperger, served as the society's main traveling missionary until his death in 1807.

against a legitimate monarch (however misguided his policies), while the Jesuit doctrine of tyrannicide, long an albatross around the neck of the Catholic party and coresponsible for the Papal suppression of the Jesuits in 1773, was obviously obsolete. The sole hope of Conservatives lay in the strength of the public opposition provoked by Joseph's doctrinaire ruthlessness and lack of ordinary human considerations —and Austrian Conservatives naturally did everything in their power to fan this opposition against the Josephine reforms. In countries and provinces where effective *Stände* bodies had survived—most notably Hungary and Belgium—Conservatives attempted to mobilize them on behalf of the threatened *status quo*. Where *Stände* bodies no longer existed—or were hopelessly impotent—there was no institutional remedy for the evils of "enlightened despotism"; here Conservatives had no choice but to suffer in resignation until the monarchs abandoned their reform programs under the panic produced by the French Revolution.

Conservatives met, finally, the organized attempt to spread *Aufklärung* through such secret societies as the Freemasons and *Illuminati* by a double program of exposing the network of Radical subversion (by the so-called "conspiracy theory") and by founding a powerful countersecret society, the Rosicrucians. The battle between *Illuminati* and Rosicrucians was a major preoccupation of the German public mind in the 1780's and will be examined in the next chapter.

CHAPTER 2

Masons, Illuminati, and Rosicrucians

The Role of Secret Societies

THE PRINCIPLES of the *Aufklärung* called for an individualistic, even atomistic structure of society; but this did not prevent the *Aufklärer* from feeling the common human need for community and membership in organized institutions—a fact proved by the rise of Freemasonry, which may be defined as an organized movement dedicated to promoting the principles of *Aufklärung*. It met man's perennial need for solidarity, mutual sympathy, and common engagement in a cause; while its secret and ritualistic character filled the psychological vacuum left by the collapse of religious miracle, mystery, and authority. Masonry also gave the *Aufklärung* an institutional outlet which neither periodicals nor enlightened despotism could provide. The journals of the *Aufklärung* were always harassed, and sometimes suppressed, by obscurantist authority; the alliance between *Aufklärung* and absolutism depended upon the personal qualities of individual rulers. Masonry provided the *Aufklärung* with a world-wide organization whose power aroused vast Conservative apprehensions. It was founded in England in 1717 as a rather simple system of lodges, without any deliberate desire to challenge the existing structure of society; it spread to the Continent in the next two decades, developing in the process a highly complex organization and an increasingly explicit desire to reform society.[1]

The purpose of Masonry was to spread *Aufklärung* in defiance of the existing patterns of social hierarchy, political authority, and traditionalist religion. No one understood this better than the Catholic Church, which consequently issued a long series of anti-Masonic bulls, beginning with one by Pope Clement XII in 1738. Both Masonry and Catholicism were universal in outlook, cosmopolitan in organization, and devoted to the brotherhood of man, but these external similarities only compounded friction between the two. The Catholic brotherhood of

[1] The literature on the origins of Masonry is endless, and cannot be listed here. The best brief introduction, written from a Masonic point of view, is Eugen Lennhoff, *Die Freimaurer. Geschichte, Wesen, Wirken und Geheimniss der Königlichen Kunst* (Vienna, 1928); the best history of German Masonry (with a full discussion of origins) is Ferdinand Runkel, *Geschichte der Freimaurerei in Deutschland* (3 vols., Berlin, 1931-32), despite its nationalist outlook and hostility to "Left wing" Masonry.

84

man, based upon the Fatherhood of God, was a far different conception from the Masonic brotherhood, based upon man's common rationality, ethical autonomy, and desire for happiness.[2]

Masonry showed its rationalist and humanitarian outlook in the promotion of tolerance, free inquiry, the bridging of class barriers, and the elimination of social injustice. The declared rationality of its goals was strangely combined, however, with an irrational mysticism in its ritualistic practices. The fact that Masonry met both the rational and the irrational needs of eighteenth-century man must be considered a major source of its wide appeal. Masonry possessed many of the qualities of an Oriental mystery cult; its members went through colorful initiation ceremonies at each stage of advance in a society based upon hierarchical principles; they searched for a "light" to promote their internal transformation; they experienced an intense sense of brotherhood as they participated in an exclusive and occult ritual in which every gesture and word had a symbolic as well as a literal meaning. Yet they differed from the mystery cults of earlier centuries—for example, the Hellenistic era—in not seeking withdrawal from a world believed to be incorrigible; the Masonic movement aimed, on the contrary, at constructing a perfect earthly society here and now through deliberate human effort. The ceremonies in the lodge had the purpose of preparing the participating brothers for the great task of building the "temple of the human race" in the world outside.[3]

The spread of Masonry throughout Germany was furthered by the prestige which English culture possessed in the age of Richardson and Sterne. The lodges did not have to contend with much institutional competition on the German scene. The atmosphere of courts was too stiff and formal to fill the emotional needs of Germans, whether "enlightened" or not; the French type of *salon* was rare in a country not noted for either wit or frivolity; while voluntary political or religious associations (like those flourishing in England) were virtually unknown in a country ruled by petty despots jealously guarding their prerogatives. The spirit of Masonic brotherhood met a genuine German need, especially since it could easily combine with the pre-romantic cult of friendship so characteristic of the age of the *Sturm und Drang*. It is small wonder that nearly everybody in Germany who was in any

[2] The conflict between Catholicism and Masonry is stated forcefully in Franz Alfred Six, *Studien zur Geistesgeschichte der Freimaurer* (Hamburg, 1942), Pt. I, a valuable book despite its Nazi prejudices.

[3] A good modern account of Masonic ritual can be found in Bernard E. Jones, *Freemasons' Guide and Compendium* (London, 1950).

way "enlightened"—and even some people who were not—joined a lodge at some time in their lives. Most of the great intellectual and political figures of the age of Goethe can be claimed by Masonry. To mention but a few: Lessing, a Mason from 1771, wrote the famous *Ernst und Falk. Gespräche für Freymaurer* (1778); Herder, a member from 1766, expressed Masonic principles in his *Briefe zur Beförderung der Humanität* (1793); Fichte, a Mason from 1794, wrote a special *Philosophie der Freimaurerei* (1802); while Goethe, a Mason since 1780, made a point of attending the Weimar lodge on important occasions for many years.[4]

The purpose of Masonry was to spread *Aufklärung*; but it must not be thought on that account that every lodge was a conspiratorial center for the transformation of German society. On the contrary, the statutes of most lodges specifically prohibited their members from engaging in political or religious controversy (though this prohibition was far from universally obeyed). The mystical and irrational Masonic ritual became, moreover, for many brothers an end in itself rather than a spur to service in the world beyond the lodge. Masonic theory emphasized the equality of man in repudiating traditional differences of class, race, or creed; but it could not prevent Masonry from degenerating at times into a snobbish parade of pseudoaristocratic follies. Many Masons craved possession of some exclusive and occult secret; they refused to accept the official explanation that dedicated service to humanity was the "real" secret of Masonry—and not much of a secret at that. The result of this craving was a series of aberrations in eighteenth-century continental Masonry which none deplored more than those who remained under the influence of the comparatively simple English mother lodges.

The most famous of these aberrations was the so-called "Strict Observance" with its colorful ritual, exclusive aristocratic appeal, and fantastic Templar genealogy. It claimed to possess special secrets based upon the assertion that it was a continuation of the old Templar Order which Philip the Fair and Clement V had suppressed in 1307. The Strict Observance Masons claimed that Jacob Molay, the last Templar Grand Master, had been able to smuggle important documents out of his final place of imprisonment. These documents had supposedly been carried to Scotland by Hugo von Salm, a canon of Mainz, and had there remained in secure hands until conditions allowed the revival of the Templar Knighthood—with its elaborate hierarchy of

---

[4] Acute observations on the spread of Masonry can be found in Ferdinand Josef Schneider, *Die Freimaurerei und ihr Einfluss auf die geistige Kultur in Deutschland am Ende des XVIII Jahrhunderts* (Prague, 1909), pp. 35ff.

degrees, with only the highest degree possessing all the secrets—
in the eighteenth century. These degrees went far beyond the simple
structure (apprentices, journeymen, and masters) which English
Masonry drew from the guild system. Four new degrees were invented in France around 1740: Scottish knights, novices, Templar
knights proper, and *Eques professus*. Only men of the upper classes
(preferably aristocrats) were ordinarily initiated into these degrees under the Strict Observance, and the initiation rites were
far more elaborate than ordinary Masonic ceremonies. Knights were required to wear elaborate armor, and the ritual was composed in a sonorous and old-fashioned Latin. The romantic and pseudo-medieval
character of the proceedings was unmistakable, and the true Masonic
"enlightened" spirit of rationality, utility, and equality had disappeared. All these characteristics of the Strict Observance were found
also in the Order of the Rosicrucians, which played an important role
in the Conservative campaign against the *Aufklärung*.[5]

The role of Masonry in the history of German Conservatism is very
ambiguous; its ordinary lodges were the institutional center of the
radical attack upon the *status quo*; its aberrations were allied in spirit,
and sometimes in practice, with the Conservative defense of German
society.

The Illuminati and Their Suppression

THE DEVELOPMENT OF THE ORDER

The degeneration of Masonry from an "enlightened" to an "obscurantist"
force left the way open for a far more cohesive and radical secret society, the *Illuminati*, to assume the leadership of the drive for *Aufklärung*. This famous organization possessed the qualities generally found
in conspiratorial secret societies forced to operate in an authoritarian
milieu which does not tolerate "constitutional opposition": clandes-
tine organization; an elitist membership sincerely devoted to the welfare of the masses, though patronizingly contemptuous of the masses
for not knowing *their own* interests; and an inflated self-importance

---

[5] A good account of the development of the "Strict Observance" is G. A.
Schiffmann, *Die Entstehung der Rittergrade in der Freimaurerei um die Mitte
des XVIII Jahrhunderts* (Leipzig, 1882). See also J. G. Findel, *Das Zeitalter der
Verirrungen im Maurerbunde* (Leipzig, 1892), and Gustav Lang, *Aus dem
Ordensleben des 18. Jahrhundert* (Heilbronn, 1929). An able contemporary
ridicule, patterned upon *Don Quixote*, is Theodor Gottlieb von Hippel, *Kreuz
und Querzüge des Ritters A-Z.*, originally published in 1792 but reprinted in
two volumes at Leipzig in 1860. We shall encounter its author again as a
Conservative foe of female emancipation in Ch. 4.

which was further stimulated by the hysterical Conservative fears which it aroused.[6]

The *Illuminati* had many specific traits obviously borrowed from Strict Observance Masonry: an exotic ritual, a strictly hierarchic organization, and the claim to possess exclusive secrets. It did, however, avoid aristocratic pretension and the taint of pseudo-medieval Catholicism. Its organization stressed the importance of obedience, discipline, and secrecy—all qualities essential in an association operating outside the framework of the law. Its existence in a twilight zone of legality attracted a variety of human types: fanatical idealists who relished the dangerous struggle of the children of light against the forces of darkness; adventurers who delighted in matching their wits against an inquisitorial police; power-hungry leaders who manipulated a docile body of followers through command, espionage, blackmail, and dire threats against traitors; and opportunists who could hope, before the order became utterly disreputable, that their careers would be fostered by the cliquish solidarity for which the order was notable. The uprooted intelligentsia of the late eighteenth century—its spiritual moorings severed by the disintegration of Christian belief, its civic impulses paralyzed by absolutist polities—could find in the order a sense of mission to promote the welfare of the human race, and a ritual calculated to satisfy the irrepressible irrational impulses which stirred even "enlightened" hearts.[7]

The external history of the *Illuminati* can be quickly told. The order was founded in 1776 by Adam Weishaupt (1784-1830), a professor of law at the Bavarian University of Ingolstadt constantly at odds with the locally dominant Jesuits.[8] It grew slowly and was at first restricted

[6] Valuable books on the general characteristics of secret political societies include Eugen Lennhoff, *Politische Geheimbünde im Völkergeschehen* (Berlin, 1932), and Georg Schuster, *Die geheimen Gesellschaften, Verbindungen und Orden* (2 vols., Leipzig, 1906), two works written by moderate Masons; Franz Schweyer, *Politische Geheimverbände* (Freiburg, 1925), a Catholic work; and Will Erich Peuckert, *Geheim Kulte* (Heidelberg, 1951), an esoteric study by a man who devoted a lifetime to the study of various mystery cults.

[7] The two standard works are Leopold Engel, *Geschichte des Illuminatenordens* (Berlin, 1906), and R. Le Forestier, *Les Illuminés de Bavière et la Francmaçonnerie allemande* (Paris, 1914). Two valuable brief studies are August Kluckhohn, "Die Illuminaten und die Aufklärung in Bayern unter Karl Theodor," *Vorträge und Aufsätze* (Munich, 1894), pp. 344-99, and Eugen Lennhoff, *Politische Geheimbünde*, pp. 17-108. The position of Illuminism in intellectual history, and especially its influence upon romanticism, is examined in an important French work: Auguste Viatte, *Les sources occultes du romantisme. Illuminisme. Theosophie 1770-1820* (Paris, 1928).

[8] There is no adequate biographical study of Weishaupt. Daniel Jacobi, "Adam

to Bavaria, with Weishaupt showing little capacity for organization and an unusual talent for antagonizing many of his immediate lieutenants. The order assumed national importance only when Freiherr Adolph von Knigge (1752-96) took charge of an organizational drive in Northern Germany in 1781 at the very time when the historical fallacies of Strict Observance Masonry were exposed—a situation which left an ideological vacuum which Illuminism was well-prepared to fill.[9] Knigge was a remarkable Hannoverian aristocrat who retains some fame today as the author of a compendium *Über den Umgang mit Menschen*.[10] He won many influential converts for Illuminism in years of indefatigable missionary labor, and soon outshone Weishaupt in the inner councils of the order. Personal rivalry was probably the main reason for the break between the two men after three years of close cooperation. Knigge's departure signalized the beginning of the end of the order; the persecution by the Bavarian government which began in 1785 was merely the *coup de grâce*.

It is important to recount briefly the aims, structure, and methods of the *Illuminati* in order to understand its influence and to explain the pathological suspicions it aroused among German Conservatives. Its immediate aim was twofold: to promote the individual perfection of its members, and to reform society as a whole in accordance with the principles of *Aufklärung*. The official statutes of 1781 declared as the order's objectives:

> to make the improvement of their moral character appear interesting and necessary to its members; to encourage a humane and sociable outlook; to inhibit all vicious impulses; to support Virtue,

---

Weishaupt," *ADB*, XLI (1896), 539-50, gives a sympathetic sketch of his life. A. Geitner, "Der Ingolstadter Universitätsprofessor Adam Weishaupt und sein Geheimbund der Illuminaten," *Gelbe Hefte*, I (1924-25), 239-57, is a sprightly but hostile account. His work as a professional philosopher is discussed in Joseph Bach, "Adam Weishaupt, der Gründer des Ordens der Illuminaten, als Gegner des Königsberger Philosophen Immanuel Kant," *Hist-Polit. Blätter*, CXXVII (1901), 94-114. Indispensable for understanding Weishaupt's intentions and motives is his autobiographical narrative, *Pythagoras oder Betrachtungen über die geheime Welt und Regierungskunst* (Frankfurt and Leipzig, 1790).

[9] The literature on Knigge is voluminous. The best modern study is Reinhold Grabe, *Das Geheimniss des Adolph Freiherrn von Knigge* (Hamburg, 1936). Two valuable dissertations are Joseph Popp, *Weltanschauung und Hauptwerke des Freiherrn Adolph Knigge* (Leipzig, 1931), and Karl Spengler, *Die publizistische Tätigkeit des Freiherrn Adolph von Knigge während der französischen Revolution* (Bonn, 1931), both including extensive bibliographies.

[10] This predecessor of Dale Carnegie's *How to Win Friends and Influence People* was republished in an abbreviated version by Hans Feigl (Munich and Leipzig, 1911).

wherever she is threatened or oppressed by Vice; to further the advance of deserving persons and to spread useful knowledge among the broad mass of people who were at present deprived of all education.[11]

This innocent-sounding official statement was calculated to conceal the fact that the *Illuminati* were pledged to engage in unremitting warfare against every form of tyranny, oppression and superstition—or, to put matters concretely, against royal absolutism, feudal exploitation, and supernatural religion. They were, of course, not pledged to destroy all these evils immediately, or to use revolutionary violence for this purpose. On the contrary, the statutes of the order declared specifically that "for the security and peace of mind of every present and future member of this association, and to disarm all unjustified outside hostility as well as agonizing uncertainty within the Order: that it does not promote any attitudes or actions hostile to religion, the state, or good morals."[12] What attitudes were in fact "hostile to religion, the state, or good morals" was presumably left to the judgment of Weishaupt and the "areopagus" which stood at the apex of the order. Of these men it can be said that they sincerely believed that the existing religion and society were incompatible with the dictates of "natural" religion and "natural" society. For them Christianity was a degenerate departure from man's "natural" religious condition; they believed that contemporary society showed a deplorable decline from an earlier condition of simplicity, equality, and rustic happiness. Their sentimental and in some ways specifically anarchist hostility to existing political and religious conditions could easily be taken for atheism and subversive intent, especially as they were prone to use the exaggerated language of the *Sturm und Drang*.[13]

The fears provoked by the *Illuminati* arose even more from their organization than their program. Weishaupt was a bitter foe of the Jesuits, but his own organization paid the Jesuits the sincere compliment of imitation. Authority in the *Illuminatenorden* proceeded from top to bottom, with Weishaupt as general and an areopagus of immediate associates claiming dictatorial authority over lesser members. They constituted a body of secret superiors whose identity was known only to their immediate subordinates. Weishaupt justified elaborate

[11] Printed in Engel, op.cit., p. 97.   [12] Ibid.
[13] An excellent account of the program of the *Illuminati*, and a refutation of the fantastic accusations directed against them, can be found in Adam Weishaupt's own *Apologie der Illuminaten* (Frankfurt and Leipzig, 1786), written immediately after the suppression of the order.

secrecy not only on prudential but also on psychological grounds. In the words of the 1781 statute:

> The Order will seek to remain clandestine as much as possible, for whatever is secret and hidden has a special attraction for men: it attracts the interest of outsiders and enhances the loyalty of insiders. It gives superiors a special opportunity to judge the conduct of men in the lower grades under circumstances where they do not know that they are being observed. It also gives the Order some protection from the impertinent curiosity of spies. Its noble purposes can be thwarted less easily and any thirst for power which may exist on the part of superiors can be repressed more easily [since there is no open acclamation, electioneering, et cetera].[14]

The order was organized into an elaborate hierarchy of nine grades. The lower grades (called novices, minervals, and lesser illuminati) consisted of small circles which met regularly to discuss "improving books" under the guidance of a superior. The junior members sometimes presented papers on "elevating topics" for criticism; the activity of the order at this level was remarkably similar to tutorial groups at present-day American colleges. The primary stress was placed, however, upon moral elevation rather than intellectual development. Self-examination was inculcated as the indispensable road to individual improvement. Members were required not only to examine themselves in accordance with elaborate questionnaires, but also to report to their superiors on the qualities of their fellow novices. This practice of espionage (the so-called *quibuslicet*) provided the leadership with detailed information on their flock, and thereby offered opportunities for the employment of blackmail in maintaining discipline. Every novice was required to swear an oath of absolute secrecy and unconditional obedience, though the odiousness of the latter was mitigated by the assurances that the order pursued neither illegal nor immoral objectives. The foes of the order asserted that novices granted their superiors the *ius vitae et necis*, but there is no documentary evidence for this charge. None of the numerous known "traitors" died as the result of organizational murder. Both discipline and a close *esprit de corps* was maintained by a colorful and awesome ritual. A sense of mystery was created by every member's assuming a classical name, with Weishaupt, for example, becoming Spartacus and Knigge Philo.

The higher grades of the order were never completed, and the entire structure gives the impression of being both improvised and poor-

---

[14] Engel, op.cit., p. 102.

ly coordinated. The middle grades consisted of masons, ordinary knights, and Scottish knights—a terminology which reveals borrowing from the Strict Observance. The highest group, or "mystery class," was to consist of the grades of priest, regent, and magus. Weishaupt and Knigge had severe differences about how to construct these topmost honors, and the order was suppressed before they actually came into existence. Members of the highest degree were supposed to possess some secret unknown to their inferior brethren, but there is no evidence that such a secret actually existed. Hostile authors assumed that the secret was nothing more or less than a deliberate plan for overthrowing the existing religion and society by revolutionary means; but, in fact, the order worked only for the eventual triumph of the principles of natural religion and natural society through the gradual perfection of the human race. Weishaupt assuredly lacked any concrete revolutionary plans; he was basically a utopian visionary rather than a practical man of affairs. The best proof of his political innocence is to be found in the fact that he spent the forty-five years of his retirement trying to refute the Kantian epistemology instead of seeking any worldly comeback.[15]

The influence which the order achieved before it was suppressed in 1785 is a tribute to Knigge's organizing genius. He seized the chance created by the collapse of Strict Observance Masonry at the Wilhelmsbad Convent (1782) to advertise the *Illuminati* as the long-sought-after true "secret superiors" of Masonry—an approach made effective by the fact that the legend of the Templar origin of Masonry had just been decisively punctured. Many of the recruits won by Knigge held positions in existing Masonic lodges, with the *Illuminati* seeking to make Masonry a "front organization" dominated by themselves. Knigge appointed as "national superiors" (*Nationalobere*), reporting directly to Weishaupt, Count Johann Martin zu Stolberg-Rössla for Germany, Prince Charles of Hessen-Cassel (who was serving as Danish governor of Holstein) for the Scandinavian countries, and Count Leopold Kolowrat, Supreme Chancellor in Vienna, for the Habsburg monarchy. A remarkable number of famous men joined individual branches of the *Illuminatenorden*. In Vienna Joseph von Sonnenfels, the eminent professor at the university; Gottfried van Swieten, president of the Com-

---

[15] The best statement of the final aims of the *Illuminati* is "Gemeinschaftlicher Schluss des Areopagus über den Zweck, die Mittel und Einrichtung der Gesellschaft" (1781), printed in Engel, *op.cit.*, pp. 108-13. The ritualistic practices were betrayed by an anonymous renegade, probably Johann Heinrich Faber, in *Der ächte Illuminat, oder die wahren, unverbesserten Rituale der Illuminaten* (Edessa [Frankfurt], 1788).

mission for Education; Count Johann Cobenzl, later foreign minister; and the poet Alxinger were all *Illuminati*. In Basel Ochs, who later headed the Swiss Jacobins; in Strassburg Dietrich, later famous as revolutionary mayor; in Stuttgart C. F. Cotta, the well-known publisher; in Munich nearly everybody that was anybody including Montgelas, later the creator of modern Bavaria; in Weimar Duke Karl August, Goethe, and Herder; in Hannover Karl von Hardenberg, the later Prussian reformer; in Braunschweig the reigning Duke Ferdinand; in Kassel Mauvillon, Mirabeau's cicerone on German affairs; in Hamburg the merchant prince Sieveking, whose country house provided the setting for the famous anniversary celebration of the storming of the Bastille in 1790—all were members. To this list must be added several minor princes, most notably Duke Ernst of Gotha, who made Weishaupt a *Hofrat* with a high pension when the founder of the *Illuminatenorden* was forced to flee from his native Bavaria. The order was strongest in Bavaria, Austria, and the small courts of West and Northwest Germany.[16]

A happy find by the archivist Josef Hansen provides us with a complete membership list for the Rhineland for the year 1784, when the *Illuminatenorden* stood at the peak of its influence. The list was drawn up by Karl Kraber, the *Hofmeister* of the sons of Count zu Stolberg-Rössla, who served—as we have seen—as *Nationalober* for the German province. Stolberg resided at the court of his brother-in-law, the Count of Wied, at Neuwied on the Rhine, and was obviously in a position to know personally all *Illuminati* in his part of the country. The list includes some 120 names, distributed geographically as follows: Mainz, 50, including Bishop Dalberg, later head of the Napoleonic Confederation of the Rhine; Neuwied, 29, headed by Count Stolberg himself; Aachen, 18; Bonn, 11, headed by the *Hoforganist* Christian Neefe, the teacher of the young Beethoven; Cologne, 4; and Koblenz, 2, including the father of Prince Metternich. This very uneven distribution is indicative of the great role played by local enthusiasm and organizing skill. Hansen also shows that nearly all *Illuminati* were simultaneously members of Masonic lodges, usually in a leading capacity, which must have multiplied the influence of the order. Membership in the *Illuminatenorden* was almost exclusively "upper class": it was dominated by princes, officials, priests, officers, lawyers, doctors, and merchants. It is certain that the common people—and especially peasants—were nei-

[16] The best analysis of *Illuminati* membership is Adolf Rossberg, *Freimaurerei und Politik im Zeitalter der französischen Revolution* (Berlin, 1942), Pt. I, a valuable book despite its disgraceful Nazi prejudices.

ther interested in, nor eligible for, membership. When the order was suppressed in Bavaria in the years after 1785, one of its leaders was asked whether peasants had participated. He replied: "That would be completely impossible. How can one drum *Aufklärung* into thick peasant skulls?"[17]

The total membership has been estimated as low as 2,000 and as high as 4,000, a remarkable number in view of its elite character. It would have warranted the fear of its antagonists if it had in fact operated as a cohesive, disciplined group under central direction. It is true that members helped one another to find jobs; there is no evidence, however, that they pursued a specific political program under centralized direction. Even their later sympathy for the French invaders expressed itself more in collaboration after, rather than treasonable activity before, the Jacobin conquest.

Their infiltration into high governmental positions was paralleled by their influence in the fields of education, journalism, and book distribution. The famous *Karlsschule* in Stuttgart (Schiller's alma mater) had several *Illuminati* on its staff. The educational movement headed by Basedow taught *Illuminati* principles, though Basedow himself apparently never joined the order. The University of Göttingen had several *Illuminati* among its professors, which led Weishaupt to exclaim with surprise that Ingolstadt was giving the law to its far more distinguished North German rival. Tutorial positions offered excellent leverage for working for the future triumph of the *Aufklärung*: the prominent *Illuminat* Leuchsenring served, for example, as tutor to the Prussian crown prince who became Frederick William III (though the later conduct of his pupil must have disappointed him). The two leading student societies (*Studentenorden*), the *Konstantisten* and the *Schwarze Brüder*, were both infiltrated by *Illuminati*. The actual influence of the order upon the education of Germany's youth obviously cannot be quantitatively defined, and statistical calculations of the infiltration of the professorate are equally impossible to make. These examples suffice to explain, however, the fact that Conservatives called for a drastic purge of educational institutions.[18]

Conservatives were even more concerned about the condition of the press and the book trade. The two leading "enlightened" journals published in Berlin, Biester's *Monatsschrift* and Nicolai's *Allgemeine*

[17] Ludwig Wolfram, "Die Illuminaten in Bayern und ihre Verfolgung," *Programm des kgl. humanistischen Gymnasiums in Erlangen* (2 vols., Erlangen 1899-1900), II, 1. For the whole paragraph see J. Hansen, *Quellen*, I, 41-74.
[18] Rossberg, op.cit., Pt. II, Chs. 2 and 3.

Deutsche Bibliothek, stood under *Illuminati* influence. Many publishers specialized, for commercial if not for ideological reasons, in *Aufklärungsliteratur*, and Conservative authors never ceased to complain that they were getting unfair treatment from booksellers, reviewers, and reading clubs. Their complaints were obviously exaggerated but received some justification from a much discussed project developed by K. F. Bahrdt, a Radical theologian, for advancing *Aufklärung* under the name of *Deutsche Union* in 1788. Bahrdt proposed the founding of a central organization embracing "enlightened" authors and readers alike. Its specific aim was to secure control over a large part of the book trade by licensing a network of four hundred reading clubs throughout Germany. These clubs would agree to purchase books exclusively through the association and would thus give its authors what amounted to large guaranteed sales, while its readers could be certain to receive only books of whose tendency they approved. The association would publish a book review recommending works to the participating clubs at regular intervals.[19]

This entire scheme—similar to the English "Left Book Club" of the 1930's—was nothing but a brain child of Bahrdt's and a bogey for Conservatives, for it never had a chance of implementation. Authors were unlikely to join an association headed by a man of Bahrdt's bad reputation, and several even protested openly that he was using their name without proper authorization in his advertising circulars; established booksellers naturally disliked the prospect of a new and powerful competitor; while readers were unlikely to be satisfied with the narrow range of publications distributed by a single source. A prominent *Illuminat*, Johann Christian Bode, took the lead in exposing the scheme as one calculated to serve only Bahrdt's tottering personal fortunes.[20] The chief organizer soon found himself in jail for the crime of having publicly ridiculed Wöllner, the powerful Prussian minister. Many Conservatives continued, however, to fear the Union as a specter, for it symbolized the advance of a Radical public opinion against which they knew themselves to be on the defensive.

[19] A good account of the Deutsche Union is the book by L. A. Hoffmann, *Aktenmässige Darstellung der Deutschen Union* (Vienna, 1796), despite Hoffmann's vehement hostility. He secured control of many key documents by pretending for some time that he was anxious to join the Union. An even more encyclopedic contemporary account is Degenhart Pott, *Pragmatische Geschichte und endliche Aufklärung der Deutschen Union der XXIIiger* (5 vols., Leipzig, 1798), based upon Bahrdt's confiscated papers.

[20] J. C. Bode, *Mehr Noten als Text, oder die Deutsche Union der Zweiundzwanziger* (Leipzig, 1789).

THE BIRTH OF THE "CONSPIRACY THEORY"

The manifold activities, real and alleged, of the *Illuminati* aroused considerable fears among German Conservatives. Some seriously began to believe that they constituted an organized conspiracy actively dedicated to the destruction of existing religion, society, and political authority. The psychological source and sociological function of this "conspiracy theory" will be examined when we deal with the German response to the French Revolution, since it assumed a broad influence only at that time. It must suffice to note here that the "conspiracy theory" was fully articulated—like so many other elements of German Conservatism—before 1789 and therefore independently of the French Revolution. The theory was the main theme of a much discussed book written by an official of the Weimar government, Ernst August Anton von Göchhausen (1740-1824),[21] under the title *Exposure of the Cosmopolitan System*,[22] in 1786.

This book was written in the epistolary manner popularized by Richardson, and it is therefore not always easy to determine which opinions expressed by which correspondent represent the views of the author. The most revealing letters are written by a young Prussian officer, called Wilhelm v. St., about his experiences as he seeks to pene-

[21] He was a *wirklicher Geheimer Kammerrat* (1784) and resided in Eisenach after joining the Weimar service in 1769 upon his retirement from the Prussian army with the rank of captain. Göchhausen's mentality appears to have been that of the typical renegade who cannot make himself psychologically free of what he once adored and now repudiates. He had joined the Philadelphia lodge in Halle as a young man (1763) and fallen victim to some of the hoaxes perpetrated by Strict Observance Masonry; it is unknown whether he was ever an *Illuminat* himself. On Göchhausen see W. Wenck, *Deutschland vor hundert Jahren*, II, 264-65, a valuable bibliographical note; *Allgemeines Handbuch der Freimaurerei* (Leipzig, 1900), I, 365-66, a bland account minimizing the anti-Masonic character of his work; J. G. Meusel, *Das Gelehrte Teutschland oder Lexikon der Jetzt lebenden teutschen Schriftsteller* (5th edn., Lemgo, 1796), II, 539-55, important for ascribing several anonymous works to him; and Heinrich Döring, "Ernst August Anton von Göchhausen," *Allgemeine Enzyclopädie der Wissenschaften und Künste* (eds. J. S. Ersch and J. G. Gruber), LXXII (1861), 41-43, still the best biographical sketch. Another early champion of the "conspiracy theory" was Joseph Niclas Count Windisch-Grätz (1744-1802), a close boyhood friend of the Emperor Josef II who became a sharp critic of the precipitate Josephine reform program. See his *Objections aux societes secrètes* (London, 1788). On Windisch-Grätz see Wurzbach, LVII (1889), 60-63.

[22] Anonymous, *Enthüllung des Systems der Weltbürger-Republik. In Briefen aus der Verlassenschaft eines Freymaurers* (Rome [Leipzig], 1786). Henceforth cited as *Enthüllung*. The book provoked a vast critical literature. Göchhausen replied to his critics in his *Aufschluss und Verteidigung der Enthüllung des Systems der Weltbürger-Republik. Nebst einer Bitte an die Leser* (Rome [Leipzig], 1787).

trate the secret of Masonry. This is how he describes to his father (a Prussian general immune to all enthusiasm) his ecstasy when he was allowed to participate in Masonic rites at last:

Our secret meetings stir our hearts (*sind hertzerhebend*). We experience sacred hours devoted to the brotherly love of mankind as we assemble in a quiet place far removed from the bustle of the world. Such a place is rightly called a "temple" since all profane relationships lose their significance there. A prince becomes a simple brother, the most humble of his subjects can communicate with him upon the basis of perfect equality. Every man is a brother to every other regardless of distinctions of rank and religion. Every meeting of the lodge strengthens me tenfold in my resolve to walk the thorny path of life as an upright and free man. My heart expands and embraces all the world—in short, I become a cosmopolitan in feeling (*es schlägt Weltbürgergefühl*).[23]

The father did not take kindly to this kind of sentimentality. He accused his son of succumbing to a fuzzy emotional exaltation. He criticized Masonic secrecy-mongering as a curious method of expressing a sense of brotherhood. "Why do you segregate yourself from other men? Do you deem yourself superior, or are you in fact inferior to other honest people?"[24] The abandonment of all social distinctions was either ridiculous or dangerous, as it tended to make Masonry a *statum in statu*. The abandonment of all religious distinctions was equally ridiculous— were Moslems, Jews, and cannibals in fact as good as Christians and was it a matter of indifference what men did believe? Was not Christianity a far better guide than Masonry on the "thorny path of life"? The father was also horrified by his son's proud "cosmopolitanism": "You are either a loyal subject or a rebel. There is no third possibility."[25] He added that "a man who repudiates sacred natural, religious, and political ties, in order to substitute ties with his exclusive confederates ... deserves to be exiled from his native country."[26] The father concluded with a warning concerning membership in a group whose real purposes he could not and did not know.

The son ignored this reprimand and continued to pursue the secrets of Masonry. He succeeded to the extent of having some exceedingly revealing discussions with one of his Masonic superiors, the revelations being made plausible by the superior's claiming to have received special permission to reveal some matters ordinarily reserved for the

[23] *Enthüllung*, pp. 172-73.   [24] Ibid., p. 175.
[25] Ibid., p. 177.   [26] Ibid., p. 178.

higher grades. These higher grades are described as a tightly organized conspiratorial group which manipulates the broad mass of Masonry for its own ends. Göchhausen obviously identified this inner group with the *Illuminatenorden*, which was persecuted by the Bavarian government even as he wrote his exposure. The *Illuminati*-Masonic superior justified his manipulation of others with the use of arguments which anticipated those used by Dostoyevsky's *Grand Inquisitor*, while he defended secrecy as essential to prevent persecution by political and ecclesiastical despots.[27]

The hero asked his superior very frankly, "What purposes do the *Illuminati* have in infiltrating and now dominating Masonry?" The reply was blunt and simple: "To emancipate all of mankind from religious and political slavery. Put specifically, to advance deism and cosmopolitanism." The young man was at first horrified by the idea that all men should become deists, and asked incredulously, "You mean to make universal this religion of pure reason—this joyless, formless, heartless metaphysical creation which has emerged from some dry brain?" The superior replied, "Precisely—only the religion of reason can be truly universal, for it alone precludes enthusiasm and its inevitable consequences: religious divisions, sectarian hatred, and the cabal of priests."[28]

The advance to cosmopolitanism, defined as emancipation from constituted political authority, parochial nationalism, and brutal militarism, was the second great objective of the *Illuminati*. In the words of the superior:

> When nations are no longer separated from one another; when citizens are no longer influenced by the exclusive interest of any state or the parochial sentiment of patriotism, which binds them to a particular plot of earth and thereby makes them useless for the great concerns of mankind; when we have finally ceased to be slaves in any sense of the word; when the whole world has become one band of brothers—will not all despots with their special interests disappear? together with the numerous evil conditions which have been created for the sole purpose of serving the interests of despots?[29]

There can be no question that Göchhausen believed in the existence of a dangerous cosmopolitan conspiracy to achieve the goals outlined by the Masonic superior. He gave, however, a confusing twist to his argument by asserting—though only as a probability—that the recently

[27] Ibid., pp. 207ff.   [28] Ibid., pp. 256-57.
[29] Ibid., pp. 235-36.

dissolved Jesuits—of all people!—had infiltrated the *Illuminaten-orden* or were at least competing with it for leadership of the Masonic movement. It would be difficult to think up a theory which was prima facie more absurd than this infiltration of the infiltrators, for the Jesuits had been unrelenting foes of Masonry and *Illuminism* from the very beginning of both organizations. Göchhausen advanced his theory in the following rather cryptic words ascribed to the Masonic superior: "Think of Rome when you think of the Church; of the Caesarist universal monarchy when of Rome; of cosmopolitanism when of Catholicism; of Jesuits when of cosmopolitans, and of Masons when of Jesuits. *That* will provide you with the true key to Masonry."[30]

To make these assertions plausible Göchhausen claimed that the (recently suppressed) Jesuits were far too intelligent to appear in the garb of superstitious monks in an age when "*Aufklärung, Publizität*, finance, industry, commerce, philosophy, tolerance and freedom of the press have become magic words."[31] He claimed that Jesuit operations in "enlightened" Protestant Northern Europe differed drastically in character from those in "obscurantist" Catholic Southern Europe:

> In the nations which are still subject to Rome the Jesuits continue to foster superstition and seek desperately to prevent the introduction of *Aufklärung*; while in "enlightened" nations they vigorously promote *Aufklärung* with the deliberate purpose of blinding the people through an excess of light.[32]

Göchhausen put the (alleged) Jesuit case in this way: The growth of *Aufklärung* will inevitably undermine Protestantism and lead men to skepticism; men cannot, however, live without religious faith for any length of time; *ergo*, the collapse of Protestantism will create a vacuum likely to be filled by a return to Catholicism; hence the seemingly strange alliance between Jesuitism and Masonry. Both believed that contemporary society was heading toward "physical and ethical bankruptcy"; both refused to take steps to stop this process but were rather promoting it "like a man who sets fire to a city so that he can the more easily plunder and murder in it."[33]

[30] Ibid., p. 271. Another example of the widespread belief that Masonry and the Jesuit Order were somehow connected is J. C. Bode, *Die Jesuiten vertrieben aus der Freymaurerei und ihr Dolch zerbrochen durch die Freymaurer* (Leipzig, 1788), a translation of N. Bonneville's *Les Jesuites chassés de la Maçonnerie* (Paris, 1788). The main thesis is that all the aberrations of eighteenth-century Masonry were due to Jesuit infiltration.

[31] *Enthüllung*, p. 273.   [32] Ibid., p. 276.

[33] Ibid., p. 311. The alliance between Jesuits and *Illuminati* is again forcefully expressed in the conclusion (pp. 441-48).

Göchhausen's sensational and fantastic book is symptomatic of a certain bewilderment characteristic of Conservatives as they faced the world of the 1780's. They were as yet unable to isolate their enemies, identify them clearly, and combat them effectively; antagonisms were not yet sharply drawn, and such irreconcilable enemies as *Illuminati* and Jesuits could be confounded one with another. Göchhausen was, however, certain of one fact—the existence of a dangerous conspiracy intended to subvert the world and composed of a self-styled elite which was manipulating the broad mass of Masons for its own ends. He called upon governments to suppress the *Illuminati*, patronize a Masonry shorn of its objectionable features, and reaffirm the traditional principles of Biblical Protestantism and patriarchal monarchy.[34]

THE SUPPRESSION OF THE ILLUMINATI

Göchhausen's call for the suppression of the *Illuminati* was no longer necessary in 1786; for the order had in fact been suppressed by the Bavarian government the previous year. This was the work of Elector Karl Theodor (1724-99), a weak and pliable prince who assumed rule in Munich in 1778. His Reactionary advisers, headed by his Jesuit confessor Ignaz Frank (died 1795)—whose special hold over his penitent must be explained in part by the latter's sensuality which required frequent absolution—convinced him that the order aimed at the assassination of all princes. Karl Theodor's hostility to the *Illuminati* was part and parcel of a general policy of obscurantism which accorded with the outlook of most Bavarians.[35]

Karl Theodor established a severe censorship under the notorious *Geheimrath* Lippert; handed over the already grossly defective school system to obscurantist clerical control; and cut the funds of the Bavarian academy when it showed some slight toleration of "enlightened" ideas.[36] His main adviser in all these policies was Ignaz Frank, about whom little is known because he shunned the trappings of power in order to operate all the more effectively from behind the scenes. It is

[34] Ibid., pp. 312ff.

[35] The best book on the Bavarian milieu is Ludwig Maenner, *Bayern vor und in der französischen Revolution* (Berlin, 1927). The prevalent obscurantism is castigated by August Kluckhohm, "Die Jesuiten in Bayern mit besonderer Rücksicht auf ihre Lehrtätigkeit," *Vorträge und Aufsätze* (Munich, 1894), pp. 239-312, an article originally published in 1873 as a contribution not only to historical knowledge but also to the *Kulturkampf* then raging.

[36] On Karl Theodor see K. T. Heigel in *ADB*, xv (1882), 250-58, an excellent sketch which makes a full biography nearly unnecessary. Heigel is hostile to the Elector but considers the persecution of the *Illuminati* (though not the specific methods employed) objectively necessary.

known, however, that *Geheimrath* Lippert was his chosen instrument and that he took a minute interest in all political questions confronting the elector. He was also the head of the Munich *Zirkel* of the Rosicrucians, but we do not know how high he actually stood in Rosicrucian councils. The elector appointed him to head the much-feared *Specialcommission in gelben Zimmer des Schlosses* which investigated the *Illuminati,* encouraged informers, and decided upon exemplary punishments.[37]

The story of the suppression of the *Illuminati* can be quickly told.[38] It was widely believed that they controlled the center of Munich Masonry, the Lodge *Theodor vom Guten Rath,* and that they had systematically infiltrated the entire Bavarian governmental apparatus. A minor poet, Joseph Maria Babo, first sounded the literary alarm against their influence in 1784 with two works which denounced the secrecy and conspiratorial purpose of the order.[39] The elector thereupon issued a proclamation directing the order to dissolve (June 22, 1784), but this was disregarded by Weishaupt and his associates. Soon thereafter the government learned a good deal about the inner workings of the order from four renegades who had left the order in 1783 and agreed to talk when requested to do so by their ecclesiastical superior. (Two of the group were priests.) The group included Joseph von Utzschneider, a man destined for a distinguished administrative career; his story appeared fully credible to the Bavarian government.[40] The series of confessions, in the form of sworn affidavits, were published in 1786

[37] On Frank see K. T. Heigel in *ADB,* vii (1878), a brief, superficial, and hostile account.

[38] I have followed the valuable archival study by Ludwig Wolfram, "Die Illuminaten in Bayern und ihre Verfolgung," *Programm des kgl. humanistischen Gymnasiums in Erlangen* (2 pts., Erlangen, 1899-1900). This study is fair-minded in its balanced condemnation of both the *Illuminati* and its persecutors; it is somewhat pedestrian in its refusal to look into motives or survey the broader background. Two apologies for the *Illuminati* are the contemporary Adam Weishaupt, *Vollständige Geschichte der Verfolgung der Illuminaten in Bayern* (2 vols., Frankfurt and Leipzig, 1786) and the modern Engel, *Illuminatenorden,* pp. 160ff.

[39] J. M. Babo, *Gemälde aus dem Leben der Menschen* (Munich, 1784), and *Über Freymaurer. Erste Warnung* (Munich, 1784). Both appeared anonymously and provoked a bitter protest on the part of the Lodge Theodor, printed under the title *Nöthige Beylage,* which in turn provoked a *Nöthige Beylage.* Space prohibits following the controversy in detail.

[40] See Carl Max von Bauernfeind, *Joseph von Utzschneider und seine Leistungen auf staats- und volkswirtschaftlichem Gebiet* (Munich, 1880), and Richard Graf Du Moulin Eckart, "Eine Ehrenrettung," *Forschungen zur Kultur und Literaturgeschichte Bayerns,* v (1897), 129-62.

and made a great impression upon German public opinion.[41] By that time the order was in full disarray under a succession of blows administered by the Bavarian government.

Weishaupt himself was driven from his professorship at Ingolstadt by his relentless Jesuit foes in January 1785—not because he headed the *Illuminatenorden* (a fact as yet unknown) but because he had urged the university library to acquire two dangerous works, Bayle's *Dictionnaire historique et critique* (1697-1702)—the source of much modern skepticism—and Simon's *Histoire critique du Vieux Testament* (1685)—the fountain of modern Biblical criticism. He took refuge in Regensburg to live with a friend named Jakob Lanz, but soon suffered a singular misfortune. As the two friends were walking in a rainstorm (July 20, 1785), Lanz was hit by lightning and killed immediately. The clergy called this a judgment of God, and were confirmed in this verdict when a list of prominent *Illuminati* was found on Lanz's body. This constituted prima facie proof that the *Orden* continued to exist in defiance of Karl Theodor's proclamation.

The elector was furious at this evidence of disobedience and issued a further proclamation on August 16, 1785. It required all members of the order to repent and register with the government within eight days, on pain of severe punishment. Those registering were promised the elector's pardon, but the proclamation naturally threw the *Illuminati* into turmoil. Many were inclined to make a clean breast and accept the elector's clemency; but could they be certain that their avowal of membership would not be held against them subsequently? On the other hand, was it not probable that the government already possessed, or might soon acquire, full membership lists? Some members— for example, Montgelas, the later premier of Napoleonic Bavaria—fled to avoid being impaled on the horns of this dilemma. Those who submitted were subjected by Frank and Lippert to endless interrogations.

The Bavarian government was fortunate in being able to confiscate some private papers throwing much light on the activities of the *Illuminati* at the house of Franz Xaver von Zwackh, a high official of the financial administration who was a close associate of Weishaupt's (October 1786).[42] These papers threw an unflattering light upon Weis-

---

[41] *Grosse Absichten des Ordens der Illuminaten, dem patriotischen Publikum vorgelegt von vier ehemaligen Mitgliedern* (Munich, 1786). The four members were Georg Grünberger, Johann Sulpitius von Cosandey, Veit Renner, and Josef von Utzschneider.

[42] The only modern study of Zwackh is Richard Graf Du Moulin Eckart, "Aus den Papieren eines Illuminaten," *Forschungen zur Kultur und Literaturgeschichte*

haupt personally (e.g., his having made his sister-in-law pregnant, after his first wife's death, in the hope that this might facilitate his getting the necessary dispensation to marry her); they included reports on some chemical experiments made by an *Illuminat* called Massenhausen which could be misconstrued as preparation to poison enemies; and much evidence of secrecy-mongering which made the order appear odious and sinister. The Bavarian government handed these documents over to a five-man commission composed of the four renegades who had made their confession in March 1785 and the archivist Eckartshausen (whom we have already encountered as a Conservative pamphleteer). The commission served as editor of an ex parte but authentic collection of documents which was published by the Bavarian government as a kind of "White Paper" to justify the persecution of the *Illuminati* ex post facto. The publication succeeded in further discrediting the *Illuminatenorden* throughout Germany.[43]

Zwackh was able to escape arrest by fleeing to Wetzlar outside of Bavarian jurisdiction; he soon published an open letter in which he protested against the publication of his personal papers.[44] He did not deny the authenticity of the documents, but insisted that their ex parte publication, with careful omissions and constant editorial innuendo, made him and the *Illuminati* appear in an unfair light. Weishaupt himself pretended that he welcomed the publication on the ground that it contained little or nothing (editorial malice apart) of which he need be ashamed.[45] The Bavarian government demanded Weishaupt's extradition from the Free City of Regensburg; this was prevented when the Duke of Gotha (a member of the order) attached him to his embassy at the Imperial *Reichstag*. To prevent a kidnaping Weishaupt soon fled to Gotha itself, where he spent the rest of his life as a pensioned *Hofrat* writing apologetic books about the *Illuminati* and ob-

---

Bayerns, III (1895), 186-239. It is almost a definitive biography, being based upon the papers made available by the family.

[43] *Einige Originalschriften des Illuminatenordens, welche bey dem gewesenen Regierungsrath Zwack [sic] durch vorgenommene Hausvisitation zu Landshut des 11. und 12. Oktober 1786 vorgefunden worden. Auf höchsten Befehl seiner churfürstlichen Durchlaucht zum Druck befördert* (Munich, 1787).

[44] Zwackh, *Anhang zu den Original Schriften des Illuminatenordens* (Frankfurt and Leipzig, 1787). A friend of Zwackh's—or possibly he himself—also published *Bemerkungen über einige Originalschriften des Illuminatenordens, welche bei dem gewesenen Regierungsrath Zwack durch vorgenommene Hausvisitation zu Landshut . . . sollen gefunden . . seyn* (Frankfurt, 1787), which not only defended the *Illuminati* against all charges but also questioned the authenticity of at least some of the papers.

[45] Adam Weishaupt, *Einleitung zu meiner Apologie* (Frankfurt and Leipzig, 1787).

scure metaphysical treatises. Those of his colleagues who were caught by the government had a less happy fate. Massenhausen, the man suspected of mixing the poisons, was thrown into prison for several months but never brought to trial; he was finally allowed to escape as the easiest way of disposing of his case. Hertel, the treasurer of the order, was harassed in the mistaken belief that he administered vast sums of money; it took him months before he could persuade his tormentors of the truth of his story that the order was in fact a shoestring organization. Dozens of *Illuminati* (confessed or suspected) were interrogated by Frank's *Specialcommission in gelben Zimmer des Schlosses*; at one time ninety-one were detained in Munich to be available for examination. Delation was encouraged and blackmail flourished; the accusation of *Illuminati* membership (or the more vague and flexible "sympathy") was long used to weed security risks out of the Bavarian government. Suspects were frequently demoted and banished to the provinces.

These measures proved effective in destroying most of the Bavarian cells of the order—the combination of persecution and exposure proved too much for an organization which had been overrated from the very beginning by friend and foe alike. The branches outside of Bavaria were also shaken. Count Stolberg-Rössla, the *Nationalober*, formally suspended all *Illuminati* activity in April 1785; he published a circular which told all members that "you are released from all duties, excepting only secrecy, which you have accepted upon entering our Order."[46] This was the end of organized activity throughout Germany; but it did not, of course, break the web of social contacts which kept *Illuminism* a force to be reckoned with. The Elector Karl Theodor continued to fear the order, if we may judge by the ferocious tenor of two further proclamations which he issued on August 16, 1787, and November 15, 1790. The former threatened the death penalty to anyone who attempted to recruit new members; the latter deplored the continued activity of the *Illuminati* and required an oath from every government official, priest, and certain other specified categories, that they were not now, and had never been, members of the order.

The Rosicrucians

Conservatives deplored the role played by secret societies in the promotion of the *Aufklärung*, even as they did the rise of modern *Publizität*. In both cases they realized, however, the futility of mere denunciation and paid their Radical opponents the sincere compliment

[46] Hansen, *Quellen*, i, 96.

of imitation. We have seen how they met the challenge of Radical journals by developing a Conservative press; we shall now see how Conservatives met the influence exercised by Masons and *Illuminati* by the development of Rosicrucianism.

The original purposes of Rosicrucianism were not political; they included two such heterogeneous activities as the promotion of religious piety and—as is indicated by the full name of the Order of the Gold and Rosicrucians—the manufacture of gold through laboratory alchemy. Both objectives appealed to mental attitudes far different from those cherished by the *Aufklärung*. A secret society with such objectives could easily become a rallying center for all the Conservative and obscurantist forces latent in Germany. We have already seen how it performed this role in Munich under Father Frank when the *Illuminati* were crushed in 1785; it did the same in Prussia after King Frederick William II, himself a Rosicrucian, succeeded the "enlightened" Frederick on the throne in 1786.[47]

A few words may be said here about the early history of the Rosicrucian Order, though it is an obscure and controversial subject happily peripheral to our main purpose. The *new* Order of the Gold and Rosicrucians was founded by unknown persons in Regensburg around 1755. They claimed a connection with the *old* Rosicrucians who had played a lively role in German intellectual life on the eve of the Thirty Years' War; this claim to continuity has not, however, been substantiated by modern research. It can be said only that both types of Rosicrucians stood in a tradition of mystical piety which had long been one

---

[47] The main secondary works on the Rosicrucians are: Will-Erich Peuckert, *Die Rosenkreutzer. Zur Geschichte einer Reformation* (Jena, 1928), the definitive work on the early Rosicrucians; Bernhard Beyer, *Das Lehrsystem des Ordens der Gold und Rosenkreutzer* (Leipzig, 1925), an encyclopedic work which is more a source collection than an analysis, and appears to have been written by a latter-day Rosicrucian; Arnold Marx, *Die Gold und Rosenkreuzer* (Berlin, 1929), a thorough dissertation; Gustav Krüger, *Die Rosenkreuzer. Ein Überblick* (Berlin, 1932), the best brief summary; and Ferdinand Runkel, *Geschichte der Freimaurerei in Deutschland* (3 vols., Berlin, 1931-32), Vol. II, Ch. 1, a hostile survey from a Masonic point of view. The best introduction to Rosicrucianism is to be found in several contemporary anonymous works. I have used the following: Carl Huberi Lobreich von Plumenoek [Bernhard Joseph Schleiss von Löwenfeld?], *Geoffenbarter Einfluss in das Wohl der Staaten der ächten Freymaurerey aus dem wahren Endzweck ihrer ursprünglichen Stiftung erwiesen* (n.p., 1777); Ketmig Vere [Adam Michael Birckholz?], *Compass der Weisen* (Berlin und Leipzig, 1779); Phoebron [Bernhard Joseph Schleiss von Löwenfeld], *Der im Lichte der Wahrheit strahlende Rosenkreuzer* (Leipzig, 1782); Chrysophiron [Johann Christoph Wöllner], *Die Pflichten der G. und R.C. alten Sistems* (Berlin, 1782); and [Johann Joachim Bode?], *Starke Erweise aus den eigenen Schrifter des hochheiligen Ordens Gold- und Rosenkreuzer* (Vienna, 1788).

aspect of German culture, generally persecuted by orthodoxy when it was not ignored. This tradition confronted dogmatism with pietism, orthodoxy with mysticism, Aristotelianism with Platonism. Its dominant traits were an inexpressible sense of wonder about the world, combined with a passionate craving for personal union with God. Its devotees proved easily vulnerable to many facets of obscurantism and superstition. One can find in their midst alchemists, astrologers, and mystics in search of the philosophers' stone, side by side with men claiming a profound pantheistic vision of the universe. The mystics range from the God-intoxicated cobbler Böhme to the racketeering alchemist Schrepfer; the outside observer is constantly struck by the narrow line dividing the sublime from the ridiculous.[48]

The disintegration of Lutheran Orthodoxy under the fire of rationalist attack left many religious minds in a disturbed condition. As Scriptural authority crumbled under the impact of the new critical scholarship it was inevitable that Catholicism—in which Scripture had never played a central role—should become increasingly attractive to men in search of authority, but the deep-rooted Protestant feeling of superiority toward "Papal superstition" made a general return to Rome unthinkable. The yearning for authority was to be satisfied by the hierarchic structure of the Rosicrucian Order; while the latter's mystical and pietist outlook made it invulnerable to the onslaught of rationalist scholarship. Rosicrucianism rose to importance because it provided an organization for what had previously been a widespread but amorphous movement. One may say that it was rather paradoxical to *organize* piety and mysticism, two essentially individualistic qualities; but organization was certainly a prerequisite for any successful attempt to combat the *Aufklärung* on a practical level.

The Rosicrucians resembled their *Illuminati* enemies in being obviously influenced by the Strict Observance Masonry which flourished during the same decades. They developed a similarly fanciful genealogy and an elaborate hierarchy of degrees. The three Masonic grades were contemptuously dismissed as mere vestibules to the (Rosicrucian) temple, though all members were required to pass through

---

[48] The best book on the Platonist mystical tradition in Germany is Ferdinand Schneider, *Die Freimaurerei und ihr Einfluss auf die geistige Kultur in Deutschland am Ende des XVIII Jahrhunderts* (Prague, 1909). A good general work on the irrationalist aberrations of the eighteenth century is Eugen Sierke, *Schwärmer und Schwindler zu Ende des 18. Jahrhunderts* (Leipzig, 1874), though its treatment is colored by the atmosphere of the Bismarckian *Kulturkampf*. A useful work on the Old (seventeenth-century) Rosicrucians is R. Kienast, *Johann Valentin Andreae und die vier echten Rosenkreutzer-Schriften* (Leipzig, 1926).

them prior to initiation into the real order.[49] There were nine specifically Rosicrucian degrees: the *juniores, theoretici, practici, philosophi, minores, majores, adepti, magistri,* and *magi.* Elaborate initiation ceremonies were used to mark passage from one to another. The order met in circles (*Zirkel*) composed of a maximum of nine members; each circle included Rosicrucians of various rank, with the chairman (*Zirkeldirektor*) usually being an *adeptus* at least. The work of the *Zirkel* consisted of reading theosophical books, making chemical experiments, and discussing common problems. Several *Zirkel* were placed under the control of an *Oberhauptdirektor.* The highest officials were several *Grosspriors,* the *Vizegeneral,* the *General,* and the *Magus,* though nothing is definitely known about the mode of operation, or even the existence, of the top echelons of the Rosicrucian Order.[50]

The initiate swore "freely and voluntarily, and after careful consideration" to abide by the following rules:

(1) to live constantly in the fear of God,
(2) to be guided in conduct by the love of my neighbor,
(3) to maintain the utmost discretion,
(4) to be attached to the Order with unshakable fidelity,
(5) to show perfect obedience to my superiors,
(6) to have no secrets from my brothers in any matter which may interest them,
(7) to devote myself completely to my Creator, His Wisdom, and this Order.
So help me God and His Holy Word. Amen.[51]

The most characteristic aspect of the order was the stipulation of absolute obedience to secret superiors. The statutes were very explicit on this point in a passage worth citing because its rhapsodical tone is characteristic of Rosicrucian literature:

> Our obedience to the Order can be expressed best by the analogy between a man and his property [which the owner can use at will] for we are the property of our Creator, of His Wisdom, and of our exalted and holy Order. We must learn to lose our individual

[49] The official Rosicrucian theory was that Masonry had been developed by Rosicrucian superiors as a *Pflanzschule* (preparatory school). Wöllner, op.cit., preface, quoted by B. Beyer, op.cit., pp. 26-27.

[50] Rosicrucian organization can be best studied in an elaborate chart printed at the end of B. Beyer, op.cit. It is claimed that in 1777 the order consisted of 909 *juniores,* 844 *theoretici,* 833 *practici,* 822 *philosophi,* 799 *minores,* 788 *majores,* 777 *adepti,* 77 *magistri,* and 7 *magi.*

[51] Beyer, op.cit., p. 77.

will in joyous subordination to the instructions of God. As His property . . . we are at the same time the legitimate property of our Holy Order, to which we have voluntarily submitted ourselves for the
sake of our happiness. The Order acts toward us only in accordance
with the instructions of our Maker. We can be absolutely certain that
our superiors will never do anything other than what God would do
Himself if he would act directly in the world.

It follows, therefore, that we must . . . obey whatever commands
are given by our superiors, promptly and without fail. How confident
and tranquil can we feel, even if some commands taste bitter to our
still unregenerate mouth. . .! How inspiring for us to know, that such
commands are invariably the expression of divine wisdom, that no
injustice can ever happen to us, since our holy superiors invariably
follow the will of God, which is perfectly known to them!

We must humbly recognize our inexpressibly good fortune, that
we have been favored out of many millions now living, with the privilege of entering into a close and precise connection with the Creator and His wisdom through this holy Order. This Order is, indeed,
a strong proof that God still extends His mercy toward sinful man
. . . and that He has reopened the gates of paradise. The superiors of
the Order are friends of God, true disciples and favorites of our Saviour Jesus Christ, and stand far above ordinary mortals. They are
masters over all of nature, they lean with one hand upon the victorious Cross of Reconciliation while the other grasps the long chain
of the Order which—O brothers, rejoice with us!—reaches down to
us since we, also, are members. Hallelujah! Hallelujah! Hallelujah!
Praise the Lord, ye servants of God, ye Rosicrucians! thank Him
and praise His most holy name! for He has done great deeds with
us, which make us rejoice! Amen![52]

Obedience was based upon the belief that the highest superiors—the
magi—possessed not only knowledge of divine mysteries but also divine powers:

Our *magi* do not carry on ordinary magic. . . . Their magic is not
necromancy, for that is the work of the Devil, and no Devil can
suffer the sight of our *magi*. They do not deal in the so-called white
magic, which achieves its aim with the help of so-called good spirits,
who yet are not sufficiently pure to show themselves in the presence
of God. Our magic is the truly divine magic, which allows us to talk
personally with God, as Moses and Isaiah did of old, or to send our

[52] Quoted in Runkel, op.cit., II, 5-6.

messages through spirits which have been purified by the fire of God. We possess the two main secrets of Jehovah, i.e., how to create and destroy all natural matter. We can transform water into blood, as did Moses; we can turn a flourishing city into debris by the sound of trumpets, as did Joshua. We can give commands to the sun, the moon, the stars and the wind, and we can raise men from the dead as did the prophets of old.[53]

Men who could believe all this were prone to be credulous in other ways as well. Many Rosicrucians spent their time and fortune in alchemical experiments, though the order officially warned against any vulgar pursuit of gold.[54] Many passages in Rosicrucian writings obviously refer to the pursuit of treasure; they could also be interpreted, however, as symbolizing the transformation of men from an impure to a more spiritual condition on the analogy of base metals being transformed into gold. Some Rosicrucians engaged in medical experiments to find wonder drugs guaranteeing perpetual youth—a search which occasionally led to the opposite result of premature death through poisoning. Others cited spirits to communicate with the living and the dead. The founder of hypnotism, Mesmer, was a Rosicrucian, and many members of the order specialized in communicating with God through the medium of hypnotized individuals.[55] Astrology, sorcery, cabalism, and thaumaturgy were all practiced in Rosicrucian circles.

It is entirely understandable that "enlightened" Germans were distressed, puzzled, and angered by the Rosicrucian outbreak of obscurantism and superstition. Many believed that the Rosicrucians were manipulated behind the scenes by members of the suppressed Jesuit Order—a theory comparable to the Conservative belief in the existence of an *Illuminati* world conspiracy. Nicolai, Biester, and Gedike all suffered from a pathological fear of the Jesuits.[56] Other "enlightened" au-

---

[53] Ibid., pp. 22-23.

[54] See, for example, Birckholz, *Compass der Weisen*, pp. 126ff., quoted in Beyer, op.cit., pp. 11-12.

[55] See Paul Schwartz, "Der Geisterspuk um Friedrich Wilhelm II," *Mitteilungen des Vereins für die Geschichte Berlins* (1930), pp. 45-60.

[56] The theory of a Jesuit conspiracy was half believed by Sierke, op.cit., as late as 1874; we have encountered it in the Göchhausen book discussed above. It is assumed in the otherwise excellent historical novel by Max Ring, *Rosenkreuzer und Illuminaten* (4 vols., Berlin, 1861). One may quote in refutation (if such is necessary) a letter from Wöllner, the prominent Rosicrucian: "May God protect us against Catholicism and the spiritual tyranny of the Pope. But may he protect us still more against the unspiritual despotism of these two scribblers [the rationalist authors Gedike and Biester]." Paul Schwartz, *Der erste Kulturkampf in Preussen um Kirche und Schule* (Berlin, 1925), 45n.

thors took the Rosicrucians with more of a sense of humor. Knigge wrote in a pamphlet in 1781 about Rosicrucian motives:

> These people, lacking the slightest familiarity with ordinary science, brought together by some unscrupulous rascal, or stimulated by some incomprehensible book, have sought to climb the cliffs of mystical wisdom. Their folly, which culminates in taking everything for revelation which is merely incomprehensible, has proved contagious. Some want to talk with spirits to learn what satisfies their passions; others want to get rich by that most miserable of arts, alchemy; while still others want to find a universal medicine which allows them to live a long life in abundance and earthly joys. They are deeply preoccupied with perpetuating the existence of their most useless selves.[57]

The different forms of Rosicrucian mysticism were all significant as reactions against the *Aufklärung*. The order appealed to men who believed that the world was far too complex and mysterious to be explicable by the limited rational tools of the human mind. Its primary hostility was to religious rationalism, but it easily opposed political rationalism as well, since both stemmed from the same kind of secularist, utilitarian, in short "enlightened" outlook. The Rosicrucians reiterated the duty of loyalty to constituted authority which had been the predominant Christian political theory since the time that St. Paul penned Romans, ch. 13. A prominent Rosicrucian put the point in the following conventional terms:

> It is one of our foremost duties to serve the state into which we have been placed by Providence—to serve it with all our power and capacity. We must be obedient and loyal to the higher powers ordained by God, and help to promote the public good even when it violates our private egotism.[58]

Adherence to these conventional maxims was accompanied by a quite novel zeal to ferret out and persecute any kind of political subversion, a zeal which fully matched that shown by the *Illuminati* against obscurantism. How effective was Rosicrucianism on behalf of

---

[57] Adolph Freiherr von Knigge, *Über Jesuiten, Freymaurer und deutsche Rosenkreutzer* (Leipzig, 1781), p. 99. A further witty ridicule is on pp. 126-27. Magister Pianco [Hans Heinrich Freiherr Ecker von Eckhoffen], *Der Rosenkreuzer in seiner Blösse* (Amsterdam [Nürnberg], 1781) is an exceedingly well-informed attack upon Rosicrucianism. A witty, once famous novel of exposure is H. C. Albrecht, *Geheime Geschichte eines Rosenkreuzers* (Hamburg, 1792).

[58] Plumenoek, *Geofferbarter Einfluss*, p. 72, quoted in B. Beyer, op.cit., p. 13.

the Conservative cause? The answer is difficult to provide, since we know very little about its membership, organization, and method of operation. The historian must regret that they were never persecuted, as Karl Theodor persecuted the *Illuminati*, by a government anxious to influence public opinion through the publication of incriminating confiscated papers.

A good deal of evidence exists, nonetheless, to show the power of the Rosicrucians. We have already seen how Father Frank, a Munich *Zirkeldirektor*, guided the suppression of the Bavarian *Illuminati*. A Vienna *Zirkel* was headed from 1780 to 1785 by Johann Baptist Karl, Prince Dietrichstein-Proskau (1728-1808), who also served as Grandmaster of the Masonic *Landesloge von Österreich*.[59] A close friend of Joseph II, he induced the emperor to issue his famous patent (1785) providing for the close governmental supervision of Masonry—a measure obviously aimed at purging "subversive infiltrators" like the *Illuminati*. A Cologne *Zirkel* headed by Franz Wallraf (1748-1824), a priest who taught at the local *Gymnasium* and was also notable as a poet, contributed to making the Rhenish metropolis a byword for obscurantism.[60] A Warsaw *Zirkel* included King Poniatowski II as its most prominent member. The clearest case of Rosicrucian influence was to be found, however, in the Prussia of Frederick William II. The king was a Rosicrucian under the name of Brother Farferus, while his two closest advisers, Wöllner and Bischoffswerder, were leading members of the order. It will be shown in Ch. 6 how they tried—and partially succeeded—to turn Prussia from the main citadel of the German *Aufklärung* into a bastion of Conservative obscurantism. Their most celebrated legal instrument was the Edict of Religion issued by Wöllner on July 9, 1788, which may be described as the specifically Rosicrucian answer to the rising current of religious Radicalism and unbelief. We must now turn to the religious controversies which were the first and long remained the most important battleground between the German *Aufklärung* and the rising forces of German Conservatism.

[59] See *Allgemeines Handbuch der Freimaurerei*, II, 263.
[60] Josef Hansen, *Quellen*, I, 68-71.

CHAPTER 3

Religious Controversies

The Religious Situation[1]

THE second half of the eighteenth century saw each of the three established branches of German Christianity—Catholicism, Lutheranism, and Calvinism—under rationalistic attack. The current of religious thought called deism or natural religion—developed in England two generations earlier by men like John Toland (1670-1722), Matthew Tindal (1657-1733), and Anthony Collins (1676-1729)—spread throughout Germany and combined with indigenous German currents —drawn from Thomasius (1655-1728), Leibnitz (1646-1716), and above all Wolff (1679-1754)—into a formidable criticism of existing orthodoxy, whether Protestant or Catholic. This criticism consisted primarily of the application of the philological-historical method to Biblical studies, begun by the Frenchmen Richard Simon (1638-1712) and Pierre Bayle (1647-1706); it was perfected with Germanic professorial thoroughness by Johann August Ernesti (1707-81), rector of the Leipzig *Thomasschule*, and Johann David Michaelis (1717-91), professor at Göttingen. The results were a piece-by-piece destruction of traditional Christian dogma and the simultaneous discrediting of those aspects of Christian morality which could be denounced as "irrational." The ensuing religious situation was accurately described by the Catholic theologian Johann Michael Sailer in a letter written a generation later as he looked over the period of his youth:

The spirit of the age (*Zeitgeist*) in the mid-1780's can be characterized in the following terms. Rationalism swept through Ger-

[1] No attempt can be made to list even the major works on eighteenth-century German religion here. I have found most valuable the following. For Protestantism: Gustav Frank, *Geschichte der protestantischen Theologie*. Vol. III: *Von der deutschen Aufklärung bis zur Blüthezeit des Rationalismus 1750-1817* (Leipzig, 1875), very hostile to neology but brilliant in its characterization of individual figures; Karl Aner, *Die Theologie der Lessingzeit* (Halle, 1929), very favorable to neology; and Emmanuel Hirsch, *Geschichte der neuen Evangelischen Theologie im Zusammenhang mit den allgemeinen Bewegungen des europäischen Denkens* (Gütersloh, 1951), IV, excellent intellectual history. For Catholicism: Carl Mirbt, *Geschichte der katholischen Kirche von der Mitte des 18. Jahrhunderts bis zum vatikanischen Konzil* (Freiburg, 1913); R. Haass, *Die geistige Haltung der katholischen Universitäten Deutschlands im 18. Jahrhundert. Ein Beitrag zur Geschichte der Aufklärung* (Freiburg, 1952); and, above all, the controversial literature provoked by the famous lecture of Sebastian Merkle, *Die katholische Beurteilung des Aufklärungszeitalters* (Berlin, 1909).

many, more especially the illusion that man's rational faculty could establish and secure a single, true, and salvation-guaranteeing religion. This rationalism expressed itself in pamphlets, in systems, in conversations, in secret societies and in many other institutions. It was not satisfied—indeed it did not even bother—to deny the distinctive doctrines of the Catholic church; its basis was rather the simple assertion: nothing in positive Christianity is acceptable except its "reasonable morality," the doctrine that God is the father of all things, and the proposition that man's soul is immortal; what goes beyond these three assertions is either poetry or superstition or pure nonsense.

The rationalists deduced from this fundamental premise the following corollaries: (1) The doctrine of original sin is nonsense. (2) Therefore, the doctrine of salvation, and more especially of a "vicarious satisfaction," is nonsense. (3) The doctrine of the necessity of immediate divine grace is nonsense: for free will can make a man virtuous and blessed through his own autonomous efforts. (4) The doctrine of the Holy Ghost as a source of grace is nonsense. (5) The doctrine of the Trinity, of three persons in one Divine Being, is nonsense. (6) The doctrine of the divine nature of Christ is nonsense. (7) Even the doctrine of the divine mission of Jesus is nonsense, if one means by it anything more than that Providence sent Him in exactly the same way as Socrates or any other wise man was sent. (8) The doctrine of Satan, as a Being who exists and tempts man, is nonsense. (9) The doctrine of the divine inspiration of Holy Scripture is nonsense. (10) The fairy tales concerning miracles and and prophecies are nonsense. (11) The doctrine of the eternal Logos becoming man, and that of the resurrection and reappearance of Jesus after death, are nonsense.

These *dogmatic* errors—which destroy the Christian religion in its very foundation—were accompanied by the following *practical* errors whose effect was to demoralize man: (12) Prayer is at best only a psychological aid to virtue (*Tugendmittel*). (13) The idea that God can hear a prayer is nonsense. (14) Pleasure is the ultimate purpose of our existence. (15) Asceticism and penance express monkish ideals and are both nonsense. These fifteen propositions expressed the spirit of the so-called "thinking world"—a spirit which has been sweeping throughout Germany from North to South for the last thirty years.[2]

[2] Letter of Sailer to an unknown correspondent, July 12, 1817. Quoted by A. Rösch, *Ein neuer Historiker der Aufklärung*, pp. 54-55. The standard work on

The disintegration, or at least discrediting, of dogma was common to Protestantism and Catholicism; but it was farthest advanced in the former because of Protestantism's lack of clear-cut ecclesiastical authority. One must also take into account some of the unintended consequences of the development of pietism since the seventeenth century. The champions of pietism certainly had no intention of furthering the *Aufklärung*, and its basic preoccupations were alien to modernity: it was in fact morbidly preoccupied with sin, personal salvation, and renunciation of the world. Yet there were tendencies in pietism which definitely paved the way for the *Aufklärung*: the stress upon personal experience in religion made dogmatic differences appear unimportant (while the *Aufklärung* went a step farther and declared them ridiculous); the direct contact between the pietistic believer and his God made any mediating clergy—in the attenuated form in which this conception had survived the Reformation—superfluous (while *Aufklärung* thinkers often declared the clergy to be positively harmful); the religious individualism of pietism showed some external similarity to the "autonomous man"—freed from traditional corporate ties, whether secular or ecclesiastical—idealized by the *Aufklärung*. It must be added that the pietists were firm champions of religious toleration, both on account of their principles—respect for religious individuality—and their situation—mostly that of a barely tolerated religious minority. They in fact produced in Gottfried Arnold (1666-1714) a great historian of religious heresy, whose recurring theme was that heretics had always been the best Christians.[3] While primarily concerned with grace, the pietists valued practical conduct above theoretical dogma; and their conduct showed a strong bent toward humanitarian and charitable effort, as in the Halle orphanage founded by August Hermann Francke (1663-1727). They also broke through traditional class barriers in their fervid belief in man's equality before God, which they turned from a pious phrase into a cardinal belief. In these various ways pietism anticipated the *Aufklärung* and was able to go a long way in alliance with it, though a breach became inevitable when rationalistic, secularistic, and even irreligious tendencies became dominant in the *Aufklärung* around 1770. Then pietism was to

---

Sailer is Hubert Schiel, *Johann M. Sailer, Leben und Briefe* (2 vols., Regensburg, 1948-52). See also Berthold Lang, *Sailer und seine Zeitgenossen* (Munich, 1932), though it is more a eulogy than a critical biography.

[3] Gottfried Arnold, *Unparteiische Kirchen und Ketzerhistorie* (2 vols., 1699-1700). On Arnold see the standard work by Erich Seeberg, *Gottfried Arnold und die Wissenschaft und Mystik seiner Zeit* (Meerane, 1923), and the excellent observations by F. Meinecke, *Historismus*, pp. 45-53.

become one ingredient of the romantic movement and an ally of the counterrevolutionary cause.[4]

It is important to remember that the full program of religious *Aufklärung* developed only gradually. The major influence upon mid-eighteenth-century Protestantism was that of Christian Wolff. This influential professor applied his pedantic but powerful logic to discredit numerous specific Christian dogmas, while having no intention to discredit Christianity as such. He in fact affirmed the complete compatibility of reason and revelation in a spirit worthy of St. Thomas Aquinas. His colleagues in the so-called "neological school" followed his lead in having more radical consequences than intentions: Johann Semler (1725-91), professor of theology at Halle, can stand for the entire school in the way he sought a *via media* between the untenable old Orthodoxy and the increasing unbelief of the more radical *Aufklärer*. The neologists, whose program was characterized quite accurately in Sailer's letter, began by repudiating those aspects of Christianity they considered nonessential. There was no stopping their campaign of hacking away at traditional Christian dogma piecemeal: original sin, predestination, the Incarnation, and the Trinity were all doomed to ultimate destruction. Only the three residual affirmations of "natural religion" were considered inviolable: a divine Creator-God, the moral law, and the immortality of the soul—a prerequisite for invoking divine rewards and punishments in support of the moral law.[5]

The rationalist repudiation of most traditional dogmas was naturally accompanied by a new conception of church organization, one best understood by confronting it with the medieval view which had largely survived in Catholicism. The medieval Church asserted that it was a divinely established institution, in which membership was automatic from the moment of baptism and disobedience to which constituted a mortal sin. The church organization contemplated by the *Aufklärung* was in principle a purely human association for cooperative worship, in which membership was voluntary and disagreement led to no graver consequences than the establishment of new competing Churches. The medieval Church was authoritarian in its internal structure, since it had to protect divinely revealed truth against rebels; the

---

[4] On pietism see the masterly monograph by Koppel S. Pinson, *Pietism as a Factor in the Rise of German Nationalism* (New York, 1934), which goes beyond its immediate subject matter and includes an exhaustive bibliography.

[5] The best book on the neological movement is the very sympathetic study by K. Aner, cited in footnote 1. An excellent contemporary exposition of the neological creed is Friedrich Germanus Lücke, *Über Toleranz und Gewissensfreiheit* (Berlin, 1774).

Church of the *Aufklärung* was democratic in its structure and tended to affirm that truth could be ascertained through the process of discussion followed by voting. The medieval Church claimed a monopoly of correct ritual needed for salvation in the next world; the Church of the *Aufklärung* was more concerned with earthly happiness resulting from virtuous conduct in this world. The medieval Church was ruthlessly intolerant in principle (and usually in practice); the Church of the *Aufklärung* minimized the importance of confessional differences and was willing to settle for (a not very strenuously) competitive coexistence. The contrast was not, of course, seen by contemporaries in the extreme form stated here; there was, nonetheless, an unmistakable trend from a divine institution to a human association, from authoritarianism to democratic autonomy, from compulsion to voluntarism, from stress upon dogma and ritual to stress upon virtuous conduct, and from intolerance to an atmosphere of "live and let live."[6]

The changed religious temper was put by a pamphleteer in the following specific terms:

> We no longer connect salvation with belief in a specific series of dogmas. We are convinced, after a careful study of the nature of man, of the impossibility of securing universal assent to any body of belief. Our better insight into the nature of religion and into the true meaning of Scripture makes us concentrate instead upon the attitudes and actions (*Gesinnungen und Handlungen*) which religion promotes.[7]

The neologists generally believed, with unquestionable subjective good faith, that their labors were strengthening Christianity by a process of accommodation—in the best style of what we have called "Reform Conservatism"—to the new needs of a new age. This point was well stated by Andreas Riem, a neological preacher who addressed the obscurantist foes of *Aufklärung* in the following words:

> Do not fear that you will lose the religion of your fathers. Reason does not undermine religion, but only its excrescences. You will lose prejudices but retain the essence of religion. The latter will, indeed, stand all the more firm in the future the more closely it approaches the light of reason. When harmonized with reason, it will no longer

---

[6] A brilliant modern exposition of the *Aufklärung* theory of the Church is found in Felix Arndt, *Zur Publizistik über Kirche und Staat vom Ausgang des 18. Jahrhunderts bis zum Beginn des 19.* (Berlin, 1918), pp. 13ff. The conceptual apparatus of this dissertation owes much to Ernst Troeltsch.

[7] K. A. E. Becker, *Über Toleranz und Gewissensfreiheit* (Berlin, 1781), p. 2.

have to fear the latter's attack. . . . If, on the contrary, you set your-self against reason—whose gradual advance is in any case irrepressible whatever you may seek to do with your usurped power—posterity will execrate your name with the same contempt with which we today execrate Torquemada.[8]

Orthodox theologians engaged in specific defense of whatever dogmas were assailed as superfluous or harmful by neologists or Radicals. Thus Goeze defended the infallibility of the Bible against Lessing's attack (see below); H. Köster, whom we have encountered as the editor of *Die neuesten Religionsbegebenheiten* in Ch. 1, defended the existence of the Devil with "proofs derived from revelation, the *consensus gentium*, and the moral necessity of his existence";[9] Georg Friedrich Seiler, the Orthodox pillar of the Erlangen Theological Faculty, defended the dogma of the redemption.[10] It would be easy, but superfluous, to add to this list of specific defenders of specific dogmas; suffice it to say that these defenses could not carry much weight with the ever more "enlightened" educated elite of Germany. The really effective opposition to neology came from simple people who resented the fact that the *Aufklärer* were depriving them of their traditional religious certitudes. This sentiment was well expressed by an anonymous poet-pamphleteer in the following *cri de coeur*:

O, wenn das alles Wahrheit wäre
Was jeder Aufgeklärte sagt:
Was wäre meine Glaubenslehre?
Ein Zweifel, der mich ewig nagt,
Denn lügt die Schrift in einem Fall,
So lügt sie wirklich überall.

O lasst mich doch bey meiner Bibel,
Lasst mich in meiner Dunkelheit!
Denn ohne Hoffnung wird mir übel
Bei dieser aufgeklärten Zeit:
Und ohne Hoffnung bin ich hier
Ein elend aufgeklärtes Thier.[11]

---

[8] Andreas Riem, *Über Aufklärung* (Berlin, 1788), p. 19.

[9] H. Köster, *Demüthige Bitte um Belehrung an die Grossen Männer, welch keinen Teufel glauben* (3rd edn., Giessen, 1775).

[10] G. F. Seiler, *Über den Versöhnungstod Jesu Christi* (2 vols., Erlangen, 1778-79). The author must, of course, not be confused with the Catholic theologian J. M. Sailer mentioned in n. 2.

[11] Anonymous, *Gerechte Klage über die aufgeklärte Zeit, doch Trost und Beruhigung aus Gottes heiligem Worte, für Nachfolger im Leben und Sterben*

This attitude seemed all the more justified when neology inevitably proved a mere halfway house toward outright unbelief (or at least theological positions so extreme as to be indistinguishable from unbelief in the eyes of the orthodox). The leader of Protestant Left-wing extremism was the notorious Karl Friedrich Bahrdt (1741-92), the *enfant terrible* of the German *Aufklärung* and as such a continuous embarrassment to his more moderate colleagues. Bahrdt, the son of a Leipzig professor of theology, was a man of very superior talents, excellent education, and superb oratorical capacity. His main troubles were thirst for notoriety, inability to get along with people, and the habit of frequenting bad company—three qualities which, when combined with Radical opinions, precluded a "respectable" career in eighteenth-century German university life. Bahrdt began as a *Privatdozent* at Leipzig when he was only twenty-five, but was soon forced to leave because of a combination of personal misconduct and intellectual heterodoxy—an experience soon to be repeated at Erfurt and Giessen. Basedow, in an inauspicious moment for the reputation of progressive education, recommended him for the headmastership of two *Philanthropine,* neither of which proved a practical success.[12]

Bahrdt next tried his hand at a new translation of the Bible, which provoked the fury of the Orthodox party headed by Pastor Goeze and was formally condemned by an imperial decree (*Reichshofratskonklusum*) in 1778. The "enlightened" Prussian government thereupon offered him a refuge at Halle, where he expounded ever more Radical religious theses in phenomenally successful popular lectures. His specialty was the rationalist debunking of Biblical miracles and the development of esoteric theories about the "true" character of the "religion of Christ."

A few examples will give the flavor of Bahrdt's teaching. He described Moses as an experimenter in explosives whose efforts on Mt. Sinai were mistaken by the credulous Jews for the thunder of God. The healings achieved by Jesus were due to secret medicines, while the

---

(Gotha and Rotenburg, 1794), pp. 29-30. A rough prose translation would run as follows: "If what 'enlightened men' say is true my faith would become nothing but a nagging doubt; for if Scripture lies in a single instance it may lie in all:—Leave me my Bible, leave me in my present state of darkness! For lack of hope would make me sick in the midst of all this 'enlightenment,' and without hope I would be nothing but miserable 'enlightened' animal."

[12] See the superb monograph written by a Lutheran pastor with admirable impartiality: Jakob Anthon Leyser, *Karl Friedrich Bahrdt, der Zeitgenosse Pestalozzi's. Sein Verhältniss zum Philanthropinismus und zur neuen Pädagogik* (2nd edn., Neustadt a.d. H., 1870).

"raising of the dead" was best explained by the supposition that the beneficiaries had been suffering from nothing worse than prolonged fainting fits. The feeding of the five thousand was made possible because the always prudent Jesus, anticipating hungry multitudes, had carefully stocked up on bread supplies in advance in a nearby cave. The report about His walking on the waves was an illusion made possible by a floating cedar beam one hundred ells in length. Most interesting of all was Bahrdt's theory that Jesus—no longer conceived as the Son of God—had been in fact the founder of a secret society akin to eighteenth-century Masonry. Jesus did not die on the cross; his strong constitution suffered, however, sufficient damage so that he was forced —after being carried out of his grave by a hidden back door—to lead a retired life as the secret superior of the Christian order. He limited his esoteric wisdom to a chosen few while his exoteric creed made broad concessions to the vulgar prejudices of Jews and Greeks alike. The distinction between an esoteric and exoteric Christianity gave Bahrdt a convenient device for repudiating everything he disliked in Biblical Christianity while continuing to claim the name of Christian.[13]

Bahrdt rounded out his career as an innkeeper and inmate of Prussian prisons. The religious reaction in Prussia which followed the death of Frederick the Great put an end to his lectures; he thereupon opened an inn located on a hilltop overlooking Halle, which was distinguished as much by the conversational as by the culinary skill of its host. Bahrdt's hopes of making his inn the center of the *Deutsche Union*, the book-distributing organization mentioned in the previous chapter, were disappointed. His fortunes took a further turn for the worse when he satirized Wöllner's famous Edict Concerning Religion.[14] The Prussian minister had him imprisoned for seditious libel in the fortress of Magdeburg; he was, however, soon released because Wöllner—whatever his other faults—was not a vindictive man. (Some

[13] Bahrdt's theological opinions in the 1780's are forcefully expressed in his popular *Briefe über die Bibel im Volkston* (5 vols., Halle, 1782-83) and *Ausführung des Plans und Zweckes Jesu. In Briefen an Wahrheit suchende Leser* (10 vols., Berlin, 1783-85). His purely utilitarian system of ethics caused equal scandal to the orthodox. See his *System der moralischen Religion zur endlichen Beruhigung für Zweifler und Denker, allen Christen und Nichtchristen lesbar* (2 vols., Berlin, 1787).

[14] Anonymous, *Das Religions-Edikt. Ein Lustspiel in 5 Aufzügen. Eine Skizze. Von Nicolai dem Jüngeren* (n.p. [Vienna, 1789]). A rather better specimen of his wit is his *Kirchen und Ketzeralmanach aufs Jahr 1781* (Häresiopel [Züllichau], 1781), a still readable ridicule of many prominent orthodox theologians and most of the famous authors of his day (including Kant, Herder, and Goethe). It caused a sensation and provoked imitations as well as replies.

say Bahrdt was released because he offered to write on behalf of the edict—an improbable story though it shows that many believed him capable of *anything*.) He spent his last years writing a sprightly and not always accurate autobiography and died a broken man, prematurely aged at fifty, in 1792.[15]

German Catholicism produced its notorious counterpart to Bahrdt in the person of Eulogius Schneider (1756-94), whose stormy career ended on the Paris guillotine when he became a victim of Robespierre's Revolutionary Tribunal. He also was a man of enormous talent driven toward religious Radicalism and unable to maintain his moral integrity amid the troubles of a checkered career. His rise was steeper than Bahrdt's—he was born the son of a Franconian vintner rather than of a professor—and his fall more precipitate when it came. He was educated in the Jesuit *Gymnasium* at Würzburg but expelled for disorderly conduct before graduation; there followed years of vagabondage which ended with his joining the Franciscan Order, presumably for worldly reasons. The order paid for the completion of his education, and he was soon ordained to the priesthood. A sermon in favor of complete religious tolerance, preached at Augsburg in 1786, made him widely disliked as an "enlightened" Catholic but helped him obtain a coveted appointment as preacher at the Ludwigsburg court of Duke Karl Eugen of Württemberg the following year. He moved to Bonn in 1789 to become professor of eloquence and poetry at the new university just established by the Elector-Archbishop Maximilian; here he became notorious for the publication of a purely rationalist catechism, the writing of libidinous poetry scarcely compatible with his ecclesiastical status, and an unbridled enthusiasm for the French Revolution. Schneider went to Strasbourg in 1791, where Bishop Brendel—a supporter of the Civil Constitution of the Clergy—appointed him preacher at the ancient cathedral.[16]

[15] The two best German accounts of Bahrdt are by Gustav Frank, "Dr. Karl Friedrich Bahrdt. Ein Beitrag zur Geschichte der deutschen Aufklärung," *Historisches Taschenbuch* (ed. F. von Raumer), 4. Folge., VII (Leipzig, 1866), 203-370, and by Rudolf Ziel, "Karl Friedrich Bahrdt 1741-92," *Zeitschrift für Kirchengeschichte*, LX (1941), 412-55. See also Bahrdt's apologetic *Tagebuch meines Gefängnisses nebst geheimen Urkunden und Aufschlüssen über Deutsche Union* (Berlin, 1790) and his insolent *Geschichte seines Lebens, seiner Meinungen, und Schicksale* (4 vols., Berlin, 1790-91). A modern abbreviated edition, by Felix Hasselberg, was published in Berlin in 1922. The recent study by Sten Gunnar Flygt, *The Notorious Dr. Bahrdt* (Nashville, 1963) is a readable and scholarly biography but comparatively weak on intellectual history.

[16] The standard book on Schneider is Leo Ehrhard, *Eulogius Schneider. Sein Leben und Wirken* (Strasbourg, 1894), a very hostile biography written by a Catholic *Oberlehrer* at the Strasbourg *Gymnasium*. While excellent on Schneider's

Schneider added to his fame by a sermon which he preached in the autumn of 1791 on *The Compatibility Between Christianity and the New French Constitution*.[17] It sought to show, with poetic eloquence, that both were rooted in the principles of equality, liberty, and virtue; and that for this reason the French constitution now—as had Christianity of old—aroused the opposition of princes, pharisees, and all men blinded by pride, egotism, and superstition. Schneider called upon Frenchmen to show the qualities of patient humility, exemplary virtue, and unshakable constancy by which the early Christians were able to overcome their Roman persecutors, though he also called for the martial virtues needed to conquer the hirelings of despotism set upon invading France. There is not a word about the divine origins of Catholicism in Schneider's sermon: salvation, grace, the sacramental system, the priesthood, and the Life to come were not even refuted; they were simply ignored. Yet Schneider had been Catholic court preacher at Ludwigsburg less than three years previously!

His subsequent career was to prove a grave embarrassment to those "Reform Conservatives" who were honest champions of *Aufklärung* within the Catholic fold. Schneider soon became a conspicuous member of the Strasbourg Jacobin Club, and he took the lead in forcing the dismissal of Mayor Dietrich, previously his sponsor but now hated as the leader of the local Feuillant party. He became a deputy in the city council in November 1792 and public prosecutor when a local branch of the Revolutionary Tribunal was established in October 1793. Here his merciless cruelty soon made him the terror of Alsace: he sent men to the guillotine for mere royalist talk, for refusing to accept at par the worthless assignats issued by the revolutionary government, for violating price controls, and for hiding nonjuror priests. His conduct showed a mixture of fanatical conviction, parvenu arrogance, and moral debasement characteristic of a man who has risen too fast in an unfamiliar milieu. His fall was as dramatic as his ascent. Some of Schneider's numerous foes denounced him to St.-Just, Robespierre's Representative on Mission, as a German, an ex-priest, and a man of great personal ambition (three facts which were all obvious and undeniable). They added, however, the preposterous charge that he was a counter-

---

Alsatian activities, it is brief and superficial on his career before 1791 and has no understanding of the Catholic *Aufklärung* of which Schneider was an extreme product.

[17] Eulogius Schneider, *Die Übereinstimmung des Evangeliums mit der neuen Staatsverfassung der Franken. Eine Rede, bey Ablegung des feierlichen Bürgereides, in der Domkirche zu Strassburg gehalten* (Strasbourg, n.d. [1791]).

revolutionary at heart whose revolutionary ferocity was that of an *agent provocateur* bent on provoking a royalist uprising. Schneider was summoned back to Strasbourg from a provincial assize on December 13, 1793, on the pretext that a reorganization of his tribunal was at hand. He may have suspected trouble, for he ostentatiously became engaged to an Alsatian girl on his return journey, a step calculated to demonstrate his total break with his clerical past. He entered Strasbourg on the evening of December 14, riding the coach and six with which he delighted to impress the public; he was received with military honors as befitted a conspicuous official of the Jacobin Republic. Schneider was, however, arrested that same evening, exhibited on the guillotine the next morning (though not decapitated), and shipped off to Paris to stand trial before the Revolutionary Tribunal in the capital. He was executed as a dangerous counterrevolutionary agent on April 1, 1794; contemporary accounts are at variance on whether he repented of his misspent life as he took his final journey to the scaffold.

Defenders of Orthodoxy frequently pointed to the horrible examples of Bahrdt and Schneider to show where religious *Aufklärung* must inevitably end. The propaganda effort of Radicals similarly centered upon attacking especially obscurantist specimens among the clergy. The following outburst by the Prussian pamphleteer Knüppeln may serve as an example of rising anticlerical sentiment:

> At present sheer superstition and outright stupid principles (*stock-dumme Grundsätze*) continue to prevail in Prussia and are deliberately encouraged by the gentlemen of the cloth—for fear that the common man will begin to think for himself and thereby end his blind obedience in spiritual affairs. The basic principle of these spiritual Don Quixotes is and remains the suppression of reason in order to be able to manipulate men with strings forged by stupidity and superstition—for fear of losing their pretended status of envoys from the deity. They have always suppressed and persecuted philosophy, because they fear its blazing torch; they have always screamed about irreligion, deism and atheism whenever anyone refused to accept their silly prattle as unimpeachable truth, or refused to defer to their ecclesiastical dignity.[18]

A polarization of attitudes increasingly characterized the German religious situation. The real struggle was no longer fought over specific

[18] Knüppeln, *Anti-Zimmermann* (Berlin, 1788), pp. 42-43. Another bitter outburst against the clergy is the unsigned article (probably by Andreas Riem) "Verdient der geistliche Stand mehrere Achtung als ein andrer?" *Berlinisches Journal für Aufklärung*, II (1789), 155-72.

dogmas, upon which disagreement was (at least in principle) possible without degenerating into mutual hatred and persecution. The battleground shifted rather to such issues as religious toleration, the freedom to discuss religious problems without restraint, the degree of diversity permissible within an established Church, and the "Josephine" efforts to impose *Aufklärung* upon the Catholic Church. We shall now examine all these controversies in some detail to show the emergence of a self-conscious and systematic religious Conservatism in the last two decades of the *ancien régime*.[19]

[19] There is a problem whether the conceptual framework developed in the Introduction, with the three types of Conservatism—Reactionary, *Status Quo*, and Reform—can be applied in the area of religious controversy. The question arises from the fact that a Church—unlike a political or social institution—may conceivably be the possessor of a unique, eternal, and unchangeable truth which must remain the same at all times and in all places. I believe, however, that this raises a difficulty more of evaluation than classification. Defense of existing religion against radical attack is an obvious case of *Status Quo* Conservatism. The attempt to return religious belief and practice to an earlier condition (e.g., the Catholic Counter Reformation in Protestant countries) fits the Reactionary category. The desire to adapt existing religion to the needs of a new age—as Riem explained the aim of the *Aufklärung* above, and as Joseph sought to do in the controversies to be discussed below—is in principle a case of Reform Conservatism, provided the intention is to conserve rather than to destroy. It is true, of course, that the Radical aim of destruction and the Reform Conservative aim of intelligent conservation are often difficult to distinguish in practice (even in the political and economic field). I believe, however, that the real problem belongs to the realm of value judgment rather than historical categorization. A reactionary program in the political or economic field—for example, the restoration of divine right monarchy after the triumph of popular sovereignty, or the return to laissez-faire capitalism after the establishment of the welfare state—is obviously silly; hence the term "reactionary" is rightly given a negative connotation in general parlance. The same cannot be said in the religious field—if Catholicism is, in fact, the true religion, its votaries were obviously justified in seeking its restoration in Protestant lands during the Counter Reformation. A reform program in the political and economic field which successfully adapts the old to new needs is generally praiseworthy, for history shows that no political or economic institution is eternal and that adaptation is the price of survival. This is not necessarily so in the religious field. If Catholicism is "true" in its existing—historical *and* eternal—form, then adaptation to a world increasingly shaped by non-Catholic forces can mean only the corruption of truth. In the eyes of believers the world must adapt to Catholicism rather than vice versa, and the Church would be untrue to itself if it sought survival by adaptation. This consideration must be kept in mind when one considers Josephinism; some view it as a case of Reform Conservatism which saved Austrian Catholicism, others as a dangerously heretical movement which came close to ruining it. It may be added that the practical problem of dealing with Catholicism in terms of our schema is not so great as this disquisition would suggest, for Orthodox Catholics generally admit that the Church must adapt itself to the modern world in a large number of "nonessentials"; while it will be remembered that the problem of determining what may be sacrificed (if sacrifice is necessary) in order to preserve what is really essential is *the* key problem for all Reform Conservatives in every area of life.

The Struggle for Religious Toleration

The cardinal demand of the *Aufklärung* in the religious field was for complete toleration of all sects—a revolutionary demand whose acceptance meant the repudiation of the principle *cuius regio, cuius religio* which had dominated German religious life since the Treaty of Augsburg in 1555. Religious toleration had made considerable *de facto* progress in Prussia since the rule of the Great Elector, and had been formally proclaimed by Frederick the Great as a principle of state policy; Joseph II had introduced a broad measure of religious toleration in the Habsburg Monarchy by his famous edict of October 20, 1781. Many of the smaller territories of Germany remained, however, woefully backward in this respect, most notably several ecclesiastical states and Imperial Free Cities. The 1780's saw several struggles for religious toleration which aroused a good deal of general interest. We shall examine two of these in detail—in Koblenz in 1783 and in Cologne in 1787—with special attention to the arguments used by the Conservative foes of religious toleration and the motives of those "Reform Conservatives" who were willing to make concessions to this modern principle.

The issue was opened in Koblenz in 1783 with a petition made to the Elector-Archbishop Clemens Wenceslas by a Protestant merchant named Richard Böcking, who asked permission to settle in Ehrenbreitstein (the town across the Rhine from the electoral capital of Koblenz).[20] The archbishop was willing to grant this petition because of the commercial and political advantage which the settlement of Protestants would bring to his electorate. He was keenly aware of the economic backwardness of his territory and was eager to attract foreign, especially Protestant, merchants, because "Protestants are forced to accustom themselves to hard work in their childhood and to concentrate upon commerce and finance since they cannot count upon benefices and other ways of being maintained by their Church."[21] The presence of such competitors would force Catholics to work harder and would probably lead to a decline of begging and theft alike. There was also a clear political advantage: the admission of Protestants would remove the long-standing stigma of intolerance from the electorate.

The archbishop's "enlightened," if rather narrowly utilitarian, argument encountered staunch opposition from the judges of his ecclesiastical court in Koblenz and his consistory in Trier, two bodies he consulted before giving a final reply to Petitioner Böcking. The Koblenz

[20] All the key documents are printed in J. Hansen, *Quellen*, i, 18-29.
[21] Ibid., p. 24.

judges admitted in a memorandum dated June 21, 1783, that (1) other Catholic states (meaning especially Josephine Austria) had already emancipated their Protestants without obvious catastrophic results and that (2) the economic gains foreseen by the archbishop were in fact likely to occur. They argued, however, that the former consideration was inconclusive and the latter irrelevant in the light of the spiritual values of the Catholic Church. Not enough time had elapsed to study the ultimate consequences of toleration where it had been granted; it was all too likely that twenty years hence a generation raised in an atmosphere of religious pluralism would succumb to skepticism. The expected increase of prosperity was irrelevant:

> It is still an unquestioned truth that the honor of God and the pres-
> ervation and spread of the Catholic religion—involving as it does
> the salvation of souls—are infinitely more important than the tem-
> poral welfare of states; therefore the latter consideration must al-
> ways be subordinated to the higher purpose of eternal happiness
> promoted by the Church. This is especially true where the person of
> the secular ruler is identical with the highest "shepherd of souls"
> (*obersten Seelenhirten*)—[as is the case in Trier]—; hence the im-
> perative necessity of protecting the Catholic flock from heresies and
> "religious dangers," of which the indifferentism inevitably wrought
> by toleration is the most horrible. We must raise, therefore, our
> warning voice against the mixing of Catholics with members of alien
> religions.[22]

The judges were also unimpressed by the argument that toleration would improve the external reputation of Trier; they argued that it would, on the contrary, lead to sharp and deserved reproaches from other Catholic states. There was also the danger that the Catholic population of Koblenz would riot against the admission of Protestants, and the judges made it perfectly clear that they would sympathize with faithful Catholics rioting in so good a cause.

The consistory at Trier, in an opinion dated June 25, 1783, was equally intransigent and even more specific in warning against the dangers of toleration:

> The Catholic religion has always been the bond of human society
> and a staunch bulwark of the authority of secular government; its
> protection has rightly been considered the first official duty of rulers.
> In this connection it must be stressed that history teaches with rare

[22] Ibid., p. 20.

unanimity that the admission of members of alien religions is dangerous to civic concord, true religion, morality, and the safety of thrones—and that the same dangers arise from veiled or open attempts to secure greater freedoms for heretics already resident, not to speak of granting their demand for full equality of rights with the orthodox. It is certain, moreover, that heretics will always appeal to their external coreligionists for support and feel a secret loyalty to some alien ruler belonging to their own religion.[23]

The argument of the Koblenz judges and the Trier consistory was vigorously supported by Archbishop Carlo Bellisomi, the Papal Nuncio who resided in Cologne from 1776 to 1786. He wrote a warning letter to Clemens Wenceslas (October 22, 1783) in which he referred to Rev. 2:14: "But I have a few things against thee, because thou hast there them that hold the doctrine of Balaam. . . ." The elector replied with some asperity six days later (October 28, 1783) that he did not expect that toleration would cause any damage to the Catholic faith; that the Protestants were not Balaamites but rather "nos frères quoique errans, ce qui doit d'autant plus animer notre charité envers eux";[24] and that he only followed the practice of the Pope who tolerated even Jews in Rome itself without thereby becoming a protector of Balaamites. The elector followed up this reply with a formal decree "concerning the introduction of a limited religious tolerance in the electoral lands" (October 31, 1783) which not only granted Böcking's petition but invited other Protestants to follow his example. The conditions governing settlement (which were partly modeled upon the Josephine edict of October 20, 1781) were deliberately drawn up in such a manner as to minimize Catholic resentment against Protestant newcomers. Protestant places of worship were henceforth permitted, but they must be inconspicuous ordinary houses without bells or towers. Protestant pastors were prohibited from wearing clerical garb in public. All children born into mixed marriages must be raised in the Catholic faith. Finally, Protestants were declared ineligible for all administrative or judicial posts unless they received a personal dispensation from the elector. It was frankly stated as governmental policy that permission to settle would be given only to wealthy Protestants after a thorough examination of their material circumstances. It would be difficult, indeed, to think of a decree of toleration narrower in scope, weighted with more safeguards, or more exclusively prompted by purely utilitarian motives.

Clemens Wenceslas nonetheless feared an explosion of clerical big-

[23] Ibid., p. 21.   [24] Ibid., p. 26.

otry against his decision and prudently gave the order to summon together, as soon as Böcking should arrive, the local heads of the Carmelite, the Dominican, the Franciscan, and the Capuchin Orders and to tell them in unmistakable language the following: "Any member of their order who should take it upon himself to preach against the decree of toleration ... will be treated as an inciter to mob violence and a rebel against constituted authority. Such conduct will result not only in individual punishment but in the ruthless expulsion from the electoral lands of *all* members of the incriminated Order."[25] The threat proved entirely effective in making a small measure of religious toleration stick in the face of vehement Conservative hostility.

The outcome of the struggle for religious toleration in the Imperial City of Cologne in 1787-88 proved less happy for the tolerationist cause. Here the long-resident, though barely tolerated, Protestant minority petitioned the city council (November 20, 1787) for permission to open a church and a school. Their wish was granted (though by a small majority only) and immediately confirmed by Emperor Joseph II (January 15, 1788). This decision aroused, however, the wrath of the Catholic clergy, the cathedral chapter, and the traditionalistic guild leadership; they pressured the city council into a formal reversal (April 22, 1788) of its concession with the argument that "Cologne has been the happiest Imperial City in Europe while governed in accordance with her old constitution. She will remain in this condition only as long as everything is avoided which prepares a revolution (*Umsturz*) in even a remote way"—for example, by permitting Cologne Protestants to attend their own schools and churches. The Catholic mob, incited by fanatical priests, threatened to lynch the protolerationist mayor and to launch violence against Masons and *Illuminati* as the champions of toleration. The emperor refused, however, to follow the craven city council in its reversal of its decision (March 29, 1789); he ordered the city government to return to its earlier resolve to satisfy the just claims of the Protestant minority. This hardpressed group was, however, by now so intimidated by mob bigotry that it withdrew its earlier petition "voluntarily." Protestant schools and churches remained forbidden for the next six years. The blessing of religious liberty was to be the fruit of French conquest rather than of the indigenous German *Aufklärung*.[26]

[25] Ibid., p. 29.
[26] See H. Oncken, "Deutsche und rheinische Probleme im Zeitalter der französischen Revolution," *Sitzungsbericht der Pr. Akad. der Wissenschaft* (Phil. Hist. Klasse, 1936), pp. 92-96, summarizing materials scattered throughout the first volume of Hansen's *Quellen*.

The Goeze-Lessing Controversy (1777-80)

The most celebrated religious controversy of eighteenth-century Germany took place between the *Aufklärer* Gotthold Ephraim Lessing, poet and critic, and an orthodox and polemical Lutheran pastor named Johann Melchior Goeze. It began with Lessing's publishing several rationalistic tracts, calculated to destroy the credibility of the Bible, which his recently deceased friend, the Hamburg deist Hermann Samuel Reimarus had written during his last years.[27] This provoked a furious pamphlet from Goeze, *Something Preliminary against Herr Hofrath Lessing's direct and indirect hostile Attacks upon our most Sacred Religion*, which was soon followed by three tracts on *Lessing's Weaknesses*.[28] Lessing replied with twelve papers published under the title *Anti-Goeze*. Goeze then became increasingly personal and demanded to know whether Lessing was still a Christian—a question to which the latter replied in *Necessary Answer to a very Unnecessary Question*.[29]

The controversy aroused enormous public interest and ultimately led the Brunswick government (which employed Lessing as a librarian) to impose a strict censorship upon his further theological writing. The poet then took refuge in "his old pulpit, the stage"—he had been a great dramatist before he became absorbed in religious controversy—and wrote *Nathan the Wise,* the greatest plea for religious tolerance in the German language. This famous play contains a malicious portrait of Goeze in the guise of the Christian patriarch of Jerusalem whose favorite phrase is: "No matter what—the Jew must be burnt at the stake (*Der Jude wird verbrannt*)." The fame and literary skill of Lessing has given Goeze an unenviable immortality as a byword for intolerant bigotry. It is assuredly a hopeless task to rehabilitate this staunch religious Conservative after six generations of obloquy; but justice is due even to the victim of a celebrated poet. Goeze was a man of sterling personal integrity, profound convictions, and great polemical skill; and there is more to be said for his position than latter-day heirs of the *Aufklärung*, and the numerous admirers of Lessing, are willing to concede.

[27] *Ein Mehreres aus den Papieren des Ungenannten, die Offenbarung betreffend* (Wolfenbüttel, 1777). The title is explained by the fact that Lessing had already published the earlier *Fragment eines Ungenannten* in 1774.

[28] *Etwas Vorläufiges gegen des Herrn Hofraths Lessings mittelbare und unmittelbare feindselige Angriffe auf unsre allerheiligste Religion*. Reprinted, together with *Lessings Schwächen*, by Erich Schmidt in his *J. M. Goeze: Streitschriften gegen Lessing* (Stuttgart, 1893). Henceforth cited as Schmidt, *Streitschriften*.

[29] *Nöthige Antwort auf eine sehr unnöthige Frage* (Berlin, 1778).

The controversy between Lessing and Goeze is interesting because it went far beyond its immediate theological problem—the validity of rationalist criticism of the Bible—to the perennial one of the extent to which society can, and ought to, tolerate criticism of its fundamental beliefs. First, however, a few words about the original controversy. Hermann Samuel Reimarus (1696-1768) was a teacher of Greek, Hebrew, and mathematics at the Hamburg *gymnasium*. He was a passionate deist in his religious views and published a treatise on *The Principal Truths of Natural Religion* (1754) which won the admiration of the young Kant.[30] In his last years Reimarus became increasingly hostile to revealed religion in general and the Judeo-Christian tradition in particular; he subjected both the Old Testament and the New to a searching criticism in a 2,000-page manuscript entitled *Apology or Defence of the Reasonable Worshippers of God*.[31] He made no attempt to publish this *magnum opus,* since he foresaw that it would stir up a hornet's nest of controversy, and preferred to end his days in peace.

Lessing secured possession of the manuscript from the family and was impressed by the power of many of Reimarus' arguments. He thought it deserved publication—though he disagreed with some of the religious positions advanced—because it would raise the level of theological controversy by forcing the defenders of Orthodoxy to reply to Reimarus' very searching questions. Lessing looked vainly for a publisher courageous enough to brave the anticipated howls of the Orthodox; when his efforts proved fruitless, he selected fragments from the bulky manuscript for a series published by his own Wolfenbüttel Library. Thus appeared in 1777 *Fragments from an Anonymous Author* with critical commentaries by Lessing as editor. This mode of publication secured, and was obviously intended to secure, a maximum of publicity, quite apart from the substance of the work as a "scandalous" attack upon "revealed Christianity." There was bound to be much curiosity about the identity of the author, whom Lessing obviously knew but refused to name; as also about the sincerity of Lessing's commentary, in which he dissociated himself from some of the argument and—even if one assumed this sincerity—the motives which prompted a publication with much of whose tendency the editor professed to disagree.

[30] H. S. Reimarus, *Die vornehmsten Wahrheiten der natürlichen Religion* (Hamburg, 1754). Kant called it the best statement of the deistic case, although he was not convinced by it.

[31] *Apologie oder Schutzschrift für die vernünftigen Verehrer Gottes.*

The substance of the *Fragments* is today only of historical interest. Its most provocative feature was the attack upon the credibility of the Biblical account of Christ's resurrection. Reimarus minutely examined the four Gospel texts and claimed to discover at least ten contradictions in the narrative. He also noted that the six postresurrection appearances of Jesus had all occurred under obscure circumstances. Would not, he asked, a single unmistakable public appearance of Christ have convinced even the most incredulous Jew of the authenticity of His mission? Reimarus obviously believed that the story of the resurrection was a complete fraud and suggested two possible hypotheses to explain what actually did happen. Either Christ did not die on the cross at all but was taken down in a debilitated condition which required a secluded life in his postcrucifixion period; this would explain his occasional later appearances to selected intimates only. Or Christ did in fact die on the cross and was duly buried; if in truth his body was missing from the sepulchre, there was much to be said for the story—current at the time and even mentioned in the Gospels— that the disciples had stolen the body to provide evidence for their propaganda tale of a resurrection. The first hypothesis deprived Christianity of its central dogma, Christ's redemption of man through His death on the cross; the second put the disciples in a decidedly unfavorable light and was bound to raise doubt about the truth of many other Biblical stories as well.

Reimarus thought that he had struck a formidable blow against "revealed religion" when he discredited its Biblical basis. This was certainly the view of many of his readers and was exactly what infuriated the Orthodox; but it was, strange to say, *not* the position of his editor. Lessing believed that both the critics and the defenders of the Biblical narrative were dealing with an essentially peripheral issue; he insisted that the accuracy of the Bible was not crucial to religion and that the criticism of its narrative could, therefore, not discredit religion as such. He formulated his own position with classic terseness in his famous *Axiomata*,[32] written at the height of the controversy, of which the third and fourth are the crux of his position: "(3) The letter is not the spirit, and the Bible is not religion. (4) Consequently accusations against the letter and against the Bible are not necessarily accusations against the spirit and against religion." Lessing added that the Christian religion had existed before, and independently of, the Bible in the first and best period of its existence. This bypassing

[32] *Axiomata* (1778). I have taken the translation from James Sime, *Lessing* (2 vols., London, 1877), II, 198.

of the Bible was bound to anger the Orthodox at least as much as Reimarus' attack upon the Biblical narrative; contemptuous indifference is often harder to answer than open hostility.

The Orthodox hue and cry against Lessing was led by Johann Melchior Goeze (1717-86), the Hamburg *Hauptprediger* known in his age as the most learned and intemperate defender of Lutheran Orthodoxy in Germany. Goeze was no mean antagonist, as Lessing—who had been on personally friendly terms with him when living in Hamburg a decade earlier—was the first to admit. He was a man of vast theological, philosophical, and literary erudition, and he possessed a sharp and precise mind with an uncanny ability to perceive weaknesses in an opponent's position. His brilliant career was evidence of his very superior talents. Predestined for the clerical calling as the son and grandson of Protestant ministers, he had won appointment as *Hauptprediger* at the *Katharinenkirche* in Hamburg in 1755 when he was only thirty-eight. He might have settled down to the respectable and uncontroversial life characteristic of successful clergymen in the eighteenth century with his devoted family (he had four children issuing from a happy marriage) and beloved books. His zeal for Orthodoxy dictated, however, a strenuous life. Goeze considered himself—exactly as did Nicolai for the opposite ideological position, and with the identical lack of humor and detachment—the watchdog of German religion who must bark whenever something went wrong. His career consisted of a never-ceasing series of controversies which made him the bête noire of the German *Aufklärung*.[33]

His polemical vigor resulted in part from a monumental self-assurance. He never doubted for a moment that Lutheran Orthodoxy constituted the truth, the whole truth, and nothing but the truth—a truth, moreover, which was absolutely essential to salvation. He annoyed his opponents by urging them repeatedly to keep better watch over their prospects in the Hereafter and to repent their errors—in their own interests—before it was too late. It would be a vain undertaking to list

[33] The best book on Goeze is still that of Georg Reinhard Röpe, *J. M. Goeze, eine Rettung* (Hamburg, 1860). The author sought to rehabilitate Goeze after nearly eighty years of continuous obloquy—unhappily from a rather narrow, dogmatic Lutheran point of view. Röpe's book provoked a furious reply: August Boden, *Lessing und Goeze. Ein Beitrag zur Literatur und Kirchengeschichte des 18. Jahrhunderts. Zugleich als Widerlegung der Röpeschen Schrift: 'J. M. Goeze, eine Rettung'* (Leipzig and Heidelberg, 1862), which scored on many points of detail but did not—in the view of this author—succeed in refuting Röpe's overall picture. An excellent brief sketch of Goeze is Carl Bertheau, "J. M. Goeze," *Realencyclopädie für prot. Theologie und Kirche* (3rd edn. by Albert Hauck), VI (1899), 757-61.

all of his antagonists here. They included Basedow, the founder of the *Philanthropine*;[34] Semler, the moderately advanced rationalist;[35] Bahrdt, the head of the ultra-Radical theological *Aufklärung*;[36] the Hamburg fellow pastor Johann Ludwig Schlosser (1738-1815), who had the temerity to defend the theater against Goeze's puritanical attack;[37] and another Hamburg fellow pastor named Julius Gustav Alberti (1723-72), who had been guilty of omitting—for reasons of misguided tolerance—a crucial passage from Ps. 79:6, in his prayer on the annual day of fasting: "Pour out thy wrath upon the heathen that have not known thee, and upon the kingdoms that have not called upon thy name."[38] In every case Goeze's polemical position was essentially simple: he pointed out that his opponents' views were contrary either to the Bible, the Symbolic Books (Lutheran creeds), ecclesiastical authority, or Christian morals. He claimed in every case to defend objective truth against the merely subjective opinion of his antagonists.

His attack upon Lessing differs from his many other polemics only in the prominence of the victim he so rashly provoked. The controversy began with Goeze's defense of the importance of an infallible Bible for the Christian religion; but this was only a prelude to the more general controversy over the respective merits of the specifically Christian religion versus the more universal "natural religion." Goeze's *Something Preliminary* included a flat defense of the literal infallibility of the Bible against Reimarus' strictures; also the assertion of the indispensability of the Bible for the Christian religion as against Lessing's distinction between the "essential spirit" and the "superfluous

[34] See the *Pastoralschreiben* mentioned in Ch. 1, n. 63. It provoked a satirical reply by Thomas Abbt which did irretrievable damage to Goeze's reputation: *Erfreuliche Nachricht von einem in Hamburg bald zu Haltenden Inquisitionsgericht und dem inzwischen in effigie zu haltenden erwünschten evangelisch-lutherischen Autodafé* (Berlin, 1766).

[35] Goeze defended the value of the Complutensian Bible, attacked by Semler, despite the fact that it had been compiled by Catholics.

[36] J. M. Goeze, *Beweis, dass die Bahrdtsche Verdeutschung des Neuen Testaments keine Übersetzung, sondern eine vorsätzliche Verfälschung und frevelhafte Schändung der Worte des lebendigen Gottes sei* (Hamburg, 1773).

[37] In the (once) famous Hamburger *Theaterstreit*, which was terminated by a senatorial decree of Nov. 23, 1769. It is interesting in our context that Goeze had explicitly excluded his—at that time!—friend Lessing from his moral strictures against the theater.

[38] Alberti published a "liberal" treatise on dogma in 1771 which enraged Goeze by its omissions. Goeze thereupon regularly used his Sunday sermons to fill in the "gaps" of the work of his fellow pastor—a cause for immense publicity. When Alberti died in 1772, after years of prolonged ill health, Goeze's enemies claimed that his bitter polemics had killed Alberti. Klose, "J. G. Alberti," *ADB*, i (1875), 213-14.

letter." The latter point led Goeze to ask Lessing with some asperity: "What is your own religion? What do you understand by that Christian religion whose independence of the Bible you so strongly maintain?" Lessing evaded answering the first question by taking refuge in a debater's trick. Since Goeze had only asked what Lessing *understood* by the Christian religion—certainly a legitimate question in the controversy about whether Scripture was, or was not, essential to Christianity—Lessing could reply, "All those doctrines of faith which are contained in the creeds of the first four centuries of the Christian Church,"[39] leaving it completely open whether or not he *believed* in those doctrines. Goeze's desire to know whether he was debating with a Christian, a deist, or a pagan was left unanswered.

The question addressed to Lessing, "Are you a Christian?" went, for Goeze, to the heart of the argument. He readily admitted that the Bible was indeed irrelevant to the truth of "natural religion" or deism; he was concerned, however, not with "natural religion" but with the Christian religion. Goeze thought that the literal inspiration of the Bible was essential for maintaining the distinctive truth of the Christian religion; and that Lessing was undermining the latter by publishing Reimarus' attack upon the credibility of the Bible.

Was Lessing in fact still a Christian? We have seen that he avoided an explicit answer; the question has been endlessly debated and obviously cannot be settled here.[40] Suffice it to say that in this author's view Lessing was a Christian only if the term is very loosely used. He did not believe in the specific dogmas of any recognized Christian Church; and he certainly thought that the traditional Protestant view of the verbal inspiration (hence infallibility) of the Bible was ridiculous. His disbelief in Lutheran Orthodoxy was, however, balanced by his simultaneous contempt for the neological criticism of Orthodoxy. Lessing thought that the latter frequently did not understand the nature of religious problems and was much too confident about its own con-

[39] The key sentence in the *Nöthige Antwort*. Trans. from Sime, op.cit., II, 221.

[40] See on this problem *inter alia* Karl Schwarz, *Lessing als Theologe dargestellt* (Halle, 1854), thorough but old-fashioned; Gottfried Fittbogen, *Die Religion Lessings* (Leipzig, 1923), learned but pedestrian; Friedrich Loofs, "Lessings Stellung zum Christentum," *Theologische Studien und Kritiken*, LXXXVI (1913), 31-64, an excellent brief discussion; Walter Nigg, *Das Buch der Ketzer* (Zurich, 1949), pp. 455-74, a deep appreciation of "the heretic who asked questions"; Karl Barth, *Die protestantische Theologie im 19. Jahrhundert* (Zillikon-Zurich, 1947), brilliant and opinionated; Helmut Thielicke, *Offenbarung, Vernunft und Existenz. Studien zur Religionsphilosophie Lessings* (3rd edn., Gütersloh, 1957), the most recent study; and, in a larger context, Hans Leisegang, *Lessings Weltanschauung* (Leipzig, 1931). All these studies remain ultimately inconclusive.

clusions in difficult and long-debated matters. The key document for Lessing's view is the often quoted letter to his brother Karl, who had reproached him for some comparatively kind words he had written about the old system of Orthodoxy. The letter is dated February 8, 1774, the very time when Lessing was editing the first installment of Reimarus' *Fragments*:

> I do not wish to maintain foul water, which has long ceased to be fit for use; I only do not wish to see it poured out before we know where to obtain clear water, and before making sure that the child will not thereafter be bathed in liquid manure (*Mistjauche*). And what is our new-fashioned theology as opposed to Orthodoxy, if not liquid manure as opposed to foul water? With Orthodoxy, thank God, we were pretty well done; there had been erected between it and philosophy a partition behind which each could go on its own way without hindering the other. But what is now done? They tear down the partition, and under the pretence of making us rational Christians make us extreme irrational philosophers. I beg you, dear brother, inform yourself better on this point, and look somewhat less at that which our new theologians throw away than at that which they wish to put in its place. We are agreed in considering our old religious system untrue, but I could not say with you that it is a patchwork made by bunglers and half-philosophers. I know nothing in the world in which human acumen (*Scharfsinn*) has been displayed and practiced more than in this. A patchwork made by bunglers and half-philosophers is the religious system which they now wish to put in the place of the old, and with far more claim to interfere with reason and philosophy than the old ever arrogated to itself.[41]

Lessing was clearly opposed to *both* Orthodoxy and neology. His affirmative position is far more difficult to state than his negations; it can be found, perhaps, in his famous *Education of the Human Race*,[42] published in 1780 and developing what one might describe as a theory of progressive divine revelation. The framework of the theory was distinctly Christian though its substantive conclusions were certainly not. God revealed Himself in proportion to the state of development reached by the human race. It was low among the Jews of the period of the Old Testament; distinctly higher in the Greco-Roman civilization of the time of Christ; still higher in the eighteenth century

---

[41] Translation from Sime, op.cit., II, 191-92.
[42] *Die Erziehung des Menschengeschlechtes* (1780).

marked by *Aufklärung*. Lessing probably believed that the rational conclusions of deism—purged of vulgarity, fanaticism, and an unhistorical condemnation of traditional Christianity—constituted the third stage of religious progress, though he was never very explicit whether that stage was already realized or still in the future. His uncharacteristic lack of explicitness was probably due to two facts (apart from want of inner certainty and self-assurance): (1) his concentration upon good moral conduct as a matter more important than adherence to specific dogma or specific authority. (This was to be the main message of *Nathan the Wise*.) (2) His supreme belief in the value of the *striving* for truth, especially religious truth, quite irrespective of whether one ever attains secure possession of the truth. Lessing put the latter point in an often-quoted passage which aroused Goeze's special ridicule:

> Not the truth which a man possesses or believes he possesses, but the sincere effort he has made to arrive at the truth, makes the worth of a man. For not through the possession but through the search for truth does he develop those energies in which alone consists his ever-growing perfection. Possession makes the mind stagnant, indolent, proud. If God held enclosed in His right hand all truth, and in His left hand simply the ever-moving impulse toward truth, although with the condition that I should eternally err, and said to me, "Choose!", I should fall into His left hand, and say, "Father, give! Pure truth is for Thee alone!"[43]

It is to Goeze's credit that he took up, at one time or another, directly or indirectly, each of Lessing's points; he thereby provided us with a clear confrontation between a Radical and a Conservative position. Most interesting of all is his reply to Lessing's choice of God's left hand in the above-quoted passage:

> What a shocking passage! It obviously contradicts the dictates of common sense, not to speak of what Holy Scripture impresses upon us with the greatest emphasis in text after text. Only a man who has never recognized nor experienced the value of truth, and the blessings which we derive from its possession, can be blinded for even a moment by this *aurora borealis* suddenly striking his eyes—and imagine that he has been hit by a ray of "higher wisdom," and lose himself in admiration of Lessing's "noble spirit."

[43] Trans. from Sime, op.cit., II, 206. It may be noted that the passage was originally directed not against Goeze, but against another of Lessing's assailants, a Pastor Ress of Wolfenbüttel.

Yet—what is the meaning of this passage? Sheer nonsense. Mr. Lessing must either think that his readers are children who will believe blindly whatever he chatters in his exalted enthusiasm, or else he thinks, writes and acts like a child himself.

Goeze then showed that Lessing's view was contradicted by innumerable Biblical texts. He readily admitted, of course, that *pretended* truth was of no value whatsoever, and led to many of the evil consequences described by his antagonist. *Real* truth was, however, a different matter. Lessing claimed that it made men's minds "stagnant, indolent, and proud." Jesus and St. Paul—to mention only two important figures—thought, on the contrary, that truth was a jewel of infinite value.

Goeze ridiculed with heavy sarcasm Lessing's statement that "not through the possession but through the search for truth does man develop those energies in which alone consists his ever-growing perfection."

What can be more silly and contradictory than the assertion that "our ever-growing perfection consists in the development of our energies"? Why have these energies been bestowed upon us? To what purpose should they be enlarged? They should be means for reaching the goal which has been set for us. What is this goal? The attainment and possession of truth. Lessing says, however, that the man who reaches this goal is most unhappy. His mind becomes "stagnant, indolent, and proud." Be satisfied, therefore, o you men! for you find yourself in the same circumstances as Tantalus [in the old Greek legend]. *He* developed his energies through his unending efforts to reach the delicious fruits which hung suspended before his mouth, and to refresh his parched tongue with the pure water which reached up to his lips. But alas! his efforts were all vain—yet *he* must have found comfort in the thought that he enjoyed the perfection which consists in an ever-increasing development of our energies. The same thought must give splendid comfort to our alchemists. The longer they stir around heaps of coal, and work blinded by smoke and steam, the more they develop their energies, the more their perfection is increased. How degraded they would become if they discovered at last the philosopher's stone! How great indeed was the advantage which pagan philosophers possessed over the Apostles and all true Christians! The philosophers searched constantly for the truth, enlarged their energies, and thereby incessantly promoted the growth of their perfection. The Apostles, by contrast, were led to the truth by the spirit of truth itself, without their own conscientious, strenuous and incessant efforts. They secured possession of the truth; but what advantage did it bring them? None, if Lessing's judgment is to be trusted. Their minds became, rather, "stagnant, indolent, and proud."

In conclusion Goeze confronted Lessing's choice of God's left hand with the following reply:

If God held enclosed in his right hand the ever-moving impulse toward truth, although with the condition that I should eternally err, and in His left hand the most horrible fate conceivable, to be reduced to nothingness (*vernichtet zu werden*), and said to me "Choose!", I should humbly bow before His left hand and say: "Father, destroy me. For if pure truth is for Thee alone, I am in eternal danger of erring; no moment is possible where I can be certain that I do not err." To be in this circumstance, and to possess at the same time the ever-moving impulse toward truth, is the most horrible condition for the human soul which I can contemplate. Yet this, if Lessing is to be believed, is the precise condition to which God has called all men in this world and the next. According to this view the assurance of faith, the joy in contemplating God, the hope of eternal life, and even the blessing of eternal life, is nothing but folly and self-delusion. According to this view it was idle boasting for St. Paul to say: "I know whom I have believed, and am persuaded that he is able to keep that which I have committed unto him against that day" (II Timothy 1:12). What a horrible doctrine, leading to utter despair! Yet such is the new wisdom through which the supposed friends of Christianity, who are declared enemies of Holy Scripture, wish to illuminate the world.[44]

We see here a classic confrontation between the Radical appreciation of effort leading toward a desired goal—even though the goal turns out to be a mirage always hovering over the horizon—and the Conservative desire for secure possession which permits relaxation of effort. Goeze was especially angered by Lessing's claim that the publication of the *Fragments* was intended to promote the Christian cause by enlivening religious discussion and providing Orthodox theologians with the opportunity for refuting clear-cut objections instead of the usual wishy-washy neological argument. Lessing argued in effect the doctrine popularized seventy years later by John Stuart Mill in his essay *On*

[44] Schmidt, *Streitschriften*, pp. 84-91 passim.

Liberty—that only opinions which have stood the test of the "free market of ideas" are worth holding and likely to possess inner vitality. Goeze tried to refute this position by presenting a series of damaging analogies which were calculated, incidentally, to enlarge the area of controversy. He wrote:

Mr. Lessing believes that the truth of our Christian religion will not be proven, and the honor of our Savior and His earliest witnesses not completely rescued, until all objections against the former, and all possible libels against the latter, have been distributed in print and in the German language to the broad masses of men—to be judged by them, and to be exhaustively discussed and refuted by scholars. He believes that he does the Christian religion and our Savior a service, and promotes the honor of both, when he serves as a midwife in publishing the most scandalous pamphlets directed against both. Does Mr. Lessing not see—or does he not want to see—the logical consequences of this principle? What would he reply to someone who says: the system of government practiced by the best and most just of rulers does not deserve allegiance until every conceivable— however stupid—objection against the system, and every conceivable libel and insult directed against the person of the ruler, has been set out in print, and placed in the hands of the mass of his subjects; until his most virtuous and benevolent actions have been presented in the most damaging light possible, and ministers have been provoked into defending the honor of their master, his system of government, and all his actions? What would Lessing reply to someone who asserts: the true nature of chastity, and the duty to preserve it and to resist all tendencies toward filth, cannot be clearly illuminated, nor adequately established, until every possible piece of pornography has been widely distributed, rare items have been reprinted, foreign items translated, and those still in manuscript put into print? These two sentences assert a principle identical with Lessing's. If he should deny them, he must show how they differ from his own principle; if he cannot do so, he must admit their truth. But in that case he cannot complain if others suspect that he would be equally willing—prudential considerations apart—to serve as a midwife in the publication of subversive and pornographic writings; since he has proven and declared himself to be willing to promote the publication of writings against the Christian religion, and the most accursed blasphemies against its divine founder.[45]

[45] Ibid., pp. 107-08.

We have seen above that Lessing considered morality, apart from the principle of free inquiry, the most important aspect of religion; and he was convinced—this is the main message of the parable of the three rings in *Nathan the Wise*—that morality was quite independent of dogma, and far more important than dogma. He frequently made a point of comparing the conduct of vicious Christians with that of virtuous non-Christians, as of Nathan the Jew. Goeze thought this kind of anti-Christian innuendo in bad taste and intellectually irrelevant. The issue had come up some years previously in the course of Goeze's controversy with his liberal clerical colleague Julius Alberti. Goeze discussed the case of the Good Samaritan in the course of a *Sermon on the Love Owed to Members of Different Religions.* He naturally praised the Samaritan but asserted that his good deed was no argument that the Samaritan creed was equal to (let alone superior over) the Jewish faith. Christ, when telling the story, had admonished his hearers, "Go thou and do likewise." He had *not* said, "Become a Samaritan." Goeze added:

> Do the errors of the Samaritan cease to be errors because one of the members of this sect once performed a meritorious deed—a deed which in fact does not require anything more than a heart which is soft and sympathetic by Nature. History shows far greater acts of humanity and benevolence even among outright pagans who lived in the most extreme idolatry. It is true that pagans, Jews, and Turks often put nominal Christians to shame—but never *real* Christians.[46]

The sermon constituted a remarkable advance answer to *Nathan the Wise.*

Goeze could not answer the profound (or fuzzy?) substantive religious views of Lessing put down in the *Education of the Human Race,* since this work remained in manuscript until 1780 and hence was unknown to Goeze at the time of the controversy. He would certainly have looked upon it, however, as a piece of subversive radicalism, indeed as a dangerous attack upon Christianity in the transparent guise of a tolerant-relativistic view of religion. He would have argued—as indeed he did argue on the basis of the limited evidence available to him about Lessing's real religious position—that Lessing lacked any understanding of the fact that correct dogma was necessary for salvation. A major difference between Lessing and Goeze was that Lessing could live in a state of permanent doubt and doctrinal skepticism, while Goeze obviously could not.

[46] *Predigt von der Liebe gegen fremde Religionsverwandte* (1768). Quoted by Röpe, op.cit., p. 97.

Goeze had all the characteristics of a fanatical bigot. He was pharisaical and patronizing—when he was not downright hostile—to men who did not share his religious certainties; his magisterial self-assurance easily degenerated into parochial intolerance; his lack of self-criticism made for a want of humor and graciousness. His sureness concerning the truth and indispensability of his own convictions made him sometimes careless about the methods employed to make them prevail. His controversies with his fellow pastors in Hamburg were unedifying, to say the least; his persecution of his rival Alberti, when the latter was already in failing health and soon to die, was inexcusable; he called upon the *Reichshofrath* to silence Lessing, thus supplementing intellectual argument with judicial coercion; and he was not above appealing to the intolerant instincts of the Hamburg mob. All these regrettable actions were products of his honest zeal in pursuit of what he believed to be the truth—truth which appeared to him absolutely essential to salvation. His exalted view of the supreme importance of "correct" religion—as also his narrowness—is glaringly shown by his honest conviction that true friendship was possible only with a man of similar religion. Goeze asked in an obviously rhetorical way:

> Would it be possible for a Lutheran Christian, and more especially a Lutheran pastor, to justify himself before God, before his fellow Christians and especially before his parish—if he entered upon, or prolonged, an intimate friendship with a Jew, or an Arian, or a Socinian—not to speak of a freethinker or someone who was openly contemptuous of religion?[47]

Goeze's narrow reaffirmation of Lutheran Orthodoxy is not without its tragic side. He recognized that piecemeal retreat before the *Aufklärung* criticism of specific dogmas would easily degenerate into a total rout; he therefore dug in and took his stand squarely upon the Lutheran Symbolic Books and the literal inspiration of the Bible. He refused to see that he had assumed an untenable position which was inevitably being eroded by the Biblical criticism and the historical scholarship of the *Aufklärung*. He lacked, unhappily, both the temperament and the imagination needed to bring German Lutheranism abreast of the religious needs of a new age. There was not a trace of the Reform Conservative in Goeze: he was incapable of differentiating between essentials which must be saved and nonessentials which were ballast to be thrown overboard. With undiscriminating zeal he clung to the *totality* of the Lutheran heritage, including the verbal infalli-

---

[47] Ibid., p. 99.

bility of every Biblical syllable. He could not follow Lessing even a small step on the (admittedly dangerous, but nonetheless necessary) path of sacrificing the letter for the spirit. He did not see that the future of Protestantism must be based more upon inner experience and less upon external dogma and authority. Goeze failed, in short, to anticipate the reconstruction of Protestant theology achieved by Friedrich Schleiermacher twenty years later, though it must be added that the time was probably not yet ripe in the 1770's for any drastic reconstruction. Neology was still riding strong; idealism could develop only after the Kantian revolution of the 1780's; romanticism was as yet only anticipated by some aspects of the *Sturm und Drang*.

It must be added also that Goeze was, by contrast with Schleiermacher, a narrow zealot rather than a man of genius with broad sympathies. There is something pathetic, as well as ludicrous, about his utterly intransigent stand in defense of an obviously anachronistic, rigid Lutheran Orthodoxy. There was no ambiguity, no flexibility, and absolutely no charity in his combative positions. His substantive theological views are only of antiquarian interest today; his importance lies rather in his being the prototype of the dogmatist who cannot stand doubt or skepticism and lashes out furiously at whoever assails his cherished positions. Goeze's criticism of the "free market of ideas" expressed a position frequently held by Conservatives: that man requires certainty in fundamentals and that this certainty is undermined if there is too much intellectual discussion. Conservatives tend to dismiss Lessing's counterposition—that certainty makes the mind "stagnant, indolent and proud," and that the incessant, never-ending and never-successful striving for truth is the proper end of man—as the aberration of intellectuals who turn an eccentric personal hobby into a categorical imperative. Goeze expressed this view with a passion and dialectical skill worthy of his great and famous antagonist; and he must be respected for sacrificing his ease and his reputation in the zealous pursuit of an obviously losing and unpopular cause. Lessing called him not inaccurately "the representative and type of whatever exists of narrow-mindedness and hostility to science and scholarship."[48] But Lessing could not understand that narrow-mindedness may to some be preferable to the broad-mindedness which leads to skepticism and rootlessness, and that science and scholarship have not brought *only* blessings to mankind.

[48] *Träger und Typus aller Geistesbeschränktheit und Wissenschaftsfeindschaft.*

The Prussian Edict of Religion

The most famous religious battle in eighteenth-century Germany was provoked by the Prussian Edict Concerning Religion issued by the Conservative minister Wöllner on July 9, 1788. It was bitterly attacked by innumerable "enlightened" writers as a tyrannical and obscurantist assault upon freedom of conscience and rational religion; it was with equal passion defended by Conservative writers as a long-overdue attempt to curb the radical subversion of the traditional Christian faith. The issuance of the edict caused the publication of innumerable books and pamphlets,[49] most of which showed more vituperation than calm discussion of issues; the best were notable, however, for a distinguished intellectual level and an honest attempt of the protagonists to reply to the arguments of their opponents. Several Conservative pamphlets went far beyond the immediate issue in stating the fundamental Conservative case for governmental support of embattled religious orthodoxy. It will be useful to outline the specific provisions of the famous edict, and the historical circumstances in which it arose, before we proceed to an examination of the controversy it provoked.[50]

The author of the edict was the Rosicrucian Johann Christoph Wöllner, who was Minister of Education and Religious Affairs under Frederick William II.[51] The minister worked extremely closely with the king; there can be no question that the Edict Concerning Religion expressed the latter's personal policy—a fact clearly expressed in the words of its preamble. Frederick William stated that he

> had observed, even before acceding to the throne, how necessary it was—following the example of our most reverend ancestors, more especially our grandfather Frederick William I [an obvious slap at his irreligious uncle, Frederick the Great]—to maintain in Prussia the Christian religion of the Protestant Church in its original purity, and where necessary to restore her authentic character; and to use our royal power to combat infidelity as well as superstition, the falsification of the basic truths of the Christian religion, as well as the ensuing licentiousness in morals.[52]

[49] See H.P.C. Henke, *Beurtheilung aller Schriften, welche durch das Religions-Edikt und andere damit zusammenhängende Verfügungen veranlasst sind* (Hamburg, 1793). The author, a professor at Helmstedt University, was hostile to the edict; the book was originally written for Nicolai's *Allgemeine Deutsche Bibliothek* and was one reason why Nicolai had to remove the place of publication from Berlin to Danish Altona.

[50] Cf. the general discussion of Prussian affairs in Ch. 7.

[51] For the aims of the Rosicrucians, cf. Ch. 2.

[52] The edict is printed in *Acten, Urkunden und Nachrichten zur neuesten Kirchengeschichte* (Weimar, 1788), I, 461-79, and many other places.

To secure these ends the king decreed that the three Confessions recognized in Prussia—the Reformed, Lutheran, and Catholic—would be protected in all their existing rights; that the established religious toleration of Jews, Mennonites, and Moravian Brethren should be maintained, provided they abstained from proselytism; that the efforts of "Catholic priests, monks and crypto-Jesuits, who furtively steal around the country to convert so-called heretics," must cease; and that the traditional liturgy of the Reformed and Lutheran Churches should be preserved, except for minor linguistic modifications required by changes in the German language since the sixteenth century. All these sections were noncontroversial;[53] indeed it could be said that the formal proclamation of religious toleration was a significant constitutional advance for Prussia, where toleration had hitherto possessed only the status of a Frederician maxim of government, not of a right based upon written guarantees.

The controversial part of the edict came in sections 7 to 10, in which the king launched a campaign against religious rationalism by requiring all Protestant preachers to adhere in their sermons strictly to their respective Lutheran or Reformed creeds, on pain of immediate dismissal from their parishes. Section 7 implemented the intention already announced in the preamble:

> We have noted with regret . . . that many Protestant pastors allow themselves unbridled liberty in the treatment of the dogma of their confession; they repudiate several essential parts and basic truths of the Protestant Church and indeed of the Christian religion; and they preach in a frivolous manner completely incompatible with the spirit of true Christian piety, and calculated to shake the foundations of the faith of their Christian flock. They are not ashamed to warm up the miserable, long refuted errors of the Socinians, deists, naturalists and other sectarians, and to spread them among the people with impertinent impudence under the much abused banner of *Aufklärung!* They denigrate the respect in which the Bible has been hitherto held as the revealed word of God, and do not hesitate to falsify, twist or even repudiate this divine guarantee of the welfare of the human race. They throw suspicion upon— or even make appear superfluous—the mysteries of revealed religion, more especially the mystery of the redemption and the work of satisfaction performed by our Redeemer, thereby shaking the

[53] The above-mentioned provisions against the missionary efforts of "Crypto-Jesuits" sound ridiculous today but did not appear so to contemporaries.

143

faith of Christians and making Christianity appear ridiculous throughout the earth. . . .

Frederick William declared that this situation called for immediate remedy, "lest the poor populace be sacrificed to the false pretences of frivolous preachers, and millions be made miserable by being robbed of dogmatic certitude during their lives and of religious comfort on their deathbeds."

Sections 8 and 9 threatened dire punishments to recalcitrant preachers who might persist in the above-mentioned rationalistic practices. All preachers that deviated from the creed of their Church would be peremptorily dismissed; for adherence to their creed "was required of them by their office, their sense of duty, and the conditions under which they were appointed to their posts." The government declared, however, that it had no intention of coercing the internal convictions of ministers (a matter recognized to be impossible), provided that they externally conformed to the creed they were appointed to teach. Wöllner did not, of course, wish to encourage hypocrisy by his edict, and he urged rationalistic preachers to resign their posts if observance of the edict should confront them with a genuine conflict of conscience. To avoid undesirable future conflicts it was decreed in Section 10 that new appointments of preachers, teachers, and university professors be limited to "subjects who provide no ground for questioning their internal adherence to the creed they are employed to teach." The remaining articles of the edict were again noncontroversial. Section 11 was a fatherly injunction addressed by Frederick William to his subjects, urging them to behave in a moral and orderly manner and to remember that only a good Christian could be a good subject. Section 12 called for the conscientious observance of religious holidays. Section 13 proclaimed measures to protect the clergy against ridicule, and to safeguard its social status by continuing to exempt its children from military service.

Such were the terms of Wöllner's edict of July 9, 1788, which were paralleled by those of several similar edicts which appeared in other German states at approximately the same time.[54] The edict signalized

[54] For example, an edict issued by Karl Eugen, Duke of Württemberg, on Feb. 12, 1780; one issued by the *Magistrat* of the Free City of Ulm on Nov. 14, 1787, threatening dismissal to all Lutheran ministers who departed from the Augsburg Confession; and several edicts issued by the Saxon *Konsistorialpräsident* Gottlieb von Burgsdorff. See M. Philippson, *Geschichte des preussischen Staatswesens vom Tode Friedrichs des Grossen bis zu den Freiheitskriegen* (2 vols., Leipzig, 1880-82), I, 198, and F. Valjavec, "Das Wöllnersche Religions-

and symbolized the complete reversal in Prussian governmental policy inaugurated by the accession of Frederick William II in 1786—a fact which helps explain the flood of hostile pamphlets which it provoked (those written by Georg Hufeland, E. C. Trapp, and Peter Villaume[55] are perhaps most notable). A brief statement of the case presented by the critics of the edict is essential for understanding the arguments of its Conservative defenders. It was denounced as a violation of the freedom of conscience long prevalent in the Prussian state; as incompatible with the libertarian spirit of Protestantism; as freezing the religious *status quo* to the detriment of progress; as an example of tyrannical Erastianism foreboding further interventions of the state in religious matters; and as likely to encourage delation, opportunism, and hypocrisy in practice. The critics found their sole comfort in the belief that the Edict Concerning Religion was bound to fail because it contravened the "spirit of the age," and that it might even create a crop of martyrs providing spiritual pathos and worldly advertising for the cause of religious *Aufklärung*.

Several writers, prominent as well as obscure, quickly rallied to the Prussian government in defense of the edict; their motives were naturally suspect since favor and preferment beckoned on their side of the controversy. Their sincerity or lack of sincerity—which might only be established, if at all, by microscopic individual examination—does not concern us here; their arguments are of interest for stating a position concerning the duty of the government to protect religion, which German Conservatives were to champion for generations to come.

Edikt und seine geschichtliche Bedeutung," *Hist. Jb. der Görres-Gesellschaft*, LXXII (1953), 386-400, especially Sect. II.

[55] Georg Hufeland, *Ueber das Recht protestantischer Fürsten, unabänderliche Lehrvorschriften festzusetzen und über solche zu halten* (Frankfurt and Leipzig, 1788); a Conservative reply was written by a Prussian judicial official (*Assistenzrath bey der Altmark*), Rudolph Anton Weyel, *Des Herrn Professor Hufelands Meynungen über das Recht protestantischer Fürsten, unabänderliche Lehrvorschriften festzusetzen und über solche zu halten* (Stendal, 1789). Hufeland was a well-known professor. E. C. Trapp, *Ueber die Gewalt protestantischer Regenten in Glaubenssachen* (Brunswick, 1788). Trapp (1745-1818) was prominent in his day as a theorist of the "progressive movement" in education. Peter Villaume, *Freimüthige Betrachtungen über das Edict vom 9. Julius 1788, die Religionsverfassung in den preussischen Staaten betreffend* (Frankfurt and Leipzig, 1788). Specific Conservative replies were written by J. S. Semler (see n. 56 below) and by Carl Heinrich von Römer, *Das Recht der Fürsten, über die Religion ihrer Unterthanen aus verschiedenen Gesichtspunkten geprüft, mit Anwendung auf das wegen der Religionsverfassung in den preussischen Landen unterm 9 ten Juli 1788 erlassene Edict* (Halle, 1789). Villaume (1746-1806), a famous progressive educator, was professor at the *Joachimsthalsche Gymnasium* at Berlin.

J. S. Semler, the great neological theologian of Halle, infuriated his former rationalist admirers by writing in defense of the edict,[56] thereby continuing the breach with religious radicalism which had begun with a sharp attack upon Bahrdt in 1779. Daniel Joachim Köppen, an otherwise obscure country parson from Zettemin in Hither Pomerania, wrote a closely reasoned pamphlet which won wide attention and constitutes perhaps the best statement of the Conservative case for the edict.[57] Wöllner's most celebrated defender was a professor of ethics at Rostock University, Jakob Friedrich Rönnberg (1738-1809), previously known for several writings on political, educational, and social questions. The weight of his opinion was enhanced by the fact that he was obviously not an out-and-out Reactionary: on the contrary, his affirmative reply, in a public speech on March 11, 1781, to the provocatively formulated question, "Is it opportune to abolish serfdom in Mecklenburg?" had made him the bête noire of the Junkers of his native state. His book *Concerning Religious Creeds in their Relationship to Constitutional Law*[58] was so pleasing to Wöllner that the Prussian minister ordered nine hundred copies for free distribution to consistories and even individual clergymen; the book also secured the special endorsement of the *Corpus Evangelicorum* at the Regensburg Diet. A further important pamphlet was written somewhat later by Simon Ludwig Eberhard De Marées (1717-1802), a Dessau superintendent famous in his day as a bitter foe of *Aufklärung*.[59] De Marées' technique was to pass from defense to vigorous counterattack, and he identified—writing in 1792—the so-called "enlightened" critics of the edict with the bloody Jacobins causing so much trouble in France. It

[56] J. S. Semler, *Verteidigung des Königl. Edikts vom 9. Juli 1788 wider die freimütigen Betrachtungen eines Ungenannten* (Halle, 1788). The *Ungenannter* was Peter Villaume mentioned in n. 55 above.

[57] D. J. Köppen, *Das Recht der Fürsten, die Religionslehrer auf ein feststehendes Symbol zu verpflichten* (Leipzig, 1789).

[58] J. F. Roennberg, *Über Symbolische Bücher in Bezug aufs Staatsrecht* (Rostock, 1789, 2nd enl. edn., 1790). The reputation of the book is something of a mystery, since it consists primarily of a rather general defense of state-enforced religious creeds and considers Wöllner's edict only as one of several praiseworthy examples. A very able counterpamphlet was written by Karl Friedrich Senff, *Bemerkungen über des Herrn Hofrath und Professor Rönnberg's Abhandlung "Über Symbolische Bücher im Bezug aufs Staatsrecht"* (Leipzig, 1790). Rönnberg's life is briefly described by Heinrich Klenz in *ADB*, xxix (1889), 131-33.

[59] S.L.E. de Marées, *Unfug sogenannter Aufklärer wider die neuen preussischen Anordnungen in geistlichen Sachen* (Berlin, 1792). De Marées (1717-1802) was *Konsistorialrat, Superintendent,* and *Hofprediger* at the court of Dessau, succeeding his father (1760) who had held the same posts; he was frequently (though unjustly) accused of being a "Crypto-Catholic."

should be noted, however, that the controversy about the Edict Concerning Religion took place, apart from the latter contribution, before the impact of the French Revolution poisoned the general atmosphere of public controversy in Germany. The action taken in defense of orthodox religion by the Prussian government, and the defense of this defense by several Conservative pamphleteers, demonstrate the rise of a Conservative outlook in Germany prior to, and hence independent of, the great events of 1789.

The Conservatives' case on behalf of the Edict Concerning Religion and their answers to each Progressive objection may be summarized as follows:

The religious argument was very simple: the edict was necessary in view of the far-from-isolated infiltration of rationalists into Lutheran pulpits—rationalists who could not possibly be described as fitting the Lutheran label. There were preachers, like the notorious Schulz of Gielsdorf,[60] who openly flaunted their rationalism every Sunday and did not even pretend to believe the dogmas of the Church which employed them. This was obviously an intolerable situation which the king was obliged to remedy both as sovereign and as *summus episcopus* of the Protestant Church.[61]

It was entirely misleading, furthermore, for critics to argue that the royal action violated religious liberty in Prussia—an argument which confused freedom of conscience for the individual believer with freedom of pastors to teach whatever they liked regardless of their employment by a specific Church defined by adherence to specific dogmas. A pastor who voluntarily accepted employment upon certain terms, i.e., with the obligation to preach in accordance with certain dogmas, could not complain that his freedom was restricted if the government forced him to adhere to the terms of his employment. It was, indeed, mandatory for the government to hold preachers to their duty lest the religious rights of parishioners be violated; for parishioners had the right to be instructed in accordance with the orthodox tenets of their Church rather than the subjective caprice of some opinionated rationalist. The Conservatives thus turned the argument

[60] A self-avowed Spinozist atheist, but of pure morals and great personal popularity, as even his enemies admitted. De Marées, op.cit., pp. 8-11, argued that if Schulz could be permitted in a Christian pulpit there was no consistent ground for rejecting either Jews or Moslems to head Christian parishes.

[61] Of the fact of widespread rationalism (incompatible with the Lutheranism of the Augsburg Confession) there can be no question; the controversy was whether it was legal, desirable, and opportune for the government to take steps against it and, if so, whether the Edict of Religion was effective in that direction.

of "freedom of conscience" squarely against the foes of the edict, while also seeking to reduce the issue to one of forcing preachers to abide by their contractual obligations.[62]

Thirdly, it was downright wrong to assert—as did the critics—that the edict was contrary to the historical spirit of Protestantism, unless Protestantism was defined as a compound of undogmatic rationalism and tolerant indifferentism. The purpose of the Protestant Reformation had been to replace an inadequate system of dogma by a refined and purified one; Luther and Calvin had not abandoned specific dogma in either practice or intention. They had been very far from wishing that every man should tailor his own religion to suit his own preferences and would have been horrified by the program and practice of eighteenth-century religious rationalism.[63]

It was not the intention of the Edict Concerning Religion to perpetuate the existing religious *status quo* for all time, or to prevent all religious improvement. Let men (especially pastors) who had improvements to suggest set them down in scholarly writings for approval by consistories; there was surely no need for trying them out directly before common parishioners lacking both judgment and religious knowledge. It was the duty of pastors to season their originality with a proper dose of humility.

> It is difficult to understand how a man can be so arrogant as to believe that his own bright idea (*Einfall*), even though it contradicts centuries of religious tradition, must be the absolute and unquestioned truth, and therefore justifies the abandonment of dogma; and that he is so infallible as to be compelled immediately to spread his opinion among the common people.[64]

It was asserted by the critics that this was precisely what Luther had done in his break with Rome; to this the Conservatives replied that, in the first place, the enlightened rationalists were not Luther and that, in the second place, the condition of eighteenth-century Protestantism was far superior to that of sixteenth-century Catholicism. It was obviously illegitimate to make an exceptional remedy applied by

[62] For the entire paragraph see Köppen, op.cit., pp. 8-13; Rönnberg, op.cit., pp. 180-81; De Marées, op.cit., pp. 44ff.

[63] De Marées, op.cit., p. 80, ridiculed the "enlightened" conception of Protestantism as meaning "the acquired freedom to destroy Protestantism itself." Rönnberg, op.cit., pp. 174-81, ridiculed the idea that the edict would lead Prussia from "free Protestantism" to a hierarchical religion akin to Catholicism. For the entire paragraph see Köppen, op.cit., pp. 132-33 and 158-59, and De Marées, op.cit., pp. 52ff.

[64] Köppen, op.cit., p. 131.

an exceptional man to exceptional abuses a norm for everyday conduct. It was added that Luther had worked closely with his prince and had certainly not been a capricious rebel contemptuous of secular authority; that, above all, Luther had not pretended that he was still a Catholic the way rationalists pretended that they were still Christians.[65]

It was entirely incorrect to describe the edict of Frederick William II as an example of royal tyranny. No informed person could question the constitutional right—nay, the duty—of German Protestant princes to protect the Protestant religion—a right specifically guaranteed by the articles of the Treaty of Westphalia as well as several electoral capitulations signed by successive emperors. The Prussian king never dreamed of claiming the power to introduce a *new* religion by absolutistic fiat, which would indeed constitute unpardonable tyranny. He only claimed the right, or rather exercised the duty, of protecting existing religious bodies against subversion from within and attack from without. This right was not incompatible with freedom of conscience; indeed, it protected the freedom of conscience (properly understood) of true believers. They were not prevented, in principle, from seceding from existing religious denominations and forming new ones subject to certain safeguards determined by the prince; and it was argued (perhaps with questionable historical accuracy) that this was precisely what Luther had done with the approval of the elector of Saxony.[66]

Several authors, while repudiating any Erastian doctrine à la Hobbes, asserted the duty of the state to supervise religion—a duty which included the right to distinguish between acceptable and unacceptable doctrines. The government must supervise the statutes (in this case, the dogmas) of religious organizations, as of all other organizations, to make certain that they did not have an antisocial tendency; this supervision was especially important in the case of ecclesiastical bodies because clergymen tended to be arrogant and opinionated and exercised exceptional influence over other people.[67] It was further argued that the welfare of society required not only re-

[65] Ibid., pp. 128-32. On the Luther analogy, ibid., pp. 68-70, and 113ff.

[66] Rönnberg, op.cit., pp. 82-104 and 144-45; Köppen, op.cit., pp. 108-27; De Marées, op.cit., pp. 31-33. For the case of Luther see n. 65 above.

[67] This anticlerical tone appears, somewhat paradoxically, quite frequently among the defenders of the edict, and easily became specifically anti-Catholic. Köppen, op.cit., p. 126, went so far as to argue, "If regents beginning with Constantine had had the insight and authority to issue an edict like that of the king of Prussia, the Roman hierarchy would never have been able to develop."

ligion per se but religion which included specific doctrines conducive to morality—for example, the immortality of the soul and a scheme of divine rewards and punishments. These were necessary to make oaths binding and to deter criminals in situations where there was little chance of detection and earthly punishment (yet no chance to escape the wrath of an omniscient God). The state must watch vigilantly over clergymen to make sure that they taught these "socially necessary doctrines" with suitable vigor and unanimity, as some rationalistic preachers certainly had not done.[68]

Conservatives readily admitted that individual men could maintain high moral standards without religious sanctions; but they denied that this was true of the broad masses, for the following reasons:

First: Religion provides the very strongest of motives for good conduct, for man can have no higher interest than to have a satisfactory relationship to God. The morality to be expected of a man is ordinarily proportionate to the strength of this motive in his conduct.

Second: It is not within the intellectual capacity of ordinary men to discover by philosophical reasoning the laws of ethics, their necessity and the appropriate motives for their certain observance— ordinary men simply lack the education to do this. The road to morality which relies upon higher authority and recognizes divine rewards and punishments is shorter, easier, and far better suited to ordinary human nature. The divine command "Thou shalt not lie," with the adjoined motive, "Because God hates liars," is far more effective than the deduction of both, command and motive, through complicated and subtle philosophical reasoning—especially since it is not only a problem of cognition but of action based upon cognition. Hence religion is in fact the only reliable foundation of morality for the broad mass of mankind.[69]

Conservatives asserted that the religious belief of a people could be maintained only if a specific religion were consistently taught as a matter of objective, long-established truth rather than subjective, recently discovered opinion. It was not sufficient to claim, as did most rationalistic preachers, that their opinions were in accordance with the Bible; all preachers of all Christian sects claimed as much for themselves. It was clear that the individual interpretation of the Bible opened the floodgates to religious subjectivism. There was no substi-

[68] Rönnberg, op.cit., pp. 9-12; Köppen, op.cit., pp. 46-54.
[69] Köppen, op.cit., pp. 56-57.

tute for historically defined dogma maintained by constituted authority.[70]

Many Conservatives argued that the right of the government to supervise religion went beyond the prohibition of obviously "antisocial doctrines" and the maintenance of a reasonable measure of religious uniformity. They claimed for the prince the right to suppress the obvious and long-refuted "errors" of deists, naturalists, and Socinians. These errors were condemned by all reputable religious parties, whether Catholic, Lutheran, or Reformed; they obviously undermined the authority of the Bible, the guarantor (if not source) of Christianity and hence of morality. (Here the argument frequently merged with the previous one.) It was claimed that only libertarian fanatics wanted to tolerate such reprobate opinions; and it was attempted to silence such fanatics by the argument *ad absurdum*:

> If they demand such toleration, they must also claim toleration for every medical quack who peddles poison. They must argue that the government has no right to curb such a quack even though it should be convinced that he distributes harmful substances under benevolent names.[71]

The entire argument differs from most of the others by being religious-dogmatic rather than pragmatic-utilitarian in character.[72]

A patriarchal conception of governmental authority was frequently expressed by defenders of the Edict Concerning Religion. Some Conservatives thought they could end the argument by the simple assertion that the government knew what was best for the people, and that any critical discussion of the actions of government was a combination of sacrilege and lese majesty. They criticized the critics for med-

---

[70] Köppen admitted that this argument led logically to the state's establishing and enforcing a single creed à la Hobbes, but refuted the logic by appealing to a pluralism of partially contradictory rights: "Here the right of authority is opposed by an equally important right, the freedom of religion of every individual." Köppen argued that the state should only control actions, not beliefs which might or might not lead to action—but he insisted that the active teaching of doctrines contrary to an established creed fell into the category of punishable actions, not innocuous beliefs. Köppen, op.cit., pp. 65-67.

[71] Köppen, op.cit., p. 85. Opinions will differ about the validity of the analogy, since governments can presumably have greater certainty in the detection of medical than religious quackery. The basic case, however, appears arguable by reasonable men: that governments must restrict certain opinions and actions even at the expense of being accused of arrogating to themselves infallibility. Readers will be reminded of the classic statement of this case by Sir Fitzjames Stephen, *Liberty, Equality, Fraternity* (London, 1874), directed against Mill's *On Liberty*.

[72] For the entire paragraph see Köppen, op.cit., pp. 16-17, 80-94, 174-76.

dling in affairs that they could not possibly understand—in short, the argument of the *beschränkter Untertanenverstand* (limited understanding possessed by subjects) was combined with a tendency to brand all criticism of government as intrinsically treasonable. This view was sometimes accompanied by a witty ridicule of the inflated pretensions advanced by the critics of the edict. Wrote De Marées:

> They claim to speak in the name of the Protestant Church, in the name of the dismayed people, in the name of the warning voice of reason, indeed in the name of all interested humanity. Truly a *plenipotentaire* such as the world has never previously seen.[73]

Some Conservatives chided the "enlightened" party for the one-sided character of its tolerance. Some years previously the Prussian government had removed a certain pastor Seyboth of Oderberg from his Lutheran parish because he had become a Crypto-Catholic; this action was cheered by enlightened public opinion. Yet when the government took steps to remove the rationalist Schulz of Gielsdorf, the same enlightened public opinion was shocked and complained of the violation of religious liberty. It was evident that the *Aufklärer* were more interested in license for themselves than in liberty for all, and that their theoretical advocacy of tolerance did not prevent them from being personally the most intolerant of men.[74]

Conservatives hotly resented the frequently made accusation that the edict aimed at subverting liberty for the benefit of a "Protestant Popery." They claimed, on the contrary, that the edict—as was clear from the preamble quoted above—was *inter alia* directed against the recognized danger of Crypto-Catholicism. It would be used impartially against both Crypto-Catholics and rationalists in order to protect the Protestant *via media*. It was also argued that it would forestall the Catholic danger inherent in the rationalistic disintegration of Protestant dogma; Köppen, for one, believed that only a firmly dogmatic Protestantism could hold its own against Catholic competition.[75]

Finally, Conservatives occasionally admitted that, regardless of the theoretical merits of the edict, there were some odious features inevitably connected with its implementation. Thus the supervision of the orthodoxy of preachers necessitated some kind of system of espionage; but the Prussian government could be trusted (it was claimed) to keep this regrettable necessity down to a minimum. There was

[73] De Marées, op.cit., p. 11. For the entire paragraph see ibid., pp. 5, 14ff., and Köppen, op.cit., pp. 23-28.
[74] De Marées, op.cit., pp. 18ff., 34-37.
[75] Köppen, op.cit., pp. 127 and 176-78. See also Rönnberg, op.cit., pp. 134-37.

danger of preachers' pretending to orthodoxy for purely opportunistic reasons. It was argued, however, that since opportunism—an ineradicable part of human nature—had worked in favor of the rationalistic party during the entire Frederician period, there could be no objection to enlisting it on behalf of the far better cause of orthodoxy. Under the old regime *all* rationalists were hypocrites since they taught rationalism despite the fact that they had been appointed Christian preachers; why get excited now about some preachers being induced to become hypocrites on behalf of what they had sworn to support? It was not immoral for a preacher to preach in accordance with an orthodox dogma which he did not fully believe personally, provided that he took a humble view toward the traditions of his Church and deemed it at least possible that tradition might be wiser than himself. This antiindividualist case lay at the core of much of the argument on behalf of the Edict Concerning Religion.[76]

It is quite impossible to measure in quantitative terms the impact of the Conservative defense of Wöllner's edict upon Prussian or German public opinion. The "enlightened" party naturally remained unpersuaded, while the government could mobilize motives, ranging from habitual obedience to outright opportunism, which must have been stronger than the most cogent rational arguments. What is, however, interesting in our context is the fact that the Prussian government did take steps in order to defend traditionalist orthodoxy against the criticism of the *Aufklärung,* and that it was interested—witness the distribution of Rönnberg's book—in building up a Conservative public opinion on behalf of its policy. The Prussian edict of July 9, 1788, is a milestone in the history of German Conservatism because it became the first occasion when a Conservative government felt it must argue its case before the court of public opinion.

The Catholic Aufklärung, Josephinism, and the Defense of Orthodoxy

THE CONDITION OF CATHOLICISM AND THE CATHOLIC AUFKLÄRUNG

There is considerable agreement among most historians that German Catholicism was in a deplorable state during the eighteenth century. Its beliefs and official practices were shot through with superstition, intolerance, and the zealous defense of anachronistic abuses. This generalization may be supported by a brief look at the training of priests, popular religious instruction, the liturgy, prevalent supersti-

[76] Köppen, op.cit., pp. 137ff., 169-72. De Marées, op.cit., p. 20.

tious practices, and widespread intolerance, not to speak of the condition of the ecclesiastical states to be examined in Ch. 5.[77]

The education of priests was dominated by a decadent scholasticism to which few additions had been made during the last four hundred years. The study of the Bible was generally considered a bad Protestant habit involving grave dangers to faith. The prevalent spirit was one of arrogant complacency which was reinforced when Catholics watched the fermentative decomposition of Protestantism. Jansenism, the last important heresy within the Church, had long ceased to be an open danger. Catholic seminaries did their best to shield their students from the disturbing blasts of Voltairean criticism, with the unfortunate result that many priests proved defenseless when they encountered the *Aufklärung* for the first time after their ordination.

Popular religious instruction was on an extremely primitive level. Reliance was placed upon the memorizing of old-fashioned catechisms, and little effort was made to explain the tenets of Catholicism in an intelligible manner. There was considerable Catholic suspicion of the dangers involved in literacy—a suspicion expressed by the bishop of Carniola in a pastoral letter in 1752:

> Rural schools should be abolished altogether. It suffices to have a few in some market towns, and they must of course be closely supervised by the clergy. It should be remembered that a knowledge of reading and writing is usually the main source for the poison of heresy, to which peasants too often cling obstinately . . . once they have been exposed to it—whereas the illiterate section . . . of the people preserves its Catholic faith intact as a matter of course.[78]

[77] The best introduction to the condition of eighteenth-century German Catholicism is to be found in the spirited controversy between S. Merkle and A. Roesch in 1909. Merkle, *Die katholische Beurteilung des Aufklärungszeitalters* (Berlin, 1909) was a pioneering rehabilitation of the Catholic *Aufklärung* and a sharp criticism of "baroque Catholicism"; it was attacked (to mention only one assailant) by Roesch, *Ein neuer Historiker der Aufklärung* (Essen, 1909) with the obvious intention of having Merkle's book placed on the index. Merkle replied with an extremely ferocious brochure, *Die kirchliche Aufklärung im katholischen Deutschland. Eine Abwehr und zugleich ein Beitrag zur Charakteristik "kirchlicher" und "unkirchlicher" Geschichtsschreibung* (Berlin, 1910). Merkle portrayed eighteenth-century Catholicism in somewhat too dark colors and minimized the heretical danger inherent in the German *Aufklärung*; Roesch attempted to whitewash eighteenth-century Catholicism and viewed all *Aufklärung* tendencies as inevitably heretical. I believe that Merkle got the better of the controversy and have generally followed his position.

[78] Quoted in F. M. Mayer, R. Kaindl, and H. Pirchegger, *Geschichte und Kulturleben Österreichs von 1493 bis 1792* (Vienna, 1960), p. 327.

German Catholicism was tenaciously attached to the old Latin liturgy and most priests instinctively opposed any proposals for liturgical reform, even one so innocent as the introduction of a German hymnbook. This was clearly demonstrated in 1785 when the government of Mainz (incidentally, be it noted, an ecclesiastical government) tried to introduce some German singing into the liturgy to increase the parishioners' sense of participation. The government soon found itself confronted by a series of mob riots instigated by the lower clergy under the battle cry that "Lutheranism was on the march." The scarecrow of Lutheranism was used, indeed, to denounce any and all reform proposals, however necessary or innocuous, throughout the eighteenth century.

Potentially superstitious practices and abuses abounded. The number of religious holidays were a heavy burden on the economy, while pilgrimages were frequently a transparent disguise for mass vagrancy. Relicmongering flourished, the veneration of local saints differed little from outright polytheism, the search for "salvation through good works" took on many superstitious forms, and monasticism was frequently decadent. There was widespread belief in numerous improbable miracles, and faith in witchcraft was still very much alive. The criticism directed against all these evils by "enlightened" writers was contemptuously dismissed by Catholic spokesmen as obviously the work of the Devil—an attitude which in turn encouraged the tendency of too many *Aufklärung* writers to substitute ridicule for argument.

German Catholicism tended to be intolerant—as we have seen in the Cologne and Koblenz controversies treated above—and to refuse to make a distinction between dogmatic and civil tolerance. The Catholic Church, claiming to be the sole depository of divinely revealed truth, could not, of course, grant any rights to dogmatic error per se; but there was nothing in Catholicism which necessarily precluded the acceptance of religious toleration as a principle of civil society. There was a widespread refusal among Catholics to recognize the unavoidability of toleration in an irreversibly multiconfessional society like Germany. This attitude was, unfortunately, symptomatic of a great deal of instinctive Catholic opposition to the "progressive tendencies" of the age; it was no accident that the ecclesiastical states of Germany were generally considered the most backward and obscurantist in the country.

Yet it was indicative of the basic vitality of German Catholicism that a Catholic Reform movement should have arisen to combat all the abuses and superstitions just outlined. A new spirit of theological

155

instruction was introduced (with whatever exaggerations) in the General Seminaries founded by Emperor Joseph; attempts were made to compete with Protestants in Biblical scholarship; while scholasticism was de-emphasized to the advantage of more modern theological currents. Inspired Catholic educators like Abbot Johann Ignaz von Felbiger promoted popular schooling upon an unparalleled scale, while a new catechism replaced mere memorizing by the liberal use of the Socratic method. There was some liturgical reform through the upgrading of the sermon and the increasing use of the German language in divine service. Numerous Catholic governments took the lead in suppressing "superstitious practices" such as excessive pilgrimages and the idolatrous veneration of saints. Some Catholic rulers, both lay and ecclesiastical, even began to seek a reputation for *Aufklärung*; we have already seen how the archbishop of Trier combated his own obscurantists in introducing a measure of religious toleration in his realm.[79]

It is difficult to judge this kind of "Reform Catholicism" or Catholic *Aufklärung* fairly, because it inevitably arose from highly heterogeneous motives and led to very mixed results. The motives ranged from a sincere and intelligent devotion to Catholicism which recognized that timely reform was the only alternative to revolution, to a passionate hatred of Catholicism which desired to hack away at specific church practices because it appeared not yet opportune to attack the Church *in toto*. The results were similarly mixed. There can be no question that many abuses and superstitions were eliminated, some piety fostered, and the general image of Catholicism improved; but there was also a continuous danger that the repudiation of so-called "superstitious abuses" would degenerate into heresy. The attack upon scholasticism and the *rapprochement* with Protestant Biblical scholarship could easily lead to interdenominationalism or even deism; new catechisms often made improper concessions to rationalism; attack

[79] The endless literature on the Catholic *Aufklärung* cannot be listed here, though a few useful books and articles may be mentioned. Heinrich Brück, *Die rationalistischen Bestrebungen im katholischen Deutschland, besonders in den drei rheinischen Erzbistümern in der 2. Hälfte des 18. Jahrhunderts* (Mainz, 1865), is a classic attack which was virtually unchallenged until Sebastian Merkle's *Die katholische Beurteilung des Aufklärungszeitalters* (Berlin, 1909), mentioned in n. 77. The impact of the *Aufklärung* upon a Catholic court is studied by J. B. Sägmüller's *Die kirchliche Aufklärung am Hofe des Herzogs Karl Eugen von Württemberg* (Freiburg, 1906); upon a Catholic university in the concluding chapters of Leo Just, *Die alte und neue Universität Mainz 1477-1798* (Mainz, 1957). The general triumph of the *Aufklärung* in the Catholic academic world is chronicled by Max Braubach, "Die katholischen Universitäten Deutschlands und die französische Revolution," *Historisches Jahrbuch*, IL (1929), 263-303.

upon superstition was too often directed not at genuine abuses but at what "enlightened" zealots chose to *consider* superstitious; while tolerance became an easy cloak for simple indifferentism. We have already seen in the case of Eulogius Schneider how the Catholic *Aufklärung* could lead to appalling results.

The problematic character of much of Germany's "Reform Catholicism" becomes especially evident when one views its inevitable clash with the Papacy—a clash provoked as much by secular absolutist ambition as by genuine religious zeal, though the two were inevitably intertwined in many reform efforts. Absolutism, whether Catholic or Protestant, enlightened or obscurantist, invariably strove for total domination over *all* elements in the state, and it naturally resented the international character of Catholicism and its allegiance to a transalpine ruler. The fact that the eighteenth-century Papacy generally sided with the party of *Status Quo* Conservatism within the Catholic Church provided a frequently welcome opportunity to cloak the desire for power in the guise of zeal for religious reform; though it is also certain that many genuine religious reformers turned to the secular state out of understandable despair at the immobile outlook of the Papacy. The desire to combine religious reform with curtailment of Papal jurisdiction appears most clearly in the so-called "Febronian movement" led by Johann Nikolaus von Hontheim (1701-90), the suffragan bishop of Trier who published a bitterly anti-Papal book, *De Statu ecclesiae et legitima potestate Romani pontificis,* under the pseudonym Justinus Febronius in 1763. It called for the establishment of a reformed "German Catholic Church" in which the Pope would be restricted to a purely nominal supremacy as *primus inter pares.* The book was immediately condemned by the Vatican, and its author was eventually induced formally to recant his heretical opinions. This could not prevent his book from becoming the political breviary of many Catholic princes, both ecclesiastical and lay, in the two decades before the French Revolution. It also aroused vast hopes among German Protestants for the healing of the sixteenth-century schism on terms satisfactory to them, and among many reformers who believed that the repudiation of Rome was the prerequisite for a German religious revival. It suffices to note in our context that Febronianism appealed to a good many "Reform Conservatives" despite the Radicalism of its program.[80]

[80] On Febronius see the numerous (but unfortunately scattered) articles of the Catholic Mainz historian Leo Just; for example, "Zur Entstehungsgeschichte des Febronianismus," *Jahrbuch für das Bistum Mainz,* v (1950). Space prohibits any

THE JOSEPHINE PROGRAM

The Josephine policy of religious reforms—or, more accurately, the policy toward the Catholic Church pursued by Habsburg rulers from Maria Theresia to Leopold II—may be defined as a specifically Austrian brand of Febronianism. It was motivated by both absolutism and a genuine zeal for religious reform, while it obviously owed much to the religious *Aufklärung* as well (although this was more evident under the "enlightened" Joseph than his rather bigoted mother). A brief outline of their religious policy will give concrete content to this characterization.[81]

Josephinism meant above all the complete domination of the Church by the Erastian state. This domination involved the curtailment of traditional Papal prerogatives and close bureaucratic supervision over all episcopal activities. Papal bulls and diocesan letters required the approval of the government before they could be read publicly. Judicial appeals and financial payments to Rome were equally prohibited. Diocesan boundaries were redrawn in accordance with political convenience to make certain that no Austrian was subject to a "foreign" ecclesiastical jurisdiction. The appointment of bishops was completely controlled by the government without regard for the wishes of either Pope or cathedral chapter; Joseph, incidentally, used this power to break the aristocratic stranglehold over the upper clergy. He braved the unanimous wrath of the Olmütz cathedral chapter by appointing a mere commoner, Lachenbauer, bishop; and defied vested interests by reducing the number of ca-

---

listing of the contemporary Febronian literature; one extreme example is Felix Anton Blau, *Kritische Geschichte der kirchlichen Unfehlbarkeit* (Frankfurt, 1791).

[81] I have followed three important recent publications on Josephinism: Fritz Valjavec, *Der Josephinismus. Zur geistigen Entwicklung Österreichs im 18. und 19. Jahrhundert* (2nd edn., Munich, 1945), very broad in its scope through defining Josephinism rather loosely; Eduard Winter, *Der Josephinismus und seine Geschichte. Beiträge zur Geistesgeschichte Österreichs 1740-1848* (Brünn, 1943), interpreting Josephinism as a laudable form of "Reform Catholicism" which was stupidly opposed by the Curia; and the monumental source collection edited by Ferdinand Maass, *Der Josephinismus. Quellen zu seiner Geschichte in Österreich* (4 vols., Vienna, 1951-59), with indispensable introductions written from the Catholic point of view. A useful but pedestrian chronicle of the Josephine measures can be found in Mary Clare Goodwin, *The Papal Conflict with Josephinism* (New York, 1938). The implementation on the local level can be studied in F. Geier, *Die Durchführung der kirchlichen Reformen Josephs II im vorderösterreichischen Breisgau* (Stuttgart, 1905). The best contemporary account is Peter Philipp Wolf, *Geschichte der Veränderungen in dem religiösen, kirchlichen und wissenschaftlichen Zustande der österreichischen Staaten unter der Regierung Josephs II* (Germanien, 1795), though it is written by a Josephine partisan.

thedral canons and requiring ten years of ecclesiastical service as a prerequisite for appointment. Any contact between monks and their superior residing abroad was placed under heavy penalties—an important matter since the heads of all the great orders (Franciscans, Dominicans, et cetera) naturally resided at Rome. The exercise of ecclesiastical discipline (excommunication, et cetera) required governmental approval. All tax exemption of ecclesiastical lands was ruthlessly abolished; new gifts to the "dead hand" were prohibited or closely controlled. The education of priests was removed from episcopal seminaries to state-controlled General Seminaries. There was, in fact, no aspect of the life of the Church immune to governmental interference.

This became abundantly clear when Maria Theresia, and even more her zealously "enlightened" son Joseph, began a process of reforming so-called superstitious practices. Holidays and pilgrimages were strictly curtailed, processions limited to the one on Corpus Christi Day. Churches were ordered cleared of superstitious or unnecessary objects such as relics; wax was saved by curtailing the number of permissible candles. New burial regulations required that corpses be placed in bags covered with quicklime in order to prevent the waste of precious wood in coffins destined for early decay. Joseph lacked the slightest consideration for tradition and was contemptuous of the wish of ordinary people to maintain the ecclesiastical services to which they had been accustomed since childhood.

The most notorious act of Josephine policy was the suppression of approximately one third of the monasteries of the Habsburg Monarchy. There were the usual charges of monastic immorality to give some justification to this policy, but Joseph was delightfully frank about his real motive: he considered all "contemplative orders" to be parasites and could not conceive of prayer as a socially useful activity. Orders engaged in education and nursing were spared in principle though not always in practice. The suppression of individual monasteries was often accompanied by the destruction of art treasures, and the appropriation of monastic buildings for secular purposes— most often for army barracks—was bitterly resented. The future of monasticism was thrown into question by first raising the age at which perpetual vows could be taken and finally prohibiting new vows altogether.

The popular resentment against intolerance shown toward Catholic monks was often compounded by the new measures of toleration introduced for the benefit of Protestants and Jews. A famous edict of toleration (October 1781) improved the legal position of Protestants although they were far from being given full equality of rights. (For example, Protestants still required dispensations before they could enter public employment; their churches were denied bells or doors facing main thoroughfares, lest Catholic sensitivities be offended; and the application of an individual to secure recognition as a Protestant entailed compulsory Catholic religious instruction for a six weeks' period to give the old Church a final chance.) The rights conferred upon Protestants were, moreover, strictly limited to Lutherans and Calvinists; Joseph had no sympathy for sectarians and went so far as to order the public whipping of Bohemian deists in 1783 on the thoroughly unenlightened ground that this might make them see the error of their sectarian ways. The improvement of the position of Protestants was followed by the formal emancipation of the Jews. They received full economic rights although some restrictions were retained upon where they could settle and build synagogues.

The Catholic-Orthodox party frequently complained against the relaxation of censorship previously directed against all anti-Catholic writings. Joseph continued to suppress outright irreligious books and pamphlets, but he welcomed publications directed against monasticism and other elements of Catholicism that he deemed superstitious. The result of this leniency was a flood of scurrilous publications which sought to carry religious Radicalism into the masses. Joseph added insult to injury by ordering his Censorship Commission to suppress "superstitious writings"—a broad and flexible category which in fact included most anti-Josephine publications. It is not surprising that many good Catholics began to believe that the emperor had embarked upon a deliberate campaign to exterminate Catholicism per se.

It is certain, at least to the eye of hindsight, that this was far from Joseph's intention. The emperor was neither a deist nor a skeptic, and in fact found harsh words against both; there is no question that he considered himself to be a Catholic believer (however subjective and selective his religious beliefs). He valued the Church as an antidote to political discontent and "crackpotism," the too frequent results of sectarianism and schism; he recognized the crucial role played by Catholicism in buttressing the Habsburg position in Europe, in the empire, and even in the heterogenous hereditary lands of the dynasty; and he saw the indispensability of established religious belief to secure morality among the masses. Joseph considered, in addition, that the existing structure of the Catholic Church was a valuable instrument in the hands of his absolutist ambitions. The emperor viewed the clergy as the spiritual section of his omnipotent bureaucracy, while he incidentally employed it frequently for purely secular ends. We have already seen how he used priests for such miscellaneous tasks as census-taking, teaching agricultural improvement, and administering relief to the poor. He provided a permanent service to the Catholic Church by increasing the number of parishes, with the purpose of bringing a priest within walking distance of every citizen. He did not squander the property of the suppressed monasteries upon favorites, or employ it for nonreligious ends; Joseph used it in part to improve clerical salaries and in part to finance educational and charitable work. His suppression of ecclesiastical pluralism at every level, from bishop to parish priest, was a salutary reform. The teaching system introduced in the new General Seminaries may have included elements of doubtful orthodoxy, but Joseph's aim of creating a learned, spiritual, and devoted clergy cannot be gainsaid.[82]

The emperor was in intention a Reform Catholic who sought to revivify what he felt was a sick Church by removing the anachronistic, abusive, and superstitious elements in her structure. Joseph was very explicit on this score, as witness the following letter to his mother:

> The service of God, our neighbor, and the state cannot be promoted so long as the clergy is not better educated and held to a higher code of morals and a more precise fulfilment of its obligations. So long as the divine promise of perfection is belied by an insipid externalization (*abgeschmackteste Veraüsserlichung*) of religion we have a situation where the Church is a stumbling block to our enemies, and provokes ridicule which too easily degenerates into outright unbelief.[83]

The spirit of Reform Catholicism was forcefully expressed in a letter written in 1782 by Seibt, a close collaborator of Joseph, to his friend Abbot Rautenstrauch, the *spiritus rector* of the Josephine party. It pointed to the necessity of a *via media* between Radical attack upon Catholicism and Orthodox Catholic defense:

> One does not know whether to weep or laugh when one sees how every egghead (*schele Strubbelkopf*) declares himself a religious

[82] My judgment on Joseph follows the estimate of Hugo Hantsch, *Die Geschichte Österreichs 1648-1918* (2nd edn., Graz, 1953), Chs. 13-14. It may be added that Joseph's Reform Catholicism naturally came under Radical attack. See the voices cited in Paul von Mitrofanov, *Joseph II* (Vienna, 1910), pp. 786-88.
[83] Quoted from Winter, *Josephinismus*, p. 143.

reformer wishing to eliminate this and that . . . and is permitted to pose with impunity as an *Aufklärer* in ecclesiastical matters. I am firmly convinced, however, that those who shout loudest about religious abuses are generally those with the least religion. The abolition of abuses is, of course, equitable, beneficial, and necessary, but that they should first be excoriated with deliberately cutting satire, and pilloried before the general public, is annoying, dangerous, and altogether disadvantageous. It is, unfortunately, given to very few men to find the *via media* between opposite extremes; the great majority is too prone to take a jump and to fall from too much [traditional religion] into too little. While disbelief (*Unglaube*) appears to be the very opposite of superstition (*Aberglaube*) the two in fact easily lead one to another.[84]

This was clearly the spirit of Joseph also. The emperor believed with obvious sincerity that he was the protector of true religion in the Habsburg realm, and that—if a nautical analogy may be allowed—the dropping of superstitious and alien ballast was the best way of refloating a Catholicism too long in dry dock. There can be no denying that he was partially successful in attaining his goal; but it is also evident that in fact, whatever his intentions, he was at least as much a Radical innovator as a Conservative reformer. His Erastianism went far beyond what the Catholic Church, claiming a direct mandate from God, could tolerate by way of governmental intervention. His cavalier ignoring of Papal remonstrances was indefensible even in an age prior to the dogmatizing of Papal infallibility. The utilitarian and secularist temper of the emperor made him contemptuous of the salvationist preoccupation of many believers, while a confident rationalism blinded him to the emotional and ritualistic needs of human nature. Joseph's interference with customary church practices was provocative; his virulent hatred of monasticism (not just the abuses of monasticism) showed that a large portion of the Catholic tradition was beyond his understanding. His belief that religion could be reinvigorated upon the command of the government revealed a basic misconception concerning the wellsprings of genuine religiosity. Most un-Catholic of all, however, was his arrogant and egotistic confidence that he himself knew what was best for the Catholic Church, even in disagreement with the Pope and the episcopate; although it is clear

[84] Quoted in ibid., p. 189, from the Rautenstrauch Papers. This deeply religious outlook of the main Josephine advisers was completely ignored by the classic attack upon them by Sebastian Brunner, *Die theologische Dienerschaft am Hofe Joseph II* (Vienna, 1868).

that his Erastian, secularist, and utilitarian brand of Catholicism was at best only *one* aspect of the totality of Catholicism. The ruthless and inconsiderate manner in which he sought to impose his views upon his Catholic subjects inevitably provoked furious opposition.

CARDINAL MIGAZZI: PORTRAIT OF AN ANTI-JOSEPHINE PRELATE

The clerical opposition to Josephinism found a great leader in the person of Christoph Anton Migazzi (1714-1803), cardinal of Vienna and a man distinguished for his learning, diplomacy, and constancy in defending the faith. He was born into a Swiss-Italian aristocratic family in Trent shortly after his father, a former adjutant to Prince Eugene of Savoy, had ruined the family fortune through gambling, taken to drink, and died at the age of forty-three. Migazzi received his worldly training at the episcopal court of Passau, his theological education at the Jesuit *Germanicum* at Rome (1732-36), and rounded out his comprehensive preparation for ecclesiastical statesmanship by taking a legal degree at Innsbruck University. There is no question that he was one of the most learned and studious men of his age, and that his Conservative views were the result of intense and disciplined thinking rather than intellectual inertia.

Migazzi was in no sense a man of the cloister. He had won the admiration of Maria Theresia as Habsburg ambassador to Spain prior to his elevation to the Viennese see, and had been by no means devoid of personal ambition in early life. His dreams were more than satisfied at the comparatively early age of forty-four, when he became archbishop of Vienna in 1757 and received a cardinal's hat four years later. His ambition was henceforth completely identified with the defense of Catholic principles, and he did not hesitate to arouse official displeasure by his unceasing opposition to the entire Josephine program.[85]

The Viennese cardinal combined the wealthy Hungarian see of Waitzen (where he generally spent the summer) with his Vienna archbishopric until Joseph forced him to resign Waitzen as part of the general campaign against ecclesiastical pluralism. Migazzi's qualities as a worldly administrator were best shown at Waitzen, where the

---

[85] This entire section is based on the encyclopedic biography of Cölestin Wolfsgruber, *Christoph Anton Kardinal Migazzi, Fürsterzbischof von Wien* (2nd edn., Ravensburg, 1897). The learned Benedictine author intended his work as a general indictment of Josephinism. The useful article on Migazzi in *Wurzbach* xviii (1868), 244-50, is respectful of the man but Josephine in its sympathies. P. P. Wolf, *Geschichte der Veränderungen*, includes a sharp Josephine attack upon Migazzi on pp. 241-81.

bishop held a dominant position in the secular as well as spiritual affairs of the city. He was admirably energetic in founding schools, establishing charities, enlarging the civic *Rathaus*, and even supervising the building of new roads, parks, and a famous promenade on the Danube; and he presided graciously over brilliant festivities when Maria Theresia visited the city in 1764. There can be no question that, in spite of the vicious accusations thrown against him by Josephine pamphleteers, Migazzi did full justice to both his sees, and that his forced resignation was deeply regretted by the clergy and population of Waitzen alike in 1785.

A further word should be said about Migazzi's personality to explain the veneration in which he was widely held. His personal piety is attested by his attending prayer services for at least two hours every day. He kept in close contact with his flock by being personally accessible to all men regardless of their social station: he could forget his aristocratic social origins and high ecclesiastical dignities in talking with the poor about their problems. Migazzi frequently visited hospitals to administer the sacraments to the sick, and he preached with regularity in an age when most ecclesiastical dignitaries freed themselves from ordinary pastoral functions. His solicitude for the clergy of his dioceses was exemplary: their number was increased to prevent overwork and allow priests to establish intimate contact with their parishioners, and a special spiritual retreat (*Exercitienhaus*) was founded where priests went every second year for a period of rest, religious exercises, and further theological training.

Migazzi saw himself as an embattled servant of Christ in a world which was rapidly going to the Devil; while never doubting the *ultimate* victory of God's Holy Church, he viewed the immediate future as dark indeed. Such old ecclesiastical weapons as excommunication had lost much of their potency in an anticlerical and secularized society, while the mobilization of popular forces on behalf of the faith was as yet unthinkable when the enemy was the established legitimate government. Migazzi no doubt rejoiced at the spontaneous opposition which the Catholic masses offered to the provocative program of Josephine innovation; but he could not give it any open lead. He knew that his efficacy depended upon maintaining good personal relations with the leading figures of the government, with the hope of influencing through negotiations what he could not prevent by force. His diplomatic training made him aware of the importance of cultivating the "right kind of people," and he had some success with the entourage of Maria Theresia though none with Joseph's. His technique was one of continuous admonition and expostulation as he engaged in piecemeal defense of whatever came under Radical attack. He may be described as an indiscriminate Defender of the *Status Quo* with little of the "Reform Conservative" in his make-up. He staunchly refused to contemplate temporary tactical withdrawals in order to prepare a position for effective counterattack; and his battle was doomed to remain a purely defensive effort.

Migazzi's opposition to the reform policies of Maria Theresia is notable for its fundamental character—its frank repudiation of the entire program of the religious *Aufklärung*—and its exhaustive thoroughness. Both qualities can be seen as early as the 1770's—a period before Joseph's extreme reforms and a time when Migazzi could still hope for a sympathetic hearing from the empress. Several examples establish the fact that Migazzi opposed *any* kind of reform, not just the excesses perpetrated by Joseph after 1780.

Maria Theresia went out of her way to ask Migazzi for his analysis of the evils of the age and prescription of remedies in October 1769. The cardinal replied with a general indictment of modernity and a clarion call for governmental repression of all undesirable tendencies. A rampant anticlericalism had long sought to subvert the position of the clergy: it must be repressed. Atheism and immorality were advancing under the guise of "natural religion": the latter must be exposed for the wolf in sheep's clothing which it was. Most modern literature, and especially recent German literature, was frankly irreligious: it must be curbed through a more vigorous censorship under more effective clerical control. Students were being corrupted by so-called "enlightened" professors at every German university: these professors must be purged. The aristocracy gave a bad example to the lower classes by its irreligion and licentiousness: it must be forced to return to religion and morality. Too many bureaucrats were irreligious, heretical, or immoral: they must be replaced by God-fearing, virtuous civil servants. Religion had fallen into contempt because the enforcement of holidays, fasts, and sexual morality had become lax: Migazzi called for the restoration of a stern moral police. His program was in fact largely limited to censorship, purges, and exhortation; it is pathetic that so intelligent a man placed so much reliance upon obviously ineffective methods for coping with the irresistible force of modernity.[86]

Migazzi's patient and resourceful defense of Catholic orthodoxy comes out best in his work as *Praeses* of the *Studien-Hofkommission*

[86] Wolfsgruber prints Migazzi's entire memorandum in ibid., pp. 263-66.

(roughly, a ministry of education), a post he held from 1760 to 1774. It should be noted that the position of *Praeses* was largely honorific, the real power being vested in the *Vice-Praeses* Gerhard van Swieten, the court physician of Maria Theresia and leader of the Viennese *Aufklärung*. Swieten headed an anti-Migazzi majority of which Freiherr von Martini, the *Generalreferent* of the commission, was the most articulate member. Migazzi did retain, however, a power to warn and a forum in which to complain, and because he was known to be *persona grata* to the empress he was initially able to check several schemes he considered subversive.

One example was a proposal made by Count Pergen (later the powerful Police Minister under Joseph) in 1770 to completely laicize the Austrian school system by dismissing all teaching monks from their posts—a proposal which Migazzi denounced as irreligious in motive and certain to paralyze Austrian education in practice, since there was no chance of finding adequate laic replacements for the dismissed clerical teaching staff. (The commission backed Migazzi against Pergen.) The commission discussed the introduction of the so-called "Felbiger catechism" for religious instruction in all Austrian elementary schools in 1772. It had been drawn up by the Silesian Abbot Felbiger, soon to be placed in charge of popular education throughout the Austrian part of the monarchy. Migazzi thought the catechism made improper concessions to "natural religion," implied unjustifiable criticism of earlier catechisms (criticism certain to be quoted by Protestants in their perennial campaign against "Catholic obscurantism"), and included crassly utilitarian economic and political commands quite out of place in a religious catechism. (The commission accepted the catechism but yielded to Migazzi's demand for substantial revisions.)[87]

Other battles were fought over the reform of theological instruction. The "enlightened" party, fearing Migazzi's opposition, prevailed upon Maria Theresia to remove him from the post of *Praeses* of the *Studien-Hofkommission* in January 1774; the pretext chosen was that the enlarged work of the commission, arising from the windup of Jesuit affairs following the recent dissolution of that order, would overtax a man already burdened by the administration of two sees. He was replaced by Freiherr von Kressel, one of the foremost Josephine *Aufklärer* at the Vienna court, who gave full support to some Radical proposals advanced by Abbot Rautenstrauch, director of Theological Faculties throughout the monarchy. The latter called for the replace-

[87] Ibid., pp. 289-309.

ment of episcopal seminaries by state-controlled General Seminaries, and the shortening of theological instruction from four years to two— a shortening to be achieved by eliminating scholastic obscurantism and replacing Latin by German as the language of instruction. The purpose was to "free young theologians from scholastic nonsense and mere school disputes and to teach them only what was useful for the salvation of souls and the welfare of the state." Migazzi protested vehemently against all these proposals in his role as cardinal of Vienna, now that he was no longer a member of the commission. Maria Theresia decided, however, for the commission and against the cardinal, though with the face-saving proviso that the new system was to be accepted only provisionally for a five-year period. By that time Joseph was emperor and the General Seminaries were to become the keystone of his entire ecclesiastical policy.[88]

Migazzi was especially concerned about the heretical tendencies found in university textbooks, and he personally composed detailed refutations of those he considered dangerous. His criticism in 1777 of the rationalist *Ecclesiastical History* of Ferdinand Stöger, covering thirty-six folio pages, so impressed Maria Theresia that the book was prohibited and its author denied a professorship. His prolonged campaign against the rationalist lectures of Joseph Sonnenfels was less successful, although the latter received a mild reprimand from Maria Theresia and was forced to submit his lecture manuscripts to the Censorship Commission. Migazzi's campaign against Paul Joseph Riegger's four-volume *Ecclesiastical Law* (1768ff.)—a treatise with a sharply Erastian outlook—proved a failure. He had better fortune in his opposition to Rautenstrauch's *Synopsis of Ecclesiastical Law* written in 1776. Migazzi's closely reasoned attack, 194 pages long, was successful in getting the empress to order substantial revisions before the book could be sold to the public. Migazzi was even more successful in his campaign against Josef Valentine Eybel's *Introduction to Ecclesiastical Law* (1777), which Maria Theresia submitted for examination to a special *ad hoc* commission dominated by Migazzi himself; the book was formally prohibited and the incriminated author dismissed from his professorship.[89]

Migazzi constantly attacked the Censorship Commission, headed by Gerhard van Swieten, because it readily passed "enlightened" books while harassing the defenders of orthodoxy. It is needless to say that Migazzi never objected to censorship as such, only censorship

[88] Ibid., pp. 309-25.
[89] All these cases are discussed in great detail in ibid., pp. 336ff.

against the "wrong" kind of people; we have seen, indeed, how he viewed censorship as a useful weapon against most of the evils of modernity. Migazzi petitioned Maria Theresia on frequent occasions to order the censor to prohibit books already passed—for example, the famous treatise of Febronius published in 1763. At other times Migazzi protested against the suppression of orthodox books which the commission considered obscurantist. Thus it had suppressed a *Life of St. Joseph of Cupertino* (1768) in which the saint was described as frequently floating in the air. Swieten declared that it was his duty to protect the Austrian reading public from such superstitious nonsense; Migazzi begged to differ. He pointed out that the saint's defiance of the laws of terrestrial gravity had been confirmed by the canonization commission appointed by the Pope. Was it not intolerable that a secular body should arrogate to itself the power to judge the work of a commission working under such unimpeachable auspices?[90]

These examples must suffice to give the flavor of Migazzi's efforts in behalf of embattled Orthodoxy. It was painstaking, detailed, undramatic work, work often unknown to his contemporaries because it had an official character in an age when official business was generally kept secret. It is probably true that Cardinal Migazzi won what rear-guard actions could be won under Maria Theresia, and that no prelate could offer effective resistance to the autocratic Joseph. His relationship to the emperor certainly proved unhappy. We have already seen that he was deprived of his Waitzen bishopric; an ultra-enlightened priest named Blaarer, who had openly expressed his contempt for the ceremony of the mass, was appointed administrator of the Viennese presbytery, with the obvious function of spying upon Migazzi; while a protest against Joseph's attack upon the jurisdiction of monastic superiors received the discourteous reply, "It is an impertinence to remonstrate with one's emperor upon the basis of mere rumors." (Migazzi had not been officially informed of the imperial action, as it did not directly affect his archepiscopal responsibilities; it is needless to say that the rumors were entirely accurate.) When Migazzi pleaded "scruples of conscience" (*Gewissensqualen*), the emperor replied: "Do not talk to me about conscience. I wish that bishops would show more conscientious scruples when it comes to accumulating benefices, receiving money, harassing honest people, and protecting obvious rascals." Migazzi proved rather helpless in the face of this kind of reproof filled with insult and innuendo. Since he obviously could not incite rebellion against the emperor, he had no choice

[90] Ibid., pp. 360ff.

but to pray for an imperial change of heart, and to place his hopes upon the rising tide of opposition provoked by Joseph's Radical actions in religion as well as other fields.[91]

THE RELIGIOUS OPPOSITION TO JOSEPHINISM

Migazzi was, of course, far from being an isolated figure. His opposition to Josephine policies was vigorously supported by Count Cardinal Batthyanyi, primate of Hungary, and Archbishop Count Heinrich Frankenberg, metropolitan of Belgium, as well as by the great majority of bishops within the Habsburg Empire. The Diets and various other *Stände* bodies (such as the Hungarian *Komitate*) declared their solidarity with threatened Orthodoxy on frequent occasions: there were protests in Bohemia, Lower Austria, Styria, Hungary, and Belgium against the suppression of the monasteries and the grant of toleration to Protestants and Jews. The attack upon the monasteries— whose abbots sat, after all, in the Diets—was especially resented as a threat to the future position of all the *Stände*:

> The principle of the inviolability of the *Stände* body is so axiomatic in a well-ordered monarchy that it is unnecessary to seek proofs to justify it. . . . What is true of the *Stände* body in its entirety must be admitted also of every considerable part thereof, such as the group of prelates and abbots. How can the entire body be sure of its continued existence if one of its main parts can be arbitrarily injured?[92]

Most significant of all was the opposition of lower-class people to changes in their customary religious ways. To give a few examples: the burial of a Protestant corpse in a Catholic cemetery in Bohemia required the presence of a whole squadron of cavalrymen to intimidate local opposition. The regulation which required burial in sacks (rather than coffins) was very unpopular; a jokester in Vienna caused much mirth by putting a dead dog in a sack and exhibiting it in one of the main squares of the city with the inscription "Hodie mihi, cras tibi." The introduction of the new church service caused a riot in the town of Bregenz, where the populace feared the loss of the mass: "The mob tore the Imperial decree from the wall and cut it to shreds, beat the Imperial commissioner and forced the district administrator and the city priest to sign a pledge that the mass would continue to

[91] For the entire paragraph see Mitrofanov, *Joseph II*, pp. 740-41.
[92] For the entire paragraph see ibid., pp. 760ff. The quotation is from a protest of the Styrian deputies in 1790, printed in n. 3 of page 766.

be celebrated in the traditional way. Some women pounced like furies upon two subordinates of the district administrator and dragged them away by their hairs into the nearest gutter."[93] It is revealing of the popular temper that when Joseph went to coordinate rescue efforts at the time of the great Danube inundation in 1785 he was coldly received: the masses viewed the inundation as divine punishment for the emperor's Godless decrees.

The popular opposition was given additional impetus by the unprecedented journey which Pope Pius VI took to Vienna in 1782. The emperor was gravely embarrassed by the arrival of his exalted uninvited guest, and visibly annoyed by the reception the Pope received from the Viennese populace. Joseph proved adamant, of course, on all major issues raised by Pius VI, and it must be said that the latter weakened his case by opposing the Josephine programs in an indiscriminate fashion. The Pope asked not only for concessions on internal Catholic matters, such as the restoration of confiscated monastic property, the return of expelled monks, the modification of the episcopal oath to the emperor to prevent conflict with obedience to the Holy See, and the teaching of Catholic theology in conformity with Papal bulls; His Holiness also asked repeal of the Edict of Toleration, which he described as a license for apostasy, and return of the censorship of books into exclusively ecclesiastical hands. The external courtesies were maintained between Pope and emperor during the former's four-week stay in Vienna, but there could be neither agreement nor a meeting of minds; the fruitless Papal journey in fact only exposed the weakness of the Orthodox Catholic position.[94]

THE CASE AGAINST JOSEPHINISM

The opposition to Josephinism was not just a question for Pope, bishop, *Stände,* and populace; it was given intellectual articulation by a series of clerical pamphleteers whose literary products are significant contributions to the history of religious Conservatism in Germany. The life of such pamphleteers was far from easy in the Josephine police state. They were harassed by the censorship and in some cases punished by being sent to the lunatic asylum. This was the fate of an obscure priest named Philipp Holzwart, author of the pamphlet *Crucifix Fernandi.* The police justified its conduct toward Holzwart with the following explanation (July 18, 1788):

[93] These examples are all taken from ibid., pp. 778-89. The quotation is on p. 779.
[94] The literature on the Papal journey to Vienna is endless. An excellent account in English is Goodwin, *The Papal Conflict with Josephinism,* Ch. 2.

It is true that this man talks and writes in a coherent fashion, yet he must be considered a most dangerous character on account of his extreme fanaticism. He must be put under lock and key lest his absurd and indecent talk arouse undesirable attention among the public.[95]

An obscure priest could be handled in this arbitrary manner; but it was otherwise with clerical writers possessing upper-class connections. The most prominent of these was the ex-Jesuit Joseph Albert von Diessbach, who not only wrote widely himself but took the lead in the dissemination of anti-Josephine literature. Diessbach (1732-98) was born into a patrician family in the Swiss Protestant canton of Berne. He followed family tradition in entering foreign military service at the Piedmontese court. (His brother entered the French army and rose to the rank of field marshal.) Diessbach became converted to Catholicism after hearing an especially striking sermon in the Turin cathedral in 1754, and decided to join the Jesuit Order (following the death of his wife) in 1759. After ordination in 1764 he worked as a missionary and itinerant preacher in the Alpine provinces of Switzerland, Northern Italy, and the Habsburg Monarchy.

The dissolution of his order (1773) only meant an intensification of his efforts on behalf of Catholicism. He was one of the first to see the need of combating the pamphlets of the *Aufklärung* with counter-pamphlets, which were circulated through a society especially founded for the purpose, the *Oeuvre de l'amitié chrétienne*. Diessbach worked closely with the previously mentioned group of Augsburg ex-Jesuits publishing the *Kritik über gewisse Kritiker, Rezensenten und Broschürenmacher* after 1787.

His work in Vienna began when Joseph II—of all people!—summoned him in 1782 to take charge of the conversion to Catholicism of the fifteen-year-old Elizabeth of Württemberg, destined to become the bride of Archduke Francis. Diessbach was a close friend of Ignaz Müller, the confessor of Maria Theresa's last years, and of Count Sigismund Hohenwart (future archbishop of Vienna), the religious tutor of the younger children of Leopold. These two connections gave him entree to Leopold after the latter became emperor in 1790; Diessbach was on sufficiently familiar terms with Leopold to submit to him a detailed memorandum calling for the total repeal of the entire fabric of Josephine religious policies (Sept. 30, 1790). The caution which Leopold showed in the face of the explosive religious legacy of his broth-

[95] Quoted in Mitrofanov, *Joseph II*, p. 743, n.4.

171

er Joseph probably owed something to this memorandum. Diessbach always stressed, however, that while true religion could be injured by government, it could be made to flourish only through the spiritual fervor of the believers themselves. He organized to this end a circle of young priests which became the nucleus of the "religious revival" associated with the name of St. Klemens Hofbauer—a circle which combined an intense religious life with militant defense of the rights and dogmas of the Catholic Church.[96]

The case pleaded by the opponents of Josephinism was partly religious and partly political in character. Their religious arguments stressed the inviolable character of the Catholic Church as a divinely created society, and the consequently sacrilegious nature of Joseph's Erastian policies. They argued that the universal mission of the Church made any—necessarily particularistic—state intervention intolerable. They asserted that the secular and utilitarian preoccupations of government tended to make rulers indifferent or hostile to truly spiritual concerns; hence Erastianism led naturally to religious atrophy.

Hostility to Erastianism in general was intensified by hostility to the particular use made by Joseph of his arrogated Erastian powers. The foes of Joseph defended the specific practices and institutions attacked by the emperor, from monasticism to Papal jurisdiction to burial in wooden coffins. They resented the distinction made by Joseph between a small core of divinely sanctioned Christianity and a far larger surrounding area determined by "human contrivance," together with Joseph's claim to set the boundary line between the two and to alter the "human area" in accordance with his own private convictions. The distinction as such could, of course, not be denied in principle, but the Orthodox party insisted that the "divine area" was far more extensive than Joseph allowed, and that the authority to set the respective jurisdictions belonged to the Pope rather than to the emperor. The defenders of established Catholic practices also denied many allegations made by Joseph, such as the existence of widespread immorality in monasteries or the superstitious character of church decorations. One of their most effective arguments, finally, was to stress the destruction and injustice to individuals wrought by Joseph's reforms. Their stories of the admittedly atrocious destruction of mo-

[96] On Diessbach see the definitive article by Ernst Karl Winter, "P. Nikolaus, Joseph Albert von Diessbach S.J.," *Zeitschrift für Schweizerische Kirchengeschichte*, xviii (1924), 22-41, 282-304. Diessbach's memorandum to Leopold is printed in full on pp. 293-304.

nastic art treasures lost nothing in the telling, and they bemoaned the fate of elderly monks who were thrown upon a hostile world with inadequate pensions after a sheltered life of prayer and contemplation.[97]

There was also much personal criticism directed against the motives and entourage of the emperor. He had allegedly suppressed monasteries in order to eliminate superstition; was it not strange, however, that his suppressions had been limited to wealthy monasteries? A pamphleteer asked and answered the rhetorical question in 1787:

> Why have the property-less Capuchin and Franciscan Orders not been suppressed, whereas those owning property—which they used to succor the poor—have been? Answer: because the former possess nothing, and hence their suppression would not have benefitted anybody economically.[98]

Surely avarice was the real motive, the desire to suppress superstition only the pretence. The emperor had, moreover, become the prisoner of an "enlightened" clique whose greed was only matched by its fanatical hatred of the Church. The clerical pamphleteers were unsparing in their denunciations of their enemies. *Aufklärer* were "monkeys, dissemblers, and infatuated people"; Jansenists, "brothers of Judas"; Freemasons, "rascals and deceivers"; and Febronians, "bad wolves who scattered the flock of Christ into every direction of the compass."[99]

These arguments and denunciations were reinforced by a general criticism directed against Joseph's despotism. What was the use of reforms (however benevolent their intention) if men were no longer permitted to live as they had long been accustomed and wanted to continue? What became of liberty under such a monarch? And what of the security of property? Did the attack upon monastic property not imperil the rights of *all* private corporations? The title by which monasteries held their land was neither better nor worse than any title held by any landowner. The pretexts used for confiscating such

[97] These arguments are summarized in the encyclopedic work of Wolfsgruber, *Migazzi*, especially pp. 282ff.; in Sebastian Brunner, *Die Mysterien der Aufklärung in Österreich 1770-1800* (Mainz, 1869), a bitterly anti-Josephine book which faithfully mirrors the pamphlet literature of the 1780's; and in Mitrofanov, *Joseph II*, pp. 789ff.

[98] Quoted in Mitrofanov, *Joseph II*, p. 791, n.4.

[99] From an anonymous pamphlet, *Wer sind die Aufklärer? beantwortet nach dem ganzen Alphabet*, published in 1787. Quoted by Mitrofanov, *Joseph II*, p. 793.

lands—such as fiscal necessity or the government's opinion that the present owners were parasites—could easily be extended to aristocratic lands as well. The sanctity of property, the very foundation of human society, was indivisible and must be defended when first challenged; otherwise the government might succeed in a program of *divide et impera* leading to Asiatic forms of despotism.[100]

Conclusion

It is impossible to exaggerate the role played by religion in German public controversy in the second half of the eighteenth century. This fact is often ignored because most historians—with their understandable concentration upon the culture of the elite and preoccupation with those tendencies which looked toward the future rather than the past—have labeled the age as one where the *Aufklärung* broke through the crust of a superstitious, traditionalist, and otherworldly Christianity. This may have been largely true in the advanced countries of Western Europe, though even there popular religious passions—especially in the form of confessional prejudice—continued to play an important role in public affairs.[101] In Germany religious topics clearly dominated intellectual controversy, and more books and pamphlets were published on religious questions than on all other questions combined. The German *Aufklärer* were preoccupied with advancing rationalist principles in both the Protestant and Catholic Churches; they thus compelled Conservatives to rally to the defense of religious Orthodoxy well before the social and political *status quo* was sufficiently challenged to make defense necessary.

Religious toleration remained anathema to many Protestants and most Roman Catholics; its introduction by "enlightened" Catholic rulers—whether the Emperor Joseph, the Elector Clemens Wenceslas of Trier, or the city council of Cologne—aroused bitter, and in some cases successful, popular opposition. The free and unfettered discussion of all religious problems, as championed by Lessing and a host of other *Aufklärer,* was opposed by the Lutheran Orthodox party. The infiltration of the Prussian Lutheran Church by Radical and "subversive" elements provoked Wöllner's edict, with its attempt to re-

[100] These arguments are summarized upon the basis of contemporary pamphlets by A. Jaeger, *Kaiser Joseph II. Reform und Gegenreform 1780-1792* (Vienna, 1867), especially pp. 85ff. A number of revealing contemporary quotations can be found in Mitrofanov, *Joseph II*, p. 791.

[101] This fact has been demonstrated recently in the brilliant book by Manfred Schlenke, *England und das Friederizianische Preussen 1740-1763. Ein Beitrag zum Verhältnis von Politik und öffentlicher Meinung im England des 18. Jahrhunderts* (Freiburg, 1963).

store Orthodoxy by a policy of censorship and purge. The edict was responsible for the first major public debate on public policy in the history of the absolutist monarchy of the Hohenzollerns—an important event in the history of German Conservatism, signifying that it could no longer rely upon the actions of the government but must justify its position before the court of public opinion.

The most bitter battles were, however, fought within the Catholic fold. The religious *Aufklärung*, though taking its origin primarily in the Protestant areas of Germany, inevitably found Catholic spokesmen as well. The deplorable condition of eighteenth-century German Catholicism invited the attention of Radical critic and Conservative reformer alike, and it proved unusually difficult to maintain the distinction between the two types of opponents of established Catholic Orthodoxy. The problem was further complicated by the frequent divergence between intention and result. The Emperor Joseph undoubtedly wished well by the Church; yet his radical actions obviously went far beyond what was permissible for a "Reform Catholic." He aroused the tenacious opposition of the Pope, the episcopate headed by Cardinal Migazzi of Vienna, the *Stände* bodies, and a whole host of pamphleteers. Their opposition was primarily religious in motive and result, but their defense of monastic property as but one species of threatened property, and attack upon despotism as an intolerable form of government, could easily lead to cooperation between religious Conservatives and defenders of the social and political *status quo*, once the latter also came under Radical attack.

CHAPTER 4

Social Controversies

The Social and Economic
Demands of the Aufklärung

THE MERCANTILIST ORTHODOXY[1]

THE SOCIAL and economic policies of the German territorial states of the eighteenth century were characterized by an uneasy mixture of traditional and modern elements. The former can be seen in the widespread, unreflective acceptance of a *status quo* which derived from the hierarchic, inequalitarian pattern of medieval society. Even rulers strongly influenced by the spirit of *Aufklärung*—such as Frederick the Great or Joseph II—did not challenge the continued existence of a pattern of society marked by aristocracy (enjoying a wide gradation of privilege), a dependent rural population (with varying degrees of servitude), and craftsmanship based upon guilds which enforced status differentiation in the towns. The "enlightened despots" worked hard to correct specific abuses as they were recognized, but their reform efforts aimed at improvement in detail *within* the framework of traditional society, not the general reconstruction of society per se.

This Conservative (or, more accurately, traditionalist) element of their policy must never be forgotten when one looks at their efforts at innovation subsumed under the general label of "mercantilism." Mercantilism may be defined as the governmental regulation of the economy in order to promote the common good or, what was often identified with it, maximum power for the state. Governmental regulation of economic life was, of course, nothing new in the eighteenth century; it had been the universal and unquestioned practice throughout the Middle Ages. What changed in the seventeenth century—when mercantilism first arose—was the *unit* of regulation and the *purposes* of the regulators. The life of medieval Europe had been dominated by municipal economies; they were regulated with

[1] Mercantilism was originally a term of opprobrium used by advocates of laissez-faire like Adam Smith to characterize what they were attacking. A favorable connotation was given to the term by Gustav Schmoller, *Das Merkantilsystem in seiner historischen Bedeutung* (Berlin, 1884). The best brief modern characterization is by A. Heckscher, "Mercantilism," *Encyclopedia of the Social Sciences*, x (1933), 333-39, summarizing the same author's standard work, *Mercantilism* (2 vols., London, 1935).

176

the primary purpose of safeguarding the moral law and preventing practices which might imperil the individual salvation of producers. The seventeenth century saw the replacement of municipal by territorial economies, while regulation for salvation yielded to regulation for maximizing the power of the state. Colbert, the great minister of Louis XIV, became the leading exponent of this policy. His system deliberately subordinated the welfare of individuals to the interest of the whole; it relied upon compulsion and minute regulation to achieve its objectives of a balanced economy characterized by ample revenues, self-sufficiency in industries essential for war, and a favorable balance of trade. To achieve these ends often required certain reforms in the *status quo,* such as some modification of aristocratic and guild privilege, but such reforms were undertaken by princes in a strictly *ad hoc* manner. The most characteristic aspect of mercantilist government was a presumed omniscience and omnipotence; its bureaucrats treated subjects as mere children with the duty to do as they were told. German princes emulated Colbertian mercantilism exactly the way they imitated all other things French.

The German version of mercantilism was called cameralism by contemporary authors. All of the great rulers of the eighteenth century— such as Frederick William I and Frederick the Great of Prussia and Maria Theresia and Joseph II of Austria—were guided by its tenets in their economic policy. It was championed by a long line of distinguished authors, of whom Johann Heinrich Gottlob von Justi (1717-71) and Joseph Freiherr von Sonnenfels (1737-1817) were the most prominent in the second half of the eighteenth century. Frederick William I of Prussia established special chairs for *Kameralistik* at the Universities of Frankfurt/Oder and Halle in 1727. All potential Prussian civil servants were expected to have a thorough grounding in the subject before they offered themselves for state employment. One must never forget the powerful position held by cameralism as an "entrenched orthodoxy" if one is to appreciate the audacity and liberating impact of the new laissez-faire doctrines taught by the French Physiocrats and by Adam Smith.[2]

[2] On Cameralism see the excellent summary by Louise Sommer, "Cameralism," *Encyclopedia of the Social Sciences,* III (1930), 158-60. The writings of the Cameralists are described by A. W. Small, *The Cameralists* (Chicago, 1909), and L. Sommer, *Die österreichischen Kameralisten in dogmengeschichtlicher Darstellung* (2 vols., Vienna, 1920-25). A full historical understanding of the practice of Cameralism will have to await systematic scholarly exploration of the social and economic history of Germany in the eighteenth century.

The great revolutionary development in economic theory wrought by the European Enlightenment was the "discovery" of the mechanism of the free market as the "natural" regulator of economic life. This "discovery" had as one of its prerequisites the great transvaluation of values sketched out in Ch. 1: it assumed the moral respectability of man's secular, rational, and hedonistic activity and presupposed the prior abandonment of such medieval and Christian values as other-worldliness, being contented with one's customary "God-given" status, and asceticism. The theory of the free market asserted that the best way to maximize prosperity was to allow free men to pursue their self-interest in open competition with other men; the free market—under which all factors of production were allocated in accordance with consumer preference—provided the "invisible hand" which guaranteed the identity of private and public interests, whereas mercantilism had believed in the necessity of state action to achieve the supremacy of the latter over the former. The change from regulation to freedom constituted a fundamental breach in economic theory, as did a new emphasis upon the personal welfare of private individuals rather than the power of the state. Yet laissez-faire also built upon mercantilism by benefiting from the latter's triumph over medieval traditionalism, and it shared with mercantilism the belief in the importance of earthly wealth where medieval people were more concerned with the problem of salvation.

The doctrines of laissez-faire and the free market required two far-reaching changes in economic policies—the dismantling of the machinery used by mercantilistic government to regulate the economy and the introduction of a substantial measure of mobility for the factors of production (land, capital, labor). To achieve these two changes became the core of the reform program advanced by the Radical critics of the eighteenth-century German socioeconomic *status quo.*

The change in the conception of the proper economic functions of the state will be noted in the next chapter, since it constituted a primarily political phenomenon. The present chapter will concentrate upon controversies provoked in part (there were, of course, other causal factors as well) by the demand for greater mobility for the factors of production.

[3] For this entire section see the classic analysis by W. Roscher, *Geschichte der National-Oekonomik in Deutschland* (Munich, 1874), Ch. 21, "Die Physiokratie in Deutschland."

Mobility in landed property required the abolition of all restrictions upon the transfer of ownership (such as family entails, the legal distinction between aristocratic and nonaristocratic lands, et cetera). The corollary of a new mobility in land ownership must necessarily be the abandonment (or at least modification) of judicial and political functions traditionally connected with such ownership. Patrimonial jurisdictions were defensible (perhaps) as part of the traditional, patriarchal order of rural society; they were obviously indefensible if exercised by parvenu owners of landed estates, men who bought and sold land as a rational investment rather than as part of a "way of life." The generalization may be ventured that every form of privilege constituted some obstacle to the mobility of the factors of production; this was one reason why the social theory of the *Aufklärung* became egalitarian and easily developed an antiaristocratic animus.

The mobility of labor required the abolition of the two basic institutions which had long restricted the efficient use of labor—serfdom and guilds. Another impediment to mobility and a survival of the medieval inegalitarian order of society consisted of the numerous restrictions upon the Jews; this proved one factor behind the demand for Jewish emancipation. Some Radical thinkers also believed that the traditional subjection of women was an anachronism unworthy of an enlightened age.

All the demands here mentioned were calculated to provoke sharp controversy because each struck at the heart of a formidable vested interest. This interest could, of course, be psychological as well as economic, though usually one detects a combination of the two. It is also important to avoid looking at the various socioeconomic controversies covered in this chapter in isolation; they must all be placed in the context of the general *Aufklärung* attack upon the existing social pattern—traditionalist and inegalitarian despite the dynamic potential inherent in mercantilism—in the name of a rationalist and egalitarian conception of a better society.

THE SPREAD OF LAISSEZ-FAIRE PRINCIPLES IN GERMANY

Laissez-faire principles had their origin in Western Europe in the writings of the French Physiocrats (especially Quesnay, Mirabeau the Elder, and Turgot) and the Scottish founder of the "classical school of economics," Adam Smith. We have already encountered the Physiocratic influence in Southern Germany in the person of *Markgraf* Karl Friedrich von Baden; of greater importance, especially in Northern

Germany, was the direct influence of the systematic work of Adam Smith.[4]

A first translation of *The Wealth of Nations* appeared as early as 1776-78[5] and became widely known through three review articles in the *Göttingische Gelehrten Anzeigen*[6] written by the influential Göttingen philosopher J.G.H. Feder. A new translation, by the Prussian philosopher Christian Garve, appeared in 1794 and enjoyed a second edition in 1799 and a third in 1810.[7] It is, of course, impossible to measure Smith's immediate impact upon public opinion, especially since his principles were not clearly distinguished from the Physiocratic doctrines coming from France at the same time. It is certain, however, that several professors at leading universities taught their students laissez-faire principles, in conscious opposition to mercantilism, by the 1790's, and that these students, becoming bureaucrats after completing their studies, reached influential positions, especially in Prussia, shortly after 1800.

Göttingen and Königsberg became the two main academic centers for the spread of Smith's ideas. All the leading Göttingen professors—Feder, Pütter, Schlözer, Sartorius, et cetera—were influenced by the great Scotsman; the latter published a special textbook on *Economics in accordance with the principles of Adam Smith* in 1796.[8] Many alumni of Göttingen were notable in later life for their advocacy of laissez-faire, including the Prussian reformers Hardenberg, Stein, Vincke, Bülow, and Sack.[9]

Königsberg stood in the shadow of the mighty Göttingen, and its

[4] The best introduction to the spread of Smithian ideas in Germany is still Roscher, Ch. 25, "Aufnahme Adam Smith's in Deutschland"; an excellent modern account is Wilhelm Treue, "Adam Smith in Deutschland: Zum Problem des 'politischen Professors' zwischen 1776 und 1810," in *Rothfels-Festschrift, Deutschland und Europa* (Düsseldorf, 1951), pp. 101-33. The following section is primarily based upon Treue, who incorporates the conclusions of dissertations by Carl Hasek (1925), Hugo Graul (1928), and Alfred Nahrgang (1933).

[5] *Untersuchungen der Natur und Ursachen von Nationalreichthümern von Adam Smith* (2 vols., Leipzig, 1776 and 1788, J. F. Schiller trans.). The translator was a cousin of the poet.

[6] March, 10, April, 5, and August 10, 1777. Other favorable reviews appeared in Nicolai's *Allgemeine Deutsche Bibliothek* and Iselin's *Ephemeriden der Menschheit*.

[7] *Untersuchungen über die Natur und Ursachen des Nationalreichtums von Adam Smith. Aus dem englischen der 4. Ausgabe neu übersetzt* (Leipzig, 1794).

[8] Sartorius, *Handbuch der Staatswirtschaft zum Gebrauch bei akademischen Vorlesungen nach Adam Smiths Grundsätzen ausgearbeitet* (Göttingen, 1796).

[9] The fact that Stein and Hardenberg began their studies well before Smith became influential (1773, 1766) is of little significance in this context since both maintained close contact with their alma mater after formally completing their studies.

professors—including Kant—frequently used the handbooks of professors who taught at the prestigious sister institution. It is not surprising, therefore, that Smithian principles spread quickly from Göttingen to Königsberg. Christian Jakob Kraus (1753-1807), the friend of Kant and most famous German spokesman of laissez-faire at the end of the eighteenth century, himself had been a student at Göttingen (1779) before joining the Königsberg faculty. He lectured on *Kameralwissenschaft* regularly after 1791 and published an abridgment of Smith's *The Wealth of Nations* in 1797. Kraus enjoyed close personal contacts with highly placed bureaucrats. The *Oberpräsident* of East Prussia, Friedrich Leopold Freiherr von Schrötter, was a close friend, as were other important officials, such as Auerswald, the curator of the university, and Theodor von Schön, later Stein's close collaborator. Schrötter decreed in 1800 that "no one would henceforth be permitted to enter the East Prussian administrative service without a certificate of having attended Kraus's lectures."[10] It was Kraus's ambition "to survive, not in dead books but through living men who owe their education to me"[11]—an ambition destined to be fully satisfied. His unoriginal and unsystematic writings have been long forgotten; but the men he influenced did not forget his principles when they began to reform Prussia—beginning with East Prussia—just after Kraus's early death in 1807. He would have rejoiced at the abolition of serfdom, the curtailment of guild privilege, and the greater mobility of landed property introduced by Stein—reforms which were recognized, by friend and foe alike, to be applications of the laissez-faire theory of Adam Smith as popularized by Christian Kraus.[12]

When the University of Berlin was founded in 1810, it became a third center for the dissemination of Liberal economic principles. The chair for *Kameralwissenschaft* was given to the Liberal Johann Gottfried Hoffmann, who had been a pupil, friend, and successor to Kraus at Königsberg;[13] the countercandidacy of the Conservative Adam Müller never had a chance.[14] Another professorship was offered to

---

[10] Quoted in Treue, op.cit., p. 115.   [11] Ibid., p. 118.

[12] The standard work on Kraus is the biography by Johannes Voigt, *Das Leben des Professors Chr. Jakob Kraus* (Königsberg, 1819). An important modern study is Erich Kühne, "Der Staatswirtschaftslehrer Christian Jakob Kraus und seine Beziehungen zu Adam Smith," *Alt-Preussische Monatsschrift*, xxxix (1902), 325ff., and xl (1903), 1ff.

[13] On Johann Gottfried Hoffmann (1765-1847) see E. R. Huber, *Deutsche Verfassungsgeschichte* (Stuttgart, 1957), i, 132.

[14] See below, where the controversy in the *Berliner Abendblätter*, dealing ostensibly with the memory of Kraus but really with who would secure the professorship, is covered.

Albrecht von Thaer, the great pioneer of "scientific agriculture," who became the special bête noir of all defenders of the traditional order of Prussian rural society.[15] The University of Berlin quickly won a commanding position in the training of Prussian bureaucrats; the influence of Hoffmann and Thaer can be traced in the thought of the generation which developed the *Zollverein* and laid the economic and financial foundations for Prussia's future greatness.[16]

The doctrine of laissez-faire originally carried Germany by storm, but there were from the very beginning warnings from men who contended that its introduction would ruin the entire established order of society. One such warning, taken from a pamphlet dealing primarily with the controversial Prussian tobacco monopoly, will suffice to illustrate this contention; it should be remembered that free trade was considered the central principle of Smithian economics:

> The three pillars of Prussian prosperity and Prussian power have hitherto been the continuous and liberal encouragement given to domestic factories; the encouragement given to the increase of cattle and population (*Vermehrung des Viehstandes und der Bevölkerung*); and a close watch over every penny which might lose its way across the border into some foreign state. Upon the maintenance of these policies depend Prussia's population, industry, fiscal resources, and preservation of the army. Let the curse of the Prussian population (*der Fluch der Brennen*) fall upon those disastrous counselors who wish to abandon them now. A nation which introduces free trade makes itself voluntarily dependent upon alien and distant states; it inflicts upon itself an incurable wound which will never cease to fester and to suck out, vampyr-like, the vital energies (*Lebenskräfte*) of the Prussian state. It will constantly withdraw money from domestic circulation and thereby diminish both con-

[15] On Thaer (1752-1828) see Wilhelm Korte, *Albrecht Thaer* (Leipzig, 1839); August Werth, *Albrecht Thaer als Nationalökonom* (Leipzig, 1905); and Theodor von der Goltz, *Geschichte der deutschen Landwirtschaft* (2 vols., Stuttgart, 1902-03), II, 3-86. He originally experimented with new forms of agriculture near his native Celle (Hannover); won a national reputation with the publication of his *Einleitung zur Kenntniss der englischen Landwirtschaft* (3 vols., Hannover, 1798-1800); and was called to Prussia in 1804 to establish a model experimental farm at Möglin (Mittelmark), which became the *Königliche Academie des Landbaus* in 1824. He was professor of agricultural science at the newly founded University of Berlin from 1810 to 1818. Thaer's main work, *Grundsätze der rationellen Landwirtschaft*, appeared in four volumes at Berlin in 1810-12. A fourth edition appeared as late as 1848.

[16] For the spread of laissez-faire principles after 1820 see the valuable study by Donald Rohr, *The Origins of Social Liberalism in Germany* (Chicago, 1963), Ch. 3.

sumption and capital investment; while it will also cause a diminu-
tion of public revenues and thereby throw the state into a condition
of serious illness.[17]

The controversy about laissez-faire was, however, primarily fought
out not on general principles but rather on specific issues concerning
the aristocracy, serfdom, and guild privileges.

The Aristocracy and Its Critics

THE CONDITION OF THE NOBILITY

The German aristocracy of the eighteenth century was an extremely
variegated body as regards rank, condition, and social usefulness. To
begin with distinctions of rank: they extended in a broad gamut from
electoral prince to petty territorial noble. The so-called "high aristocracy" consisted of all princes with the right to sit in the *Reichstag*,
a body which was sometimes called the "aristocratic council" of the
empire; from a technical point of view the electors of Prussia and Bavaria were both aristocrats subordinated to their imperial sovereign
(though in practice they felt and acted like sovereigns themselves).
The "lower aristocracy" consisted of Imperial Knights who knew no
superior but the emperor (but lacked representation in the *Reichstag*) and of territorial nobles (*Landadel*) who owed allegiance to a
member of the "high nobility" (for example, the Junkers of Prussia
owed allegiance to the king). The Imperial Knights deemed themselves
far superior to the Junkers, though the latter in fact often held more
land and exercised similar governmental functions over their social
inferiors in such fields as justice, police, and tax collection. The legal
and political distinction between Imperial Knight and territorial noble
was in fact of comparatively small sociological importance and can be
diregarded for the purpose of our analysis.

The following section will be devoted primarily to controversies
dealing with the position of the "lower nobility" in German life; controversies involving the "higher nobility" were *political* in character
and will be considered in the next chapter. The group we intend to
cover was defined by an author writing in 1791 in the following
terms:

> that class of citizens which is raised, by generally visible character-
> istics, above the middle classes. . . . Its characteristics are defined by

[17] Anonymous, *Was ist für und was ist gegen die Generaltabaks-Administration
zu sagen* (Berlin, 1786), quoted by Karl Adolf Menzel, *Zwanzig Jahre preussische
Geschichte 1786-1806* (Leipzig, 1849), p. 32.

the authority of law as supported by public opinion. Membership in the class is usually derived from birth into a "superior family" whose aristocratic origin goes back to the remote past; it may, however, also be due to the specific conferment of a patent of nobility by a specific sovereign prince at a specific time. It must be accompanied in either case by wealth, social prestige, and intermarriage with similarly situated families.

A recent patent of nobility conferred genuine—as opposed to *pro forma*—membership only when it was combined with

possession of wealth, the holding of important offices, and the enjoyment of princely favor—and it must be followed by intermarriage with families of acknowledged aristocratic status.[18]

The most important sociological distinction to be made when looking at the lower nobility is between those who lived on their estates in the countryside and those who sought employment from territorial princes as courtiers, bureaucrats, or officers. The former tended to be patriarchal, parochial, tough, and uncultivated, though there were of course many exceptions to this stereotype. The latter's qualities were naturally shaped by the atmosphere of court life and tended to take on both the virtues (refinement, aesthetic interests) and the vices (flattery, moral degeneracy) characteristic of much of German court society in the eighteenth century. Their estates (when not lost through extravagance or mismanagement) were run by bailiffs for their absentee owners—a situation usually incompatible with traditional patriarchal codes of behavior.

It is obviously impossible to make blanket generalizations about the social "usefulness" of either type of aristocracy in eighteenth-century Germany. There were local squires (and Imperial Knights) that exemplified the best patriarchal traditions, supplemented in some cases by leadership in undertaking agricultural improvements; others were boorish local tyrants who made life miserable for their subjects and serfs. The court nobility provided many of the best ministers and generals of Germany's various territorial states; but it also provided an abundant supply of degenerate courtiers, lazy bureaucrats who attained high posts without professional qualifications, and

[18] Friedrich Wilhelm von Ramdohr, "Über das Verhältniss des anerkannten Geburtsadels deutscher monarchischer Staaten zu den übrigen Klassen ihrer Bürger in Rücksicht auf die ersten Staatsbedienungen," *Berlinische Monatsschrift*, xvii (1791), 124-74, 250-83. Henceforth quoted as Ramdohr, *Verhältniss*. The quotation is from page 127.

officers better known for martial pride than proficiency in the increasingly technical profession of soldiering. A good many nobles alternated, finally, between state service and local residence (this was true, for example, of most Prussian Junkers); they tended consequently to possess an inextricable medley of the virtues and vices of both types mentioned above.

The German aristocracy possessed in abundance the qualities usually characteristic of aristocracy and all the more pronounced when aristocracy comes under bourgeois attack: caste consciousness, best exemplified by the doctrine of "blue blood" and contempt for those born mere commoners; a tenacious resolve to defend inherited privilege, no matter how parasitic it had become through the passage of time; a loose attitude toward money, with economy being considered a shabby bourgeois virtue; a still looser attitude toward morals (especially sexual morals), since morality was a matter for commoners rather than their blue-blooded superiors; and a preoccupation with refined manners that were valued as a status symbol if nothing else. The personality of the young aristocrat was usually shaped by consciousness of tradition and family obligation, the stress upon dignity and *noblesse oblige,* and the inculcation of the maxim that aristocrats must master circumstances rather than adapt to them. All these qualities were perpetuated by exclusive schools (such as the *Ritterakademien* and the Prussian *Kadettenanstalten*) where young aristocrats were educated in sharp segregation from commoners. These schools were more successful in breeding class consciousness than general culture, and had the unfortunate result of divorcing their pupils from popular outlook and feelings.

The general position of the European aristocracy had been undermined for centuries by certain irresistible historical forces. The nobility had lost its distinctive military function with the collapse of the feudal system during the later Middle Ages. Knights became an anachronism when infantry successfully challenged cavalry and gunpowder made castles militarily obsolete. The development of absolute, centralized government in the seventeenth century chipped away at aristocratic control of local governmental functions; and it sometimes championed the rights of the lower classes against their aristocratic oppressors in the name of Reason of State. The economic basis of aristocratic life was undermined by inflation in those parts of Western and Southern Germany where labor services had been commuted for money. The traditional functions of the aristocracy—military and political—had originally justified such privileges as tax exemptions; but by the eighteenth century the functions had disappeared while the privileges remained. All these facts were increasingly pointed out by numerous "enlightened" writers after 1750 and brought to the consciousness of the nobility itself. Its usual reaction was, however, one of defiant resistance rather than accommodating renunciation, and frivolity in enjoying traditional privileges rather than justifying their survival by the performance of onerous duties.[19]

CRITICISM OF THE NOBILITY

The privileges possessed by the German nobility provoked increasing criticism throughout the eighteenth century, criticism fueled by a new vigor of bourgeois self-assertion and by the increasing spread of the principles of the *Aufklärung*. The *bourgeoisie*—ever more conscious of its cultural and moral superiority over the nobility—increasingly resented aristocratic privilege though this privilege was objectively no more onerous in, say, 1785 than it had been half a century earlier. The fully developed egalitarian doctrines of the *Aufklärung* now began to strike, not only at the abuses connected with aristocracy, but the principle of aristocracy per se. The aristocracy found itself, therefore, increasingly upon the defensive before the court of German public opinion; and this public opinion may be described as a "loaded jury" dominated by bourgeois readers and writers.

The following specific points were frequently made: The aristocracy did not carry its fair share of public burdens because it was traditionally exempted from numerous taxes. The monopoly possessed by aristocrats to own so-called "aristocratic lands" restricted the mobility of landed property in defiance of sound economic principles, and impeded agricultural improvement by restricting credit and investment.

---

[19] The best contemporary description of the eighteenth-century German aristocracy is to be found in Johann Michael von Loen, *Der Adel* (Ulm, 1752). Loen, a prolific man of letters who lived most of his life (1694-1776) in Frankfurt, urged many reforms upon the nobility but was not opposed to nobility in principle. He had contact with the rural nobility after he purchased an estate at Mörfelden in 1733, and entered the "bureaucratic nobility" by accepting appointment as *Regierungspräsident* of the Prussian territory of Lingen in 1752 (just after completing the above-mentioned treatise). He married the sister of Goethe's grandmother Textor and was therefore the poet's grand-uncle by marriage. See W. Stricker, *ADB*, xix (1884), 86-88. On the problem of aristocracy in general see the excellent introduction by Georg von Below, "Adel," *Handwörterbuch der Staatswissenschaften*, i (2nd edn., Jena, 1898), 47-53. The sociological exploration of the German aristocracy is still in its infancy, even in the case of the much-discussed Prussian Junker class. Two pioneering studies are Fritz Martiny, *Die Adelsfrage in Preussen vor 1806 als politisches und soziales Problem* (Berlin, 1938), and H. Brunschwig, *La crise de l'état prussien* (Paris, 1947).

Other abuses connected with aristocratic privilege were the survival of patrimonial jurisdictions and police powers, which prevented the agrarian lower classes from direct contact with the government; rights of ecclesiastical patronage, which made the clergy servile toward its nobiliar patrons; and hunting rights which placed the pleasures of the nobility above the necessities of the poor. All these abuses were over and above the fundamental abuse that many aristocrats lived idle and essentially useless lives at the expense of the lower classes for no better reason than their ancestors' participation in the now-defunct feudal system. The aristocracy enjoyed, moreover, a privileged legal status incompatible with modern principles of equality before the law. They could be tried only by central, not ordinary local, courts; were exempted from torture where it was still practiced; their word sufficed in lieu of an oath; and they suffered smaller (or at least different) penalties compared to commoners convicted of identical crimes. (For example, nobles were executed by beheading rather than hanging, in the rare cases where they were sentenced to capital punishment.)

These financial, economic, and legal privileges were reinforced by those of a political and social nature. Individual aristocrats possessed an inherent and hereditary right to sit in *Stände* bodies where these survived, and aristocrats as an order possessed a predominant voice within these bodies compared to other represented estates. (The famous case of the Württemberg Diet, dominated by the municipal and ecclesiastical oligarchies, was one of the rare exceptions to this rule.) Aristocrats claimed, and generally received, privileged access to court, bureaucratic, and military positions even when they did not possess educational qualifications comparable to those of their bourgeois competitors. They were frequently permitted to skip the junior grades when entering the civil service, and thereafter promoted faster than their personal accomplishments warranted. Bourgeois criticism was especially severe where aristocrats received highly remunerated sinecures and then appointed bourgeois clerks to do the actual work at a fraction of their own salary. The frequently narrowly aristocratic definition of *Hoffähigkeit* (i.e., eligibility to be presented at court) was a further bourgeois grievance, as was *Stiftsfähigkeit* (i.e., eligibility for ecclesiastical canonries) in the Catholic (and a few Protestant) parts of Germany. There were, finally, certain external marks of aristocratic superiority which caused irritation far beyond their substantive importance: in this category were special seats reserved for nobles in churches, theaters, and even the lecture halls of universities; certain sumptuary privileges like the wearing of swords and coats of arms in public; and the exclusive right to certain special forms of address (e.g., *Fräulein* for unmarried young ladies). It will be seen from this extended catalogue that criticism of the aristocracy was variegated, comprehensive, and fueled by bourgeois class resentment and self-interest; and that the defenders of the aristocratic *status quo* faced no easy task in the second half of the eighteenth century.[20]

THE CONSERVATIVE DEFENSE OF ARISTOCRACY

The defenders of aristocracy developed several different types of arguments, most notably the frank assertion of aristocratic superiority over ordinary mortals; the general defense of hierarchic over egalitarian society; and the specific defense of many (though by no means all) aristocratic privileges previously mentioned. These were all arguments advanced by *Status Quo* Conservatives. There were, however, also Reform Conservatives who admitted the force of many Radical criticisms and accepted the historic obsolescence of many aristocratic positions. They were willing to surrender indefensible points in order to make the residual aristocratic position less vulnerable to attack; and combined prudent withdrawal with proposals to improve the composition of the aristocracy in order to make it more capable of per-

---

[20] Good summaries of the criticisms levied against the aristocracy can be found in Ernst Brandes, *Ueber den Einfluss und die Wirkung des Zeitgeistes auf die höheren Stände Deutschlands* (2 vols., Hannover, 1810), II, 75-123, contemporary remarks by a candid friend of the aristocracy, and W. Wenck, *Deutschland*, I, 28ff., a good modern survey. Literary voices critical of the aristocracy are, of course, legion. For an example in prose see the *Erziehungsroman* by Christian Salzmann, *Carl von Carlsberg, oder Über das menschliche Elend* (4 vols., Karlsruhe, 1778) especially II, 188ff. Numerous poetic examples are printed in Emil Horner, *Politische Dichtung*, especially Leopold F. G. von Goecking's *Die Parforcejagd*, Bürger's *Der wilde Jäger* and *Des Pfarrers Tochter von Taubenheim*, and Voss's *Frohndienste*. Criticism of aristocracy sometimes took the indirect form of praising American equality, as in the following stanza in the frequently quoted anonymous "Die Freiheit Amerikas" in the *Berliner Monatsschrift* of April 1783:

> Wo süsse Gleichheit wohnet und Adelbrut
> Europans Pest, die Sitte der Einfalt nicht
> Beflickt, verdienstlos bessern Menschen
> Trotzt und von Schweisse des Landmanns schwelget.

Ibid., pp. 87-90. Cf. also the useful survey of Johanna Schultze, *Die Auseinandersetzung zwischen Adel und Bürgertum in den deutschen Zeitschriften der letzten drei Jahrzehnte des 18. Jahrhunderts 1773-1806* (Berlin, 1925), which specializes in "content analysis" (theories of the state, theories about aristocracy, theories about the difference between the aristocracy and the *bourgeoisie*) but also includes valuable tables about authors, trends in magazine publishing, et cetera.

forming those social functions which it could still retain. There was as yet no powerful Reactionary party among German aristocrats, for the simple reason that aristocracy was still everywhere socially predominant. (Reactionary sentiments usually arise only within a dispossessed social class.) Only in the political sphere did many nobles resent the advance of absolutism and look back nostalgically to the pre-absolutist *Ständestaat*. This attitude will be covered when we deal with political controversies in the next chapter.

The simplest defense of aristocratic privilege consisted of a categorical assertion that it was founded upon the inherent, hereditary biological superiority of the nobility. This point of view was stated with delightful frankness by *Markgraf* Karl Friedrich von Baden, otherwise known for his enlightened theory and practice. He called the often-advanced dictum of the *Aufklärung* that "nobility is intrinsically a chimera"

> an extremely unphilosophical position. If there are races among animals there are races among men; for that reason the most superior must put themselves ahead of others, marry among themselves and reproduce a pure race: that is the nobility.[21]

The argument was buttressed by looking at the historical nature of aristocracy. Opinions differed on whether it was as old as the human race itself (and therefore a natural and indelible condition of all human society), or whether it was based upon specific recognition of the specific achievement of unusually gifted men and subsequent hereditary transmission. This achievement might be military, as in the "feudal aristocracy"; political, for princes often conferred patents of nobility upon distinguished ministers and civil servants; or even economic, as in many recent ennoblements of merchants and financiers. It was asserted that ability was, to some extent at least, hereditary; and as aristocrats tended to marry other aristocrats, or else the choicest members of the upper *bourgeoisie*, it stood to reason that their average biological quality stood somewhat above the average of the population. Heredity was in any case reinforced by a favorable environment, since aristocrats possessed "all the advantages" for developing all their talents; while the incessant challenge of "living up to a great name," and fulfilling the claims of great positions sur-

---

[21] Karl Obser, "Aus Karl Friedrichs hinterlassenen Papieren," *ZGOR*, xxvi (1911), 466. Quoted by Helen Liebel, "Enlightened Bureaucracy v. Enlightened Despotism in Baden 1750-92," *Transactions of the American Philosophical Society* 55 (1965), p. 22.

rounded with great expectations, was a stimulus likely to provoke a maximum response.[22]

A further proof of the innate superiority of the nobility was seen in its remarkable evolution from medieval robber baron to modern Junker.

> No other estate in history has transformed itself as much, and as successfully, as has the lower nobility since the abolition of club law *(Faustrecht)*. The nobility consisted formerly of crude, restless, unbridled protectors of princes and their own independence—ever ready pugilists *(Klopffechter)* with a notorious contempt for all the arts and sciences and those who practice them. Yet they adapted themselves, in a remarkably short span of years, to all those forces primarily responsible for the loss of their earlier position: princely absolutism, new methods of warfare, and Roman law.[23]

The general case for aristocracy was reinforced by the great advantages allegedly possessed by a hierarchic society (where aristocrats formed the "top of the pyramid") over modern egalitarian society with its "war of all against all." In a hierarchic society with stable classes and limited social mobility everybody "knew his place," men were not consumed by insatiable ambitions, and the social mobility of a few did not occasion feelings of inferiority among the many. The frustration suffered by a few divinely gifted swineherds born to a station beneath their true abilities was a small price to pay for these general advantages. A hierarchic society had the further advantage of guaranteeing that all socially necessary functions were performed by lifetime (often even hereditary) professionals who had no occasion to develop talents outside of their chosen line of activity. An egalitarian society led, on the contrary, to slipshod work and the understaffing of many necessary—albeit unattractive—professions because men were constantly "on the make." It was argued that the attack upon aristocracy was really much more than a mere attack upon a class; it was part of an attack upon the principle of hierarchic order of society per se, a principle worth defending even if this led incidentally to defense of the particular demerits which a particular aristocracy might on occasion possess.[24]

[22] A good summary of this case can be found in Loen, *Der Adel* (Ulm, 1752), especially Ch. 1, "Von dem Ursprung des Adels," and Ch. 7, "Wie der Adel erlanget wird."

[23] P.A.F. von Münchhausen, *Über Lehnherr und Dienstmann* (Leipzig, 1793), pp. 101-02.

[24] Ibid., pp. 107-12. The most notable champion of a hierarchic order of society was Justus Möser, whose thought will be covered in Ch. 6 below.

Conservatives also claimed that lower-class deference to aristocracy was a natural feeling and that there was nothing intrinsically unjust about aristocrats possessing superior privileges irrespective of their individual merit.

> Why should it be unjust when the state shows its gratitude to the posterity of distinguished men by conferring privileges upon them? Should the heir of a great name be deprived of the right to be proud of his ancestors? After all, no one ever questions the right of the most mediocre son of a rich father to use his inherited wealth exactly as he wishes.[25]

It was untrue, moreover, to say that aristocrats were not—or no longer—performing useful functions in society. The rural nobility was ruling over ignorant peasants quite incapable of taking care of themselves. The nobility which served princes was performing functions which commoners were unlikely to perform half so well. Nobles made excellent officer material because rural life gave them good physiques; the role of landlord, the habit of command; and family traditions, a refined conception of loyalty and chivalry. (Frederick the Great was a well-known champion of this view.) Nobles made excellent statesmen and bureaucrats because they were accustomed to approach public questions in a broad spirit free of pedantry and narrow self-seeking. Nobles were indispensable as court officials because their breeding, refinement, and sense of delicacy gave them—and them alone—a reliable instinct for what was done and what was not done. The Hannoverian nobleman Münchhausen argued that aristocratic privileges were necessary to provide the social milieu in which alone qualities required for public service could develop:

> It is salutary for a state if a distinctive class devotes itself primarily to matters which are public-spirited, dangerous, and rarely lucrative; it is only right and proper that it should enjoy certain privileges in return, privileges which provide the leisure and the means for making its members prepared and suited for the performance of such functions.[26]

To allow men of bourgeois origins to attain high office was to encourage parvenus with all their odious qualities—ambition, vulgarity,

---

[25] Münchhausen, op.cit., pp. 105-06.

[26] Ibid., pp. 106-07. For the whole paragraph see the contemporary pamphlet by August von Kotzebue, *Vom Adel. Bruchstück eines grösseren historisch-philosophischen Werkes über Ehre und Schande, Ruhm und Nachruhm, aller Völker, aller Jahrhunderte* (Leipzig, 1792), and the modern summary by Wenck, *Deutschland*, I, 28-39.

and the shallow aping of standards and customs whose inner spirit they could not share. Parvenus were often notable for nepotism in order to carry their near relatives into their newly acquired status. Some aristocratic writers noted rather mischievously that failure to practice nepotism also created problems. "A landlord, even though far from proud, would scarcely want to have among his serfs any whose sons were his judges or the powerful ministers of his prince."[27] If the "natural order" was disturbed, it was best to disturb it for the whole family.

Another Conservative argument frequently heard stated that nobles constituted—as Montesquieu had forcefully argued in his *Spirit of the Laws*—a powerful bulwark against princely despotism: their independent position and capacity for resistance made autocrats unable to establish despotism, a form of government which presupposed a total leveling of society into an egalitarian potpourri. Yet while checking despotism aristocrats were simultaneously reliable bulwarks of the throne against republican subversion or the intrigues of ambitious demagogues. The battle cry, "No aristocracy, no king," faithfully expressed the truism that a king was defenseless against popular demagogy if he was not surrounded by a broad body of aristocratic intermediaries whose existence prevented his isolation.[28]

It was further argued that aristocracy constituted an indispensable counterweight against the single greatest danger confronting the modern world—plutocracy. A plutocracy was selfish, grasping, and utterly indifferent to the welfare of the nation as a whole; whereas aristocracies were generally public-spirited and filled with the ethos of *noblesse oblige*. Money was vulgar and its possession gave impersonal power, whereas landownership (the economic basis of aristocracy) was traditionally conducive to an intimate, patriarchal relationship between the upper and lower classes. Aristocrats were in a far better position to check plutocracy than either king or people, since they were more numerous than the former and not anonymous like the latter.[29]

[27] Münchhausen, op.cit., p. 111.

[28] See ibid., pp. 122-26; L. T. Spittler, "Über das ausschliessliche Recht des alten Adels auf Domherrnstellen" (1788), *Sämtliche Werke* (ed. K. Wächter, Leipzig, 1836) XI; and J. G. Schlosser, "Vom dem Adel" (1789), *Kleine Schriften* (Basel, 1793) VI. The proaristocratic writer Ernst Brandes, whose views will be examined in the next paragraph, concluded—however reluctantly—that special circumstances prevented the German aristocracy from being a reliable bulwark against despotism. Ernst Brandes, "Ist es in den deutschen Staaten vorteilhaft, dass der Adel die ersten Staatsbedienungen besitzt?" *Berliner Monatsschrift*, x (1787), 395-439. See especially pp. 429ff.

[29] Münchhausen, op.cit., pp. 118-22.

The preference given to aristocrats in appointment to high state office was defended in the 1780's by two distinguished Conservative pamphleteers, Ernst Brandes[30] and Friedrich von Ramdohr. Brandes presents the interesting case of a bourgeois official who defended the very system which precluded his reaching a bureaucratic position commensurate with his high abilities in his native Hannover. His argument ran as follows: The problem of getting the right people for the top positions boils down to who is to make the selection; this problem must be solved differently in different states according to their different conditions. In England with its vigorous parliamentary system the House of Commons provided an excellent judge of the qualifications for high office; hence there was no objection to allowing the advancement of commoners like Edmund Burke or William Pitt. In Germany, however, with its atrophied representative bodies this form of selection was impossible. Selection must, therefore, be left either to public opinion, which is a poor judge of political capacity and rarely speaks with a clear-cut voice, or to individual princes, of whose capacity for choice Brandes also had a poor opinion. The advantage of limiting the competition for high office to aristocrats derived from the fact that they were well known from birth, whereas commoners had to employ discreditable means in order to call attention to their own eligibility.

Aristocrats were usually raised in a tradition stressing the value of public service, and possessed economic independence irrespective of office, whereas commoners were usually motivated by vulgar ambition and clung to their jobs because they had nothing to fall back upon if they were dismissed by their prince. Their rule was, moreover, frequently resented by their former equals, whereas aristocratic rule was still widely accepted as a "natural" fact. The prince's choice of ministers should be restricted to aristocratic candidates.[31]

Brandes' position was restated, with some amplification as well as qualification, by another Hannoverian official (this time, however, an aristocrat), Friedrich Wilhelm von Ramdohr (1757-1822), *Oberappellationsgerichtsrat* in Celle.[32] He admitted the force of the abstract case in favor of "equality of opportunity" in appointment to high positions,

[30] More about Brandes will be found in Ch. 11 dealing with A. W. Rehberg, his closest friend.

[31] This paragraph paraphrases the argument of Brandes' article cited in n. 11. Many of Brandes' contentions, more especially the crucial point that neither prince nor public opinion was a good judge of ministerial candidates in Germany, were contested by Ramdohr, *Verhältnisse*, pp. 250-84.

[32] Ramdohr, *Verhältniss* (see n. 18).

and in placing more value upon industry and ability than the mere fact of aristocratic birth; but he thought there was an excellent concrete case for leaving the existing German aristocratic quasi-monopoly undisturbed. His argument may be summarized as follows:

To change the *status quo* would cause much discontent among present ministers (who would resent having to work with parvenu commoners as their equals) and young aristocrats aspiring to become ministers (who would henceforth have to reckon with bourgeois competition unknown to their fathers).[33]

Furthermore, the change would stimulate ambition and restlessness among the middle classes by spreading the idea that everybody could henceforth become anything. This would destroy the spirit of hierarchy (*Geist der Stände*) so essential for a well-ordered society. Ramdohr insisted that the state needed a large body of men, especially in its middle ranks, who were satisfied to perform the duties of their customary status without jealousy, frustration, or personal ambition. The living of life in accordance with a quasi-hereditary *Standesehre* (conception of honor dictating the performance of the duties of every status) was what Ramdohr admired in the "middle rank" of public servants—judges, medium-level officials, clergymen, and their families. He depicted them in the following "ideal portrait":

Look how these men find pleasure in performing their chosen tasks and are armed by their industry against any temptation to engage in vice! Look how their wives nourish no sentiments in their hearts which do not belong to the household they serve! Look how they educate their children from infancy to become the best friends of their parents! Happy people! Their heart is not enflamed by excessive ambition; their avarice is not stimulated by abundance of material goods. A moderate prosperity spreads fruits which are enjoyed with deliberate pleasure. They rejoice in the cabbage, flowers, and trees which they personally plant in their garden; they delight in the leisure hours devoted to the arts and sciences. . . ; they are free of the obligation to "shine" at boring aristocratic gatherings, and never experience the nagging doubt about whether they have not by chance displeased the whims of the mighty.

They gather together, instead, a small circle of intimate friends with whom they exchange noble thoughts and true sentiments; when they leave a party they are at ease with themselves and the world.

[33] Ibid., p. 135.

Who does not feel the dignity, who does not feel the happiness of such a status even if one's social position (or perversity of character) make one unable to participate in its joys and advantages? It is certain, in any case, that morality and sound policy are equally served by the preservation of a class of men whose mode of life is a conspicuous example of the virtues which Our Creator intended *all* men to practice.[34]

But this idyllic mode of life would necessarily be destroyed if access to the highest posts became possible for commoners and middle positions therefore became mere posts of transit. It was often forgotten, moreover, that the qualities desirable in a middle position—precision, pedantry, austere virtue, routine—were very different from, and often incompatible with, the qualities desirable in a statesman—large views, imagination, prudence to temper morality (*Klugheitslehre*), and the gift for improvisation. Was it not an empirical fact that the former qualities were most frequently found in the *bourgeoisie*, the latter in the aristocracy? And was it not better, therefore, that each class prepare itself deliberately and exclusively for the place in life it was best able to fill?[35]

The aristocracy possessed additional claims upon the highest positions in the state. It was born with a sense of dignity, honor, propriety, and fear of degradation and shame—indeed, it set the *standards* for what was proper and desirable, irrespective of whether it held the leading positions. It tended to be free of narrow parochialism, to develop good judgment about men through its broad experience of life and ease and self-assurance in the transaction of business. Its independence evoked the respect of princes. (Louis XIV, flushed with anger at the Duke of Lauzan, exclaimed, "I would cudgel you now if you were not an aristocrat!") A fallen aristocratic minister could retire to his country estate without the degradation of being powerful one day and an obscure nobody the next.[36]

A further reason why aristocratic ministers were preferable to commoners was that most ministers were necessarily personally ordinary men. Ramdohr argued that "the advantage of birth made the elevation of aristocrats tolerable to commoners possessing equal abilities" because their elevation was due to an objectively identifiable criterion

[34] Ibid., pp. 148-49.
[35] Ibid., pp. 150-52. Note that the argument presupposed that the average qualities of classes were a relevant factor in filling even the highest posts—presumably because there was no man or body competent to judge the individual merits of candidates for these offices.
[36] Ibid., pp. 135-44.

which did not reflect upon those passed over. The rule of aristocrats also had the advantage of being naturally accepted by the broad mass of people. The vanity of the German nation, a sentiment which relieved much "civic suffering" *(bürgerliche Leiden)* among the weak and the poor, was flattered by being ruled by the highborn only.[37]

One other consideration could be pleaded in favor of maintaining the present aristocratic monopoly of the highest bureaucratic posts. Once social mobility were granted to the middle charges there was no telling where social mobility would stop. The lower classes would obviously "get ideas" and press into the middle positions exactly as the middle incumbent would press for the top. The decision on whether to terminate the aristocratic monopoly could not be made exclusively by considering the respective merits of aristocrats and members of the *bourgeoisie,* collectively or individually; it must also consider the respective merits of a static-hierarchic vs. a mobile-egalitarian society.[38]

It was a merit of Ramdohr's argument (though it also led him to some inconsistency) that he did not plead for an absolute and exclusive aristocratic monopoly of top government posts. He did not want to discourage *all* political ambitions in the middle class, but desired only great, but not insuperable, obstacles to political advancement. He deplored a situation where birth would count for everything, talent and energy for nothing, because it must have a paralyzing effect upon society as a whole. Even if only meritorious aristocrats became ministers, the world would believe that it was blue blood rather than merit which had brought them to the top. The natural scarcity of statesman-like talents made it occasionally imperative to look to other strata of the population. A little nonaristocratic competition was an excellent device for "keeping aristocrats on their toes" and checking the nefarious idea that aristocrats possessed a God-given right to rule humanity irrespective of personal merit. There was the additional consideration that an aristocratic monopoly in office-holding would force princes—in a Germany where innumerable courts required innumerable ministers —into the undesirable practice of drawing upon the petty nobility which desired office more for private gain than *noblesse oblige.* Yet— despite all these reasons, fully and fairly stated—Ramdohr believed that the present aristocratic predominance in the foremost public offices—which in many states amounted to a monopoly—was on balance to the advantage of the German nation, and could be made still more so through the gadfly effect of a small but controlled increase of

[37] Ibid., p. 145.   [38] Ibid., p. 152.

competition from below. Ramdohr was more a Defender of the *Status Quo* than a Reform Conservative, though he did make several specific reform suggestions.[39]

The most bitterly attacked survival of aristocratic privilege, next to preferential entry into top governmental posts, was the continued aristocratic exemption from several different kinds of taxes. This exemption was defended by Carl Häberlin,[40] a well-known professor of public law at Helmstedt University, in a skillfully argued article in 1793.[41] Häberlin admitted that the demand for the taxation of nobiliar lands appeared prima facie just, since tax exemption had formerly been a *quid pro quo* for now obsolete personally performed military service. A moment's reflection showed, however, that prima facie appearances did not exhaust the subject. Häberlin admitted that tax exemption could no longer be a *quid pro quo* for an obsolete military service; but he argued that it was *now* the *quid* for the new *quo* of restrictions imposed by the government upon landlords as to how they could treat their dependent peasants. Most rulers now issued strict regulations which prevented landlords from gobbling up peasant land *(Bauern-legen)* or raising peasant rents; in some cases they even compelled landlords to reduce the level of existing dues. Governments did this in order to maintain their own fiscal and military interests, for such regulations had proved necessary to keep the peasantry in a condition to pay heavy taxes and to be available for military service in adequate numbers. Häberlin argued that the heavy taxes now paid by the peasantry were in fact made possible *only* by the curtailment of the rights of aristocrats to handle their property as they saw fit—and that therefore the landlords were in reality the payers of taxes formerly paid by their peasants. It would obviously constitute unjust "double taxation" if the landlords were additionally compelled to pay taxes for their own lands.

Häberlin pursued his point in the following analogy. To yield to the popular clamor for the taxation of aristocratic lands

> would be inequitable; indeed it would be as inequitable as if a decree had been issued a hundred years ago, that all tenants renting apartments from realtors should deduct a certain portion of their rents to pay as taxes; soon thereafter a further decree was issued that

[39] Ibid., pp. 153-74.
[40] On Carl Friedrich Häberlin (1756-1808) see Ernst Fischer, *Carl F. Häberlin, ein braunschweigischer Staatsrechtslehrer und Publizist* (Göttingen, 1914).
[41] Carl Friedrich Häberlin, "Worauf beruhet die Steuerfreiheit des Adels, und ist sie ungerecht?" *Braunschweigisches Magazin*, Feb. 9, 1793, pp. 82-91.

house owners could no longer terminate a lease, or raise rents, or even compelling them to lower rents by a third or even a half [in order to protect the tax-paying capacity of their tenants]. House owners would, in short, lose the full control of their property; yet there arose soon a clamor among tenants that it was unfair that they alone should pay taxes, while their landlord houseowners lived free of tax liability in the other part of the house. It was said that justice required that the house owners pay the taxes now paid by their tenants in complete disregard of the fact that the tenants enjoyed the use of apartments at exceptionally low rents because of the arrangement dictated by the government through its earlier decree.[42]

The argument is a tribute to Häberlin's ingenuity. While leaving bourgeois critics unconvinced, it must have stifled the conscience of many an aristocrat who felt disturbed by the continuation of feudal tax exemptions in a postfeudal world.

The Silesian philosopher Christian Garve offered a still different kind of justification for aristocratic tax exemption and the consequent regressive taxation of the poor:

It appears inequitable, indeed, to a man arguing from general principles, irrespective of concrete conditions, that those least able to pay should bear the greatest burden of taxation. A philosopher, however, who reflects upon existing conditions instead of dreaming about how to create a new utopia, will easily find reasons to justify this *apparent* anomaly. . . . It may be said that all types of inequality are equally just or unjust. An estate like the aristocracy is advantaged over other estates in honor, wealth, and legal privileges: why should it not also be advantaged through exemption from certain types of taxes? If the happiness of the lower classes is not injured through differences in honor, wealth and legal position: why should it be incompatible with the continued existence of regressive taxation?[43]

[42] Ibid., p. 90. The following implied premises of Häberlin's argument are interesting: (1) that protection of the peasants against nobiliar exploitation required a *quid pro quo*; (2) that nobiliar rights could in principle never be curtailed, even when curtailment was dictated by the common good.

[43] Christian Garve, "Über den Charakter der Bauern und ihr Verhältniss gegen den Gutsherrn und gegen die Regierung," *Vermischte Aufsätze*, I, 180-81. Garve cautiously added, "All this argument is true only up to a point" (p. 181). Christian Garve (1724-98) was, together with Moses Mendelssohn, the most widely read *Popularphilosoph* in Germany in the second half of the eighteenth

Garve added as a further argument that tax liability (or lack of it) was always included in calculating the purchase value of an estate. As property became mobile any injustice which may have existed originally would be cancelled after the first transfer; likewise the abolition of tax exemption would work injustice and hardship upon recent purchasers of property who had paid a high price for the property in the expectation that they would continue to remain tax-exempt.[44]

Several Conservatives understood the weight of the criticisms directed against the aristocracy, and saw that its present condition would prove untenable in the long run. They urged the aristocracy to buttress its sagging position—or at least to save what could still be saved—by reforming its mode of life and also reforming its composition. The Conservative writer J. M. von Loen urged his fellow aristocrats to abandon such fashionable vices as idleness, arrogance, caste consciousness, and sexual immorality; and to cultivate such characteristic aristocratic virtues as military courage, political leadership, zeal for the public welfare, and *noblesse oblige*. He urged nobles to attend universities to make themselves objectively as well qualified as their bourgeois competitors for any governmental post. Aristocrats must above all abandon the caste pride which was the source of most of their degeneracy. Loen himself combined a hierarchic with a Christian-egalitarian outlook in the following passionate appeal to his fellow nobles:

> No civil society can exist without hierarchic differences of rank where some hold a higher position than others; but there must be a reciprocal relationship based upon help and protection. . . . The rich and well-born person has no reason to despise the poor and humble, in as much as our status and happiness in life is independent of our personal merits. An aristocrat must be foolish indeed if he forgets the dependence of all men upon a Higher Being; and he should re-

---

century; his popular reputation far exceeded that of Immanuel Kant. He was professor of philosophy at Leipzig from 1768 to 1772, but returned to his native Breslau as a free-lance author when he was only 30 because of ill-health. His ambition was to become the German Hume; he shared with the Scottish philosopher an outlook characterized by skepticism, distrust of systems, empiricism, utilitarianism, interest in political and social systems, and practical Conservatism, while lacking the latter's depth and originality. He quarreled with Friedrich Nicolai (see Ch. 2) over Nicolai's pathological fear of the Jesuits, and was on close terms of friendship and correspondence with Friedrich Gentz (see Ch. 17). (Their correspondence was published in 1857.) Garve's views on serfdom will be analyzed in detail in the next part of this chapter.

[44] Ibid., p. 181.

member that contempt for his more humble fellow-men loosens the very bonds of society itself in an intolerable manner. An aristocrat must always remember that he is a mere mortal creature whose corpse will rot exactly like the corpse of a despised pauper.[45]

Loen urged nobles to show their usefulness and prove their vigor by excelling at every type of public employment, military, civil, or diplomatic; and he urged them personally to direct agricultural operations if they preferred rural to court life. They should live lives which could serve as exemplary models for their peasants, and Loen prudently advised them to avoid contact with their fellow aristocrats, "for it happens not infrequently that the nobility of an entire area collectively ruins itself through feasting, extravagance, and what is called simply 'friendly neighborliness.'"[46] The author added much specific advice on how aristocratic landlords should treat their peasants with justice and firmness—advice which will be considered in the next section of this chapter.

Thus Loen demanded that aristocrats should cease to be arrogant, immoral, and idle; then they could maintain, with relatively little controversy, most of their traditional functions in German society, for most of the "enlightened" criticism was directed more against prevalent vices of aristocrats than the principle of aristocracy per se. Another way to disarm criticism was to open the ranks of the nobility to distinguished commoners who possessed the manners and wealth necessary for assimilation into the old aristocracy. Loen favored the prevalent practice under which a patent of nobility could in fact be bought from the emperor for a specified sum, provided the total number of annual sales was limited and the purchasers were subjected to some scrutiny as regards manners, character, and the willingness to take up the duties as well as the privileges of aristocracy. He also favored the practice of young nobles' marrying the daughters of the wealthy *bourgeoisie,* a process which had the double advantage of bringing new blood and new wealth into the aristocracy at one and the same time. He favored relatively frequent ennoblement of distinguished non-noble bureaucrats to open top posts to conspicuous merit without formally breaching the principle that high state service should be monopolized by aristocrats governing in an aristocratic spirit; every ennoblement must, however, be accompanied by a sufficient "material base" to allow the family to become blended with the old nobility. Loen and other "reformers of the aristocracy" had a horror of

[45] Loen, *Der Adel,* pp. 287-88.   [46] Ibid., p. 300.

impoverished, petty nobles compelled to use their nobility as a pass-key to public employment, in order to maintain—in pretence, if not reality—their nobiliar status; yet he no more found an answer to this perennial problem than did most of the *Adelsreformer* who followed in his footsteps.[47]

Critics and Defenders of Serfdom

THE CRITIQUE OF SERFDOM

The attack upon aristocracy was usually accompanied by an attack upon the serfdom which constituted the economic foundation of the aristocratic society of large parts of Germany. This attack relied upon arguments partly humanitarian and partly economic in character. Humanitarians deplored the misery and exploitation of servile life, and considered the survival of "medieval serfdom" a scandal in a supposedly "enlightened" age. They attacked the lord's possession of large and essentially arbitrary power over the dependent agricultural population. The economic position of the lords was based upon the compulsory field labor of serfs (usually three days a week), heavy dues paid in money or kind, and the unpaid domestic labor of the minor children of serfs. While serfal obligations were supposedly regulated by custom, the custom was subject to interpretation by patrimonial courts standing under the lord's control. Discontent was crushed by the lord's police power, with even minor delinquencies being often punished with draconic severity. Village public opinion was controlled by the parish priest, who was invariably a creature of the lord to whom he owed his appointment. The serf was legally bound to the soil; his marriage required the lord's approval; his children could choose a profession other than serfdom only with the permission of their lord. The lot of the serf was, in fact, virtually indistinguishable from slavery.[48]

Serfdom not only degraded the vast majority of the rural population, but also made for an extremely inefficient rural economy. The serfal labor obligations were inflexible, demoralizing, and often performed in a spirit of sullen obstinacy not conducive to efficiency. The rational

---

[47] Ibid., especially Ch. 7, "Wie der Adel erlanget wird."

[48] For one of many contemporary attacks upon serfdom see an anonymous pamphlet presented to the East Prussian diet in 1798: "Über die Aufhebung der Leibeigenschaft, Erbunterthänigkeit oder Gutspflichtigkeit in Preussen. Ein Geschenk für den preussischen Adel zur Beherzigung bei dem Landtag 1798," paraphrased with long quotations in *Jahrbücher der preussischen Monarchie unter der Regierung Friedrich Wilhelm III*, III (1800), 213-44, especially 226-28. Henceforth cited as *Über die Aufhebung* (1798).

direction of servile labor was difficult if not impossible. The serfs were kept—often deliberately—in a condition of ignorance lest they become discontented with their traditional lot in life. They had little incentive to work hard or to invest in any kind of agricultural improvement; on the rare occasions that a good harvest gave them extra money it disappeared into an unproductive stocking when not spent on drunken orgies at the local alehouse. It was clear that serfdom constituted a formidable obstacle both to efficient agriculture and to the freeing of redundant rural labor for industrial development.[49]

The following philippic, written by the Hannoverian nobleman P.A.F. von Münchhausen, has the bitter tenor characteristic of much of the argument against serfdom. It uses the demagogically effective technique of concentrating fire upon extreme (though probably untypical) excesses which were possible under the attacked institution. Münchhausen listed the following intolerable abuses connected with serfdom:

That a peasant should be obligated to cart the lord's harvest to market while *his own* urgently requires his attention.

That he must help build a luxurious mansion for his lord while his own hut decays.

That he must carry a letter, probably containing polite nothings, from his lord to some other lord while his dying mother may call for her son.

That a peasant must travel hours with two or even four horses, in order to cart a small load a small distance, when a single local horse could have undertaken the local haulage just as well.

That he must travel miles to make some trifling, anachronistic payment, which symbolizes his servitude, in person.

That he must act as night watchman for his lord, even when he is so exhausted from a day of field work that he can scarcely keep his eyes open.

That he must perform his labor services in the lord's field, even if his house burns down in the meantime.

Who, when contemplating these irrational horrors, is not re-

[49] Three pamphlets pointing out the economic disadvantages of serfdom are: G.F.G. Westfeld, *Über die Abstellung des Herrendienstes* (Lemgo, 1773); P.A.F. Münchhausen, *Über Lehnherrn und Dienstmann* (Leipzig, 1793), especially pp. 29ff.; and Josias von Qualen, *Schreiben eines vornehmen holsteinischen Gutsherrn, darin die Abschaffung der Hofdienste auf seinem Gute und die Folgen dieser Veränderung nach einer zwanzigjährigen Erfahrung beschrieben werden* (Hamburg, 1775). The latter pamphlet was distributed by the *Gesellschaft zur Beförderung der Künste und nützlichen Gewerbe*.

minded of [a prisoner in] some dark Gothic dungeon with walls ten feet thick . . .—whose strength and energy go to waste and who shudders in discomfort and creeping dread of things to come?[50]

It was argued, finally, that serfdom was not only unjust and uneconomic but anachronistic as well. It arose in the Dark Ages when central and orderly government had collapsed in Europe, and local lords performed a valuable social function in preventing chaos by setting up a decentralized pattern of authority. At that time the lord gave his serfs much-needed protection and livelihood and there was some *reciprocal* element in the obligations of manorialism. Serfdom also allowed knights to perform a valuable military function in the age of feudal monarchy. All of these "original justifications" of serfdom had, however, lost their meaning by the end of the eighteenth century. The apologists forgot, moreover, that serfdom—whatever its justification in Western Europe during the Dark Ages—had never had a real justification in those parts of Eastern Germany where it still existed in maximum force. It had been instituted in the late medieval and early modern times by German conquerors dominating a defeated Slavic population; it had been perpetuated by agreements between Hohenzollern princes and Junker aristocrats in the seventeenth century. Even if an original flaw in the peasantry—such as the refusal to accept Christianity at the time of the Teutonic conquests—had given some *ad hoc* justification to serfdom, there was no excuse for its hereditary character after the original flaw had disappeared. This hereditary character made it the main ingredient of that hierarchic-inegalitarian structure of society now challenged by the rise of the *Aufklärung* and the *bourgeoisie*.[51]

The reformers did not deny that the abolition of serfdom would constitute a social revolution and violate historical rights consecrated by tradition. They insisted, however, that justice constituted a far stronger title deed than mere historical prescription: "A thousand years of injustice cannot establish a single moment of legitimacy."[52]

[50] Münchhausen, op.cit., pp. 23-24.
[51] *Über die Aufhebung*, p. 226; Münchhausen, op.cit., pp. 16ff. For an excellent historical survey of serfdom, written from a point of view hostile to it, see Ernst Moritz Arndt, *Versuch einer Geschichte der Leibeigenschaft in Pommern und Rügen. Nebst einer Einleitung in die alte teutsche Leibeigenschaft* (Berlin, 1803). See also the summary of this work in the same author's *Geschichte der Veränderung der bäuerlichen und herrschaftlichen Verhältnisse in dem vormaligen Schwedischen Pommern und Rügen vom Jahre 1806 bis zum Jahre 1816* (Berlin, 1817), pp. 1-14.
[52] Münchhausen, op.cit., p. 26.

THE DEFENSE OF SERFDOM

The formidable Radical attack upon serfdom naturally provoked a comprehensive defense of that institution. Three types of arguments were used: those claiming that serfdom was not nearly so bad as its critics charged; those showing that, whatever its evils, its abolition would cause greater evils still; and those that stressed the danger of injustice to landlords and of creating precedents for the spoliation of other types of property and violation of contractual obligations. All these Conservative arguments are worth examining in some detail.

It was asserted by most Conservatives that the lot of the serfs was not nearly so bad as the "do-gooders" charged. The reformers erred in putting themselves, with their very different sensitivity and life experience, into the place of the peasants and thinking that the latter suffered in the same way that the reformers would suffer if they suddenly became serfs:

> The misery experienced by the peasant is not particularly severe, both because he is accustomed to it and because his capacity for suffering remains undeveloped. He is fortunate, indeed, because his work takes place in the open air, amidst all the beauties of Nature; it gives him good health, the most priceless gift of man and the prerequisite for happiness; he never knows, moreover, the thousand artificial needs whose stimulation creates unhappiness for the so-called upper classes, and in fact poisons their existence.[53]

Conservatives claimed that the real wages of serfs, if one included the patriarchal services rendered by their lords, were not significantly below the wages paid to free laborers in countries where serfdom had been abolished. They also noted that landlords had no difficulty in finding applicants willing to take over vacant *Bauernstellen* under conditions of serfdom—surely prima facie evidence that the lot of the serfs was not *generally* considered to be intolerable.[54]

[53] Karl Fischer, *An den Herrn Philipp Adam Custine, Neufränkischen Bürger und General* (Germanien, 1793), p. 99. Fischer was a well-known Württemberg publicist.

[54] These arguments were paraphrased by Garve, *Über den Charakter der Bauern*, pp. 135-43. Radicals replied that Conservative statisticians were wrong about the comparative wages of free and servile labor, and that the competition for vacant *Bauernstellen* did not mean peasant happiness but rather overpopulation and want of alternative employment opportunities. Arndt, *Versuch einer Geschichte der Leibeigenschaft*, p. 245, was unusually drastic in criticizing the argument based upon voluntary acceptance of serfdom: "What men do is not always what they ought to do. Otherwise gaming clubs and whorehouses would be admirable institutions, although promising young men are daily ruined by

Conservatives argued that the poverty which admittedly characterized Germany's countryside was due primarily to the sluggishness and apathy of the peasants, not the exploitation by their landlords. The peasants were tenaciously hostile to innovations in agricultural technique. What little progress had been made in farming techniques was largely due to the vigor and modernity of the landlord class, and it was freely predicted that peasant emancipation would lead to total agrarian stagnation:

> The opposition of peasants to innovation results partly from sheer *laziness*—any innovation requires some intellectual effort to grasp and some practical energy to implement; partly from *stupidity*—the peasant is not capable of following an argument showing the value of innovation, and therefore clings firmly to experience as his only guide; partly from *suspicion directed against his superiors*—most suggestions for innovation come from bureaucrats and landlords, or else from scholars: the peasant thinks that the latter lack all practical competence, the former all good-will toward himself; partly from *the utter lack of any real desire for a better condition* than he has now.[55]

The sole remedy for this deplorable sluggishness was coercion from above, such as some landlords were able and willing to apply under the existing agrarian system. The entire argument attempted to meet the widespread view that serfdom stood in the way of economic progress.

Conservatives frequently depicted the existing agricultural order in idyllic colors. While Radicals overstressed atypical cases of brutal oppression, Conservatives tended to concentrate unduly upon equally atypical cases of genuine patriarchal relationships. They described landlords acting as the stern but just guardians of serfs whom Nature had designed for perpetual nonage. The landlord's wife combined the role of social worker and visiting nurse. The domestic labor of the children of serfs was an admirable institution for "socializing" young savages in a refined atmosphere far superior to the parental hearth. The

---

both. No one will praise Hell or the gallows although men transport themselves there every day of the year."

[55] Garve, op.cit., pp. 64-65. Radicals replied to the argument by insisting that peasant laziness, stupidity, suspiciousness, and inertia were the results of serfdom and would disappear once serfdom disappeared. The argument raised the fundamental question whether peasants were inferior by their (unchangeable) nature or whether their admitted present inferiority was due to an environment subject to improvement.

serf enjoyed social security from the cradle to the grave, and never had an opportunity to acquire the neuroses frequently connected with social climbing. It never occurred to him—unless his tranquillity was disturbed by some Radical agitator—that he might be anything but a serf, and he genuinely accepted the landlord as a superior type of human being. His labor was healthy and diversified and did not stunt his personality in the manner of factory work under the industrial system just developing in England. Did he not have reason to be happy, and to be grateful to the landlord for making his Arcadian type of life possible?[56]

It was easy to foresee that the abolition of serfdom must inevitably introduce a long catalogue of evils. Serfs would be shaken out of their moorings and given wild ambitions about entering professions for which they were unsuited. The intoxication of freedom could easily compound their habitual laziness; freedom of movement must lead to a nomadism indistinguishable from vagabondage, while estates became derelict for want of labor. Cities would become overcrowded with ex-serfs eager to try the life of artisans and to taste the diversions of urban life. The resulting disorder and misery could be curbed only by governmental measures far sterner than the essentially patriarchal authority now exercised by landlords over their serfs.[57]

Conservatives argued—as has been argued against *every* social reform ever proposed—that the emancipation of the serfs would be unjust to the dispossessed landlord class: "It is unjust to deprive landowners and aristocrats of their labor supply, and to deprive them of rights which they or their ancestors have acquired in a perfectly legitimate manner."[58]

It was further argued that serfdom had arisen originally from voluntary contracts, and that the compulsory dissolution of such contracts by governmental fiat would create a dangerous precedent. Serf-

---

[56] This theme was to be taken up by the romantic movement in the 1790's, but it was also given full expression by the non-romantic Conservative Junker Ludwig von der Marwitz. Radicals frequently admitted that many serfs were quite happy with their existing condition and did not desire any change; but they considered this the very worst possible indictment of serfdom, because it indicated that it had numbed "the spirit of man" by turning the serfs into mere vegetative machines. *Über die Aufhebung*, pp. 238-39.

[57] *Über die Aufhebung*, pp. 238-43. Radicals replied to these gloomy apprehensions by stressing that the abuse of freedom was a manageable police problem; nomadism a scarecrow because the serfs lacked all means of travel; while the overcrowding of artisan professions could—if necessary—be met by a temporary *numerus clausus*. Estates would not become derelict, since they could be operated very efficiently with comparatively few free laborers.

[58] *Über die Aufhebung*, p. 235. See also Arndt, op.cit., pp. 247-52.

al obligations were a species of property; if it were violated, any other kind of property could be violated just as well. Was not the sanctity of contract and of property the very foundation of society? And was not, therefore, the proposed abolition of serfdom far more than mere injustice, namely, a blueprint for anarchy by striking at the very foundations of society?[59]

CONSERVATIVE PROPOSALS FOR REFORM

Several men with a genuinely Conservative temperament agreed with the Radicals in considering serfdom doomed, and refused to devote themselves to a quixotic defense of an obvious anachronism. They strove instead for an orderly evolution of rural society through the commutation of servile labor obligations into money payments for the use of part of the lord's land. The Hannoverian aristocrat Münchhausen argued as follows:

Let labor obligations be commuted into money obligations; let the landlord use the money received in order to hire laborers to work that part of the estate not rented to his former serfs. Some ex-serfs would become freehold proprietors as they eventually saved enough money to buy the land they were now renting; others would become comparatively well-paid rural laborers whose per capita yield would certainly far exceed that of inefficient present servile labor; still others would welcome the opportunity of leaving agriculture altogether to try their fortune in the cities. Much thought must, of course, be given to planning the pattern and terms of commutation; there could be no rules universally applicable to the very variegated existing conditions. Münchhausen favored making the entire commutation process voluntary, and he anticipated that many aristocrats would fail to see that their own self-interest would benefit from the process. He urged princes to try an appeal to the sense of patriotism of the landlords by calling upon them to cooperate with a state-approved policy of commutation. He further suggested that princes offer a small bribe to commuting landlords by freeing them of the few remaining burdens of feudal vassalage; and he was willing in the last resort to coerce

[59] This was one of the favorite arguments of the Prussian reactionary von der Marwitz and will be examined further in Vol. II. It is needless to add that Radicals replied—when they deigned to take the argument seriously—that coercion rather than voluntary contract had been the original basis of serfdom, and that the property rights connected with it were illegitimate *ab ovo*; moreover, that origins were in any case irrelevant when dealing with an obvious case of injustice here and now. Garve, op.cit., pp. 135ff.

landlords by the "use of the absolute power of a wise and benevolent prince" who had himself set a salutary example of commuting all servile obligations owed to him upon crown domains.[60]

The philosopher Christian Garve warned aristocratic landlords against two arguments which were frequently being urged by fellow aristocrats to deter them from cooperating with the reform measures of the government. One was that landlords owed it to their posterity to bequeath their estates in a condition identical with that which they themselves had inherited. This argument, appealing to the sense of family obligation, undoubtedly had some merit; but Garve insisted that it must yield both to self-interest properly understood (which necessarily included the interest of posterity) and of the just claims of the existing peasantry for a better life. Everybody had an interest in the agricultural improvements which only commutation could bring; while the landlord class had an interest (however little understood by some of its members) in the timely replacement of anachronistic serfdom by a durable labor system based upon free contract.[61]

The second argument often advanced to stifle needed reform stressed the solidarity of the landlord class. If one landlord took the plunge from servile to free labor it must inevitably create embarrassment for the owners of neighboring estates. Would not their serfs become restless and troublesome? Garve admitted the force of the argument but thought that it should be overridden by considerations of justice and economic rationality. It also ignored the fact that peasant obligations were already extremely diverse at the present moment without provoking major discontents; and Garve believed that the existing police system was prepared to cope with any discontent which might arise from a differential application of the principle of commutation.[62]

Garve insisted upon one point which was absolutely crucial to the case for peasant reform, namely, that the presently prevalent laziness, ignorance, and boorishness of the peasantry was the result of environment (more especially the institution of serfdom) rather than any hereditary defect. Garve engaged in a remarkable venture in what we today call class sociology to establish his point. He said that the character of serfs was formed by three conditions over which the serf had no control: the parochial and monotonous mode of life of the rural village; the serf's utter dependence upon a landlord class which treated

[60] Münchhausen, op.cit., pp. 41-86. The quoted phrase is from p. 65.
[61] Garve, op.cit., pp. 158-64.   [62] Ibid., pp. 164-66.

him with harshness and contempt; and the close-knit solidarity of the village group with its collective personality, settled status for every member, and suspicious hostility toward all outsiders. The result of these conditions must be sloth, since there was much to discourage and nothing to encourage industry. Monotonous physical work easily led to exhaustion and encouraged an escape to the bottle. Want of education prevented the rise of ambition; lack of imagination made serfs incapable of envisaging desirable consumer goods; while age-old poverty bred a mood of hopelessness concerning the very possibility of ever attaining better conditions of life. Industry was discouraged by the arbitrary and indefinite character of labor services and the precarious security of all peasant tenures. Laziness frequently had a purely constitutional cause, namely, overwork and undernourishment in childhood. Was it surprising, in the light of all of these factors, that peasants were lazy? Or, in view of their extreme parochialism and want of educational opportunity, ignorant? Or, in view of their utter lack of occasion to acquire manners, boorish?

Garve insisted that peasants would lose many of their unattractive qualities if they were provided with a change of environment. Given land of their own, incentives to industry would be maximized; given geographical mobility, parochialism would diminish; given education, ambition would be stimulated; given agricultural progress, the present backbreaking monotony would cease. Garve said that many Conservatives made the fundamental mistake of confusing cause with consequence. They argued that peasant primitivity caused and necessitated serfdom, when in fact serfdom was the cause—or at least the needless perpetuator—of peasant primitivity. It was high time to try the long-overdue experiment with free labor.[63]

Conservative reformers did not confine themselves to suggesting a timely abolition of serfdom; they also offered much advice on how landlords should live and treat their peasants in order to maintain their position in an age increasingly critical of the traditional order of rural society. Garve suggested the following rules for conduct: Aristocratic landlords should reside in the country and take a personal interest in the management of their estates. They should enforce their rights *personally*—at least on occasion—because serfs felt a natural respect for their real lords which they could not feel for mere bailiffs. There was danger when aristocrats came to depend too exclusively upon bailiffs, who tended to dilute authority by not standing sufficiently "above" the peasantry; they also sometimes promoted discord between peasants

[63] The entire argument is developed in Bk. I of ibid., 3-84.

and lords by denouncing the former as lazy and the latter as stern to the other party. The aim of a landlord must be to secure an obedient, willing, industrious, and prosperous peasantry; the means, steady, scrupulous but just enforcement of all obligations—in short, applying the maxims animating any good government. While promoting measures of mutual benefit—such as the commutation of servile labor—landlords must avoid making mere gifts to the peasantry; these would not arouse gratitude but only stimulate an appetite for further gifts. Punishment of peasant transgressions should be prompt and severe but only when the peasants were aware—or could be made aware—of the justice of punishment: Garve urged landlords to apply to their peasants all the rules governing the sound education of children. The authority of landlords could be enhanced by acts of benevolence (something very different from showering gifts) and acts of successful leadership, such as the introduction of agricultural improvements whose value would eventually be apparent to the peasantry. It could also be enhanced by leading a life of conspicuous virtue evoking peasant respect; still more important, however, was the avoidance of conspicuous vice—especially in such common matters as sex and drink—whose invariable consequence was the total loss of peasant respect for their social betters.[64]

It must be stressed that Conservative reformers, in contrast to Radical reformers, had no intention of terminating aristocratic domination of the countryside; on the contrary, they aimed at perpetuating it by giving it a modernized form appropriate to the world of the eighteenth century. They had every intention of "keeping the peasantry in its place" and maintaining the traditional hierarchic form of rural society. Reforms must be undertaken *for* but never *by* the peasantry; and peasant disorder must be firmly repressed by every device, political, social, and even ecclesiastical. Loen, whom we have encountered in the previous section as a proponent of aristocratic reform, put the point in the following terms:

> Territorial governments should concentrate their attention upon improving the rural police system whose efficiency has declined in recent years: any evil conduct and all disorder must be met with exemplary repression. Clergymen must use their sermons to make their parishioners aware of the civil duties taught by religion instead of elaborating—as they do now—upon the mysteries of the Holy Trinity and . . . the endless polemics which this dogma has aroused since the beginning of Christianity. Aristocrats must personally con-

[64] Garve gives copious advice to landlords in ibid., pp. 85-134.

cern themselves about the moral welfare of their dependents and give them an example of a Christian and well conducted life.[65]

Loen, like Garve and other Conservative reformers, pleaded for a judicious mixture of cautious reform from above and firm repression of any rebellious discontent emerging from below. Such a policy offered the best hope of preserving as much as possible, for as long as possible, of the traditional order of German rural society. Conservative reformers appealed to the aristocrats' sense of benevolence and justice, but also to considerations of what constituted economic self-interest properly understood. Behind these arguments loomed the general contention which lies at the root of all Reform Conservatism: that timely reform and adaptation is the only alternative to revolution in an increasingly dynamic world. Münchhausen stated this point in the following graphic manner:

A modern constitution (Staatsverfassung) must twist and contort itself in a forced and convulsive manner if it is confined by the chains wrought by the customs and laws of earlier centuries: shall we keep these chains around the expanding body until they either choke it to death or the growing giant breaks them with destructive but possibly at the same time suicidal exertions?[66]

FREDERICK'S ATTEMPT TO ATTACK SERFDOM IN 1763
It remains to note a little-known attempt made by Frederick the Great to abolish serfdom in Pomerania. The attempt is interesting for showing both the concrete application of many of the arguments outlined above and the power of the Pomeranian Junker class which first sabotaged and finally defeated the royal plans. Frederick embarked upon it as part of his herculean effort to promote Prussian economic recovery after the devastation of the Seven Years' War. The great king issued the following decree, dated Colberg, May 23, 1763, to *Finanzrath* von Schöning (Pomeranian *Kammerpräsident*):

Serfdom *(alle Leibeigenschaften)* is to be absolutely and immediately abolished wherever it exists—be it on royal, aristocratic, or municipal lands. Let this decree, issued by His Royal Majesty for the benefit of the entire province, be implemented immediately. All opponents should be persuaded gently (*mit Güte*) of the value of this

[65] Loen, *Der Adel*, pp. 301-02.
[66] Münchhausen, *Über Lehnherr und Dienstmann*, p. 16.

211

decree, but coercion may also be resorted to, in the last resort, if necessary.[67]

The latter threat failed to intimidate the Junkers of Pomerania. The *Ritterschaft* of Vorpommern met at Demnim on July 29, 1763, to memorialize the Crown against the emancipation decree. They claimed, in the first place, that the dependent peasantry consisted of *Gutspflichtige* rather than *Leibeigene*, and that *Leibeigenschaft* could not be abolished for the simple reason that it did not exist. They asserted, in the second place, that the relationship between landowner and peasant had been created through a "voluntary and honest contract" bringing reciprocal benefits. The landowner had pledged himself to "feed and maintain the peasant family, including children and servants, even when they became invalids through accident or old age; to supply the peasant with house, stable, crop land, cattle, and garden for his use; to pay equitable wages to domestic servants; and to build and maintain central buildings for residential and economic purposes." The peasants had pledged themselves and their posterity, in return, "never to leave the lord's estate without the permission of the landowners, and to provide, for as long as bodily powers permitted, the economic services, by hand and team of oxen, necessary to cultivate and maintain the lord's estate." The *Ritterschaft* protested against the royal attempt to break up this long-tested relationship and asserted categorically: "Serfdom is a positive benefit which many peasants desire because it makes the lord responsible for their maintenance. It is certain that freedom would make most peasants presumptuous."[68] Among the many merits of serfdom was that it kept the peasants "in their proper place."

It was argued, finally, that the economic details of emancipation created nearly insoluble problems for administrators and judges. The Junkers considered it axiomatic that they should receive full compensation for all labor services, judicial rights, manorial dues, et cetera, while simultaneously being freed of their traditional patriarchal obligations. Within these premises they could argue that the abolition of serfdom would bring few benefits to the peasant population, and that the attempt would only stir up unnecessary trouble.[69]

Frederick was convinced—or at least intimidated—by these argu-

[67] Quoted from Arndt, *Versuch einer Geschichte der Leibeigenschaft*, p. 229, an illuminating account of the entire episode.

[68] Arndt characterized this general defense of serfdom as "a pack of historical lies" presented in a spirit of "stupid, sophistic hypocrisy." Ibid., p. 232.

[69] *Über die Aufhebung*, pp. 230-32.

ments; he henceforth limited his efforts on behalf of the serfs to decreeing that a nobleman must settle a new serf upon every serfal plot which became vacant for any reason. This prohibition of *Bauernlegen* (i.e., driving peasants off the land) was only partially motivated by benevolence; its primary purpose was to preserve a numerous peasantry capable of providing recruits and taxes for the Prussian army and treasury. The king was not prepared to face the hornet's nest of complications which emancipation would bring; he preferred to maintain the traditional alliance between the Hohenzollern crown and the Junker class. The collapse of the Frederician state was to prove a necessary prerequisite for Stein's emancipation of the Prussian serfs in 1807.

The Guild Controversy

The most bitterly contested social controversy, after that involving the aristocracy and the serfs, concerned the position of the guilds, which continued to dominate Germany's urban economy. Several proponents of laissez-faire, most notably the economic writer Johann August Schlettwein,[70] asserted that guild defects were not accidental excrescences but rather essential ingredients of the structure of guilds, and that nothing short of the total abolition of guilds could cure Germany of their evil influence. The suppression of the French guilds by the reform ministry of Turgot in 1774, and their restoration in 1776, aroused much interest in Germany. The guild issue was debated intensively throughout 1776 in the Basel journal *Ephemeriden der Menschheit,* which translated all the key documents of the French controversy and added several German contributions, most notably a defense of the guilds by the Badenese official J. G. Schlosser.[71]

The best statement of the Conservative case was, however, provided by an otherwise obscure author, J. H. Firnhaber, whose book (published in 1782) is a learned compendium of the entire guild contro-

[70] Schlettwein (1731-1802), a close friend of Markgraf Karl Friedrich, was for some years in charge of introducing Physiocratic principles in a part of Baden. After leaving the Badenese service he became a professor at Giessen. His main Physiocratic works are *Die wichtigste Angelegenheit für das ganze Publicum, oder die natürliche Ordnung in der Politik* (2 vols., Carlsruhe, 1772-73; 2nd re. ed., 1776-77) and *Grundveste der Staaten, oder die politische Oekonomie* (Giessen, 1778), an outline of his Giessen lectures.

[71] The *Ephemeriden der Menschheit* (7 vols., 1776-83) were edited by the Basel *Aufklärer* Isaak Iselin (1728-82), a close friend of Schlosser's. Successive issues of the *Ephemeriden* brought Schlettwein's criticism of the guilds, Schlosser's defense, the proguild speech by the French official Segrier (Aug. 1776) and some antiguild observations by a German bureaucrat named Müller.

versy. The author honestly sought to meet all the arguments advanced by the critics of the guilds, and freely admitted that the guilds required extensive reforms. His central thesis was characterized by the spirit of Reform Conservatism: reform of abuses was the only way of preventing the total abolition of the incriminated institution. Firnhaber believed that the Radical attack upon the guilds went far beyond their real faults while ignoring their equally real merits; he invoked patriotic pride as he accused the Radicals of mechanically applying French formulas to German problems; and he fell back upon a standard Conservative argument when he asserted that the evils criticized in connection with the guilds—laziness, selfishness, jealousy, et cetera—were really not due to the guilds, but rather due to human nature, and as such certain to persist even if the principles of laissez-faire were ever to replace the still dominant guild spirit.[72]

It is appropriate to make a rather thorough paraphrase of Firnhaber's arguments because he covered the entire controversy with admirable lucidity and exhaustiveness. He sought to refute, or at least minimize and place in proper perspective, every significant argument advanced by the Physiocrats against Germany's guilds.

They argued that guilds restricted the "natural freedom" of every man to use his labor power in any way not obviously harmful to his fellow men. Firnhaber replied that society, by its very nature, required a good many restrictions upon "natural freedom" for the sake of the common good—and his entire book argued that existing guild restrictions (subject to reforms to be noted later) *were* in fact defensible in terms of the common good.[73]

The Physiocrats argued that the minute regulations of technical processes and materials impeded the industrious and inventive master and precluded technical progress. Firnhaber admitted part of this charge, but pleaded countervailing considerations. Guild regulations guaranteed a high *average* quality of product; they prevented the demoralization of craftsmen resulting from cutthroat competition; and they eased the life of a beginning master, who was spared the killing task of establishing a personal reputation for craftsmanship among potential clients. The evil of technical stagnation could easily be remedied if the government kept a watch over guild sluggishness, encouraged inventions, and if necessary even compelled the introduc-

[72] J. H. Firnhaber, *Historisch-politische Betrachtung der Innungen und deren zweckmässige Einrichtung* (Hannover, 1782).
[73] Ibid., pp. 112-26.

tion of new methods where they were proved clearly superior to the old.[74]

The Physiocrats argued that the guilds charged outrageous prices by exploiting their monopolistic powers over the consumer. Firnhaber replied with elaborate cost calculations which tended to show that profits were generally not unreasonable, and that guild production was economical by developing specialized expertize and encouraging bulk purchase of materials; he also insisted that the guild (unlike the laissez-faire) system allowed public authority to control excessive prices in the public interest.[75]

The Physiocrats attacked excessively the admittedly irrational guild practices which restricted entry into apprenticeship. Firnhaber pleaded "substantially guilty" for the guilds on this score, but claimed that these faults were partly exaggerated and wholly remediable through governmental action. The Physiocrats complained of the needlessly long duration of apprenticeships (seven years in some crafts), the frequent abuse of apprentice labor for menial domestic services by the master's wife, the useless and often humiliating ceremonies required to pass from apprenticeship to journeymanship, and the total exclusion of illegitimate and so-called "dishonorable" children from the possibility of apprenticeship. Firnhaber replied that the acquisition of craft skills was usually a longer and more difficult process than the Physiocrats thought, especially when one considered the callowness of most fourteen-year-olds at the time when they began their apprenticeship; the length of apprenticeship could, furthermore, not be exclusively governed by the time needed to require craft skill, as a certain over-all maturity of personality was essential before a young man could safely become a journeyman. He also defended the moderate use of apprentices for housework as good for discipline and a preventive of mischief arising from apprentice idleness. Firnhaber found, in short, that the existing pattern of guild practices was more reasonable than the critics thought; he admitted, however, that certain abuses existed which required reform, and urged the following reforms himself: Mistreatment of apprentices must be prohibited by firmly enforced laws; the improper diversion of apprentices to domestic duties (at the expense of craft training) should be eliminated by requiring a certain level of professional knowledge at the end of the apprenticeship period (with punishment for masters whose apprentices were found to be substandard); all unnecessary ceremonies upon entering journeymanship, which at present formed a lucrative source of income

[74] Ibid., pp. 134-50.   [75] Ibid., pp. 150-83.

215

for masters who granted dispensations, should be abolished; while the exclusion of illegitimate and dishonorable children (e.g., those of shepherds) should be mitigated by the government's declaring such children eligible upon a selective basis. Firnhaber did not, however, want the government to declare the last two categories to be admissible for craftsmanship *en bloc;* he thought that considerations of individual justice must yield to the necessity of guilds' maintaining their *esprit de corps,* which would surely disintegrate if there were a mass infusion of "dishonorable elements" in violation of traditional prejudices.[76]

The Physiocrats denounced the vagabondage, disorderliness, and begging usually connected with the life of journeymen. Firnhaber again admitted much of the charge and urged the total prohibition of journeyman begging and the exemplary punishment of the ringleaders of journeyman riots. He insisted, however, upon the basic principle underlying journeymanship: the value of having a number of itinerant years between apprenticeship and masterhood. Traveling contributed to general maturity besides allowing the journeyman to become acquainted with the different productive techniques practiced in different places. The availability of journeymen was indispensable in certain crafts, such as metal-working, where an efficient workshop required the employment of several men with skills beyond the apprentice stage; it also provided for the needs of sick masters (and widows of masters) whose shop could be kept going by skilled journeymen.[77]

The Physiocrats denounced the many arbitrary practices which made it needlessly difficult for journeymen to become masters. Most guilds required the production of a useless masterpiece and expensive feasts (paid for by the journeyman) before the journeyman could become a master craftsman; some required either that masters be sons of masters or that they marry the widow or daughter of a master; while others excluded journeymen for such irrelevant factors as sexual offenses. Firnhaber admitted the existence of these abuses and wanted the government to suppress all of them by law—as some "enlightened" governments like that of Frederician Prussia had already done.[78]

The Physiocrats argued that the lack of competition inherent in the guild system necessarily made for inferior products. Firnhaber flatly denied this and praised the spirit of craftsmanship for being oriented around product quality, whereas entrepreneurs under laissez-faire

[76] Ibid., pp. 185-205, 271-91. [77] Ibid., pp. 205-13, 338-54.
[78] Ibid., pp. 291-323.

were oriented toward profits; he reminded his readers that the guilds had as one of their purposes the protection of the consumer against shoddy goods; it was quicker and more effective, furthermore, for a cheated consumer to complain to the guild than to a judge or police official (even assuming that society did not settle for a *caveat emptor* principle). Guild officials held the terrible power of expulsion over dishonest or incompetent members; expulsion meant total ruin of livelihood, since entry into another profession was virtually impossible under the prevalent guild system.[79]

The Physiocrats rightly accused the guilds of wasting much time and effort upon jurisdictional squabbles and the harassment of nonmembers. Firnhaber suggested as a simple solution to these problems the compulsory amalgamation of guilds working in neighboring fields: the frequency of disputes was to serve as prima facie proof of the need of amalgamation. The problem of ferreting out nonmember producers (the so-called *Pfuscher* or *Bönhasen)* would be minimized as entry into the guilds became facilitated through the above-sketched reforms.[80]

Firnhaber thought that he had an answer to every objection and a reform proposal to cover every abuse; but he was also at pains to avoid being driven into an exclusively defensive position. He argued that the guilds possessed many merits which their critics generally ignored, merits which must be considered in any general evaluation of the institution. Firnhaber placed himself upon solid Physiocratic ground—valuing agriculture above all other activities—when he praised the guilds for preventing the exodus of rural labor into the cities, since desirable urban employments were monopolized by guild members. The guilds were essential for the smooth working of the valuable institution of journeymanship: they provided social centers, employment exchanges, unemployment payments, and sickness benefits which would otherwise have to be established by the state. The tradition of journeyman wandering was especially important since the present, degenerate generation of young men would otherwise be inclined "to remain home sitting behind mummy's warm stove."[81] The guilds also played a useful role in guaranteeing a steady and reliable supply of goods and services, an important matter especially in small towns. The absence of guild specialization would inevitably lead to the establishment of jacks-of-all-trades who might or might not be available whenever a particular customer wanted a particular service.

[79] Ibid., pp. 213-20, 247-54.   [80] Ibid., pp. 220-21, 354-72.
[81] Ibid., p. 244: "bei der Mamma hinter dem Ofen bleiben."

Under the guild system one could go to a cobbler or smith or wheelwright and find him in his workshop at regular guild hours without fearing that he might be out mending fences or collecting taxes.[82]

To these advantages of guilds must be added the disadvantages attendant upon their abolition. Firnhaber thought that abolition was probably impracticable and certainly unjust, and in any case fraught with grave (and too often unanticipated) consequences. The territorial division of Germany confronted guild abolitionists with a difficult dilemma, for abolition must obviously occur on a *national* scale if hopeless confusion were to be avoided. Yet it was most unlikely that the Regensburg *Reichstag* would rouse itself to so revolutionary a deed: it had labored for decades to produce the *Reichspolizeiordnung* of 1731 which curbed, feebly and ineffectively, some widely recognized guild abuses. A coordinated suppression of the guilds by *all* the states was obviously impossible; while a suppression by *some* states would lead to the mass migration of artisans who benefited from the existing system to those territories which still permitted guilds.[83]

Even if suppression were possible it would be unjust. The privileges of guilds had been voluntarily conferred by governments, frequently in return for a *quid pro quo* which possessed all the sanctity of a contract. To destroy these contracts without absolute necessity was to undermine the very foundations of society. To minimize this injustice it would be necessary for the government to "fork out" vast sums of money to the guild masters who had paid heavily for guild membership in entrance fees and other charges. To raise money for these compensation payments would provoke an unforeseen dilemma: the necessary taxes would either fall upon the entire population, masters included, so that the masters could legitimately complain about being taxed to compensate themselves; or they would fall recessively upon the nonmaster population which was least able to pay and likely to be stirred into rebellion.[84]

To risk these consequences would be justified only if the guilds constituted an intolerable evil now, and if their admitted abuses categorically defied all reform efforts. Firnhaber argued that neither was the case. His program was Conservative in intent because it aimed to *preserve* the guilds by pruning them of the excrescences which had developed in the course of time. The program was thoroughly practicable. In fact, most of it had already been realized in such "enlightened" states as Frederician Prussia, where the government had

[82] Ibid., pp. 228-58.   [83] Ibid., pp. 258-60.
[84] Ibid., pp. 260-64.

successfully eliminated such abuses as arbitrary restrictions upon apprenticeship and the difficulties placed in the way of achieving masterhood. The already-mentioned *Reichspolizeiordnung* of 1731 had aimed in the same direction though it had unhappily proved something of a dead letter. Vigorous reform action by individual states could count upon the support of "enlightened" public opinion. Firnhaber obviously wanted an *ad hoc* alliance between Radicals, who wanted the total abolition of the guilds but might prove willing to settle for their reform, and his own brand of Conservatism, which wanted reform in order to prevent complete abolition. This alliance was to prove a great historical success; the guilds, shorn of their abuses, were to play a major role in the German economy until the onset of the Industrial Revolution in the 1840's.

It must always be remembered that the German economy was still very backward in the last third of the eighteenth century. Industrialization was the fascinating—or horrible—subject matter of books written by travelers to England, not an immediate problem confronting Germany. There was, however, already—or still—a widespread transfiguration of the conditions of artisan life when it was contrasted with merchant activity or what was reported about the hectic pace of English industrialization. Dohm, a Prussian diplomat whom we will soon encounter as the famous champion of Jewish emancipation, wrote as follows in 1781:

> The life of a skilled artisan craftsman is perhaps the most happy one possible in our civil society. His soul is troubled by neither nagging fears nor delusive hopes concerning the future; he enjoys the present with a pure and perfect joy, and expects tomorrow to be exactly like today. His strenuous labor keeps him healthy, while its uniformity brings his spirit the satisfactions of quiet tranquillity. . . . He is happy with his own lot in life, and suspects at least dimly that the upper classes are less so with theirs. He is honest and just in the prices he charges; both because this is dictated by the honor of his craft and because he does not aspire to a life which places him above his fellow craftsmen. His product is sound because he cannot maintain his credit and status if he does not follow customs and regulations in producing only articles of standardized excellence.[85]

Dohm's description may be considered the swan song of the static, customary, and predictable world which was soon to be overthrown by the inexorable force of industrialization.

[85] Christian Wilhelm Dohm, *Ueber die bürgerliche Verbesserung der Juden* (Berlin, 1781), p. 100.

The Debate on Jewish Emancipation

DOHM'S ADVOCACY OF JEWISH EMANCIPATION

The argument for human liberty and equality could not stop short of championing the claims of even the most hated and despised group living in Germany—the utterly miserable Jews confined in filthy ghettos since time immemorial. Their right to equal citizenship began to be argued by several obscure German authors in the second third of the eighteenth century;[86] it came to the general attention of the German reading public, however, only with the publication of Dohm's famous *On the Civic Improvement of the Jews* in 1781.[87]

Christian Wilhelm Dohm (1751-1820) was one of the most influential writers of the German *Aufklärung*, although his official responsibilities as a Prussian diplomat made literature his hobby rather than his profession. The son of a Lutheran clergyman, he had developed his "enlightened" principles at Göttingen under Schlözer and lived for a year with Basedow in Altona before entering the Prussian foreign service as a protégé of Hertzberg in 1779. Frederick the Great employed his fluent pen to defend the *Fürstenbund* in 1785,[88] and he served as Prussian ambassador to several West German courts during the period of the revolutionary wars. He was famous throughout Germany for his encyclopedic knowledge of political problems; though he himself attached far greater importance to his work on behalf of the sacred cause of *Aufklärung*. Dohm possessed a genius for friendship; his friends included such diverse figures as the Swiss historian Johannes von Müller, the Prussian poet Gleim, the mystical Christian philosopher Jacobi, and the rationalist Jewish philosopher Mendels-

[86] For example, J. F. Kayser, *Über die Autonomie der Juden* (Giessen, 1739); Heusch, *Über die öffentliche Lage der Juden* (Strassburg, 1745); and J. F. Fischer, *Über die Lage und Rechtsprechung der Juden* (Strassburg, 1763). The "lag" in German development compared to Western Europe is attested by the fact that the basic English tract in favor of Jewish emancipation had been published as early as Queen Anne's time: John Toland, *Reasons for Naturalising the Jews in Great Britain and Ireland, on the same foot with all other Nations. Containing also, A Defence of the Jews, against all vulgar Prejudices in all Countries* (London, 1714).

[87] Christian Wilhelm Dohm, *Ueber die bürgerliche Verbesserung der Juden* (Berlin, 1781). An important second part, containing Dohm's arguments against his critics, appeared under the same title in 1783. Henceforth cited as Dohm, I, and Dohm, II. A useful survey of the entire controversy is the Leipzig dissertation by Franz Reuss: *Christian Wilhelm Dohms Schrift, "Über die bürgerliche Verbesserung der Juden," und deren Einwirkung auf die gebildeten Stände Deutschlands* (Kaiserslautern, 1891). Reuss is impatient with Dohm for his numerous concessions to his "unenlightened" Conservative critics.

[88] See Ch. 5 below.

220

sohn. The latter aroused his interest in the Jewish question when he asked Dohm's help in drafting a memorial to the French government asking for the redress of the grievances of some Alsatian Jews who had appealed to Mendelssohn in 1781.[89]

Dohm seized the opportunity to write a general book on Jewish emancipation which went far beyond the needs of the immediate occasion. He wanted to argue the case on the plane of fundamental principle as a question of public policy rather than of humanitarianism; his argument was deliberately drafted to appeal exclusively to the "enlightened" self-interest of non-Jews and their princes.[90] It is not surprising, therefore, that his book is notable among philo-Semitic writings in depicting the character and qualities of contemporary Jews in a most unfavorable light. He almost went out of his way to admit the validity of the criticism leveled against contemporary Jews on the grounds of clannishness, low and one-sided Talmudic culture, physical degeneracy, prevalent dishonesty, and cringing cowardice. Dohm insisted only that these qualities were not due to an indelible and unchangeable Jewish character but rather were the inevitable consequence of having lived for a millennium in a hostile environment. He argued that *any* people, similarly treated, would develop the same unattractive characteristics; the responsibility for these qualities of the Jews must be placed primarily at the door of the Christian community which had been responsible for anti-Judaic policies during the past fifteen hundred years.[91]

Accepting the undesirable condition of the Jews as a fact, Dohm saw three possible approaches for dealing with the "Jewish problem." One might, in the first place, maintain the *status quo*—but neither Jew nor Christian could desire this; one might, in the second place, seek "to

---

[89] On Dohm see the elaborate but ill-digested family biography by his son-in-law W. Gronau, *Christian von Dohm nach seinem Wollen und Handeln, ein biographischer Versuch* (Lemgo, 1824); the lively sketch in Reuss, op.cit., pp. 8-16; and the excellent brief biography by Max Braubach, "Christian von Dohm," *Westfälische Lebensbilder*, v (1937), 238-58. His still readable memoirs, *Denkwürdigkeiten meiner Zeit* (5 vols., Lemgo, 1814-19), covering the years 1778-86, are an invaluable source for the Germany of the *ancien regime*. His reputation was under some cloud in the "age of nationalism" because he "collaborated" with the French after Jena and became Westphalian ambassador to Dresden before ill-health forced his retirement in 1810. His cosmopolitan conception of *Aufklärung* and want of nationalist intolerance—both conspicuous in his advocacy of Jewish emancipation—made "collaboration" with the "progressive" Westphalian state entirely natural for him.

[90] See especially Dohm, II, 151-52.

[91] Dohm, II, 152ff., though the "environmental thesis" can be found throughout the book.

eliminate the Jews from the face of the earth" if, Dohm added, "such a thing could still be contemplated in our enlightened age"; the third, and obviously most desirable, policy was to "seek to make the Jews better citizens" by encouraging their better nature through an improvement of their environment. Dohm was optimistic about the chances of this third policy although he warned against the expectation of quick results. He thought that centuries of oppression had made the Jews so utterly degenerate as to require a transition period of three to four generations before they could be brought up to the level of other human beings.[92]

Dohm proposed several specific suggestions calculated to bring the Jews, in both rights and qualities, to the point of equality with their Christian fellow citizens. The Jews must secure, in the first place, legal rights and obligations equal to those of non-Jews; this required not only the elimination of all special taxes, residence permits, and other legal disqualifications but also their dispensation from such civic obligations as military service. Dohm believed, in the second place, that the undesirable qualities of the Jews were largely due to their exclusive absorption in commerce; he favored, therefore, far-reaching measures to encourage Jews to enter agriculture and the crafts, and even contemplated "illiberal" transition steps (such as tax exemption for new Jewish farmers and a *numerus clausus* for Jewish merchants) to achieve a better occupational balance.

"I believe," wrote Dohm, "that the problem of the moral and civic improvement of the Jews would completely disappear within fifty years if it were possible to turn the majority of the Jews into farmers and artisans."[93] Dohm further called for the elimination of the present housing ghettos which impeded social and business intercourse between Jews and non-Jews; he called for a mutual conquest of prejudice, while he urged the Jews to give up certain habits not essentially connected with their religion, such as the keeping of business records in Hebrew, which needlessly complicated contact with Gentiles. Effective Jewish emancipation also required that the Jews break out of their narrow Talmudic culture and enter the main stream of German intellectual life; to this end Dohm wanted Jewish schools to accommodate their curriculum (except, of course, for religious instruction) to that of German schools. Such a reform would permit Jews to enter the universities and gradually qualify them to enter public employment on equal terms with Gentiles (though Dohm cau-

[92] The entire paragraph, with the quoted phrases, is based upon Dohm, II, 214.
[93] Ibid., II, 298.

tiously thought that Jewish public ambitions should be discouraged at first). Dohm also wanted the Jewish community to secure complete freedom to build synagogues and otherwise openly exercise its faith; and he called upon all governments to create a favorable climate for Jewish emancipation by requiring all Christian ministers to preach on the virtues of religious toleration.[94]

Dohm welcomed discussion of his specific proposals, although he refused to argue with those who denied his basic premise that the Jews *could* be improved. "I must confess that I cannot conceive of a human group which is incapable of improvement. Such an idea stands in stark contradiction to all psychology, all history, and all experience."[95] He was eager, however, to answer the arguments of those critics who shared his environmental thesis but claimed there were special difficulties in applying it to the case of the Jews; Dohm insisted that these difficulties made it all the more imperative to begin the long-drawn-out battle of overcoming them here and now. The Jews were clannish and intolerant toward their neighbors—but centuries of Christian intolerance had made them so. The Jews clung with fanatical parochialism to formalistic rituals and anachronistic dietary laws—but Dohm thought this natural in a community hitherto immune to the liberating wind of the *Aufklärung*. The Jews lacked any conception of citizenship—but their Christian environment had never allowed them to develop loyalties transcending loyalty to their coreligionists. The Jews had one-sidedly developed the qualities of an exclusively commercial people—but their exclusion from artisan guilds and agriculture had left them no alternative.[96] This catalogue of obstacles to Jewish emancipation could easily be extended; Dohm insisted, however, against all his critics that their arguments showed only the difficulty, not the impossibility, of the Jews eventually attaining equal citizenship. There was nothing in either the Jewish character or the Jewish religion which could ultimately preclude successful emancipation.

OPPOSITION TO JEWISH EMANCIPATION

Dohm's powerful arguments—all the more persuasive because he was willing to admit difficulties raised by his critics—won much support

[94] Dohm's proposals are outlined in Dohm, I, 110-27.

[95] Ibid., II, 23-24.

[96] While admitting all these faults, Dohm also stated that the present-day Jews possessed—for the same environmental reasons—a host of virtues, such as high intelligence, industry, flexibility, a pure family life, and solicitude for the Jewish poor. He especially praised their staunch refusal to purchase temporal advantage by religious apostasy. Dohm, I, 91ff.

and encouraged a host of pamphlets arguing a similar position.[97] Yet it was inevitable that his challenge to a powerful prejudice should also provoke bitter opposition to both his basic premises and his specific proposals. A few authors condemned Dohm's entire approach *sans phrase;*[98] most critics preferred to make a bow to Dohm's benevolent intentions while seeking to refute his arguments in detail.[99] The following survey will summarize both kinds of Conservative arguments against Jewish emancipation.

Some authors maintained the incorrigible wickedness of the Jewish race and thought this documented by the Old Testament (chronic rebellion against God, cruelty toward other people), New Testament (killing Christ), and contemporary experience (all the unattractive Jewish qualities admitted by Dohm).[100] They saw no reason to believe that this wickedness could be altered by a change of environment, arguing on the contrary that it expressed certain fundamental qualities of the Jewish race and religion. It was argued that the Jewish "Asiatic temperament" led to restlessness, ruthlessness, and acquisitiveness—all qualities especially useful in commerce; the Jewish concentration upon commerce was more due to native bent than to legal exclusion from other professions.[101] It was further argued that the Jewish religion was intrinsically unsocial, intolerant, and hostile to honest dealings between Jews and non-Jews. The dietary laws made social intercourse difficult; the Jews took an intolerant pride in the exclusive truth of their religion;[102] while that religion allegedly taught that Jews were

[97] For example, H. F. Diez, *Über Juden* (Dessau, 1783), by a Prussian civil servant, and Wolf Davidson, *Über die bürgerliche Verbesserung der Juden* (Berlin, 1798), by a Jewish doctor. For a list of other titles see Reuss, op.cit., pp. 104-05.

[98] Most notably, Friedrich Traugott Hartmann, *Untersuchung, ob die bürgerliche Freyheit den Juden zu gestatten sey* (Berlin, 1783), and a review of Dohm's book by Professor Hissmann in the *Göttinger Gelehrten Anzeigen* (1781), pp. 753-63, reprinted separately as *Anmerkungen über Dohms bürgerliche Verbesserung der Juden* (Vienna, 1782).

[99] Dohm replied to these critics in his second volume. The study of the controversy is facilitated by the fact that Dohm usually printed the case of his critics *in extenso* before proceeding to refute it. The most interesting criticisms were those by Professor Michaelis of Göttingen, first printed in the *Orientalische Bibliothek* (reprinted in Dohm, II, 31-71); and by Pastor Schwager, first printed in *Minden'sches Intelligenzblatt* (reprinted in Dohm, II, 89-111).

[100] This is the main theme of Traugott, op.cit. Dohm expressed his disappointment with this view and the uselessness of arguing against it, in Dohm, II, 23-28.

[101] Dohm ridiculed the view that Jews had an indelible "commercial temperament" by observing that they had been successful farmers in antiquity. Dohm, II, 220-21.

[102] Dohm noted this was true of all religions, and had been especially true of Christianity when it was still a persecuted minority. He argued that all re-

not required to keep an oath toward non-Jews.[103] If these arguments were correct—as Dohm denied—they provided an irrefutable case against Jewish emancipation; they logically suggested—as Dohm pointed out polemically—that appropriate steps be undertaken to eliminate the Jews altogether for the benefit of humanity.

The Göttingen professor Michaelis seized upon Dohm's admission that Jewish emancipation would take some three to four generations to argue that this process, however desirable ultimately, would be most unfair to the intervening Christian generations, which would be doomed to suffer from contact with emancipated but as-yet unimproved Jews who remained grasping, clannish, hostile to Christianity, incapable of military service, et cetera, yet enjoyed full equality of rights.[104] (This was an argument which skillfully exploited Dohm's cautious willingness to meet his opponents part way; it refused to admit that the remedy of millennial wrongs sometimes requires considerable sacrifices, and certainly exaggerated those in the present case.)

Some authors argued that the lot of the present Jews was not so intolerable as the champions of emancipation claimed. They pointed out that rich Jews could mitigate the practical effect of Jewish disabilities by exploiting their close relationship to reigning princes. "I believe that rich and refined Jews do not feel much pressure, while the rabble among the Jews is as insensitive (*abgestumpft*) to it as are our serfs to the pressure of their masters."[105]

Another argument held that the pretended right of the Jews on such matters as equal access to public office in fact created real wrongs to non-Jews. Many of the latter felt, rightly or wrongly, that it was intolerable to be governed by Jewish bureaucrats or judged by Jewish judges. This feeling was a social fact which could not be argued away. Furthermore, did not majorities have rights as well as minorities, especially if the latter were felt to be alien?[106] It was also argued, with

---

ligions lose their sharp edges when they achieve a tolerated and respected position in a pluralistic community. Dohm, II, 187ff., compares the Jews to the early Christians, and states the general proposition on pp. 214-15.

[103] Dohm patiently refuted this vulgar misconception in Dohm, II, 300-48. He admitted that if the charge were true, then all Jews would deserve to be banished regardless of any good qualities they might otherwise possess. Pages 304-05.

[104] Dohm, II, 54-56.

[105] This was argued by one of Dohm's anonymous correspondents. Dohm, II, 149.

[106] Michaelis stated as a general proposition, "A people that cannot eat and drink with us—as is true of the Jews so long as they cling to their dietary laws—remains in our and its own eyes an alien people (*sehr abgesondertes Volk*)." It

somewhat greater sophistication, that it was not in the interest (properly understood) of Jews to seek bureaucratic or judicial office. So long as anti-Semitic feeling persisted (and this would be for a long time), it was inevitable that the controversial acts of Jewish officials would be judged as Jewish, not *individual*, acts; it could not be in the interests of the Jewish people as a whole to be subjected incessantly to controversy just to allow a few of their members to rise into positions of public responsibility.[107]

Many authors argued that certain Jewish traditions or qualities prevented Jews from fulfilling some of the normal obligations of citizenship; it was therefore illogical to give them the full measure of corresponding civic rights. Thus it was frequently asserted that Jews could not perform military service. Their poor physique and alleged cowardice might be terminated by several generations of emancipation; not, however, several factors connected with their religion. It was impossible to maintain the Jewish dietary laws in a mixed army; there was also the Talmudic prohibition against fighting any but defensive battles on the Sabbath.[108] Dohm himself admitted that these difficulties justified imposing for some time a special tax upon Jews *in lieu* of military service. There were, however, other difficulties which could not, according to the critics, be so easily resolved. Since noncombatant Jews would not be killed in wars, there would be a disproportionate increase in Jewish population, which would add to the defenselessness of the country in future wars; while Dohm's proposal to allow Jews to enter agriculture might even allow Jews to purchase the estates of heirless Christian warriors killed in defense of their country.[109]

Much ingenuity was spent demonstrating that the Jews could not succeed in agricultural operations. It was claimed that they lacked both the physical strength and the psychological steadiness required in a farmer, while the dietary laws would require Jewish landowners to hire exclusively Jewish farm laborers (who were unlikely to prove

---

was not surprising, then, that Germans were reluctant, in Michaelis' view, to be governed by "aliens." Dohm, II, 61.

[107] For the entire paragraph see Dohm, II, 60-63.

[108] Dohm denied the practical importance of these difficulties. Rabbis could dispense Jewish soldiers from the dietary laws as, in fact, Dutch rabbis had done for Dutch Jewish sailors during the recent war; while the Talmudic prohibition about fighting on Saturdays was far more flexible than the critics believed. Dohm, II, 222ff.

[109] For the entire paragraph see Dohm, II, 46-51 (Michaelis), 104-06 (Schwager).

available). The agricultural economy of Northern Germany was, moreover, dependent upon pig-raising, which Jews—with their religious prohibition against eating pork—would probably refuse to do. It was also asserted that no empty lands were available for new farmers, and that if such lands were available it would be more rational to give them for settlement to non-Jews, who were more likely to succeed in farming and also available for other civic functions (such as military service) which Jews allegedly could or would not perform.[110]

Conservatives similarly asserted that there were insuperable obstacles to Jews' becoming artisans. The existing guilds would never admit them, while Christian masters were most unlikely to accept Jewish apprentices. How, then, were Jews supposed to learn crafts? And were there not reasons to believe that the much-cited "Jewish temperament" was in any case incompatible with the steady exercise of craftsmanship.[111]

It was inevitable, therefore, that Jews would remain confined to their present mercantile pursuits, and this meant continued friction between Jews and non-Jews; while the economic friction would always be compounded by the fact that the Jews were considered by others, and believed themselves to be, an "alien" people. This alien status was enhanced by the Zionist dream about the coming of a future messiah who would lead his "chosen people" back to Palestine. How could Jews develop a genuine loyalty to their countries of residence so long as they remained faithful to this Zionist creed? How could they expect to develop a feeling of genuine patriotism? And how could non-Jews, knowing this Zionist messianic tradition, cordially accept Jews as fellow citizens?[112]

Conservatives pointed out the special danger which confronted any country which took the lead in Jewish emancipation. Would not the Jews from all the world flock to it to enjoy advantages they had scarcely believed possible? Each country had enough difficulty man-

---

[110] Dohm stated and refuted these arguments in Dohm, II, 247-65.

[111] Dohm stated and refuted these arguments in Dohm, II, 266-99. He wanted to meet the difficulty by the temporary employment of illiberal governmental policies, such as special tax exemptions for Jewish artisans. He answered his liberal-egalitarian critics with the assertion: "Methods of compulsion are sometimes indispensable in order to remedy an evil which has developed over the centuries. What man's meddling has confused cannot always be cleared up by the unassisted efforts of Nature." Dohm, II, 295.

[112] Dohm stated and refuted this argument in Dohm, II, 215-20, admitting its theoretical force but denying its practical importance. The expectation of the Messiah and the implementation of the Zionist program was remote; it would become still more remote if Jewish emancipation increased the happiness and prosperity of Jews in their present countries of residence.

aging its own Jews to permit the entry of immigrants whose religion and temperament created—to say the least—special problems.[113] This was all the more true because the Jews tended in any case to multiply faster than non-Jews because of their habit of early marriage and exemption from military service. Most Conservatives felt an instinctive shudder at the thought of being forced to live in the same country with a large proportion of Jewish fellow citizens.[114]

It was argued, finally, that Jewish emancipation would *eo ipso* do grave injuries to existing Christian interests. The loss of princely revenue from special Jewish taxes was perhaps a minor matter;[115] the increased competition for attractive jobs in administration, education, and the professions was not. The Lutheran pastor Schwager, who thought he was benevolent toward the Jews, put the question, "Why should we undertake strong steps to transform the spirit of the Jews, and thereby make them eligible for certain posts, for which we already possess a sufficient number of candidates with the proper spirit?"[116] (The question heralded those middle-class fears and resentments which have done so much to keep anti-Semitism alive in the modern world despite the atrophy of its original religious roots.)

These various Conservative arguments—despite their frequently tortured character—must be presumed to have exercised some influence upon governments in postponing Jewish emancipation. It is impossible, of course, to state in quantitative terms what "public opinion" thought about the entire controversy; it is clear only that there was henceforth in Germany an articulate group of philo-Semites, favoring Jewish emancipation as a matter of prudence and justice, and a somewhat less articulate group of anti-Semites whose poverty of argument was more than compensated by a large reservoir of popular prejudice. The cause of emancipation made some progress through "enlightened absolutism," which was contemptuous of popular prejudice. Joseph II substantially enlarged the rights of the Jews in 1781, with Dohm hailing this action in his concluding pages.[117] Prussia lagged behind for a few years until the body tax upon Jews (*Leibzoll*) was abolished in

---

[113] Dohm admitted the force of the argument by favoring special immigration barriers to meet this contingency. His general argument was, however, that the maximizing of population—Jewish or non-Jewish—was always an advantage to a country. Dohm, II, 154-71.

[114] Michaelis spoke of the danger of the development of "a defenceless and most contemptible Jewish state" (*den wehrlosesten, verächtlichsten Judenstaat*).

[115] Dohm, I, 130-32. Dohm thought this an advantage, as Jewish merchants were able to pay these only by fleecing the consumer, which in turn led to increased anti-Semitism.

[116] Dohm, II, 107. [117] Dohm, I, 151-54.

1787 and the obligation to purchase unneeded royal porcelain in 1788. Complete freedom of worship was attained in 1792, while Jews were admitted to the stock exchange *(Börsenkorporation)* on terms of full equality in 1803. The king granted full rights of citizenship to selected Jewish families in 1792; but genuine emancipation had to await Hardenberg's edict of March 11, 1812.[118] The Jews of Southern and Western Germany won their emancipation under the influence of France, only to lose some of their rights upon the fall of Napoleon. The relics of legal discrimination were to survive in Germany until the National Liberal ascendancy of the 1870's.

It may be noted in passing that emancipation entirely transformed the character of anti-Semitism. Religious hatred of the Jews diminished with the advance of secularism, but the breakup of the ghetto created new dangers for the relationship between Christians and Jews. The Jews of the ghetto had been despised rather than feared; the emancipated Jew striving for equality threatened the social position of groups hitherto little affected by competition. The entry of capable Jews into politics, the professions, industry (going beyond their traditional role in banking), and the new world of journalism was to be exploited by Conservative elements in their defensive struggle against a Radicalism for which Jews provided numerous leaders. The eighteenth-century bogey of an *Illuminati* conspiracy was to be supplanted by (or in some cases merged with) the theory of a Jewish world conspiracy toward the end of the nineteenth century.

The Debate About the Emancipation of Women

We have seen that the egalitarian principles of the *Aufklärung* could not stop short of the emancipation of the Jews, the most despised of races. It is not surprising, therefore, that at least a few people carried egalitarian principles to their logical conclusion by demanding the emancipation of women as well—though this constituted a still sharper break with the social traditions hitherto dominant in Europe. Some authors even explicitly drew a close connection between the two types of emancipation. Thus Theodor Gottlieb von Hippel, a prominent judge of Königsberg and governing mayor after 1780, wrote an (anonymous) book called *On the Civic Improvement of Women*,[119]

---

[118] For an excellent account of the miserable condition of the Prussian Jews and their gradual emancipation see Hugo Rachel, *Das Berliner Wirtschaftsleben im Zeitalter des Frühkapitalismus* (Berlin, 1931), pp. 42-52.

[119] Anonymous [Theodor Gottlieb von Hippel], *Über die bürgerliche Verbesserung der Weiber* (Königsberg, 1792). Henceforth cited as Hippel, *Weiber*. The book produced an interesting reply in an anonymous article, "Über die

whose title was an obvious imitation of Dohm's *On the Civic Improvement of the Jews.*

Hippel made his point with the following words: "Some contemporary authors have recommended the civic improvement of the Jews; should a people *truly* chosen by God—I mean the fair sex—be less worthy of solicitude than the *so-called* 'people of God'?"[120] The author also criticized—writing in 1792—the French revolutionaries for neglecting the cause of women; they had failed to destroy "the bastilles of gallantry, the prisons of domesticity, and the civic dungeons in which the fair sex continues to find itself."[121] Hippel urged equal legal rights, equal educational chances, and equal job opportunities for women. He did not, of course, believe that these could be achieved overnight by a simple act of legislation; he insisted, however, that the long-overdue first steps in this direction must be taken now. His aim was to make women ready for emancipation by enlarging educational opportunities immediately. "I do not believe that the other sex can be freed from its long-standing servitude by a single blow; I am satisfied with encouraging it with steps which will make it deserving of this emancipation."[122]

Hippel argued that women should be emancipated as a matter of right; he based this argument upon the contention that men and women were identical in their nature except for certain sexual differences irrelevant to their civil condition. He surveyed the reasons which had hitherto made for male domination in all known societies, to show that

---

politische Würde der Weiber," *Berlinisches Archiv der Zeit*, i (1799), 403-12, 502-10, written in the form of a dialogue and thus presenting both the pro- and anti-feminist arguments. (The latter invariably won out.) Henceforth cited as *Würde der Weiber*. Hippel (1741-96) studied theology and law, became one of the leading lawyers of Königsberg, and entered royal service in 1765. His appointments included membership in the blue-ribbon commission which drafted the *Allgemeine Landrecht* after 1780 (see Ch. 7), *dirigirender Bürgermeister* of Königsberg, and *Kriegsrath* in charge of incorporating Danzig after the third partition of Poland in 1795. Hippel wrote two widely read novels, *Die Kreuz-und-Querzüge des Ritters A-Z* (1792-93), ridiculing all secret societies (already referred to in Ch. 2), and *Die Lebensläfe in aufsteigender Linie* (1778-81), popularizing the philosophy of his friend Immanuel Kant. The article about him by Brenning in *ADB*, xii (1880), 463-66, includes a remarkably hostile character sketch. He praised marriage while remaining a bachelor; denounced rapacity and ambition while being notorious for both; and ridiculed secret societies while being an active Mason. Most of his writing was anonymous, with authorship of many pieces becoming known only long after his death when his collected works, in fourteen volumes, were published at Berlin in the years 1827-38.

120 Hippel, *Weiber*, pp. 24-25.   121 Ibid., p. 19.
122 Ibid., p. 21.

male domination was a remediable *historical,* not an unalterable *natural* fact. Hippel's book also included detailed suggestions about how to improve the condition of women here and now, and concluded with a refutation of many objections which Conservatives advanced against the emancipation of women.

Hippel put the core of his case in the following rhetorical question: "Is it not inexcusable that half of the abilities of the human race should be allowed to remain dormant: unknown, unappreciated, and unused?"[123] Women possessed the same intelligence and character structure as men. Why should God have given them intelligence if they were not supposed to use it? Had they not responded to every intellectual challenge which history had presented to them? They had produced outstanding rulers, like Queen Elizabeth of England and Empress Catherine of Russia, when women were permitted to mount the throne. They had produced many examples of extraordinary patriotism, of willingness to sacrifice their all to the Fatherland, in numerous heroines described by Plutarch and other ancient authors. The paucity of similar examples in European history was obviously due to the prevalent policy of "degrading women to a position half way between the human and the animal condition."[124]

Why had women been long kept in such a degraded condition? Traditionalists claimed subjection was due to the "natural fact" that women were the "weaker sex" and were especially vulnerable during the period of pregnancy and birth. Hippel replied that this fact at best only expressed the primitive "right of the stronger"—and was it not the very essence of society to replace this primitive so-called right by the claims of justice? Traditionalists also referred to the Old Testament story that woman was created out of Adam's rib; this provoked the exclamation, "O! spare us a stupid myth created by a barbarous, still nomadic Hebrew."[125] There were many specific reasons why women had been kept in subjection throughout the Dark Ages and well into the modern period, but such historical reasons could not prevent an "enlightened" century from testing a long-standing historical wrong at the bar of reason and justice and finding it wanting.[126]

Hippel expected glowing advantages from the emancipation of women. The pace of progress would be quickened by eliminating an obstacle which had kept mankind back for ages:

[123] Ibid., p. 25.
[124] *Würde der Weiber*, pp. 301-02. On the entire paragraph see Hippel, *Weiber*, Ch. 2 and pp. 235ff.
[125] *Würde der Weiber*, p. 407.
[126] On the whole paragraph see Hippel, *Weiber*, Chs. 3 and 4.

If one reckons . . . the fact that half of the human race has hitherto been without all education, or has been miseducated; and that the major role in training the young has been left to this very half. Is it not some kind of a miracle that we are at this moment human beings at all?[127]

Educational progress would be accompanied by a general humanitarian advance. Though Hippel—in this anticipating many future feminist writers—had just asserted that the characters of men and women were substantially identical, he now claimed that women were especially benevolent and sympathetic toward all kinds of suffering; to give them full human rights (including political rights) must therefore lead to great humanitarian advances in prison reform, outlawing war, improving manners, et cetera. Women also possessed a special aptitude for certain professions (for example, medicine and teaching, both of which required "female patience") from which they had been hitherto excluded. Hippel believed that the availability of women doctors would significantly reduce maternal mortality because many pregnant women refused to go to a male obstetrician. He cited figures to show that of women who went to a (male) obstetrician one out of every 130 died in childbirth, while the mortality rate among those who went to a (female) midwife was one out of every 70.[128] A further advantage to be expected from the emancipation of women was a reduction of immorality, as such professions as hairdressing and the teaching of music and dancing (all fields traditionally offering great dangers of seduction) became accessible to women.[129]

The first step necessary was to provide women with educational opportunities equal to those of men. Hippel was, however, no friend of any "separate but equal" doctrine; he argued strongly for coeducation especially during the decisive early years until about the age of twelve. The function of education was to turn animals into humans and humans into citizens, and this task was exactly the same whether one dealt with boys or girls. Whatever sex differences existed were certainly irrelevant before twelve and (in Hippel's view, at least) only marginal thereafter. The result of coeducation would be a mature adult relationship between men and women, who could henceforth understand and solve all their problems jointly instead of allowing

[127] Ibid., pp. 215-16.
[128] Hippel obviously assumed that sex rather than pocketbook was the basic factor in the decision of whether to go to an obstetrician or a midwife. It is impossible to say whether he was right or wrong in this view.
[129] Ibid., pp. 377ff.

marriage to become degraded into a relationship between master and slave. Coeducation would provide a great stimulus to the primary task of turning both men and women into refined, intelligent human beings and citizens worthy of the name, instead of concentrating upon a narrow, somewhat dehumanizing education aimed at preparing women exclusively for domestic life.[130]

Hippel gave systematic and eloquent expression to many views which were already "in the air" and had been discussed for years in pamphlets and articles. The Conservative case against female emancipation was best stated by Ernst Brandes, whom we have already encountered as a defender of privileged aristocratic access to office, in a special book entitled *Concerning Women* in 1787.[131] His argument may be summarized in the following terms:

The assertion that men and women possessed identical (or at least equal) natures was contrary to all experience, science, and history. Women were generally small in stature and inferior in physical strength. They were incapable of logical reasoning because of their weak brain nerves *(schwache Kopfnerven)* made it impossible for them to see the connection between different ideas. There was also a chemical difference in blood between men and women: the former contained more iron, the latter more fluids. Doctors and morticians were agreed that "female corpses burnt to ashes far more quickly than those of males; the female body had fewer solid but far more loose parts than the male body."[132] These anatomical and psychological facts were supported by the historical evidence which showed that men had dominated women since time immemorial. Was it not a typical failing of the arrogant eighteenth century that it felt free to ignore millennia of human experience in order to implement a favorite a priori prejudice?[133]

Brandes insisted that women possessed their own distinct—and highly important—functions, for which Nature had predestined them by giving them the appropriate qualities.

> I do not, indeed I cannot, wish to make any value judgment in comparing male with female qualities. Suffice it to say that Nature gave distinct vocations to each sex and that each can attain perfection only to the degree that it lives up to its own vocations.[134]

[130] Ibid., pp. 217ff.
[131] Ernst Brandes, *Über die Weiber* (Leipzig, 1787).
[132] Ibid., p. 44.
[133] For the entire paragraph see ibid., pp. 39-47.
[134] Ibid., p. 55.

The most characteristic female qualities were "gentleness, refinement, attachment, and tender and deep sensitivity,"[135] as well as the capacity to bear pain: "Female heroism shows itself best in patient endurance."[136] These qualities suggested the following distinctive functions for women: bearing children; raising children (with Brandes insisting especially on the importance of nursing babies); managing the household; refining social intercourse by taking the roughness off male conduct (for example, in codes of chivalry); providing men with a domestic refuge from the trials of life; and smoothing human relations by insisting upon the proper nuances of human conduct.[137]

It followed from all this that women should devote themselves to finding their true fulfillment in marriage rather than the "unnatural" pursuit of emancipation. Brandes' prosaic nature broke into poetic expressions when he described the proper relationship between husband and wife. The perennial analogy of sun and moon was not missing, and forestry came to the aid of astronomy: "If I may be permitted to write in images I would say that man is a strong elm, woman the tender grape-vine which winds around its tall stem."[138] Man and wife supplemented each other perfectly when the man represented the qualities of reason and will, the wife those of emotion and spontaneity. The proper division of function made for the maximum happiness of all:

> While man creates society, woman safeguards humanitarian values. When man goes to war against his enemies his fighting zeal is animated, and his fatherland becomes most dear to him, as he contemplates the wife he left behind at the domestic hearth. When he educates his intellect and enters into the rarified realm of science his wife alone has the power to pull him back down to earth. When—intoxicated by consciousness of superior talent—he craves appreciation, he finds in his wife enough understanding to pay incense to his greatness (*seiner Grösse hinlänglich Weihrauch zu zollen*). This appears to be the order of Nature which I see observed wherever man can lay some claim to happiness.[139]

Woe, however, unto the country where this natural harmony has been destroyed—a destruction symbolized by the consequences which fell upon Adam and Eve when Eve, that first champion of female eman-

[135] Ibid. [136] Ibid., p. 65.
[137] For the entire paragraph see ibid., pp. 54-83.
[138] Ibid., p. 47. [139] *Würde der Weiber*, pp. 64-65.

cipation, sought to transcend her allotted vocation by demanding knowledge of good and evil![140]

Brandes was bitterly contemptuous of the social role played by the few emancipated women which Germany had so far produced. As hostesses of the few *salons* they sought to imitate their French models. This sometimes had a favorable impact upon conversation by discouraging the national sin of learned pedantry. The over-all effect of mixed company upon culture was, however, disastrous. Women were incapable of serious, sustained conversation on any one topic; their ignorance unfortunately did not prevent them from seeking to participate in talk, if only to draw attention to their physical charms; while the reduced wine consumption produced by their presence froze many otherwise brilliant tongues. Society women had other disastrous qualities as well. Their habit of "constantly stimulating male desires while having no intention to satisfy them"[141] drove many men to prostitutes in despair. The daughters of such women often turned out even worse than themselves: mothers tended to tyrannize over their pretty daughters out of jealousy, and to heckle their ugly daughters out of anxiety of being stuck with a household of old maids.[142]

Brandes was especially caustic in denouncing the half-educated women produced by female emancipation. Their vanity was inflated by the reading of novels with heroines suited to their tastes. (The rise of a female reading public had, in Brandes' view, been a powerful force in the degradation of German literature. He thought that books written for female readers tended to be *ipso facto* trashy.)[143] Brandes also thought that emancipated women tended to neglect both their domestic obligations and the rules of financial prudence through their "love of ornament and craving to attract attention."[144] The bacheloric Brandes concluded his argument with some ninety-six pages denouncing the sexual looseness to be expected from emancipated women.[145]

Another writer supplemented this picture of female degeneracy with the following portrait:

[140] Ibid., pp. 507-10.   [141] Brandes, *Weiber*, p. 125.
[142] For the entire paragraph see ibid., pp. 108-44.
[143] Ibid., pp. 163-88.
[144] The heading of a chapter in ibid., pp. 188-95.
[145] Ibid., pp. 196-293. (Even an amateur psychoanalyst can have a field day with the light which these pages throw upon Brandes' personality. It is, perhaps, not gratuitous to refer in this connection to Brandes' earlier description of the position of women in classical civilization, and the remarkable praise of the glorious consequences wrought by homosexuality in Socrates among the ancients and Winckelmann among the moderns. Ibid., pp. 25-39.)

The true picture of the educated female shows vanity rather than principles; ostentation rather than knowledge; arrogance rather than dignity; intrigue rather than prudence; and deceit rather than honesty. They want to look like men in external appearance; they affect a masculine unconstraint in their morals; and wish to outdo men at their own game through superior elasticity. They become in fact *caricatures* who drag themselves about on stilts.[146]

Intellectual women found themselves relegated to a social ghetto where they were estranged from their own sex while not being fully accepted by men:

Such women must defy the jealousy of fellow-women and meet masculine pride with contempt when they cannot humble it with the art of coquetry or the science of intrigue. Such a situation inevitably distorts a woman's character, and rare indeed is an intellectual woman who does not cross your way as a fury.[147]

This, then, was the indictment directed against the proposed emancipation of women: it was contrary to Nature by distracting women from their proper vocation of raising children, managing households, and being a helpmeet to their husbands; it did not make women happy, since it alienated them from both men and their fellow women; and it had disastrous effects upon society as a whole by ruining culture and creating a group of half-educated women who neglected their proper function while dragging others down to their own level of useless dilettantism. Brandes appealed to women to realize the error of their emancipatory ways and return to their true role as good wives and mothers; he promised them that this role would bring them far greater satisfactions than the idle life of the flirt and the society woman. His real appeal was, however, to men, since women were most unlikely to listen to reason, least of all in a matter where their own vanity was involved. Men must continue to exercise their natural domination over women, or to resume it where they had abandoned the reins; the only alternative was a topsy-turvy society marked by social chaos and moral disintegration, since Nature had a way of avenging even the slightest violation of its eternal laws.[148]

[146] *Würde der Weiber*, p. 507. [147] Ibid., p. 505.
[148] Brandes, *Weiber*, pp. 293-300.

CHAPTER 5

Political Controversies

THE INCREASING criticism of German political conditions by "enlightened" thinkers after about 1770 led to numerous public controversies interesting in themselves but also significant for preparing the Napoleonic Revolution of the first years of the nineteenth century. Men became accustomed to questioning previously unquestioned institutions, with the result that their minds were being prepared for the overthrow of those political entities that lacked any vital relationship to the dynamic forces of eighteenth-century Germany. The Holy Roman Empire, the ecclesiastical states, the Imperial Free Cities, and small principalities were all vulnerable to attack; while even the "living force" of monarchical absolutism was not unaffected by the increasing habit of thinking about political conditions, even as the princes prepared themselves for territorial aggrandizement at the expense of their anachronistic neighbors. Isolated voices of republican criticism from the Left were a sign that the princes' aggrandizement was taking place in a climate of Indian summer. The persistent criticism of absolutism from the Right—by champions of the *Ständestaat* and by old-fashioned supporters of patriarchal government— showed that absolutism could never completely win the allegiance of even the upper classes. Sometimes, indeed, the common adherence to an ideal of self-government, however divergently interpreted, led to an *ad hoc* alliance between critics of the Left and Right. The fact that absolutism was placed on the intellectual defensive compelled rulers to put their own houses in order through various reforms. It is no accident that the years after 1770 saw the heyday of an "enlightened absolutism," with princes becoming vigorous reformers and conceiving of themselves as the "first servants of the state" rather than beneficiaries of monarchy by divine right.

The present chapter will begin with a survey of the major anachronistic institution soon to be swept away—the Holy Roman Empire of the German nation. It will then discuss the vigorous type of polity which had grown up within the imperial shell, and was already the dominant political institution in Germany—the territorial principality ruled by an absolute monarch. The next sections will deal with two anachronistic polity types doomed to early annexation by the monarchical principalities—ecclesiastical states and Free Imperial Cities. The concluding section will analyse two major controversies which did much to stir Germany out of a prolonged period of political apathy—debates dealing with militarism and with the attitude to be taken toward the American Revolution.

The Empire[1]

THE STRUCTURE OF THE EMPIRE

The venerable institution of the Holy Roman Empire of the German nation provided a loose framework for the vast diversity of states which existed in Central Europe. Its name—so Voltaire had mocked in an oft-quoted aphorism—was as anachronistic as its substance was feeble; there was in fact nothing either Holy or Roman about the Empire, while its imperial and national character proved increasingly questionable. If the concept of empire implies effective central institutions, there was little that was imperial about eighteenth-century Germany; while the boundaries of the empire did not coincide—in fact, had never coincided—with the linguistic frontier of the German nationality. There were many German-speaking peoples outside its boundaries, most notably the Swiss and the inhabitants of East Prussia; there were many non-Germans inside its boundaries, such as Czechs, Italians, Walloons, and Flemings. This multinational reality did not prevent the empire from evoking a good deal of German national pride—a pride, however, that had little to do with politics and was in fact suffused with the spirit of cosmopolitanism.

All the institutions of the empire were notable for their inability to perform the functions for which they were originally designed. The elected emperor (usually the head of the Habsburg family) could not provide national leadership. He possessed only infinitesimal power and revenues by virtue of his imperial office. His power was limited to issuing patents of nobility and urging the appointment of certain canons to certain cathedral chapters; his revenue, to receiving some

---

[1] The literature on the empire in the eighteenth century is endless and only a few titles can be listed here. The best general surveys are to be found in K. Biedermann, *Deutschland im 18. Jahrhundert* (1854, i), Ch. 2, and F. Hartung, *Deutsche Verfassungsgeschichte* (7th edn., Stuttgart, 1950), Ch. 4. A good modern analysis of the constitutional development after 1648 is H. E. Feine, "Zur Verfassungsentwicklung des Hl. Römischen Reiches seit dem Westfälischen Frieden," *Zeitschrift für Rechtsgeschichte*, LII (1932). The standard contemporary account, still worth reading today, is J. S. Pütter, *Historische Entwicklung der heutigen Staatsverfassung des Teutschen Reiches* (3 vols., 2nd edn., Göttingen, 1788). There is an English translation by Josiah Dornford under the title *An historical Development of the present political constitution of the Germanic empire* (3 vols., London, 1790).

customary "coronation presents" and collecting regular "protective dues" from the Jews *(Judenschutzgeld)*. A host of other powers and revenues had been whittled away over the centuries by successive "capitulations" imposed by the electors upon newly chosen princes; while the prescribed coronation oath pledged the emperor to protect all the customary rights of all the *Stände*. An emperor bent upon breathing life into the imperial office must begin with perjury and end with civil war. It must be said, however, that the actual influence of the emperor was greater than this analysis of his powers would suggest. He could rely upon the formidable *Hausmacht* possessed by the head of the House of Habsburg; the majority of the small *Stände* knew that their survival was closely linked to the imperial office; as the leading Catholic prince he was the natural head of the Catholic party throughout Germany; and he was surrounded by all the pomp and circumstance of the most venerable secular office in Europe.[2]

The *Reichstag*, sitting at Regensburg, was practically incapable of legislation: it was a permanent congress of ambassadors strictly bound by instructions, not an elected parliamentary body performing normal legislative functions. For the sake of economy it was customary for several states (even of variegated size and interest) to pool resources and appoint a single ambassador—a practice which sometimes led to the ridiculous situation of an ambassador contradicting himself in the course of a single debate as he followed the different instructions of his various employer governments. Though Germany contained some 159 states with the right to representation, there were rarely more than 25 ambassadors active in Regensburg. The *Reichstag* was divided into three houses *(Curiae)* composed respectively of the representatives of 8 electors, 100 princes (of whom 63 were secular, 37 spiritual), and 51 cities. Representation in the princely chamber did not follow the principle of "one state, one vote"; those states which had annexed territories possessing a vote annexed the vote along with the territory. Thus Prussia possessed eight and Hannover six votes. Since both the king of Prussia and the king of England (the ruler of Hannover) were also electors, they possessed a powerful voice not only in their own electoral chamber but also in that of the ordinary

---

[2] It is a strange fact that some Radical contemporary authors thought that the imperial office was still too powerful. See the much discussed anonymous pamphlet, *Warum soll Deutschland einen Kayser Haben?* (n.p., 1787), which argued that Germany would be better off if the imperial office were abolished altogether. Among several replies the most notable was the vigorous pamphlet by Count Julius von Soden, *Teutschland muss einen Kaiser haben* (n.p., 1788), one of the best defenses of the imperial constitution and as such frequently cited below.

princes. The only thing to be said for this complicated system was that it faithfully mirrored the cumbersome political structure of eighteenth-century Germany.

The conduct of business at the *Reichstag* was proverbial for endless delays caused by procedural debates and adjournments to allow delegates to receive new instructions from their governments. The agenda dealt primarily with disputes between princes or between princes and their own *Landstände*; many of these were judicial in nature since the *Reichstag* acted as an appellate court for the two imperial courts (to be discussed below). Religious questions could only be settled by agreement between the *corpus catholicum* and *corpus evangelicum* (American readers will be reminded of Calhoun's doctrine of the concurrent majority): when Catholics and Protestants could not agree, the result might be total paralysis of the *Reichstag,* as happened for five years (1780-85) on account of a ridiculous dispute as to whether certain Westphalian counts (possessing a single vote jointly) should be represented by a Catholic or a Protestant delegate. The inadequacy of the *Reichstag* as a national parliament was demonstrated most glaringly by the perennial controversy on whether *Stände* were legally or morally obligated to pay taxes which they had opposed in the *Reichstag* before being outvoted. Legislation had become practically a lost art at Regensburg. This had not always been the case: the experience of the sixteenth century, with its code of criminal law (the *Carolina* of 1532), its religious peace (1555), its great coinage reform (*Reichsmünzordnung* of 1559), and its various police codes (*Reichspolizeiordnungen*) of 1530, 1548, and 1577, showed that the *Reichstag* could achieve legislative results provided the *Stände* put their hearts into the effort. They certainly failed to do this in the eighteenth century, which saw only two major pieces of national legislation, the *Zunftordnungen* of 1731 and 1772 (necessitated by the fact that guild abuses were national rather than local in scope). Only a determined optimist could expect any revival of legislative activity from the Regensburg *Reichstag*, not to speak of its becoming an instrument for reforming the entire structure of the empire (barring coercion from the outside, as was to happen in 1803).[3]

The judicial institutions of the empire were quite incapable of enforcing general rules of justice. There were two Imperial High Courts with no clear-cut division in jurisdiction—the *Reichskammergericht* in

[3] The working of the *Reichstag* machinery is explained in an excellent monograph, Johannes Schick, *Der Reichstag zu Regensburg im Zeitalter des Baseler Friedens 1792-95* (Bonn, 1931), Ch. 1.

Wetzlar and the *Reichshofrath* in Vienna. The former consisted theoretically (since 1719) of twenty-five judges elected by the various *Kreise,* though salaries paid out of the so-called *Kammerzieler* were available for only seventeen. The delays of imperial justice were proverbial, the court having a backlog (around 1770) of some 60,000 cases which continued to grow from year to year. The only way to bring a case to trial was by what was quaintly called the "solicitation" of one of the parties—a procedure involving presents for court officials which were practically indistinguishable from bribes. Emperor Joseph II appointed a commission to undertake a "visitation" of the court in the 1770's. This resulted in an increase in the number of judges and the dismissal of some corrupt officials, but the court remained basically unreformed. Yet many Conservatives denounced the emperor's reform effort as a "revolutionary innovation" and feared the remedy far more than the disease.[4]

The *Reichshofrath* had the reputation of being less corrupt and somewhat more speedy than the *Kammergericht,* while being on the other hand suspect of yielding too easily to imperial pressure and being overstaffed with Catholic judges (although Joseph increased the number of Protestant *Hofräthe*). Both courts suffered from the absence of any effective executive which could be relied upon to enforce their judgments; also from the right of any defeated party to appeal to the *Reichstag* on the plea that the disputed matter was one of "general interest." One must also remember that most major states possessed the privilege *non appellando,* i.e., cases could not be appealed beyond their own territorial courts. The result was that both the *Kammergericht* and the *Reichshofrath* were preoccupied with unimportant cases usually involving petty princes. On this level they performed a valuable function in checking tyranny; the far-more-important tyranny of major states unfortunately knew no legal remedy.[5]

The ineffectiveness of imperial institutions was revealed most clearly by the condition of the imperial army (*Reichsarmee*), a body obviously incapable of defending the empire against external foes. Nonexistent in time of peace, it was mobilized in time of war upon the basis of the *Kreis* organization defined in 1521 and last revised in 1681. Each *Kreis,* indeed nearly each prince in each *Kreis,* equipped,

[4] There is no monograph on the *Reichskammergericht* in the eighteenth century. Its earlier history is covered exhaustively in R. Smend, *Das Reichskammergericht* (Vol. I, Weimar, 1911. No more appeared).

[5] The definitive monograph on the *Reichshofrat* is O. von Gschliesser, *Der Reichshofrat. Bedeutung und Verfassung, Schicksal und Besetzung einer obersten Reichsbehörde von 1559 bis 1806* (Vienna, 1942).

paid, and *supplied* its own contingents separately—a system which inevitably created a chaotic supply situation. The contingents from major states, consisting of regular army units earmarked for imperial service, had a well-justified contempt for the miscellaneous rabble brought together by the lesser states of the empire. Officers were appointed by particular *Stände* to particular posts, a practice which precluded either promotion or the development of an *esprit de corps;* appointment to the higher posts was governed by confessional parity rather than military competence. The officers had an interest in furloughing their men from the army during any slack campaigning season, since officers were paid flat sums for feeding their units, which gave officers a vested interest in commanding men not regularly under arms. The results of this system were revealed in the Seven Years' War, when the imperial army—fighting against Frederick the Great, who had been placed under the ban of the empire—proved no match for the Prussian grenadiers.[6]

It will be clear at this point that to describe the constitution of the Holy Roman Empire is the same thing as to criticize it, for each of the institutions mentioned—emperor, *Reichstag, Kammergericht, Reichshofrath, Reichsarmee*—was a byword for inadequacy. Their interaction with one another led to total paralysis, a condition also promoted by other factors still to be mentioned. While the empire was collectively weak, it included several strong states among its component members, most notably Austria and Prussia. These two powers could not be expected to subordinate their individual interests to the general welfare of the empire as a whole. The same was true of several medium states—Bavaria and Württemberg, for example—notable for a high degree of political self-consciousness. Genuine loyalty to the empire existed only among its "rotten" and anachronistic members: petty states, ecclesiastical states, Free Cities, and the Imperial Knighthood, all entities doomed to extinction if the imperial framework should ever collapse. These "rotten" members abounded in South and West Germany, and for this reason imperial sentiment was largely a *regional* phenomenon. All the larger states were instinctively anti-imperial, since the empire still put some small measure of restraint upon their tenaciously cherished "sovereignty." These large and medium states turned the Regensburg *Reichstag* into an organ of

---

[6] The classic description of the imperial army is M. Jähns, "Zur Geschichte der Kriegsverfassung des Deutschen Reiches," *Preussische Jahrbücher,* xxxix (1877), 133ff.

permanent opposition against Emperor Joseph when the latter appeared to threaten the "liberties of Germany."

In this endeavor they could count upon the by-no-means disinterested support of France, long desirous of perpetuating those German divisions which were the prerequisite for French hegemony upon the Continent. The prevalent *Kleinstaaterei* had (as we shall see below) considerable advantages; but many of its immediate results were prima facie undesirable. There was an obvious waste of man power and resources in the multiplication of courts with their court officers, lackeys, mistresses, et cetera; while rational administration was quite impossible in a country divided into hundreds of units separated by arbitrary boundaries. These boundaries were an obvious handicap to economic development, as they limited markets and impeded the free flow of the factors of production. The result was comparative poverty and a strong tide of emigration to America and the Balkans, especially from the petty territorial units of the Southwest. The existence of numerous petty pseudo states, headed by princes who claimed to rule by the grace of God, did more than economic damage to the German nation; it led in fact to a general distortion of national values. Too many Germans, as they lived under the direct shadow of petty courts, became affected by such court foibles as the hunting for titles and decorations and such court vices as flattery and servility. These conditions were quite incompatible with the development of public spirit and civic virtues; while the servility owed to petty princes at local courts led to an unbelievably parochial outlook upon life.[7]

This parochialism was only very partially corrected by a continued loyalty toward the Holy Roman Empire as a whole. We have already examined the weakness of the imperial constitution in practice; it remains to note the most fundamental source of this weakness—the virtual nonexistence of German national feeling on a political plane. Germans were proud to belong to a *Kulturnation* with a common language, literature, and history; but only a few believed in the existence of a German *Staatsnation,* or identified it with the people living within the boundaries of the Holy Roman Empire. Princes knew no political loyalty higher than their dynasties; even the emperors usually placed the claims of their Habsburg territories before the obligations of the Imperial Crown. Subjects owed their primary allegiance to their

[7] These faults of *Kleinstaaterei* are attacked in an anonymous article, "Betrachtungen über den Einfluss der deutschen Reichsverfassung auf das Nationalglück der Deutschen in Bezug auf zwei Aufsätze von Mirabeau und Wieland," *Berliner Monatsschrift,* xix (1792), 268-95. Largely reprinted by W. Wenck, *Deutschland,* ii, 237-48.

princes rather than the emperor, to their immediate "country" like Bavaria or Württemberg rather than Germany as a whole; *Staatspatriotismus* was a far stronger force than *Reichspatriotismus*. It may be added that the intellectuals of Germany were imperial patriots only in rare cases. They were usually tied to the interests of some ruling prince, hence unable and unwilling to champion the general interests of Germany; or else they were ostentatiously unpolitical in their outlook, or proud of their supranational cosmopolitanism. Only a few writers, most notably the Hessian publicist C. F. Moser, can be described as an exception to this rule.[8]

THE CONTROVERSY ABOUT THE EMPIRE

Carl Friedrich von Moser[9] called for a revival of somnambulent imperial institutions in a much discussed pamphlet, *Concerning the German National Spirit*,[10] in 1765. While deploring in earnest language

---

[8] On the problem of national feeling in the eighteenth century and its connection with *Reichsbewusstsein* see F. Meinecke, *Weltbürgertum und Nationalstaat* (most recent edn. ed. Hans Herzfeld, Berlin, 1963); P. Joachimsen, *Vom deutschen Volk zum deutschen Staat. Eine Geschichte des deutschen Nationalbewusstseins* (n.e., J. Leuschner, Göttingen, 1956); Gerhard Masur, "Deutsches Reich und deutsche Nation im 18. Jahrhundert," *Preussische Jahrbücher*, CCXXIX (1932); Wilhelm Mommsen, "Zur Bedeutung des Reichsgedankens," *HZ*, CLXXIV (1952); and, above all, two articles by E. R. Huber, "Reich, Volk und Staat in der Reichsrechtswissenschaft des 17. und 18. Jahrhunderts," *Zeitschrift für die gesamte Staatswissenschaft*, CII (1942), and E. R. Huber, "Der preussische Staatspatriotismus im Zeitalter Friedrichs des Grossen," ibid., CIII (1943).

[9] Carl Friedrich von Moser (1723-98), the famous son of the still more famous political writer Johann Jacob Moser, lived in Frankfurt before becoming chief minister of the Duke of Hessen-Darmstadt in 1770. His abrupt dismissal in 1780 led to a celebrated lawsuit which was finally ended through a compromise settlement a decade later. Moser combined practical experience with literary skill in a manner rare in eighteenth-century Germany. His name will reappear frequently in the course of this chapter, notably as a champion of "enlightened absolutism" and critic of the ecclesiastical states. On C. F. von Moser see Heidenheimer in *ADB*, XXII (1885), 764-83, and H. H. Kaufmann, *F. C. von Moser als Politiker und Publizist* (Darmstadt, 1931).

[10] Anonymous [C. F. von Moser], *Von dem deutschen national-Geist* (Frankfurt/Main, 1765). This pamphlet provoked much controversy, which is described in B. Renner, *Die nationalen Einigungsbestrebungen Fr. C. von Mosers 1765-67* (Königsberg, 1919), and in the especially valuable recent work of Wolfgang Zorn, "Reichs- und Freiheitsgedanken in der deutschen Publizistik des ausgehenden 18. Jahrhunderts," *Darstellungen und Quellen zur Geschichte der deutschen Einheitsbewegung im 19. und 20. Jahrhundert* (ed. Paul Wentzcke, Heidelberg, 1959), II, 20-34. The most important publications provoked by Moser's essay were Johann Jacob Bülau, *Noch etwas zum deutschen Nationalgeist* (Frankfurt and Leipzig, 1767), written by a *Stadtschreiber* in Zerbst who criticized Moser for identifying *Nationalgeist* with the subordination of the *Stände* to the Emperor; and Friedrich Carl Casimir von Creutz, *Neue politische Kleinigkeiten II. An-*

the widespread ignorance of, and indifference to, the venerable German constitution, he traced these evils to the following causes: the miserable instruction in public law provided at the universities by professors tied to a particular territorial state; confessional squabbles which prevented consciousness of a common fatherland; and the development of territorial states with absolute princes demanding exclusive loyalties. He suggested essentially simple remedies for all these causes: the teaching of public law must be reformed through the appointment of professors filled with a spirit of national patriotism; young men must be encouraged to travel through all parts of Germany to wear off their confessional prejudice and political parochialism; while leading administrators of various states should arrange for regular meetings to draw up common political plans in a common spirit of German patriotism, and remain in correspondence between meetings. Moser pointed to the example of Switzerland, where loyalty to the thirteen individual cantons did not preclude loyalty to the *Eidgenossenschaft* as a whole. These well-meant suggestions certainly fell far short of any realistic program for breathing life into the paralyzed imperial structure.[11]

The attempt made by Emperor Joseph II to reinvigorate the German constitution through political action went far beyond Moser's purely literary proposal. We have already mentioned that his efforts at reforming the *Reichskammergericht* and the *Reichshofrath* yielded little practical success, while he considered the *Reichstag* and the *Reichsarmee* as beyond the possibilty of effective reform. He set his mind instead upon the aggrandizement of Austria in Germany—a project which would indirectly augment the influence of the emperor even if unaccompanied by formal changes in the imperial constitution. His specific program looked to the acquisition of Bavaria in exchange for the Belgian provinces of the House of Habsburg, and he won the approval of Karl Theodor, the elector who acceded to the Bavarian throne in 1777, for this plan. Karl Theodor, a native of the Palatinate without Bavarian roots, was attracted by the lure of a Belgian crown; Joseph, by the consolidation of his territories as he exchanged a far-

---

merkungen über die Blätter eines Ungenannten vom deutschen National-Geiste (n.p., 1767), written by a Hessen-Homburg *Staatsrat* who protested against the application of the concept of the nation to the structure of the existing *Reich*.

[11] Two years later Moser made a concrete proposal for the creation of a German House of Commons, elected by the people directly to give Germany a vigorous national parliament; the existing Regensburg *Reichstag* should simultaneously become a House of Lords. See Moser's *Patriotische Briefe* (n.p., 1767), pp. 62ff. No one took this utopian proposal seriously.

away and indefensible territory for one adjoining his central realm. The project was stopped by Frederick the Great in the so-called Potato War of 1778; its revival in 1785 led Prussia to initiate the negotiation of the famous *Fürstenbund*. This league had the strictly Conservative aim—in Frederick's own words—of "protecting the rights and liberties of German princes, to guarantee the possessions of each and to prevent an enterprising and powerhungry Emperor from overthrowing the entire German constitution piece by piece." To this end it specifically pledged resistance to territorial exchanges or imperial interference with either the *Reichstag* or the imperial courts, and drew up plans for a stringent electoral capitulation which would curtail the already minimal imperial power still farther after the next election.[12]

The *Fürstenbund* overcame many long-standing German antagonisms by including powers large and small (for example, Prussia and Weimar), Protestant and Catholic (though predominantly North German and Protestant in character, it was joined by the archbishop of Mainz, who by tradition headed the *corpus catholicorum*). Its heterogeneous membership inevitably meant that the participants had somewhat divergent aims in mind. Some of the smaller states, most notably Weimar, hoped to make the league an instrument for reforming the imperial constitution, and it is possible to interpret the *Fürstenbund* as a forerunner (though of course not a deliberate one) of the Prussian unification of non-Austrian Germany in 1866.[13] Frederick the Great for one had no such intention; he viewed the league as a simple

---

[12] The standard work on the *Fürstenbund* is still Leopold von Ranke, *Die deutschen Mächte und der Fürstenbund. Deutsche Geschichte von 1780-90* (2 vols., Leipzig, 1871-72), marvelously objective though written at the height of the Bismarckian struggle for unification. The decline of the *Fürstenbund* is definitively analyzed by Wilhelm Lüdtke, "Der Kampf zwischen Österreich und Preussen um die Vorherrschaft im 'Reiche' und die Auflösung des Fürstenbundes (1789-1791)," *MIÖG*, xlv (1931), 70-153. The most succinct contemporary statement of the purposes of the *Fürstenbund* is the official Prussian *Erklärung der Ursachen welche Se. Königl. Majestät von Preussen bewogen haben, Ihren hohen Mitständen des Teutschen Reichs eine Assoziation zu Erhaltung des Reichs-Systems anzutragen und mit einigen derselben zu schliessen* (Berlin, August 1785), 10 pp. It provoked the semiofficial Austrian *Prüfung der Ursachen einer Assoziazion zu Erhaltung des Reichssistems, welche in der Erklärung Seiner Königl. Majestät von Preussen an Derohohe Reichsmitstände und andere Europäische Höfe sind vorgelegt worden* (n.p. [Vienna?], 1785), 32 pp. The two pamphlets are conveniently bound together in a copy of the Göttingen University Library which I have used. A portion of the *Publizistik* provoked by the *Fürstenbund* crisis is surveyed by Zorn, op.cit., pp. 49-66.

[13] This is brought out recently in the important publication edited, with an excellent introduction, by Hans Tümmler, *Politischer Briefwechsel des Herzogs und Grossherzogs Carl August* (2 vols., 2nd edn., Stuttgart, 1954).

dictate of Prussian *Staatsräson* requiring that Austria be prohibited aggrandizement, though he found it convenient to cover Prussia's power interests with the transparent clothing of Conservative and patriotic phrases about the "venerable German constitution." There was irony in the fact that Frederick, whose entire career had been devoted to making Prussia a Great Power in defiance of the imperial constitution, should end his life posing as the loyal defender of that very constitution.

The *Fürstenbund* provoked much political pamphleteering dealing with such subjects as territorial exchanges, the intentions of Joseph, and the legitimacy of organized opposition to the emperor.[14] The apologists for the *Fürstenbund* argued that Joseph was a potential tyrant bent upon overthrowing the traditional "liberties of Germany"; they viewed the plan to absorb Bavaria as but the first step in a long-range program of aggrandizement where the appetite must grow with the eating. Once Bavaria was digested, Joseph would inevitably seek to absorb the numerous small principalities which lay between Bavaria and the Habsburg part of the Black Forest *(Vorderösterreich)*. This dangerous prospect alarmed numerous Free Cities, ecclesiastical states, and petty princes and tended to break their customary alliance with the emperor—clear proof that Joseph had departed from all imperial traditions in becoming the disturber rather than guardian of the German *status quo*.

The most interesting aspect of the *Fürstenbund* controversy is that it stimulated several explicitly Conservative defenses of the Holy Roman Empire from both a national and a cosmopolitan point of view. Christian Dohm, a Prussian diplomat whom we have already encountered as the champion of the emancipation of the Jews, provided an eloquent defense of the existing imperial structure in his *Ueber den deutschen Fürstenbund*. He argued that Joseph's designs were incompatible with either the German equilibrium or the equilibrium of the European state system, two equilibria whose value he assumed to be axiomatic. Dohm was astonishingly frank in putting his point in purely military terms. Bavaria had served for over a hundred years as a French military outpost on the borders of Austria, indeed an inva-

---

[14] An important defense of Joseph's policy is Otto Freiherr von Gemmingen, *Ueber die königlich Preussische Assoziation zur Erhaltung des Reichssystems* (Germanien, 1785). It was reprinted, with a hostile commentary, in Anonymous, *Freymüthige Anmerkungen zur Schrift des Freyherrn Otto von Gemmingen über die Königl. Preussische Assoziation zur Erhaltung des Reichssystems* (Teutschland, 1785), and by Christian Dohm in the pamphlet mentioned in the next footnote.

sion gate leading to Vienna; while the Habsburg possessions in Belgium had been a virtually indefensible Austrian strategic liability on the borders of France. The proposed exchange would, therefore, greatly improve Austria's military position in any future war against France to the detriment of the European equilibrium. This argument was indicative of the prenational, cosmopolitan, European outlook of many German writers of the late eighteenth century. In Dohm's case it obviously provided a cover for the interests of Prussian *Staatsräson;* but it is significant, nonetheless, that this kind of cover appeared appropriate to an experienced publicist who aimed to convince a broad reading public of the value of the *Fürstenbund.*

Dohm's view of the interdependence of the German and the European equilibrium is worth quoting in his own words because it became the favorite Conservative argument on behalf of the imperial *status quo* until the dissolution of the empire in 1806.

> Some think that "German freedom and equilibrium" are empty sounds! exactly as there are some who declare that the "equilibrium of Europe" is a political chimera whenever it is challenged. . . . It is a fact, however, that the continued existence of the Imperial constitution depends upon the preservation of the "German liberties" which protect everyone in his rights as defined by law and tradition; exactly as the European international system requires that everyone be left undisturbed in the possession of his lawfully acquired rights, and that all treaties be scrupulously observed. How can this be achieved? Knowledge of human nature has led to the wise precaution that no state be permitted to enlarge its power to such an extent that the freedom of others becomes exclusively dependent upon its own moderation. . . . One can count upon the sacrosanctity of treaties only when all the contracting parties know that they cannot break them with impunity. It is clear . . . that an equal respect for justice and equity can be expected only if the distribution of power is not too unequal, and that forces must be joined in common against any power which so far exceeds others in strength that its respect for justice becomes dependent upon its own will.

Why should this maxim of the general European state system not apply to the specific German state system as well? Are the fundamental laws which bind Germany together more firmly established than the treaties which bind together the states of Europe? Does membership in the Empire *(Reichsstandschaft)* strengthen the sense for justice and equity and weaken the passion for ambition and aggrandizement more effectively than membership of the European equilibrium?[15]

Dohm clearly did not think so: he had many reasons for distrusting the power and intentions of the Austrian emperor, and he viewed the *Fürstenbund* against Joseph II as analogous to the international alliances which had humbled the pride of Louis XIV a century before.[16]

A similar argument was developed by Nicolaus Vogt, professor of history at Mainz University,[17] in his celebrated magnum opus, *Concerning the European Republic*,[18] published in 1787 when the *Fürstenbund* crisis was still fresh in the mind of the German reading public. He set himself to answer the specific question, "Whether it will be best for our German Empire to maintain its present constitution, or whether it should develop into a strong monarchy."[19] Vogt saw some obvious advantages in the extension of the monarchical authority planned by Joseph II. It would stimulate commerce and industry; end the collisions and jealousies now prevailing between the various German *Stände*; enhance the role of Germany in the councils of Europe; eliminate the extravagance and tyranny of Germany's many petty despots; and lead to the creation of an effective imperial army. These were prima facie great advantages; Vogt insisted, however, that they must not be overrated and must be balanced against other considerations which made it essential to preserve the empire substantially in its present form.

A close examination of these advantages removes most of their glitter in the eyes of a patriot, and almost all in the eyes of a cosmopolitan. The German patriot says: Trade from one province to another within a single monarchy frequently suffers from as many restrictions as trade between the component states of the present

---

[15] Christian Dohm, *Über den deutschen Fürstenbund* (Berlin, 1785), a specific reply to Gemmingen's pamphlet mentioned in the previous footnote.

[16] Dohm, op.cit., pp. 28-30.

[17] Vogt (1756-1836) has a niche in history as the close collaborator of Archbishop Dalberg in the period of the Confederation of the Rhine, as the collector of Rhenish fairy tales (*Rheinische Geschichten und Sagen*, 4 vols., 1817-36), and as the teacher of Prince Metternich, at whose Johannisberg estate he lies buried. Metternich wrote upon his gravestone, "Dem treuen Verfechter des alten Rechts, dem eifrigen Beförderer der heimatlichen Geschichte widmet diesen Grabstein sein dankbarer Freund und Schüler C.W.L. Fürst von Metternich." See the article by Bockenheimer in *ADB*, XL (1896), 189-91, and the dissertation by Magdalene Herrmann, *Niklas Vogt. Ein Historiker der Mainzer Universität* (Giessen, 1917).

[18] Nicolaus Vogt, *Ueber die europäische Republik* (5 vols., Frankfurt, 1787-92).

[19] Ibid., I, 90.

empire. A prince or a republic within our empire will usually protect local interests better than a monarch and his centralized ministry ruling from afar. The extravagance and tyranny of our princes are perhaps not as oppressive as would be the despotism of appointed provincial governors. A hereditary prince certainly has more reason to spare his country than a governor whose interest can disappear at any time through death or removal. . . . Let us, however, assume for a moment the invalidity of all these arguments, and admit that the present constitution is harmful in many respects —it still does not follow that our constitution ought to be replaced by an absolute monarchy. The evils of such a monarchy would be at least as great as the evils from which we now suffer, while its introduction would in addition lead inevitably to frightful convulsions. . . .

Any doubt about the proper answer to our initial question [which is preferable, the present empire or a centralized monarchy?] is removed when one looks at the question from a cosmopolitan point of view. . . . It is certain that a single monarch, if he possessed the power to bring all Germany under his sceptre, would be sufficiently powerful to establish a universal monarchy. . . . Simple reflection and historical experience tell us to expect little from powerful monarchies in the way of enlightenment and freedom. It is a well-known fact about human nature that the powerful do not easily tolerate contradiction . . . while historical experience shows that all big monarchies easily degenerate into despotism. . . . [A long series of historical examples follows.]

The same point can be demonstrated negatively by looking at the recent history of freedom and *Aufklärung*. Both have flourished best in Germany or other free states (such as Holland, England and Switzerland). These countries have become the natural refuge for the champions of freedom persecuted in monarchical lands. Germany is especially well suited by her constitution to offer shelter to the oppressed, and to become the center of vigorous thought on public affairs (*Publizität*). Freedom is protected in Germany by the multiplicity of small states, with escape to a neighboring state being always easy; by the jealousy and hostility which most princes feel toward one another (they rather like to see their rivals denigrated *connivendo* in public journals); by the mutual zeal of all small states to be on the same cultural level as their neighbors; finally by the focusing together of all of the quarrels of Europe in this small microcosm: all these factors, and many others which

250

might still be mentioned, make the German constitution, crippled as she may appear, venerable in the eyes of a far-sighted cosmopolitan.[20]

Most of the arguments advanced by the defenders of the imperial constitution are mentioned by Nicolaus Vogt in this long quotation. It may prove useful to restate them in a systematic manner since they provide the first comprehensive defense of the political *status quo* in the history of German Conservatism. The obvious inadequacy of the empire placed its defenders in an intrinsically difficult position, for they were forced to admit that imperial institutions were far from satisfactory. They argued, therefore, that these conditions were in fact somewhat more satisfactory than was generally thought, that changes were unlikely to bring substantial improvements, and that changes— even assuming that they were attainable—would inevitably be accompanied by undesirable political convulsions.

Much stress was laid upon the advantages of the existing pattern of *Kleinstaaterei*. It allowed patriarchal government in which princes were close to the people and easily accessible to complaints. "In most territories of Germany a subject only has *to wish* to speak to the prince in order to be able to do so." Escape from an unusually tyrannical prince was always possible over a nearby frontier; princes were forced to watch over their reputation lest they lose out to their neighbors. There was widespread freedom of political discussion, if not in every territory yet in Germany as a whole. There was no effective system of literary censorship, and the power for good which was wielded by critical journals like Schlözer's *Staatsanzeigen* was immense. The princes had, in short, every incentive to provide good government: patriarchal ties to a small area known intimately since childhood; fear of emigration of discontented subjects; and vigorous public criticism. To these factors must be added the jurisdiction of the two imperial courts to which appeal was possible in cases of flagrant tyranny.[21]

The latter fact showed that imperial institutions were certainly better than their reputation. However paralyzed in their *working*, they were still valuable by their mere *existence*. The *Reichstag* symbolized the fact that Germans possessed a national unity transcending the

[20] Ibid., I, 96-101.

[21] A systematic statement of the advantages of *Kleinstaaterei* is to be found in Wilhelm A. F. Danz, "Deutschland, wie es war, wie es ist und wie es vielleicht werden wird. Eine ungedruckte Vorlesung gehalten am 11. Feb. 1792 am Geburtstage des regierenden Herrn Herzogs Carl zu Württemberg," *Neues Patriotisches Archiv für Deutschland*, II (1794), 150-58. The quotation is from p. 152.

limits of particular states—a national unity which was, moreover, in full accordance with the principles of "German freedom." Count Julius von Soden, an able defender of the imperial constitution writing in 1788, put this point in the following words:

> I find a shield of German freedom and an unshakeable foundation of our wise constitution in the mere fact that there exists an assembly of the representatives of the entire nation. This assembly is an ever present symbol of our constitutional system, even though the matters discussed may be few and unimportant and political collisions paralyze the constructive forces latent in the assembly.[22]

Germany's complicated constitution had the merit of faithfully mirroring the existing diversity of the German people in the vast area which they inhabited. The strong articulation of local life had predestined Germany to become an "aristocratic republic." Political decentralization led to a marvelous multiplication of local centers of culture and personal opportunity. The confessional pluralism since the Reformation had strengthened particularism and made any kind of ecclesiastical unity unthinkable. The comparative absence of political nationalism made a loose imperial structure the best possible Central European polity. Count Soden put this point with his customary precision:

> The geographical variety to be found within the German Empire, the original diversity of the peoples who inhabit it, and its vast geographical extent—all these factors have led to a diversity in climate, in manners, in political and economic interests, and in many other factors which militate against the introduction of a system of centralized monarchy.[23]

It was also argued that the excellence—or at least adequacy—of the existing German political structure was attested by the general growth in population, political security, economic prosperity, and spread of *Aufklärung* which characterized the eighteenth century.[24]

Many writers followed Dohm and Vogt in viewing the empire above all as a *European* necessity. Germany's large population and its central location in Europe threatened to give it—if its power were ever consolidated into a centralized monarchy—a hegemonial position which would prove intolerable to neighboring countries. This basic

---

[22] Anonymous, *Teutschland muss einen Kaiser haben* (n.p., 1788), p. 32.
[23] Ibid., pp. 6-7.   [24] Ibid., pp. 21-24.

reason made a centralized German state either a chimera or a nightmare. It must not be thought, however, that Germany's interests were being sacrificed to the interests of Europe as a whole. A decentralized, loosely federated Germany possessed not only the advantages of *Kleinstaaterei* mentioned above; it also avoided the disadvantages inherent in any centralized monarchy per se. These disadvantages included the propensity to wage aggressive war and to suppress domestic liberty, two evils known in individual states within the empire but not in the Holy Roman Empire as a whole. That empire was, on the contrary, an expression of the deeply rooted German sense for liberty.[25]

A final argument in defense of the existing imperial structure was that there was no satisfactory alternative. The various states and institutions of Germany were so interlocked in an intricate pattern that the removal of individual pillars must bring the entire structure tumbling down. The collapse of the present empire would invite civil war and foreign intervention. There would be no way of preventing the annexation of weak states by the strong and the intensification of the already disastrous dualism between Austria and Prussia. Was it not far better to "make do" with the existing constitution, inadequate though it was, rather than work for its overthrow and thereby provoke a deluge leading to results no man could foretell?[26]

Absolutism and Its Critics

THE POSITION OF PRINCELY ABSOLUTISM[27]

Princely absolutism was the prevalent form of government within the Holy Roman Empire, whether one thinks of large states (e.g., Prussia),

[25] The classic statement of this point of view is Johannes Müller, *Darstellung des Fürstenbundes* (1787), esp. Bk. III, "Vom Reich der Teutschen." Reprinted as Vol. IX of Johannes von Müller, *Sämmtliche Werke* (ed. Johann Georg von Müller, Tübingen, 1811). The early history of the idea that Germany had a distinctive libertarian heritage which made her especially immune to absolutism has been analyzed by Erwin Hoelzle in a valuable monograph, *Die Idee einer altgermanischen Freiheit vor Montesquieu. Fragmente aus der Geschichte politischer Freiheitsbestrebungen in Deutschland, England und Frankreich vom 16. bis 18. Jahrhundert* (Munich and Berlin, 1925).

[26] This theme is elaborated by both Vogt and Dohm.

[27] The discussion of absolutism has generally centered upon the genesis and meaning of "enlightened absolutism." Its genesis is explored by Peter Klassen in *Die Grundlagen des aufgeklärten Absolutismus* (Jena, 1933), a work of miscellaneous but not very relevant erudition; its position in modern history by R. Koser, "Die Epochen der absoluten Monarchie in der neueren Geschichte," *HZ*, LXI (1889), 246-88, and by F. Hartung, "Die Epochen der absoluten Monarchie in der neueren Geschichte," *HZ*, CXLV (1932), 46-52. See also the same author's

medium states (e.g., Bavaria), or small principalities (e.g., Weimar). The fact of absolutism may be defined by the absence (or impotence) of the historic *Stände* bodies, in other words by the elimination of the constitutional dualism between prince and *Stände* which had characterized earlier German government. Dualism survived in only a very few "exceptional" states such as Württemberg or Mecklenburg. The rise of absolutism had been the central fact in German constitutional history since the Reformation. Many factors were responsible for, or at least connected with, this development. The Reformation strengthened the state by giving it control over the Church in Protestant and Catholic states alike, and confirmed the traditional Christian duty of obedience to "constituted authority." The rise of standing armies provided princes with a reliable instrument of coercion against refractory subjects (including aristocrats organized in *Stände* bodies). Mercantilistic policies transcended the parochialism of the urban guild economy and provided ever-increasing revenues; trained bureaucrats replaced amateur administrators in collecting those revenues and administering ever-increasing state activities. It may be added that a stream of new laws overrode much local custom and brought the ordinary citizen increasingly into direct contact with the government. All these factors may be viewed as part cause and part effect of the rise of monarchical absolutism in Germany as well as other countries of Europe. By the middle of the eighteenth century the government (as headed by the prince) possessed a concentration of institutionalized power unknown since the time of the Roman emperors in the first Christian centuries. The achievements of absolutism are too well known to require detailed treatment here. Suffice it to say that they included the development of administrative centralization, trained bureaucracies, religious toleration, mercantilistic prosperity, standing armies, rational justice, and the suppression of at least some class privileges.

The establishment of absolutism originally followed the dictates of *Staatsräson,* but it was increasingly justified by the principles of the *Aufklärung.* Both called for religious toleration, the breakdown of aristocratic privilege, and the development of rational administration. The marriage of absolutism and *Aufklärung* led to the "enlightened

---

"Der Aufgeklärte Absolutismus," *HZ,* CLXXX (1955), 15-42. Wilhelm Mommsen, "Zur Beurteilung des Absolutismus," *HZ,* CLVIII (1938), 52-76, provides a very favorable verdict. An excellent recent study is E. Walder, *Zwei Studien über den aufgeklärten Absolutismus [Schweizer Beiträge zur allgemeinen Geschichte,* XV (1957)].

despotism" of figures like Frederick the Great, Joseph II, and Karl Friedrich of Baden. This marriage proved (as we have seen above) the single most important force in the active promotion of *Aufklärung;* yet it was a marriage more of convenience than mutual love. Many princes adopted "enlightened" policies not for the humanitarian motives approved by "enlightened men," but rather in pursuit of Great Power ambitions abhorred by the latter. Such princes were ready to abandon the program of the *Aufklärung* the moment it came into conflict with power considerations. A case in point is Frederick's attitude toward the aristocracy, a body he considered indispensable as a reservoir for his officer corps: he confirmed its privileged access to state positions and willingly tolerated serfdom (the bête noire of all "enlightened men") because he viewed a servile peasantry essential for the maintenance of an officer-producing Junker class. The demand of the *Aufklärer* for civic equality left him completely cold when it conflicted with the interests of the Prussian states as he understood them.

There was, on the other hand, no absolute commitment to monarchical absolutism on the part of the champions of *Aufklärung.* Its advocates valued strong monarchy insofar—and *only* insofar—as it promoted "enlightened policies" of religious toleration, legal equality, and rational administration; they valued it not for itself but for what it could do for them. They increasingly saw some form of self-government—patterned upon the example of republican antiquity or such modern communities as England, Holland, and Switzerland—as a desirable alternative to monarchical absolutism, and argued that the community itself was a better judge of its own true interests than even an "enlightened" monarch; for the latter could never completely disregard the claims of his princely position, though they were founded on nothing more rational than the accident of biological descent. The political outlook of the *Aufklärer* could easily change from support of "enlightened" monarchy to calling for the introduction of republican self-government. Those who criticized monarchy in the name of self-government sometimes evoked the reminiscence of the old historic *Stände;* this could bring them into an *ad hoc* alliance with the Reactionary critics of monarchical absolutism whose ideal remained the preabsolutist *Ständestaat.* (It must be remembered that self-government is not necessarily a democratic ideal, for self-governing institutions have often been aristocratic or plutocratic in character.) It will prove useful to survey the criticism directed against monarchical absolutism from both the Radical Left and the Reactionary

Right before analyzing the defense offered by the champions of monarchy against both kinds of criticism.

CONTROVERSIES ON PRINCELY ABSOLUTISM

Historians with their propensity to concentrate upon general trends rather than individual events have tended to stress the achievements of absolutism and to ignore the tyrannical caprice with which it was often associated. Contemporaries standing under or near the yoke of a tyrant naturally stressed the immediate tyranny more than the long-range achievements. There were endless complaints in eighteenth-century Germany of the "Sultanism" which prevailed in many territories, especially the petty principalities where rulers were less likely to develop an austere conception of being "servants of the state" than in Great Powers like Austria and Prussia. Local tyranny was usually met by flattery and accommodation, but it also evoked two kinds of critical response: some critics simply castigated individual tyrants in the hope that they might repent and see the error of their ways (as happened, for example, to some extent in the famous case of Karl Eugen of Württemberg in the latter part of his reign);[28] others took the further step of calling for *institutional* restraints upon princely power, whether in the form of the restoration of the old *Ständestaat*, the advance to "constitutional monarchy," or even the establishment of a republic.

The first kind of criticism is one of the major themes of German literature after about 1770. It is usually directed against tyrants in general rather than any particular tyrant, though specific allusions were of course common.[29] Johann Voss (1751-1826), later famous as the translator of Homer, wrote a *Drinking Song for Free Men* in 1774. It castigates a prince for stealing a subject's young bride, sending his men into an unnecessary war, and mercilessly taxing the poor to maintain his frivolous court.[30] Johann A. Leisewitz (1752-1806), later famous as the author of the melodramatic *Julius von Tarent* (1776), attacked the widespread practice of seizing the goods of poor subjects to pay tax arrears in a poem called *The Seizure*. It describes the tearful protests of a miserable couple whose family bed has just been

[28] The fact of the "conversion" is readily admitted even in the bitterly hostile work by A. E. Adams, *Herzog Karl Eugen und seine Zeit* (Stuttgart, 1903).

[29] Numerous other examples from Klopstock, Stolberg, Claudius, Schubart, et cetera are cited by W. Wenck, *Deutschland vor hundert Jahren* (Leipzig, 1887), pp. 11-12.

[30] Cited by Emil Horner, *Politische Literatur. Vol. I. Vor dem Untergang des alten Reichs 1756-1795* (Leipzig, 1930), pp. 56-58.

pawned by the ruthless police officers of the prince; their bitterness is enhanced by the thought that their taxes support an idle and extravagant court.[31]

The best-known criticism directed against princely tyranny can be found in the early dramas of Friedrich Schiller (1750-1805). *Don Carlos* (1787) may serve as an example. The figure of King Philip is the incarnation of everything that Schiller found repulsive in tyrannical absolutism. The Spanish king confuses his private caprice with the public welfare. His absolutism does not prevent him from being dependent upon a selfish entourage composed of flatterers and intriguers. He is pathologically prone to jealousy and suspicion, and becomes precipitate and brutal whenever he believes his position threatened. His view of human nature is one of utter contempt, and this serves as a rationalization for his exercise of absolute power. He suppresses freedom of speech because his pride cannot tolerate contradiction, and gladly cooperates with bigots like the priest Domingo, a treacherous and insinuating intriguer, and the Inquisitor, a man utterly devoid of human feelings, in the brutal repression of religious freedom. Schiller's *Don Carlos* is a powerful indictment of princely absolutism; yet the poet shows his artistry by evoking a measure of sympathy for the king's terrible loneliness and isolated position. The hero of the drama, the marquis of Posa, is full of patronizing pity for those so unfortunate as to be born princes.

What remedy does Schiller advance for the evils of monarchical tyranny? The marquis of Posa is willing to contemplate rebellion as a last resort, but evidently has little confidence in this remedy. He knows that rebellion usually creates as many problems as it solves, and specifically condemns "the ridiculous rage for innovation":

> "Der Neuerung, die nur der Ketten Last
> Die sie nicht ganz zerbrechen kann, vergrössert
> Wird mein Blut nie erhitzen."[32]

His real remedy is limited to the hope that the throne will soon be occupied by an enlightened prince (Don Carlos) advised by an enlightened minister (himself). Such a prince will voluntarily recognize the rights of man and "return to the people," by a simple stroke of the pen, such blessings as freedom of speech and religious toleration. The welfare of mankind is, in Schiller's view, dependent upon the individual qualities of particular princes.

Schiller's political program is notably devoid of any institutional

---

[31] Ibid., pp. 58-59. [32] Schiller, *Don Carlos*, lines 3057-79.

element. He presents no specific plan (either in *Don Carlos* or elsewhere in his work) for perpetuating "good absolutism," even supposing that it can be established in the first place through the individual virtue of an individual prince. There are no details on how good princes can be secured and bad princes avoided. There is no demand for self-government, whether through old-fashioned *Stände* or newly fashioned parliamentary bodies. There is at best a germ of democratic sentiment when Schiller defends human nature against the misanthropic views of King Philip; but his generous view of ordinary human nature does not serve as the basis for any specifically democratic political program. A strong element of elitism can be found in the outlook of Marquis Posa: he clearly believes that the welfare of the people is best served when power is held by enlightened individuals like himself.

Not all critics of absolutism were so politically helpless as Schiller. There were authors with a specific program for educating good princes;[33] there were others who called for specific institutional restraints upon princes through either the codification of the *Rechtsstaat* or the revival of *Stände* life. Both types will be discussed below, but first it is necessary to mention briefly those ultra-Radicals who proposed to abolish the evils of monarchy by abolishing monarchy itself. These republican voices were of course thoroughly unrepresentative of German public opinion as a whole; they made no attempt to translate their theoretical wishes into practical action; and they were obviously not taken seriously by the governments they attacked with extreme language. Their significance must be sought in the fact that they expressed the logical culmination of one strand of political *Aufklärung*.[34]

The sources from which German writers derived republican ideals were variegated, ranging in literature from the works of the ancients (the staple reading of German schoolboys) to the novel *Contrat Social* doctrine of Rousseau, and in practice from the cantons of Switzerland to the American colonies which had successfully defied George III. The American struggle was followed with intense interest by German public opinion (as will be shown below), with republican ideals sometimes arising as a corollary of enthusiasm for the Americans. Thus an (anonymous) German professor published a poem,

[33] A representative example is Christoph Martin Wieland, *Der Goldene Spiegel* (1782). See the excellent analysis by O. Vogt, *Der Goldene Spiegel und Wielands politische Ansichten* (Berlin, 1904).
[34] A good survey of these voices is provided by W. Wenck, op.cit., pp. 9-20.

American Freedom, in the *Berliner Monatsschrift* of April 1783, in which he called upon Europe to imitate America and predicted a future republican sweep over the old Continent:

> Und du, Europa, hebe das Haupt empor.
> Einst glänzt auch dir der Tag, da die Kette bricht,
> Du, Edle, frei wirst; deine Fürsten
> Scheuchst und ein glücklicher Volksstaat grünest.
> Noch immer schreckt die rasende Despotie
> Die, Gottes Rechte lügend, nur Grossen frönt
> Den Erdkreis.
> Doch die eiserne Fessel klirrt
> Und mahnt mich Armen, dass ich ein Deutscher bin.
> Euch seh' ich, holde Szenen schwinden,
> Sinke zurück in den Schacht und weine.[35]

The author was, however, confident that this state of affairs would not last much longer.

The same journal published another article two years later in which a prince was urged to win immortal fame by voluntarily introducing a republican form of government. This was the only way in which he could hope to match the fame of Frederick the Great. It was argued that the prince would not thereby lose any real power, for his grateful former subjects (now advanced to the status of fellow citizens) would certainly elect him president for life.[36]

Some Radicals did not stop at republican demands but went on to advocate outright anarchist ideals. We have already encountered such views in our discussion of the *Illuminati* movement, and need not repeat what was said there. Suffice it to say that the *Aufklärung* carried the germs of extreme Radicalism within it, but that the practical importance of political Radicalism was as yet infinitesimal. It is evident, indeed, that there was an intimate connection between the extreme language employed by Radicals and the objective weakness of Radicalism: men speculated all the more freely when they saw no need (or even possibility) of implementing their ideas; governments

---

[35] Cited in the anthology of E. Horner, op.cit., pp. 87-90. A rough translation is as follows: "You, Europe, raise your head! Your day will also come when you can break your chains and become free. You will expel your princes and establish a happy and flourishing republic. Today, however, raging despotism which belies the law of God and flatters the great, still defiles our Continent. The clanging of iron chains reminds me—poor man that I am—that I am a German. I see the pleasant vistas disappear as I sink back into the pit and weep."

[36] *Berliner Monatsschrift,* I, 1785, 139ff.

tolerated such speculation because it constituted no immediate danger to themselves.

Far more important than the Left-wing critics of absolutism were the critics on the Right, who condemned eighteenth-century absolutism because it violated *Stände* rights (or, worse still, had been consummated upon the ruins of those *Stände* rights) and pursued objectives far different from the traditionally patriarchal objectives of German princes. The conflict between absolutism and *Stände* rights was especially acute in Württemberg, where the ambitious Duke Karl Eugen stood in perennial feud with the *Stände*. The latter found a distinguished leader and spokesman in their *Landschaftskonsulent* Johann Jakob Moser (1701-85),[37] who became the classic defender of surviving *Stände* rights in action as well as words. The constitutional struggle in Württemberg was closely followed by all Germans interested in political affairs.

There has been a tendency, especially among critics of Germany's belated advance to self-government, to romanticize the *Stände* bodies of the eighteenth century and to exaggerate their constructive potential.[38] There is an obvious temptation to regret the failure of the so-called "lost opportunity," that the neomedieval *Stände* might have developed into modern "representative bodies" without any breach in constitutional continuity.[39] It is important, however, to remember that the old *Stände* were very different from modern parliaments and that the evolution from one to the other encountered formidable obstacles which were only overcome in some exceptionally fortunate countries like England. A *Landstand* (member of a *Stände* body) owed his position to the ownership of a particular piece of property or the holding of a particular clerical or urban office (abbot, mayor, et cetera); a modern representative is elected by the people of a particular district. He is usually given some kind of mandate and faces the constant threat of losing the next election; a *Landstand* was virtually independent of external pressures. The *Stände* were usually separated into dif-

[37] On J. J. Moser see the biography by Oskar Wächter, *J. J. Moser* (Stuttgart, 1885), which is primarily a compilation and paraphrase of Moser's own voluminous autobiographical writings. A good modern introduction to his *Weltanschauung* is Marianne Fröhlich, *J. J. Moser in seinem Verhältnis zum Rationalismus und Pietismus* (Vienna, 1925). Father and son (Carl Friedrich von Moser) are presented together in the popular study by J. Herzog, *Moser. Vater und Sohn* (Stuttgart, 1905).

[38] This is notably true of the recent book by F. L. Carsten, *Princes and Parliaments in Germany from the Fifteenth to the Eighteenth Century* (Oxford, 1959).

[39] See H. Christern, *Deutscher Ständestaat und englischer Parlamentarismus am Ende des 18. Jahrhunderts* (Munich, 1939).

ferent *curiae,* each deliberating in secret and then negotiating with other *curiae* upon equal terms; a modern parliament deliberates in public and, if multichambered, usually provides for the clear-cut preponderance of one chamber in cases of conflict. The *Stände* were part of a dualistic polity where the prince and the *Stände* were expected to cooperate voluntarily upon an equal basis for the good of the state; a modern parliamentary body will seek, on the contrary, direct control of the executive in a manner incompatible with the spirit of dualistic polity. Dualism worked reasonably well in an essentially static society where men were content with the *status quo;* it could not survive when princes sought to establish thoroughly integrated and centralized polities capable of meeting the needs of dynamic modern society. Princes found *Stände* an obstacle on the road to modernization because they tended to rally to the defense of every kind of anachronistic privilege, whether aristocratic, plutocratic, clerical, or regional. The *Stände* discredited the cause of self-government by identifying it with social reaction; while the cause of absolute monarchy was with good reason hailed by "progressive" forces as the best hope for modernizing society.

The "irrepressible conflict" between the *Stände* and the prince had been fought out in most of the major states of Germany in the seventeenth century, and had generally resulted in the clear-cut victory of the prince (most notably in Austria, Prussia, and Bavaria). In Württemberg, on the other hand, the battle had ended in a draw and was repeatedly resumed during the eighteenth century. The Württemberg *Stände* were for several reasons in a comparatively strong position. They were, in the first place, remarkably homogeneous in composition because the aristocracy of the region, consisting primarily of Free Knights, did not sit in the *Landtag* (since they proudly owed allegiance directly to the emperor). The *Stände* consisted of about sixty-five lay representatives (elected by rural districts or city corporations) and about fifteen prelates. Prelates and laymen were united in defending the Protestant character of the Württemberg state against a ducal house recently turned Catholic; their position was strengthened by the guarantee of several foreign Protestant powers (Prussia, England, Denmark) which did not hesitate to intervene on behalf of the *Stände* in Württemberg constitutional struggles. The rights of the *Landtag* were unusually well established as a result of the Tübingen Treaty of 1514, and had been confirmed recently after a constitutional struggle extending over the years 1737-39. The major weakness of the *Landtag* to modern eyes lay in its strictly oligarchic character, which meant

261

that it opposed any kind of democratic reform; but this had the contemporary advantage of providing respectability and a close association with class interests more formidable (as yet) than democratic theory.[40]

The perennial battle between the duke and the *Stände* was resumed when the young and vigorous Duke Karl Eugen (reigned 1739-93) personally assumed the reins of government in 1755. Karl Eugen had the temperament of a tyrant and the ambition of an absolute prince. He conducted an anti-Prussian foreign policy during the Seven Years' War (1756-63) without bothering to consult the *Stände*, and similarly collected unprecedented taxes without securing the approval of the *Stände* required by the constitution. His generally arbitrary conduct provoked the firm opposition of the *Landtag;* their grievances were ably formulated and publicized by Moser. It throws a glaring light upon the *de facto* absolutism which existed in Württemberg that the duke was able to imprison Moser in the Hohetwiel fortress without any formal accusation or trial for a period of five years (1759-64). The *Stände* were able to protest but not prevent this arbitrary act; the loss of their leader did not, however, cow the *Stände* opposition as a whole. Eighteenth-century constitutional conflicts were fought out with a certain restraint upon all sides: it would have been unthinkable for the duke to destroy the *Stände* by imprisoning *all* its members, even as it would have been unthinkable for the *Stände* to aim at the deposition of the duke.

The moderation of the struggle was not only due to the "spirit of the age" which—prior to the French Revolution—sought to avoid any sharp conflicts between contrasting political principles; it was also due to international considerations and the availability of the *Reichshofrath* as a judicial remedy. The Protestant powers which had guaranteed the Württemberg religious *status quo* in 1733 sent special

[40] This account of the Württemberg constitutional struggle is based upon the following standard works: Albert Eugen Adam, *J. J. Moser als württ. Landschaftskonsulent* (Stuttgart, 1887); idem, "Herzog Karl und die Landschaft," in *Herzog Karl Eugen von Württemberg und seine Zeit* (2 vols., Esslingen, 1907-09), I, 193-310; Friedrich Wintterlin, "Die Altwürttembergische Verfassung am Ende des 18. Jahrhunderts," *Württ. Vjh.*, XXIII (1914), 195-209; Ludwig Timotheus Spittler, "Zur Geschichte des Erbvergleichs," *Sämtliche Werke*, XIII (1893), 255-78, a classic early treatment still worth reading; and, above all, the two modern works which synthesize the most recent scholarship: Erwin Hoelzle, *Das alte Recht und die Revolution. Eine politische Geschichte Württembergs in der Revolutionszeit 1789 bis 1805* (Munich and Berlin, 1931), which includes a brilliant background survey, and Walter Grube, *Der Stuttgarter Landtag 1457-1957. Von den Landständen zum demokratischen Parlament* (Stuttgart, 1957), Bk. III, significantly entitled "Gegen den Strom."

envoys to Stuttgart as soon as they were freed of more pressing pre-occupations by the end of the Seven Years' War. These envoys encouraged the *Landtag* to take its grievances to the *Reichshofrath* sitting in Vienna. The grievances were succinctly summarized on November 16, 1764, under six headings, and may be enumerated here because they give an excellent impression of the eighteenth-century absolutist encroachment upon *Stände* rights:

(1) *Constitutional complaints*: violation of the right of the *Landstände* to give assent to taxation and legislation; confiscation of funds held by the *Landschaftskasse*, i.e., the treasury administered by the *Landschaft* in accordance with the traditional dualist polity; and arbitrary judicial actions (such as the imprisonment of Moser).

(2) *Ecclesiastical complaints*: violation of Protestant rights by the Catholic prince, especially in the maladministration of church property. (This was especially important because it provided the "Guarantee Powers" with a clear-cut reason for intervention.)

(3) *Military complaints*: arbitrary recruitment and quartering, levying unconstitutional taxes to maintain unauthorized military units. (This had happened at the very beginning of the constitutional controversy.)

(4) *Fiscal complaints*: apart from arbitrary taxation, the ruthless exploitation of royal monopolies and the inefficient administration of ducal domains (leading to gaps in the exchequer which the *Stände* were expected to fill).

(5) *Forest complaints*: arbitrary increase of *corvées* in connection with the ducal forests; incalculable damage wrought by roaming ducal game.

(6) *Ducal intervention in the rights of local self-government*: especially the attempted reorganization of the communes in 1762. (This had struck at the basis of *Stände* power because the communes were the bodies which elected *Stände* representatives.)[41]

The *Reichshofrath* announced two judgments on the issues submitted by the *Landtag* of Württemberg (Sept. 6, 1764, and May 15, 1765). They both proved very favorable to the *Stände* and consequently enraged Duke Karl Eugen. He refused to submit unconditionally to the judgment, knowing well that it would never be enforced; but he realized that he had been driven into a defensive position and could not refuse participation in a mediatory *Hofkommission* appointed by the Emperor Joseph II (July 1765). This special commission did not resolve the controversy; but it induced Karl Eugen

---

[41] I have taken this summary of the grievances from Grube, op.cit., p. 440.

263

to resume negotiations with the *Stände* in Stuttgart (September 1766). Another three and a half years of bargaining proved necessary before settlement could be reached on the famous *Erbvergleich* of January 15, 1770. Its terms must be considered an important defensive victory for the *Stände,* whose traditional rights were reconfirmed and guaranteed anew by the three Protestant powers. Karl Eugen formally promised henceforth to obey the constitution; while the *Stände* in return agreed to higher taxes and also accepted joint responsibility for the vast debts which the duke had accumulated during his fifteen years of unconstitutional rule. The *Stände* in effect repurchased their violated rights by voting solid cash—an unsatisfactory bargain but nonetheless a check on absolutism and a victory for *Ständetum.* The only trouble was that there was no guarantee that a born tyrant like Karl Eugen would keep his word; but he had in fact learned that he could not violate the constitution with impunity, and curbed his absolutist temperament for the rest of his reign.

The check on absolutism had been made possible, it must be repeated, by the special conditions of Württemberg, where *Stände* institutions had especially deep historic roots; were buttressed by indigenous confessional as well as constitutional forces; and could count upon outside international intervention and the judicial action of the imperial *Reichshofrath.* All these special reasons meant that the Württemberg case could not become a precedent for other German defenses of *Stände* power against absolutist encroachment.

The opposition to absolutism from the Right was not confined to defense of *Stände* rights where these still existed; it also included defense (or reaffirmation) of the old-fashioned, patriarchal conception of the state, under which the prince promoted the general happiness of his subjects instead of the policy of modern princes of sacrificing this happiness (if necessary) to the impersonal goal of the greatness of the state. The Prussian monarchy of Frederick the Great was often singled out for attack from this direction, for nowhere else was the happiness of the individual (including that of the king himself) sacrificed more ruthlessly in the pursuit of the status of a Great Power. In Prussia everything was subordinated to the power and greatness of the state: militarism flourished under the motto of *toute en vendette*; 80 per cent of the taxes collected went for support of the army; mercantilistic policy aimed at self-sufficiency in the event of war; while the administrative system was primarily geared to military needs. The organization of the resources of the entire community for the sake of power was the primary end of absolutism, and this end re-

quired that the historic variety and differentiation which characterized the medieval patriarchal state be swept away. Put in a
nutshell: the pursuit of Great Power status was a revolutionary goal
which necessitated the application of revolutionary means in foreign
and domestic policy. A good many Conservatives were opposed to
ends and means alike.[42]

How did German Conservatives defend princely absolutism against
its critics from the Left and the Right? It is necessary to distinguish
sharply between defense on a popular and on an intellectual level.
The former consisted of a simple reaffirmation of the old theory of the
divine right of princes; the latter, of an attempt to refute new Radical
arguments by an appeal to experience while simultaneously developing the ideal of a "reformed absolutism" which maximized its constructive potential and minimized its tyrannical features. The former,
however intellectually "uninteresting," is of great historical importance; it will be surveyed before passing on to the more sophisticated
arguments presented on behalf of absolutism for the narrow strata
which appreciated intellectual argument.

A famous, not to say notorious, example of popular defense of
princely absolutism was the political catechism (*Volkskatechismus*)
issued by August Styrum, the strong-minded bishop of Speyer, in
1785.[43] Its argument, presented in question-and-answer form, was
calculated to hammer simple truths into uncomplicated minds. The

[42] See, for example, Ernst Brandes' attack upon the "soulless despotism" of
Prussia, where the state had become a pure machine for attaining Great Power
status. *Betrachtungen über den Zeitgeist in Deutschland* (Hannover, 1808), pp.
50-67. Other examples will be found in the chapters on Möser and Rehberg below.

[43] It was frequently reprinted, usually with a hostile commentary. I have used
the edition, "Probe eines Deutschen politischen Volcks-Catechismus: 'Pflichten
der Unterthanen gegen ihren Landesherrn. Zum Gebrauch der Trivialschulen im
Hochstift Speier. Auf Gnädigsten Befehl Bruchsal, 1785'. Nebst einem Prolog
und Anhang," *Neues Patriotisches Archiv für Deutschland* (ed. C. F. von Moser),
I (1792), 309-402. Henceforth cited as *Volcks-Catechismus*. Moser commented
on the catechism (p. 318), "die ganze Schrift könnte eben so leicht Lehrbuch des
Christ-Fürstlichen Sultanismus heissen und in den trivial-Schulen der Moldau
und Wallachey eingeführt werden." Schlözer was equally sharp in his comment
in his *Staatsanzeigen*, IX (1786), 501ff., and XII (1788), 118ff. Bishop Styrum's
practice was as bad as his theory, and provoked a protest by his Speyer subjects
to the *Reichskammergericht* in Wetzlar. The latter declared Styrum's method
of rule to be "contrary to all law and equity, as well as the principles of German
civic freedom" (*der deutscher bürgerlichen Freyheit ganz entgegen*). Moser,
ibid., p. 313. For a balanced portrait of the bishop, who reigned from 1770 to
1797, see Jakob Wille, *August Graf von Limburg-Stirum, Fürstbischof von Speyer.
Miniaturbilder aus einem geistlichen Staate im 18. Jahrhundert* (Heidelberg,
1913). The author stresses the unpleasant personal character of the bishop but
admits that he was an able administrator not lacking in benevolent intentions.

obvious purpose was to buttress the evidently failing loyalty of the common people of Speyer. Appeal was made to Holy Scripture, whose infallibility in all political questions was an unchallenged axiom, and to the certainty of both divine and human punishment for all who dared to defy the prince.

The catechism begins with an uncontroversial statement concerning the indispensability of authority (*Obrigkeit*) if men are to live an orderly and civilized life. The distinctive argument begins with the second section, with its assertion that *Obrigkeit* has been vested by God in the hands of existing princes. The real ruler of mankind is God: "God is, however, invisible; for this reason he has appointed princes as his visible regents, so that he may govern through them."[44] As proof of this proposition the bishop cites various Biblical authorities from both the Old and the New Testament, including the Sayings of Solomon (8:15-18), the explicit statement of Jesus (John 19:2) and St. Paul's Epistle to the Romans (Rom. 13:1).

God has decreed that men must faithfully perform the obligations of their station in life, whether exalted or humble, on pain of temporal unhappiness and eternal punishment. The catechism makes this explicit for every station. Take, for example, the case of the peasants:

> What happens to lazy, dissolute, and drunken peasants? Lazy, dissolute, and drunken peasants remain poor, are held in contempt by their neighbors, die an early death, and suffer the most horrible punishment available to God, eternal damnation.[45]

It does not suffice for men to perform their social duties externally; they must perform them in a religious spirit: "A man who lacks religion does not fear God; a man who does not fear God cannot be a good (*rechtschaffenes*) subject."[46]

God wants all subjects to love and honor their temporal rulers; and this love and honor must not be purely external:

> To bow down to the ground in the presence of princes is only an external honor which does not suffice to fulfil the divine command. God wishes that they be honored also in the internal recesses of every heart. How does one honor them properly? By valuing and loving them; by wishing them long life, a happy government and all other blessings; and by obeying all of their commands. . . . One also honors them by fearing them.[47]

[44] *Volcks-Catechismus*, p. 327. [45] Ibid., pp. 331-32.
[46] Ibid., p. 333. [47] Ibid., p. 335.

Obedience is the highest duty of a subject, and it is owed to evil princes as well as good: "Disobedience is a sin, disobedience in an important matter a mortal sin."[48] While, on the other hand, "God rewards obedient subjects with temporal blessings on earth and eternal bliss in the Hereafter."[49]

The catechism was very specific on the duties of subjects in peace and war. Their main peacetime duty was to pay taxes faithfully: "Whoever is able to pay his taxes and does not do so commits a sin."[50] And who is most likely to be able to pay his taxes? "Subjects can most easily pay their taxes if they are industrious, avoid unnecessary expenses, and live modestly."[51] Their main duty in time of war is to keep quiet and suffer (if suffer they must) with resignation. Subjects should abstain from discussing the various events of war. "Why, indeed, should they judge and talk about them at all? It is best for them to neither judge nor talk, for they cannot be adequately informed about the true state of affairs; and chatter can easily confuse the common people."[52] This applies even when the subject is adversely affected by the course of war: "If subjects suffer losses through enemy action they must be patient and reflect that they have experienced what can only be considered a deserved divine chastisement for their sins."[53] The catechism presents war as the business of the prince rather than the people; hence military service is contemplated only as a last resort: "Burghers and peasants are obligated to take up arms if hired mercenaries do not suffice to defend the borders and fortresses of the state."[54]

The catechism describes the duties of soldiers in inordinate detail although the strength of the Speyer army never exceeded three hundred men. Soldiers must be obedient, acquire military skill, and conquer the fear of death by contemplating the heavenly reward which God has promised to the faithful soldier. The positive side of the Christian-patriarchal political conceptions underlying the catechism is revealed by the strict injunction against killing noncombatants, plundering, or molesting the civilians with whom soldiers are quartered: "Soldiers must conduct themselves quietly in their quarters and be satisfied with the food which their hosts provide in accordance with princely regulations. It is sinful for soldiers to pick quarrels, and even more sinful for them to deceive their hosts or to come to blows with them."[55] Soldiers must cheerfully bear hunger, illness, and

[48] Ibid., p. 339. [49] Ibid., p. 341. [50] Ibid., p. 344.
[51] Ibid., p. 343. [52] Ibid., p. 346. [53] Ibid., p. 347.
[54] Ibid. [55] Ibid., p. 352.

wounds by remembering—exactly as must suffering civilians—"that they have deserved these temporal evils as a punishment for their sins . . . and must humbly subject themselves to the will of God."[56] Desertion is one of the gravest of sins, and as such punished by God and prince alike: "God punishes deserters with temporal and eternal penalties. The temporal penalties are illness, poverty, shame, and ridicule; the further penalty eternal damnation."[57] Princes punish deserters through the lash or even capital punishment. Those so punished have no right to curse their prince, but must rather recognize that "they have brought this penalty upon themselves by committing perjury [in fleeing from the colors]; and in recognizing this they will worship the divinely-established just order of the world, and suffer their punishment with patience."[58] Parents who give support to their deserter sons also make themselves guilty of a grave sin.

A final section of the catechism deals with the general duties of all subjects. They are obligated to perform unlimited *corvées*, such as road-building or transmitting government letters, unless they have been specifically exempted from these obligations. It is sinful to perform these obligations in an unwilling or refractory spirit, for this implies criticism of the prince appointed by God. Subjects must above all love their princes as children love their parents, and this must be an exclusive love: "Pious children love their parents more than their neighbors."[59] The reward of such love, and the performance of the duties consequent upon such love, are "fame, praise, and honor with God and man alike."[60]

Styrum's statements were no doubt extreme, but the significance of his catechism lay in the fact that he *expressed* with delightful frankness what many other princes only *thought*. This point was stressed by C. F. von Moser in an indignant accompanying note to his reprinting of the catechism:

> The so-called *popular* catechism is in fact a *princely* confession of faith, as held by many princes whether their territory be big or small, ecclesiastical or secular. It expresses how they *think* about the real and pretended duties of their subjects, and what they wish and demand that their subjects should *believe* in the crucial question of obedience. The catechism maintains a deep and well-considered silence about the general rights of man and the particular principles of German freedom; about the reciprocal duties of

[56] Ibid., p. 354.   [57] Ibid., p. 358.   [58] Ibid., p. 360.
[59] Ibid., p. 370.   [60] Ibid.

princes toward their subjects and subjects toward their neighbors.
. . . Many of the assertions of the catechism are not only philosophically false and breathe the spirit of the most bare-faced despotism,
but they are also contrary to the constitution and laws of the
Empire.[61]

A more sophisticated defense of monarchy was undertaken by
several authors who set out to show that European absolutism had
never been absolutism in the sense of Asiatic despotism, and that the
two other possible forms of government—monarchy limited by *Stände*
and republicanism—possessed important drawbacks. It was easy to
show that several factors in European history had tended to counter-
vail tyrannical absolutism in theory and practice alike—for example,
the independent spiritual position of the various Christian Churches,
the independent social position of the landowning nobility, and the
humanitarian legacy of classical civilization. To these factors must be
added the strong legal tradition of Europe which, while not incompatible with absolutism in principle (witness the influence of Roman
law!), yet tended to preclude arbitrariness in detail. This legal tradition was to come to a fine flowering in eighteenth-century Prussia with
its ideal of the *Rechtsstaat* and its great codification of the *Allgemeines Landrecht*—a Prussia, be it noted, in which *Stände* bodies
had ceased to play a significant role in the seventeenth century.

It is no accident that a Prussian author, writing anonymously in the
Berlinisches Archiv der Zeit,[62] denounced *Stände* bodies for being
either harmful or, at best, useless. He asserted that the defenders of the
Stände usually wrote ex parte, with J. J. Moser, for example, having
been the employee of the Württemberg *Stände*. Moser had praised
the principle of consultation between *Stände* and prince as the distinctive virtue of a dualistic polity. The author argued, on the contrary,
that while consultation was in principle desirable there was no reason
to believe that *Landstände* made good consulting partners. "Their
counsel does not rest upon the intellectual and moral base of wisdom,
experience, and patriotism, but rather upon the physical base of the
possession of a certain status in ecclesiastical, aristocratic, or urban
affairs."[63] The composition of the *Stände* almost guaranteed Reactionary bias. Bishops did not belong in a secular assembly at all; aristocrats were usually preoccupied with narrow defense of their own class
privileges; urban representatives were rarely heard and then only as

[61] Ibid., pp. 317-18.
[62] "Mit oder ohne Landstände," *Berlinisches Archiv der Zeit*, II (1799), 13-28.
[63] Ibid., p. 18.

champions of municipal privilege.[64] There could be little question that bureaucrats were generally superior to *Stände* members as princely counselors. They possessed an intimate understanding of public affairs through careful training and long experience, and a professional ethos which gave them a patriotic devotion to the whole community and a superiority over regional and class privilege.[65]

More frequent than criticism of the *Landstände* was criticism of republicanism on both theoretical and practical grounds. It was argued that republican regimes tended to be ignorant and obscurantist if democratic, selfish and exclusive if aristocratic. Venice and Poland (the latter being generally considered a republic because its king was really an elected president) were constantly mentioned as warning examples for the evils inherent in oligarchic and aristocratic republicanism. Venice was a byword in eighteenth-century Germany for decadent sloth, while Poland was so badly governed that it proved incapable of defending its national integrity. Many German authors also pointed to phenomena nearer home, namely, the Imperial Free Cities, well known for their stagnation, and the ecclesiastical states, viewed as elective monarchies and generally believed to be less well-governed than neighboring hereditary monarchies. The internal turbulence of the oligarchic Dutch republic in the 1780's was also a frequent exhibit in the "republican chamber of horrors."[66]

Democratic republics fared no better than oligarchies in the eyes of Conservative champions of monarchy. Critics of the American Revolution (an articulate minority among German publicists, but headed by the great Schlözer) found in republican aspirations the source of the perennial American turbulence—the fact that it would subside after the launching of the federal constitution could not be foreseen in the mid-1780's. Schlözer also made a much-discussed attack upon what German republicans hailed as the democratic freedoms of Switzerland. He had reason to be critical of the Swiss conduct of public affairs, for one of the informants of the *Briefwechsel*, the Zurich pastor Waser, was executed by his government after being convicted

[64] Ibid., pp. 21-24. The author realized the possible democratic implications of his argument, for the evils he criticized could in theory be corrected by a popularly elected legislature; he thought, however, that the French experience of the years 1789-99 was discouraging in this respect (p. 24). His view is a good example of how the "horrors of the French Revolution" strengthened the case for enlightened absolutism by discrediting the republican alternative.

[65] Ibid., p. 25.

[66] These and other examples are mentioned by W. Wenck in his useful survey of German critics of republicanism in *Deutschland vor hundert Jahren*, pp. 20-28.

of illegal possession of a document connected with the financial administration so bitterly criticized by Schlözer. This celebrated affair, notorious for what Schlözer called, in a new word coined by himself, a "Justizmord" (judicial murder), was widely interpreted as showing that republicans had a propensity toward tyranny. Democrats could argue that the conduct of the Zurich government was due to its oligarchic character, but it was soon shown that the completely democratic canton of Glarus had no greater regard for the rights of man than oligarchic Zurich. It burned as a witch a domestic servant, Anna Goldin, as late as 1782, to the great indignation of German publicists like Schlözer and Wekhrlin. The latter engaged in a sharp personal controversy with the Glarus government after he had reported on the case in his journal, *Die Chronologen*. As a responsible journalist he naturally refused to name the informant to whom he owed his detailed description of the case. The Glarus government thereupon issued a warrant for Wekhrlin's arrest and put a price of 100 thalers upon his head. This was an empty gesture—Wekhrlin lived outside Swiss jurisdiction—but it was widely denounced as a typical example of democratic tyranny.[67]

Much hostility to republican governments was based upon more theoretical grounds. Niklas Vogt, whom we have already encountered as a defender of the imperial constitution, was also a sharp critic of republicanism. He admitted that there was a case against monarchical rule based upon the "accident of heredity," but believed that this (possible) evil was smaller than the (certain) republican evil arising from open competition for the leading position in the state. Such a competition led to factionalism and put a premium upon demagogic arts, while leading to resentment among citizens who believed themselves at least as well qualified to rule as their rulers but deprived of rulership by mere want of demagogic skills. Was it not psychologically preferable to be ruled by a man whom God (or even accident) had placed in a position beyond one's own reach?

[67] The cases of Waser and Goldin are discussed in Wenck, ibid., pp. 21-22 and 24-25. They placed a brake upon the widespread enthusiasm for Switzerland described in E. Ziehen, *Die deutsche Schweizerbegeisterung in den Jahren 1750-1815* (Frankfurt, 1922). Wekhrlin's conflict with the Glarus government is described in F. W. Ebeling, *Wekhrlin. Leben und Auswahl seiner Schriften* (Berlin, 1869). Wekhrlin's summary judgment of democratic republics was unflattering: "Nowhere is freedom more talked about and less practiced than in republics. . . . Those who direct governmental affairs in democracies have only in the rarest cases a knowledge of affairs and of the true interests of the state. Jan Hagel [German archetype for the common man] will more readily learn to dance on a rope than to govern." *Das Graue Ungeheuer*, IV (1785), 234.

271

No reasonable man will feel curtailed in his liberty if he is impeded—while walking in the country—from making progress by a precipitous rock or a drenching rain. These are obstacles set by Nature, and even the freest of creatures remain subjected to the laws of Nature and God.[68]

Vogt's argument was directed against all republics, whether oligarchic or democratic. There were others more specifically directed against democratic republics. Even its champions—for example, Rousseau—admitted that this form of government was best suited to small and primitive communities—what Vogt polemically called pseudo states quite incapable of the most elementary function of the state, namely, self-defense. The Swiss cantons had tried to cope with this problem by forming a confederation, but all federations were cumbersome and ineffective. It was clear that the larger political units required to survive in the competitive European state system called for monarchical government; and that the actual conduct of foreign policy required a secrecy and continuity difficult to achieve in a republican regime.[69]

Another prominent defender of monarchy, the Halle *Popularphilosoph* Johann August Eberhard (1739-1809),[70] argued that there was no connection (or rather an inverse relation) between civil freedom (i.e., immunity from state interference) and political freedom (i.e., participation in government). The extent of civil freedom depended upon the quality and self-restraint of those who wielded political power. Was there any reason to believe that a properly trained king would exercise less self-restraint than a democratic mob or an oligarchic clique? The already-cited examples from recent Swiss history suggested the contrary, a view that was to receive much supporting evidence during the French Revolution.[71]

The defenders of monarchy did not, of course, restrict their argu-

---

[68] N. Vogt, *Über die europäische Republik* (1787), i, 108.

[69] Ibid., pp. 102ff.

[70] Eberhard was a prominent member of the Berlin *Aufklärung* before winning a professorship of philosophy at Halle in 1778. He won notoriety as one of the most vigorous critics of Kant, immortality by provoking the latter's sarcastic *Über eine Entdeckung, nach der alle neue Kritik der reinen Vernunft durch eine ältere entbehrlich gemacht werden soll* (1790). See the biographical articles by A. Richter, *ADB*, v (1877), 569-71, and L. Gabe, *NDB*, iv (1959), 240-41.

[71] Johann August Eberhard, *Über Staatsverfassungen und ihre Verbesserungen* (2 vols., Berlin, 1793-94), i, 115-22. He had already expressed the same views in his "Ueber die Freiheit des Bürgers und die Prinzipien der Regierungsformen," in *Vermischte Schriften* (n.p., n.d.), i, 1ff. His views are discussed in detail in Ch. 9 below.

ment to criticism of republicanism; they also developed an ideal of monarchy purged of all its (admitted) present evils. They argued that there were forces at work which already made monarchical government and good government virtually identical, and would increasingly do so in the future. The argument, as developed by Vogt, insisted that the self-interest of princes required that they behave as "enlightened" rulers. The precarious position of all states in the European and German equilibrium made security dependent upon strength, and strength was in turn dependent upon a prince ruling over free, contented and prosperous subjects. Only a *Rechtsstaat* could develop the internal sources of strength in an optimum manner: "Only a people whose property, rights and liberties are secure against arbitrary intervention will labor for more than its immediate necessities; for otherwise a citizen possesses no guarantee that he can harvest in the future the fruits of his present efforts."[72] Religious toleration strengthened the state by raising its population through the admission of religious refugees. Only a virtuous prince could earn the affection of his people essential in times of adversity, and evoke the spirited support which often made the difference between survival and extinction of the state.[73]

There was much to be said in favor of this objective identity of interest between ruler and ruled; but what reason was there to believe that princes would see matters in this light? All these arguments had been valid for centuries, ever since Europe had developed a state system based upon the principle of competitive equilibrium. The new factor which gave rise to maximal hopes was the spread of the principle of *Aufklärung* even to the throne itself. The example set by devoted and enlightened monarchs like Frederick the Great and Joseph II was putting their less enlightened monarchical colleagues to shame. Enlightened rulers were now expected by the public opinion of Germany, tyrannical rulers castigated by public opinion guided by influential journals like Schlözer's *Staatsanzeigen*. Rulers increasingly identified their own happiness with the happiness of their subjects, and accepted the "enlightened" identification of virtue with happiness. The wish for posthumous fame (thoroughly characteristic of a secularist age) worked in the same direction: only a virtuous monarch had a chance of having his measures outlive him through the continuity of a stable dynasty. All these factors minimized the possibility that an absolute monarch would act as a capricious despot.[74]

[72] N. Vogt, *Über die europäische Republik* (1787), i, 119.
[73] Ibid., i, 109ff. [74] Ibid., i, 111ff.

"Enlightened absolutism" based itself increasingly upon the doctrine of the social contract rather than the divine rights of kings. The Halle philosopher Eberhard, the critic of republicanism, was one of many authors who used the social contract theory to provide an intellectual foundation for monarchical rule rather than direct democracy. He did not deny that popular sovereignty lay at the root of the social contract theory, but argued that the people must, for convincing utilitarian reasons, *delegate* their power to an absolute and hereditary monarch. The people obviously could not govern themselves; they must, therefore, delegate their power either to an aristocracy or to a monarch. Delegation to an aristocracy was undesirable, since it possessed a selfish interest distinct from that of the community; while a monarch could readily identify himself with the interests of the entire community. King and people were equal contracting partners, and their contract was mutually binding unless cancelled by mutual consent. The contract could be implied (through prolonged prescription) as well as expressed: Eberhard was far too intelligent to believe in any historical social contract as the basis of existing governments. The terms of the contract must be those of absolute hereditary monarchy. No king could be expected to accept the difficult commission to govern unless he was given absolute authority; a people was no more able to supervise a ruler than to govern itself. Only hereditary authority could secure the instinctive adherence of broad bodies of men. Elective monarchy was discredited by the example of Poland and several other countries; hereditary monarchy stood justified by the splendid achievements of modern absolutism. We have already examined the various reasons which were given why it was most unlikely to degenerate into despotism.[75]

Eberhard's use of the rationalist and secularist doctrine of the social contract in arguing upon behalf of hereditary monarchy was more likely to impress intellectuals, seeking a synthesis between old political practice and new political doctrine, than the broad mass of the people who were more likely to be attracted by a simple doctrine, whether that of popular sovereignty or the divine right of kings. This was clearly understood by Carl Friedrich von Moser, who was no great friend of monarchical absolutism (as we have seen) but also feared that a purely rationalist approach to political questions would

---

[75] Eberhard's argument is developed in the already cited popular lectures, *Über Staatsverfassungen und ihre Verbesserungen*, Vol. i, Chs. 1-12. His axiom that the people "obviously" could not govern themselves ignored the possibilities of representative government; and he never frankly faced the rational arguments easily advanced against absolute hereditary monarchy.

shake the foundations of all government. He argued that belief in the divine (rather than purely utilitarian) basis of authority was essential for the preservation of existing thrones. Moser quoted Rom. 13:1-5 with approval, adding:

> Here is the true "social contract." Its meaning is "God has so decreed! He has put an obligation upon the conscience of man." If we abandon this thread, this basic conviction, *that all authority is derived from God;* if we make it dubious or suspicious in the eyes of the common people, or even tear it out of their hearts: we will then find that there is no human bond sufficiently strong so that it cannot be philosophized, reasoned or demonstrated away *(wegphilosophiren, wegraisonniren, wegdemonstriren)*—and that means the end of all security for all thrones.[76]

There remained the problem of what to do if princes remained obstinately unenlightened, if they persisted in refusing to see their own interest in the terms defined by the *Popularphilosophen.* Monarchical writers naturally continued to express abhorrence of rebellion, an abhorrence soon to be increased by the spectacle of the French Revolution. The duty of obedience to bad as well as good princes was persistently reaffirmed; but obedience did not preclude several remedial steps short of rebellion, and even rebellion as the very last resort:

> The attitude of obedience does not preclude firm attachment to the rights of man, protests by *Landstände* and even individual subjects, sermons by court preachers calling upon the prince to show repentance, specific treaties between the prince and his subjects, appeal to Imperial courts in case of violation—and, as a last desperate measure, to be employed only in the most extreme cases, self-help against a deliberate, persistent, and incorrigible exploiter of the people.[77]

The necessity for contemplating such extreme cases seemed, however, remote. The champions of "enlightened monarchy" were confident that arbitrary despotism was rapidly becoming an atavistic anachronism. The substantive demands of *Aufklärung* were largely identical with those previously sought by absolutism; and their implementation did not require any institutional changes so long as monarchs were willing to act in an "enlightened" manner. Radical

[76] C. F. von Moser, "Von dem göttlichen Recht der Könige, vom Ursprung der Landesherrlichen und Obrigkeitlichen Gewalt und von der Natur und Gränzen des Gehorsams," *Neues Patriotisches Archiv für Deutschland,* i (1792), 539.
[77] Ibid., i, 548.

policies on religious and social questions within a Conservative political framework—this long remained the ideal of most of the champions of the German *Aufklärung*.

The Debate About the Ecclesiastical States

The thirty-five odd Roman Catholic ecclesiastical states of Southern and Western Germany were a remarkable anachronism in eighteenth-century Germany. They included 20 bishoprics and some 40 abbeys (or other ecclesiastical foundations) with a total population of about 2,650,000, including 70,000 monks and secular clergy. The distinctive characteristic of these states was the union of ecclesiastical and secular office: the bishop (or abbot) was not only the ecclesiastical head of his diocese (or monastery) but simultaneously the secular prince of a territorial state whose boundaries tended to coincide with those of his diocese. The dual function exercised by the prince-bishop was also characteristic of his cathedral chapter, which performed not only the ecclesiastical duties of an ordinary chapter but played a secular role analogous to the *Stände* in a secular territorial state (or, more accurately, the role they had played prior to the triumph of absolutism). The dualistic constitution, which had been overthrown in most states by princely absolutism, continued to prevail in the ecclesiastical states. The cathedral chapters had exactly the same vices (aristocratic narrowness, blind attachment to the *status quo)* which observers criticized in the surviving secular *Stände*—a matter not surprising since they were recruited from exactly the same strata (specifically the so-called *"stiftsfähige Familien"*). The power of these chapters tended to be greater than had been that of their secular analogues even in palmier preabsolutist days, since it included the right to select bishop-rulers when a see became vacant. The celibacy of the Catholic clergy precluded ecclesiastical states from becoming hereditary monarchies. They were in fact elective monarchies of a highly oligarchic type, whose ruler was selected by and from a narrow body of *stiftsfähige* families.[78]

The years before the French Revolution saw violent discussion throughout Germany concerning the condition and future of the ec-

[78] The best account of the ecclesiastical states is still C. T. Perthes, *Das deutsche Staatsleben vor der Revolution. Eine Vorarbeit zum deutschen Staatsrecht* (Hamburg, 1845), Pt. I, Ch. 2, Sect. 2. Max Braubach, *Maria Theresias jüngster Sohn Max Franz, letzter Kurfürst von Köln und Fürstbischof von Münster* (Vienna, 1961), an expanded version of a study originally published in 1925, provides an extremely readable introduction to the special problems confronting prince-bishops in the last phase of the Holy Roman Empire.

clesiastical states—a discussion set off by the widespread belief that the ecclesiastical states were on the average less well governed than their secular neighbors. It is significant that a Catholic editor, Freiherr von Bibra, himself a *Domcapitular* and leading official of the ecclesiastical state of Fulda, should have announced in 1785 a prize essay contest in his *Journal von und für Deutschland* in the following terms:

> Since the ecclesiastical states of Germany generally cover the most fertile regions of the country, and are elective monarchies [frequently held to be an excellent form of government], they should by all rights enjoy the wisest and happiest governments. If they are not as happy as they ought to be the responsibility cannot rest with the individual rulers but must rather rest with the basic constitution. What are the fundamental faults of this constitution, and how can they be remedied?[79]

Bibra received some twenty entries into his contest, many of which did not confine themselves strictly to the subject matter of proposing remedies for evils in the constitution of ecclesiastical states.[80] The most famous of the replies was that by Carl Friedrich von Moser, who suggested the total abolition of the ecclesiastical states and their replacement by elective secular governments. His book is a useful compendium of all the criticisms which were advanced by "enlightened" writers against Germany's ecclesiastical states.[81]

Moser's case rested partly upon anti-Catholicism pure and simple. He viewed the Catholic Church as the incarnation of superstition and

[79] See the excellent article by Max Braubach, "Die kirchliche Aufklärung im katholischen Deutschland im Spiegel des 'Journal von und für Deutschland,'" *HJb.*, LIV (1934), 16. It should be noted that the Protestant Justus Möser was made one of the two judges of the essay contest. Bibra (1750-1803) was a "Reform Catholic" who aimed at strengthening the ecclesiastical states through reforming their abuses, not a Radical bent upon abolishing them. *Ibid.*, pp. 5-18. He was surprised and indignant when he was widely condemned as a "traitor to his class": "Heaven knows that I love my clerical estate and my small (Fulda) as well as my greater Fatherland (Germany), and do not wish to exchange either for a different one; but to remove evils in both (and where are evils unknown?) is the wish, and must be the duty, of every patriot." *Journal von und für Deutschland*, v (1788), *Vorbericht*.

[80] The prize was won by the rather colorless Josef Edler von Sartori, *Eine statistische Abhandlung über die Mängel in den geistlichen Wahlstaaten und von den Mitteln, solchen abzuhelfen* (n.p., 1787). Sartori argued that the ecclesiastical states did not suffer from any fundamental flaws, and that any existing evils could be easily remedied through the application of a few "enlightened" measures.

[81] C. F. von Moser, *Ueber die Regierung der geistlichen Staaten in Deutschland* (Frankfurt and Leipzig, 1787).

could not conceive that a government animated by Catholic principles could promote the real interests of its subjects. His words are worth quoting as an example of how easily hostility to superstition (real or alleged) could degenerate into sheer bigotry:

A religion which confines the spirit of man, which weakens his elasticity and deprives him of some of his powers, which prohibits him from exploring or thinking about certain questions, which imprisons his reason with the shackles of a blind faith and a blind obedience, which keeps the heart of man in restless fear concerning his fate in the Hereafter and therefore makes him melancholy in the present and apprehensive about the future—such a religion cannot possibly make a people joyous, happy, contented with its lot, and filled with an understanding of itself. A people shaped and led by such principles cannot possibly be called *wise*, while government over a people destined (as a matter of principle) to remain *stupid* cannot be called happy, whether one looks at the matter from a moral or a political point of view.[82]

How did these principles reveal themselves in the government of Germany's ecclesiastical states? Moser thought these states notable for religious intolerance, lack of intellectual freedom, hostility to education, and prevalence of beggars and other poor people; he thought that the latter were encouraged by the Church in order to allow the faithful to perform the good works required by Catholic superstition.[83] All these evils derived from the Catholic faith were compounded, Moser thought, by certain specific evils inherent in the governmental structure of ecclesiastical states. He noted the following:

The brevity of episcopal reigns made for a lack of system and continuity. The cathedral canons frequently elected elderly men as stopgap figures in order to provide themselves with an early second chance at personal elevation. The bishops could not be motivated by dynastic feeling to work for a long-range future; their high officials were too often preoccupied with the next succession rather than the immediate problems of government. The uncertainty about who would be the next ruler, and what his maxims of government would be, chronically demoralized the entire administration.[84]

The effectiveness of a good bishop—that *rara avis*—tended to be

[82] Ibid., pp. 35-36.   [83] Ibid., pp. 37-54.

[84] Ibid., pp. 54ff. This complaint did not preclude the opposite complaint that children were sometimes advanced to bishoprics through family pressure. The latter was an occasional, the former a characteristic evil.

paralyzed by opposition from his cathedral chapter, whose concurrence was constitutionally necessary for many governmental steps. The dualistic polity was far better suited for preventing evil than achieving good. An additional difficulty arose from the fact that the composition of the chapters combined the characteristic faults of clergy and aristocracy alike. As priests the canons were likely to be superstitious and intolerant; as aristocrats they were likely to be narrow-minded defenders of traditionalism and class privilege. These factors together militated against the introduction of enlightened policies in ecclesiastical states.[85]

The prevalent method of training and electing bishops was unlikely to lead to the elevation of suitable rulers. Certain theoretical advantages pointed out by clerical writers were only rarely attained in practice. Men preparing for an ecclesiastical career were (generally) in no danger of early elevation before their training was completed (a constant danger in hereditary monarchies); while the uncertainty about whether they would eventually secure high office prevented the pride which too frequently disfigured the personality of crown princes. These advantages did not, however, necessarily lead to the availability of a large number of well-trained, humble, and suitable episcopal candidates among the canons, for they were countervailed by other factors. Canons were usually appointed by their aristocratic parents to family canonries while they were still in the cradle, before there was evidence of a clerical calling. Their early education was entrusted almost exclusively to clerics, more especially Jesuits, and gave them only rarely a broad outlook upon life. Their aristocratic family pride made them too often immune to Christian humility, while their worldliness of life—not excluding hunting, wine, women, and song—gave little opportunity for developing true spirituality. The elections to a bishopric were too often influenced by extraneous factors which had little to do with either spiritual depth or administrative capacity (two qualities in any case only rarely combined in one and the same person). Such irrelevant factors were family influence, imperial pressure, shabby intrigue, and even outright simony—factors which frequently led to the selection of unsuitable candidates, includ-

[85] Ibid., pp. 69ff. It speaks for Moser's fundamental fair-mindedness that he nonetheless gave the following general judgment about life in the ecclesiastical states: "Taken as a whole, the proverb 'One lives well under the crozier' (*Unterm Krummstab ist gut wohnen*) is legitimate when one compares the lot of ecclesiastical subjects with that of the subjects of the big secular monarchies of Germany" —though perhaps this shows more about Moser's hatred of Prussia (and other Big Powers) than genuine appreciation of life under ecclesiastical princes.

ing even minors from the Houses of Habsburg and Wittelsbach (though the usual tendency, noted above, was to elect men of advanced years).[86]

The faults of Catholic prince-bishops and canons were not corrected by the employment of Protestant bureaucrats, for the ecclesiastical states were naturally loath to give jobs to heretics. Confessionalism in administrative appointments had demonstrably disastrous results in Catholic states. In the words of a polemical writer who gave Moser vigorous public support in the following ex parte language: "Protestants are on the average far more active, industrious, reflective, enterprising, tougher, attentive to business, and economical than Catholics." They were not corrupted by superstitious fasts followed by unhealthy gluttony, and by the demoralizing preoccupation with frivolous good works undertaken in a sordid attempt to purchase salvation from God.[87]

The failure to tolerate Protestants was only one example of Catholic principles leading to misgovernment. The failure adequately to tax clerical property was another; the multiplication of lazy, vicious, or at least useless monks a third. There was, moreover, an ineradicable fault in the personal combination of spiritual and temporal power. The cares of secular government encouraged worldliness and love of power incompatible with apostolical simplicity; the spirit of ecclesiastical function made for bigotry and superstition. It was hard to say whether spiritual or secular rule suffered more from the unnatural combination of the two; suffice it to say that the combination generally maximized the evil potential of both and minimized the blessings which either could bring in its pure form.[88]

How could all these evils be remedied? Moser was categorical in demanding a series of drastic remedies: the introduction of absolute freedom of thought (which he expected would soon lead men to abandon Catholicism in favor of his own form of pietist Protestantism); a break with Rome in the spirit of the Bad Ems *Punktation* (1786), desirable since Rome was the foundation of all superstition; the gradual suppression of monasteries; and complete equality of civil rights for Protestants. Moser realized that these measures were

[86] Ibid., pp. 87-154.

[87] Andreas Joseph Schnaubert, *Ueber des Freiherrn von Moser's Vorschläge zur Verbesserung der geistlichen Staaten in Deutschland* (Jena, 1788). The quotation is from p. 188. Schnaubert (1750-1825) is an ex parte source. The son of a Catholic wine merchant in the Rhineland, he was originally destined for the clergy but became a Protestant convert around 1776. He became a professor of law at Jena in 1785. *ADB*, xxxii (1891), 83-84.

[88] Moser, op.cit., pp. 160ff.

quite incompatible with the spirit of Catholicism, and that their introduction could scarcely be expected from Catholic prince-bishops; he nonetheless believed that they would be achieved because they were dictated by the irresistible tide of *Aufklärung*. They would, however, not cure the evils connected with ecclesiastical government per se: for this Moser suggested the drastic step of complete separation of the episcopal from the princely office, i.e., the end of the ecclesiastical states. Bishops must again (as they had done in apostolic times) devote themselves exclusively to their religious responsibilities; their governmental functions must be transferred to secular persons under a new constitutional pattern of elective monarchy. Moser proposed to minimize any revolutionary upheaval by giving the existing *stiftsfähige* families the exclusive right to elect a secular prince and to compose the new secular *Stände* to be established; the first task of the first elective prince must be to implement the anti-Catholic program outlined above.[89]

Moser lacked specific ideas as to how the replacement of ecclesiastical states by elective monarchies could be legally and constitutionally implemented; this point was well argued by Andreas Joseph Schnaubert, a writer favorably disposed toward Moser's project. Schnaubert's argument is an example of what one might describe as "reluctant Conservatism"—the spirit of "It would be nice to do it, but unfortunately it can't be done."

Schnaubert showed that there was no constitutional method of changing ecclesiastical into secular states. It could not legally be done by the bishop, or the cathedral chapter, or both in combination: the bishop was the agent, not the owner, of the diocese-principality; the cathedral chapter was a committee of the *stiftsfähige* aristocracy and not its master. Neither possessed the right to commit political suicide. Even if they should, by a miracle, possess the inclination to implement a nonexisting right, they would require the approval of both the emperor (whose sovereignty included supervisory powers over the Church, as well as feudal overlordship) and the *Reichstag* (since such an act would change the basic structure of the German constitution). There was no chance whatsoever that all these groups and persons would work together to implement Moser's scheme.[90]

[89] Ibid., pp. 157-95. It may be noted that Moser's program did not meet the objections he himself had advanced against the elective principle. If it led to short reigns and a want of dynastic continuity in the existing ecclesiastical states, this would prove true of elected secular princes as well.

[90] Schnaubert, op.cit., pp. 113-49. The author argued convincingly that Mo-

Schnaubert thought equally poorly of the practicability (not desirability) of some of Moser's other reform suggestions. His desire for absolute freedom of thought was incompatible with the infallibility of the Church and the authoritative interpretation of Scripture—he was asking the Catholic Church to cease to be Catholic.[91] The same was true of his call for repudiation of the Papal supremacy.[92] The prince-bishops could, however, introduce a greater measure of freedom of thought (in all areas not covered by infallibility) and considerable religious toleration for Protestants; he also thought nothing stood in the way of curbing the Papal supremacy (as had already been attempted at Bad Ems in 1786) and suppressing superfluous monasteries (as had already been done by several German princes and bishops). The general point made by Schnaubert was that the ecclesiastical states needed reform and could be reformed, but that they could not be eliminated without shaking the legal and constitutional foundations of the empire.[93]

Schnaubert's reluctant defense of the continued existence of the ecclesiastical states must be supplemented by looking at the arguments of more enthusiastic defenders. They could, of course, not hope to refute the general spirit of anti-Catholicism which underlay most of Moser's argument, but they could attempt to answer his specific points:

The argument concerning the brevity of reigns, and lack of continuity from reign to reign, was partly false (since comparatively young men were often elected) and in any case much exaggerated. The lack of dynastic feeling—so much deplored by Moser—prevented a good deal of politics centered upon the welfare of the reigning family rather than of the common people; while the frequent occurrence of new starts and new perspectives often resulted in good government. There were obvious advantages to the elective process which usually elevated men only after they had reached mature years—old enough to have spent the passions of youth and to be primarily concerned with the reputation they would carry with posterity.[94]

The dualistic constitution—however Reactionary the cathedral

---

ser's principles required the transformation of ecclesiastical states into hereditary, not elective monarchies. Ibid., pp. 97-109. Cf. n.89.

[91] Ibid., pp. 7-31.   [92] Ibid., pp. 31-84.

[93] This conclusion is a summary of the major theme of Schnaubert's book.

[94] Anonymous [Peter Anton Frank], *Etwas über die Wahlcapitulationen in den geistlichen Wahlstaaten* (Frankfurt, 1788), p. 4. The author (1746-1818) was professor of history and law at Mainz (1780) before entering into Austrian service (1791).

chapters—had at least the merit of preventing the despotism so characteristic of Germany's absolutist princes. This was no mean advantage when one contemplated the horrors of despotism which the ecclesiastical states were spared: "No commerce in cannonfodder to America or the Indies; no compulsory military service; no taxes to support princes and princesses in the state to which they have become accustomed; none of the endless fiscal harassments which secular states have refined to perfection in order to torture their subjects."[95] The ecclesiastical states were still animated by the traditional conception of the state where the welfare of the subject was not subordinated to the necessities of achieving and maintaining Great Power status.

The criticism directed against the training of future bishops was only partly justified. It was true that the Jesuits played a large role; but were the Jesuits not noted, by friend and foe alike, for combining religious orthodoxy with mastery of secular affairs? What better educators could there be for future prince-bishops? There was the additional advantage that future bishops usually secured, while cathedral canons, a good deal of administrative experience before they were seriously considered for episcopal advancement. They could earn this administrative experience without being frustrated by the jealousy which kings usually felt for crown princes.[96]

The criticism directed against the religious intolerance of the ecclesiastical states was rapidly becoming out of date. Several Catholic prince-bishops, most notably those of Trier and Mainz, were imposing religious toleration upon their bigoted subjects and cathedral chapters. The latter even went so far as to finance an interconfessional university with revenues secured from the suppression of superfluous monasteries. The University of Bonn, founded by the archbishop of Cologne, was notorious throughout the Catholic world for employing an "advanced" spirit such as Eulogius Schneider. It was significant that nearly all ecclesiastical rulers sought a reputation for *Aufklärung* and tolerance; the old-fashioned view that heretics should be expelled (let alone burnt) had obviously become obsolete in the second half of the eighteenth century.[97]

Several writers defended the much-criticized union between Church and state which was the distinctive hallmark of ecclesiastical

[95] Fabritius, *Ueber den Werth und die Vorzüge geistlicher Staaten* (n.p., 1799), p. 3.
[96] This point was admitted even by Moser, op.cit., pp. 87ff.
[97] The best survey of these trends is the important article by Max Braubach, "Die kirchliche Aufklärung," cited in n.79.

territories. It was claimed that this was the best way to avoid the perennial quarrel between *imperium* and *sacerdotium* which had bedeviled so much of European history. Both Church and state were magnified and dignified by their close union. The Church could move quickly against irreligious tendencies before the disease could spread too far; the state was clothed with the aura of supra-mundane authority, a matter all the more important in an increasingly skeptical age. The separation of Church and state was viewed as a symptom of modern decay, and the surviving ecclesiastical states congratulated for avoiding this evil. It was also pointed out that the union of Church and state was by no means an exclusively Catholic practice, for it was the dominant pattern throughout Lutheranism; hence it was unfair to criticize it only in the Catholic parts of Germany.[98]

Catholic writers stressed that the suppression of the ecclesiastical states would endanger the position of every other state in Germany, for the legal position of ecclesiastical states was as well founded as that of secular ones. The ecclesiastical states could (as we have seen above) be suppressed only by application of brute force in violation of the imperial constitution. If the ecclesiastical states were suppressed, the small secular states would certainly be next, "for their existence does not rest upon any pillars more firm or more holy than that of the ecclesiastical states. The right of the stronger is like an insatiable hyena which searches for new prey day and night."[99]

The ecclesiastical states were, indeed, an essential part of the constitutional structure of the Holy Roman Empire. They were devoted to it—far more than were any other group of *Stände,* even the Imperial Knights and the Free Cities—by the double bond of interest and principle. Their existence in the face of rapacious neighbors depended upon the survival of the venerable imperial framework; their principles stressed allegiance to the "holy empire"—a relic of the Christian civilization of medieval Europe—and the emperor as the "anointed of God," protector of the Church, and natural head of the Catholic party within the empire. The ecclesiastical states were outspoken in their imperial patriotism and prided themselves for standing above the crude Machiavellian egotism of the secular princes.[100]

Finally, the defenders of the ecclesiastical states castigated in strong words the motives of many of the champions of secularization. These included, to be sure, some philanthropic reformers like Moser, though

[98] Fabritius, op.cit., pp. 43-45.
[99] Frank, op.cit., i; Fabritius, op.cit., pp. 140-43.
[100] Fabritius, op.cit., vii-xv.

even he was motivated by bigoted anti-Catholicism. Most of them were, however, the hired lackeys of secular princes desirous of rounding out their territories at the expense of their ecclesiastical neighbors. The call for secularization also appealed to

> the rapacity and yearning for sacrilege of all anarchists, scoundrels, ne'er do-wells and have-nots (*Anarchisten, Bösewichter, Taugenichtse und Habenichtse*)—in fact that whole army of desperate men who have lost their honor, health and property. They hope to exploit the storms of anarchy to seize the goods of the aristocracy and the clergy in order to be again in a position to eat, drink and be merry without work or fear of punishment.[101]

Such were the arguments offered by the Conservative defenders of Germany's ecclesiastical states. They carried comparatively little weight with public opinion. The dynamic forces of German public life—the territorial princes and the Radical intellectuals—were not open to persuasion concerning the merits of what they viewed a priori as intolerable anachronisms. The position of the ecclesiastical states was, however, secure so long as the general imperial fabric remained intact; if the empire collapsed, or suffered an external defeat, it was certain that the ecclesiastical states would be the first to be thrown into the ensuing territorial melting pot. This was to happen in the early stages of the Napoleonic Revolution in Germany. It is important to note, however, that the ecclesiastical states proved a permanent rather than a temporary casualty of that revolution. Their position had been undermined before the court of public opinion by a quarter century of controversy, and there was no significant public demand for their restoration after Napoleon's overthrow in 1814.

The Imperial Free Cities

The condition of the Imperial Free Cities has already been characterized in Ch. 1, in connection with the Reactionary outlook of the urban patrician class. Suffice it to repeat here that most of these Free Cities were in a state of hopeless decay. They were governed by narrow oligarchies, composed of patrician or (less frequently) guild elements, with an inefficiency and egotism unique even in the Germany of the eighteenth century. Their religious intolerance frequently exceeded that of the worst ecclesiastical states. They were generally economically stagnant and in consequence financially bankrupt. The tenacious adherence to anachronistic guild regulations paralyzed economic de-

[101] Fabritius, op.cit., XVI.

velopment within their walls, quite apart from the hostile policies of neighboring territorial states which aimed at economic strangulation preparatory to annexation. The widespread discontent of the middle- and lower-class population of the Free Cities was firmly repressed by police action and (if necessary) appeals to the imperial courts or the *Reichskreise.*

These evils were widely discussed in the journal and pamphlet literature of the period;[102] it is notable, however, that the Free Cities, unlike the Empire and the ecclesiastical states, found practically no literary defenders. The beneficiaries of the existing abuses were quite inarticulate; they presumably knew that their privileged condition could not stand the heat of public discussion. Their strategy was to suppress criticism by censorship and to denounce all critics as wicked and abominable rebels.[103]

Two specific examples will serve to illustrate the oligarchic practices of the cities and the controversies to which they gave rise; they both show the tenacity of patrician defense against the claims advanced by the semiprivileged citizen body (let alone the common people). The Free City of Cologne saw a sharp struggle in the early 1780's between the *Magistrat* (consisting of the patrician *Rat* and the *Bürgermeister* selected from its midst) and the *Bürgerschaft* (i.e., the body of full-fledged citizens, composed of house owners, guild masters, and established members of reputable professions). The *Bürgerschaft* complained of a wide range of evils (characteristic of oligarchy), such as graft, maladministration of municipal property, neglect of hospitals and other charitable institutions, and the voting of extravagant salary increases to themselves by city officials and their friends. There were also constitutional complaints: it was asserted that the *Magistrat* suppressed political rights guaranteed by two famous charters, the *Verbundbrief* of 1396 and the *Transfixbrief* of 1513; and that the *Magistrat,* which was constitutionally required to be renewed each year, had in fact established the practice of being re-elected only every three years, and at that through the use of corrupt methods. The *Ratsherren* of the *Magistrat* were supposed to be controlled by the body of *Bannerherren,* a group composed of hon-

---

[102] Schlözer took special pleasure in exposing the abuses which flourished in the Free Cities. See, as one example of many, *Staatsanzeigen,* IV (1784), *Vorbericht,* 3ff.

[103] I have been unable to find any general defense of the Free Cities comparable to the defenses of the Empire (Vogt, Müller, et cetera) and the ecclesiastical states (Frank, Fabritius, et cetera) for the period before 1789.

orary *Zunftvorsteher* elected for life; but they had long ceased to perform this control function because two thirds of the *Zunftvorsteher* were also *Ratsherren* with little inclination to control themselves and their immediate partners in the racket of living off the city trough.

The *Bürgerschaft* began with complaints which were ignored, then encouraged popular riots which were suppressed, and finally tried appeal to the *Reichshofrat* in Vienna to secure redress of grievances. It justified its appeal in the following words in January 1784:

> It is not necessarily due to a spirit of discord, obstinacy, disobedience or other evil qualities that subjects raise complaints against properly constituted authority; for unfortunately these authorities sometimes abuse the power which God and the Emperor have entrusted them with. Instead of being fathers of the fatherland they exceed their powers, show contempt for law, and become the scourge of their subjects. Can a subject remain silent under such circumstances? Should he not rather speak up with a firm voice so that his complaint may penetrate even to the sacred throne of the highest judge? Is it fair to call him a rebel when he only wants to prevent the destruction of the fatherland of which he is a member? The *Bürgerschaft* of the Imperial and Free City of Cologne on the Rhine finds itself precisely in this position. It finds its constitution violated, its members mistreated in the most shameful manner, the city treasury exhausted, commerce perishing, the seeds of discord scattered broadcast, and the city overwhelmed with debts—in short, the entire city stands on the verge of destruction. How could any citizen justify himself before either God or Emperor if he remained silent and did not loudly clamor for the exemplary punishment of the author of these evils?[104]

The *Bürgerschaft* demanded that the *Reichshofrath* establish an Imperial Commission of Inquiry to examine the abuses connected with the Cologne city administration. This the *Reichshofrath*, fearing to establish a dangerous precedent, refused to do; but it at least criticized the Cologne *Magistrat* for its financial mismanagement and called for the elimination of at least some abuses. The *Magistrat* took this reprimand in its stride and continued to misgovern in its customary manner, for it knew that the *Reichshofrath* lacked the power to enforce its judicial decisions. The *Bürgerschaft* of Cologne could do nothing but resign itself to a situation for which no legal remedy ap-

---

[104] Josef Hansen, *Quellen zur Geschichte des Rheinlandes im Zeitalter der französischen Revolution 1780-1801* (Bonn, 1931), I, 38.

peared available; it is not surprising, however, that this same *Bürgerschaft* showed little eagerness to defend its Cologne fatherland against the French invaders a few years later.[105]

A similar struggle occurred in the Imperial Free City of Ulm, which was also governed by a narrow patrician oligarchy justifiably apprehensive about public inquiry into its affairs. The *Bürgerschaft* (here also consisting primarily of guild masters and professionals) protested to the *Reichshofrath* in 1782 against a new system of taxation which continued the traditional tax exemption of patrician-owned rural lands; it demanded a new and more equitable system of taxation, the introduction of an open budget, and the appointment of a fiscal control body *(Revisionsausschuss)* drawn from its own ranks. The *Bürgerschaft* did not dream of raising these demands in the name of popular sovereignty or the rights of man (which might give ideas to the lower classes); it appealed rather to the *Schwörbrief* (charter) of 1558 with its specific guarantee that the *Bürgerschaft* had the right to be consulted on important governmental affairs.

The *Magistrat* protested to emperor and *Reichshofrath* about the rebellious demands of its subjects, and denounced as an illegal body the commission *(Deputat)* which the *Bürgerschaft* had elected to champion its claims. The *Reichshofrath* nonetheless called for negotiations between the *Magistrat* and the *Deputat,* but these failed in view of the intransigence of the former body. When a decision of the *Reichshofrath* could no longer be avoided, it proved generally favorable to the *Magistrat* (1782). The *Bürgerschaft* was censured for its rebellious conduct, and condemned to pay all trial costs. The *Deputat* was, however, to be tolerated as an *ad hoc* body, although the desire of the *Bürgerschaft* to make it a permanent control body was specifically condemned. It would be unfair to say that the *Reichshofrath* sided completely with the *Magistrat* against the *Bürgerschaft;* but its judgment was marked by an unwillingness to become the instrument for imposing major reforms upon the anachronistic structure of the Imperial Free Cities.[106]

---

[105] The main documents connected with the Cologne controversy are printed by Hansen, op.cit., pp. 38-41, 74-75, 107-08. The general Cologne situation is described in Arnold Stelzmann, *Illustrierte Geschichte der Stadt Köln* (Cologne, 1958), pp. 197ff.

[106] The so-called Ulmer *Bürgerprozesse* are described by Vierhaus, *Deutschland,* mss., pp. 91-93, on the basis of two unpublished Tübingen dissertations: G. Gansslen, *Die Ratsadvocaten und Ratskonsulenten der freien Reichsstadt Ulm, unsbesondere ihr Wirken in den Bürgerprozessen am Ende des 18. Jahrhunderts* (1950), and K. Lübke, *Die Verfassung der freien Reichsstadt Ulm am Ende des alten Reiches* (1955).

The Imperial Cities remained in fact unreformed until the Napoleonic period, when their problems were solved in a fashion through the simple device of annexation by their territorial neighbors. It is doubtful whether timely internal reforms would have prolonged their external independence, since the period of the city state was obviously over; but it is a noteworthy fact that the annexed cities caused remarkably little trouble to the states into which they were incorporated after 1803. Their citizens had little reason to yearn back to an imperial immediacy of which only a small patrician clique had been the beneficiary.

Two Specific Controversies

It remains to note briefly two specific controversies which aroused wide attention in pre-1789 Germany, namely, the prevalence of militarism and the attitude to be taken toward the American Revolution. The former is interesting for showing both the utopian strain of the *Aufklärung* and the Conservative willingness to defend even obvious evils in the *status quo*. The latter is important for stimulating a political consciousness hitherto largely dormant in Germany; it is significant that public opinion could be stirred more easily by criticism of the alleged tyranny of a British king over an America four thousand miles away than by the far-more-obvious tyranny of innumerable despots much closer home.

THE CONTROVERSY ON STANDING ARMIES AND WAR

The emphasis which the *Aufklärung* placed upon humanitarianism and enhancing individual happiness inevitably led to a criticism of war and standing armies. War caused unparalleled suffering to individuals, devastated fertile fields, removed tens of thousands of young men from economic pursuits during their most productive years, and paralyzed industry by requiring heavy taxes. To what end? Only to gratify the ambitions of despots, the martial instincts of aristocrats, and the rapacity of a few army contractors. The common people, on the other hand, did much of the fighting and most of the suffering, while their royal and aristocratic superiors garnered what glory was to be had. Many of the criticisms directed against war applied to the existence of peacetime standing armies as well. Their members were brutalized by a ferocious discipline considered necessary to prevent desertion in peace and guarantee fighting efficiency in war. They were removed from useful economic work and their maintenance was a heavy charge upon the taxpayer. It is small wonder that the thinkers of the *Aufklärung* confronted a Europe constantly in arms with the vision of a future world where harmony had replaced strife as the rule of international intercourse; where war had become an anachronism associated in the public mind with an earlier barbarous state of society; and where standing armies had been superseded by minuscule police forces exclusively devoted to the maintenance of internal order.[107]

Conservative authors did not question that war was a scourge and armies a heavy charge upon the resources of the state; they insisted only that both possessed compensatory merits and that the proposal to abolish them was far too utopian to merit serious discussion. The Prussian diplomat Dohm—whom we have previously encountered as prominent champion of Jewish emancipation and defender of the *Fürstenbund*—argued the case for standing armies against Radical critics in the following words:

> Much has been said against standing armies, and it must be admitted that they constitute a great misfortune for humanity when they take up too large a proportion of the population of a state and deprive agriculture and industry of too many hands. Many critics have, however, overlooked the fact—amply demonstrated by the experience of Prussia ever since the days of King Frederick William I—that the maintenance of a large army brings solid advantages wherever these mistakes are avoided: it increases the circulation of money, creates many employment opportunities, and becomes a stimulus to agriculture and industry alike. It must be added that war encourages many virtues (though the suffering it causes admittedly more than outweighs their value); but it must be remembered that even the peace-time standing army provides an opportunity to exercise certain qualities, and to develop certain capacities, which would atrophy but for the existence of standing armies, though they are important and beneficial to mankind. I reckon among these not only the refinement of the sense of honor, the training of the intellect, and the sharp eye for reality which differentiate officers from other members of the upper class; but the common soldier also benefits from military service through the improve-

[107] Literary criticism of militarism and war abounds in the last third of the eighteenth century. See, for example, M. Claudius, *Kriegslied* and *Ein Lied nach dem Frieden in Anno 1779*, printed in Emil Horner, *Politische Dichtung: Vor dem Untergang des alten Reichs 1756-95* (Leipzig, 1930). The dreams of perpetual peace can be studied in Kurt von Raumer, *Ewiger Friede; Friedensrufe und Friedenspläne seit der Renaissance* (Freiburg, 1953).

ment of his physique in strength and endurance; a better appreciation of the value of discipline, precision, activity, and subordination;
and an enlargement of his intellectual horizons. The peasant who
has spent several years with the colors is usually a better peasant
for that very reason.[108]

The well-known Cameralist writer Johann H. G. Justi took the lead
in demonstrating that eternal peace was a chimera.[109] He ridiculed
the dream of a European federative polity advanced by numerous
writers since the Abbé Charles de St. Pierre's (1658-1743) *Projet pour
rendre la paix perpetuelle en Europe* (1713). Justi argued that princes
possessed—and would always possess—an ineradicable desire for conquest, and that war was the only possible method to achieve territorial
gains since alternative methods (for example, purchase or international arbitration) were rarely efficacious. He took a dim view of the
functioning of all federations, ancient and modern: strife was perennial whether one looked at ancient Greece or contemporary Germany.
The only effective basis for federation was common consciousness of
an external menace, as in the cases of Holland and Switzerland.

It is impossible, however, to name any common interest which
could prompt all the princes of Europe to join into a federation
based upon equal membership. Europe as a whole has nothing to
fear from any external enemy; while the preservation of the existing
territorial *status quo* cannot possibly become an equal interest of
both the strong and the weak.[110]

Even supposing, however, that all European powers should, by a miracle, agree upon the establishment of an international tribunal, it
would nonetheless be impossible to make it an effective instrument for
settling all outstanding disputes. If a settlement required unanimity,

[108] Christian Dohm, *Über die bürgerliche Verbesserung der Juden*, II, 234-36.
Dohm added that militia services brought many of the same advantages; for a
minimum it brought men into the open air out of alehouses, which destroyed
both their health and their fortunes.

[109] Johann Heinrich Gottlob Justi, "Untersuchung: Ob Europa in eine Staatsverfassung gesetzt werden könne, wobei ein immer währender Friede zu hoffen
ist," *Historische und juristische Schriften* (Frankfurt and Leipzig, 1760), I, 171-
84. On Justi (1720-71) see W. Roscher, *Nationaloekonomik*, pp. 444-65, and
Louise Sommer, *Die österreichischen Kameralisten in dogmengeschichtlicher Darstellung* (2 vols., Vienna, 1920-25), II, 170-318. Justi was a professor at the
Theresianische Ritterakademie in Vienna (1750-53) and at Göttingen University
(1755-57) before entering the Prussian mining administration. He died in the
prison of Küstrin while under investigation for financial irregularities.

[110] Justi, op.cit., p. 177.

one could only expect permanent paralysis; if one relied upon majority voting, there would be no way of avoiding voting coalitions where political interests would play a larger role than the dictates of justice. There was, furthermore, the problem of how to enforce judgments levied against powerful offenders whose punishment would demand a police action indistinguishable from war. Justi prophetically foresaw all the problems inherent in international organizations, collective security, and the attempt to judicialize political disputes. He was extremely pessimistic as he placed his sole hope in a far-from-imminent improvement in human nature: "ruinous wars will only end if we truly make place in our hearts for brotherly love."[111]

Justi regretted that the abolition of war was impossible; others went farther to argue that it was *undesirable* as well. Johann Friedrich Wilhelm Jerusalem (1709-89), the famous court preacher of Brunswick, deplored the horrors of war but was certain that war played a providential role in the divinely created benevolent order of the world. He drew the following picture of eternal peace:

> How degenerate would the human race become! How licentious every vice, how tyrannical the pride of the great, how inhuman the luxury of the rich, how poisonous the general mode of thinking! Where would the austere teachings of Virtue still find entry into the human heart? How could God continue to remain in the eyes of men? The Creator of the world protects the atmosphere from pestilential rottenness through thunderstorms; He has created volcanoes to give an outlet to the miasmas stored in the bowels of the earth; likewise He sporadically requires the scourge of war in order to prevent serious outbreaks of immorality in the world. War shakes up the entire constitution of men; when the paroxysm is over they feel their weakness and moderate their sensuous drives. The long-prevalent spirit of frivolity is broken; there arises, at least for a time, a more serious way of looking at the world; there is a revival of the feeling for religion and for virtue; and men resume the search for the Unknown God.[112]

[111] Ibid., p. 183.
[112] Johann Friedrich Wilhelm Jerusalem, *Betrachtungen über die vornehmsten Wahrheiten der Religion* (Leipzig, 1768), p. 143. This work was the most widely read treatise on theology written in German during the eighteenth century; it was translated into French, Dutch, Swedish, and Danish. On Jerusalem (1709-89) see Wagenmann, *ADB*, XIII (1881), 779-83. He was a native of Osnabrück, a cousin of Justus Möser, and for almost fifty years (1742-89) the leading ecclesiastical and intellectual figure at the court of Brunswick.

Jerusalem found further additional benefits as he contemplated war. It stimulated certain virtues—the spirit of sacrifice, greatness of soul, and discipline—which inevitably atrophied during long periods of peace. It prevented the tyranny of the great by providing them with employment away from home; while simultaneously enlarging the horizons of the lower classes through foreign travel and challenging experiences. War prevented mankind from degenerating into provincialism by leading to a mixture of peoples and civilizations; often it provided unexpected cultural benefits, as when Greek culture was brought to the West as a consequence of the Turkish conquest of Constantinople in 1453. Even the devastation caused by war brought the incidental benefit of stimulating employment, encouraging invention, and checking unemployment. The reader suspects that there is a certain amount of special pleading in Jerusalem's argument as he added disarmingly, "You see, I am describing the benefits wrought by a fever."[113] His treatise nonetheless reveals what kinds of arguments were considered respectable in opposition to one of the noblest aspirations of the *Aufklärung*—the abolition, or at least the discrediting of, the age-old scourge of war.

THE DEBATE ON THE AMERICAN REVOLUTION

The criticism of war was partly derived from a thorough pacifism; but it was sharpened by being directed against the specific dynastic wars of aggrandizement so characteristic of the eighteenth century. That many Radicals were willing to distinguish between "good" and "bad" wars, instead of criticizing all wars indiscriminately, was shown by their frequent enthusiasm for the American Revolution. Here was an event calculated to touch the German imagination by its color and drama; it allowed vicarious identification with the cause of liberty and equality whose prospects appeared well-nigh hopeless in Germany itself; and it was far enough away to provide a harmless outlet for the most extreme political sentiments. Small wonder, then, that there was widespread enthusiasm for the American cause. The Americans were seen as revolting against despotism in the name of the inalienable rights of man. They were building a society based upon the principles of liberty and equality. They were blessed by the absence of all the forces which were perpetuating the German *status quo* so deplored by Radicals—monarchy, aristocracy, and ecclesiastical tyranny. The enthusiasm for the American cause was widespread throughout all of Germany, though there was also a measure of regional differentiation.

[113] Ibid., p. 145.

It was strongest in the Southwest, which had long had close ties to America as the home region of most of Germany's emigrants; here the Radical publicist C. F. Schubart, himself a victim of the absolutist caprice of the Württemberg ruler Karl Eugen, gave especially eloquent expression to the cause of American independence. A good many poets—Klopstock and Stolberg, for example—penned odes to the spirit of liberty arising in the New World; while the prosaic philosopher Kant found himself for once in full agreement with the men of the *Sturm und Drang*. The journals of the Berlin *Aufklärung*—the *Allgemeine Deutsche Bibliothek* and the *Berliner Monatsschrift*—were solidly on the American side; so was Frederick the Great, who never forgave the British their so-called "desertion of 1762." The main pocket of resistance against the "American disease" proved to be Hannover—a fact in part explained by that country's being ruled directly by the very George III whom the Americans had deposed as a "tyrant" in 1776.[114]

The leader of the anti-American position was A. L. Schlözer, the Göttingen professor whom we have previously encountered as one of the main champions of the *Aufklärung* as editor of the famous *Staatsanzeigen*. (This fact shows the impossibility of dividing even leading German figures in terms of any clear-cut Radical-Conservative scheme.) Schlözer believed that he had good "Liberal" reasons for opposing the American cause. His argument may be summarized as follows:[115]

The American colonists were both hypocrites and ingrates. They wanted independence from the motherland, an understandable desire in view of their "grown-up" status; but instead of saying so openly they advanced constitutional grievances as transparent pretexts. Schlözer thought the Americans were dead wrong on the entire con-

---

[114] This entire section is based upon the two standard works by H. P. Gallinger, *Die Haltung der deutschen Publizistik zu dem amerikanischen Unabhängigkeitskriege (1775-83)* (Leipzig, 1900), and Henry Stafford King, "Echoes of the American Revolution in German Literature," *University of California Publications in Modern Philology*, xiv (1929), 23-193. The earlier literature is listed in ibid., v. Two closely reasoned works favorable to the American cause were Matthias Christian Sprengel, *Geschichte der Revolution von Nord-Amerika* (Frankenthal, 1785), by a professor teaching at the Prussian University of Halle, and the anonymous article "Ist es gut, dass die englischen nordamerikanischen Kolonien unabhängig werden?" *Deutsches Museum* (1782), pp. 440-69. The author argued that Europe would suffer some economic disadvantages from American independence, but asserted this was more than balanced by the political advantage of providing mankind with a refuge from despotism.

[115] Gallinger, op.cit., pp. 24-46; King, op.cit., pp. 46-51.

stitutional issue; all the precedents showed that parliament was legally competent to legislate and tax everywhere within the British Empire: the contention of some Americans that it was necessary to break positive law in the name of a supposedly higher "natural law" was simply anarchical. The issue of "no taxation without representation" was an ingrate's device for avoiding the payment of a fair share of the revenue needed to service the debt piled up during the Seven Years' War fought largely for American interests. The Americans had been happy about the imperial connection when they needed imperial help against French aggression from Canada; they were prepared to throw it off the moment that it ceased to bring any direct advantage, whatever the benefits it had brought in the past.[116]

Schlözer viewed revolution as an intrinsic evil to be resorted to only after all other means had failed to redress intolerable wrongs. He ridiculed any attempt to glorify revolution as an expression of "natural rights"; only very great grievances could possibly justify a reluctant call to arms.[117] He was certain that the Americans had risen upon insufficient provocation, and he was highly critical of the lawless violence which had preceded the formal insurrection. The Boston Tea Party aroused his special anger: "Could one possibly describe the conduct of the Bostonians as responsible? Were disguised criminals, or undisguised protectors of disguised criminals, instruments appropriate for suffering subjects appealing for justice to their overlord?"[118] Did the Americans, while invoking the spirit of liberty, not in fact succumb to the spirit of anarchy and license?

Schlözer was, incidentally, convinced that the Americans could not win, as is shown by his incautiously printing a communication which sought to demonstrate in ten points why England must emerge triumphant from the war.[119] He expected a long-drawn-out struggle which must inevitably discredit the cause of moderate freedom throughout the world. Schlözer's hostility to the American Revolution must be partly explained by his fear that it would henceforth be more

[116] These points were made by the Dutch publicist Isaac Pinto in his article "Aufruhr in Amerika. Schreiben über die Empörung der Nordamerikaner," translated and printed by Schlözer, with approving comments, in *Briefwechsel*, I (1776), 29-53. They provoked a furious reply from the Brunswick publicist J. Mauvillon, "Anmerkungen über der Herren Pinto und Schlözer sophistische Verteidigung des englischen Ministeriums gegen die Kolonien," *Aufsätze über Gegenstände aus der Staatskunst* (2 vols., Leipzig, 1776-77), I, 139-88.

[117] *Briefwechsel*, I (1776), 383.

[118] Ibid., p. 53.

[119] "Politische Weissagungen des Herrn von Pinto über Nordamerika," ibid., pp. 103-10. Pinto did not prove to be much of a prophet.

difficult to persuade German princes to embark upon moderate reforms:

> The most disastrous result [of the American Revolution] lies in the conclusions which servile politicians, serving in the palaces and cabinets of princes, will draw from it. They will argue with an air of plausibility, that all the maxims of moderation, humanity and freedom, which have recently been accepted by numerous princes, are in fact part of a false political theory, since experience now shows that their application leads to rebellion, disorder, and anarchy. Despotism and tyranny will now be erected on the ruins of the principles of freedom, humanity, and sound policy reared through untold effort in the past. . . . Wise and moderate men, friends of humanity, champions of liberty will no longer be permitted to open their mouths; they will now have no choice but to sigh about the misfortunes of their fellow men in secret. Some, I fear, will even be so weak as to doubt the truth of their principles after their abuse has caused so much trouble.[120]

It is impossible, of course, to make any quantitative judgment about the impact of the American Revolution upon German public opinion. All that can be said is that it quickened interest in public questions, and helped to break the political torpor which was the legacy of two centuries of monarchical absolutism. It was without question one factor in the increasingly widespread Radical attack upon some key elements of Germany's political structure; though it occasionally also served—as Schlözer feared—as an element of retardation. Its most unfortunate effect was to perpetuate the German legacy of divorcing opinion from action, for many Germans combined fervid sympathy for the American cause with total apathy toward German conditions far more intolerable than those against which the American colonists rebelled.[121]

[120] Quoted by King, op.cit., p. 47. The Swabian publicist L. Wekhrlin, usually an *Aufklärer* with "advanced" tendencies, fully agreed with Schlözer's argument. See Gallinger, op.cit., pp. 57-61.

[121] For a Europe-wide survey of the impact of the American Revolution see R. R. Palmer, *The Age of the Democratic Revolution* (Princeton, 1959), Ch. 9.

CHAPTER 6

Justus Möser: Portrait of a Prerevolutionary Conservative

Biography and Milieu

WE HAVE hitherto treated many Conservative voices which defended specific dogmas, social conditions, or political institutions against the attacks of the *Aufklärung;* we have not yet, however, encountered any figure that can be described as championing a comprehensive Conservative *Weltanschauung* embracing all aspects of life. Such a figure was Justus Möser (1720-94), the administrator of the small Westphalian state of Osnabrück who won widespread fame in his day as the author of a series of urbane essays, and still interests us today because of his position at the beginning of Germany's self-conscious Conservative tradition. His broad impact upon his contemporaries is documented by Goethe in a famous passage in *Truth and Poetry*.[1] Herder admired Möser and printed part of the latter's *History of Osnabrück* in the famous collection of essays, *Von teutscher Art und Kunst,* the strident manifesto of the *Sturm und Drang*.[2] The most prominent German historians of the late eighteenth century—men such as J. S. Pütter, A. L. Schlözer, J. G. Eichhorn, and Johannes Müller—were all deeply influenced by Möser. The same can be said about the leading champions of the historical school of law, Savigny and Niebuhr.[3] Of subsequent Conservative writers the Hannoverian A. W. Rehberg was an acknowledged pupil; the thought of Adam Müller shows remarkable

---

[1] J. W. von Goethe, "Dichtung und Wahrheit," *Goethes Werke*, Vol. IX (ed. H. Kurz), Pt. II, Bk. XIII, 511-13. Möser may, in fact, have played a decisive role in Goethe's life. The latter had one of Möser's books displayed in his Frankfurt living room when Karl August of Weimar, his future patron, first called in 1775. The conversation turned to political topics treated in Möser's book; perhaps this suggested to the duke that the author of the *Sorrows of Werther* had potential as a practical statesman as well as a melancholic poet. Goethe's first conversation with Karl August is described in ibid., pp. 552-53. See also Georg Kass, *Möser und Goethe* (Berlin, 1909).

[2] *Von deutscher Art und Kunst, einige fliegende Blätter* (1773). Herder and Goethe were the other two contributors.

[3] See the excellent study by Ernst Hempel, "Justus Mösers Wirkung auf seine Zeitgenossen und auf die deutsche Geschichtsschreibung," *Mitteilungen des Vereins für Geschichte und Landeskunde von Osnabrück*, LIV (1933), 1-76, esp. 9-15.

parallels to that of Justus Möser;[4] Karl Ludwig von Haller's conception of politics as a series of private law relationships was taken straight from the pages of the Osnabrück author.[5] Of Conservative statesmen both Stein and his antagonist Marwitz stood under the influence of Möser's ideas; while he had a moderating effect upon such West German Liberals as Hardenberg's publicistic champion Benzenberg and Karl T. Welcker, coeditor of the famous *Staatslexicon*.[6] The romantic school considered Möser too prosaic and down to earth to reckon him as an honored forerunner; yet it owed more to his organic and evolutionary conception of society than it was generally willing to acknowledge.

While Möser contributed much to Germany's Conservative tradition, this is but part of his work, for he was one of the best-known and most-distinguished literary figures in Germany during the second half of the eighteenth century. He knew, personally or through correspondence, just about everybody worth knowing in the cultural world.[7] He won the admiration of the entire German republic of letters by entering the lists against the great Frederick's ignorant attack upon German literature in 1781.[8] His attractive and tolerant personality allowed him to have friendly relations with men of very diverse views: thus Friedrich Nicolai, the very incarnation of the German *Aufklärung*, was not only Möser's publisher but frequent correspondent and sympathetic first biographer.[9] This fact deserves to be remembered because it shows that the battle line between Radicalism and Conservatism was not as yet firmly drawn in the years before the French Revolution. We tend to see Nicolai and Möser as intellectual opposites, but it is certain that they did not view each other in this light. There were many ingredients of the *Aufklärung* in Möser him-

---

[4] Jakob Baxa, "Justus Möser und Adam Müller. Eine vergleichende Studie," *Jahrbuch für Nationalökonomie und Statistik*, CXXIII (1925), 14-30.

[5] See F. Meinecke, *Historismus*, p. 344.

[6] Hempel, op.cit., esp. pp. 40ff. On the relationship of Möser to Marwitz see K. Mannheim, "Conservative Thought," pp. 144-45; the influence on the Liberals is documented by Heinz Boberach, *Wahlrechtsfragen im Vormärz. Die Wahlrechtsanschauung im Rheinland 1815-49 und die Entstehung des Dreiklassenwahlrechts* (Düsseldorf, 1959), esp. pp. 18-35.

[7] His contacts are chronicled in the popular biography by Ludwig Bäte, *Justus Möser: Advocatus Patriae* (Frankfurt, 1961), pp. 206-24, and the somewhat pedantic compilation by Heinrich Schierbaum, "Justus Mösers Stellung in den deutschen Literaturströmungen," *Mitt. des Vereins f. Gesch. u. Landeskunde von Osnabrück*, XXXIII (1908), 167-216, and XXXIV (1909), 1-43.

[8] Möser, *Ueber die deutsche Sprache und Literatur* (1781). Reprinted in a critical edition by Carl Schüddekopf (Berlin, 1902).

[9] Friedrich Nicolai, *Leben Justus Mösers* (Berlin and Stettin, 1797).

self; he stands, indeed, at the watershed of two intellectual worlds which he was still able to fuse into a harmonious though distinctly personal synthesis. While our analysis will concentrate upon those aspects of his thought which contributed to Germany's emergent Conservative tradition, it should be remembered that these by no means embrace the *whole* Möser.

First, however, a few words about his life and local milieu. Justus Möser was born in Osnabrück in 1720 and spent his entire life there until his death in 1794 (excepting only four years at the Universities of Halle and Göttingen, and eight months on a mission to England in 1764). He had the good fortune to be born into the urban patriciate which constituted part of the ruling class: his father, descended from a long line of lawyers and Protestant clergymen, was *Kanzleidirektor* and *Konsistorialpräsident,* two high administrative posts; Justus' mother was the daughter of the *Bürgermeister* (mayor). Young Justus was appointed through family influence to the post of secretary of the *Ritterschaft* (i.e., the corporate organization of the territorial nobility) while he was still at the university, and he therefore had little incentive to engage in laborious study to pick up a degree. His student years were devoted at least as much to literature—his great love—as to the law that was destined to become his profession. Möser returned to Osnabrück in 1744 to settle down as a lawyer and to embark upon a brilliant public career that was to make him the leading citizen and the soul of the administration of his native state for more than thirty years.[10]

It is essential to know the main facts about the constitutional and social structure of the principality of Osnabrück to understand the thought of Justus Möser, for rarely has any writer drawn so much upon his local milieu in the development of his principles. Osnabrück may be described as a venerable museum where much of Germany's medieval past had survived into the eighteenth century. It was a small state even in the parcellated world of Western Germany, with

[10] All biographical information is taken, unless otherwise stated, from Nicolai's biography cited in n.9. The recent study by Ludwig Bäte, *Justus Möser; Advocatus Patriae* (Frankfurt, 1961), is a useful work of popularization while sometimes degenerating into a local chronicle. It is conventional and superficial in its intellectual history. The best brief summary is still Wegele, "Justus Möser," *ADB*, xxii (1885), 385-90. An indispensable source on Möser's life is the collection of Möser's *Briefe* edited by E. Beins and W. Pleister (Hannover, 1939). Two valuable studies centered on his early intellectual development are Paul Göttsching, *Mösers Entwicklung zum Publizisten* (Frankfurt, 1935), and Werner Pleister, "Die geistige Entwicklung Justus Mösers," *Mitt. des Vereins f. Geschichte und Landeskunde von Osnabrück,* L (1928), 1-89.

an area of forty-five square miles and a population of about 125,000. The form of government may be described as "theocratic," since a bishop, assisted by his cathedral chapter, exercised the power of temporal sovereignty. Under a curious stipulation of the Treaty of Westphalia (1648) there was an alternation between Catholic and Protestant bishops (the latter in practice taken from the royal Hannoverian House). For the first half of Möser's life the ruler was the Catholic Klemens August, a pluralist more famous as elector-archbishop of Cologne and builder of the palace of Brühl. When Klemens August died in 1761 he was succeeded by the Protestant Frederick Duke of York, the second son of the British King George III. The personal power of the bishop was closely circumscribed by the aristocratic cathedral chapter composed of twenty-one Catholic and three Protestant canons; while the aristocratic element in the constitution was further enhanced by the position of the surviving *Stände*. This body was composed of the highly privileged *Ritterschaft* and the *Städtekurie* (i.e., city representatives elected by the various municipal oligarchies). The capital city of Osnabrück (from which the entire state took its name) had a popular form of government since the city council (*Magistrat*) of sixteen members was elected annually. The franchise was broad but limited strictly to citizens, a group sharply distinguished from mere inhabitants. (This distinction was to play a central role in Möser's thought.) It will be seen that this constitutional framework combined ecclesiastical, aristocratic, patrician, and democratic features in a unique blend; and that it was in every way the antipode of that monarchical absolutism which was relentlessly pulverizing the old *Ständestaat* in other parts of Germany.[11]

The social structure of Osnabrück was also characterized by the continued existence of medieval elements. The countryside knew a good many nobles whose estates were worked by servile labor; but it also contained numerous independent peasants who owned and farmed their own homesteads—survivors (or so Möser thought) of that

[11] The classic contemporary description of the constitution of Osnabrück is J. E. Stüve, *Beschreibung und Geschichte des Hochstifts und Fürstentums Osnabrück* (Osnabrück, 1789). A dry modern analysis is M. Bär, *Abriss einer Verwaltungsgeschichte des Regierungsbezirks Osnabrück*, Vol. v of *Quellen und Darstellungen zur Geschichte Niedersachsens* (Hannover and Leipzig, 1901). The peculiar provision for the alternation of bishops is described in Johannes Freckmann, "Die Capitulatio perpetua und ihre verfassungsgeschichtliche Bedeutung für das Hochstift Osnabrück (1648-50)," *Mitt. des Vereins f. Gesch. u. Landeskunde von Osnabrück*, xxxi (1906), 129-203.

"golden age" of German social history when free peasants combined farming with militia (*Heerbann*) and jury service prior to the general degradation caused by the introduction of the feudal system in the age of Charlemagne. Serfdom still existed in Osnabrück at the bottom of the rural pyramid, but it was in a comparatively lenient form of which Möser was to become a somewhat reluctant defender. The towns were dominated by guild artisans little affected as yet by the Commercial Revolution; the "putting out" system had developed only in a few crafts. Foreign trade had declined since the days when Osnabrück had been a member of the Hanseatic League. The eighteenth-century state was a parochial backwater where most men contented themselves with traditional subsistence rather than striving for prosperity, and where the medieval idea that every man should seek no more than a customary scale of living was only beginning to break down. In Möser's native milieu traditionalism was for most people still an unquestioned fact; dynamic innovation, a remote rather than a present danger. This may serve to explain Möser's remarkably good temper in his combat with the modern forces that threatened to destroy his cherished world—they were unlikely to do so in his own lifetime and did not personally affect him in an adverse way.[12]

When Möser returned from the university to his native city, he began his public career. This career proved notable for the plurality of seemingly incompatible jobs which he held in combination at one and the same time. We have already seen that he was appointed secretary of the *Ritterschaft* while still a student (he took up his duties in 1744 at the age of twenty-four). He was promoted to the post of syndic in 1755, which made him the main spokesman for aristocratic interests in Osnabrück. The *Ritterschaft,* using its traditional prerogative of recommending a candidate, nominated him for the office of *advocatus patriae* in 1747; the romantic name has kindled the admiration of Möser's later admirers, but in fact the post only made Möser the most junior member of a three-man commission charged with protecting the financial interests of the government. One might describe him as a district attorney specializing in fiscal cases; some of these might be

---

[12] The best analysis of the social condition of Osnabrück is to be found in the background description of two works devoted to Möser's social policies and views: Otto Hatzig, *Justus Möser als Staatsmann und Publizist* (Hannover and Leipzig, 1909), and Heinz Zimmermann, *Staat, Recht und Wirtschaft bei Möser* (Jena, 1933). The former is based upon minute archival research (but virtually unreadable); the latter a brilliant summary despite some unnecessary polemics against modern Liberal society and the author's grotesque belief that the suffering mankind of 1933 had much to learn from Möser.

directed against the *Ritterschaft* or its members; hence there was a constant possibility of conflict of interest (though one built into the Osnabrück constitution). Möser accepted an additional job in 1762 as *Justitiarius beym Kriminalgericht*, i.e., court official charged with investigating the facts in pending judicial cases. He was appointed to this post by the cathedral chapter which governed Osnabrück during the vacancy between the death of Klemens August in 1761 and the election of Frederick of York. The appointment reveals the confidence which Möser inspired even among the Catholic canons—unless it was by chance an attempt by the canons to bribe an influential citizen with office on the eve of the inevitable constitutional struggle between prince and chapter. The Hannoverian House nominated Frederick, who was still an infant, to the episcopal vacancy in order to control Osnabrück for a maximum length of time. The chapter claimed the powers of regency in competition with the prince's father King George III. Möser, who had established personal contact with His Majesty while in England on official *Ritterschaft* business in 1763-64, sided with the king and helped him to prevail over the canons. While retaining his earlier posts of *Ritterschaft* syndic, *Justitiarus,* and *advocatus patriae* Möser became in fact (though as a commoner he could not in name) the leading official of the new Protestant government. He served the royal regency first as *Consulent* (1764) and then as *Referendar* (1768) until Frederick of York came of age in 1783; thereafter he was given the title of *Geheimer Justizrath* and continued to govern Osnabrück until his death in 1794.[13]

Möser was singularly successful during all these years in enjoying the confidence of all of his masters—king, *Ritterschaft*, and cathedral chapter—no matter how much they were at odds with one another. When the *Stände* assembled in Osnabrück, all royal rescripts were drafted ex officio by Justus Möser, *Consulent* to George III, regent for Bishop Frederick of York. The replies of the *Ritterschaft*, which dominated the *Stände corpora*, were drafted ex officio by Justus Möser, syndic of the *Ritterschaft;* while disputes arising between king and *Stände* might very well be investigated ex officio by Justus Möser, *Justitiarius beym Kriminalgericht* (until he resigned that post, and that post alone, in 1768). There was no pretence at maintaining any separation of powers so far as Möser was concerned.

[13] Möser's political role is covered by Otto Hatzig, "Justus Möser als Politiker," *Zeitschrift des historischen Vereins für Niedersachsen,* LXXVI (1911), 102ff., and Bruno Krusch, "Justus Möser und die Osnabrücker Gesellschaft," *Mitt. d. Vereins f. Gesch. und Landeskunde von Osnabrück,* XXXIV (1909), 244-73, both based upon exhaustive archival researches.

Möser's disciple Rehberg described the formidable administrative problems constantly confronted by his master in the following passage:

The conduct of public business in Osnabrück—for which Möser stood primarily responsible—was far more complicated than is the case in other states, whether large or small, where a sovereign will issue orders which are automatically obeyed. The princely government was constantly involved in endless entanglements: with the Emperor and the *Reichstag;* with the various Imperial courts; with the authority of the Pope and the chancery (*Vikariat*) of the Archbishop; with the cathedral chapter and the *Ritterschaft;* and with the city of Osnabrück, a curious hybrid of Imperial Free City and territorial town. Möser held the most variegated and finely spun threads of government in his own hand; guided the movement of the most disparate forces through the power of his intellect and the justice of his character, which was always scrupulous in protecting all existing rights; and was able to evoke both love and admiration from all with whom he came into contact.

The cathedral chapter had claimed, on the basis of some electoral capitulations, participation in the regency during the minority of the prince; Möser was compelled to oppose the claim as the guardian of the princely prerogative. The canons, especially those who were Roman Catholics (21 out of 24), were suspicious toward the Protestant government but had full confidence in Möser personally. The *Ritterschaft*, which claimed—under the protection of the laws of the Empire—extreme privileges against both the government and the broad body of its fellow-citizens, stood under the domination of a very few "family connections." Möser, who had served as guardian to the orphan scion of one of the oldest families (von dem Bussche), was able to exercise a moderating influence upon [aristocratic pretensions]. Relations with the city of Osnabrück required extremely cautious handling. As a corporation it could claim privileges far outdating the establishment of princely sovereignty (*Landeshoheit*), privileges which approximated those claimed by the Imperial Free Cities. Its citizens were notable for all the qualities which one expects to find in Free Cities: attachment to corporate privilege, civic consciousness (*Gemeinsinn*), family connections, and obstinate prejudice in the defense of communal and private rights. Möser was able to moderate contentions through his admirable talent, based upon his perfect knowledge of history and law, for circumventing constitutional disputes: fully knowing that such disputes, when once brought into the open, are only rarely resolvable.[14]

Möser was never satisfied with merely operating the cumbersome constitutional machinery of his native state with a minimum of friction. He desired in addition to educate his fellow citizens in the ways of their government in order to enhance their patriotic allegiance:

> I always thought it insufficient that a ruler should impose good government upon his people by decree: this objective should rather be achieved by the consent and satisfaction of those for whose sake good government exists.[15]

The best way of promoting consent was through the frank and full explanation of the reasons for governmental actions:

> It was my intention to inform the public about all public business and thereby promote love of our prince and confidence in the skill and honesty of his officials. My fellow-countrymen should know how the prince speaks to his *Stände* and how they reply; what the reasons are why some taxes are granted and others rejected; the scrupulous care given to even the smallest matters affecting the public welfare; the precise way in which taxes are spent; and everything else which pertains to the conduct of the government and the state of our constitution.[16]

To achieve these ends—which reveal how sharply Möser stood outside of Germany's predominant absolutist tradition—Möser founded and edited a weekly newspaper, the *Wöchentliche Osnabrückische Anzeigen,* in October 1766, and retained his editorship, over and above his multifarious other responsibilities, for the next sixteen years, until 1782. The weekly was conceived as a combination of governmental bulletin, local gazette, and forum for Möser's lay sermons. Most of its columns were filled with news about births, deaths, marriages, and visiting foreigners. There were many official announcements about new laws, regulations, and taxes; and a large amount of space was devoted to the advertisements which soon made the paper a money-earning enterprise. The most interesting feature of nearly every issue was, however, a descriptive or exhortative article on some public theme; almost 60 per cent of these were written by Möser him-

[14] A. W. Rehberg, *Sämmtliche Schriften* (Hannover, 1831), ii, 22-23.
[15] From the preface to the collected edition of the *Patriotische Phantasien,* ii, 3.
[16] Ibid.

self. (It is clear that his newspaper, like nearly all German journals in the eighteenth century, was substantially a one-man affair.) The articles (some 848 in 16 years, of which Möser personally wrote 458) deal with the greatest variety of topics, but they are all characterized by an appeal to the reading interests of the local population. Möser wrote for his Osnabrück contemporaries, not Germany as a whole or posterity. This simple fact explains why most of his articles have only an archaic interest today and often require the commentary of an antiquary to be fully understood.[17]

Nevertheless, at least some of his contributions are still interesting and readable today, and they aroused excitement among many contemporaries who lived far from the parochial concerns of Osnabrück. Möser had the essayist's gift of extracting a maximum of general significance out of any specific situation; his worldly wisdom and dry humor, compared by Goethe to Benjamin Franklin's, had a direct appeal to many readers; and he possessed one of the most distinguished prose styles in Germany. The German public must, above all, have appreciated the man behind the work—a man who possessed a well-rounded and consistent view of the world which found expression in miscellaneous observations on the most variegated subjects. It is not surprising that there arose a widespread demand for reprinting his articles in book form; Möser yielded in 1774 and gave his collection the title *Patriotische Phantasien*,[18] under which his name has

---

[17] The definitive monograph on the *Wöchentliche Osnabrückische Anzeigen* is Wolfgang Hollmann, *Justus Mösers Zeitungsidee und ihre Verwirklichung* (Munich, 1937), valuable despite its Nazi outlook and arrogant contempt for most previous Möser scholarship.

[18] Four volumes appeared in all: 1774, 1775, 1778, and 1786. They were edited by Möser's daughter, J.W.J. von Voigts. Successive editions are listed by Hollmann, op.cit., pp. 225-27. I cite after the reissue of 1842 in Vols. I-IV of Möser's *Sämmtliche Werke*. Henceforth cited as Möser, *Werke*. This edition, published in Berlin in ten volumes in 1842-43, was edited by Bernhard Rudolf Abeken (1780-1866), after 1812 the rector of the Osnabrück *Humanistisches Gymnasium* and the foremost authority on Möser in the nineteenth century. His editorial methods were rather too sharply criticized by Erich Haarmann in a pedantic article, "Über Mösers Art zu schaffen, mit einer Bemerkung über B. R. Abekens editorische Tätigkeit," *HZ*, CXL (1929), 87-99. A definitive edition is now in preparation: *Justus Mösers sämtliche Werke, Historisch-kritische Ausgabe* (eds. Werner Kohlschmidt, Ludwig Schirmener, et cetera; 7 vols., to date, Oldenburg and Berlin, 1943-58). (It has seemed preferable to cite the completed earlier edition to avoid a mixed system of references.) There are two excellent anthologies which include everything of interest for the nonspecialist: Karl Brandi, *Justus Möser, Gesellschaft und Staat* (Munich, 1921), and Curt Loehning, *Advocatus Patriae, Justus Möser. Schriften* (Berlin, 1948). It is no accident that both were published after disastrous World Wars when Germans were rethinking their political heritage.

entered German literature. The four-volume collection constitutes our main source for Möser's Conservative *Weltanschauung*.

This fact presents certain problems which confront every historical treatment of Möser. His articles were frequently hastily written to meet his weekly deadline and he did not bother to correct them later in more than a perfunctory manner. They are often written in a dialogue form in order to stimulate thought about controversial questions; it is not always clear with what party (if any) Möser wished to identify himself. He had, moreover, the habit of mind of the trained lawyer who can argue all sides with equal facility while concealing his personal convictions. A further problem is created by Möser's acknowledged lack of frankness when dealing with locally contentious themes. His qualified defense of serfdom—to mention only the most notorious example—scandalized his "enlightened" contemporaries. When Nicolai queried him on this matter Möser pleaded in extenuation the following prudential considerations:

I do not wish to be suspected of having presented the pro and contra about many issues [such as serfdom] in any spirit of wanton indifference. I have been forced to write in this manner because of local circumstances *(wichtige Lokalgründe)*. I certainly would have declared open war upon serfdom if the ministry and the estates *(ganze Landschaft)* had not consisted exclusively of serf-owners *(Gutsherren)*. If I were to lose their admiration and confidence I would seriously impair my future usefulness to the public.[19]

Möser enlarged upon this point in his introduction to the third volume of his *Patriotische Phantasien*, commenting wryly that "it is peculiar that I am known at home as the most intransigent foe, abroad as the most earnest defender of, the institution of serfdom."[20] He frankly avowed that he wrote not to advance general truth but rather to promote specific objectives in specific situations.

I would gain no advantage by the honor of having spoken my opinion freely if I thereby antagonized my fellow-citizens; and I confess that I value the love and confidence of my fellow-citizens as much as I do truth and justice. In order to simultaneously not lose the former yet avoid violating the latter I have often spoken more ambiguously than if I had written for a larger public.[21]

[19] Nicolai, op.cit., pp. 57-58. Nicolai rather transcended his customary pharisaism in sympathizing with his friend's genuine predicament.
[20] Möser, *Werke*, III, 3.   [21] Ibid.

Whatever he wrote, Möser was above all a busy and practical administrator; writing was his hobby, not his profession. He did not strive for the logical consistency and systematic development of a complete view of the world obligatory for a professional philosopher. He was in fact not a professional intellectual of any kind and the farthest possible character from the "rootless intellectual." His feet were always planted firmly on the ground, and even when he advocated irrationalism there was not a trace of fuzziness or mysticism in his pleading. His temper and cast of mind were distinctly prosaic and utilitarian. His finest quality was his minute knowledge of the society which he governed as well as described. The descriptions of peasant life are dripping with the mud of the Westphalian countryside; those of town life show how closely he observed his Osnabrück neighbors irrespective of their station in life. His analyses of legal problems reveal the keen eye of the practicing lawyer, that of governmental problems, a mastery of administrative processes which made Möser understandably contemptuous of the abstract generalizations which often passed for political thought in the age of the *Aufklärung*.

Möser possessed an uncanny gift for simultaneously standing both inside and above the society of his native Osnabrück. He enjoyed being in the center of its affairs, increasingly monopolized all strings of power in his hands, and worked hard at cultivating personal relationships in that small patrician, aristocratic, and bureaucratic circle which alone counted. He was evidently satisfied with his comfortable and inherited niche in this remarkably small world, and never seriously contemplated leaving it for a larger stage more commensurate with his abilities.[22] Yet he could also laugh at the foibles of this Lilliputian state, was intellectually stimulated by the large perspectives opened up by his eight months' stay in London (1763-64), and took a keen interest in the literary affairs of all the leading European countries (France, England, Germany, and Italy). It was his consciousness of the relativity and parochialism of all human endeavor—not an intrinsically parochial outlook—which prevented him from viewing and judging Osnabrück *sub specie aeternitatis*. There were no Olympian heights from which one could look down on, or absolute standards by which one could judge, any society. Möser's descriptions of his native

[22] The Hannoverian government offered Möser an attractive position as *Oberappellationsrath* in Celle in the early 1750's, which might have become the stepping stone to a career in the leading state of Northwest Germany; but he preferred to remain in the service of his native Osnabrück.

Osnabrück often illustrate Meredith's definition of humor—to laugh at what one loves while never ceasing to love it.

It is idle to search for intellectual influences to explain Möser's Conservatism. He stands at the very beginning of Germany's Conservative tradition, before there were forerunners upon whose writings he could draw. His opinions must be described as autonomous in the sense that they were the original and spontaneous response to his specific environment of a man of unusual intelligence and personality. While we stress his unique qualities we must not forget, however, that much of this response was what one might expect from a Westphalian patrician. He showed many qualities often considered specifically Westphalian: robustness, an earthy sense for realities, the capacity to pierce through shams, and a high sense of his own individuality—all qualities explicable perhaps by the long survival of a freehold peasantry (*bäuerliches Hofsassentum*) in Westphalia, whereas in many other parts of Germany peasant proprietorship succumbed to the feudal system with its artificial chivalry and brutalized servility. Möser's self-assurance came naturally to a born patrician whose smooth and unexciting life was devoid of conflict, frustrated ambition, or dramatic alterations of fortune. His sense of civic responsibility—of passionate concern for the *res publica*—was characteristic of the best type of German burgher in cities whose public spirit was neither crushed by princely absolutism nor paralyzed by oligarchic stagnation.

Möser's most conspicuous trait was his identification with his native milieu and satisfaction with it. He was fortunate in never having to struggle for a livelihood, social status, or an interesting career; he had reason to be contented and in fact *was* contented. It is certainly true that his greatness was not appreciated by his Osnabrück fellow citizens; it is far from certain that he recognized it *himself*. He lived and died as the main administrator of a petty principality in Northwest Germany, differentiated from many other administrators, like Fürstenberg in neighboring Münster, only by the publication of a weekly newspaper whose articles impressed contemporaries by their shrewdness and charm. They interest us today because they gave expression to nearly every theme advanced by German Conservatives for the next century. This fact, and their direct influence upon many of the figures subsequently treated in this volume, serve to justify a detailed analysis of Möser's ideas, quite apart from their intrinsic interest and Möser's historic position as the first German Conservative writer possessing a comprehensive and well-defined *Weltanschauung*.

The Break with the Aufklärung

It will be convenient to analyze Möser's Conservatism under three different headings: his hostility to much of the general spirit of the *Aufklärung;* the outlines of his general political theory; and his specific defense of the specific Osnabrückian *status quo.* The fragmentary and *ad hoc* character of his thought makes its presentation in orderly sequence especially desirable if a coherent picture is to emerge from his welter of miscellaneous observations. This systematization is, however, introduced purely to serve the convenience of the reader, who must never forget that in real life Möser was a busy administrator and part time newspaper columnist, not a systematic philosopher.

We have seen in Ch. 3 that the *Aufklärung* tended to be hostile to the principle of religious revelation, and sought to replace Orthodoxy —whether Catholic or Protestant—by a deistic "religion of nature" comprehensible through Reason alone. Möser was sufficiently a child of the eighteenth century to appreciate, and indeed share, much of the criticism directed by *Aufklärung* thinkers against traditional Christianity: he knew that critical scholarship had discredited some of the Biblical foundations of Protestantism, believed that Catholicism was a congeries of obscurantist superstition, and deplored the evils wrought by religious intolerance and bigotry throughout the history of Christianity. What Möser's personal religion was is difficult to say with any certainty, since he was a reticent man who did not wear his heart on his sleeve. It appears probable—on the basis of rather scattered evidence—that his own beliefs were a curious compound of rationalist theism and traditionalist reverence for the faith of his Protestant fathers, a faith certainly no less "reasonable" than any other. Möser's worldliness, absorption in practical affairs, and robust temperament make it unlikely that he brooded much about his personal salvation. He viewed religion rather as a statesman who recognizes its crucial importance as a social phenomenon, and seeks to mobilize it, in a frankly utilitarian spirit, for the cause of social order, moral discipline, and keeping the poor contented with their lot in life.[23]

What kind of religion was most likely to perform best these utili-

[23] The attempt of Franz Blanckmeister, *Justus Möser, der deutsche Patriot und Apologet des Christentums* (Heidelberg, 1885), to portray Möser as a believing Lutheran rather than one who approached religion in a purely utilitarian spirit must be considered a failure.

tarian functions? Certainly not the dry deism of Voltaire, whom Möser criticized in 1750 for his failure to understand the Protestantism propagated by the earthy, colorful, flesh-and-blood figure of Martin Luther;[24] nor the rather ethereal, undogmatic enthusiasm of Rousseau's Savoyard vicar, whose religious conceptions must always remain incomprehensible to the broad masses of men.[25] What the masses needed was a simple, authoritative religion based upon divinely revealed dogma (not argument), one which gave firm and uncomplicated ethical commands and which possessed an impressive ritual to appeal to the emotional side of man. There was no substitute for a unique religious revelation authenticated by miracles geared to the credulity of mankind, even if such an exclusive religion showed a tendency toward intolerance. It may be said in summary that Möser wished to strengthen and preserve for the lower classes a traditionalist type of Christianity in which he personally did not believe. Even more than that: Möser disliked some crucial features of Christianity—for example, the stress upon love rather than honor, and the egalitarian implications of the universal Fatherhood of God, which could easily give men misguided ideas about equality. He considered these personal dislikes, however, to be inconsequential in view of the fact that Christianity was the established religion with a mass appeal, and that its replacement by another—or a selective purge of its doctrines—must be considered a quixotic enterprise certain to stir up undesirable controversies.[26]

He was much concerned about the connection between religious belief and effective performance of civic duties. This preoccupation was clearly revealed in a series of essays, purportedly consisting of "Letters from Virginia," which he published in the *Berlinische Monatsschrift* in the late 1780's under the title *Concerning General Toleration*.[27] The satirical and extravagant style of these pieces makes it impossible to take them completely seriously; but Möser obviously identified himself with their general argument: that there must be

[24] Justus Möser, *Lettre à M. de Voltaire, contenant un Essai sur le caractère de Dr. Martin Luther et sa Reformation* (Hamburg 1750). Reprinted in *Werke*, v, 215-29.

[25] Justus Möser, *Schreiben an den Herrn Vicar in Savoyen, abzugeben bei Herrn Johann Jacob Rousseau* (Hamburg, 1763). Reprinted *Werke*, v, 230-51. It was immediately translated into English by J.A.F. Warnecke, *Letter to the Vicar of Savoy wherein Mr. Rousseau's Emile is examinated* (London, 1763).

[26] The best discussion of Möser's religion is in F. Meinecke, *Die Entstehung des Historismus* (n.e., Munich, 1959), pp. 347-51.

[27] "Über die allgemeine Toleranz. Briefe aus Virginien," in *Werke*, v, 293-315.

some limits to religious toleration, and that the government must have the right to differentiate between permissible and impermissible religious beliefs. A religion which taught obviously immoral practices—such as polygamy, incest, and infanticide—or doctrines incompatible with the established political and social order—such as the abolition of private property or absolute pacifism—must be outlawed and its adherents forced to emigrate. Certain slightly less dangerous opinions should be tolerated but their advocates penalized by being given second-class citizenship. Möser placed atheism and the denial of immortality in this latter category. He argued that the oaths of atheists could not be trusted since they did not believe in an omniscient deity who punishes perjury known to himself alone; their signature on commercial contracts was worth less than the signature of God-fearing men; and they were comparatively useless as soldiers because their fear of death was not neutralized by the hope of a happier life in the Hereafter. Atheists should be tolerated in society only if they accepted, in writing, such disabilities as ineligibility to testify in court and to negotiate mortgages; and they must pledge themselves to hire a substitute to perform their military service in case of war. These illiberal conclusions struck at the heart of the "enlightened" principle that citizenship should be completely independent of religious status.

Möser differed, however, from an orthodox zealot like Goeze in his refusal to get unduly excited about the neological attack upon traditional Christianity, for he was certain that it must ultimately fail since the common man would always require an authoritative traditionalist religion. He wrote in an open letter to a friend who feared that Orthodoxy was crumbling under *Aufklärung* attack:

> Do not worry, dear friend, religion will survive no matter how hard pressed: the ordinary man needs her too much to dispense with her completely. If Herostrat should ever succeed in burning her temple it is certain that man would immediately start to search for her traces amidst the ruins.[28]

Or again:

> You ask where we will stand when revelation and miracles will have been reasoned away by philosophy. Let me rejoin that it is improbable that things will ever go that far: the men who earn their daily bread by the sweat of their brows—and they will always compose the greater part of mankind—will refuse to surrender either

[28] "Über Toleranz," in ibid., p. 73.

311

revelation or miracles so long as the fact of human suffering persists
—that is forever.[29]

Möser foresaw that deism could never satisfy either the emotional
needs of the masses, the intellectual needs of the educated elite, or the
political needs of the state. In his view it was but a temporary, though
typical, religious aberration produced by the one-sided rationalism of
the intellectuals of the *Aufklärung*.

Möser's distrust of rationalism—or at least "one-sided rationalism"
—placed him in opposition to the great body of *Aufklärer*. Several
factors serve to explain this distrust. It arose in part from his responsible absorption in practical affairs; administrators usually reject and
resent the blueprints for a better society drawn up by their armchair
critics. Another factor was Möser's passionate interest in history and
reverence toward its results (to be discussed below); he knew that
history did not conform to any rational pattern, at least in the conventional meaning of "reason." He deplored the attacks made upon
existing society in the name of reason, and spent much time and effort
to combat them with the use of "better" rational argument. It is a
measure of his shrewdness that he anticipated, moreover, the main
conclusion of the antiintellectualists of our own century (Pareto,
Freud, et cetera)—that reason has little efficacy when it seeks to refute
what men want to believe. Möser saw men as creatures of emotion,
faith, custom, tradition, and habit; this view gave him, incidentally, a
rather cheerful attitude toward the world, and made him free of
hysteria when viewing the impact made by *Aufklärung* rationalism.
He deplored it as he deplored deism, its inevitable religious offspring;
saw its consequences as predominantly bad; but refused to take it
very seriously because one could rely upon human nature to prevent
its triumph.[30]

In the demand that all institutions should conform to a single pattern discovered by "true reason"—which was so characteristic of the

[29] "Die Religion, das beste Hausmittel," in ibid., pp. 71-72.
[30] Möser's most vigorous ridicule of rationalism is in a fragment entitled "Anti-
Candide," which is not a refutation but rather a continuation of Voltaire's famous
tale. Möser agreed with Voltaire that one "must cultivate one's garden" and that
a rational explanation of the universe was vain. *Werke*, IX, 252-64. The necessity
of stressing nonrational counterweights to pure rationalism is one of the main
themes of his "Der Werth wohlgewogner Neigungen und Leidenschaften," *Werke*,
IX, 3-54 (written in 1756), an essay which owes much to Shaftesbury. Möser
also opposed rationalism, in the more narrow sense of logical reasoning, from the
standpoint of "common sense." See Wilhelm Spael, *Common Sense, oder gesunder Menschenverstand und sein Ausdruck by Justus Möser* (Essen, 1947).

political thought of the *Aufklärung* and the political practice of enlightened absolutism—Möser saw a deplorable tendency toward uniformity. One of his best essays is entitled "The Current Tendency towards general Laws and Administrative Decrees is Inimical to Freedom."[31] Möser used as the springboard for his discussion Voltaire's observation that it was ridiculous that laws should change as travelers changed horses—"that someone might lose a law suit in accordance with the customs of one village which he might have won under the customs of the neighboring village."[32] What Voltaire found ridiculous Möser declared desirable, since it was a faithful reflection of the "natural" variety of the world produced by history and Nature. He refused to accept uniform law codes as the dictate of justice, common sense, or simple convenience, but ascribed them rather to the despotic ambitions of lazy bureaucrats:

> The gentlemen of the central government *(Herren beim Generaldepartment)* desire to regulate everything in accordance with simple principles. If matters conformed to their wishes altogether the state would be governed according to the prescripts of an academic theory, and every bureaucrat sitting in the capital would have authority to direct the work of local officials in conformity to a general plan. They naturally wish to regulate everything by a printed rule book . . . in order to make the art of government easy for themselves. . . . I can certainly understand how such a scheme flatters the vanity, and promotes the ease of these gentlemen. . . . It is a simple fact, however, that [if we should comply with their demands] we depart from the true plan of nature, which reveals its wealth through its manifold character; and that we would clear the path to despotism which always seeks to strait-jacket life by confining it to a few rules, and to abandon that variety which constitutes the richness of life.[33]

Möser was especially fearful of general philosophic theories which claimed that some single principle, such as popular sovereignty, could alone give legitimacy to political and social institutions. Such a theory threw into question all the "original contracts, privileges, liberties, and prescriptive rights"[34] which Möser saw as the foundation of all states. It tended to produce anarchy by declaring that all historic institutions, rights, and duties were anachronisms unworthy of respect. Apart from

---

[31] "Der jetzige Hang zu allgemeinen Gesetzen und Verordnungen ist der gemeinen Freiheit gefährlich," *Werke*, ɪɪ (1772), 20-26.
[32] Ibid., p. 20.   [33] Ibid.   [34] Ibid., p. 23.

this practical consideration he intensely disliked, on "aesthetic" grounds, the uniformity which *Aufklärung* theory sought—in his view —to impose upon the colorful variety of the world.

Möser's love of variety was clearly one of the fundamental matrices of his Conservatism. Its earliest manifestation is to be found in the literary field in the repudiation of the uniform art canons of the Gott-schedian school.[35] The connection between his aesthetic and political views comes out most clearly in the following series of analogies presented in the above-mentioned essay:

> Critics praise the sculptors of ancient Greece for modelling their figures after the specific beauty of specific figures instead of guiding their chisels after certain *general* rules of beauty. Critics admire the laws of the Romans because they were designed to cope with specific cases, with each law being applied only to completely analogous situations. It is a commonplace how general rules confine men of literary genius, and how difficult it is for modern poets to transcend mediocrity unless they break through the tyranny of rules. Yet the most precious work of art of all, the constitution of a state, should be patterned after a general rule! it should conform to the uniform beauty of a French drama! and one should be able to describe its essential features upon a single sheet of paper, so that the gentlemen of the central department can perform their work without undergoing any exertions.[36]

By way of contrast Möser asserted in an essay entitled "Should not every little town have a political constitution distinctive to itself?" that many advantages accrued from the cultivation of individuality. Great energies and extraordinary loyalties were characteristic of communities possessing their own distinctive institutions, laws, and schools. Such communities possessed a spirit of patriotic solidarity which societies organized in accordance with abstract rational maxims could not equal.[37]

Möser's view of Nature was very different from that prevalent in "enlightened" circles in his day. He did not, of course, question the achievements of Newtonian science; but its conception of a mechan-

[35] Peter Klassen, *Justus Möser* (Frankfurt, 1936), argues—in my view convincingly—that Möser never sympathized with the Gottschedian school and that therefore there was no occasion for a break, as postulated by several earlier authors. See esp. p. 431.

[36] *Werke*, v, 21.

[37] "Sollte man nicht jedem Städtchen seine besondere politische Verfassung geben?" *Werke*, iii (1777), 67-72.

ical and rather static universe, ordered in accordance with mathematical formulae, did not dominate his *Weltanschauung* as it did that of most of his contemporaries. He refused consistently to apply the methods of the natural sciences to the study of man. His antiquarian love for historical origins made him sharply hostile to any static view of the world, and gave him a well-defined sense for the fact that every institution, legal system, and class relationship develops over centuries in accordance with laws peculiar to itself. He thought that the search of *Aufklärung* thinkers for simple general laws to explain society—the search for a "social physics"—was doomed to failure. On one point only did he agree with the conception of Nature propagated by the thinkers of the *Aufklärung*: the belief in its over-all beneficence. Yet there was a characteristic difference about how the principle of beneficence worked itself out. For many champions of laissez-faire Nature would do its beneficent work (defined as the "invisible hand" which harmonized egotism and the common good) only after man had swept away a vast array of historical institutions (guilds, entails, tariffs, et cetera); for Möser beneficent Nature was *embodied* in those very institutions which had grown up over centuries to serve the needs of man. It was unnatural to wish to sweep them away in the name of an abstract theory which was nothing more than a contrivance of the human mind.[38]

Möser differed from the *Aufklärung* in the enormous importance which he attached to history and the belief that it was the story of man's wise accommodation to the world—not, as Gibbon thought, a chronicle of the crimes and follies of mankind. His interest in history was not escapist—as was so clearly the case with many of his romantic successors—nor did he usually romanticize the past, though his idealization of the old German peasantry was certainly not devoid of romantic features. His relationship to the past was above all an intimate relationship. In the words of Karl Mannheim, "The past is not something that lies behind him; it is an integral part of his life, not as a memory and a return, but as the intensified experience of something

---

[38] See the excellent observations on Möser's view of Nature in Peter Klassen, *Möser*, pp. 23-46 (in a discussion devoted to Möser's early publications), and in Ulrike Brünauer, *Justus Möser* (Berlin, 1933), pp. 82ff., in her concluding summary. Möser's refusal to interfere with Nature sometimes took on perverse forms. He never consulted doctors, putting his faith in the recuperative forces of a beneficent Nature (from what we know about eighteenth-century medicine, not an irrational attitude); but he also opposed smallpox vaccination because smallpox was part of Nature's plan of preventing overpopulation. "Also sollte man die Einimpfung der Blattern ganz verbieten," *Werke*, IV (1779), 63-67.

that he still possesses and is merely in danger of losing."[39] Möser's interest was partly the love of the antiquary, partly the utilitarian outlook of the practical statesman who knew that existing institutions could best be understood in terms of their origins. He was completely free of the patronizing contempt with which many of his "enlightened" contemporaries viewed the Middle Ages; it was his deep conviction that our ancestors were no less rational than ourselves:

> Whenever I encounter an old custom or habit which does not square with our modern notions I tell myself: there is no reason to believe that our ancestors were fools. I then explore the problem until I find a reasonable explanation of the old (which is available usually, though not always); having found it I can return the ridicule of those who have ignorantly attacked old customs and sought to humiliate those who are attached to them by prejudice.[40]

A further word may be said about Möser's historical outlook, for recent interest in him has centered around his position in the rise of Historicism.[41] Friedrich Meinecke placed him in the exalted company of Herder and Goethe because of his opposition to the "unhistorical" outlook of the *Aufklärung*, which tended to judge all periods in the name of a uniform code of static and eternal natural law. Möser's conception of Nature and history stressed, on the contrary, the importance of individuality and the need for specific understanding of specific institutions, instead of judging them contemptuously by the standards of one's own age. He applied this principle in his one major historical

[39] Karl Mannheim, "Conservative Thought," p. 140.

[40] *Werke*, v, 144, in a fragment "Über den Leibeigenthum" (not published in Möser's lifetime). Cf. Burke: "Many of our men of speculation, instead of exploding general prejudices, employ their sagacity to discover the latent wisdom which prevails in them. If they find what they seek (and they seldom fail), they think it more wise to continue the prejudice, with the reason involved, than to cast away the coat of prejudice and to leave nothing but the naked reason." *Works*, iii, 346.

[41] See the brilliant essay by Meinecke, *Historismus*, pp. 303-54. Möser's principle of individuality is discussed by Hans Baron, "Justus Mösers Individualitätsprinzip in seiner geistesgeschichtlichen Bedeutung," *HZ*, cxxx (1924), 31-57. Georg Stefansky, "Justus Mösers Geschichtsauffassung im Zusammenhang der deutschen Literatur des 18. Jahrhunderts," *Euphorion*, xxviii (1920), 21-34, rightly stresses Möser's "collectivist realism" in overcoming the *Aufklärung* tendency of ignoring the state and economic conditions, but he errs in denying to Möser any real understanding of individuality. Clemens August Hoberg, " 'Historische Logik.' Ein Beitrag zu Mösers Geschichtsauffassung," *HZ*, clviii (1938), 492-503, is a confused medley of little value. The "break-through" character of Möser's historical thought was emphasized by W. Dilthey in his still valuable essay in *Gesammelte Schriften*, iii (21959), 247-57.

work, whose subject matter was characteristically limited to his own native Osnabrück from its early Germanic origins to the year 1192.[42] Möser described the specific institutions of Osnabrück with loving care, and was cautious about larger generalization. He always asked himself, "How did this particular institution arise in this particular milieu?" and he relied upon a completely empirical method in seeking answers. The general causes operating through a uniform human nature—so beloved by many historians of the *Aufklärung*—play no role in Möser's *History*.

The *History of Osnabrück* is not only a pioneering work of Historicism; it is also a precocious contribution to the "economic interpretation of history." Möser had a remarkable grasp of the "total configuration" of each successive period of Osnabrückian history; and he anticipated latter-day Marxist historians in viewing economic conditions as the key to the configuration—a key which explains such derivative phenomena as laws and governmental institutions. He arrived at this point of view because of his passionate interest in the condition of the peasantry, whose status was his main preoccupation in studying any period of history. (This concern with the peasantry was moral and aesthetic in origin; it certainly had nothing to do with Möser's own class position.) The major theme of his work is how the free peasantry, which dominated society in the happy prefeudal period before Charlemagne, fared under feudalism, the late medieval *Ständestaat*, and the modern territorial period.[43]

Möser found the condition of his beloved peasantry most satisfactory in the early Middle Ages and he no doubt idealized this period when hailing it as a vanished "golden age." This placed him in sharp opposition to all "enlightened" thinkers, who viewed the period between the fall of Rome and the empire of Charlemagne as the darkest portion of Europe's "dark age"—a period characterized by barbarous superstition and the prevalence of primitive club law *(Faustrecht)*. Möser did not hesitate to scandalize his contemporaries

---

[42] Part I, 1768; Pt. II, 1780. Reprinted in Vols. VI and VII of *Werke*. The best discussion of the *History* is Peter Klassen, *Möser*, Pt. II, where each of Möser's four stages of German history is exhaustively analyzed.

[43] The accuracy of Möser's view of the stages of German social history is irrelevant in our context; it is his over-all conception of history which must be reckoned a great achievement. His specific views upon early German history have exercised a vast influence (chronicled in Hempel, op.cit., Pt. II, "Die historischen Lehrmeinungen Mösers im einzelnen und ihre Fortwirkung"), but are no longer accepted today. See, for example, Karl Siegfried Bader, *Dorfgenossenschaft und Dorfgemeinde* (Weimar, 1962).

by a frank defense of club law which contradicted the fashionable doctrine of progress.

He began with the observation that the critics of club law, then as now, were primarily "timid chroniclers who viewed life from behind cloister walls, or armchair scholars who wore night caps."[44] Möser argued in his reply to these critics that decades of medieval club law caused far less suffering than did a single eighteenth-century military campaign; that it involved only those directly affected, whereas now an insult offered to a prince could lead to a war where thousands not directly involved in the insult were killed; and that club law had been regulated by elaborate rules aimed at preventing harm to non-combatants, who were inevitably injured by the vast devastation characteristic of modern warfare. The age of club law was notable for individual combat determined by individual courage, skill, and honor, whereas modern fighting had become deplorably mechanical and impersonal. The early Middle Ages believed, moreover, that single combat involved a judgment of God; this gave victory an ethical sanction which it could no longer possess in a secular age where victory merely expressed the brute superiority of stronger battalions. Möser concluded his argument with the characteristic words:

> Unfortunately no power in the world is able to restore the "good old law" of the club; but this consideration ought not to deter us from at least *praising* the "good old times" when club law was still the generally accepted custom.[45]

Möser also differed from the thinkers of the *Aufklärung* in his avowal of the comparative unimportance of truth and justice. He explained his point of view in an article, "Concerning the important difference between real and formal justice," as follows:

> Everybody knows what is meant by real justice *(wirkliches Recht)* and real truth *(wirkliche Wahrheit)*, however difficult it may be to identify one or the other in any particular case; but many people do not have a clear idea of what is meant by formal justice or truth. . . . I will give a few examples: What a Church, or an assembly of properly consecrated bishops, declares to be religious truth is formal truth for all members of this particular Church; formal justice for contending private parties is what the properly appointed judge says it is. The formal decision of either Church council or

---

[44] "Von dem Faustrecht," *Werke*, i, 395-99. The quotation is from p. 395.
[45] Ibid., p. 399.

individual judge *may* accord with real truth and real justice, and in all probability will do so. It is in fact, however, not crucial whether they do so or not. Both are infallible (provided they observe proper procedure) so far as *formal* truth is concerned. Their decision turns real white into formal black and vice versa. The basic human need for authoritative certainty makes it necessary to accept formal truth and formal justice whenever it has been declared and decided; otherwise men would never cease to quarrel. . . .

If, however, the two concepts [real and formal justice] are confounded an intolerable situation is created, with individuals being tempted to implement immediately whatever they believe to be real justice. A prince would be able to fire and punish arbitrarily any official at will, if persuaded that he is a dishonest man; the judge would be able to immediately execute his judgment without awaiting the test of its formal correctness [as determined by appellate courts]; and every clergyman would have to hesitate before he signs the creed of his Church until personally convinced of the truth of every article: whereas [the distinction between "formal" and "real" truth] allows him to sign it as soon as he is certain that it has been promulgated by the properly constituted body.

All men can err, the King as much as the philosopher, and indeed these two groups are more likely to err than others, because their elevated position and the vast range of subjects to which they have to turn their attention, makes it difficult for them to examine any matter in detail at leisure. For this reason all nations are agreed on the following foundation of their freedom and property: that whatever a given individual believes to be truth and justice shall be considered to be such only after it has been sealed by the observance of proper forms.[46]

Möser concluded with the assertion that the world could if necessary dispense with real justice and truth, provided that formal truth and justice remained unimpaired. This attitude bespoke the statesman above all concerned with maintaining peace and order, and the Conservative with his instinctive hostility to rebels who protest against the formally sanctioned *status quo* in the name of *their* conception of truth and justice. It also indicated a skepticism concerning man's ability to attain the truth, and to know once it had been attained; hence a willingness to "make do" with whatever was established be-

---

[46] "Von dem wichtigen Unterschiede des wirklichen und förmlichen Rechts," *Werke*, IV (1780), 110-12.

cause—though it was probably no more "true" than the principles by which it was challenged—it had the supreme merit of being *established*. Möser was a Conservative because he was a skeptic; he accepted the precepts of *Lokalvernunft* because he found them at least as reasonable, and far more familiar, than the dictates of abstract and universal Reason and Justice.

Outline of Möser's Political Theory

Given Möser's hostility to deism, his distrust of rationalism, his hatred of uniformity, his emphasis on variety and individuality in Nature and history, his rejection of the doctrine of progress, and his skepticism, it is hardly surprising to find Möser disagreeing sharply with his Progressive contemporaries also on political and social matters. He used the vocabulary of the *Aufklärung*, but, just as in the case of Rousseau, this served mainly to conceal his differences with the true children of the *Aufklärung*. Möser believed in an organic theory of the state (in contrast to the individualistic-mechanistic theory of the *Aufklärung*); he was preoccupied with the position of the peasantry (while Progressives hailed the expansion of urban industry); he championed a hierarchic-inequalitarian pattern of society (while Radicals affirmed equality, especially equality of opportunity); he opposed liberty in the name of specific liberties, abstract conceptions of property in the name of concreteness, and cosmopolitanism in the name of national sentiment; and he desired to maintain the existing *Ständestaat* in opposition to all attempts at leveling, whether emanating from absolute monarchs or revolutionary Jacobins. On each of these questions his position was far from a simple, conventional opposition to the Radical view.

Möser's organic conception of society and the state is obscured at first glance by his use of the formula of the social contract and the unfortunate analogy between the state and a joint-stock company. He explained the origin of the state in the following terms: A number of strong men individually occupying plots of land in a given territory agreed to make a contract with one another to set up a government and reciprocally guarantee possession of their several properties. They, and they alone, became full-fledged citizens of the newly established state, their citizenship being based upon their possession of land *(Landaktie)* in the same way as participation in a commercial joint-stock company is based upon stock ownership. The state so constructed was composed, however, not only of full citizens: there were also landless agricultural laborers, men too weak or too stupid to participate in the original appropriation of land, and immigrants who arrived after all the land had already been appropriated. The last two categories of people were called *Nebenbewohner,* whose strictly limited rights were determined by a "secondary contract" between themselves and the full citizens. This condition prevailed so long as the pattern of society remained purely agricultural; upon the rise of industry it became impossible to keep *Nebenbewohner* (who might be guild artisans or even rich merchants) in a completely subordinate position. To accommodate their justified claims Möser developed the idea that money shares *(Geldaktien)* could provide a basis for citizenship as well as *Landaktien.* The important point was to keep the unpropertied inhabitants "in their place," and to maintain the two principles that citizenship must be based upon property and that the rights and duties of citizenship should be proportionate to the amount of property owned.

This theory constituted an excellent rationalization for the inegalitarian structure of Osnabrück society. It was realistic in avoiding the untenable contention that the beginning of society had been egalitarian; it provided an explanation for the perennial fact of human differentiation and frankly accepted the role played by power (in the original appropriation of land) and luck (in the fact of timely arrival in a territory while vacant lots were still available) in determining social status. It postulated a close connection between rights, duties, and capacities, with Möser always correlating the *right* of citizenship with the *capacity* to perform certain civic duties (such as equipping oneself for militia service, leaving one's farm for duty as juryman or dike inspector, paying taxes upon property, et cetera). It could explain the emergence of aristocracy out of the ranks of the larger peasant landowners without postulating any fundamental cleavage between noble and peasant. All this was done, moreover, without abandoning the principle of the voluntary social contract which had become an unavoidable shibboleth in eighteenth-century political thought.[47]

[47] Möser stated his theory of the state as based upon *Landaktien* most explicitly in "Der Bauerhof als eine Actie betrachtet," *Werke,* iii (1774), 291-309. His theory led to a fruitful controversy (mostly in the columns of the *Berliner Monatsschrift*) in the early 1790's, when Möser attacked the French Constituent Assembly for basing the new French constitution upon the rights of man rather than the possession of *Land* or *Geldaktien:* "Wann und wie mag eine Nation ihre Constitution verändern," *Werke,* v, 177-80; and "Über das Recht der Menschheit, als den Grund der neuen Französischen Constitution," *Werke,* v, 190-95. The latter article provoked a reply from a certain Eduard von Clauer, "Auch etwas über das Recht der Menschheit," *Berliner Monatsschrift,* xvi (1790), 197-

This mechanistic language concealed, however, Möser's vivid conception of society and the state as a vital, interdependent organism developing through a process of gradual historical growth. He used on occasion the organic analogy, more especially when he warned against arbitrary reforms. An example is a letter to "a young statesman" too much affected by the reformism of the *Aufklärung*:

> Any mature state tends to possess a certain number of stiff, misshaped, hardened and fragile members due to faulty treatment in the period of its youth; if you seek to twist them into shape through heroic remedies you will run the danger of disintegrating the whole and even destroying outright certain members which have until now willy-nilly done their duty, however imperfectly. There was above all a special danger in forcing an old body to do what it could no longer be trained to do properly: it is easier to turn a stiff old man into a cripple than into a rope dancer.[48]

Möser followed the organicists—and indeed the stereotyped medieval view of society—in stressing the interdependence of the various classes of society and preaching the social ethos that every man must take pride and find honor in performing his customary role in society. He never saw the state as an aggregation of equal individuals claiming the protection of *rights;* he always viewed it as a differentiated, hierarchical organism where every member should be preoccupied with the performance of his customary *duties.* Möser insisted that society must always be viewed as a whole, and that mistaken views usually result from looking at one part in isolation. He used the analogy that parts of bodies, when put under a microscope, frequently look ugly and grotesque though they appear perfectly normal and harmonious when viewed with the naked eye. (He did not, however, apply this observation to his own concentration upon the freehold peasantry.)[49]

Möser anticipated the romantic school in realizing and cherishing

---

209, with an important dissociating postscript by Erich Biester, the editor (pp. 209-20). Möser thanked Biester and continued the controversy in "Über das Recht der Menschheit, in so fern es zur Grundlage eines Staates dienen kann," *Werke*, v, 196-203.

[48] "An einen jungen Staatsman," *Werke*, v, 204-05.

[49] The microscopic analogy is made in "Von dem moralischen Gesichtspunkt," *Werke*, i (1767), 196. The importance of Möser's "wholistic" view of the state (*Totaleindruck*) is stressed by F. Meinecke, *Historismus*, pp. 309-10. It is characteristic of Möser that he differed from the *Aufklärung* in stressing both the importance of individuality and the necessity of viewing the whole through a *Totaleindruck.*

the totality of any given society, not only in the interdependence of its parts but also the interdependence of all of its purposes (political, social, military, economic, et cetera). Thus—to give only one example —he deplored the discussion of economic activity in terms of what maximized wealth in isolation from other considerations. Möser insisted that economics must always be discussed with reference to the general welfare of society, which dictated that virtue was at least as important as prosperity; hence the danger of unleashing inherently vicious acquisitive appetites even if they did in fact produce prosperity. Yet this truism was ignored by the entire laissez-faire school, with its habit of analyzing economics as an autonomous field of human activity apart from the general configuration of society.[50]

All of Möser's political and economic theory was centered upon the landowning peasant, the typical possessor of the *Landaktie*. It should be stressed that this preoccupation had nothing in common with the mawkish sentimentality of Rousseau and little with Physiocratic principles: it was based rather upon the conviction that a society dominated by freehold peasants—such as he conceived prefeudal Germany to have been—was the healthiest kind of society possible for man. Such a society was characterized by the virtues which Möser admired most: frugality, simplicity, hard work, and the contented performance of one's duties. The social and economic policies which he advocated (in both his practical and his literary work) aimed at preserving what still existed of a freehold peasantry in Osnabrück; to this end he advocated many measures calculated to prevent the division or alienation of peasant property by restricting the right to mortgage, the provision of cheap agrarian credit, et cetera. His ideal was a self-sufficient agricultural society where farming was a "way of life" rather than a market-oriented "business"; though he accepted the development of wider markets as an irreversible fact and even supported the free circulation of grain (a favorite demand of laissez-faire economists) on the ground that grain embargoes tended to be unenforceable in practice.

It would be wrong to suggest that Möser's special love for the peasantry made him actively hostile to commerce or manufacture; all that may be said is that he was very far from seeing in them—as most *Aufklärer* tended to do—the key to a glorious future far superior to

[50] H. Zimmermann, *Staat, Recht und Wirtschaft bei Möser* (Jena, 1933), pp. 73ff. Möser's constant view of the totality of life—in contrast to the atomistic views of the *Aufklärung*—is stressed especially well by F. Meinecke, *Historismus*, p. 309, and Ulrike Brünauer, *Justus Möser* (Berlin, 1933), Ch. 1, Sect. i.

the present. He admired large-scale commerce and had glowing words for the vigor and enterprise developed by the old Hanseatic League; he insisted, however, that trade, like any other activity, must be subordinated to the general welfare. There was danger in the irresponsible international power exercised by big commercial companies; Möser suggested that they should be influenced from the inside through the governmental purchase of stock, which would give the state influence upon management, and from the outside through mercantilistic regulation. He tended to view retailers and petty traders (Krämer) as parasites upon the community whose peddling had a depressing effect upon local handicrafts. He disliked the spread of the "putting-out" system of manufacture (as well as the incipient factory system) because it destroyed artisan handicrafts, though he also had respect for the vigor and industry of the new type of manufacturer. His ideal remained the craft shop where small family or patriarchal units produced for an essentially self-sufficient community. In all these views (including the admiration expressed for Hanseatic greatness) Möser looked backward rather than forward, and aimed at preserving what still survived from a golden past instead of succumbing to any vision of future economic utopias. He favored a "balanced economy" and pointed to Holland (with its exclusively commercial economy) and Poland (with its primitive agrarian stagnation) as two extremes to avoid. The best balance was one between frugal guild artisans running their small shops and freehold peasants owning their land and working it with the help of a limited number of Nebenbewohner.[51]

Möser's admiration for a society of peasants and guild artisans (with the former enjoying predominance) has a Jeffersonian flavor; it did not, however, imply any bias toward egalitarianism. On the contrary, Möser explicitly favored a hierarchic order of society where everybody knew and kept his place. He expected that a large group of Nebenbewohner would always provide a necessary reservoir for agricultural laborers, journeymen, domestics, petty civil servants, and

[51] Möser's economic views are surveyed in detail in the following works: Wilhelm Roscher, Geschichte der National-Oekonomie in Deutschland (Munich, 1874), Ch. 22, an extravagant eulogy; L. Rupprecht, Justus Mösers soziale und volkswirtschaftliche Anschauungen (Stuttgart, 1892), treating Möser's economic views too much in isolation and exaggerating their "Medieval" character; Otto Hatzig, Möser als Staatsmann und Publizist (Hannover and Leipzig, 1900), very important in correlating his administrative work with his writings, but so encyclopedic as to be unreadable; C. W. Ouvrier, Der ökonomische Gehalt der Schriften von Justus Möser (Giessen, 1928), a pedestrian dissertation; and, above all, Zimmermann, op.cit., Pt. III.

retailers too small to qualify for a *Geldaktie;* and he accepted the fact that the owners of large parcels of *Landaktien* constituted an original aristocracy, which was reinforced by those ennobled for special services. (Möser wished, however, to retain a close connection between nobility and land; he wanted ennoblement to be accompanied by the conferment of landed estates.) He valued aristocracy provided it was not too numerous, possessed concrete functions, and was motivated by a spirit of *noblesse oblige.* It should possess distinctive, self-enforced ideals of honor (which should preclude entering certain "nonaristocratic" professions, especially those connected with trade); also a distinctive educational experience, preferably including service as court pages, qualifying it to exercise in later life a special political role. (Möser had no objection to certain high governmental posts being monopolized by the aristocracy.) He was critical of the condition and conduct of much of the eighteenth-century German nobility, and admired such British practices as primogeniture (which prevented the multiplication of aristocrats) and the participation of aristocratic JP's in local administration and justice. Möser did not, however, develop any specific program for making the German aristocracy conform more to his ideal of what an aristocracy ought to be; he went no farther than to preach moral homilies in favor of curbing idleness and luxury by a return to old-fashioned virtues.[52]

Möser admired a society marked by a great diversity of status and condition, where everybody was content to perform his traditional function for the common good. He looked upon inequality as a positive good, not a necessary evil, and wanted as much differentiation as possible even within major occupational groups (peasants, guildsmen, et cetera). Differentiation was the source of a sense of honor; pride in status, a major motive for valuable human conduct. Both must be fostered if possible by separate courts serving separate groups (*Standesgerichte*). Möser saw no merit in general courts serving the entire population regardless of status.[53] With this belief in maximum differentiation Möser quite logically disliked the idea of individual

[52] Möser's scattered views on aristocracy are brilliantly assembled by Zimmermann, op.cit., Pt. i. The most important source is Möser's "Der Staat mit einer Pyramide verglichen, eine erbauliche Betrachtung," *Werke,* ii, 250-54, and "Warum bildet sich der deutsche Adel nicht nach dem englischen?" *Werke,* iv (1780), 236-47.

[53] Möser's belief in differentiation is best expressed in his "Antwort auf verschiedene Vorschläge wegen einer Kleiderordnung," *Werke,* i (1768), 231-35; his desire for *Standesgerichte* in "Ueber die Art und Weise, wie unsre Vorfahren die Prozesse abgekürzt haben," *Werke,* i (1770), 347-85.

social mobility. The possibility of mobility made for restlessness among those men—the vast majority—who did *not* rise above the status of their fathers; while it gave rise to the dangerous notion that social status ought to be based upon individual merit rather than parentage. Möser was deeply hostile to two new, related principles championed by the reformers of the *Aufklärung*: equality of opportunity and promotion according to merit. His argument against the latter, written to an officer who had complained about being "passed over," is acute in its psychological insight, whatever one may think of the over-all value of the argument:

> Your demand that the State should solely look to true merit [in promotions] is . . . the strangest product of an hour's idle contemplation. I, for one, should—paid or not—never remain within a State in which it is a rule to award all honors solely on the basis of merit. Rewarded, I should not have the heart to appear before a friend for fear of humiliating him; and unrewarded, I should live under some sort of public calumny, because everybody would say of me, *That man has no merits.* Believe me, so long as we remain human, it is better that from time to time fortune and favor distribute the prizes, than that human wisdom award them to each according to his merit —birth and age are better determinants of rank in this world than is true worth. Yea, I shall dare to say that public service could not even exist if every promotion were based solely on merit. For all those who shared the hopes of the promoted—and this would quite naturally include all who had any sort of a good opinion of themselves—would consider themselves offended and calumniated. Their minds would turn against him, against the service, and even against their chief; they would erupt in hate and enmity. . . . On the other hand, contemplate the case where this man is promoted because of high birth, that man because of his seniority in service, and from time to time, other men are promoted by happy chance: here, everybody will be free to flatter himself that merit is not the measure of the world; nobody can regard himself as calumniated; self-love acquiesces, and we think that time and fortune will bring up our turn, too. With these thoughts, we drive away our grief, get new hopes, continue to work, suffer the fortunate; and public service is not impeded.[54]

[54] "Keine Beförderung nach Verdiensten," *Werke*, II, 187-91. There is an English translation, with a valuable introduction, by Hans W. Baade, "No Promotion based on Merit," *Journal of Public Law*, XII (1963), 185-92. I have used Professor Baade's excellent translation. There is reason to believe that Möser

Möser also added the further argument that the objective choice of merit could not fairly be left to any single individual or body of men: certainly in eighteenth-century Germany neither prince nor counselor could claim infallibility in exercising so weighty a responsibility.[55] There was also the consideration that competition for promotion would naturally stimulate the development of unpleasant qualities calculated to draw attention to oneself. These were good arguments against the principle of "meritocracy"—though unfortunately Möser did not show how the increasing modern impatience with status-based promotion could be eliminated, and the ever-more-complicated modern world dispense with the superior efficiency connected with a merit system. How could a state which dispensed with the merit system possibly survive in the struggle with other states in Europe's competitive multistate system? Möser showed some of his fundamental limitations in failing to anticipate and answer these rather obvious objections to his position. It may be added that his failure to consider problems of foreign policy, while characteristic of citizens of small states like Osnabrück sheltered within the walls of the venerable Holy Roman Empire, was an outstanding example of his being a victim of a parochial milieu despite his transcendent intellectual abilities.

Möser's hostility to the principle of equality—whether of opportunity or condition—was paralleled by his sharp dislike for the abstract principle of liberty. The right to liberty, derived by the *Aufklärung* from the fact of participation in the human race, could be no part of a political theory built upon the joint-stock analogy. Möser knew only specific people with specific liberties in the plural. He believed that liberty was always a function of status, and insisted that it must be connected with property, obligation, and a conception of honor which combined both. Möser has much to say about the liberties of aristocrats, freeholders, and guildsmen, but never anything about liberty per se. His world, with its multifarious historical rights and its can-

---

practiced what he preached, even to the point of outright nepotism. He had a ne'er-do-well younger brother, Johann Zacharias Möser (1726-67), who had a checkered career as an alchemist, secretary to the Dutch consul in Tripoli, and retailer of goods captured by the Barbary pirates. Möser finally got him a job as *Criminal-Aktuar* in the Osnabrück judicial service, a post for which he possessed no obvious qualification. See Abeken in his introduction to Möser's *Werke*, I, 44-45 and n.51.

[55] Here Möser contradicted himself; for the baneful results of promotion based upon merit assumed that such promotion actually did take place. If princes (or whoever determined promotion) were in fact unreliable judges of merit no one need feel inferior for having been passed over.

onization of the *Ständestaat*, had no place for the leveling and abstract conception of natural rights. He was convinced, moreover, that gradations of rank were the best barrier against despotism:

> I will never be attracted by a state where the King is a lion and all other citizens are ants: a good state is one characterized by soft gradations extending from the poor man's hut to the throne, and where there are men other than the King who possess distinctive rights.[56]

Möser was opposed to the abstract, generalized conception of property which was so congenial to capitalist society. This conception saw individual pieces of property, whether land, utensils, or shares of stock, as something which was readily transferable from one person to another and expressible in monetary terms. Möser viewed property, on the contrary, as a reciprocal relationship between an object and a particular person (or family)—a relationship which included values, sentiments, and attitudes of a nonmonetary, nontransferable kind. Thus ownership of a landed estate—to give only one example—was not primarily an economic investment but rather a "way of life" involving patriarchal obligations and local leadership—all qualities which could not readily be transferred from one owner to another. Möser wished that other forms of property would involve a similar web of obligations, and distrusted mobile forms of property (money, shares of stock, et cetera) because of their abstractness and transferability. His conception of property was clearly more suited to the feudal past than the capitalist future.[57]

Whatever *Aufklärung* ideal one mentions—equality, liberty, or property—one finds that Möser took a hostile view toward it because he was rooted in an earlier age. The same may be said of his hostility to the cosmopolitanism of the eighteenth century, though his nationalist counterdoctrine possessed modern as well as anachronistic features. His love of nationality, more especially German nationality,

[56] *Werke*, I, 25 (fragment, published posthumously). Möser's correlation of liberty, property, and honor is excellently analyzed by Zimmermann, op.cit., Pt. I. Many of his essays seek to illustrate the specific *Standesehre* of nobles, burghers, bureaucrats, peasants, et cetera; Möser's ethical ideal is obviously that every person should enjoy the liberties, and perform the functions of, his customary status. He was profoundly aware that few words have had such a dubious history as "liberty"; his observations on this point (*Werke*, x, 149, written in 1767) are a remarkable example of the use of the philological method to gain historic insights.

[57] The best statement of Möser's view of property is "Von dem echten Eigenthum," *Werke*, IV (1778), 158-62.

was the result of his love of whatever was concrete, specific, and original; its aesthetic roots lay in the hostility of the *Sturm und Drang* to the alien literary tyranny of French classicism with its universalist pretensions. Möser's nationalism was more cultural than political in its concern, though he occasionally indulged in the invocation of Germany's glorious political position in the Middle Ages when the Holy Roman Empire had given the law to Europe. It is certain that his national feeling did not lead him to envisage the creation of a German national state in the future; it was oriented essentially toward the early German past. The following question posed and answered by Möser is significant:

> Where do we find the true German nation? We certainly do not find it at the court of princes. Our cities today are filled with misshapen and spoiled copies of humanity; our armies with carefully dressed machines *(abgerichtete Maschinen);* our countryside with exploited peasants. How different was our nation [in the early Middle Ages], when every Franconian or Saxon peasant cultivated and defended in his own person his *paterna rura,* that is his hereditary allodial lands, free of feudal ties or manorial obligations; and when every freeholder went from his homestead to participate in the work of a popular assembly. At that time every person without a freehold—though he be the wealthiest shopkeeper—was reckoned to belong to the class of poor and dishonored people. At that time it was easy to say who constituted the German nation—today it is impossible.[58]

He clearly despaired of any early rebirth of Germany. Möser's nationalism placed him in opposition to the *Aufklärung;* but it must be repeated that his nationalism—with its orientation toward the past, agrarian bias, and want of specific political content—was very different from the German nationalism which triumphed in the second half of the nineteenth century.[59]

One occasionally encounters in Möser the thought—so comforting to German Conservatives for the next century and a half—that the forces bent upon subverting the German *status quo* were in essence alien, and especially French, in origin. The historically evolved Ger-

---

[58] From Möser's review of C. F. von Moser's book, *Vom deutschen National-geist, Werke,* IX (1765), 241.

[59] An excellent brief account of Möser's nationalism is Robert Ergang, "Möser and the Rise of National Thought in Germany," *J.N.H.,* V (1933), 172-96. His attitude toward the old empire is examined by H. U. Scupin, "Volk und Reich bei Justus Möser," *Zeitschrift für öffentliches Recht,* XIX (1940), 561-639.

man *Ständestaat* was being challenged first by absolutism (whose prototype was Louis XIV) from above, and after 1790 by the French-inspired German Jacobins from below. Both were bent upon a general process of leveling which was utterly destructive of the manifold variety which constituted the distinctive character of Germany's historical development. Möser's hostility to centralized tyranny in general and meddling bureaucracy in particular permeates all his work, and he was proud that he lived in a state where absolutism was unknown. His hostility to Jacobin leveling is the dominant theme of the writings of his last years; it is best expressed in several essays written for the *Berliner Monatschrift* between 1790 and 1794. His ideal of the "old German" peasant state gave him an unshakable *point d'appui* from which to offer opposition equally to Frederick the Great and to Robespierre. Admiration for self-government and respect for tradition made royal absolutism anathema to Möser; belief that a healthy society must be traditionalist and hierarchic made the Jacobins appear as anarchical fanatics to him. Möser insisted above all that the aims of both were essentially similar: the destruction of the variegated *Ständestaat* in the name of a centralized, leveled uniformity.[60]

Möser's two-fronted war against the forces promoting change marks him out clearly as a *Status Quo* Conservative. He refused to see that the reforms championed by "enlightened" absolutism from above—which were in some cases imbued with the spirit of Reform Conservatism—constituted a relatively acceptable alternative to the otherwise inevitable revolution from below. He refused in fact to see the inevitability of *any* far-reaching changes in the world with which he was familiar. There is an element of tragedy in this sterile outlook, and surprise since Möser possessed a pioneering understanding for the principle of historical development—a principle which ought to have prevented him from idolizing the ephemeral Osnabrückian conditions with which he was familiar. His love of his customary milieu and deference to local interests proved far stronger than his willingness to accept the corollaries which flowed from his fundamental premises. Given many of his ideas, he might have been expected to develop a program of reform for an age marked by change; he preferred instead the role of defender of anachronistic abuses in his native Osnabrück.[61]

---

[60] Möser's simultaneous hostility to enlightened absolutism and the bourgeois-democratic *Aufklärung* is brought out especially well by Meinecke, *Historismus*, p. 317.

[61] This point is powerfully elaborated, from a Liberal rather than Reform Conservative point of view, by J. K. Bluntschli, *Geschichte der Neueren Staatswissenschaft* (Munich, 1864, 3rd edn., 1881), pp. 463-76.

The Defense of Osnabrück Conditions

Möser's defense of the particular *status quo* of Osnabrück, with its parochial institutions, has little general interest and cannot be analyzed in detail here. A few examples will reveal, however, the flavor of Möser's style of thought.

Although his defense of serfdom, which caused such a scandal, was inspired partly by his private interests, it was entirely consistent with his fundamental principles. It fitted perfectly into the hierarchic, differentiated society which he cherished. His idealization of the free peasant proprietor did not mean that he intended to exclude either aristocrat or serf from society. Even a serf had a status with particular rights and obligations (mostly the latter) attached to property rights protected by custom; his being tied to the soil was not in principle different from other restrictions upon social mobility. It should also be noted that the actual economic condition of the serfs of Westphalia was comparatively tolerable; indeed, it was probably superior to that of the free rural population of England, whose freedom included the freedom to be driven off the land by the enclosure revolution.[62]

Möser was especially concerned about preserving the guild economy and restoring the guildsman to his former position of honor. He deplored the vicious circle under which artisans had increasingly fallen into contempt and respectable people refused to allow their children to become artisans:

> When a craft is once held in contempt it will be carried on only by poor and simple people; and whatever is done by poor and simple people will seldom win prestige or be conducted with excellence.[63]

The remedy was to have the sons of rich people become craftsmen and thereby raise the prestige of the craft which they honored by their entry; Möser also thought that this would be the best way of bringing capital into the craft shop and perhaps allowing it to develop into

[62] Möser's famous (qualified) defense of serfdom is in "Über den Leibeigenthum," *Werke*, v, 136-47. It may be noted that Möser contemplated *Leibaktien* to supplement the *Geldaktien* and *Landaktien* which were the basis of his state, but he never developed the concept in such a fashion as to give the serfs a convincing stake in the community. *Werke*, III, 295, and VI, 69. Möser provided a historical defense of serfdom in his essay, "Über Theorie und Praxis," IX, 158-75, especially pp. 168ff., written in reply to Kant during the last year of his life. The fullest discussion of his attitude toward all agrarian questions is Otto Hatzig, *Möser als Staatsmann und Publizist*, pp. 35-89.

[63] "Reicher Leute Kinder sollten ein Handwerk lernen," *Werke*, I (1767), 113.

a small factory. He admired the—perhaps somewhat mythical—English master craftsman who supervised the work of forty journeymen while also finding time "to sit in parliament to decide the fate of the East and the West Indies and to conduct his business on the stock exchange."[64]

The honor of craftsmanship must be restored through encouraging social infusions from above and discouraging undesirable infusions from below. Möser was adamantly in favor of maintaining the prevalent harsh practices of excluding bastards from guild membership. In one of his most characteristic passages he ridiculed the humanitarian efforts made by the *Aufklärung* to give illegitimate children all the advantages of legitimacy:

> More has been done, in the last ten or twenty years, for whores and their children than has been done for wives in the last millennium. Every philosopher . . . has done his best to free illegitimate children and their mothers from any kind of shame, and thinks of himself as a benefactor of humanity when he frees the poor, innocent fruits of a forbidden but ever seductive love from all reproach. I do not deny that there are plausible arguments for this point of view. Nature, humanity, and philanthropy all speak loudly in favor of elevating the position of bastards; and yet it is primarily the *unpolitical* philosophy of our century which is here revealed. It is a case of the new-fangled philanthropy *(Menschenliebe)* triumphing at the expense of love of one's fellow citizens *(Bürgerliebe)*. . . .[65]

Möser insisted that such a policy struck at the basis of the institution of marriage, the very foundation of human society. He demanded that this institution be protected even if such protection incidentally meant injustice to individuals. Marriage inevitably involved inconvenience, which must be compensated by corresponding advantages:

> It is unpolitical to give the children of whores the same honor as children born in wedlock, for this would destroy the single strongest motive making for marriage. . . . It is unpolitical to give the unmarried condition the same honor as the married one, since a firmly united family is of far greater value to the state than a group of men and women living in fluctuating free love. Our forefathers, who did not judge after theories, but were rather guided by experience,

---

[64] Ibid., I, 120.

[65] "Ueber die zu unsern Zeiten verminderte Schande der Huren und Hurkinder," *Werke*, II (1772), 164.

always demanded proof of legitimate birth before allowing entry into a guild.[66]

Möser believed it was part of the inescapable divine order that innocent people were condemned to suffering: "Why does the philosophic legislator presume to improve upon the divinity itself?"[67]

Möser was always a defender of "old-fashioned morality" against what he believed were the fashionable modern vices of license, frivolity, and extravagance. He never lost an opportunity to praise the "good old days" when discipline, seriousness, and frugality were still the order of the day. He pointed out, in a fine essay entitled "How much does one need in order to live?"[68] that consumption tends to rise faster than salary because every salary increase is accompanied by a disproportionate increase in pretension—the net result being that men often feel subjectively more cramped as they objectively rise in the income scale. As a born misogynist he was certain that female vanity was the main factor driving prosperous families into bankruptcy. The emancipation of women aroused his abhorrence. He urged women to be good cooks and mothers rather than social climbers and half-educated dilettantes. One of his most stinging anti-feminist tracts is entitled "She danced well but cooked badly"[69]—for Möser a disastrous combination but one too often found in modern women. He even half-seriously pleaded for female illiteracy: "As regards girls I certainly do not want to marry one who can read and write."[70]

Möser's views on education were naturally sharply opposed to Basedow's principles. He thought that progressive education tended to spoil the character of children and to ignore the importance of conveying substantive information, whereas traditional education was on the right track in stressing the importance of knowledge and simultaneously building character through stern discipline.[71] He was critical of the spread of education to the countryside, complaining that literacy gave the sons of peasants unrealistic pretensions and incapacitated them for practical work: "Children today . . . think that if they can read and write and possess a pat answer to all questions they

---

[66] Ibid., 165.   [67] Ibid., 167.

[68] "Wie viel braucht man, um zu leben?", *Werke*, II (1774), 298-303.

[69] "Sie tanzte gut und kochte schlecht," *Werke*, II (1771), 79-83.

[70] *Werke*, II, 309. In this matter Möser's practice was better than his theory. Abeken describes Möser's wife as "eine Frau von grossem Geiste und herrschender Willenskraft." *Werke*, I, 50.

[71] "Die Erziehung mag wohl sclavisch sein," *Werke*, III (1776), 133-34.

are superior to those whose main skill lies in knitting three stockings a day."[72]

Möser showed his remarkable immunity to the humanitarian movement of his age by his advocacy of the retention—or reintroduction—of barbarous punishments for crime. He was a confirmed believer in the "deterrence theory" of punishment, and was convinced that mild penalties only led to the multiplication of crime.

> The blinding of convicted criminals has been a very prevalent form of punishment among many peoples in former times. It served in place of capital punishment, and I believe it is in fact the most horrible of all punishments. We have abandoned it now because we believe that, though it is proper to hang the image of God on the gallows, it is improper to rob it of its eyes. Whether this belief is correct appears to me to be an open question. Would it not have a salutary deterrent effect if we blinded a few criminals and sentenced them to tread a wheel *(Radlaufen)?* There are many situations . . . where cheap criminals could serve more effectively than expensive horses. Such blinded criminals also could not escape and would not pose disciplinary problems for their masters.[73]

Aristocratic *Selbstverwaltung* and *Stände* bodies took a conspicuous place among Osnabrück institutions defended by Möser. His position as the leading bureaucrat of Osnabrück did not prevent his detesting bureaucrats as the plague of mankind and pleading for as much self-administration as possible in political and economic affairs. We have already seen how he admired the role played by the English squirearchy in providing vigorous lay administration through the JP's, and he never uttered a word against surviving patrimonial jurisdictions. He wanted guilds to take an active part in the governing of towns. Möser deeply abhorred any kind of acquiescence in monarchical absolutism: his ideal was that of a self-governing, civic-minded, public-spirited community, and he identified this ideal with the

---

[72] "Ueber die Erziehung der Kinder auf dem Lande," *Werke,* II (1771), 308. There are several monographs summarizing Möser's views on education. See, for example, E. Bender, "Justus Möser als Volkserzieher," *Ztschr. d. historischen Vereins für Niedersachsen,* LXXX (1915), 38ff.

[73] "Etwas zur Verbesserung der Zuchthäuser," *Werke,* IV (1778), 142. It goes without saying that Möser was a firm champion of capital punishment: "Ueber die Todesstrafen," *Werke,* IV (1780), 126-30. On the survival of torture he evidently wavered, but thought it could be dispensed with in a country with a well-functioning jury system: "Von der Tortur," *Werke,* V, 118-19.

"golden age" of prefeudal Germans. He stands in the German tradition of the *Genossenschaft* rather than the *Obrigkeitsstaat*.[74]

Self-government should, moreover, not be confined to the local level; Möser also desired it at the central level through *Stände,* which he thought would generally cooperate harmoniously with their prince. Osnabrück constituted an excellent example of how the most heterogeneous bodies could work for the general welfare and compromise whatever differences arose between them. Möser's desire to perpetuate the "dualistic polity" led him to ignore completely the rationalist conception of sovereignty: he assumed that public-spirited princes and *Stände* could work together indefinitely without the question of sovereignty being fought out. He did not envisage any democratization of the *Stände* or any social changes which would make democratization inevitable. It must always be remembered that Möser expected the future to be not very different from the present and past, and that he had no understanding of the forces which were to make both monarchy (except constitutional monarchy) and *Stände* institutions obsolete in the near future. His political thought remained tied to the world of a parochial *Ständestaat* like Osnabrück; his conception of change was strictly limited by his belief that the world moved very slowly, had mostly moved in the wrong direction during the last fifteen hundred years, and by preference ought not to move at all.[75]

Conclusion

In viewing Möser one must never forget that he stood at the threshold between an unreflective traditionalism and a self-conscious Conservatism.[76] He lived in the age when the thinkers of the *Aufklärung* first criticized the established pattern of German society, politics, and religion; this criticism appeared as yet, however, as a series of *ad hoc* criticisms rather than a general plan to reconstruct German society. It was natural, therefore, that defense would take on an equally *ad hoc* character, and that the time for Conservative

[74] See the excellent summary of Möser's views on self-government in Brünauer, *Möser,* Ch. 1, Sect. II.

[75] There are remarkably few specific references to the work of the Osnabrück *Stände* despite the avowed aim of the *Osnabrückische Anzeigen* to enlighten the citizenry about their work (see pp. 304-305). Presumably Möser felt too close to their work to feel comfortable in reporting about them. Möser's views on *Stände* are summarized by Hatzig, *Möser als Staatsmann und Publizist,* pp. 173-79.

[76] This is the fundamental theme of Karl Mannheim's assessment of Möser in his essay, "Conservative Thought," *Essays on Sociology and Social Psychology* (New York, 1953), pp. 138-45, although I believe that Mannheim overdraws the contrast between Möser and Müller.

system-building had not yet come. What is significant about Möser's Conservatism is that he did not confine his defense to particular institutions under attack, but struck against many of the fundamental premises which stood behind the *Aufklärung* assault upon German society. We have seen him attack deism in the name of revelation (or at least the utility of revelation), rationalism in the name of the plurality of human faculties, uniformity in the name of variety, natural law in the name of history, progress in the name of cherished medieval institutions, and the passion for truth and justice in the name of the importance of observing existing legal forms. In the more narrowly political field he opposed the mechanistic theory of the state, abstract liberty, leveling equality, the impersonal conception of property, and a cosmopolitanism which defied the difference between French and German. His consistency on all these questions—the mark of a well-integrated personality with great intellectual power—is impressive; and the elements for future Conservative systematization were all present in his work.[77]

The time was not yet ripe for a systematic Conservative theory; but Möser was also not the man to elaborate such a system even if the time had been more advanced. His instinctive dislike of theory was developed even beyond that customary in a Conservative; his administrative work led to preoccupation with the specifics of every problem; his range of experience was largely confined to the parochial world of his native Osnabrück; and his writings were journalistic columns written for his fellow townsmen rather than an audience of trained thinkers. His personality and milieu cooperated in making him a born writer of fragments—probably the greatest such in German literature—but the genre does not allow for the highest achievements.

Most of the criticisms conventionally delivered against him appear justified.[78] He was a pioneer historicist yet lacked the talent for writing great history; his *History of Osnabrück* was marred by carelessness in the use of sources and undue idealization of the free peasantry of prefeudal Germany. His intuitive understanding of the organic character of the state was marred by his use of the mechanistic jointstock analogy; his theory of the state was, moreover, a rather crude

[77] It may be noted that the unsystematic, *ad hoc* character of Möser's thought receives special praise in Hans Mühlenfeld's eulogy, "Die Entstehung des Konservativismus: Möser," *Politik ohne Wunschbilder* (Munich, 1952,) pp. 188-204. The author's thesis is that the systematizing undertaken by post-Möserian Conservatives led to an undesirable "pseudo-Conservatism."

[78] The most trenchant criticism is still J. K. Bluntschli, *Geschichte der Neueren Staatswissenschaft*, pp. 463-76.

justification of the existing hierarchic *Ständestaat*. His defense of obvious anachronisms—such as the discrimination against bastards, barbarous punishments, and the survival of serfdom—made him appear ridiculous to a later age; while the defense of serfdom exposed him to the charge of opportunism and insincerity. His failure to consider problems of foreign policy, or to transcend the horizons of a petty territorial state like Osnabrück, marked him as an indelibly parochial figure.

His Conservatism was largely inspired by a love for the existing order and by an idealized picture of the past, though he was too practical a man to develop any general Reactionary program. It cannot be denied, moreover, that his idealization of the ancient Germans provided him with an entirely anachronistic standard for judging the affairs of his own time. The worshipful gaze directed toward a remote past made him unhelpful in dealing with the problems of the present and indifferent to those of the future. There was remarkably little of the Reform Conservative in Möser's outlook, except for a few insights on such problems as the adaptation of guilds to the factory economy and the preservation of peasant homesteads in the age of agrarian laissez-faire. These occasional gleams of light fell far short of a Reform Conservative program aiming at a constructive synthesis of the old and the new.[79]

This fact is rather paradoxical in view of Möser's precocious grasp of the principle of historical development and understanding for the need of all institutions to adapt themselves to the total configuration of society. His interest in historical origins, and nostalgic regret for the passing of the old German peasantry, made him in principle aware of historical change. What precluded him from understanding his own —and, even more, the coming—age was his failure to appreciate that dynamism of the modern world which required that adaptation be made a deliberate and manipulated process. Möser was intellectually handicapped by too close identification with—verging on idolization of—his Osnabrückian milieu. The result was an inability to understand the specific historical changes which were to mold Germany's future. Möser failed to assess the correct strength of secularism, egalitarianism, and nationalism and had no idea of their irresistible character; hence he developed no plans, and could not be expected to develop any plans, for taming them through incorporation into those aspects of the *ancien régime* which could still survive.

[79] Meinecke, *Historismus*, p. 353, calls Möser "einen reformerisch gesinnten Konservativen," but all the evidence is against this surprising statement.

All these limitations are not surprising in a citizen of a small German state who grew up before 1770. Möser was in many ways a child of his age and milieu; it is, indeed, a remarkable tribute to his intellectual power that he was able to transcend both as he replaced an unreflecting traditionalism by at least the beginnings of a self-conscious Conservatism. One must also remember that his limitations, as is true of most men, were but the reverse side of his virtues. Möser's identification with his milieu gave him the encyclopedic mastery of detail which gives such authoritativeness to his writings; his immersion in the concrete and the specific allowed him to write with unusual trenchancy, vigor, and color. He succeeded in making eighteenth-century Osnabrück interesting for posterity because it provided the solid earth which gave strength to his Anteuslike qualities. There is something touching about Möser's devotion to his native city, and his restless endeavors on behalf of his fellow citizens. We owe his *Patriotic Phantasies* not to any desire to instruct posterity but rather to the immediate desire to provide his countrymen with a civic education to go along with his benevolent administration. These fragments written for a local public nevertheless influenced some of the greatest of his contemporaries and still attract attention two centuries later. A whole generation was to pass before German Conservatism found again a writer of comparable stature in the person of Adam Müller.

PART TWO

THE CHALLENGE OF THE
FRENCH REVOLUTION AND NAPOLEON
(1790-1806)

CHAPTER 7

Prussia from Frederick the Great to Frederick William III

Frederician Prussia

PRUSSIA'S STRENGTH AND WEAKNESSES[1]

THE PRUSSIA of Frederick the Great enjoyed enormous prestige in Germany and Europe. It had succeeded in the difficult task of transforming a small North German margraviate into one of the five Great Powers of Europe—a success demonstrated to an astonished world when Frederick survived the hostility of the coalition composed of Russia, Austria, France, the Holy Roman Empire, and Sweden in the Seven Years' War. The Prussian army was generally considered the best in the world; the victories of Rossbach, Leuthen, and Minden put into the shade all military exploits since the days of Marlborough. Yet Prussia was renowned for the arts of peace as well as those of war: the structure of its internal polity evoked as much admiration as did its military triumphs. Frederick's absolutism was probably the least arbitrary and the most enlightened in Europe; the bureaucracy had begun to win an enviable reputation for efficiency and incorruptibility; and the administration of justice was comparatively independent of governmental pressure. (A famous exception, Frederick's punishment of the judges of Miller Arnold, was more often hailed for its motives—protecting a poor miller against the antisocial legalism of the court—than denounced for its arbitrariness.) The mercantilistic policies pursued by the Prussian government after 1763 had promoted rapid recovery from the extensive devastation caused by the Seven Years' War. Berlin was the unchallenged capital of the German *Aufklärung*. Prussia's religious toleration was famous for embracing Huguenots, Jews, and Jesuits alike. The state had proclaimed the principle of universal education and made greater progress toward its practical implementation than any of its neighbors. The dominant aristocratic class was not without faults, but it was devoted to the

---

[1] The discussion of Prussia's problems in this chapter is based on Max Lehmann, *Freiherr vom Stein* (3 vols., Leipzig, 1902-05), II, 11-65, a well-known indictment of the Prussian *ancien régime*, and the reply by Ernst von Meier, *Französische Einflüsse auf die Staats- und Rechtsentwicklung Preussens im 19. Jahrhundert* (2 vols., Leipzig, 1907-08), Vol. II, Sect. I, "Der preussische Staat des 18. Jahrhunderts."

king's service and personally active in the management of its own estates: it was far different from the decadent French nobility, which lived in pampered idleness at Versailles. Clearly there was much for Prussians to be complacent about.

Prussia's greatest glory was, of course, its unmatchable sovereign. Frederick's untiring industry on behalf of his people, his craftiness in diplomacy and heroism in war, and, above all, the radiant star of his personality—all these qualities made him a legend while he was still alive. Their influence was enhanced by the sheer length of his reign—forty-six years (1740-86), as well as by Frederick's gift for expressing his conception of kingship in trenchant language:

> A true prince exists only to work and not to enjoy himself. He must be dominated by the feeling of patriotism, and the only goal to which he aspires must be: to achieve great and benevolent measures for the welfare of his state. To this goal he must subordinate all personal considerations, his self-love as well as his passions. . . . Justice must always be the primary concern of the prince; while the welfare of his people must have precedence over every other interest. The ruler is far from being the arbitrary master of his people; he is, indeed, nothing other than its first servant.[2]

There can be no question that Frederick succeeded in living up to his own ideals; his rule constitutes the finest flowering of "enlightened absolutism" in European history, with most of its virtues but also all its limitations.

The historian of today has no difficulty in perceiving what only a few acute contemporary observers—for example, Mirabeau, whose views will be outlined below—could see even dimly: that Prussia, for all its surface splendor, was in fact seriously ill and in need of drastic reforms if it was to survive in the dynamic, competitive world of the late eighteenth century. Its political, military, and social structures were all hopelessly anachronistic in the face of the challenge to be presented by the French Revolution only three years after Frederick's death. The political system was one of pure monarchical absolutism —an efficient system when wielded by a superman, but a feeble and unreliable one when men of ordinary talents sat on the throne. Neither Frederick William II nor his son Frederick William III possessed the capacity or the temperament to govern a state of Prussia's size and complexity autocratically. Their inadequacy was left uncorrected by a

[2] From Frederick's *Anti-Machiavel*, quoted by H. J. Schoeps, *Das war Preussen*, p. 138.

strong body of ministers, for Frederick had feared to train such a body lest it threaten his personal control. He and his successors relied, instead, upon humble cabinet secretaries with neither prestige nor status, who were expected to be faithful errandboys for the king, and in fact screened him not only from regular contact with his ministers but also from many unpleasant realities.

Prussia was an *Obrigkeitsstaat* where the affairs of government were held to transcend the understanding of mere subjects. An elaborate, carefully trained, and rigidly supervised bureaucracy governed the country in the name of the king. Its government was benevolent in intention if not always in practice. The bureaucrats never doubted that they possessed a monopoly of wisdom in all matters concerning the public welfare. Subjects were encouraged to mind their own business as they fulfilled the functions of their customary status. The very conception of a state entity called Prussia still stood in its infancy. The various provinces united under the Hohenzollern dynasty differed markedly from one another, and men felt themselves to be more Pomeranians or Silesians than subjects of a common monarchy. There was no civic spirit, no widespread interest in political affairs, no concern about Prussia's position in Europe. When the catastrophe of Jena came twenty years later, the Prussian population met it in a spirit of helpless apathy, as if an unexpected disaster had struck from the moon—a disaster which it was somebody else's business to repair. The state was essentially a machine receiving impulses from above, not yet an organism with an articulate life and will of its own. It scarcely occurred to either rulers or ruled that Prussia might become a self-governing country; the virtues of self-government (and the prerequisites of its success)—initiative, spontaneity, willingness to assume responsibility—were certainly not Prussian virtues.

The military system was as obsolete as the political. The officer corps was recruited almost exclusively from the Junker class, in itself not a bad reservoir for military leaders, but an insufficient one at a time when France was about to open careers to the talents of every class. The military efficiency of the Junker officers was handicapped by a combination of arrogance and complacency which made them reluctant to see that conditions of warfare had changed since the glorious days of Rossbach and Leuthen. The rank and file were conscripted from among the serfs of the country, a thoroughly degraded, exploited, and brutalized group of men who could understand only a discipline based upon the whip. The common soldier was not attached to military service by any patriotic ties, and desertion was the major problem confronting the military administration in peace as well as war. How could such an army compete with the levies soon raised by France, which combined devotion to the fatherland with zeal to bring the blessings of the French Revolution to less happy lands?

The Prussian social system was still characterized by a hierarchic division of society in which nobles, burghers, and serfs all held their appointed place and social mobility was disapproved in theory and rarely seen in practice. The nobility was far from being degenerate, but many of its members were both uncultured and poor. Nobles were not permitted to enter "burgher" professions, with the result that younger sons either divided the paternal estate with their older brothers or sought state employment, to secure maintenance for themselves rather than to serve the public. The fruitful English intermixture of money and birth in an "open" aristocracy was virtually unknown.

The power exercised by the Junker nobility over its serfs remained very great. The Junker usually appointed the village official, the *Schulze*, who exercised the local police power and administered the local court. The serfs owed labor obligations and banalities, while minor children were held to domestic service (*Gesindezwang*). They could marry, or leave the village, only with the lord's permission. The village clergyman and schoolmaster were both appointed by the Junker lord. It is true that the exercise of these despotic powers was in practice sometimes mitigated by a spirit of paternalism and adherence to local custom, but the possibility of abuse was ever-present. The state also required that Junkers help their serfs in time of distress, and strict laws prevented serfs from being driven off the land. The fact remained, nonetheless, that the spirit and law of feudalism continued to prevail in Prussia at a time when Western Europe was already well advanced toward capitalist development.

The Prussian burgher class lived a sheltered and parochial life under the fetters of mercantilistic and guild supervision. Prosperity at the king's command was the official slogan; that private initiative and the free breath of competition might be the key to maximum prosperity was outside the ken of regulating bureaucrats. The vigorous municipal life of earlier periods had decayed first into oligarchy and corruption, later into political apathy as royal control made a mockery of what survived of municipal self-government.

The atrophy of political life had been accompanied by cultural sterility. Prussia was able to produce utilitarian authors like Nicolai, but it stood somewhat outside of the main stream of Germany's budding national literature. Winckelmann had fled from the uncivilized "Sparta of the North"; Lessing had been rejected for the post of Frederick's librarian. Frederick's ignorant attack upon German poetry had provoked a well-deserved rebuke from Justus Möser. Weimar and Potsdam stood in a position of antagonism which boded ill for the future of Germany. The cleavage between the Prussian power state (*Machtstaat*) and German national culture (*Nationalgeist*) deprived Prussia of a great potential reservoir of power, for the rising consciousness of nationality—though largely nonpolitical in its origins and intentions—in fact provided a new basis for political power of incalculable import. The French Revolution was to show that the spirit of nationality could rouse hitherto dormant energies and provide a bond of cohesion for previously heterogeneous provinces and classes. German national consciousness was fostered by the end of the eighteenth century by the imperial glories of the past as well as the cultural achievements of the present; but Prussia naturally lacked imperial consciousness, as its rise to Great Power status had been accompanied *pari passu* by defiance of the imperial constitution. The empire had condemned Frederick as the aggressor in the Seven Years' War, while hostility to Austria—whose ruler held the Imperial Crown—was the keynote of Frederick's foreign policy. It may be added that Prussia lost its national homogeneity through the fateful partitions of Poland begun by Frederick in 1772.

More important than all these weaknesses was the problematical character of Prussia's ambitions and the qualities which were required to realize those ambitions. To turn a small margraviate into a Great Power, and to secure the newly won status against a host of jealous neighbors, required the constant attempt to do too much with too little. The result was an atmosphere of incessant exertion and strain scarcely compatible with the development of a healthy polity. It required a disproportionate diversion of resources to military ends, the predominance of a narrow military spirit, and excessive prestige for the officer class. All the institutions of the state—the monarchy, the administration, the fiscal system, and the privileged position of the Junkers—were geared with primary emphasis upon military efficiency and the needs of the army. It may also be noted that the position of *toute en vedette* encouraged the development of estimable rather than lovable qualities: industry, economy, discipline, and a cult of duty. All these Prussian virtues were widely if grudgingly acknowledged; but there was also much complaint that they were too often accompanied by a want of graciousness, cultivation, adaptability, and sensitivity to the needs and interests of other people.

No one could expect Prussians to question the *raison d'être* of Prussia and to conclude that the sacrifices entailed by the winning of Great Power status might not be worth the cost; but there was no excuse for failure to work at remedying the fundamental weaknesses outlined above. The fact that all these weaknesses—political, military, social, and national—were interconnected made a policy of comprehensive reform at the same time more imperative and more difficult. Absolutism was based upon, and in turn perpetuated, the total want of civic spirit; both rested upon the survival of an essentially anachronistic feudal structure of society. The aristocratic monopoly of the officer corps reflected the dominant position of the Junkers in the civil polity; while the power of the officer class likewise mirrored the fact that in civilian life the conscript serfs were more subjects of the local Junker than of the remote king. The rigid and caste-ridden class system was natural in a society where the *bourgeoisie* as yet lacked economic vigor, culture, and self-consciousness. The want of national spirit was but a function of the absence of any kind of civic spirit: Prussia was essentially a loose agglomeration of territories which dynastic statecraft had brought together and external disaster might well destroy.

THE PRAISE OF PRUSSIA

The worst of the Frederician system was that it bred an enormous complacency which made men incapable of seeing, much less tackling, the formidable weaknesses here analyzed. Prussians were spoiled by success, unable to recognize the precariousness of their situation, and more willing to lend their ears to flatterers than to critics. Frederick himself had been too contemptuous of public opinion to care much for flattery; this matter changed when his insecure nephew Frederick William II ascended the throne in 1786. Two birthday orations of 1788, honoring the new king and the state he ruled, give us an excellent indication of what Prussians believed about themselves (or at least wanted to hear). The two orations were read respectively before the Literary Society of Halberstadt[3] and the *Joachim'thalische Gymnasium* in Berlin.[4] They are most convincing

---

[3] Anonymous [signed "J.T.F."], "Über das Eigenthümliche der Preussischen Monarchie," *Berlinisches Journal für Aufklärung*, II (1789), 54-75; III (1789), 148-61; IV (1789), 43-49. Cited henceforth as *Das Eigenthümliche*.

[4] Brunn, "Der preussische Staat, der glücklichste unter Allen in Europa," *Ber-*

when they expatiate on the virtues of the Frederician monarchy, least convincing in their almost Byzantine flattery of Frederick William II.

One of the eulogists, Professor Brunn, set out to demonstrate the proposition that "Prussia was the happiest country in Europe." His method of proof began with an interesting European *tour d'horizon* showing the unhappiness of every other country. Russia was a vast and barren land, plagued by needless wars of conquest, an unstable throne, and a universal primitivity once one excepted the enlightened court of the personally admirable Catherine. Turkey was a corrupt and unstable despotism where the stagnant character of Islam precluded cultural progress. The Habsburg Empire had an excellent ruler in Joseph II, but his benevolent intentions were paralyzed by Catholic obscurantism, feudal intransigence, and the centrifugal revolts of Hungary and Belgium. France, which misguided souls deemed a model for the rest of Europe, could not compare with Prussia: it had been ruled for several reigns by vain, sensuous, or incompetent kings; its religious toleration was incomplete (witness the case of Calas); its financial mismanagement was evident in its high and unfair taxes which yet could not eliminate the deficit, much less the swollen national debt; its judicial system was marred by arbitrary imprisonment *(lettre de cachet),* royal interference with the courts, and a barbarous criminal code; while the incompetence of French diplomacy and soldiering had led to a great decline in French prestige since the days of Louis XIV. The condition of England was not much better. It was true that Englishmen were proud of their wealth and freedom. Their wealth was, however, badly distributed, heavily taxed, and accompanied by a base spirit of materialism and luxury; while freedom easily degenerated into license, as in the Gordon riots and the scurrilous tone of the public press. Nor did English government deserve the praise too frequently bestowed upon it by foreign admirers. The king, the aristocracy, and the Anglican bishops joined together in oppressing the nation; the House of Commons was a plutocratic, corrupt, and turbulent body; while the opposition was more noted for its factiousness than its public spirit. English foreign policy was characterized by numerous senseless wars started to promote selfish mercantile interests; domestic conditions, by a chaotic welter of archaic laws.

The small countries of Europe were no more fortunate than the great. Holland was notorious for being a nation of shopkeepers dom-

---

linisches Journal für Aufklärung, v (1789), 104-61. Cited henceforth as *Der preussische Staat.*

inated by a spirit of avarice and luxury; the anarchical factionalism of its politics had just required curbing by the benevolent military intervention of Prussia. Denmark and Norway suffered from economic backwardness, a bigoted Protestant clergy, and the painful consciousness of having declined since the days when their Viking forebears swept over Europe. Sweden had similar cause for unhappiness, while its government was rent by factionalism verging upon chronic civil war. Poland was a European byword for ridiculous government, feudal oppression, and religious intolerance; while its weakness had been dramatically illustrated by the Partition of 1772. Even Switzerland had lost much of its former simplicity, freedom, and patriotism: the Swiss aristocracy was oppressive, French gallantry had corrupted manners, and the export of mercenaries was demoralizing. The various states of Italy were known for their degeneracy, banditry, and monkish superstition; the soil was exhausted and life was made insecure by the activity of volcanoes; while national pride was humiliated by the knowledge that the days of the Caesars were gone forever. Spain had an unenviable notoriety throughout Europe for its bigotry, despotism, and laziness; the Portuguese were likewise notorious for being "a lazy, degenerate, poverty-struck, bigoted and spiritless people."[5]

How happy was Prussia's lot when seen against this dark European background! Though comparatively small in territorial extent, population, and wealth it had yet succeeded in winning secure Great Power status. This greatness had not been the gift of the gods but the result of strenuous work by king and people acting together. The people of Prussia had the good fortune of belonging to the German race:

> a people (*Volk*) which combines adaptability and receptivity for everything great with a happy disposition at least the equal of that of any other people; which is still free from serious national vices yet possesses already great national virtues or at least a propensity to virtue; and which is characterized as much by a sense for lawful freedom as for rational obedience.[6]

The Prussians were, furthermore, not only Germans but predominantly German Protestants, "without question the most noble and enlightened part of the human race."[7]

This noble breed of men possessed exactly the government which

[5] Ibid., pp. 109-52, provides a country-by-country survey of Europe.
[6] *Das Eigenthümliche*, p. 71.
[7] Ibid.

it deserved. Prussia had been ruled by a succession of great princes famous for their austere sense of duty. The factionalism of republics and the turbulence of parliamentary bodies were alike unknown. The king felt himself bound by the law, and the laws were now in the process of modernization through the codification of the *Allgemeines Landrecht*. The administration was efficient and honest, the fiscal system economical and equitable. The government's skillful encouragement of economic activity had led to a comparatively high standard of living, while religious toleration had made Prussia the haven of the oppressed of other lands.[8]

Prussia was unique in combining excellence in military and civilian affairs alike. Its military greatness, and the tremendous exertions required to win and maintain Great Power status, were always balanced by careful attention to enlightened policies at home. The honesty of a bureaucrat was honored as much as the bravery of the soldier, the happiness of the subject as much as the security of the state. It was also claimed that Prussia had shown an unusual rectitude in her conduct of foreign affairs—a most dubious claim but one which showed that a bragging and self-advertising Machiavellianism, the great political sin of the Wilhelmine period of German history, was still a matter for the future.[9]

It was complacently believed that Frederick had laid the foundations of Prussia's greatness upon a permanent basis although her rise had occurred with dizzying rapidity.

> Frederick has given Prussia foundations which are as strong and unshakable as those of any monarchy, insofar as anything human can be made unshakable; he has given such an impetus to the driving wheels of his handiwork as to secure it for a long time against disintegration and disaster.[10]

This future was guaranteed by a unique synthesis between opposed conditions and qualities rarely found together: military virtues were combined with a superior civilian administration; monarchical rule did not preclude an almost republican freedom of opinion; absolutism did not prevent close adherence to natural law. Prussia's virtues were matched by the avoidance of many evils much too prevalent in less

---

[8] The merits of Prussia are best summarized in Brunn, *Der preussische Staat*, pp. 152-58, while the criteria for excellence are explicitly set forth in pp. 108-09.
[9] *Das Eigenthümliche*, pp. 68-69.
[10] Ibid., p. 59.

happy lands: internal conflicts, party feuds, corruption, exploitation, extravagance, poverty, arbitrariness, and clerical intolerance.[11]

THE CRITICISM OF PRUSSIA

It is easy to find examples of the praise of Prussia, like the two birthday orations just paraphrased; it is far more difficult to find criticism, not because there was no dissatisfaction but because its expression was restrained by the general spirit of Prussia's absolutist polity and specific censorship over the discussion of public affairs. It is true that Prussia—and especially the capital city Berlin—was proud of the freedom of opinion which allegedly prevailed; but the real limits upon that freedom were set forth in a famous letter written by Lessing to Nicolai on August 25, 1769:

> Please do not talk to me about your Berlin freedom; it is really confined to the single freedom of bringing to market scurrilous antireligious pamphlets to one's heart's content. . . . Just wait until someone should appear at Berlin to raise his voice for the rights of subjects and against exploitation and despotism, as happens now in countries like France and Denmark—you will then see what country in Europe is in fact characterized by the worst slavery at the present day.[12]

It is not surprising, then, that critical voices should appear more readily outside than inside Prussia; it must be assumed, however, that these voices spoke also for suppressed voices within the country. The criticism came from two opposite positions of the political spectrum, though the same things were often criticized. The Hannoverian publicist Ernst Brandes attacked Prussia from the Right in the name of *altständisch*-patriarchal Reactionary ideals; the French statesman Mirabeau from the Left in the name of Progressive Physiocratic Liberalism.

Brandes hated the Frederician state because he saw in it a soulless mechanical machine which had replaced the flourishing organic life of the patrimonial monarchy of the late Middle Ages. The royal will had made the powers of the *Stände* vestigial; mercantilism had paralyzed all spontaneous economic activity; while militarism consistently sacrificed individual happiness to the (pretended) welfare of the state. Brandes admitted that absolutism, mercantilism, and militarism had yielded remarkable material results in the short run;

---

[11] Ibid., pp. 154-61.
[12] Quoted in K. Aner, *Theologies der Lessingzeit*, pp. 169-70.

he insisted, however, that the long-run result must be nothing short of a degradation of men through servility, atrophy of individual thought, and a decline in the sense of social responsibility. These results would be deplorable in any country: Brandes thought them especially deplorable in a country like Germany whose national character already tended toward pedantry, love of routine, and want of self-reliance. The creation of a petty, cringing, and unimaginative type of man in Prussia must be further encouraged through the spread of irreligion following the skepticism of the great king himself.[13]

The most celebrated Liberal criticism of the Frederician state was advanced by Mirabeau, who had spent the year 1786-87 in Berlin as a semiofficial French agent, in an open letter to King Frederick William II upon his accession. He criticized the just deceased Frederick for having engaged in too many wars, having paid undue honor to the military at the expense of deserving civilians (for example, by always wearing uniform), and having maintained a system of "military slavery" based upon conscription when a militia system based upon the spirit of patriotism would have been far more abreast of the ideals of the age. (The criticism fell just short of a general indictment of Prussia's Big Power ambition and the militarism which it necessitated.) Mirabeau, while carefully avoiding a direct attack upon serfdom, criticized various forms of aristocratic privilege, such as semiautomatic access to state employment and the legal distinction between noble and nonnoble property in estates. His main objection was, however, directed against the meddling omnicompetence of the government expressed in its mercantilistic policies: Mirabeau urged the introduction of Physiocratic principles of laissez-faire, as in the abolition of monopolies and the termination of all restrictions upon emigration. He did not attack royal absolutism per se in the name of self-government, but wanted to improve the caliber of royal administration through advancing nonnobles to ministerial posts. Mirabeau also criticized the residual censorship and the purely *de facto* character of religious toleration; and he possessed an instinct for the future by demanding workshops for the unemployed and the rational planning of urban expansion.[14] In all these ways he presented a chal-

---

[13] Ernst Brandes, *Betrachtungen über den Zeitgeist in Deutschland* (Hannover, 1808), pp. 38-44, 50-67. Though written only in 1808 this work faithfully describes views the author already held thirty years earlier, while his avowed purpose is to chronicle *Zeitgeist* currents in the period 1770-1800.

[14] H.G.R. Mirabeau, *Schreiben an Friedrich Wilhelm II, itzt regierenden König von Preussen, am Tage seiner Thronbesteigung* (Paris, 1787). It should be noted that this is an *ad hoc* letter, designed to influence the king, not a balanced presen-

lenge to King Frederick William II when the latter succeeded his famous uncle in the summer of 1786.

The Reign of Frederick William II (1786-97)

THE KING AND HIS ADVISERS

Frederick William II has fared ill both in popular memory and the judgment of serious historians. He lacked both the political genius of his predecessor Frederick II and the private virtues of his successor Frederick William III. It should not be forgotten, however, that he faced a nearly impossible situation at the beginning of his reign. The Prussian governmental machine was tailored to suit the herculean capacity of a Frederick: it was no fault of his nephew that he was not a Hercules. Yet the machine was hallowed by the prestige of Frederick, and there was no alternative readily available: Frederick William cannot be blamed for being both unable and unwilling to replace absolutism by some form of constitutionalism. He attempted to rule as an absolute monarch in the Frederician tradition while really lacking both the strength and ability required for playing this role.

It is necessary to say a few additional words about the personal qualities of the king. He was not without the gift of winning popularity: his stately physique, gracious manners, personal charm, and desire to please all contrasted favorably with Frederick. He was, unfortunately, poorly prepared for his kingly office: Frederick had neglected his education, refused to give him steady governmental responsibilities after he came of age, and wounded his self-esteem by not bothering to conceal the contempt he felt for him. Frederick William was unable either to conceive long-range policies or to pursue them steadily. Vacillation was the keynote of his reign; personal insecurity, its cause. He alternated, as weak men in authority often do, between obstinate self-assertion and pliant accommodation to the wills of others. He was overdependent upon his advisers, and as his advisers advocated divergent views his policies necessarily lacked consistency. He sought release from the burden of kingship in two seemingly incompatible ways: sensuality and religion. His sexual con-

---

tation of Mirabeau's views. This fact probably explains why Mirabeau pressed neither for self-government through revitalizing the old estates nor for ending serfdom—two proposals which certainly would have shocked the king. Mirabeau's over-all views are presented in his classic *De la Monarchie prussienne sous Frédéric le Grand* (7 vols., London, 1788). The standard secondary work on the subject is H. Welschinger, *Mirabeau in Berlin* (Leipzig, 1900).

duct was the talk of the age. His first marriage (1765-69) had ended in divorce under scandalous circumstances involving both spouses; his second marriage (1769) did not prevent a permanent liaison with Wilhelmine Enke (1753-1820), the daughter of a trumpet blower, technically married to a royal valet named Rietz, and later raised to the dignity of a Countess of Lichtenau. Even this unusual arrangement—unusual at least for the Prussian court, where an influential mistress had never been known before—did not satisfy the king's libidinous drives; he insisted, after ascending the throne, upon a bigamous marriage with the Countess Voss and, following her early death (1789), a second bigamy with the Countess Dönhoff (1790). The latter was incidentally banished from court after she had quarreled with the still powerful Lichtenau.[15]

These unedifying personal circumstances did much to undermine the prestige of the Prussian crown; they were all the more scandalous because Frederick William combined private license with public zeal for the restoration of religion *and* morality (both allegedly fallen into sad decay under Frederick). We have already noted that Frederick William and his closest advisers were important members of the Rosicrucian Order; the king had a typically Rosicrucian sense of mission about the extirpation of rationalism and all its evil works. He also had need of mystical religious experiences, and his entourage did not scruple to employ séances in order to gratify him and at the same time maintain their own ascendancy in the royal councils.[16] Two of these

[15] There is no satisfactory biography of Frederick William II. The best substitute is the remarkably full article by von Hartmann, *ADB*, VII (1878), 685-700, though it concentrates primarily upon foreign policy. Friedrich Paulig, *Friedrich Wilhelm II, König von Preussen. Sein Privatleben und seine Regierung im Lichte neuerer Forschungen* (Frankfurt/Oder, 1895), is an unsuccessful attempt at rehabilitation. G. Stanhope, *A Mystic on the Prussian Throne: Frederick William II* (London, 1912), is an unscholarly popularization. The standard work on the reign is Martin Philippson, *Geschichte des preussischen Staatswesens vom Tode Friedrichs des Grossen* . . . (2 vols., Leipzig, 1880-82), though it is more a compilation of materials than a readable history; its hostility to every kind of "obscurantism" marks it as a product of the still confident Liberalism of the 1880's. The court of Frederick William is the subject of two works: Friedrich von Oppeln-Bronikowsky, "Die Rosenkreuzer, Bischoffwerder, Wöllner, Gräfin Lichtenau," in *Abenteurer am preussischen Hofe 1700-1800* (Berlin, 1927), pp. 140-74, popular, and Erich Bleich, *Der Hof des Königs Friedrich Wilhelm II und des Königs Friedrich Wilhelm III* (Berlin, 1914), scholarly. Johannes Schultze, "Die Rosenkreuzer und Friedrich Wilhelm II," *Mitteilungen des Vereins für die Geschichte Berlins* (1929), pp. 41-51, is important for using Bischoffwerder's letters to Wöllner (his Rosicrucian superior) now deposited at Wolfenbüttel.

[16] See the revealing article by Paul Schwartz, "Der Geisterspuk um Friedrich Wilhelm II," *Mitteilungen des Vereins für die Geschichte Berlins* (1930), pp.

counselors have left their distinctive mark upon Prussian history: Rudolf von Bischoffwerder and Johann Christoph Wöllner. Both were men of Conservative principle who knew—far better than the king himself—what they wanted in politics; they may, indeed, be described as the first self-consciously Conservative politicians in German history, politicians in the honorable sense of the term—men eager for power for the sake of implementing their principles.

Both men have suffered severely at the hands of five generations of predominantly Liberal historians. Posterity has been somewhat kinder to Bischoffwerder than to his colleague, partly because his name is not so intimately linked to the bitterly hated Edict Concerning Religion of 1788. Bischoffwerder also had the good fortune of not being a parvenu: while Wöllner was the son of a humble country parson, Bischoffwerder (1741-1803) came from Thuringian noble stock. His father, an officer in various armies, died early (in 1754) after having been A.D.C. to the famous Marshal de Saxe. The son first studied law but soon decided to follow the same career as his father; the last period of the Seven Years' War (1760-63) found him a cornet in the Prussian cavalry. After the war Bischoffwerder became stablemaster and chamberlain to Charles Duke of Courland, a son of the Saxon king who headed the Saxon branch of "Strict Observance" Masonry.[17]

Bischoffwerder had been passionately absorbed in Masonic mystery-mongering since early manhood. His thirst for occult knowledge was as incorrigible as his superstitious credulity. He became the victim of most of the impostors who plagued German Masonry in the second half of the eighteenth century. His disappointment at the failure to secure full initiation into alchemy while a Mason led him to the Rosicrucian Order, which he joined on Christmas Eve, 1779. He intensified his study of cabalistic writings but despaired of ever winning full understanding: "I sometimes see a speck of light but it is too weak to penetrate to the truth." His proneness to superstition did not preclude a genuine Christian piety, and he could say truthfully of

---

45-60, based upon the protocols of the commission which interrogated Countess Lichtenau in 1798 and on the king's letters to her.

[17] On Bischoffwerder see the excellent sketch by Johannes Schultze, "Hans Rudolf von Bischoffwerder," *Mitteldeutsche Lebensbilder*, III (Magdeburg, 1928), 134-55, with the thesis that he was an honest fanatic; the same author's valuable "Die Berichte Hans Rudolf von Bischoffwerders an seine Ordensvorgesetzten 1777-81," *Quellen zur Geschichte der Freimaurerei* III (Leipzig, 1921), 49-73; von Hartmann in *ADB*, II (1875), 675-78, still the best brief account of his diplomatic activities; and the balanced sketch by Count Stolberg-Wernigerode in *NDB*, II (1955), 266.

himself, "I beg the Eternal-Allmighty daily, nay hourly, to bestow upon me a Christian rebirth."[18]

He had rejoined the Prussian army in 1778 as a major to participate in the so-called "Potato War" against Austria. His friendship with the prince of Prussia, the future Frederick William II, dated from this campaign. The head of the Berlin Rosicrucians, Duke Frederick August of Braunschweig-Oels (Brother Rufus), instructed Bischoffwerder to win the prince for the Order sometime in 1780. The mission was easy to accomplish in view of the prince's mystical-superstitious temperament: Frederick William became Brother Ormesus Magnus on August 8, 1781, in an impressive ceremony in which Wöllner gave the initiation oration. Bischoffwerder became the immediate superior of the royal novice and was henceforth the inseparable companion of the prince.

The secret of his ascendancy, which fascinated contemporaries and led to wild gossip about sorcery and correct talk about the employment of spiritualist mediums, is to be found primarily in Bischoffwerder's personality. His social qualities evidently impressed the as yet somewhat gauche prince. Bischoffwerder was "a tall man with regular and attractive features, experienced in all sports and knightly arts. He was an expert swimmer, fencer and marksman, while his perfect cavalier manners made him the favorite of women."[19] These qualities were made more impressive by the maintenance of a certain distance in social intercourse; his aloofness gave him a nimbus of mystery and authority. His voice was deep and rather imprecise, "as if his tongue were located in his stomach." It is clear that Bischoffwerder was made to be envied and admired by a weak and insecure prince like Frederick William.

Bischoffwerder became a very influential political figure when Frederick William became king in 1786. Since there was nothing in his background to justify the exercise of political power, he inevitably aroused the jealousy of old servants of the Prussian crown. Stein spoke for this group in one of his characteristically harsh judgments: "Bischoffwerder is clever, observing, secretive, imaginative, and pleasure-loving. He lacks both the specific knowledge and the professional training required for public business."[20] Yet, unlike Wöllner,

[18] Quoted in Schultze, *Lebensbilder*, p. 144.

[19] Theodor Fontane, *Wanderungen in der Mark Brandenburg*. Pt. III, *Ost-Havelland* (Berlin, 1873), pp. 259-77, includes an excellent description of Bischoffwerder in connection with his Marquardt estate. The quotation is from p. 269.

[20] Quoted in Schultze, *Lebensbilder*, p. 154.

he was not generally accused of self-seeking; there was no question of his fanatical Rosicrucian zeal. He even tried to induce the king to give up his long-standing liaison with Wilhelmine Enke, surely a courageous step whose failure showed the limits of his personal influence.[21] He neither held nor sought a post in the civilian government, being quite content to serve as A.D.C. to the King. (He became *Generaladjutant* in 1789.) His military promotion, while rapid, was neither spectacular nor scandalous; he was a major general in charge of the *Feldjägerkorps* at the age of fifty-six when his royal friend died in 1797. Bischoffwerder's influence was strongest in the field of foreign policy, where he successfully championed a counter-revolutionary crusade against French Jacobinism—a policy which owed more to Rosicrucian Conservatism than adherence to the traditions of Prussian Reason of State.

The dominant figure in domestic affairs during most of the reign was Bischoffwerder's Rosicrucian superior, Johann Christoph Wöllner (1732-1800), a much-hated figure whose magnitude must be judged by his success in converting obscurantist Rosicrucianism into the semi-official ideology of the once "enlightened" Prussian state.[22] His spectacular rise from humble beginnings was bound—quite apart from his substantive policies—to make him a host of enemies. The son of a Lutheran pastor, he also undertook a clerical career but soon abandoned it to administer the landed estates of the socially prominent widow of General von Itzenplitz, whose husband had been killed in battle in 1759. His spare time was devoted to writing books and reviews on agricultural subjects, and he became an acknowledged authority. It is strange to note that Wöllner's favorite outlet was

---

[21] It throws a characteristic light upon the Prussian court to note that Lichtenau counteracted Bischoffwerder's influence by claiming contact with the spirit of the deceased Count of Mark, the favorite natural son of the king.

[22] There is no biography of Wöllner. The best study is the detailed and fair-minded article by Paul Bailleu in *ADB*, XLIV (1898), 148-58. The pioneering study by J.D.E. Preuss, "Zur Beurtheilung des Staatsministers von Wöllner," *Zeitschrift für preussische Geschichte und Landeskunde*, II (1865), 577-604, 746-74, and II (1866), 65-95, first "discovered" Wöllner's remarkable pre-1786 "reform program" and gives a thorough account of his ministry; it contains, however, little on his Rosicrucianism and condemns Wöllner unhistorically for "betraying" the heritage of Frederick the Great. The account in Philippson, op.cit., I, 69-75, shows the same tendency. Max Lehmann, "Wöllner und die auswärtige Politik Friedrich Wilhelm II," *HZ*, LXII (1889), 285-86, prints an important *Immediatbericht* from Wöllner to the king (Oct. 7, 1794) which shows that he opposed the counterrevolutionary war (herein differing sharply from Bischoffwerder). Reinicke, "Johann Christoph von Wöllner der Rosenkreuzer," *Jahrbuch für brandenburgische Kirchengeschichte*, XII (1914), 342-47, is an insignificant article favorable to Wöllner.

Nicolai's *Allgemeine Deutsche Bibliothek;* he lived for several years on cordial terms with the man who was to be persecuted by his system twenty years later. There was little open indication of his future mysticism in these early years—a fact which frequently led to charges of opportunism when his later Rosicrucianism provided the basis for a phenomenal rise.

Wöllner's tranquil rustic life was disturbed when he married the only daughter of General Itzenplitz in 1766—an extraordinary social advance for the son of an impoverished pastor, but one approved by the bride's mother. Other members of the Itzenplitz family took a less complacent view of this intrusion into the old Junker family; they went so far as to induce Frederick to forbid the marriage as a violation of established class barriers. The royal messenger arrived, however, twenty-four hours after the marriage had been consummated, and royal tyranny did not go so far as to insist upon an immediate annulment. Yet the bride was put under arrest for a month while the husband was investigated to see if her hand had been won by improper pressure (it had not); the couple was to live happily together for the next thirty years despite their different social antecedents. The wrath of Frederick remained, nonetheless, unappeased, and he indignantly refused to give Wöllner a patent of nobility: he labeled him "a deceitful and intriguing *Pfaffe*"—a judgment which has been parroted by five generations of historians—and placed the administration of the Itzenplitz estates under the supervision of the *Ober-Pupillencollegium.* Wöllner had personal reason to hate Frederick's system of rigid maintenance of class barriers.

He found a living as *Rentmeister* of the *Domänenkammer* of Prince Henry from 1770-86, collecting rents and administering forests—a job which left much leisure for the work in secret societies which was henceforth his major preoccupation. A Mason in 1765, he rose to be *praepositus* of the Berlin prefecture (consisting of five lodges) by 1773 through his drive, industry, and oratorical ability. He became a Knight of the Strict Observance in 1776, but soon expressed disappointment at his failure to learn either deep secrets or to acquire supernatural power. A Rosicrucian in 1779, he quickly became chief organizer for Northern Germany and *Oberhauptdirektor* in charge of twenty-six *Zirkel* (including approximately two hundred members). He entered the eighth Rosicrucian degree *(magistri)* but complained to friends that the Magi refused to initiate him into the final mysteries. It is uncertain who these Magi were, or whether they in fact existed:

it is equally uncertain whether Wöllner was an honest fanatic, an unscrupulous opportunist, or a mixture of both.

Wöllner worked closely with his fellow Rosicrucian Bischoffwerder in establishing an ascendancy over Frederick William in the years before 1786. He gave private lectures to the crown prince on many current questions during the last years of Frederick's reign. These lectures show Wöllner not only as a Rosicrucian but also as a far-sighted, reforming Conservative who had precise ideas on what timely reforms were desirable to buttress the rigid and fragile Frederician polity. He wanted to liberalize mercantilistic policies by promoting free trade and abandoning royal monopolies in accordance with the teachings of Adam Smith and the Physiocrats. Wöllner did not, however, advocate complete laissez-faire but favored a truly Conservative paternalist social policy: the state must protect the worker against the profit drive of "manufacturers with immoral souls,"[23] a group just emerging in Prussia at that time. He saw the obsolescence of serfdom, and favored the creation of peasant proprietors on royal domains and church lands twenty years before Stein's reforms; he even contemplated the breakup of Junker estates in favor of the peasantry. Wöllner wanted to abolish the hated *Regie* (the Frederician tax system operated by French collectors) and replace taxes which fell primarily upon the serfs with taxes imposed upon the wealthy classes of the community (land tax, progressive income tax, and various luxury taxes). It appears probable that this remarkably coherent program was dictated by an enlightened Conservative recognition that Prussia could not maintain its customary ways in a Europe in which far-reaching changes were inevitable. Frederick had led Prussia into a European position which far exceeded her real strength: only vigorous reforms, leading to an increase in population, wealth, and contentment, could reduce the dangerous gap which still existed between the claim to Great Power status and the inadequacy of Prussia's resources.

Wöllner saw the crucial importance of secular reforms, but deemed them nonetheless secondary to a Rosicrucian program of rescuing Prussia from the chains of irreligion wrought by Frederick and his "enlightened" ministers. Wöllner wrote for the crown prince a remarkable *Abhandlung über die Religion*, dated September 15, 1785, in which he set out in detail the entire ecclesiastical program of the coming reign. It included a statement of the utility possessed by religion

[23] Quoted by Bailleu, op.cit., p. 53. The entire account of Wöllner's reform program is a paraphrase of Bailleu's analysis.

for the greatness of states, an explanation of why Prussia had sunk into deep irreligion, and a constructive program for remedying this near-mortal flaw.

On the first point Wöllner argued—taking up a standard point of all utilitarian defenders of religion—that religion was indispensable to guarantee morality. Wöllner understood, of course, that these utilitarian considerations would never make men religious; but he insisted that their importance made it imperative for government to shield men as far as possible against dangers to their religious faith. He condemned—now as always—any persecution of men for their religious opinions, but insisted on the propriety of restraining antireligious or—that which he deemed the same thing—rationalist propaganda.

Why had Prussia become the center of European irreligion? Partly because of the evil example of Frederick, who never went to church and never bothered to conceal his own agnosticism. His government had shown a completely misguided tolerance toward a murky flood of irreligious pamphlets. Worse still was the fact that Lutheran church matters had been placed in the hands of a nonbelieving Minister for Ecclesiastical Affairs, Count Zedlitz. Zedlitz had appointed some extreme rationalists, like the notorious Bahrdt, to theological lectureships; he had placed a complete rationalist like Gedike, editor of the *Berliner Monatsschrift*, in an influential post in the administration of Prussia's schools; and he encouraged every ambitious opportunist to become a rationalist to further his career. Wöllner completed this one-sided denunciation of the policies of a man he obviously wanted to replace by a sharp attack upon his personal character.

How could Prussia be brought back to religion? Primarily by the new king's counteracting the evil example of Frederick by setting a good example himself. Frederick William must be ostentatious in his piety and leave no opportunity unturned to demonstrate the importance of religion to his subjects. He must prohibit irreligious writings through a reinvigorated censorship. He must, above all, appoint an "honest man to the direction of the Department of Ecclesiastical Affairs," and Wöllner drew a picture of such a man which was obviously intended as a self-portrait. The new minister must be provided with a new set of instructions aimed at segregating orthodox sheep from rationalist goats among the existing clergy. The whole program of Wöllner's administration is here set out some three years before he secured his post: the Edict Concerning Religion of July 9, 1788, requiring orthodoxy among preachers; the Edict of Censorship of December 19, 1788, repressing irreligious writings; the *Immediat-*

Examinations-Kommission of May 1791, enforcing the Edict Concerning Religion against rationalists; and the new *Landeskatechismus* of 1792, serving as a guidebook on what really *was* orthodox.[24]

WÖLLNER AND RELIGIOUS POLICY

Wöllner received the opportunity to pass from planning to implementation when his friend and Rosicrucian brother Frederick William ascended the throne in August 1786. It was not, however, at first in the field of ecclesiastical affairs: it is probable that the king, always fearful about his popularity, did not want to offend public opinion by the brusque dismissal of the distinguished Count Zedlitz. Frederick William preferred to employ Wöllner in the financial and economic fields, where he was an acknowledged master. He made him *Geheimer Oberfinanzrat* in charge of the *Dispositionskasse*, minister in the *Generaldirektorium* with special responsibility for factories, trade, and tariffs, and head of the building department *(Oberhofbauintendant)* with special responsibility for beautifying Potsdam. More important than these official positions was Wöllner's role—along with Bischoffwerder—as daily confidant of the king. He drafted royal speeches and cabinet orders, accompanied Frederick William on all his journeys, advised on appointments, and made himself especially unpopular with all other ministers by drafting the searching questions which the king directed at all department heads in the annual *Ministerrevue*. The king provided Wöllner with an external sign of favor by elevating him into the nobility in October 1786—a demonstrative step since it was known that Frederick the Great had adamantly refused to do so.

Wöllner must be given a large measure of credit for the promising beginning of the new reign. Some of the economic reforms he had suggested earlier were now implemented: the hated *Regie* was terminated; several monopolies were abolished; and the transit trade in grain freed of some of its fetters. There were notable improvements in the administrative system. The *Generaldirektorium* received new instructions aimed *inter alia* at limiting joint responsibility to general matters—a major improvement; the independence of the *Oberrechenkammer* (general accounting office) was increased; while school administration was for the first time placed in predominantly lay

[24] This account of Wöllner's "plan of campaign," as well as its implementation, draws heavily upon the standard work by Paul Schwartz, *Der erste Kulturkampf in Preussen um Kirche und Schule 1788-98* (Berlin, 1925), which combines a massive amount of detail with remarkable readability. It is bitterly hostile to Wöllner.

hands through the creation of a new *Oberschulkollegium*. There was a much-needed relaxation of the rigors of Frederician government, as in righting the wrong committed against the judges of Miller Arnold; and an admirable attentiveness to long-overdue social and humanitarian reforms, such as the improvement of the lot of the common soldier and the provision of pensions for the widows and orphans of deceased officers. Wöllner even planned some mitigation of serfdom, and an attack upon the tax exemption of the landed nobility through the introduction of a progressive income tax *(Classensteuer)*; the king, however, was afraid of so much courage and refused to follow his minister on this audacious path. The greatest achievement of the reign lay in the cultural sphere: a beginning was made in that *rapprochement* between the Prussian state and the "German national spirit" which was the prerequisite of Prussia's future domination of Germany. German literature, which Frederick had held in ignorant contempt, was at last discovered at the Prussian court; the monopoly held by the French language at the Academy of Science was broken. There was discerning patronage of the architect Langhans (designer of the Brandenburg Gate built 1788-94), the sculptor Schadow (creator of the Victoria above the gate), and the painter Chodowiecki; and Mozart was invited to Berlin for concerts.

Wöllner had a part in many of these measures; his real ambition was, however, to replace Zedlitz as Minister of Ecclesiastical Affairs. He wanted nothing less—as he had written to Bischoffwerder on March 18, 1786—than "to become an unworthy instrument in the hands of Ormesus [Rosicrucian name of the king], to save millions of souls from perdition and to lead the entire country back to faith in Jesus Christ."[25] His initial attempt to win influence over educational matters by appointment to the new *Oberschulkollegium* in February 1787 proved a failure, for he found himself an isolated Conservative on a board dominated by convinced rationalists. He pressed the king to order Zedlitz to abandon his patronage of rationalism, but the latter replied by evasion and procrastination. Wöllner finally succeeded, after nearly two years of incessant intrigue, in replacing Zedlitz on July 3, 1788, as *Staats- und Justiz-Minister* and *Chef des Geistlichen Departements* (Minister of Ecclesiastical Affairs); he rejoiced at finally receiving "the general command in the campaign against the *Aufklärung*."[26]

The Edict Concerning Religion, setting the keynote to Wöllner's

[25] Bailleu, op.cit., p. 154.
[26] Ibid., p. 155.

administration, appeared only six days after his new appointment (July 9, 1788). We have already discussed in Ch. 3 the literary controversy to which it gave rise; here it remains to recount the political struggles provoked by its practical implementation. They reveal in a dramatic fashion the difficulties encountered by a Conservative minister at the end of the eighteenth century, when he embarked upon a policy disapproved by an "enlightened" public opinion and sabotaged by an "enlightened" bureaucracy.

It will be recalled that the basic purpose of the edict was to require Lutheran ministers to preach in accordance with the Lutheran confession—a seemingly innocuous matter. The difficulty lay in defining what was Lutheran, drawing a clear line identifying nonpermissible religious opinions, and then enforcing this line against rationalist clergymen already in office. Wöllner was wise enough to wish to avoid a crop of rationalist martyrs, and he specifically directed his edict only against the actions (more especially the sermons), not the beliefs, of rationalist clergymen. The edict said that they were expected to resign their parishes if they felt that they could not conscientiously adhere to the creed they had sworn to uphold, but that the government would not compel their resignation provided they gave no external cause for offense. This policy was attacked for being an open invitation to hypocrisy—a rather uncharitable interpretation of Wöllner's leniency; its real fault was, however, that no provision was made for the material needs of clergymen who felt compelled to abandon their posts because of their rationalist convictions. The edict confronted honest rationalists with the unpleasant alternatives of hypocrisy or dismissal without pension. Could a pastor burdened with family obligations be expected to resign his living for conscience's sake? Much needless suffering could have been prevented if clergymen had been allowed to retire without complete loss of livelihood. The failure to make such a provision meant that many rationalists bent to the wind and stayed on the job—a fact which inevitably led to a good deal of delation and espionage to make sure that suspected rationalists stayed within the terms of the edict. Wöllner was determined to see to it that the Church and future clergymen would not be confronted with this kind of unpleasant situation; hence his insistence upon a thorough screening of all new theological candidates prior to their ordination.

Wöllner experienced a great deal of difficulty in enforcing his edict. Five of the six clergymen sitting in the *Oberkonsistorium* of the

Lutheran Church (the highest ecclesiastical body) entered an official protest against it (September 10, 1788)—clear proof how far the rationalists dominated the institutional structure of the Church. Their protest was rejected by the king in a sharply worded cabinet order drafted by Wöllner. The rationalist *Oberkonsistorialräte* refused at first to take "no" for an answer; their renewed protest (October 1, 1788) was answered by the king in an insulting reprimand (November 24, 1788). Meanwhile the pamphlet war described in Ch. 3 began to rage, and Wöllner saw the need to intensify the censorship, lest his edict be drowned in a sea of hostile ink. It soon proved, however, that the new Edict of Censorship (December 19, 1788) provided little protection for the government—or at least for Wöllner—for the censors were in some cases the same rationalist *Oberkonsistorialräte* who had opposed the edict in the first place. In rare cases where books were actually prohibited, the authors appealed, sometimes successfully, to the *Kammergericht* or the *Staatsrat*, two bodies packed with rationalist sympathizers and only too eager to humiliate Wöllner. The minister had no more luck with his plan to introduce a *Landeskatechismus* of undoubted orthodoxy—a most necessary step, since it alone could end uncertainty and arbitrariness about what was permissible under the edict and what was not. It was at first vetoed by the *Oberkonsistorium;* when Wöllner finally overrode this veto with the king's support, the rationalist opposition nonetheless continued to sabotage the introduction of the new catechism in most provinces. Wöllner saw that he must create a loyal enforcement body if his policies were not to be completely checked by the holdovers from the Zedlitz regime.

This was the origin of the five-man *Immediat-Examinations-Kommission* established in May 1791 for the purpose of examining the orthodoxy of preachers and theological candidates, as well as censoring theological books. Its two most active members were Hermann Daniel Hermes and Gottlob Friedrich Hillmer. Hermes (1731-1807) was a prominent Silesian preacher and Rosicrucian, who came to the attention of the king because his son-in-law Ostwald hypnotized an obscure woman into citing spirits for the benefit of Frederick William in 1790. The king was so impressed that he called Ostwald to Potsdam as librarian and reader-aloud, while Hermes was instructed to work out a scheme for the examination of all theological candidates.[27]

---

[27] G. Hoffmann, *H. D. Hermes, der Günstling Wöllners* (Breslau, 1914), is one of the best biographies of the period dealing with a minor figure; the author considers him to have been a misguided fanatic.

Hillmer (1756-1835), a Rosicrucian like Hermes, had gone through a variegated career as schoolteacher, tutor, and travel companion of princes before he was appointed to the new commission. He was an honest fanatic who shared Wöllner's desire to extirpate rationalism. All the other members of the commission were equally fanatical and their clumsy zeal was soon to embarrass even Wöllner himself.

The commission was widely feared by the rationalist party, though its bark proved much worse than its bite. It was certainly far from omnipotent; Hillmer joked, "People say we are powerful, but in fact we have not yet succeeded in dismissing a single neological preacher."[28] It played some role in the dismissal, by royal decree (May 21, 1792), of the notorious preacher Schulz of Gielsdorf, but even this triumph did not pass uncontested. The *Kammergericht* had earlier dismissed charges against Schulz (though he was obviously guilty of violating the Edict Concerning Religion); it even sought to thwart the king directly by ordering the preacher's return to his Gielsdorf parish—surely an unusual step in a supposedly absolutist state. The judges added insult to injury by specifically admitting that Schulz's views did not square with the Augsburg Confession; it is small wonder that their order was specifically canceled by the king with a sharp reprimand directed against the bench (June 10, 1792). The only way Wöllner could ever prevail was by the direct invocation of the royal prerogative.

It would be wrong, however, to think that the work of the *Immediat-Examinations-Kommission* (henceforth abbreviated IEK) was a failure because it did not achieve a purge of rationalists; for it largely succeeded in its general objective of transforming the general ecclesiastical climate of Prussia. A system of espionage was set up to collect information about the conduct of theology professors, preachers, and schoolteachers throughout the land. A specific new set of preaching instructions (May 13, 1793) required preachers to show their true colors (or become hypocrites) by preaching on assigned Biblical texts on specified Sundays, thereby ending the prevalent neological practice of avoiding those parts of the Bible which dealt with miracles, the incarnation, and other parts of orthodox dogma of which they disapproved. All new candidates for ordination were henceforth examined in accordance with a scheme drawn up by Hermes (and imposed, it will be recalled, by Wöllner upon the ra-

[28] Quoted in Colmar Grünhagen, "Der Kampf gegen die Aufklärung unter Friedrich Wilhelm II mit besonderer Rücksicht auf Schlesien," *Zeitschrift für Geschichte und Altertümer Schlesiens*, xxvii (1893), 23.

tionalist *Oberkonsistorium*), while the new *Landeskatechismus*, also drawn up by Hermes, was made the standard for orthodoxy. The candidates were required to sign a written pledge *(Revers)* that they would preach only in accordance with the Augsburg Confession; this was followed by a special oath of orthodoxy imposed upon all Lutheran clergymen (October 1, 1794). They were further required each year to send in the written text of a sermon on a given topic (usually selected to cause maximum embarrassment to rationalists). The IEK drew up lists of reliable, half-reliable, and unreliable preachers to serve as a guideline for appointments, transfers, and promotions. The information for these lists was provided by the twelve provincial branches of the IEK, though Wöllner found it hard to staff these with suitable personnel despite the bait of promotion after three years of service. He was compelled to rely primarily upon opportunists—men who had previously gravitated toward rationalism but now became orthodoxists unless they were very farsighted opportunists. It must be remembered in this connection that the Prussian clergy in the eighteenth century was not staffed by spiritual zealots but rather by men, usually from humble ranks of life, who had succeeded in going to a university but lacked the connections to enter more prestigious careers. It is probable that intense personal conviction, whether orthodox or rationalist, was the exception rather than the rule, and hence the soil was congenial to the sprouting of opportunism. What applied to the parish pastor went equally for the schoolteacher, who indeed was most frequently a clergyman waiting for a parish and hence all the more eager not to offend the powers that held control over his professional future. The new educational instructions issued by the IEK on December 16, 1794, made it perfectly clear what was expected of teachers and pupils. The emphasis was placed upon the memorizing of the catechism, Biblical passages, and church hymns; while instruction in reading, writing, and arithmetic was obviously deemed a lesser matter.

The essential strength of Wöllner's position—so long as he possessed the support of the king—is proven by his success in silencing the leaders of the Prussian *Aufklärung*, including such distinguished figures as Nicolai, Gedike, Biester, and even Kant. Nicolai was forced to take his *Allgemeine Deutsche Bibliothek* to Danish Altona after a cabinet order of April 17, 1794. Gedike and Biester removed their *Berliner Monatsschrift*, long the spokesman of the Berlin *Aufklärung*, from the Prussian capital. The case of the silencing of Kant deserves more extensive treatment because it has been frequently misunderstood. The Könisberg philosopher published his *Religion Within the Limits of Pure Reason* in October 1794 with the approval of the Philosophical Faculty of his university. (Kant took advantage of the fact that professors had the option of exemption from the ordinary censorship if they submitted their work to the judgment of their academic colleagues.) A part of this work had, however, been previously submitted for publication to the *Berliner Monatsschrift* and been rejected by the censor (who happened to be Hermes). Wöllner and Hermes could not possibly tolerate Kant's sleight-of-hand publication of a manuscript previously vetoed by the official censorship. The desirability of censorship per se or the merit of Kant's opinions are not at issue here; any government which wanted to be taken seriously *had* to reprimand Kant's conduct. The philosopher's craven apology, accompanied by the promise of future silence on religious topics (subject to the mental reservation that this applied only during the lifetime of Frederick William II), make a rather painful impression.[29]

It is strange to relate that Wöllner fell into disfavor because his vigilance fell short of the persecuting zeal of Frederick William. It is probable that Hermes used his position in the royal household to intrigue against his chief by accusing him of lukewarmness in the campaign against rationalism. A peppery cabinet order to Wöllner, dated March 8, 1794, deplored the insufficient progress made in the war against the *Aufklärung*. It deprived Wöllner of his job in the Building Department (which he had continued to hold even after his advance to the Ecclesiastical Department), so that he could henceforth give his undivided attention to the religious struggle. It was followed by a new cabinet order directing the fullest compliance with the Edict Concerning Religion (April 12, 1794). The chastened minister replied by a profession of zeal but also continued to assert the advisability of a moderate policy:

> I am more and more convinced that it is best to make haste slowly, where the choleric Hermes is inclined to proceed with violence; but impatience and severity in fact only lead to bitterness and ferment which must eventually lead to disorder. God does not

[29] It should be noted, however, that—in the words of Schwartz, Wöllner's sharpest critic—"the I.E.K. acted in accordance with the demands of progressive pedagogy as far as its obscurantist spirit permitted." *Der erste Kulturkampf*, p. 289. It prohibited side employment for teachers and encouraged the use of new methods of instruction. Its examination of theological candidates aimed, likewise, not only at orthodoxy but at maintaining a high intellectual standard—including proficiency in Greek and Hebrew—for clergymen.

demand more of us than what we can give in accordance with our strength and prevailing circumstances. The rest is His task, and it is part of His secret design for our sinful world that our Saviour Jesus Christ should continue to be widely misunderstood and rejected even in our day.[30]

The mature wisdom of Wöllner's views was quickly demonstrated by the experiences of Hermes and Hillmer at Halle, their first station on a proposed tour of Prussian universities to check upon the orthodoxy of all faculties of theology. A student riot, tolerated if not instigated by the faculty, smashed the windows of their hotel and threatened their lives. The two inquisitors, thinking discretion the better part of valor, left town to avoid bloodshed while denouncing the "spiritual and temporal Jacobins" of the university and calling upon the faculty to hand over the riot leaders for punishment. The faculty replied with a plea of ignorance and inability, and counterattacked by accusing Hermes and Hillmer of libeling the orthodoxy of their honorable university. Wöllner publicly backed his subordinates while privately deploring their clumsiness to the king:

> The good cause suffers infinite harm when unskilful instruments ruin the implementation of the best-laid plans; more especially if they refuse to follow orders and think their own judgment best.[31]

Wöllner gave strict orders that the theological teaching at Halle must henceforth conform to the Edict Concerning Religion, thereby identifying himself with the accusations levied by Hermes and Hillmer (which soon became a formal decision of the entire *Immediat-Examinations-Kommission*). The university replied with a flaming affirmation of academic freedom, and appealed to the *Staatsrat* on the ground that the IEK was a partisan body acting as both accuser and judge. The *Staatsrat*, well known for its rationalist sympathies and detestation of Wöllner, first procrastinated on the case and then arranged a face-saving compromise (January 22, 1795) which proved eminently satisfactory to the Halle faculty. The vacillating king had meanwhile wearied of the entire matter and allowed it to be dropped.

Wöllner was never fully restored to favor after the reprimand of the spring of 1794. He was conspicuously ignored in the distribution of South Prussian booty after the Second Partition of Poland, when all other royal favorites (including Bischoffwerder) received estates.

[30] Schwartz, op.cit., pp. 347-55, gives a well-balanced account of Kant's reprimand.

[31] Wöllner to King, May 19, 1794, quoted in Hoffmann, *Hermes*, p. 115.

The unsatisfactory outcome of the Halle affair was symptomatic of the fact that Wöllner was no stronger than the strength of the royal will behind him. He could not rely upon any kind of organized party in either the bureaucracy or public opinion. His instruments consisted primarily of fanatics like Hermes and Hillmer, whose bad judgment and excess zeal was sometimes turned against even Wöllner himself. The opportunists who rallied to his side were by their nature unsteady supporters who began to desert as soon as he had appeared to lose the favor of the king. The bureaucracy remained overwhelmingly against him, and a mass purge was unthinkable for want of adequate replacements. The Junkers joined the old Frederician officials in hating him as a parvenu. It is remarkable, in the light of all these adverse circumstances, that he accomplished as much as he did in his brief years of never-uncontested power; and this fact surely indicates that he possessed very unusual abilities indeed.

It is hard to pass a final verdict on so controversial a figure. That he loved power is certain, but what effective politician does not? That he used unscrupulous means—including Rosicrucian hocus-pocus—to achieve and maintain his ascendancy over the king is equally certain, but what other method of holding power was available to him under Prussian conditions? That he was more than a mere flatterer is proven by his fall from favor in 1794 and his continued adherence to a measure of moderation even after the persecuting zeal of the king and Hermes ran completely amuck. He certainly did not use power for personal enrichment, for he died a poor man and received far fewer material favors than other royal favorites. It is impossible to say whether he sought power primarily for power's sake, or valued it chiefly as a means for implementing certain Conservative principles. There is much reason to believe that his Rosicrucianism was fervidly sincere to the point of flagrant superstition.[32] He evidently believed that the *Aufklärung* ruined religion and developed a sense of mission about extirpating principles he considered pernicious. He certainly showed ruthlessness in pursuing his goal, but the power of his rationalist foes left him no alternative; his choice of methods cannot be considered always happy, though he was at least more moderate than several of his subordinates. If governmental intervention on behalf of specific religious beliefs is ever permissible, it can scarcely be denied that Lutheran orthodoxy stood in need of support against rationalist infiltration in 1786; and it must be admitted that Wöllner achieved a measure of success for the cause he championed. This much can be

[32] Grünhagen, op.cit., p. 24, reports a revealing example of Wöllner writing

said on Wöllner's behalf; but it must also be said, on the other hand, that police measures are rarely—at least prior to our own totalitarian age—effective against major intellectual currents and that they tend to do grave injury to the cause they are supposed to protect—a fact which Bischoffwerder understood better than Wöllner when he wrote to the king on March 31, 1795:

> I remain of the opinion that error cannot be prevented by mere prohibition any more than can contraband. The only way the pure doctrine can prevail is when it is advanced by God-fearing teachers who carry the conviction of truth in their face and support their convictions by the example of a pure life.[33]

THE CAMPAIGN AGAINST THE FRENCH REVOLUTION

The Prussian struggle against rationalism, begun well before the outbreak of the French Revolution, naturally became intensified after 1789. Some Frederician holdovers, like Foreign Minister Count Hertzberg, openly favored the work of the revolution; but this was naturally not the attitude of the Rosicrucian clique around Frederick William II. Bischoffwerder was an early champion of a counterrevolutionary crusade against France, while Wöllner—perhaps because of his knowledge of Prussia's precarious financial condition—was a farsighted champion of the cause of peace. There was no difference of opinion, however, upon the necessity of stamping out any trace of Jacobinism that raised its head in Prussia itself. A royal cabinet order of February 4, 1792, criticized the ministry for its laxity in suppressing subversive books and journals; the ministers replied by claiming that they had exercised proper vigilance, and congratulated the king on the fact that there was happily no revolutionary danger in his realm. This did not, however, prevent the anti-Jacobin panic from sometimes going to ludicrous extremes. To give only one example out of many: Count Hoym, the powerful minister for Silesia, ordered the arrest of all men who *talked* about the French Revolution without making any distinction between those who talked for, against, or merely about the greatest event of the age. Hoym's decree of March 7, 1794, stated:

> His Majesty has graciously agreed to my request that all such troublemakers *(Ruhestörer)* should be brought to reason through running the gauntlet *(Spiessruthenstrafe)* without bothering first

---

to a Rosicrucian brother that he should stop doubting that the magi of the eighth degree have the power to hatch chickens out of boiled eggs.

[33] Quoted in Hoffmann, *Hermes*, p. 117.

about any regular trial *(ohne viele prozessualische Weitläüfig-keiten)*. This will set a deterrent example to all simple country folk.[34]

Hoym had panicked because some social disorders had broken out among the tailor-journeymen, weavers, and peasants of his province, though these were crushed with minimal effort by the military and had little connection with the French Revolution. Their main consequence was that they intensified the king's already strong hostility to social reform, especially the reform of serfdom. Frederick William declared his views on this subject in an unmistakable manner on Sept. 5, 1794:

> The abolition of serfal labor obligations *(Hofdienste)* could never be squared with the wise and just principles of government held by His Majesty. These principles protect everyone, without distinction of class, in all his property and rights, and preclude the application of pressure against anyone for the surrender or renunciation of his established rights; for this reason His Majesty will never deprive the lords *(Gutsherrschaften)* of the services of their subjects *(Unterthanen)* or to urge their cancellation or commutation into monetary obligations against the will of their owners.[35]

Clearly Reform Conservatism was dead for the duration of the reign; yet the fact that the king had found it necessary to make a statement at all showed that the foundation of serfdom was tottering. When a government declares that it will *not* do something demanded by a section of public opinion, it admits that the issue has become controversial and hence possibly subject to future reform efforts.

The attitude of *quieta non movere* in domestic affairs did not characterize Frederick William's foreign policy. In this field there was a sharp conflict between the Frederician Foreign Minister Count Hertzberg, pursuing Prussia's traditional policy of aggrandizement in opposition to Austria, and the Rosicrucian Bischoffwerder, favoring a reconciliation with Austria preparatory to a counterrevolutionary crusade against Jacobin France. Hertzberg pursued a somewhat artificial "Great Design" during the Austro-Turkish War begun in 1788. The Prussian minister wanted to compel Austria, by war or the threat of war, to yield Galicia to Poland in return for Balkan compensations; Poland would in turn yield Danzig and Thorn to Prussia. This complicated scheme might have been achieved by a resolute king

---

[34] Quoted in Philippson, op.cit., II, 35.
[35] Ibid., II, 39.

combining ruthless diplomacy with the willingness to strike a military blow; but for this Frederick William was not the man. He compromised instead with Austria at the Convention of Reichenbach (July 1790), preferring the advice of his favorite Bischoffwerder over that of his foreign minister (who was soon dismissed in disgrace). Bischoffwerder was now able to pursue his policy of "burying the hatchet" between Austria and Prussia; his secret mission to Vienna in February 1791 brought the first steps on the road to a *rapprochement*. Bischoffwerder negotiated a treaty defining a common policy toward France and Poland (July 25, 1791) on a second mission to Vienna; the new solidarity between Prussia and Austria was soon revealed to the public in the joint declaration of Pillnitz (August 27, 1791) censuring the work of the French National Assembly. A military alliance was signed on February 7, 1792, and it was under its terms that Prussia entered the Franco-Austrian War on the side of Austria in April of that year. The Brunswick manifesto, issued three months later, showed that the allies aimed primarily at overthrowing the revolution and restoring legitimacy in France—an ideologically Conservative aim which was only remotely connected with the dictates of Prussian Reason of State.

The war revealed all the weaknesses of the unreformed Prussia of Frederick William II. Its army had lost its former offensive capacity; its finances were exhausted after a single campaign; its population was completely apathetic in the face of momentous events; while its diplomacy proved incapable of exploiting the great opportunity of dominating Northern Germany opened by the Treaty of Basel (April 5, 1795). The Second and Third Partitions of Poland, besides distracting Prussia from the western war, saddled the state with some two and a half million unassimilable Polish subjects; the Prussian army could not cope with Polish rebels without Russian help, and the Prussian ruling class and bureaucracy soon disgraced themselves by the racketeering administration of the newly won provinces.

The rule of Frederick William, who died of premature old age in 1797 when only fifty-three, ended on this note of failure. The reign, surely one of the most unfortunate in Prussian annals, left the country exhausted, discredited, and unreformed. An irresolute foreign policy had made only dubious gains and led Prussia into total isolation. Its army had fought with equal ineffectiveness in the west and in the east. The monarchy was discredited by an unsavory monarch who kept an influential mistress, practiced bigamy, and allowed his court to be dominated by a fanatical Rosicrucian clique. The religious reaction under Wöllner had curbed some rationalist excesses but had degenerated into a witch-hunt and robbed Berlin of its reputation as the leader of Germany's *Aufklärung*. None of the basic reforms which Prussia needed had been attempted, much less achieved. The principle of monarchical absolutism left her policy still dependent upon the accident of heredity; aristocratic privilege was uncurbed; serfdom continued as the basis of Prussia's social structure; and the loosening of mercantilistic fetters had only begun. The only gains achieved under Frederick William were some minor humanitarian reforms at the beginning of the reign; some relaxation of the rigorous Frederician spirit, though this had its reverse side in a certain moral flabbiness for which the king set a bad personal example; a reaction against the aggressive rationalism of the Frederician period, though this degenerated easily into obscurantism and persecution; and the great codification of Prussia's laws, discussed in the following section.

The Controversy About the Allgemeine Landrecht

The desirability of a codification of Prussia's laws had become increasingly evident to Frederick the Great in the course of his reign. The existing legal structure could only be described as utterly chaotic: Prussia's different provinces—acquired by the dynasty at various times—possessed variegated systems of law; the substantive law of every province was based upon a heterogeneous mixture of customary German law and a feudalized Roman law (as interpreted by a host of modern and not-so-modern commentators—the so-called *usus modernus pandectarum*); the survival of endless varieties of local, institutional, and class privileges made law the secret of the antiquary and the despair of every rational jurist; while judicial decisions were usually narrowly specific and *ad hoc* for fear of creating precedents—a practice which led to the further accumulation of legal rubbish. New laws were issued by virtue of the absolute power of the king, who was not constitutionally bound to consult anybody in legislation—a practice conducive neither to consistency nor continuity.

The system of courts (if one can speak of a system where there was in fact a historically developed pattern of concurrent jurisdictions) was as chaotic as the substance of the law. At the bottom stood a strictly feudal structure of patrimonial courts, the only courts with which the ordinary rural Prussian ever came into contact; these courts were supervised by the government only in the most shadowy manner. "Governmental justice" was administered on the provincial level by two very different bodies, both of which were unspecialized: the

Regierungen, which also controlled school and ecclesiastical affairs, and the *Kammern,* which also administered the royal domains. The *Regierungen* were traditionalist bodies standing under strong aristocratic influences and bent upon checking the trend toward state omnipotence; the *Kammern* were bureaucratic bodies interested in serving as the local agents of an ever-stronger centralizing absolutism. Since neither was an exclusively judicial body, the clear-cut separation between justice and administration remained unknown in Prussia until the Steinian reform of 1808. Their respective jurisdiction had been delimited (somewhat imperfectly) by a regulation of June 19, 1749, which assigned all questions connected with domains, taxes, et cetera to the *Kammern.* Frederick's ruthlessness in raising revenue made his *Kammerjustiz* something of which the individual subject had reason to be afraid. There was also considerable direct intervention of the central executive in purely judicial affairs. The king frequently appointed special commissions to try special cases; royal edicts often dealt with specific cases in a thinly disguised manner; the Ministry of Justice had the right to issue binding instructions to the *Regierungen;* while successive kings at times overthrew specific judgments which they considered unjust (the so-called *Machtsprüche* spoken by Frederick in the case of Miller Arnold in 1779 and by Frederick William II in the case of Pastor Schulz in 1792).[36]

The need to reform this chaotic structure should be apparent from this brief outline. Prussia needed a common law for all its provinces if it was to be integrated into a single state instead of remaining a congeries of heterogeneous provinces. Prussia needed a simplification of the variegated substantive laws through an intelligent synthesis of German, Roman, and (most important as a simplifying instrument) "natural law." Prussia needed to advance to the principle of legal equality which would sweep away the anachronistic survivals of local and class privilege. Prussia required, finally, a clear-cut hierarchy of government courts staffed by professional judges freed from distracting administrative responsibilities. Such relics of feudalism as patrimonial courts and aristocratic influence upon the *Regierungen,* and such absolutist practices as the personal intervention of the king in judicial cases, must be considered anachronisms. It was further neces-

[36] The weaknesses of Prussian judicial administration are exposed in the valuable book of Uwe-Jens Heuer, *Allgemeines Landrecht und Klassenkampf. Die Auseinandersetzung um die Prinzipien des Allgemeinen Landrechts Ende des 18. Jahrhunderts als Ausdruck der Krise des Feudalsystems in Preussen* (East Berlin, 1960), pp. 54-77. The entire study is path-breaking in correlating legal with social history, and can be used with profit despite its intolerable Marxist jargon.

sary that the personal legislative power of the king be given some kind of institutional restraint.

Neither Frederick nor his successor could be expected to tackle this kind of reform program in its entirety; it is remarkable, indeed, how far these two Prussian kings were in fact willing to go in their reform work. This will emerge most clearly from a brief survey of the effort which went into the preparation of the *Allgemeine Landrecht* (henceforth abbreviated ALR)—the great law code begun in 1780 but promulgated only in 1794. The launching of the codification (if one ignores some abortive work in the 1740's associated with the name of *Grosskanzler* Samuel von Cocceji)[37] dates from the cabinet order of April 14, 1780, which gave *Grosskanzler* Heinrich Casimir von Carmer (1721-1801) broad responsibility for "reforming justice and renovating Prussia's laws" *(Justizreform und Gesetzerneuerung)*. Frederick specifically directed that the law should be simplified, freed from legal subtleties, and made comprehensible to the layman; that it be unified for Prussia's diverse provinces; and that there be a synthesis between old German, Roman, and natural law. It was realized that this ambitious program would take years to complete; to prevent further legal confusion in the pending interval Frederick established, by royal patent of May 29, 1781, a Commission on Law *(Gesetz-Kommission)* with the duty to advise upon all future legislation prior to its promulgation. This patent did not eliminate the right of the king (by virtue of his absolute power) to issue new laws by arbitrary fiat, but it voluntarily bound him to seek expert advice before he exercised this right. The personnel of the law commission was largely identical with the personnel assembled by Carmer to prepare the work of codification—a fact which thus guaranteed that new laws would be in concordance with the ALR then in preparation.[38]

[37] On Cocceji's reforms see the useful recent study by H. Weill, *Frederick the Great and Samuel von Cocceji. A Study in the Reform of the Prussian Judicial Administration 1740-1755* (Madison, 1961).

[38] An excellent recent introduction to the creation of the *Allgemeine Landrecht* is Hermann Conrad, *Die Geistigen Grundlagen des Allgemeinen Landrechts für die preussischen Staaten von 1794* (Cologne and Opladen, 1958). Conrad prints the cabinet order of April 14, 1780 (n.9, pp. 13-15) and the patent of May 29, 1781 (n.23, pp. 22-23). Three important historical introductions to the ALR are Wilhelm Dilthey, "Das Allgemeine Landrecht," in *Gesammelte Schriften*, XII: *Zur preussischen Geschichte*, 131-204, valuable despite some metaphysical nonsense about the ALR being the "objectivation of the Frederician spirit," and Hans Thieme, "Die preussische Kodifikation. Privatrechtsgeschichtliche Studien II," *Zeitschrift der Savigny-Stiftung für Rechtsgeschichte*, LVII (1937), 355ff., valuable despite some Nazi jargon; and, above all, Uwe Jens Heuer, op.cit., in my opinion the best work on the subject despite its procrustean ideological framework.

Carmer's main assistant in the work of codification was the indefatigable Carl Gottlieb Svarez (1746-98), who may be described as the real author of the ALR.[39] His career shows the opportunities for constructive work Frederician Prussia offered to a man of talent even if he was of comparatively humble birth. Svarez' father was an obscure provincial lawyer; the son had to struggle to complete his university education in the confused aftermath of the Seven Years' War. He entered the judicial service under Carmer (then Minister of Justice for Svarez' native province of Silesia) in 1770 and accompanied his chief to Berlin when Carmer was appointed *Grosskanzler* in 1780. Little can be said of his personality, since he was completely absorbed in his work, though it is clear that he was also a man of wide political and literary culture. His political theories have only recently been rediscovered by the publication of some lectures he delivered to the crown prince, the later Frederick William III, in 1791-92.[40] His friendship with and influence upon many leading contemporaries is attested by his prominent role in the select *Mittwoch-Gesellschaft*.[41]

Svarez' political ideals are worth sketching because they reveal, if not what he achieved through the ALR, at least what he intended to achieve. He believed in the doctrine of "enlightened absolutism" in the following terms: An intolerable state of nature must be superseded by means of a social contract; a first contract creating society is followed by a second contract under whose terms absolute power is irrevocably conferred upon a hereditary monarch; this monarch has an interest identical with that of the community. "The regent can never, provided he has correct conceptions *(richtige Begriffe)*, possess interests different from, let alone hostile to, the interests of the people."[42] Svarez knew, of course, that regents frequently did act as if they did have separate interests of their own, but he thought this prima-facie evidence of either weakness or stupidity. In such a

[39] On Svarez see the definitive if old-fashioned biography by Adolf Stölzel, *C. G. Svarez. Ein Zeitbild aus der 2. Hälfte des 18. Jahrhunderts* (Berlin, 1885); Eberhard Schmidt, "C. G. Svarez," *Schlesische Lebensbilder*, II (Breslau, 1926), 29ff., an excellent brief sketch; and, above all, Erik Wolf, *Grosse Rechtsdenker der deutschen Geistesgeschichte* (3rd edn., Tübingen, 1951), pp. 421-63.

[40] C. G. Svarez, *Vorträge über Recht und Staat*. (eds. Hermann Conrad and Gerd Kleinheyer, Cologne and Opladen, 1960). This is an extremely important source for the political theory of the Prussian *Aufklärung*. A valuable introduction and analysis is Gerd Kleinheyer, *Staat und Bürger im Recht. Die Vorträge des C. G. Svarez vor dem preussischen Kronprinzen* (1791-92) (Bonn, 1959).

[41] He sometimes spoke in the *Mittwoch-Gesellschaft* about codification problems. See his lecture, "In wie fern können und müssen Gesetze kurz sein?" printed in the *Berliner Monatsschrift* (1788).

[42] Svarez in *Kronprinzenvorträge*. Quoted by Conrad, op.cit., p. 35.

case they became despots (defined as regents following their subjective caprice rather than the objective needs of the state) and lost their moral right to rule, though Svarez naturally did not draw institutional consequences from this analysis, either by advocating parliamentary bodies or by clearly defining a right of resistance. (How could he as a high Prussian official and tutor to the crown prince?) He concentrated instead upon the education of the future ruler and the establishment of an actually (if not formally) binding pattern of voluntary restraints upon absolutism—two factors which made it unlikely that Prussian kings would act as despots in the future.[43]

His faith in Prussian "enlightened absolutism" as the best form of government was partly based upon his belief in the irresistible forward march of *Aufklärung*, which even an obscurantist like Wöllner could only curb rather than check; it was strengthened by the experience of the French Revolution, which confirmed Svarez in the view that the democratic revolutionary alternative to enlightened absolutism was most undesirable. Democracy in France had led to frivolous and destructive legislation, an incompetent executive, an administration of justice influenced by popular passion, and a never-ending pattern of mob violence—all evils unthinkable in the Prussia of Frederick William II. It had led to the proclamation of anarchical rights of man against the state which ignored the simple fact that any kind of right can be enjoyed only within a state possessing a properly functioning legitimate authority. It had proclaimed a principle of equality going far beyond the simple affirmation of equality before the law and thereby had thrown man back into the state of the "natural man" and had ignored the fact that "social man" was characterized precisely by social differentiation. It is entirely understandable that Svarez saw little hope for mankind from democracy, whereas the historical experience of the Prussian state showed the possibility of great progress through enlightened absolutism. Prussia certainly lacked the defects of tyrannical democracy, while Svarez believed that it could avoid the dangers of royal tyranny through the elaboration of the principles of the *Rechtsstaat*.[44]

The perfection of the *Rechtsstaat* was for Svarez and his main collaborator, Ernst Ferdinand Klein[45] (1744-1810), their major goal as

[43] This political theory is analyzed briefly by Conrad, op.cit., and at length by Kleinheyer, op.cit.

[44] Conrad, op.cit., pp. 30-35.

[45] He edited the *Annalen für Gesetzgebung und Rechtsgelehrsamkeit in den preussischen Staaten* (Berlin, 1788ff.), invaluable for the light it throws upon the outlook of the authors of the codification; and wrote a revealing dialogue, *Freyheit*

they codified Prussia's anarchical laws into a single comprehensive code of some 19,000 paragraphs (each of a single sentence), organized in two parts under a total of forty-three titles and covering some 2,500 printed pages. They believed that they were not just codifying laws but were giving Prussia a surrogate for her nonexistent constitution. This was most apparent in the famous introductory articles dealing with "Law in General" *(Von den Gesetzen überhaupt)* and "General Principles of Law. The Relationship of the State to its Citizens" *(Allgemeine Grundlage des Rechts. Verhältniss des Staates gegen seine Bürger).* Here could be found such maxims as, "The purpose of the law is to further the general welfare" (paragraph 50 of draft of 1784) and, "The state is permitted to restrict the natural freedom of its citizens only insofar as this is required by the welfare of society as a whole" (paragraph 56). All new laws required the approval of the *Gesetzeskommission* (paragraph 13), while ex post facto laws were specifically prohibited (paragraph 19). Most important was the elimination of royal *Machtsprüche*: "Arbitrary fiats, or decrees issued by higher powers *(der oberen Gewalt)* in judicial disputes without the observation of judicial procedure, can create neither rights nor obligations" (paragraph 6 of the draft of 1791). The royal power was further curbed by protecting bureaucrats against arbitrary punishment or dismissal.

These antiabsolutist maxims (or better, these voluntary limitations upon absolute monarchy) represent the highest aspirations of the creators of the ALR. They constitute, however, only a small portion of the whole work; the whole was characterized by the desire to codify rather than to reform the Prussian *status quo* from a political, administrative, social, and moral point of view. A brief enumeration of some of the titles (major sections) of the ALR will give an impression of its encyclopedic scope. It is best to concentrate upon Part II, whose highly specific codification of the most various aspects of Prussian affairs make it the best introduction to the study of German society in the eighteenth century. For example, Title 7 regulated the condition of the peasantry, including the pattern of rural government (in 548 paragraphs); Title 8 the condition of the urban population, including municipal government and the structure of the guilds; Title 9 the condition of the aristocracy; Title 10 the rights and duties of bureaucrats;

---

und Eigenthum abgehandelt in acht Gesprächen über die Beschlüsse der Französischen Nationalversammlung (Berlin and Stettin, 1790), in which Svarez appears as Kriton, Klein himself as Kleon.

Title 11 ecclesiastical affairs (a monster section with 1,232 paragraphs); Title 12 school affairs; Title 13 the general rights and duties of the state; Title 14 the taxing power of the government.

A few examples of the substantive content of the ALR may serve to reveal its fundamentally Conservative character. It was imbued, in the first place, with a patriarchal spirit of old-fashioned morality. An often-cited example is the famous paragraph 67 of Part II, Title 2: "Every healthy mother is obligated to nurse her own infants." There was no attempt to modify the existing social structure of Prussia, especially in the crucial matter of serfdom. The reader finds in Part II, Title 7, an elaborate codification of all the traditional practices of serfdom: labor obligations, the pursuit of escaped serfs, patrimonial jurisdiction, and the right to whip refractory domestics. The Conservative character of these provisions of the ALR was underlined by making them strictly subsidiary to the existing (or to be created) provincial provisions governing serfdom. "The regulations of the ALR concerning the services and dues owed by peasants to their *Gutsherrschaft* are applicable only insofar as specific provincial constitutions do not provide for exceptions" (Title 7, paragraph 90). The exception was in fact intended to be the rule, for paragraph 87 called for the creation of provincial codes wherever they did not already exist. The authors of the ALR were extremely careful lest they be accused of challenging serfdom, a charge which could easily ruin the entire work of codification. When some peasants got the mistaken idea that the ALR aimed at improving their condition, Carmer instructed that they be told that "the ALR did not bring the slightest change in the relationship, duties, and obligations which they owed to their *Gutsherrschaft*."[46]

The Conservative character of the ALR is confirmed by several other features. There is very little evidence of the application of the rational and humanitarian doctrine of natural law, apart from the comparatively mild punishments meted out in Part II, Title 20, dealing with Crimes and Penalties; yet even here there was not even equality before the law, since insults directed against aristocrats were punished more stringently than those directed against mere commoners. The extremely detailed provisions of the ALR tended to make it a very faithful chronicle of the social *status quo*, and embarrassed any future Progressive interpretation; while interpretation was specifically declared the monopoly of the *Gesetzeskommission*, a body un-

---

[46] Quoted in Heuer, op.cit., p. 115, in the course of an excellent discussion of the ALR and the peasant question.

likely to fall under Radical influences. It is further notable that professors—as we have seen, a potentially Radical class—were specifically prohibited from writing any commentaries upon the ALR. It is clear in the light of these circumstances that the ALR, whatever may have been the ultimate intentions of some of its creators, was most unlikely to alter the social *status quo;* indeed, it was calculated to buttress it against Radical attack by its work of codification, rationalization, and consolidation. It appears rather surprising that it provoked in fact so much sharp Conservative opposition; but this opposition was based upon the essentially correct instinct that, however Conservative the substance of the ALR, there was something profoundly un-Conservative about the fact of codification per se. Codification was symptomatic of the fact that custom and prescription no longer reigned unchallenged, since it was now necessary for men to organize and collate what previously had been accepted as a mere given. The ALR codification might be satisfactory in its specific terms, but it set a dangerous precedent for future codifications of a potentially Radical character.

The procedure used to create the ALR also aroused Conservative apprehensions. A first draft of the entire ALR was published on March 24, 1784. Carmer called at that time for public discussion and criticism of its provisions, an unheard-of procedure in an absolute monarchy; and he even offered gold and silver medals to all those who submitted valuable suggestions for improvements. Carmer sought, though only with limited success, to keep the discussion within bounds both as regards participants and subjects discussed. He specifically called for contributions from legal experts (*Justizbeamte*) and practical men of affairs (*Kaufmänner*) and wanted them to answer such specific questions as: Did the ALR depart from Roman law? Were the gaps which existed in Roman law well filled? Were important matters omitted from the ALR? Was the code as clear and precise as possible? Carmer received a total of sixty-two replies to his public request for improvements. All were carefully read in his ministry and twenty-five received either gold or silver medals. Many of them inevitably criticized the ALR from the Left for its failure to abolish either serfdom or absolutism. Johann Georg Schlosser, the Badenese official whom we have previously encountered as a foe of progressive education, wrote and published five letters of criticism to which Klein replied in successive issues of the *Annalen.*[47] A certain Professor Eggers of Copenhagen was critical of

[47] The most important criticism from the Left is Johann Georg Schlosser,

the failure to abolish serfdom. He received a prize—a fact which suggests the real sympathies of the authors of the ALR; but Svarez wrote that Eggers "had not always remembered that the intention of the new law code was not total abolition or alteration *(Aufhebung oder Umschmeltzung)* of the existing laws, but only their improvement, correction and supplementing *(Verbesserung, Berichtigung und Ergäntzung)*."[48] Svarez on another occasion put the point in more fundamental terms. His enlightened critics forgot that the ALR

> did not seek to provide laws for a state still to be created, but for one which had existed already for a long time. . . . It was better to repair an already existing road, than to lead the traveler into a completely new and unknown region, and to demand from him that he enter with confidence upon the dark road ahead; which even his guides had never trodden previously, but had only claimed to see in birds' eye perspective from the heights of speculation.[49]

Carmer and Svarez suffered the usual fate of the moderate (perhaps too moderate) reformer when they were bitterly attacked by the intellectuals of the Left.

The death of Frederick had no perceptible effect upon the ALR; for, contrary to the legend that seeks to make him a great legislator as well as a great general à la Napoleon, the great king had taken only a perfunctory interest in the implementation of his cabinet order of April 14, 1780. The new King Frederick William II deserves credit for giving a new impetus to the work begun by his predecessor: he issued no less than three cabinet orders dealing with the ALR in the first days of his reign (August 21, 23, and 27, 1786), though these included the potentially dangerous request that Carmer and Svarez consult the surviving Prussian *Stände* about the terms of the new code.[50] The creators of the ALR pretended to accept this instruction with enthu-

---

Fünfter Brief über den Entwurf des Preussischen Gesetzbuchs insbesondere über dessen Apologie in den Annalen der preussischen Gesetzgebung (Frankfurt, 1790). Schlosser had, incidentally, turned down an offer to enter Prussian services to work on the ALR. His criticism may have been sharpened by a case of sour grapes, for he had earlier declared codification to be an impossible "labor of Sisyphus." See his *Vorschlag und Versuch einer Verbesserung des deutschen bürgerlichen Rechts ohne Abschaffung des römischen Gesetzbuchs* (Leipzig, 1777).

[48] Quoted by Heuer, op.cit., p. 99.

[49] Ibid.

[50] This cannot be described as a departure from the Frederician tradition, for it but repeated an order of Frederick's dated May 21, 1749, at the time of the Cocceji reforms. Heuer, op.cit., p. 162.

siasm, with Carmer announcing, in a memorandum issued April 30, 1787, that

> the citizens of Prussia will be able to boast [following *Stände* approval of the ALR] that they live under laws which they have themselves examined and approved. . . . The social contract, invented by wise men with philanthropic impulses as the ground why men owe obedience to the laws, will henceforth be something more than a beautiful hypothesis.[51]

Carmer proposed to hold a meeting of deputies from all the different provincial *Stände*, but no such body ever assembled in fact. The *monita* (suggestions) of the various provincial *Stände* were examined by the Justice Department exactly as were all other suggestions, and had the same insignificant influence upon the final result. Carmer and Svarez were resolved to create an ALR cast by themselves out of a single mold; they resisted the idea of a compromise patchwork expressing the parallelogram of pressures and suggestions showered upon them.

The final polishing of the draft was completed only after extensive negotiations between the *Gesetzeskommission* and various governmental departments. Questions involving guilds, factories, and the police were discussed with the *Generaldirektorium;* financial matters with the *Bankdirektorium;* mining problems with the *Bergwerksdepartment;* the much-controverted question of duels and officers' debts with the *Oberkriegskollegium.* Carmer was able, on December 18, 1790, to submit the entire code to the king as a comparatively little revised version of the first draft published six years previously. Within three days Frederick William had given his general approval (December 21, 1790), while objecting to a few provisions (e.g., the limitation of his rights to fire bureaucrats at will). Carmer hastened to make some minor changes and was thereupon allowed to issue a patent of publication on March 20, 1791: the ALR was to become the law of the land on June 1, 1792, and 10,000 printed copies of the ALR were distributed throughout Prussia in the autumn of 1791. Carmer and Svarez could relax with a sigh of relief since the battle for codification appeared to be won.

This feeling proved, however, premature, for the enemies of the ALR were by no means willing to surrender as yet. It is hard to identify these enemies as a specific group, since Prussia did not possess parties engaged in open political combat; but it is clear that they in-

---

[51] Quoted by Heuer, op.cit., p. 164, n.45.

cluded influential figures at court and in the bureaucracy with close ties to the aristocracy and the *Stände* bodies dominated by the latter group. They were helped by the general constellation of European affairs. The French Revolution was degenerating into violence and anarchy—facts which the foes of the ALR claimed were due to the very *Aufklärung* whose principles had infiltrated the proposed code. The Polish constitution of May 3, 1791, with its Liberal provisions, appeared a threat to the absolutist principles of Prussian monarchy. Was not the ALR a kind of dangerous surrogate for a Liberal constitution? There was some peasant discontent in the eastern provinces of Prussia and neighboring Saxony which the foes of the ALR blamed upon expectations aroused by the new code. This point was made very emphatically by the *Regierungspräsident* of Küstrin, von Poser, in reports to the king; he complained that the peasant discontent was due to "the wide-spread popular belief that new laws must bring new advantages to themselves—for otherwise it would have been best to leave old things as they were."[52]

The aristocratically dominated *Stände* of Minden-Ravensberg, an outlying western province of Prussia, issued a sharp protest against certain ALR paragraphs affecting the nobility (December 29, 1791). They complained about the provision that permitted legitimate marriages between nobles and girls from the lower classes. Such marriages must ruin certain aristocratic foundations and cathedral chapters by leading to a shortage of candidates for positions which required an impeccable escutcheon of sixteen noble ancestors; while it would also corrupt the nobility by the introduction of the spirit of usury and infidelity *(Wuchergeist und Untreue)*. To permit such marriages was a dangerous concession to "the spirit of the now unhappily fashionable so-called theoretical philosophy, of which the equalization of all *Stände* is one of the main principles." The application of such principles could only lead to

> the abominable anarchy which is now devastating France. Who will deny that similar results will sooner or later occur in the rest of Europe, if even the legislators [of respectable monarchies] support such principles, however incapable of realization they may be?

The *Stände* of Minden-Ravensberg also complained about the new obligation, imposed upon young nobles who had made peasant girls pregnant, to pay some measure of economic support to the mothers of their children. They further protested that restrictions upon dueling

[52] Reports of April 6 and 19, 1792. Quoted Heuer, op.cit., p. 196.

were incompatible with military honor, and that a provision which handed the property of bachelors to charitable foundations was a blow at the principle of private property. Some similar complaints were brought to the king in April 1792 by Count Finckenstein, distinguished as one of the martyrs of the Miller Arnold case, as spokesman for the *Stände* of the Kurmark. There was general complaint that the *Stände* had not been sufficiently consulted in the preparation of the ALR.[53]

The die-hard supporters of a Reactionary position were joined by men out to make a career by discrediting the authors of the ALR. Goldbeck, the Minister of Justice who was angling for Carmer's job as *Grosskanzler* (which he got in January 1795), denounced his rival as a dangerous foe of absolutism and the established social order. The Silesian provincial Minister of Justice, von Danckelmann, who probably had similar ambitions, took the lead in formally urging the suspension of the ALR in a letter dated April 9, 1792, on the ground that it was still too little known throughout Prussia—a ridiculous argument in view of the fact that successive drafts had been published and discussed for seven years since 1784. The king yielded to these cumulative pressures and formally suspended the ALR in a cabinet order to Carmer on April 18, 1792. Carmer vainly replied the next day, "I am completely convinced that all the insinuations which have been made to your Royal Majesty against the new law code have come from a very few heads pregnant with aristocratic forms of government" *(mit einer aristocratischen Regierungsform schwanger gehenden Köpfen.)*[54] The king proved, however, dead to the chancellor's arguments; he formally and publicly decreed on May 5, 1792, the indefinite suspension of the ALR. It is clear that Danckelmann's letter of April 9, 1792, was only the occasion, not the cause, of the suspension; for the argument that the ALR was still insufficiently known could have been met by merely postponing the effectiveness of the code to some specific date later than June 1.

What were the real reasons behind the king's decision? We cannot know with any certainty, but there was probably a combination of factors leading to the tentative suspension of April 18 and the definitive suspension of May 5. The opposition of aristocratic and court figures must have left their mark on the pliable Frederick William, especially in the general atmosphere of increasing hysteria about the course of the French Revolution in the early spring of 1792. France

[53] Heuer, op.cit., pp. 193-95. Martin Philippson, *Geschichte*, II, Ch. 1.
[54] Quoted in Heuer, op.cit., p. 201.

declared war upon Austria on April 20, and it was certain that Prussia would soon be involved in the same struggle: the argument must have been persuasive that "this was no time for social experiments." There was a further specific factor which must have strengthened the king's resolve finally to suspend the ALR. He was extremely indignant at this time about the way in which the Berlin *Kammergericht* handled the case against Pastor Schulz, the first man to be prosecuted for violating Wöllner's Edict Concerning Religion. The king issued a *Machtsprych* on April 27, 1792, against Pastor Schulz, whom the *Kammergericht* had refused to punish—precisely the kind of *Machtsprych* which was prohibited by the ALR. A code which would have prevented the king from doing what he did to Schulz must have appeared especially suspect at that particular moment.[55]

It took a remarkable combination of circumstances to save the ALR and finally bring it into force—with two years' delay—on June 1, 1794. Carmer and Svarez refused to despair about bringing the king back to their side. Svarez joined a colleague in publishing a popular exposition of the ALR calculated to meet Danckelmann's objection that it was insufficiently known;[56] they certainly did not consider the ALR a "dead matter." The *Gesetzeskommission*, in which Svarez played the key role, frequently referred to the ALR in its approval of new laws, as if it had never been suspended. The great second chance for the code came in the summer of 1793 following Prussia's annexation of large Polish territories in the Second Partition. The Prussian Government was bent upon Prussianizing the new territories, and this could best be done by introducing Prussian law in such matters as taxation, administration, and military discipline. Where could one find a better statement of Prussian law than in the ALR? Even Danckelmann, a sharp foe of the introduction of the new code in April 1792, saw the force of the argument and began to consult Carmer on the question whether parts of the ALR should not be introduced in Prussian Poland (July 1793). Carmer seized the opportunity to suggest introduction in its entirety (August 3, 1793), and he gradually won over Danckelmann, though the latter insisted upon the prior necessity of making some revisions to free the code of its Radical features. Carmer wisely allowed Danckelmann to take the lead in a memorial to the

[55] Heuer, op.cit., p. 203, shows that the Schulz case was not the main cause of the suspension of the ALR; but he probably goes too far in asserting that it had *little*—and Wöllner, the main opponent of Schulz, *nothing*—to do with the suspension of the ALR.

[56] C. G. Svarez and Christoph Gossler, *Unterricht über die Gesetze für die Einwohner der preussischen Staaten von zwei preussischen Rechtsgelehrten* (Berlin, 1793).

king urging the revocation of the suspension of the ALR if certain changes were made (November 5, 1793). The king thereupon instructed Goldbeck, the other major opponent of the ALR in the previous year, to identify and excise offending paragraphs, and then proclaimed on February 5, 1794, that the revised code would finally go into effect on June 1, 1794. His earlier opposition was now so far forgotten that he decreed its introduction for the entire monarchy and not just for the newly acquired Polish conquests.[57]

What changes had been deemed imperative by the king, Danckelmann, and Goldbeck before the ALR was fit to be introduced? They are worth listing because they reveal what the Reactionaries had found most objectionable in the earlier draft. The king was most concerned about purging the "constitutional paragraphs" contained in the introduction. The right to make *Machtsprüche* was reinserted to allow future action against future Schulzes; paragraphs 77-79, which had defined the general welfare as the object of all legislation, were eliminated. Of lesser importance were three changes dealing with three particular groups: the right of officers to contract valid debts without the permission of their superiors was curtailed—a change which symbolized the special position which the officer corps continued to hold as servants of the king, who must not be economically encumbered; the contraction of "left-handed marriages," i.e., those in which the children did not secure the father's status, was made somewhat more difficult—a change important for its partial concession to aristocratic demands; and, finally, there was elimination of the provision that the property of bachelors go to charitable foundations. Carmer disliked all of these changes but accepted them gracefully as a comparatively small price to pay for achieving the belated introduction of the ALR in Prussia. His diplomatic flexibility must be reckoned an important factor in his final triumph.[58]

[57] The thesis of the importance of the Polish question in the final decision to introduce the ALR is convincingly developed by Heuer, op.cit., pp. 226ff., though he does not show clearly how the desirability of introducing it into the new Polish provinces of the monarchy overcame opposition to introducing it in the old.

[58] The study of the changes made in the "constitutional articles" is facilitated by the synoptic printing of the texts of 1784, 1791, and 1794 in parallel columns by Conrad, op.cit., pp. 44-49. The best historical survey is still Stölzel, *Svarez*, Bk. III, Sect. II, Ch. 4, "Die Umwandlung des Allgemeinen Gesetzbuchs in das Allgemeine Landrecht," 320-403. Meier, *Französische Einflüsse*, II, 142-49, gives a good summary of the over-all changes while ridiculing their significance. One change not mentioned in the text was the royal decision (Jan. 5, 1794) to change the name of the new code from *Allgemeines Gesetz Buch* to *Allgemeines Landrecht* because the latter name smelled less of a constitution. I have permitted myself the terminological inexactitude of referring to the ALR throughout.

It is not surprising that the completion of the great work of codification should have been accompanied by further protest from both the Right and the Left. The *Stände* of the Kur and Neumark issued a new protest against the fact of codification, the inclusion of too many abstract expressions, and the use of the German language (June 17, 1794, i.e., seventeen days after the ALR went into effect); but they only received a sharp reprimand from the *Staatsrat* for their pains.[59] Leftist intellectuals continued to criticize the ALR as a miserable, Reactionary patchwork unworthy of a truly enlightened age;[60] their protest has, however, aroused more interest with posterity than it did with their contemporaries. The simultaneous attack from both Reactionaries and Radicals is a good indication of the Conservative character of the work of Carmer and Svarez.

The ALR succeeded in achieving some of the reform objectives outlined at the beginning of this section. It provided Prussia with a high measure of legal uniformity despite the fact that many of its provisions (for example, those dealing with serfdom) were strictly "subsidiary" in character. It achieved a remarkable synthesis of Roman and Germanic law, and, above all, succeeded in firmly establishing what the actual law was without the necessity of antiquarian researches in every particular case. It aimed, cautiously and tentatively, at some substantive concessions to justifiable Radical demands—for example, the curtailment of absolutism and the facilitation of intermarriage between different classes—though its authors had to abandon much reformist ground before the king could be persuaded to sanction final publication. Greater than any specific achievement was, however, the general fact of codification as such. Codification inevitably meant rationalization of and choice between different aspects of the highly complex legal legacy of the past. It meant the abandonment of a legal Conservatism oriented purely to the *status quo* in favor

---

[59] M. Philippson, op.cit., II, 58; Stölzel, *Svarez*, pp. 398-400.

[60] See, for example, the anonymous attack upon the ALR by Ernst Gottlob Morgenbesser, a prominent Königsberg judge destined to play a considerable role in Stein's reforms: *Beyträge zum republikanischen Gesetzbuch, enthalten in Anmerkungen zum allgemeinen Landrecht und zur allgemeinen Gerichtsordnung für die preussischen Staaten* (2nd edn., Königsberg, 1798, 1800). Morgenbesser criticized the ALR for its failure to establish (1) popular sovereignty and the election of officials, (2) rational law administered by a hierarchy of courts exclusively staffed by the central government, (3) separation of Church and state, (4) the elimination of inheritance, and (5) the abolition of aristocratic and every other form of privilege. These views are hailed by Heuer, op.cit., pp. 259-70; they are ridiculed by Meier, *Französische Einflüsse*, II, 173-83, who has a field day in describing Morgenbesser's very "advanced" views upon marriage and sex, including the view that parents have no duty to support their children.

of a deliberate attempt to adapt Prussia's often anachronistic laws to the needs of the society of the 1790's.

We have seen that the authors of the ALR did not have any intention of overthrowing the general pattern of Prussian society in favor of some doctrinaire theory, and that social and political conditions would not have allowed them to do so even if they had been so inclined. They deserve great credit for their accomplishments in the face of bitter Reactionary opposition; but it must nonetheless be said that their efforts fell considerably short of what was objectively needed. Prussia's judicial organization remained chaotic and its anachronistic patrimonial courts intact. There was practically no attack upon class privilege: the position of the aristocracy remained unshaken, serfdom unreformed, and the guild structure a continued source of economic paralysis. The proposed curtailment of royal absolutism was specifically abandoned when the prohibition of *Machtsprüche* was eliminated from the final version of the ALR: the goal of a full-fledged *Rechtstaat* remained an aspiration instead of becoming a reality. There was no trace of any advance toward self-government, though a law code was perhaps not the place to look for any advance in this important area of public life. Suffice it to say that the ALR served admirably to enhance Prussia's reputation as the most efficiently conducted monarchical absolutism in Europe, but that Prussia remained a state characterized by two qualities which must be considered anachronistic in the year 1794, the fifth year of the French Revolution: authoritarian monarchy in its political life and Junker domination in its social life. It required the catastrophe of Jena before a vigorous reform minister like Stein—not a group of well-intentioned bureaucrats like Carmer and Svarez—could make some progress toward self-government and legal equality; and even then Stein went no farther than he could drag a reluctant King Frederick William III, and fell from power before he had gone very far.

Frederick William III and the Road to Jena

PORTRAIT OF A STATUS QUO CONSERVATIVE

In 1797 Frederick William III ascended the Prussian throne, which he was to occupy with conspicuous lack of distinction for the next forty-three years.[61] His main quality was lack of self-confidence. His intel-

---

[61] There is no satisfactory biography of the king. A good substitute is to be found, however, in the two excellent biographical articles by von Hartmann, *ADB*, VII (1878), 700-29, and H. Haussherr, *NDB*, V (1961), 560-63. The standard biography of the queen is Paul Bailleu, *Königin Luise. Ein Lebensbild* (Ber-

lectual abilities were mediocre, as none knew better than the king himself; he hated, above all, to make decisions, a fault which led variously to irresolution, vacillation, and obstinacy when decisions became unavoidable. It was not only Stein who despaired of Prussia's future in 1807 because it was governed by "a mediocre, inactive, and cold man."[62] The king lacked any real understanding of the great political forces which were transforming Europe in his lifetime: his political ideal was limited to preserving as much of the Frederician legacy as possible instead of seeking a fruitful synthesis between the old and the new. He lacked the vision or imagination to plan long-range policies, or the perseverance to pursue them consistently: he preferred to absorb himself in routine detail, especially military detail, and allowed Prussian policy to drift with the tide of events instead of trying to shape them. Frederick William sought escape from the burden of kingship by an Arcadian idyll of domesticity; he loved nothing better than to live the life of a simple country squire at the estate of Paretz (near Potsdam) with his lovely and devoted Queen Louise (1776-1810).

His merits, as is the case with most men, were closely connected with his defects. His exemplary family life restored a moral example to his Prussian subjects, one urgently needed in view of the bacheloric Spartanism of his great-uncle Frederick and the bigamous epicureanism of his father Frederick William II. The romantic cult of monarchy developed by a poet like Novalis was made possible only by the combination of a pure king and a beautiful queen. Frederick William III also differed from his father in an almost pedantic devotion to duty, an eminent sense of decorum, and an unfailing common sense which was closely connected with his lack of imagination and his mediocre intelligence. His incapacity for flights of heroism stood the Prussian state in good stead in its darkest hour in 1811; when Gneisenau penned a burning memorandum favoring a desperate insurrection against Napoleon, the king made the classic marginal comment, "Good as poetry." Gneisenau's retort that "Your Majesty's throne rests upon poetic sentiments also" was not a sufficient answer, for the loyalty of Prussia's subjects was in fact a simple matter of tradition and habit— two pillars which dethronement after an unsuccessful war might

---

lin, 1908), though it has remarkably little to say about her political influence and is somewhat reticent about her personal weaknesses (e.g., her infatuation with Tsar Alexander in 1802).

[62] Freiherr vom Stein, *Ausgewählte Politische Briefe und Denkschriften.* (eds. Erich Botzenhart and Günther Ipsen, Stuttgart, 1955), p. 108. Henceforth cited as Botzenhart-Ipsen, *Stein.*

easily shake.[63] Frederick William was resolved, above all, to preserve the dynasty; for this end he bore shame and humiliation in a spirit of Christian resignation. His constancy was rewarded by his remarkable success in steering Prussia through the turmoils of the most tragic period of its history.

It is a commonplace to say that the successes of his reign were largely due to the efforts of men larger than himself. The king should, however, be given some credit for the instruments that he chose, and for the admirable abnegation which made him overlook qualities personally odious to him because he believed that the men possessed great value for the Prussian state. He long suppressed his anger at Stein's impertinences which no king could be expected to suffer in silence; he tolerated Hardenberg's scandalous private morals, bad entourage, and disorderly financial habits because he rightly saw in him Prussia's greatest diplomat. He could truthfully say of himself, in the celebrated letter dismissing Stein (Jan. 3, 1807), that he had long "suppressed his prejudices [against Stein], because he had always sought to select the servants of the state not after his personal caprice but in accordance with sound reason."[64] Frederick William thereby showed that he was imbued with the Frederician ethos of subordinating his subjective wishes to the objective dictates of state necessity. The same consideration made him occasionally open-minded about the reform needs of Prussia after he ascended the throne; an active reformer taking broad initiatives he could not become, for he was timid and never free of his Reactionary court entourage; but his impressionability in the face of advisers, and his basically benevolent outlook, made him sometimes accessible to reform impulses. These impulses crystallized into deeds only very inadequately before 1806; it required the fiasco of the *ancien régime* at Jena to override temporarily the formidable obstacles blocking any fundamental transformation of a Prussia which had fallen asleep on the laurels of Frederick the Great.

THE BEGINNING OF THE REIGN

The first actions of the new king were hailed by public opinion and

[63] Gneisenau replied to Frederick William's comment, "Als Poesie gut," with the unforgettable words: "Religion, Gebet, Liebe zum Regenten, zum Vaterland, zur Tugend sind nichts anderes als Poesie, keine Herzenserhebung ohne poetische Stimmung. Wer nur nach kalter Berechnung handelt, wird ein starrer Egoist. Auf Poesie ist die Sicherheit der Throne gegründet." Quoted Hans Delbrück, *Das Leben des Feldmarschalls Grafen Neithardt von Gneisenau* (2 vols., Berlin, 1882), I, 217.

[64] Botzenhart-Ipsen, *Stein*, p. 88.

gave Frederick William even more than the usual popularity of a newly crowned king. The Countess Lichtenau—who had, incidentally, nursed her dying lover with admirable devotion when prudent friends vainly urged her to emigrate—was immediately arrested and subjected to prolonged interrogation; her record proved, however, clear, and the king was compelled to agree to her release in 1798. Frederick William next dismissed the entire Rosicrucian clique which had dominated the court of his father. Bischoffwerder was prematurely retired from the army at the age of fifty-six, in January 1798, with full pension rights; he withdrew to the Polish estate conferred upon him by the former king, and lived there, virtually forgotten by his contemporaries, until his death in 1803. Wöllner suffered a harder fate. The *Oberkonsistorium*—too long pushed aside by the imperious minister—petitioned the king (Dec. 25, 1797) for the restoration of its full powers, many of which had been usurped by Wöllner's *Immediat-Examinations-Kommission*; it received a favorable reply two days later and resumed its earlier control of the censorship, the examination of theological candidates, and the approval of ecclesiastical appointments. The hated IEK was soon formally abolished and its members retired with pensions.[65]

Wöllner himself acquiesced in what he could not prevent, but showed his unshaken belief in the rightness of his policies by specifically reaffirming the Edict Concerning Religion by a most untimely new decree. This provoked an unusually sharp cabinet order (Jan. 11, 1798), drawn up by the influential new *Kabinettssekretär* Mencken, which constituted a general indictment of the entire "Wöllner System." The minister thereupon offered, with a certain lack of dignity, "to obey the will of the King most strictly, and to implement all orders of his royal master";[66] but this offer did not suffice to save his position. He was ungraciously dismissed, without pension, on

---

[65] Hermes had a remarkable and controversial subsequent career. He lived in Berlin writing antirationalist pamphlets until 1805, when he was rather surprisingly appointed by Count Reventlow, curator of Kiel University, as professor of theology and director of the teacher training seminar, although he was already seventy-three. The appointment was widely criticized because—other reasons apart—Hermes had never won a theological doctorate. The staunchly orthodox theology faculty of Tübingen came to the rescue by making him a doctor of theology on April 23, 1805. His lectures at Kiel were considered scandalously low-grade and popular, and his appointment was one factor in the fall of his patron Reventlow that same year. Hermes was retired after only a year's teaching in 1806, and died in Kiel the next year. This footnote is based on the concluding pages of Hoffmann's excellent *Hermes*.

[66] Bailleu, *Wöllner*, p. 157.

March 11, 1798, and retired in rather straitened circumstances to his estate of Gross Rietz (Kreis Beeskow), which he had bought with his wife's money in 1790. The man who had recently been Prussia's nearly omnipotent minister spent his last years as a struggling landlord, and died—embittered and depressed, but respected by his neighbors—in 1800. The Edict Concerning Religion, the capstone and symbol of his policy, was never formally repealed, but it was allowed to fall quietly into desuetude.

Few people in Prussia regretted the fall of the Rosicrucian clique, though it cannot be said that the new king's advisers were significantly superior to the old. Frederick William III relied heavily upon the judgment of his mediocre *Generaladjutant* Karl Leopold von Köckritz (d. 1821), the daily companion of his table); his advisers in foreign policy were the equally incompetent Count Kurt von Haugwitz (1752-1832), a Rosicrucian holdover, and his bosom companion Johann Wilhelm Lombard (1767-1812), son of a barber in the French Huguenot colony; military affairs were the province of the undistinguished General Friedrich Wilhelm Zastrow (1752-1830). Civilian affairs, at least, were in the capable hands of two successive cabinet secretaries, Anastasius Mencken (1752-1801) and, after 1800, Karl Friedrich von Beyme (1765-1838), both of whom favored reform while not being able to influence the king far in that direction. The regular ministers had even less direct access to the king than had been the case under Frederick William II, though at least two successive finance ministers, Karl Gustav von Struensee (1735-1804) and Karl von Stein, were men of exceptional capacity. Struensee had already suggested broad reforms in the previous reign but failed to override Conservative obstacles; this had led to a notable exclamation in 1791 which remained valid until the debacle at Jena fifteen years later:

How is one to convince XYZ that glaring abuses must be reformed? I can neither alter nor abolish ten anachronistic budgets, twenty pigeon holes, fifty constitutions, one hundred privileges—not to speak of endless purely personal considerations [which stand in the way of reform]. I am not a Prime Minister, and even my own department is inextricably interwoven with the prevalent governmental system of ineffectual scribbling.[67]

Struensee was not always so pessimistic. He is reported to have told the French chargé d'affaires in 1799:

[67] Quoted in Philippson, *Preussische Geschichte*, II, 98.

The beneficial revolution which you Frenchmen gave conducted violently from below we Prussians will conduct gradually from above. The King is a democrat in his own way: his constant pre-occupation is to restrict the privileges of the aristocracy. . . . A few years hence Prussia will no longer possess a privileged class.[68]

This proved a highly inaccurate prophecy but one characteristic of the high hopes aroused by the various reforms proclaimed—but only rarely implemented—in the first decade of the government of Frederick William III.

An *Immediat-Kommission* on military reforms discussed such proposals as introducing universal military service, reducing the number of foreigners in the army, setting up a militia reserve, opening the officer career to nonnobles, and revising the barbarous code of military discipline—all anticipations of Scharnhorst's great work after 1807, yet significantly only verbal anticipations, not concrete deeds. A special Finance Commission sitting in 1798 discussed the abolition of guild privileges, the reform of the excise (hitherto an obstacle to economic progress by raising an artificial barrier between town and country), and the termination of aristocratic tax exemptions—all useful reforms which were to be achieved (except for the last) by Stein and Hardenberg after 1807. Serfdom remained untouchable so far as the private Junker estates were concerned; but the government achieved a great reform (its only major success before 1807) when it emancipated some 50,000 crown serfs, though there was no satisfactory accompanying land settlement. There was endless discussion of reforms needed in Prussia's governmental structure, with suggestions for establishing a ministry with collective responsibility, decentralizing administration by strengthening the provincial *Staats-und Domänen-kammern*, and strictly separating administration from justice. None of those useful reforms went, unfortunately, beyond the discussion stage before 1806. The government remained in fact under the personal control of a king whose personality precluded effective rule; his main advisers remained irresponsible cabinet secretaries rather than responsible ministers. The so-called "reform before the reform," stressed by some Conservative historians in a vain attempt to maximize continuities in Prussian history, never amounted to much.[69]

[68] Quoted in Otto Hintze, *Die Hohenzollern und ihr Werk* (Berlin, 1915), p. 427.

[69] The standard article on the "reform before the reform" is Otto Hintze, "Preussische Reformbestrebungen vor 1806," *HZ*, LXXVI (1896), 413-43, stressing the wide gap which existed between idealistic aspiration and concrete achieve-

It may be repeated once more that Frederick William III was essentially a stupid and unimaginative Defender of the *status quo* who only rarely and tepidly saw the need for reforms and completely lacked the drive to implement what he deemed desirable in the face of opposition built into the unreformed structure of the Prussian monarchy. It required the catastrophe of Jena to create a situation where reforms became possible because they had become obviously necessary, and even then the king did not prove a stanch champion of the reform cause. His merit was limited to appointing reform ministers and allowing them—temporarily—to impose their policies upon him; but this was no small merit in an absolute monarchy where reforms could occur only if decreed "from above." His historic position is assured because he acquiesced after 1807 in one of the most successful experiments in Reform Conservatism in history, and thereby made an indispensable contribution to the greatness of Prussia in the nineteenth century.

---

ments; the continuity is overstressed by Ernst von Meier, *Französische Einflüsse*, II, Sect. II.

CHAPTER 8

The Habsburg Monarchy
from Maria Theresia to Francis II

Prussia and Austria Compared

WHEN ONE compares Prussia with Austria in the middle of the eighteenth century it is fascinating to observe how fundamentally similar tendencies worked themselves out in states very different in geographical condition, governmental structure, and historical tradition. Prussia was a unitary-centralized state despite the variety of its provinces, and it was composed (at least until the First Partition of Poland in 1772) of purely German territories; the Habsburg Monarchy was a congeries of provinces inhabited by various nationalities held together by an as-yet very imperfectly centralized administration. Both states tended toward a monarchical absolutism which degraded the historic *Stände* bodies from political to purely ceremonial functions, but the process had advanced much further in Prussia. Here the *Stände* power had already been broken by the Great Elector, whereas in some sections of the Habsburg Monarchy (most notably Hungary) the *Stände* remained politically very much alive well into the nineteenth century. In both states centralization and absolutism served primarily military needs, though this fact was most evident in Prussia. The Hohenzollerns maintained an army of 160,000 men out of a population of about four million, with the military budget constituting some five-sevenths of the total; the Habsburg Monarchy maintained about the same number of soldiers out of a population more than three times as large, with a requirement of less than half the annual budget. Under Frederick the Great, Prussia's fiscal machinery proved very efficient in providing constant surpluses except in time of war; the Habsburg Monarchy was handicapped by chronic deficits and poor credit until its budget was finally balanced—temporarily—in the 1770's.

Prussia might be compared to a hard-working, economical, tightly disciplined parvenu who can maintain a recently won position only by laborious effort; the Habsburg Monarchy had much of the lassitude of a *grand seigneur* who looks back upon centuries of glory and cannot really take new rivals very seriously. (The shock of 1740, when the monarchy stood on the verge of dissolution after the failure of the Pragmatic Sanction, was quickly forgotten following the brilliant

394

successes of Kaunitz' diplomacy.) Prussia was a dynamic and expansive power, though Frederick had become cautious after completing the wars provoked by his Silesian adventure; the Habsburg Monarchy was essentially a static and defensive power despite Joseph's ill-starred enterprises in seeking annexations in Bavaria and the Balkans. Prussia was a predominantly German state which could appeal to the rising sentiment of national pride, though Prussia's rise had constituted a continuous revolt against the fabric of the Holy Roman Empire which expressed (however inadequately) the historic unity of the German nation; the Habsburg Monarchy was a European state whose multinational composition precluded any exclusive identification with German nationalism despite the usual union between the Imperial and Habsburg Crowns.

The greatness of the Habsburg Monarchy was especially notable outside the political field. Its citizens prided themselves upon the flourishing music, architecture, and painting in cosmopolitan Vienna, where German, Italian, Spanish, and French elements had produced a style of baroque art of special distinction. The Viennese viewed Berlin as a provincial city on the periphery of the cultivated world; they sneered at the thin veneer of alien French culture which Frederick had introduced to cover up the cultural poverty of his backward lands; and they saw little reason to envy Berlin as the literary capital of the German *Aufklärung*. This complacent sense of cultural superiority made it difficult for Austrians to take Prussia seriously despite the triumphs of Prussian arms in successive wars: the psychological gap between an Austria, which viewed its traditional primacy in Central Europe as an axiomatic fact, and a Prussia which must strive for parity of status with Austria (if not something more) proved a powerful factor in promoting Austro-Prussian friction throughout the entire period covered by this volume—and beyond.

Contemporaries often noted the sharp difference in religion as the most important difference between the lands of Habsburgs and Hohenzollerns. The Habsburgs had been closely identified with the Counter Reformation of the sixteenth century and the Thirty Years' War, and in no European capital did the Jesuits carry greater weight than in Vienna. Religious toleration was frowned upon in principle, although in fact a good deal of subsurface Protestantism had survived. Jews were treated with extreme harshness. Maria Theresia never made her peace with the *Aufklärung*, and regretted the suppression of the Jesuit Order. Prussia had, on the other hand, become Lutheran in 1539, and had acted as the informal head of the Protestant party in

Germany following the decline of Saxony and the Catholic conversion of the House of Wettin. The Hohenzollern family had become Calvinist in 1613 but had made no attempt to impose its new brand of Protestantism upon its subjects: its subsequent position as a Calvinist dynasty in a Lutheran country gave it a vested interest in the principle of religious toleration. The promotion of this principle caused no embarrassment to the skeptical Frederick. While the bigoted Maria Theresia harassed Protestants and Jews, he welcomed men of any and no faith (including Jews and members of the suppressed Jesuit Order) to swell the population, and hence power, of his state. His greatest pride was to make Prussia a center of the *Aufklärung,* and his encouragement of science and scholarship—fields in which Maria Theresia had no personal interest—started Berlin on the road which was to make it the future intellectual capital of Germany.

The socioeconomic structure of the two monarchies was similar in essentials. The landed aristocracy possessed a dominant position in both, but the two aristocracies were sociologically very different: in Prussia the dominant type was the hard-working, economical, parochial Junker who sent his sons into the army at the king's command; in the Habsburg Monarchy a far more variegated aristocracy was headed by magnates who often possessed leisure and a wide view of the world and were much less militarized than their North German fellow nobles. The Junkers were utterly intransigent in defense of their class privileges, whereas the Austrian aristocracy accepted taxation of its lands in 1749 with only minor opposition. We have already seen how the Pomeranian Junkers defied the attempt of Frederick to abolish serfdom, whereas the Austrian nobles accepted the Josephine abolition in the 1780's with remarkably good grace. Both governments pursued mercantilistic policies aimed at promoting both the power of the state and the welfare of the individual. Their attempt to create "prosperity at the King's command" was only partially successful, and both monarchies remained economically backward by the standards of Western Europe.

Most of the problems confronted by the two monarchies were analogous and provoked a similar Radical challenge and Conservative response. The autocratic pattern of government was opposed by the *Stände* (where they survived) in the name of medieval constitutionalism and by a body—as yet insignificant—of advanced thinkers in the name of popular sovereignty. A small group of merchants, bureaucrats, and economists resented the surviving relics of feudalism and the meddling policy of mercantilism, in the name of equality and laissez faire. In both countries the existing religious orthodoxy was questioned by the *Aufklärung*—a situation which led to attempts at reform as well as impassioned defense of the old orthodoxy. In Prussia the Frederician government engaged itself on the side of *Aufklärung*, absolutism, and (to a lesser extent) laissez faire; the Austrian government did the same, hesitantly under Maria Theresia but with full conviction under her son Joseph. Both countries were to see a change in their general policy through a change in sovereigns within a period of six years: in Prussia the religious *Aufklärung* was repudiated by Frederick William II in 1786; in Austria the reform spirit was drowned in every field by the accession of the obscurantist Francis II in 1792. This chapter will attempt to characterize the main stages of Austrian policy from Maria Theresia to Francis II, and provide the background for the understanding of the Franciscan system which was to merge into the famous system identified with the name of Metternich, the dominant figure of German Conservatism in the post-Napoleonic world.

Maria Theresia: A Reluctant Reform Conservative

Maria Theresia was the creator of the modern Habsburg Monarchy. In 1740 she assumed rule over miscellaneous provinces united only by the fragile tie of the Pragmatic Sanction and threatened by numerous foreign foes; the great achievement of her reign was that she not only successfully defended her inheritance but also consolidated it through a series of administrative, social, and religious reforms. Her policy strengthened absolutism by replacing *Stände* with bureaucratic institutions; enlarged the role of the central government in such fields as finance, economics, and education; weakened the power of the feudal aristocracy; and placed the Church under the domination of the state. Although these were all *Aufklärung* objectives it is certain that Maria Theresia was not prompted by *Aufklärung* ideas, of which she remained, indeed, an avowed foe throughout her long reign of forty years (1740-80).[1]

Her reforms were strictly *ad hoc* in character. The War of the Austrian Succession (1740-48), which she had been compelled to fight when her neighbors had refused to abide by the Pragmatic Sanction, had ended in the loss of Silesia to her Prussian rival. Maria Theresia

---

[1] I have used the following standard works on Maria Theresia: Alfred von Arneth, *Geschichte Maria Theresias* (11 vols., Vienna, 1863-79); Eugen Guglia, *Maria Theresia* (2 vols., Munich, 1917); H. Kretschmayr, *Maria Theresia* (Gotha, 1925); Karl Tschuppik, *Maria Theresia* (Amsterdam, 1934). An attractive introduction in English is Constance Lily Morris, *Maria Theresia, the last Conservative* (New York, 1937), despite its grotesque subtitle.

had been quick to recognize that she had much to learn from Prussia about organizing the resources of the state for war. To strengthen the external power of the monarchy became the primary objective of all the Theresian reforms; the extension of absolutism was more a means than an end, though it certainly accorded well with belief in her divine right to rule. Maria Theresia's deep devotion to the welfare of her subjects, the fruit of her maternal personality rather than any conscious adherence to the humanitarian outlook of the age, added a moral mandate to the absolute form of government she wielded with remarkable success.

Her greatest reform was the creation of a new administrative system which overrode many privileges long possessed by the *Stände* of her various provinces. These *Stände* had made efficient war finance impossible by insisting upon their right to vote taxes on an annual basis; they in fact collected completely inadequate sums by maintaining the traditional tax exemption of all aristocratic lands. The *Stände* had been in charge of recruiting and equipping the troops, a field of administration where their record appeared miserable when compared with that of the centralized Prussian war machine. They had used their domination of provincial administrative bodies to place in leading positions aristocrats with no special bureaucratic training, and with no loyalties larger than those to their native province. The conduct of local affairs was traditionally left in the selfish, inefficient, and unsupervised hands of the aristocracy in the countryside and the patriciate in the towns.

Maria Theresia set out after 1747 to remedy these defects with the help of her great reform minister, Count Friedrich Wilhelm Haugwitz (1700-65). Most of the provincial *Stände* were pressured into voting taxes for a ten-year period, a change which promoted long-range planning and put the ax to the constitutional power of the *Stände*. The principle of tax exemption for lands owned by the nobility was eliminated in the name of "equality pleasing to God" (*gottgefällige Gleichheit*), though the fact that nobiliar lands were taxed at 1%, rather than the peasant rate of 2%, proved that equality before the law still had a long way to go in the Habsburg dominions. The military administration was centralized under the direction of the Viennese *Hofkriegsrath*, while the various supply obligations of the *Stände* were commuted into regular money payments. The exercise of traditional governmental power on the local level by nobles and patricians was henceforth regulated by the establishment of bureaucratic *Kreisbehörden* on the county level. The lower class was everywhere encouraged to appeal to these bodies in case of exploitation or injustice, and Maria Theresia took care that they did not fall under the control of local magnates.

Of even greater importance was the reorganization of the provincial and central administration. The *Stände* had previously dominated provincial government by indirectly electing (or at least suggesting) the key officials; these now became strictly bureaucratic appointees with a clear-cut responsibility to the empress rather than to their former *Stände* master. The *Stände* had also exercised much influence over certain parts of the central administration—for example, the Bohemian *Hofkanzlei* (Royal Chancellery); this was now eliminated through the union of the Bohemian and Austrian *Hofkanzleien* into a single body known as the *Vereinigte Hofkanzlei* (United Court Chancellery) after 1761. Its detailed work was done through a number of high-powered committees, of which the most important were those charged with education (the *Studien Hof Kommission*), ecclesiastical affairs (the *Geistliche Kommission*), and the codification of laws (the *Compilationskommission*). The entire work of domestic administration and legislation was planned and coordinated by a small *Staatsrat* (Council of State), first established in 1760. This new administrative structure was second in excellence only to Prussia's among the Great Powers of Europe, and it stood the test of time until the rise of Liberalism in the second quarter of the nineteenth century.[2]

The improvement of administrative institutions was accompanied by a great extension of the functions of government. In Ch. 3 we have already examined the most important of these, the "Josephine" ecclesiastical program, in fact launched by Maria Theresia after about 1760. The creation of an "enlightened citizenry" was made as much the obligation of the schoolmaster as the priest, and the Theresian government sought to create a system of universal education on the primary level. The effort proved premature, and illiteracy remained a serious problem for another hundred years; but a few steps forward were made under the inspiring direction of Abbot Felbiger. Vigorous economic policies showed that the empress was as much concerned with the economic as the spiritual welfare of her subjects. A new *Universalkommerzdirektorium* (in many ways a centralized Ministry of Commerce) was created in 1749. It sought to promote manufactures and develop a transportation system so that the Habsburg

---

[2] The best modern account of the administrative reorganization is F. Walter, *Die Geschichte der österreichischen Zentralverwaltung in der Zeit Maria Theresias* (Vienna, 1938).

economy could begin to compete with those of Western Europe. In her social policy Maria Theresia criticized serfdom and desired to transform the agrarian structure in the direction of peasant proprietorship and long-term leaseholds. She did not, however, dare to pursue such revolutionary plans actively, and in fact concentrated upon the lesser aim of regulating the labor obligations of private serfs and of commuting servile obligations altogether on the royal domains. Some progress was also made in the field of law reform, an area where the Habsburg Monarchy was woefully backward. Maria Theresia appointed several commissions to draft new codes in different fields of law (civil, criminal, court procedure, et cetera), only to find—as had the Prussian legal reformers from Cocceji to Svarez—that law reform was more easily talked about than achieved. A new penal code, the famous *Nemesis Theresiana*, was promulgated in 1769. Many of its specific terms—for example, the retention of torture—remained, however, far behind the best thought of the age; but the fact of a single code for the entire monarchy (excepting only Hungary and the outlying provinces of Belgium and Lombardy) was in itself a forward-looking achievement.[3]

The remarkable extent of the Theresian reforms appears all the more surprising when one remembers that the empress was in outlook a defender of the *status quo* with many Reactionary hankerings. She believed firmly in the Catholic faith of her fathers, regretted the suppression of the Jesuits, and was anxious to avoid any open clash with the Papacy. She was opposed to the toleration of Protestants advocated by her son Joseph, and believed that a Catholic monopoly was essential for the secular welfare of Austria as well as for the salvation of souls. Her hatred of the Jews must be considered extreme even in a generally anti-Semitic age: thus she ordered the expulsion of all Jews from Prague in 1744 because some Jews had sympathized with the Bavarians and Prussians during their brief occupations of the city. This ferocious decree was sabotaged by city officials who were fearful of economic disaster, and finally rescinded upon the demand of the Bohemian *Stände* in 1748. The empress' sentiments toward the Jews remained, however, unchanged. Some thirty years later (June 14, 1777) she asserted that the Jewish community of Vienna was a nuisance and a danger to the general welfare, and decreed as follows:

[3] An excellent account of Maria Theresia's educational, economic, and legal policies can be found in Mitrofanov, *Joseph II* (Vienna, 1910), pp. 802-07, 396-406, 503-14. (Each section provides an introductory background to the reforms of Joseph II.)

No Jew shall henceforth be permitted to live in Vienna without my written permission. I know of no pestilence worse for any state than this people of cheaters and usurers, which constantly throws honest men into misery through its money transactions; a people capable, moreover, of actions which make every decent person shudder with disgust. For these reasons it is essential to keep the Jews far away from Vienna. I wish to have submitted to me a list of how many Jews live here now, and another in four years' time with explanations concerning whether and why they have increased or decreased in numbers.[4]

The empress was dead four years later—the year of the publication of Dohm's *On the Civic Improvement of the Jews* (1781)—and her son Joseph did not share his mother's views on the Jews.

Maria Theresia frequently ridiculed the modern demand for freedom and the principles of the *Aufklärung* of which it was an essential part. She was convinced that the ideas of the *Aufklärung* produced private unhappiness and public misfortune. Witness the following letter to her youngest son, the Cologne Archbishop and Elector Maximilian:

Nothing appears more attractive, nothing is more calculated to flatter our self-esteem, than the idea of freedom without any restrictions whatsoever. Freedom is, indeed, a word which our enlightened century puts too often in place of the word "religion." It is fashionable today to denounce the entire past for its ignorance and prejudice without bothering even to be informed about it. . . . I would willingly plead guilty to prejudice, pride, and obstinacy for my refusal to join these so-called scholars and philosophers, if I could only observe that they are happier in their enterprises or more content in their private lives [than those devoted to religion]. But daily experience confirms me in the contrary view. . . . No one is weaker or more easily discouraged, no one more depressed in the face of even small misfortune, than these so-called "strong spirits." They make bad fathers, sons, husbands, ministers, generals, and citizens. Why? Because they lack solid foundations. For they draw all their philosophy, all their principles from self-love alone; and the slightest accident makes them downcast because they have nothing external to lean upon.[5]

[4] Quoted in ibid., p. 668.
[5] Quoted by F. Walter, *Männer um Maria Theresia* (Vienna, 1951), pp. 127-28.

401

Maria Theresia's attitude toward government was also essentially traditionalist despite her policy of vigorous administrative reforms. She viewed absolutism as the traditional way of governing the Habsburg Monarchy, and could scarcely conceive of any other. She never doubted her own divine right to rule and never felt any need to rationalize her absolutism through the theory of the social contract (or any other theory). Her entire outlook prevented her from thinking of herself as the "first servant of the state," though in practice she was no less selflessly devoted to the general welfare than her rival Frederick or her son Joseph. She disliked the *Stände* for the trouble they caused in raising and financing troops for war, but she never dreamed of attacking *Stände* rights per se. Her advisers could win her for pressuring the *Stände* to meet obvious governmental needs, but this did not prevent her adherence in principle to the fundamental maxim of dualist polity: that monarchy and *Stände* were natural partners in the promotion of the welfare of the state. This attitude was strengthened by her inherent moderation and instinctive grasp of what was possible and what was not. Thus she never attempted to tackle the Hungarian problem—a problem created by the fact that the Magyar aristocracy used its control of age-old institutions to avoid paying its fair share of the common burdens of the monarchy. It may be said, indeed, that the empress' failure to apply her numerous administrative reforms to Hungary encouraged the Magyars in their favorite notion that Hungary was a completely independent kingdom united to Austria by a personal union alone, a notion which was to cause endless trouble to her successors.

Maria Theresia had, as we have seen, reservations about serfdom and did much to alleviate the condition of the serfs. She was, however, bitterly opposed to any quick or violent termination of serfdom. She was deeply shocked when the Bavarian Elector Charles Albert, challenging Maria Theresia's dynastic rights in 1742, promised to emancipate any serfs who should take up arms upon his behalf; the Bohemian serfs who had spread his emancipation proclamation were summarily executed by the Habsburg government. At that time she made the following categorical statement from which her own policy was to deviate in later years:

> It is most inappropriate to think about eliminating serfdom *(Unterthänigkeit)*, since there is no country in the world which does not differentiate between lords and serfs [sic]. To free the serf of his obligations to the lord would only make the former unbridled

and the latter discontented, quite apart from the fact that it would violate every canon of justice.[6]

Maria Theresia had a similar traditionalist and moralistic outlook in her conceptions of foreign policy. Her famous letter to her Foreign Minister Kaunitz, opposing Austria's participation in the Partition of Poland in 1772, gives eloquent expression to her dislike for the newly fashionable theory of Reason of State:

> I readily confess that I have never, throughout my entire life, felt as sorely troubled as I do now. When I was challenged in the position of my hereditary lands [in 1740] I relied upon my good right and the support of God; but in the present situation, where not only justice is not on my side, but law, equity, and the respect owed to treaties are all against me, I cannot feel at ease for a moment, but suffer from the reproach of a heart which has never been able to narcotise itself, or make duplicity assume the guise of integrity. We shall lose once and for all our reputation for good faith, which is surely not only the most precious jewel of a monarch, but also an element of true strength in the face of all adversaries. I would be lacking in my duty if I did not present my point of view once again; but must also confess that I feel no longer strong enough to manage affairs by myself; hence I must let them, though with the greatest regrets, go their way.[7]

Maria Theresia's reluctant acquiescence in the Polish partition was due to the fact that she no longer had the strength to curb strong men like Joseph and Kaunitz. It provoked Frederick's famous remark that "she burst into tears, but grabbed nonetheless"; but this remark did too little justice to the empress' deeply felt Conservative scruples in the face of the European international practice of grabbing whatever could be grabbed.

The fundamental Conservatism of the empress expressed itself, finally, in her deep dislike of the Radicalism and impetuosity of her son Joseph, whom she had made coregent in 1765. Their chronically unpleasant relationship was, of course, primarily due to a conflict of personality, for both were born autocrats; but there were deeply rooted differences in principle as well. Joseph pursued a vision of a centralized, omnipotent governmental machine wielded by himself, in which *Stände* bodies had no place. Maria Theresia, insisting only

---

[6] Quoted in Adam Wolf, *Österreich unter Maria Theresia, Josef II und Leopold II 1740-1792* (Berlin, 1884), p. 98.
[7] Quoted in A. von Arneth, "Maria Theresia," *ADB*, xx (1884), 358.

upon the essentials of absolutism, generally respected historic rights and was tolerant of existing diversity. Joseph wanted complete equality of all men before the law and took an almost sadistic delight in humiliating the ancient nobility; Maria Theresia moved slowly and cautiously to curb some of the most anachronistic privileges of the aristocracy. Joseph wanted to abolish serfdom quickly; Maria Theresia was satisfied with some modification of servile obligations. Joseph pressed for the abolition of torture and capital punishment; Maria Theresia thought both essential for the protection of society against criminals. Joseph wanted religious toleration for Protestants and civic emancipation for Jews; Maria Theresia abhorred both reforms on political and religious grounds alike. Joseph rejoiced at the suppression of the Jesuit Order; Maria Theresia gave only her reluctant acquiescence. It would be easy to enlarge this catalogue of differences, but it must also be remembered that there was a broad measure of continuity between the two reigns and that Josephine policies often represent simply a Radicalization of those pursued by Maria Theresia. There was, however, a world of difference as regards the methods to be employed to achieve agreed common objectives— for example, the implementation of absolutism and the Erastian control of the Church. Maria Theresia was a prudent woman with a natural penchant for *suaviter in modo;* Joseph, a rash, impatient man who wanted to get things done and cared little who was antagonized in the process. His Radicalism in aim and impetuosity in method made it certain that he would arouse far greater antagonisms than his mother did in her long and fruitful reign.

The Reaction Against the Josephine Reforms

The main policies of Joseph may be classified under the following headings: the reform of religious "abuses" and the establishment of religious toleration; the centralization of the monarchy and abolition of all obstacles to absolutism; the taxation of the nobility on terms similar to those of commoners; the encouragement of manufacturing through the suppression of guild privileges; the improvement of the lot of the peasantry; and the creation of a uniform and modern system of justice. All these policies evoked vigorous and articulate opposition. Having already discussed the opposition to Joseph's religious policies in Ch. 3, we shall now survey the opposition to his other policies.[8]

[8] I have used the standard works on Joseph II: Paul von Mitrofanov, *Joseph II. Seine politische und kulturelle Tätigkeit.* Trans. fom the Russian by V. von Demelic (2 vols., paged consecutively, Vienna and Leipzig, 1910), encyclopedic

Joseph's centralization was felt with an especially heavy hand in Hungary, where the emperor ended his mother's prudent moderation by introducing the administrative reforms hitherto confined to the other parts of the monarchy. He refused to be crowned at Pressburg lest he be forced to swear an oath to the Hungarian constitution, and angered Hungarian public opinion by transferring the crown of St. Stephen from Pressburg to Vienna in 1784; Joseph was either oblivious to the symbolic importance of the transfer or chose deliberately to ignore it. He did not summon a single Hungarian *Reichstag* during his ten years' reign. Another unpopular innovation was the introduction of German as the "language of administration" throughout the entire monarchy. For Joseph, who was free of German nationalist feeling, this was a matter of utilitarian convenience, not deliberate Germanization; he was probably surprised that the proud and sensitive Magyars refused to see the matter in this light. Joseph also refused to respect the venerable structure of the Hungarian counties *(Komitate)* with their tradition of aristocratic self-government. He sought to destroy aristocratic power by replacing the elected *Vicegespane* (the main county official) with appointed bureaucrats surrounded by large staffs (composed too often of German "carpet-baggers"), while simultaneously dividing Hungary into ten districts headed by appointed *District-Kommissionäre*, which replaced the *Komitate* as the effective centers of administration.

These administrative reforms, the general policy of treating Hungary as an integral part of the Habsburg Monarchy, and the specific application of new social and fiscal measures (to be discussed below) brought Hungary to the point of open rebellion by the autumn of 1789. At that time Joseph lay in his last illness and his army was preoccupied with an unpopular and inglorious war against the Turks. The Hungarians felt that they could oppose the now impotent emperor with impunity. The suppressed county diets met in defiance of the Viennese government; royal officials ceased to be obeyed; German bureaucrats appointed by Joseph had to flee for their lives; the language ordinance became a dead letter; while taxes ceased to be

---

and balanced in its treatment; Saul K. Padover, *The Revolutionary Emperor. Joseph II 1741-1790* (New York, 1934), good as a biography but superficial on reforms; V. Bibl, *Kaiser Joseph II. Ein Vorkämpfer der grossdeutschen Idee* (Vienna, 1943), excellent despite its occasional lapses into Nazi jargon; H. Benedikt, *Kaiser Joseph II, 1741-1790. Mit Benutzung ungedruckter Quellen* (Vienna, 1936), a solid but conventional biography; and Francois Fejtö, *Un Habsbourg revolutionnaire. Joseph II, portrait d'un despote éclairé* (Paris, 1953), the brilliant but undocumented study of a gifted amateur.

paid on the ground that they had never been properly voted by any Hungarian *Reichstag*. There was much popular clamor for the return of the Hungarian crown to Pressburg, a clamor to which the dying emperor yielded upon the unanimous advice of his Hungarian counselors. He also promised the assembling of a new *Reichstag* (the first since 1765) and the return to the constitutional position of 1780. His brother Leopold, in implementing these belated concessions, was able to prevent the armed insurrection which threatened in the winter of 1789-90.[9]

Joseph's policy of centralization was part and parcel of his policy of absolutism. His autocratic temper found the traditional prerogatives of the *Stände* intolerable, and he sought their direct abolition instead of simply continuing the silent "hollowing out" so skillfully begun by his mother. The customary act of coronation (or homage) was omitted in the Austrian provinces as well as in Hungary. The *Landesausschüsse*, committees which looked after *Stände* rights between the sessions of the plenum, were officially abolished on April 4, 1784; the *Stände* were given little comfort by the conferral of the right to appoint two counselors (*Gubernialräte*) to participate in the work of each provincial government. The *Stände* were also deprived of their traditional right to suggest nominees for several honorific provincial posts (*Marschälle, Provinzialhauptleute,* et cetera)—a matter deeply resented by the old aristocratic families from whose ranks they had been drawn. It goes without saying that Joseph also continued his mother's policy of undermining the fiscal rights of the *Stände,* and that he refused to tolerate any kind of *Stände*-controlled administrative organs competing with his own.

Joseph insisted, indeed, upon building up an effective bureaucratic apparatus extending from the local *Kreis* to the central administration in Vienna. He systematized the government's hitherto sporadic supervision over the exercise of patrimonial justice and seignorial administration; enlarged the staff and functions of the bureaucratic *Kreisbehörden;* and increased the efficiency of the *Gubernien* (chief administrative bodies) of the various provinces, now quite free of *Stände* influence despite the nominal concession of the appointment of two *Gubernialräte*. Even more important than these institutional reforms was the general spirit with which Joseph tried to imbue his bureaucrats. They were expected to follow orders with military precision,

[9] The indispensable book on Hungary under Joseph is Henry Marczali, *Hungary in the Eighteenth Century* (Cambridge, 1910). Joseph's clash with Hungarian nationalism is analyzed by Mitrofanov, *Joseph II*, pp. 299ff.

were supervised by an elaborate spy apparatus, and were graded by notorious *Conduitenlisten* (a kind of annual report card). They were expected to work long hours at low pay, and find their reward in the consciousness that they were instruments of progress and *Aufklärung*. Joseph viewed them as extensions of his own omniscient and omnipotent self, and they were destined to share the emperor's unpopularity in full measure.[10]

These Josephine policies aroused furious though at first rather muted opposition. The *Stände* were cowed by Joseph's control of the army and police; the full force of the long-repressed opposition became apparent only during the first few months of the reign of Leopold. At that time nearly every *Landtag* passed resolutions condemning Joseph's tyranny ex post facto; the most celebrated of these protests, that of the Bohemian *Stände*, will be discussed in detail below. Here it will suffice to quote the "remonstrance and petition of the *Stände* deputies of Tyrol concerning the confirmation of their traditional liberties *(Landesfreiheiten)*" of December 2, 1790, which is especially revealing because it shows that opposition to absolutism and centralization was one and the same thing:

> The *Stände* ask most humbly for the abandonment of the pattern of uniformity *(angenommenen Gleichheitssystem)* recently introduced [in the entire monarchy]. All future decrees should be exclusively framed with reference to the constitution, local circumstances, and other conditions of the *Land* of Tyrol, which all differ sharply from those of the other hereditary provinces; they should not be derived from any abstract and uniform norm, or from what has been found useful in some other province.[11]

This provincial outlook was also expressed forcefully by *Landeshauptmann* Franz von Lodron:

> What does it concern the people of Tyrol what happens in Bohemia, Moravia, and other countries? The Tyrolese have their own sovereign, their own laws, their own constitution, and their own country. It is a matter of pure accident that their prince also happens to rule over other countries. They are flattered, of course, that they have a prince-protector who is a great monarch and rules over

---

[10] All these administrative matters are covered exhaustively by Mitrofanov, *Joseph II*, Bk. II, Ch. 3. A more recent treatment is F. Walter, *Die Geschichte der österreichischen Zentralverwaltung unter Joseph II und Leopold II* (2 vols., Vienna, 1950).

[11] Quoted in Mitrofanov, *Joseph II*, pp. 307-08, n.3.

numerous provinces, but they do not wish to pay for this honor by the loss of their fundamental laws, which are guaranteed to them by God and *Stände* alike *(worüber ihnen Gott und die Stände Bürgschaft leisten)*.[12]

Joseph's attempt to apply equal tax rates to aristocratic and peasant lands in his decree of February 10, 1789, provoked sharp opposition from the nobility. Joseph unveiled the Radical character of his proposal in the introductory sentence: "One must go to the bottom of things and determine a general principle, disregarding whatever customs and prejudices have been established in the course of centuries."[13] Joseph's general principle was that all land should be taxed equally, regardless of whether it was owned by noble, peasant, Church, or state. The equal treatment of land by the tax collector was only a corollary of the equal treatment of men—a principle which required the elimination of all aristocratic privilege in fiscal matters:

> From a fiscal point of view aristocrats are, as regards their lands, no different from peasants or cattle merchants; in cities they are ordinary house owners [in paying real estate taxes] and consumers [in paying excises]; on the road and on ferry-boats they are ordinary road users and passengers [in paying dues]. In each of these cases they must be treated on an identical footing with all other inhabitants.[14]

A good many high Josephine officials, including the respected *Oberst-Hofkanzler* Count Kolowrat, found it hard to accept this principle and remonstrated with the emperor while the tax decree was still in preparation. Joseph was very abrupt with the count: "I consider your objections to be empty talk and a total waste of time *(leeres Geschwätz und überflüssiger Zeitverlust)*. They are scarecrows and their circulation can only stimulate discontent and create a completely artificial panic."[15] The promulgation of the decree led to remarkable protests from several *Stände* bodies which happened to be in session. The *Stände* of Styria called the new tax both ruinous and unconstitutional and demanded its immediate suspension. Its novel and severe character would destroy the economic basis of aristocracy; its imposition without prior *Stände* approval, and collection by bu-

[12] Quoted in A. Wolf, *Österreich unter Maria Theresia etc.*, p. 370.
[13] Quoted in Mitrofanov, *Joseph II*, p. 417.
[14] Quoted in ibid., p. 421, from a Hungarian tax decree of Feb. 10, 1786.
[15] Quoted in ibid., p. 470.

reaucratic bodies not subject to *Stände* control, was a clear violation of the Styrian constitution (June 9, 1789):

> We are prompted to present this petition out of the love of truth and justice which we owe to our Fatherland and to Your Majesty. . . . If this humble petition, which we present with a heavy heart to the best, most gracious, and most just of monarchs . . . should be rejected there would be no limit to our despair. We would be confronted by a most terrible situation: robbed of our property, deprived of our prosperity, we would also lose our (collective) credit and appear to the world as an unreliable debtor.[16]

The last point was intended as a threat since the *Stände* had always underwritten governmental debts.

The *Stände* of Krain were even more categorical in their protest. They passed a fiery resolution when Joseph lay dying and was no longer in a position to retaliate (Jan. 9, 1790):

> We cannot accept the new tax register since it undermines public and private credit, robs landowners of half their income, destroys the existing equilibrium of society, and shakes the foundations of our constitutional life.[17]

The strength of these protests succeeded in inducing Leopold to cancel the tax decree formally on April 19, 1790.

Joseph's desire to promote manufactures by curtailing guild restrictions inevitably aroused resentment among the injured guildsmen. They pointed to the disastrous multiplication of tradesmen which resulted from free entry into a given craft, and the collapse in product quality when guild regulations were no longer enforced. Their main point was, however, that they were unjustly and without compensation deprived of long-standing rights—a special injustice in view of the fact that they had always tried conscientiously to serve the public. This point was made, for example, in the following protest delivered by the Viennese butchers' guild to the city magistrate on Nov. 30, 1782:

> We do not wish to elaborate upon the care we have taken for so many years to serve the public without complaint. The public was not allowed to notice the difficulties caused by cattle sickness in Hungary, war, or numerous other misfortunes. . . . It is all the more bitter for us to lose all at once, our property, our economic position,

[16] Quoted in ibid., pp. 471-72.
[17] Quoted in ibid., p. 474.

and the hope of maintaining our wives and children, and especially the hope of raising the latter as honorable citizens.[18]

The emperor's emancipation of the serfs (1782) was protested by the aristocratic *Stände* and several Conservative pamphleteers. It was argued that serfdom was a mutually beneficial institution in view of the primitive outlook of the peasantry, a class which could not possibly use its freedom wisely. The lord's loss of banalities and various other traditional dues constituted an obviously unjust confiscation of private property by despotic fiat. The economic and moral result of the abolition of serfdom must prove disastrous. The peasants, once freed from the lord's direct pressure, would lapse into their natural laziness; the inevitable result would be the return of ploughland to grass and the frequent spoilage of crops due to the unavailability of harvest hands. The idle peasant would know nothing better to do with his time than to patronize the local alehouse to the point of bankruptcy and physical degeneration. It would be foolish for the government to expect gratitude from such a group; on the contrary, their newly won idleness would multiply their discontent and promote rebelliousness against whatever obligations still survived.[19]

Joseph's judicial reforms, which aimed at centralizing and modernizing the administration of justice throughout the monarchy, provoked many Conservative complaints. On the administrative side there was protest when Joseph set up six courts with appellate jurisdiction which ignored provincial boundaries; several *Stände* bodies complained about lawsuits being appealed to "foreign" courts—another example of how a tenacious localism was the strongest obstacle to the emperor's reform program. Aristocrats complained about a new policy which made the exercise of patrimonial justice a burden rather than a privilege: the lords who maintained patrimonial courts were required to appoint a university-trained judge (not, as had too often been the case, some untutored bailiff) and pay him out of their own pocket.[20]

Joseph's reform of the substance of the law provoked controversy upon several points. Aristocrats complained about a provision establishing equal inheritance rights for all the children in a family, because it violated the hallowed institution of primogenitive entail; clericals were aroused when Joseph decreed that illegitimate children receive rights equal to those born in wedlock. Even more vociferous

[18] Quoted in ibid., p. 490n.
[19] Numerous sources elaborating these points are quoted in ibid., pp. 628-47.
[20] Ibid., pp. 549-55.

was the aristocratic protest against the abolition of special aristocratic courts long notorious for dealing out lenient penalties to aristocratic offenders. Joseph insisted upon the identical treatment of noble and commoner in the punishment of crime, even when the punishment involved degrading exposure in the pillory and street-cleaning by convicts chained together. The *Stände* of Lower Austria declared their opposition to this:

> Such punishments as corporal beating, exhibition in the pillory, etc. hit the upper classes with special severity on account of their education, refined sentiments, and accustomed comfort of life; the low-born find these punishments severe *only* on account of the physical pain involved. The aristocrat loses, on the other hand, everything—all of his status and former position of privilege.[21]

It should be noted that these various protests against the religious, administrative, fiscal, economic, and judicial policies of Emperor Joseph tended to reinforce one another and to create a widespread sentiment of opposition to Joseph's reforms in their totality. Most aristocrats, clergymen, and urban patricians were convinced that the emperor aimed at a complete subversion of traditional society in doctrinaire conformity with the most Radical principles of the *Aufklärung*. We already saw in Ch. 3 that this charge was untrue in the field of religion, and it appears certain that there was a Reform Conservative *intention* in many of Joseph's other policies as well. In conversations with his entourage he himself defended his reforms as the only alternative to revolution.

Joseph's *Hofkanzler,* Count Rudolf Chotek (1748-1824), was a sharp foe of the tax reform of 1789 because he considered it unjust to the aristocracy. Chotek carried opposition to the point of resigning his high office and writing to the emperor, "My conscience does not permit me to put my name under a decree which does so much injustice to the nobility." The emperor replied, "My dear Chotek, is it not better to give some timely relief to the peasantry instead of creating a situation where they will eventually refuse to pay landlords anything at all?" Chotek replied that matters would never come to such a pass since recalcitrant peasants could always be *compelled* to pay their dues. "Compelled?" replied the emperor. "You must remember that the third estate possesses, collectively, the greatest physical power

21 Ibid., p. 569.

in the state. Believe me, if the peasants ever refuse to pay we will all be ruined" (*Wenn der Bauer nicht will, sind wir alle pritsch*).[22]

A further piece of evidence for Joseph's Reform Conservatism is that he encountered opposition from the Left as well as the Right. The intellectuals of the Left criticized the limited character of Joseph's religious toleration, the survival of censorship however attenuated, the failure to accept the Physiocratic program of total free trade, the continued *de facto* ascendancy of the aristocracy in government (58 out of 65 *Kreishauptleute* were aristocrats), and the general neglect of cultural enterprises. They also joined Conservatives in denouncing Joseph's militarism and policy of imperialist aggrandizement, and were critical of his despotism while not, of course, sharing the aristocratic hankering after the anachronistic *Stände*. The discontent was not confined to intellectuals, for there was mass resentment in the face of extensive conscription, price increases resulting from the termination of internal price controls, the abolition of the usury laws, and the too slow pace of agrarian reform. This popular discontent, based upon economic grievances, easily merged with opposition to the emperor's interference with customary ecclesiastical ritual.

The opposition of the Left gave Joseph a sense of bitterness, frustration, and anger against the ingratitude of the beneficiaries of his reforms. He met it by reorganizing the police under the efficient Count Pergen, whose main task was to watch over, and if possible influence, public opinion. The censorship was tightened to protect the public against the horde of Radical scribblers (*Broschürenschmierer*), and a new stamp tax aimed deliberately at placing newspapers out of the reach of lower-class citizens. Booksellers who dealt in foreign literature were closely supervised and in some cases arbitrarily harassed; thus Georg Wucherer (to give only one example), the Viennese agent of Bahrdt's proposed *Deutsche Union*, was fined, his book supply pulped, and he was finally banished. There is some evidence that Joseph's deathbed concessions to his Reactionary opponents, as in the revocation of most of his Hungarian reforms, were due in part to fear of the Radical genii he had aroused, and not just a capitulation to his Conservative entourage.[23]

[22] Quoted by Albert Jäger, *Kaiser Joseph II und Leopold II* (Vienna, 1867), p. 168. The essential Conservatism of Joseph is also argued in the slight and fragmentary article by F. Valjavec, "Die Josephinischen Wurzeln des österreichischen Konservatismus," *Südost-Forschungen*, XIV (1955), 166-75.

[23] The best treatment of the opposition from the Left is the study by Ernst Wangermann, *From Joseph II to the Jacobin Trials* (Oxford, 1959), Bk. I, Ch. 3. The much discussed problem of Joseph's attitude toward the censorship has

The life of the "enlightened" emperor ended in sadness and tragedy. He died, prematurely aged at forty-nine after a reign of only ten
years, of an illness caught while campaigning against the Turks in the
unhealthy Danubian swamps. His foreign and domestic policies were
both in shambles. The Turkish war had exposed serious weaknesses in
Habsburg military organization, and a new war threatened against a
Prussia unwilling to allow Austrian gains in the Balkans without generous Polish compensations for herself. The French Revolution had
just destroyed the value of the Bourbon-Habsburg alliance, the keynote of Austrian foreign policy since 1756. Hungary stood on the
verge of rebellion despite the appeasing concessions, considered too
little and too late, made by the dying emperor. Belgium, whose affairs
have not been treated here because peripheral to our subject, had
successfully proclaimed its independence. Habsburg finances had
been ruined by the war despite numerous new levies (widely considered unconstitutional) imposed by the government. The long-
cowed *Stände* were preparing to ventilate their grievances. The aristocracy smarted under a decade of humiliation and was resolved to
prevent the implementation of the tax decree of February 10, 1789.
A large part of the clergy supported Cardinal Migazzi in his opposition to the Josephine reform program, while dispossessed monks
viewed Joseph as the incarnate Antichrist. To add to the monarchy's
troubles there was also much discontent among the champions and
beneficiaries of Joseph's reforms, especially intellectuals and peasants.
Leopold assumed a difficult inheritance when he succeeded Joseph in
the spring of 1790.[24]

The Reign of Leopold[25]

LEOPOLD'S PRINCIPLES

Joseph's younger brother Leopold was in many ways ideally suited to
"clean up" the difficulties left behind by the dead emperor. The new

recently been given fresh treatment by Oskar Sashegyi, *Zensur und Geistesfreiheit
unter Joseph II. Ein Beitrag zur Kulturgeschichte der habsburgischen Länder*
(Budapest, 1958).

[24] The position of Joseph in Austrian public opinion at the time of his death
is analyzed by F. Engel-Janosi, "Josephs II Tod im Urteil seiner Zeitgenossen,"
Mitt. d. Inst. für Österreichische Geschichtsforschung, XLIV (1930), 324-46.

[25] All earlier treatments of Leopold have been superseded by the classic biography of Adam Wandruszka, *Leopold II. Erzherzog von Österreich, Grossherzog
von Toskana, König von Ungarn und Böhmen, Römischer Kaiser* (2 vols., Vienna,
1963-64). A concise summary of the author's conclusions is "Die Persönlichkeit
Kaiser Leopolds II," *HZ*, 192 (1961), 295-317. For Leopold's foreign policy the

ruler in fact agreed with most of Joseph's objectives, especially the subordination of the Church to the state and the breaking of the privileges of the aristocracy. But he was free of his brother's doctrinaire outlook and ruthless disregard for human feelings; rather, he followed their mother, Maria Theresia, in a policy of *suaviter in modo*. He was exceptionally well qualified to assume heavy responsibilities on the basis of his experience as Grand Duke of Tuscany during the preceding quarter century (1765-90). Leopold had long followed Habsburg affairs closely in the expectation that he would eventually succeed Joseph, since the latter had no direct heir and refused to contemplate another marriage after the death of his second wife in 1768. His position of junior member of the House of Habsburg had precluded open opposition to Joseph's policies, though privately he was sharply critical of such blunders as the invasion of Hungarian and Belgian constitutional rights and the launching of the war against the Turks while the army was poorly prepared. His personal relations with Joseph were also clouded by the emperor's despotic temperament and his interference with the education of Leopold's children. (Joseph had gone so far as to take the future Emperor Francis with him to Vienna in 1784, away from his parents, when he was only 15, in order to supervise personally his further training.) A brooder like Leopold also must have agonized over his position as younger brother whom the accident of primogeniture reduced to a secondary role—a bitter fate, since he felt far better qualified to rule than the impetuous and imprudent Joseph, and must have felt that the latter's folly was ruining his future inheritance.[26]

Leopold's personality repelled most of his contemporaries, and he has generally won but grudging admiration from modern historians. He was abnormally suspicious of his fellow men, and gave much personal attention to developing an elaborate espionage network. He took a malicious delight in ferreting out the weaknesses of others and had little generosity of spirit. His effectiveness was often paralyzed by

---

indispensable source is Adolf Beer, *Leopold II, Franz II und Catherina. Ihre Correspondenz, nebst einer Einleitung: zur Geschichte der Politik Leopold's II* (Leipzig, 1874).

[26] The relationship between Joseph and Leopold, and the latter's attitude toward the reforms of the former, is analyzed by Alfons Huber, *Die Politik Josephs II beurteilt von seinem Bruder Leopold von Toscana* (Innsbruck, 1877). The basic source is A. von Arneth (ed.), *Joseph II und Leopold von Toscana. Ihr Briefwechsel von 1781 bis 1890* (2 vols., Vienna, 1872), though the official correspondence naturally minimizes the friction between the two. The best psychological analysis of the relationship is in Wandruszka, *Leopold II*, passim.

bouts of melancholy. Leopold's greatest asset was his cold, piercing intelligence and an uncanny ability to differentiate between the possible and the merely desirable. He was fully abreast of the most enlightened thought of his age, and eagerly sought the approbation of the men of the *Aufklärung*. There can be no question of his deep devotion to the principles of religious toleration, legal equality, and—in this departing from his brother Joseph—constitutional self-government.

Joseph was an autocrat by temperament, principle, and practice. Leopold wanted, on the contrary, to limit the power of the prince through a written constitution protecting the inviolable rights of man, and he favored strong parliamentary bodies to distribute the burden of governmental responsibility. Leopold stated this position most eloquently in the remarkable "political confession of faith" sent to his sister Marie Christine on Jan. 25, 1790, on the very eve of his mounting the Austrian throne:

> I believe that any ruler, even one succeeding by hereditary right, is only a delegate or official of the people, and that it is his vocation to serve the people no matter how great the trouble and labor this involves. I believe that every country ought to possess a constitution based upon a contract between people and ruler, a contract which defines the authority and sets limits to the competences of the latter; that a ruler who fails to abide by that contract in fact abdicates his position (since it has been conferred upon him subject to specific stipulations), and that no man is thereafter morally bound to obey him; that while the executive power belongs to the ruler the legislative power belongs to the people and their representatives. . . . The ruler must never interfere, directly or indirectly, with the administration of civil or criminal law, whether by giving instructions or altering penalties. The ruler is obligated to give an account of the state of the public finances and his expenditure of public revenues. He must never arbitrarily collect taxes or dues, for this right belongs exclusively to the people and may be exercised only after the ruler has explained the needs of the state and the people's representatives have accepted his explanation as justifiable and reasonable. . . . I believe, in conclusion, that the ruler must rule in accordance with the law, and that the people—his sovereign (*Vollmachtsgeber*)—may neither silently renounce its natural, inalienable rights, nor be deprived of them. The people gives itself a ruler, i.e. it confers upon a specified individual powers to promote its happiness and welfare not in accordance with his will, but in accord-

415

ance with *its own;* for the sole purpose of government is to promote the happiness of each individual.[27]

The origins of Leopold's political outlook, unique even in an age when many rulers prided themselves upon being "enlightened," have been endlessly discussed. It appears that several factors were at work. Leopold had been deeply influenced by the teachings of his "enlightened" tutor Karl Anton Martini while he was still an adolescent, and this influence was deepened by the reading of French Physiocratic authors (especially Turgot). Leopold was interested in the American Revolution and maintained an indirect contact with Benjamin Franklin. Some personal experiences were probably also relevant: his unhappy dual position as sovereign prince of Tuscany while simultaneously remaining a "subject" of the despotic Joseph II made him appreciate the value of constitutional guarantees. Several members of his court entourage were closely tied to the aristocratic world of Carinthia, where the preabsolutist *Stände* still exercised much power, and they probably encouraged Leopold's "constitutional consciousness." In his ideas on government he sought a synthesis between the virtually dead world of the medieval *Stände* and the as-yet only embryonic Liberal-democratic aspirations of his age. There is reason to believe that Leopold's advocacy of constitutionalism also owed something to his detached assessment of contemporary forces; he could joke about monarchy's becoming an increasingly bankrupt profession, and saw that educated, prosperous Europeans would not permanently tolerate being governed by absolute monarchs, no matter how enlightened. Leopold wanted to distribute the burden of governmental responsibility, and was fond of enumerating the advantages which strong parliamentary bodies brought to princes willing to cooperate with them. His rationalist temperament provided him with the comforting but false belief that strong monarchy and independent legislatures could long coexist in fruitful harmony.[28]

LEOPOLD'S GOVERNMENTAL MEASURES

The major achievements of the brief reign of Leopold (1790-92) were the restoration of the diplomatic position of the Habsburg Empire, the pacification of Hungary and Belgium, and the defeat of the domestic Austrian opposition against the centralized absolutism set up by Joseph. In the field of foreign policy Leopold saw the imperative

[27] Quoted by Wolf, *Österreich unter Maria Theresia*, pp. 325-26.
[28] The entire question is discussed exhaustively by Wandruszka, *Leopold II*, ɪ, 368ff.

necessity of terminating the Turkish war and preventing the Prussian attack which threatened in 1790. He courageously reversed Austria's anti-Prussian policy of the past fifty years by offering the olive branch to Frederick William II. The result was the famous Convention of Reichenbach (July 27, 1790), ostensibly a humiliation for Austria because it was compelled to renounce Balkan conquests despite its recent military exertions; but in reality it was a master stroke because it deprived the disaffected elements in Belgium and Hungary of their Prussian patron, insulated these "internal problems" from "foreign" influences, and thereby created a situation where monarchical authority could be restored.

We have seen above how Joseph himself had canceled many of his Hungarian reforms on his deathbed; Leopold carried this policy of concession still farther. He summoned the *Reichstag* promised by the dying Joseph, the first to be held since 1764, and swore fidelity to the Hungarian constitution prior to his coronation at Pressburg on Nov. 15, 1790. Yet there were limits to his concessions, as was shown by his adamant refusal to accept a proposed new "coronation diploma" whose terms were less favorable to the Crown than those granted to his mother, Maria Theresia, in 1741. Leopold succeeded in overcoming the opposition of the proud Hungarian nobility by a skillful mixture of flattery and threats; the latter included but slightly veiled sympathy for the aspirations of non-Magyar nationalities (especially Serbs and Rumanians), the fanning of burgher and peasant discontent against the Hungarian *status quo* (to be discussed in the next chapter), and the exposure of treasonable contacts made by some leading Magyars with Prussian emissaries while they were preparing their rebellion against Joseph in 1789.

Leopold proved equally skillful in appeasing discontent within the Austrian provinces of the monarchy. While maintaining most of the Josephine ecclesiastical program he encouraged the bishops to submit complaints directly to him; and he offered the abolition of the hated General Seminaries as a major concession. Leopold also cracked down upon irreligious literature through new censorship regulations issued on August 10, 1790. The morale of bureaucrats was improved by the abolition of the hated *Conduitenlisten,* public opinion appeased by the firing of the unpopular Police Minister, Count Pergen (though Leopold refused to alter Josephine espionage practices). There was also general relief at the abolition of the severe and degrading pun-

417

ishment of criminals to which Joseph had shown such an unenlightened attachment.[29]

Most important of all was Leopold's partial appeasement of the Reactionary aristocracy by the formal cancellation of Joseph's controversial land tax edict of Feb. 10, 1789. Leopold tried hard to avoid making this step look like a slap at the memory of his dead brother:

> We have been convinced, after examining the consequences upon the welfare of the landlords *(Grund-Obrigkeiten)* and their subjects, that the system introduced by my late beloved brother is not likely to fulfill his benevolent intentions *(landesväterliche Absichten)*. We are certain that he would have himself repealed it if all the evil consequences now evident had already shown themselves while he was still alive.[30]

This reasoning could not have sounded very convincing in view of the fact that it was dated April 19, 1790—less than two months after Joseph's death.

The aristocracy was also pleased by Leopold's consent to the restoration of some of the powers of the provincial *Stände* bodies. We have seen above how he cherished the principle of self-government and valued the *Stände* as a restraint upon monarchical tyranny. Leopold was, however, far from blind to the fact that the surviving *Stände* were dominated by aristocratic privilege, and he was resolved both to enlarge their composition and to minimize concessions to their Reactionary demands. The *Stände* were allowed to assemble in most provinces in the summer of 1790, and passed—as we have already seen by several examples—numerous ex post facto denunciations of the tyranny of Joseph. It would be wearisome to examine the work of all these bodies; we will instead describe in detail the composition and resolutions of one of the most important, the Bohemian Diet of 1790-91, whose records are unusually well preserved. It has received modern monographic treatment by a distinguished American historian, and is unusually well suited to bring out the full scope of Reactionary desires in the Habsburg Monarchy of the early 1790's.[31]

[29] The concessions of Leopold are carefully chronicled in Ernst Wangermann, op.cit., Bk. II, Ch. 1: "The Continuation of the Retreat from Enlightened Absolutism."

[30] Quoted by Mitrofanov, *Joseph II*, p. 478, n.3.

[31] An excellent survey of the revival of *Stände* life under Leopold can be found in Wolf, *Österreich unter Maria Theresia etc.*, Bk. IV, Ch. 3: "Die Restauration der erbländischen Verfassungen." Two of the diets have received somewhat old-fashioned scholarly treatments in Heinrich Ignaz Bidermann, "Die

THE BOHEMIAN STÄNDE AND THE LEOPOLDINE GOVERNMENT

It will be recalled that the powers of all the *Stände* bodies of the various Habsburg provinces had fallen into virtual desuetude under Maria Theresia and, more especially, Joseph. They had continued to meet on rare occasions to hear the financial demands *(Postulata)* of the government, but usually only to grant them after a minimum of discussion. Their administrative functions had been almost completely eliminated through the advance of bureaucratic absolutism, their earlier domination of provincial government had shrunk to the right to nominate two *Gubernialräte* to serve in the *Gubernium*. The impotence of the *Stände* had been shown by Joseph's refusal to be crowned in their presence; by the formal abolition of the *Landes-ausschüsse* (committees to protect *Stände* rights between regular sessions) as useless bodies in 1784; and by the fact that they were not consulted by the emperor when he introduced the famous land tax of 1789.

The right to sit in the Bohemian Diet belonged in the 1780's to some one hundred nobles, upper clergy, and representatives of towns. Actual attendance during the Josephine period had rarely exceeded twenty-five, of which at least two thirds held bureaucratic posts which made them subject to pressure by the royal governor. The government possessed, in short, a working majority in the unlikely case that there was serious resistance to royal demands. Yet it was this rather unpromising body which briefly stirred to life to become an instrument of opposition to Leopold's government. The news that Hungary had been successful in its agitation for the restoration of a powerful Diet induced several Bohemian nobles to meet informally to talk about the organization of opposition to Joseph's fiscal and economic policies in the winter of 1789-90. They hoped to revive the moribund Diet as an instrument for defending aristocratic powers over the peasantry and maintaining traditional tax exemptions. The moment Joseph was dead they gave themselves formal status as a so-called "Little Diet" in March 1790. The adjective "little" was a euphemism covering the irregularity arising from the absence of a royal summons; the number

---

Verfassungskrisis in Steiermark zur Zeit der ersten französischen Revolution," *Mitt. d. hist. Vereins für Steiermark*, XXI (1873), and D'Elvert, "Die Desiderien der mährischen Stände und ihre Folgen," *Schriften der hist. statist. Section der Mährisch-schlesischen Gesellschaft*, XIV (1864). The following section is based upon the exhaustive and lucid monograph by Robert J. Kerner, *Bohemia in the Eighteenth Century, a study in political, economic and social history with special reference to the reign of Leopold II* (New York, 1932).

attending was in fact seventy-five, whereas the last regular Diet (1789) had been attended by only twenty-five participants. The Little Diet elected a new *Landesausschuss* of sixteen members (to fill the void left by Joseph's abolition of that body six years previously), and instructed it to draft grievances *(Desideria)* for submission to a "Big Diet" and subsequent presentation to the emperor. The leading spirit of the committee was Baron William Hugo MacNeven (1734-1814), the scion of a distinguished Irish-Bohemian family which combined aristocratic status with middle-class connections. (His father had been a professor of medicine at Prague University.) MacNeven was an ideal spokesman for the Reactionary party because of his expert knowledge, *savoir faire,* and residual moderation. A passionate antiquary, he authored an erudite *Historical Exposition* of the rights of the *Stände* which denied all the premises of Habsburg absolutism. His preabsolutist outlook had not been shaken by active participation in the work of Josephine government as one of the two Diet-appointed *Gubernialräte* sitting with the Bohemian *Gubernium.* MacNeven knew the government he was attacking from the inside out.

A "Big Diet" met on July 12, 1790, with the full membership of about a hundred in attendance. That times had changed was demonstrated by the fact that it was invited to submit its grievances *(Desideria)* to the government instead of merely receiving the customary *Postulata.* (The *Postulata* were in fact presented only on November 10, 1790, long after the *Desideria* had been formulated though not yet presented to the emperor.) The *Landesausschuss* selected by the Little Diet had worked hard to draw up a long list of *Desideria,* which was reported to the plenum by MacNeven as committee reporter. They were then subjected to debate in the liveliest political discussions known in Bohemia since the early seventeenth century. An ultra-Reactionary party under a certain Count Buquoy could usually muster some 40 votes, enough to goad but not to outvote the more moderate Reactionaries headed by MacNeven. After being voted, the *Desideria* were submitted to the Bohemian *Gubernium,* which in turn sent them to the chancellery in Vienna *(Böhmisch-Österreichische Hofkanzlei).*

The *Hofkanzlei* thereupon commissioned advisory opinions from its own standing commissions on education, religion, et cetera, and a newly appointed *ad hoc* Commission on *Desideria* before replying to the Diet. Additional opinions were solicited from the *Staatsrat* and the *Oberste Justizstelle* before the official replies were worked out by the *Hofkanzlei-Konferenz.* These would become official *Hofdekrete* or *Patente* after approval and signature by the Emperor Leopold, whose personal touch is revealed by many last-minute alterations. The historian must be grateful to this somewhat cumbersome process because it has led to the survival of much fascinating material on the clash between Bohemian Reactionaries and the Leopoldine government.

The *Desideria* were consolidated by the *Stände* into three major documents which received separate answers from the emperor. They deal respectively with constitutional, economic, and miscellaneous (mostly religious) questions, and we will examine them in this order. The *Desideria* illustrate the substance of Reactionary discontent in the early 1790's; the Leopoldine answers, the measure of the "retreat from absolutism" considered prudent by the emperor.

The constitutional demands of the *Stände* were preceded by the previously mentioned *Historical Exposition,* which chronicled the glorious record of the Bohemian Diet through half a millennium of history. The exposition relied strongly upon ex parte sources to claim inflated precedents of *Stände* power in the fields of administration, taxation, and legislation; it flatly denied the Habsburg contention that medieval *Stände* rights had been forfeited by the rebellion of 1620; and argued, citing the social contract doctrine (here put to Reactionary uses), that the Bohemian crown was elective rather than hereditary. The exposition, to be sure, explicitly repudiated any desire to restore the full historic rights of the *Stände,* but it wanted to state them at length in order to convince Leopold of the moderation of the Diet's actual demands.

The Bohemian *Gubernium* replied to this *Historical Exposition* by a royalist counterpamphlet drawn up by *Gubernialrat* Joseph Paul von Riegger. (The sharp difference between his views and those of his colleague MacNeven was presumably not unconnected with the fact that one was a royal, the other a Diet nominee to the *Gubernium.*) Riegger showed that much of MacNeven's historical lore was inaccurate; that he had drawn most of his precedents from the Hussite period of the fourteenth century, when the *Stände* had usurped many a royal prerogative; and that his denial of the forfeiture of rights, following the crushing of the rebellion by Ferdinand II in 1620, was bad history and worse law. Riegger argued further that constitutional rights must always be interpreted in the light of historical developments, and that the course of Bohemian affairs during the fifty years of effective absolutism under Maria Theresia and Joseph could not be lightly disregarded.

Of greater immediate importance than these theoretical controversies was the specific demand that the consent of the Diet should again become necessary for the validity of either new laws or new taxes. In his reply Leopold refused to renounce the by-now traditional Habsburg right to issue new laws by virtue of his prerogative, though he willingly accepted the right of the *Stände* to petition against any law so promulgated. (He rejected, however, the suggestion that such laws should be suspended for a year pending the royal reply to any *Diet* petition.) While willing to grant that taxes ordinarily required Diet approval, Leopold insisted that his tax prerogatives be maintained to cope with emergency situations. The emperor's reply was in fact firm to the point of insult, for it struck at the very foundations of *Stände* power by adding the suggestion that the latter did not necessarily represent the Bohemian nation, but only a small, privileged, aristocratic-oligarchic part of that nation. Leopold, thinking of himself as a spokesman for the entire Bohemian people, considered his mandate to be at least as representative as that possessed by the *Stände* magnates.

Leopold was willing to concede several demands aiming at the regularization of the constitutional position of the Diet. Meetings were henceforth to be held annually every spring, emergency meetings whenever necessary (though Leopold, with a slap at the Little Diet, declared these illegal if held without a royal summons). The attendance of forty members would henceforth be necessary to constitute a quorum, a change desired by the magnates to diminish the danger of royal domination. The Diet received (in slightly obscure language) the right to initiate legislation without seeking prior approval of the government, and to appeal over the head of the Bohemian *Gubernium* directly to the emperor in Vienna.

There was more controversy about the restoration of the regular *Landesausschuss* which, it will be recalled, Joseph had suppressed in 1784. It was clear that effective *Stände* institutions presupposed an interim body to represent the *Stände* between Diet sessions, formulate grievances as they arose, and supervise the parts of the administration still under Diet control. We have seen how the appointment of an irregular *Landesausschuss* had been the first work of the irregular Little Diet which assembled in March 1790. Leopold agreed in principle to the permanent restoration of such a committee though he was unwilling to give it the large powers it had exercised in the past and was exercising in 1790-91. Detailed discussion of its future role was postponed by Leopold because of the comparatively weak position of the monarchy at the moment; the *Stände* were to suffer defeat later when the issue was taken up again during the Franciscan period. The traditional supervision over *Stände*-controlled administrative bodies was in any case obsolete despite Leopold's symbolic restoration in 1791 of a *Ständekasse* (treasury controlled by the *Stände*), earlier abolished by Joseph. Leopold successfully opposed the *Stände* demand for the appointment of nobles drawn from its ranks to the leading positions in the Bohemian administration. The conciliatory emperor was quite willing to restore the sonorous titles which had accompanied such appointment in the past, but he refused to restore the functions abolished by Joseph in the course of his policy of bureaucratic centralization. His agreement to consult with the *Stände* before making major appointments likewise proved a concession of form rather than substance.

It may be said in summary that Leopold, while clinging to the essence of absolutism, was willing to tolerate a limited revival of *Stände* rights. He opposed all extreme *Stände* claims, and encouraged *Gubernialrat* Riegger to ridicule *Stände* pretensions, but he nonetheless acquiesced in the restoration of the conditions which had existed during the later reign of Maria Theresia. There was to be regular consultation on legislation and taxation, but more as a matter of royal courtesy than constitutional law, and always with the clear implication that the king could promulgate by royal edict what the *Stände* denied to his persuasion. Leopold's concessions were in fact so limited as to make the attempted aristocratic counterrevolution against two centuries of absolutist advance a complete failure.

The same may be said of the Diet demand for a repeal of some aspects of the Josephine judicial system. The Diet was bitterly opposed to the principle of equality before the law, and more especially the idea that all people should be tried before the same courts. The *Desideria* demanded the establishment of a special aristocratic senate in every Appellate Court, to be staffed by certain ex officio nobles, with exclusive jurisdiction over aristocratic offenders. This proposal was ridiculed by the *Gubernium, Hofkanzlei,* and *Oberste Justizstelle* alike, and never seriously considered. On the substance of law (as contrasted with its administration) Leopold was willing to make a few concessions to aristocratic demands and clerical prejudice. To give only two examples: the institution of entails (so important for preserving the material basis of aristocracy) was again permitted; while the Josephine inheritance law dictating equal shares to legitimate and illegitimate children was repealed.

Financial and economic grievances loom large in the *Desideria* of the Bohemian *Stände*. The financial grievances of the Diet were partly provincial in character, i.e., the complaint that Bohemia carried an excessive share of the total tax burden of the monarchy; partly aristocratic in character, i.e., the complaint that the nobility had been arbitrarily deprived of much of its traditional tax exemption. Bohemia paid between 25% and 30% of total Habsburg revenues although it contained only 10% of the area and 14% of the population of the empire —a fact which reflected, of course, Bohemia's position as the wealthiest and economically most developed part of the monarchy. The demand for a general redistribution of provincial burdens was, however, bound to fall upon deaf ears in Vienna because the Habsburg Monarchy had to cope with an over-all deficit of 26 million florins in 1790 despite the fact that Bohemia contributed a surplus of 3 1/2 million. The Diet complained to Leopold that some 11,200 nonexistent farmers had been assessed for tax liability in Bohemia ever since the inauguration of the Haugwitz financial reforms in 1748; as a result the province carried an unfair additional annual obligation of 570,000 florins. Leopold admitted the grievance but stated that he simply could not do without the money. There was a similar refusal to consider any general change in the allocation of tax quotas among the various Habsburg provinces. Leopold insisted that the needs of the central government must override the grievances (however justified) of any particular province, or even the promises rashly made by his predecessors. Leopold's mother, Maria Theresia, had promised in 1748 and again in 1767 to use part of the Bohemian surplus revenue to establish a sinking fund for the provincial Bohemian debt; but Joseph and Leopold refused to honor this commitment so long as a deficit persisted in the finances of the monarchy as a whole. The basic issue was whether Bohemia was a separate kingdom with but limited obligations to the Viennese government or whether it was an integral part of a centralized Habsburg government; and on this issue Leopold would not yield.

The greatest bitterness of all was produced by the controversy over the taxation of the landed property of the nobility. We have seen how Maria Theresia had terminated the traditional tax exemption of aristocratic lands in 1748, and that in 1789 Joseph had introduced the Radical principle that aristocratic lands should be taxed at the same rate as peasant lands. Joseph had ordered the creation of a new tax register which revealed that aristocratic lands had been scandalously undervalued in most cases and sometimes left totally untaxed because their existence was concealed (!) from the tax collector. Leopold, in his reply to the *Stände*, proved unwilling to abandon the principle of the equal taxation of all land, but in effect he surrendered part of the principle by agreeing to the abandonment of the Josephine tax register (with its fair valuations) in favor of the restoration of its inequitable Theresian predecessor. Henceforth all land, whether held by noble or peasant, was to be taxed at the uniform rate of $33\frac{1}{3}\%$; but, in view of the Theresian overassessment of peasant and underassessment of nobiliar land, this Leopoldine compromise—which was to last until 1867—must be considered a great victory for the aristocratic *Stände*.

Many of the economic demands of the Diet were flagrantly Reactionary and were opposed by Leopold insofar as he dared. Examples are the restoration of guild privileges, which Leopold granted in principle though implementation was postponed; the restoration of usury laws to provide cheap credit for noble landowners, which Leopold rejected as impracticable; and the restoration of some of the serfal obligations commuted or abolished in 1781 and 1789, which Leopold met with tactical finesse. We have already seen how he had canceled the tax patent of 1789 (with its famous provision limiting serfal obligations to 17 2/9% of total product) soon after his accession to the throne, but this concession only whetted the appetite of the Reactionary nobility for further concessions. Robot services were frequently reimposed upon the serfs, though this led to peasant riots; the panicky landlords thereupon called for draconic penalties to be imposed by martial law, a step which the government wisely avoided. Leopold urged free bargaining between landlord and serf to commute robot into money obligations, and pressed the Diet to set up a general formula to serve as a guideline for individual negotiations. The Diet refused, obviously preferring to retain the traditional robot; only one third of the landlords arranged for voluntary commutation by 1794, and thereafter the Franciscan government pressed them no farther. The survival of robot as a usual mode of serf exploitation in Bohemia must be reckoned one of the "accomplishments" of the Diet. There can be no question, on the other hand, that Leopold wished to continue Joseph's proserf policy, and he even contemplated the representation of the peasantry in future Diets, a step which horrified all the privileged classes of Bohemia.

On educational questions the Diet was critical of several Theresian and Josephine policies. It petitioned for the abolition of the bureaucratic school commissioners established in 1787, a step which would have returned the schools to aristocratic and clerical control; this was flatly refused by Leopold. It also desired to restore Czech as the major language of instruction, although Joseph had determined upon German in 1774; this vexatious issue was settled by a sensible compromise. A plan to found a special academy for the Czech nobility in Prague (comparable to the Viennese *Theresianum*) was cold-shouldered by the government; Leopold followed his brother Joseph in being hostile to purely aristocratic schools which inculcated class pride rather than a spirit of "enlightened" citizenship.

On religious questions the Diet was deeply divided. An ultra-clerical party desired a general repeal of the Josephine system. It demanded a restoration of thirty-nine monasteries suppressed by Joseph (including their right to representation in the Diet) and the repeal of the toleration granted to Protestants and Jews. The majority of the Diet refused, however, to go so far as that: it was willing to live with the "private rights" conferred upon non-Catholics, such as the right to hold religious services and to be buried in public cemeteries, while agreeing with the ultras in demanding withdrawal of such "public rights" as equal access to office and the right to own all kinds of property.

The Leopoldine government was resolved to hold firm against clerical demands. The Bohemian *Gubernium* defended Josephine toleration against the clamor of the clerical party, and was fully supported by the Viennese Commission on *Desideria* (July 23, 1791). The emperor's final reply to the Diet (Oct. 21, 1791) reaffirmed the principle of religious toleration as one of the foundations of the monarchy. We have seen above that he was willing to abolish the general seminaries and to tolerate the monasteries which still survived, but this was the limit of his concessions; he categorically refused to restore those which had been suppressed.

It may be said in conclusion that the *Desideria* of the Bohemian Diet in 1790-91 did not affect the general course of Habsburg history, despite a few imperial concessions to the nobility in matters of taxation and the relationship between landlord and serf. The interest of the Diet lies not in what it accomplished but rather in what it reveals about the objectives of the aristocratic Reactionary party in one of the leading provinces of the Habsburg Monarchy. The constitutional demand for a powerful Diet, led by a permanent *Landesausschuss* and exercising a dominant voice in administration, aimed to reverse the trend of two centuries toward bureaucratic absolutism. The fiscal demand for lowering the Bohemian share of the total tax burden of the monarchy flew in the face of the centralization achieved by Maria Theresia and Joseph. The demand for aristocratic tax privileges and special courts, and the veto exercised upon commuting servile labor obligations into monetary dues, ran contrary to Joseph's encouragement of legal equality and the monetization of economic relationships. The demand for the restoration of guild privilege and the usury laws revealed a refusal to accept the new policy of laissez-faire. The demand for terminating lay and bureaucratic control of the school system was symptomatic of the clerical and aristocratic distrust of the *Aufklärung* produced by Josephine schoolmasters. The demand for the repeal of the religious toleration granted to Protestants and Jews showed that bigotry still possessed great residual strength.

The spirit of class privilege, aristocratic constitutionalism, and religious intolerance expressed by the Bohemian *Desideria* could not prevail in the face of Leopold's determination to defend the egalitarian, absolutist, and "enlightened" heritage bequeathed by his brother Joseph. Leopold's willingness to make concessions in detail, and the Diet's unwillingness to contemplate rebellion on the pattern of Belgium and Hungary, gave the emperor a strong position in his disputes with Bohemia. He was in fact defending an absolutist *status quo,* not aiming at any aggressive farther advance on the course charted by Joseph; whereas his opponents were Reactionaries in the strict sense of the term, who wished to return to pre-Josephine conditions. Their major weakness was that they represented only a small crust of aristocrats, clerics, and urban patricians; the bulk of the peasantry was hostile to them, and they were dependent upon the government for protection against the potentially rebellious lower classes. The day of aristocratic frondeurs in the Habsburg Monarchy was over, except in Hungary; absolutism was too firmly entrenched to be shaken, though it could still be forced on occasion into retreats. This was the situation before the forward-looking Leopold was replaced by the standpat Francis in 1792. Thereafter an aristocratic fronde became unnecessary in any case, for Francis had no desire to engage in social reforms, and monarch, aristocrats, and clerics terminated their long-standing conflicts in the face of their common fear of the Jacobin danger.

Leopold died, suddenly and unexpectedly, at the early age of forty-five on March 1, 1792. The last year of his reign saw him preoccupied with the problems raised by the French Revolution, and Austria stood on the verge of an unwanted war with France when he died. While striving to maintain peace and opposing any kind of counterrevolutionary crusade, he had nevertheless "cleared the deck" by the *rapprochement* with Prussia initiated at Reichenbach. It may be reckoned his greatest achievement that he solved the most pressing problems confronting Austria before she became absorbed in the prolonged revolutionary wars. While Leopold was a friend of *Aufklärung,* legal equality, and self-government, he had wisely seen his task to be one of consolidation rather than of farther advance to the goals plotted by Joseph. Leopold saw that his brother had rashly advanced to a good many exposed positions which it was imprudent to defend, and he skillfully retreated wherever retreat appeared necessary to disarm opposition to the fundamental substance of Joseph's reforms. The success of his policies during his brief reign suggests that with a longer reign he would have proved a great Conservative reformer in Austria. To an unusual degree he combined progressive goals with political skill, and, while an effective wielder of absolute power, he looked toward the eventual curtailment of absolutism through the establishment of a measure of self-government. In all these respects he was far superior to his son and successor Francis, who was a stupid and unimaginative defender of the *status quo.* The premature death of Leopold was the greatest disaster suffered by the cause of German Reform Conservatism toward the end of the eighteenth century.

Francis II: Portrait of a Status Quo *Conservative*[32]

Francis II may be described as the single most influential Conservative in Germany throughout his long reign of forty-three years (1792-1835). There was never any question about his role as tenacious defender of the *status quo,* and he was consistently able to put his personal imprint upon the policy of the Habsburg government. Many of his ministers were exceedingly able men with strong individual views—for example Thugut, Stadion, Metternich, and Kolowrat; yet he used them all without ever falling under the complete domination of any single adviser. The Habsburg Monarchy was governed in accordance with the "Franciscan System" while he occupied the throne, and indeed for another dozen years under his successor until the debacle of 1848.

[32] There is no adequate modern biography of the Emperor Francis. Victor Bibl, *Kaiser Franz, der letzte römisch-deutsche Kaiser* (Leipzig, 1937), is a passionate attack by a professional historian; Walter Tritsch, *Metternich und sein Monarch; Biographie eines seltsamen Doppelgestirns* (Darmstadt, 1952), a strained apologia by a gifted amateur. There are two excellent studies dealing with his early life, both unfortunately ending with the year 1792: Cölestin Wolfsgruber, *Franz I, Kaiser von Österreich* (2 vols., Vienna and Leipzig, 1889), and W. C. Langsam, *Francis the Good. The Education of an Emperor 1768-92* (New York, 1949).

So strong and influential a ruler surely does not deserve the belittlement to which he has been subjected by historians who cannot forgive his hostility to Liberalism and Nationalism. Francis was a man of considerable talent and numerous virtues, though both were countered by strong weaknesses and conspicuous faults. The emperor's industry was legendary; fourteen hours at his desk became the rule rather than the exception after he had overcome a youthful tendency toward indolence and apathy. His greatest weakness as an administrator was his inability to differentiate sufficiently between the important and unimportant. The emperor's working day was about equally divided between paper work and the granting of audiences. Much of his paper work could just as well have been performed by a secretary, and his absorption in petty detail was incompatible with efficient administration. His accessibility to even his lowestborn subjects was certainly a tribute to his patriarchal conception of government, and had the advantage of keeping Francis close to the concerns of his people; it had the disadvantage, however, of leaving little time for self-improvement and intelligent study of the great problems which confronted the Habsburg government. When Francis acceded to the throne in 1792 he possessed an admirably detailed knowledge of his realm and its people, for Joseph and Leopold had sent him on frequent journeys, arranged apprenticeships on several official bodies, and consulted with him on all major questions of policy. The only trouble was that all this knowledge was stored up passively instead of being really digested and used as the basis for an enlightened program in the tradition of his predecessors. His memory for facts and faces was superb. Francis spoke most of the languages current in his multinational empire, and his use of the Viennese dialect was especially ingratiating to the populace of the capital. It contributed to the remarkable popularity which characterized at least the second half of his long reign. The "good Emperor Francis" *(der gute Kaiser Franz)* was liked for his simplicity, happy family life, industry, accessibility, and obvious benevolence toward his subjects. His constancy in the face of endless misfortunes during the revolutionary and Napoleonic wars further contributed to his popularity. There can be no question that he sincerely strove to be just to all men, and considered *Justitia regnorum fundamentum* the principal maxim of his reign. His desire to mitigate individual misfortunes when they were brought to his attention did not, however, prevent him from being exceedingly severe with all who challenged the bases of his system of government; Francis considered the exemplary punishment of troublemakers essential to protect the interest of the vast majority of his quietly contented subjects.

Many of Francis' qualities were akin to those of his father. He frequently suffered from bouts of melancholy, lack of self-confidence, and jealousy of men blessed with less complicated personalities. His abnormal suspiciousness of all men made police reports his favorite reading, and there was a similar lack of generous human feelings. Both father and son loved minute bureaucratic paper work and won a reputation for incorrigible pedantry. Both were completely lacking in military qualities and abstained from commanding their armies personally in time of war: they were unable to provide the dynasty with the military laurels needed to compete with the Hohenzollerns before the court of German public opinion.

Yet the differences between father and son were historically more important than the similarities. The latter were largely confined to the area of personality; the former predominated in the area of public policy. Leopold was a widely cultivated man with a deep understanding of the forces of his age and a deliberate program of Reform Conservatism; Francis, a man of pedestrian intelligence who was blindly attached to the *status quo* and saw no reason why it could not be maintained indefinitely against all challengers. Leopold saw himself as the contractual servant of the sovereign people whose right to self-government was indelible; Francis believed in his divine right to rule over people whose real interests he felt he understood far better than they themselves possibly could. Leopold wanted to revive and modernize the *Stände* as part of a general program of leading Austria from absolutism to a harmonious cooperation between prince and people; Francis believed that subjects were most happy when they attended to their private affairs, while the government attended to all public business. Leopold delighted in thinking up projects for administrative reform; Francis concentrated upon drawing maximum advantage out of the existing bureaucratic machinery. Leopold wanted to promote the happiness of his subjects by increasing their prosperity through the encouragement of modern forms of industry; Francis thought it sufficient to maintain traditional standards of living and feared the presumptuousness likely to accompany a newly won prosperity. Leopold preserved the Erastian ecclesiastical policies launched by his brother; Francis was more conciliatory to the Church and made broad concessions to Ultramontanism in his later years. Leopold wished in principle to deprive the aristocracy of its remaining privileges (though he proceeded cautiously in practice); Francis believed in the desirability of a hierarchic society marked by steep gradations in rights. It may be said in conclusion that Leopold was molded by the thought of the *Aufklärung* in his political, social, and religious policies; while Francis—despite, or perhaps because of, the fact that he was educated in these same principles—reacted sharply against the ideas of his uncle Joseph and father Leopold, two men who had badgered him in his unhappy childhood and given him a deep feeling of inadequacy. Leopold looked upon the French Revolution, which broke out when he was a man of forty-one with opinions firmly fixed, as a basically justifiable movement, however much he deplored its excesses; Francis, an impressionable young man of twenty-one in 1789, reacted violently to the attack upon the throne of his uncle Louis XVI. He was to devote the rest of his life to the antirevolutionary cause.

The key to Francis' reign is provided by his hostility to the French Revolution and his confounding of every Progressive movement with it. He refused to distinguish between Radical innovation and Conservative reform, and proved vulnerable to the "conspiracy theory" and the witch-hunting to which it naturally led. His blind resistance to change, and panicky hatred of men who advocated change, was to be intensified after the discovery of the Viennese Jacobin conspiracy of 1794 (to be discussed in the next chapter). Francis was convinced that to yield to reform demands would only open the floodgates to revolution, since the appetite of Radicals would always prove insatiable. He put this point in the following words in rejecting an Italian petition for specific political reforms:

> I must say "no" since *every* concession is always dangerous. Since the nature of man is insatiable, he will always ask for something more. Give him the hand, and he wants the arm; give him the arm, and he wants the whole body. I do not wish to give up my head.[33]

With this kind of outlook Francis was bound to remain faithful to the maxim which he bequeathed to his successor on his deathbed in 1835: "Govern and change nothing." *(Regiere und ändere nichts!)*[34] He refused to adapt the eighteenth-century institutions of the Habsburg Monarchy to the needs of the nineteenth century, though these needs were made ever more imperative by the irresistible and irreversible development of economic forces, political demands, and a

[33] Quoted by W. C. Langsam, "Emperor Francis II and the Austrian Jacobins 1792-1796," *AHR*, L (1945), 471.
[34] Quoted by Hugo Hantsch, "Franz II," *NDB*, v (1961), 360.

climate of opinion shaped by the *Aufklärung*. The full emancipation of the peasantry, so farsightedly begun by Maria Theresia and Joseph, was adjourned throughout Francis' reign and achieved only by the revolution of 1848. Modern forms of industry and commerce were permitted to develop, but the government refused to provide any systematic lead because it feared their moral and political results; the emperor failed to see that Austria's consequent economic backwardness compromised the maintenance of the Great Power status to which he was deeply attached. No attempt was made to pass, however, gradually, from anachronistic divine right absolutism to at least the beginnings of modern self-government through altering the historic *Stände* bodies by adding burgher and peasant deputies. The bureaucracy remained top-heavy, rigid, inefficient, and unresponsive to the needs of the people. Worst of all was the brutal repression of the intellectual life throughout the Habsburg Monarchy: Francis never lost his suspicion that thinking was an intrinsically dangerous activity, and he was blind to the elementary truth that repression is usually the mother of extremism. The emperor's program for coping with those of his subjects who persisted stubbornly to use their minds consisted of censorship, espionage, and, as a last resort, government-directed propaganda. This program was given classic expression in a famous circular letter which Police Minister Count Pergen—who had been fired by Leopold but reappointed by Francis—sent to all provincial governors on April 5, 1793:

> Your Excellency will . . . tolerate no reading clubs or other secret gatherings, no matter what their name. These rarely aim at anything good, and because of their potentialities for evil may become dangerous in spite of any laudable intentions they may possess. This has been amply demonstrated by experience. . . .
>
> The provincial chiefs . . . must keep themselves constantly informed on the state of public opinion within the areas under their control and on the actions of any suspicious individuals who may be living in the land. . . . This information, furthermore, must regularly be sent to [Count Pergen] so that he may keep His Majesty posted on conditions prevailing in the entire monarchy. . . .
>
> It only remains to make one additional observation regarding the precautions necessary to maintain peace and quiet in the cities and especially in the rural districts. Ordinary security measures do not suffice for the current delicate situation, in which the freedom-racket [*Freyheits-Schwindel*] has gained so much ground and all

monarchical governments are facing unrest. Every chief must secretly set in motion all levers for converting those in error and for wiping out all subversive views with which individuals or classes may have been infected by sneaking agitators. This can best be done through the agency of well-disposed citizens who possess the confidence of, and have influence over, the public; through the unostentatious distribution of patriotic writings by officials of the provincial administration; through a strict watch over privately and publicly circulated tracts; and above all, through the forthright cooperation of all teachers.[35]

The personal government of Francis was marked by stubborn adherence to the existing structure of society; refusal to see that far-reaching changes, while they cannot be prevented, can be made at least relatively harmless when they are guided from above; indiscriminate hatred of Radicals and Reformers, with refusal to see that the ultimate aims of the two groups differed sharply; and the naïve faith in police repression as the panacea for political troubles—in short, all the characteristics of a Status Quo Conservative. Yet it must be admitted that Francis was remarkably successful from his own point of view. He was born to the purple and died peacefully in bed, though his era saw exceptional vicissitudes for the Habsburg Monarchy. After fighting four unsuccessful wars against revolutionary and Napoleonic France he rebounded to become the arbiter of Europe at the time of the Congress of Vienna. He selected in Metternich, his chancellor for over a quarter of a century, the ablest statesman of the age. The "Metternichean System"—which could just as well be called the "Franciscan system"—dominated the politics of Central Europe for more than a generation. Francis maintained the Austrian Status Quo Conservatism throughout his long reign of forty-three years. Yet his "success" proved utterly sterile in the long run, for he left an impossible legacy to his successor—a fact which but illustrates the commonplace that a too successful defense of the *status quo* in an age filled with dynamic political and social forces usually sets the stage for a violent explosion in the future.

[35] Quoted by W. C. Langsam, "Emperor Francis," pp. 465-66.

CHAPTER 9

The Challenge of the French Revolution

THE TRADITIONAL view of German political life during the period of the French Revolution has been that the great events of 1789 first roused an apathetic country into political consciousness.[1] This theory can only be accepted with reservations in the light of the materials surveyed in the earlier chapters of this book. We have seen that there was vigorous religious, social, and political controversy in Germany before 1789, as witnessed by the articulation of a Radical challenge and a Conservative defense of the *status quo.* Yet there is obviously a core of truth in the traditional view, for the French Revolution did have a great impact upon German political development. This impact was threefold: it enlarged the circle of Germans interested in political questions; it raised the temperature of political discussion several degrees; and it led some to the "un-German" belief that political consciousness should manifest itself not only in theoretical discussion and utopian exclamation, but in occasional practical activity as well. These were certainly significant changes, but even their combined force left Germany's political condition far "behind" that of the "advanced" countries of Western Europe. Political consciousness, though enlarged, remained confined to a comparatively small upper- and middle-class elite; the largely illiterate masses, though capable of occasional riots with political overtones, did not take a sustained interest in politics. Passionate interest in French affairs did not preclude the survival of a "spectator psychology" under which Germans cheered and booed with only a vicarious sense of participation; one frequently encounters the phenomenon of Germans approving of the Jacobins' most Radical measures without supporting (much less expecting) similar measures at home. The various factors which had long been responsible for German civic apathy—*Kleinstaaterei,* absolutism, the political heritage of Lutheranism, absorption in nonpolitical cultural pursuits, and a comparatively stagnant economy—were still at work.

The present chapter will analyze in successive sections the initial response of German public opinion to the French Revolution; the

[1] This traditional view is explicitly challenged by F. Valjavec in his remarkable book *Die Entstehung der politischen Stromungen in Deutschland 1770-1815* (Munich, 1951), though unfortunately not without the exaggerations too often characteristic of "revisionist" historiography.

problem of whether there was any serious revolutionary danger in the Germany of the 1790's; the official response to the Revolution in the various forms of intensification of repression, encouragement of counterrevolutionary propaganda, and support of the war against revolutionary France; the Jacobin conspiracy of 1794 in the Habsburg Monarchy and its repression; the main Conservative voices against the revolution; and, finally, the feeble attempts of Reform Conservatives to make themselves heard at a time when hysterical fears of Radical conspiracies threatened to obliterate any distinction between revolutionaries and Reform Conservatives. The rise and spread of theories of conspiracy will form the subject of the following chapter.

The Initial Response to the Revolution

It is extremely difficult in our age, with its disillusionment with past efforts to achieve utopia and its doubts about the future progress of humanity, to recapture the generous enthusiasm which swept through politically conscious Germany in the summer of 1789. Politics monopolized the attention of the educated classes of the country. Archenholz, the editor of the *Minerva*, complained that "the tremendous interest aroused by the French Revolution crowds out all other concerns; the best poems remain unread, men are interested only in newspapers and in writings which satisfy their voracious political appetite."[2]

The initial response to French developments was overwhelmingly favorable, as a look at almost any political magazine or the writings of all but a very few writers will demonstrate. Germans hailed the French Revolution as the dawn of a new era in history when mankind would triumph at last over its age-old enemies—tyranny, bigotry, injustice, and oppression. This was the view—to mention only the most famous figures—of such poets as Klopstock, Wieland, and Schiller, and such philosophers as Kant, Herder, and Fichte; even many writers who subsequently became foes of the revolution—such as August Rehberg and Friedrich Gentz—went through an initial period of enthusiasm. Of Germany's major intellectual figures only Möser and Goethe were foes of the revolution from its very beginning. The overwhelming weight of German public opinion welcomed the replace-

[2] Quoted in K. T. Heigel, *Deutsche Geschichte vom Tode Friedrichs des Grossen bis zur Auflösung des alten Reiches* (2 vols., Stuttgart, 1899-1911), I, 275. The entire chapter 1 of Bk. II, "Die französische Revolution und der deutsche Volksgeist," is a succinct summary of the problem by no means superseded by the standard works cited in n.3.

ment of Bourbon despotism by constitutional liberty, the downfall of aristocratic privilege through the achievement of equality before the law and "career open to talent," and the curtailment of Catholic privilege and superstition in the name of rational religion and the too-long-denied principle of religious toleration.[3]

Even more important to Germans than these specific achievements was the inspiring fact that their western neighbors made a deliberate attempt to reconstruct the totality of national life in accordance with the dictates of the *Aufklärung*. This effort, though made initially by Frenchmen for France, inevitably had universal significance: its success would provide an enormous impetus, its failure a heavy handicap, to *all* Progressive effort everywhere. The twenty-six-year-old Friedrich Gentz, soon to become an influential opponent of the revolution, gave eloquent expression to this attitude in a letter to the philosopher Christian Garve on Dec. 5, 1790:

> The Revolution constitutes the first practical triumph of philosophy, the first example in the history of the world of the construction of government upon the principles of an orderly, rationally-constructed system. It constitutes the hope of mankind and provides consolation to men elsewhere who continue to groan under the weight of age-old evils. All these evils would, moreover, become ten times more irremediable if the Revolution should fail. I can foresee most vividly that many men would be forced to concede—after Reason had been silenced by despair—that men can be happy only as slaves; and how all tyrants, whether big or small, would use this terrible confession to revenge themselves for the panic to which they succumbed upon first hearing of the awakening of the French nation.[4]

[3] The single best work about the impact of the French Revolution upon Germany is J. Droz, *L'Allemagne et la Révolution française* (Paris, 1949). G. P. Gooch, *Germany and the French Revolution* (London, 1920), is catalogic but superficial; A. Stern, *Der Einfluss der französischen Revolution auf das deutsche Geistesleben* (Stuttgart and Berlin, 1928), is too exclusively concerned with the attitude of "great thinkers." An exhaustive recent treatment is Kurt von Raumer, *Deutschland um 1800* (Konstanz, 1962), pp. 24-119. The response of "popular opinion"—as revealed in ephemeral pamphlets, songs, dramas—is treated in the compilation of Eberhard Sauer, *Die französische Revolution von 1789 in zeitgenössischen Flugschriften und Dichtungen* (Weimar, 1913), valuable despite the dubious thesis that German public opinion was less aroused than has usually been thought.

[4] *Briefe von und an Friedrich von Gentz* (ed. F. C. Wittichen and Ernst Salzer, 3 vols., Munich, 1909-13), I, 178.

The "French gospel" was championed in Germany by a number of distinguished authors and pamphleteers who became, collectively and individually, the bête noire of German Conservatism. Among those who remained faithful to the revolution to the end were Adolf Freiherr von Knigge, the former organizer of the *Illuminati*; Johann Heinrich Campe, a Braunschweig educator who had succeeded Basedow at the famous Dessau *Philanthropin* and made a celebrated "pilgrimage" to Paris in 1789; Jakob Mauvillon, best known as Mirabeau's German collaborator on the famous book about the Prussian monarchy (1788); Georg Forster, the distinguished naturalist who joined the Jacobin Club in Mainz and died in Paris, where he had gone in 1794 to plead for French annexation of the Rhineland; Johann Gottlieb Fichte, the idealistic philosopher; and Georg Friedrich Rebmann, a gifted satirist and editor who fled Germany to enter the French judicial service in 1798.

There is no difficulty in explaining the passionate and widespread German enthusiasm for at least the early stages of the French Revolution: the French had finally done what philosophers had long talked about as needing to be done, and what Progressive Germans approved even when they saw no prospect of achieving it in their own country. The enthusiasm for the French Revolution constituted an obvious parallel to the enthusiasm felt for the American Revolution fifteen years earlier.

It should be remembered that Germans had little reason to resist French principles because of pride in indigenous German conditions. We have seen that the institutions of the country were in a hopeless state of disintegration, both in the empire as a whole and most of its component parts—Free Cities, Imperial Knights, ecclesiastical states, and petty states generally. Social conditions were marked by obsolescence and injustice. To many the religious situation appeared deplorable, whether one looked at the corrosive rationalism of Bahrdt in the Protestant Church, the Febronian and Josephine movements in Catholicism, or the obscurantism and intolerance associated with Wöllner.

The one popular and successful German institution—enlightened absolutism—contributed to the acceptability of French revolutionary ideas both by its past triumphs and its present weaknesses. Many Germans were proud of the parallelism which existed between the work of Frederick the Great and the French Constituent Assembly in such matters as religious toleration, efficient administration, judicial reform, and explicit affirmation of the "rights of man." (There are, in-

437

deed, some striking similarities between the French revolutionary legislation and the Prussian *Allgemeine Landrecht*.)[5] The French Revolution appeared attractive, however, not just because of its similarity in aim with enlightened absolutism; the attraction was enhanced by the contrast between the dynamism of the French and the loss of impetus, not to say outright failure, of German absolutism around 1790. Joseph II's reckless extremism had brought much discredit to reforming monarchy as his career reached its tragic close. Frederick William II had symbolically turned against the program of the *Aufklärung* with Wöllner's Edict of Religion. Karl Theodor of Bavaria had persecuted the *Illuminati* with Rosicrucian zeal, and there were many other despots whose *Aufklärung* was nonexistent or only skin-deep. Apart from these specific examples of failure stood the larger fact that the alliance of absolutism and *Aufklärung* had never been anything other than a marriage of convenience. Absolutism, by its nature, could not easily concede the demand for self-government inevitably made by a rising *bourgeoisie;* and it never sought to attack the principle of social hierarchy per se. The French revolutionaries' advocacy of popular sovereignty and legal equality inevitably placed reforming absolutism in the shade so far as the Radical sections of German public opinion were concerned.

The general prestige enjoyed by eighteenth-century French society and culture was a further aid in the rapid spread of French principles. Most educated Germans knew French, which, in fact, was the language of several German courts; and they had long looked to the country of Montesquieu, Voltaire, and Rousseau for political inspiration. (This generalization remains valid despite the fact that some German Conservatives had already used German nationalism as a political weapon before 1789.) A sharp decline in the popularity of England, associated with her fighting on the "wrong side" in the American Revolution, also contributed to German political sympathies turning toward France in 1789.

An additional factor to keep in mind is that German enthusiasm for France was not a completely spontaneous phenomenon: it was carefully fostered by a stream of deliberate revolutionary propaganda

[5] Droz, op.cit., Pt. II, Ch. 2, "La Prusse et la Révolution française," cites several contemporary authors who argued this position. The most prominent example is E. F. Klein, *Freiheit und Eigentum* (Berlin, 1790), especially notable because Klein was one of the main authors of the Prussian *Allgemeine Landrecht* (see Ch. 7 above). The thesis has been argued by many distinguished historians. See, for example, A. de Tocqueville, *The Old Regime and the French Revolution* (New York, 1955), pp. 226-31.

which began to inundate Germany in 1790. Numerous German visitors to France—the so-called "pilgrims of revolution," of whom the Brunswick educator J. H. Campe was the most prominent—were afforded every opportunity to observe French developments, and their glowing accounts were gobbled up by a German public opinion eager to believe the best. A former secretary of the Prussian embassy in Paris, Karl Wilhelm Theremin, became adviser on German affairs to the French foreign ministry and exercised a key role in France's "propaganda offensive" across the Rhine. The German-speaking city of Strasbourg provided an excellent base of operations; here congregated numerous German refugees like the notorious Eulogius Schneider and the Württemberger Christoph Friedrich Cotta (1758-1838), editor of the *Strassburger Politisches Journal für Aufklärung und Freiheit*—both dedicated to spreading the French gospel of liberty in their native land. The French embassy in Basel was also used to flood Germany with propaganda. A number of French agents roamed throughout the country establishing contact with French sympathizers. These were naturally most numerous in those institutions which had already spread *Aufklärung* principles before 1789, especially reading clubs and Masonic lodges. The surviving evidence does not, of course, permit any definitive assessment of the impact of French propaganda, but two observations may be ventured. First, its success was partly due to its skillful technique—it was often written by Germans for Germans—but mostly due to the fact that it told Progressive Germans exactly what they wanted to hear. (It is impossible, therefore, to talk about "alien impact" as an independent variable in German political development.) Second, its success was certainly exaggerated both by the propagandists—eager to magnify their work and to prepare Frenchmen for war by fostering the illusion that French armies would be greeted as liberators—and by the German governments—eager to believe that the discontent of their subjects was exclusively due to alien agitators rather than the result of indigenous grievances.[6]

[6] Much information on French propaganda, and the German response to that propaganda, can be found in the encyclopedic work of Heinrich Scheel, *Süddeutsche Jakobiner. Klassenkämpfe und republikanische Bestrebungen im deutschen Süden Ende des 18. Jahrhunderts* (East Berlin, 1962), a valuable study despite its Marxist jargon and doctrinaire exaggeration of the importance of German Radicalism in the 1790's. The same may be said of the similar work of Hedwig Voegt, *Die deutsche jakobinische Literatur und Publizistik* (Berlin, 1955), which centers on the figure of A.G.F. Rebmann. Rebmann, perhaps the most interesting of the German Radicals, was rediscovered by Nadeschka von Wrasky, *A.G.F. Rebmann. Leben und Werke eines Publizisten zur Zeit der grossen Französischen*

One additional point, obvious but sometimes forgotten, remains to be made about the German attitude toward the French Revolution: the opinions of many Germans changed as the revolution changed. Many who had cheered the springtime of liberty in 1789 turned their backs when they saw the emergence of a despotism more arbitrary than that of the Bourbons. The revulsion was strengthened when war broke out between France and the German Powers, and when French armies invaded the Rhineland in 1792. It was at that point that German public opinion, increasingly divided since 1789, became sharply polarized between antagonistic groups. A large but somewhat inert majority opposed the revolution, supported the war, and, in most cases, accepted the German *status quo;* a small but (insofar as censorship permitted) articulate minority retained its sympathy for the revolutionary cause (or at least was ready to make excuses for the crimes of the revolutionaries), called for an early peace, and insisted upon the need to reform Germany's political and social institutions. There was ferocious recrimination between the intellectual spokesmen for these opposite positions. The former claimed a monopoly of patriotism and denounced their opponents as traitorous Jacobins; the latter claimed a monopoly of virtue and denounced their opponents as the hired lackeys of Reaction. The two parties—or, to be more precise, loose groupings of men of roughly similar views—stood in a line of continuity with the Radical and Conservative elements analyzed in earlier chapters. The main difference was that the comparatively re-

---

Revolution (Heidelberg, 1907). R. R. Palmer, *The Age of the Democratic Revolution* (2 vols., Princeton, 1959-64), II, 443, devotes an informative bibliographical footnote to the *Rebmannfrage* (n.32). Several regional studies dealing with Bavaria are important: Richard Graf Du Moulin Eckart, "Bayerische Zustände und die französische Propaganda im Jahre 1796," *Forschungen zur Kultur und Literaturgeschichte Bayerns*, II (1894), 168-211; Anton Ernstberger, "Nürnberg im Widerschein der französischen Revolution 1789-96," *Zeitschrift für bayrische Landesgeschichte*, XXI (1958), 409ff.; K. T. Heigel, "Das Project einer süddeutschen Republik im Jahre 1800," in Raumer's *Historischen Taschenbuch* (ed. W. H. Riehl, Leipzig, 1871), pp. 119-75; and especially August Fournier, "Illuminaten und Patrioten," *Historische Studien und Skizzen* (Leipzig, 1885), which includes a fascinating report about Bavarian conditions written by the Austrian agent Armbruster in Oct. 1801. (Armbruster seeks to demonstrate the omnipotence of the old *Illuminaten* clique and finds them challenged by a still more Radical group of patriots with connections among the common people. He admits, however, that the *Illuminaten* confined themselves to Bavarian affairs and did not possess international connections.) The most thorough coverage of the topic of French propaganda is to be found in the monumental, but rather dry and unimaginative work of Sydney Biro, *The German Policy of Revolutionary France. A Study in French Diplomacy during the War of the First Coalition* (2 vols., Cambridge, Mass., 1957).

laxed pre-1789 atmosphere yielded to one marked by bitterness and suspicion; that Radical utterances were no longer made in a political vacuum but were increasingly feared in the light of what had happened to the apparently secure French *ancien régime*; and that Conservatives became panicky in the face of a "revolutionary danger" where domestic Radicalism could count upon the support of a powerful foreign ally.

Was There a Revolutionary Danger in Germany?

THE PATTERN OF DISORDER[7]

The belief of Conservative Germans during the 1790's in the existence of a serious danger of domestic subversion provides the key to much Conservative theorizing and the call for repressive action. This belief was not prima facie irrational. Conservatives pointed to what they considered an alarming pattern of popular disorder, discontent, and rebelliousness. The spring and summer of 1789 saw a good deal of lower-class rioting in several parts of the Rhineland. The worst outbreak occurred in the Rhenish town of Boppard in May 1789, when peasants protested against some of the relics of feudalism; the riot was quelled only after the arrival of five hundred soldiers armed with heavy artillery. The successful "popular revolution" against the bishop of Liége in 1788-90, which paralleled the Belgian rising against Joseph II, aroused a good deal of interest throughout the Rhineland, for Liége was part of the empire; the attempt made by several Rhenish princes to suppress it by executing a decision of the Wetzlar *Reichskammergericht* proved an inglorious failure. (Order was finally restored only by Austrian troops after Leopold had quelled the rebels in neighboring Belgium.) A threatened insurrection in the Austrian Breisgau against the new conscription system of Joseph was bought off by Leopold's timely concessions in 1790. In the Prussian province of Silesia large numbers of serfs rose against their Junker masters between 1790 and 1792 after their hopes of emancipation, originally inspired by the preparation of the *Allgemeines Landrecht,* had been postponed again and again before being finally frustrated; King Fred-

---

[7] The best recent summary is K. von Raumer, *Deutschland,* pp. 73-77. A synthesis of the evidence is scattered in numerous articles published in local journals. The most interesting instance of disorder was the Liége Revolution and the attempt of the Rhenish princes to suppress it. See the contemporary Johann Melchior Hoscher, *Beyträge zur neuesten Geschichte der Empörung deutscher Unterthanen wider ihre Landesherrschaft* (Giessen, 1790), and the modern H. Strothotte, *Die Execution gegen Lüttich 1789-92. Ein Beitrag zur Geschichte des Heiligen Römischen Reiches deutscher Nation* (Bonn, 1936).

erick William II was forced to use the army and martial law to defend the social *status quo*. A bloody uprising of journeymen in the Silesian capital of Breslau in April 1793 showed that discontent was by no means confined to the countryside of Silesia. The weaving villages of the *Erzgebirge*, threatened by the competition of the cheap products of the English Industrial Revolution, rose in open rebellion at the same time; Hoym, the minister in charge of the province, estimated the number of armed rebels at some twenty thousand men as he again called for troops to restore law and order. Most dangerous of all was the Saxon agrarian revolt of the summer of 1790, which deserves to be examined separately.

THE SAXON PEASANT REVOLT OF 1790[8]

The importance of the Saxon revolt to the historian lies in the fact that it provides a perfect case study in the interaction of long-standing domestic grievances with the new excitement produced by the developments in France. It may be said at once that there is no evidence that the revolt was instigated by French agents, or that French revolutionary propaganda played a direct role. The influence of the French Revolution was nonetheless important though it was limited to reflections provoked by news of its course and early achievements. Information concerning the revolution was circulated throughout Saxony by the primitive newssheets of the day; a certain part of the rural population was at least semiliterate, while others heard pamphlets and broadsheets read aloud by the "village elite" of schoolmasters and discontented clergymen. The peasants were initially incredulous when they learned that the French had abolished corvées and other relics of feudalism, and then had gone farther and abolished aristocracy as such. If this had occurred under the comparable circumstances of France, why should the Saxon aristocracy continue to oppress the peasantry with corvées and dues, hunting and grazing rights, and innumerable other relics of feudalism? The burden of these

---

[8] The standard work on the Saxon disorders is Percy Stulz and Alfred Opitz, *Volksbewegungen in Kursachsen zur Zeit der Französischen Revolution* (East Berlin, 1956), an important study despite its Marxist jargon and customary bows to the historical wisdom of Lenin and Stalin. It supersedes the pioneering archival study by Hellmuth Schmidt, "Die sächsischen Bauernunruhen des Jahres 1790," *Mitteilungen des Vereins für die Geschichte der Stadt Meissen*, VII (1909), pp. 261-427. The contemporary diary of F. E. von Liebenroth, *Fragmente aus meinem Tagebuche, insbesondere die sächsischen Bauernunruhen betreffend* (Dresden and Leipzig, 1791), provides a vivid expression of the attitude of the upper class toward the rebels. Liebenroth was an officer in the army which crushed the peasantry.

oppressive privileges had been recently magnified by the two harsh winters of 1788-89 and 1789-90 and the prolonged drought of 1789, which had ruined crops and forced the slaughter of cattle as soon as fodder supplies became exhausted. Yet the landlords, hit equally hard by these climatic disasters, refused to consider even a temporary lowering of the obligations owed them by their peasants.

Several lower-class agitators began to formulate concrete political programs in this flammable situation. The most notable leader was one Christian Benjamin Geissler, a ropemaker in the village of Liebstadt (Kreis, Pirna), who had followed French developments through the columns of Wieland's *Teutscher Merkur*. He had been especially impressed by the march of the women to Versailles on October 5, 1789, which had resulted in removing King Louis XVI from his aristocratic court clique and had made him a virtual prisoner of the French people. Geissler developed the plan that a peasant mob should bring the Elector Frederick August from Pillnitz, the summer retreat of the Saxon dynasty, to Dresden and use him there as a figurehead to promote a series of Radical measures. His program, which he drew up in writing, called for the purge of existing officials and judges, the establishment of a civic guard, the reform of religious abuses, the limitation of peasant dues, the elimination of oppressive game laws, and the drastic reorganization of the fiscal system. When Geissler began to distribute printed copies describing this program in the neighborhood of Liebstadt, he was promptly arrested on July 10, 1790, and subsequently sentenced to twenty years' imprisonment.[9]

There were sporadic peasant disorders throughout the spring of 1790, caused mainly by the destruction wrought by deer driven by the harsh winter into the flatlands—deer which the peasants were not permitted, under the existing game laws, to kill. The real insurrection began, however, on Aug. 3, 1790, in the village of Lommatzsch, northwest of Meissen, when a group of peasants refused to perform any further corvées and chased away the lord's sheep grazing on the common fallowland of the village. The peasants in neighboring villages began to do likewise, usually spontaneously but in some cases under the coercion of rebels who sought safety by maximizing the number of accomplices. The government attempted a quick arrest of the ringleaders, but its troops were thwarted by mobs of peasants armed with stolen guns, pitchforks, and other weapons available. Court sum-

---

[9] On Geissler see "Christian Benjamin Geissler. Ein Beitrag zur Geschichte der Bauernunruhen des Jahres 1790," *Neues Archiv für Sächsische Geschichte und Altertumskunde*, xxviii (1907), 253ff. His program is analyzed by Stulz-Opitz, op.cit., pp. 57-65.

monses were ignored. Panicky landlords fled to Dresden in a mood little different from that of the French émigrés; those who remained behind were forced by threats of murder and arson to sign documents in which they renounced all their surviving feudal rights. The renunciations were often followed by the burning of the legal documents of servitude in a public ceremony. It is estimated that some ten thousand peasants stood under arms by the last week of August, and that they controlled most of central Saxony.

The government responded to the crisis with firm and intelligent countermeasures. It concentrated its best troops—some three thousand men under the command of General von Boblick—in the Meissen area to stamp out the center of the insurrection. The regulars had little trouble dispersing the peasant mobs which lacked military training, equipment, discipline, and experienced leadership. A royal decree (*Tumultmandat*) of Aug. 26, 1790, threatened death to armed rebels but promised amnesty and examination of grievances to those who laid down their arms voluntarily. The danger of a spread of rebellion to nonpeasant strata was met by measures lowering food prices in the cities and inaugurating public works to employ the unemployed miners of the mountain regions. These measures sufficed to crush the central rebellion by early September, though spontaneous outbreaks continued elsewhere for another month. A special *Regierungskommission* under Chancellor Friedrich Adolf von Burgsdorff, appointed to punish the rebels, showed commendable moderation: there were no death sentences and only about a hundred cases of imprisonment. The government wisely decided to minimize the extent of the insurrection, both to assuage the panic of the upper classes and to diminish lower-class feeling of power in case of future trouble. The attempt to prevent the circulation of any extensive information about the actual course of the rebellion was remarkably successful: the full story was discovered only when twentieth-century historians began to explore the Dresden archives.

The researches of Hellmuth Schmidt and Percy Stulz have shown that the Saxon government was genuinely alarmed by the rebellion and that it embarked upon a deliberate program of preventing any recurrence through a triple policy of Conservative propaganda, threats of severe punishment, and an attempt to remedy the legitimate grievances of the peasantry. We shall examine the themes of Conservative propaganda in the next section, but something should be said here about the policy of combining draconic warnings with constructive reforms. The threat of punishment took the form of a new Decree

Against Tumult and Insurrection.[10] (Jan. 18, 1791), which announced dire punishment to "all unlawful self-help, all unauthorized refusal to perform traditional obligations, and all violence directed against others in exercise of their rights and privileges." There was a specific paragraph aimed against groups of persons who "jointly sought to exercise illegal violence against other persons or their property, or to defy with their common strength the implementation of governmental decrees or to coerce the government to act in a manner contrary to its spontaneous will." All these provisions must be read in the light of the specific events of the rebellion, which had seen peasants refusing to perform their corvée obligations, forcing loyal peasants at gun point to join their cause, organizing self-help against the plague of sheep, defying bureaucrats, judges, and soldiers by force of arms, and aiming to compel the government to abolish all the surviving relics of the feudal system. The Saxon government also tried to strike at future troublemakers by prohibiting the distribution of all libels (Schmäh-schriften) directed against the existing social order and declaring illegal all village meetings called for mutual consultation—two prohibitions of a dangerously elastic character. Death, to be inflicted in ordinary cases by the sword, under aggravated circumstances by the wheel, was decreed for organizing tumult; the attempt to organize tumult was to be punished by ten years in jail, under aggravated circumstances by life imprisonment. Complicity in plans to stimulate tumult was declared the equivalent of participation, while those who informed the government of conspiratorial plans were to be awarded with one hundred thalers.[11]

Some officials of the Saxon government realized, however, that the threat of punishment was not enough to prevent future rebellions unless an attempt was also made to remove the legitimate grievances of the peasantry. The above-mentioned Burgsdorff recommended limiting corvées, dues, and the grazing rights of lords; he also wanted to increase the minimal wages paid to children of peasants during the compulsory years of domestic service (Zwangsgesindelöhne). The Privy Council, in which landowners predominated, opposed these proposals as an unjust invasion of landlord rights, and declared them most inopportune at that moment in view of the excited state of mind

[10] Mandat wider Tumult und Aufruhr, issued in thirty paragraphs covering seventeen pages. The government ordered it to be read annually from all pulpits, a measure rescinded only in 1816.

[11] This paragraph draws heavily upon the invaluable study by Percy Stulz and Alfred Opitz mentioned above. See especially Ch. 3, Sect. 1, "Repressiv-massnahmen der Regierung."

of the rural population. The benevolent but weak elector failed to give adequate support to Burgsdorff in the Privy Council, and the *Landtag,* also dominated by landlords opposed to reform, was a further obstacle. Burgsdorff reluctantly conceded that reforms could not be carried out under the prevalent constellation of political forces, and he did not wish to court a rejection of governmental measures by the *Landtag.* Such a rejection would be certain to increase peasant defiance of landlords in the belief that the government was on the side of the peasants, had sanctioned peasant claims, and had no intention of opposing peasant self-help in the face of aristocratic intransigence. Was it not far better to let sleeping dogs lie? Suffice it to say that the reform intentions of the government were not implemented. The penalty for this passivity came promptly in new peasant disorders in 1793 and 1794.[12]

THE GERMAN IMMUNITY TO REVOLUTION

The Saxon disorders of 1790, and the pattern of disturbances mentioned earlier, should not obscure the fundamental fact—clear at least in retrospect—that Germany's political, economic, social, and religious structure provided her with a substantial immunity to domestic revolution in the 1790's. The best way of demonstrating this point is to compare the situation of Germany with that of France: the forces which made for the genesis of the French Revolution were either absent or at least comparatively weak in Germany.[13]

By 1789 France had developed a dynamic and quantitatively important commercial and manufacturing *bourgeoisie* able and ready to become the dominant force in society. It was based upon colonies and maritime commerce, whereas Germany had largely withdrawn into its continental shell when it failed to adjust to the "oceanic revolution" during the sixteenth century. The French *bourgeoisie* was angered by the contrast between its real socio-economic weight and its formal lack of legal rights and political influence; it aspired to become the dominant class within French society. The German *bourgeoisie,* on

---

[12] The entire paragraph is based on Stulz-Opitz, op.cit., Sect. 3, "Reformbestrebungen," and the pioneering study by W. Behrendts, *Reformbestrebungen in Kursachsen im Zeitalter der Französischen Revolution* (Leipzig, 1914), passim.

[13] See the brilliant summary by K. D. Erdmann in *Deutsche Geschichte im Überblick* (ed. P. Rassow, Stuttgart, 1953), pp. 366-67. A remarkable contemporary statement of the contrast between Germany and France, written to reassure German princes fearful of indigenous revolution, is Adolph Freiherr von Knigge, "Über die Ursachen, warum wir in Deutschland vorerst wohl keine gefährliche politische Haupt-Revolution zu erwarten haben," *Schleswig'sches Journal,* II (1793), 273-90.

the other hand, had little economic power; it demanded only, at the very most, some share of power alongside of the aristocracy. Its economic activity was largely dependent upon state support, and its political impotence was essentially a reflection of its inability to stand on its own economic feet. Both countries had a potentially discontented rural lower class, but this fact became explosive only in France because there the expression of rural discontent could be synchronized with an effective urban revolution; whereas in Germany the various rural disorders "sputtered out" for want of guidance from bourgeois agitators.

The political condition of Germany as much as the economic precluded revolution. The pattern of extreme decentralization meant that organized revolutionaries, if such existed, lacked a specific target whose capture would ensure their triumph on a national level. In a centralized nation like France the control of Paris meant a long step toward the control of the entire country; in decentralized Germany a revolutionary triumph in Saxony, Silesia, the Rhineland, or Liége (to mention the places of major disorder in the five years between 1788 and 1793) would leave intact many centers for launching a counter-revolution.[14]

The political achievements of enlightened absolutism illustrate the general rule that timely reforms are usually the best method of deflating revolutionary pressures. Many Germans believed that enlightened absolutism made a revolution unnecessary because it had already achieved much in the past and would achieve still more in the future; while the French Revolution had been made possible only because the Bourbon Monarchy had ceased to be enlightened since the early days of Louis XIV.[15]

The specifically unpolitical character of much of Germany's cultural life also served as a protection against indigenous revolution. The greatest and most influential writers of France in the eighteenth century—such men as Montesquieu, Voltaire, and Rousseau—had been passionately interested in politics and done much to educate the French nation on political matters. By contrast many leading German writers—Lessing, Winckelmann, and Goethe may serve as examples—

[14] This point was expressed forcefully at the time by the Liberal publicist August Hennings in his *Annalen der leidenden Menschheit* in 1796. Quoted by H. Voegt, *Die deutsche jakobinische Literatur*, p. 189.

[15] A brilliant statement of the role played by absolutism in preventing revolution in Germany can be found in Rudolf Stadelmann, "Deutschland und die westeuropäischen Revolutionen," in *Deutschland und Westeuropa* (Laupheim, 1948), pp. 11-34.

were either ostentatiously disinterested or only marginally interested in political problems; they preferred to devote themselves to the ideal world of beauty found in philosophy, poetry, and art. This kind of escapism was not unnatural in the stultifying and parochial world of the Holy Roman Empire, where a frozen political structure (incorporating the apparently irremovable political rubbish of centuries) precluded effective political work; but an escapist attitude certainly did much to perpetuate the very anachronisms from which it originally arose (or which had at least encouraged its rise). Cause and effect proved self-perpetuating as inadequate political institutions promoted an unpolitical culture, which in turn buttressed existing institutions against any kind of effective protest.

When Germany's intellectual leaders did devote themselves to politics, their ideas too often had little relationship with the actual world in which they lived. R. R. Palmer, who has studied the Germany of the 1790's from a comparative point of view, comes to the following judgment:

> There was an eagerness to consider the state in the abstract, but no chance to plan courses of action, assume responsibilities, weigh alternatives and probable consequences, or form alliances with persons of different ideas from one's own. Political thinking became idealistic; it fell not on the contending interests of conflicting groups, nor the actual dilemmas of justice, nor the illogicalities of empirical problems, nor the imperfections that attend the result of all human effort, but on the pure essence of the state itself, or of liberty, right, law, human dignity, perpetual peace, or the general movement of history.[16]

The prevalent nonempirical, nonpragmatic political outlook was accompanied by fantastic notions concerning the importance which ideas—and especially the ideas of German philosophers—had, or ought to have, upon human affairs. Many German intellectuals, by way of assuaging their potential sense of national inferiority as they contrasted the achievements of the French Revolution with the obsolete structure of the unreformed German polity, pointed with pride to Germany's "revolution of the mind." A prominent Rhenish journalist, the ex-Franciscan monk J. B. Geich, wrote in 1798: "Our nation has produced a revolution no less glorious, no less rich in consequences than the one from which has come the government of the (French)

[16] R. R. Palmer, *The Age of the Democratic Revolution* (2 vols., Princeton, 1959-64), II, 430.

Republic. This revolution is in the country of the mind."[17] He meant that Kant's revolution in philosophy, signalized by *The Critique of Pure Reason* published in 1781, was an event comparable to the revolution wrought by the French in political affairs since the summoning of the Estates-General; perhaps it was a revolution of even superior importance, for what were purely external transformations as opposed to a revolution in man's spiritual and moral outlook? The philosopher Fichte had a similar view concerning the importance of his own *Wissenschaftslehre* (Theory of Knowledge). He wrote in 1795: "My system is the first system of liberty. As the French nation liberated man from external chains, my system liberates him from the chains of the Thing-in-Itself, or of external influence, and sets him forth in his first principle as a self-sufficient being."[18]

This exalted conception of intellectual achievement frequently led to exaggerating the influence which it could exercise upon political affairs. To give only a single example, Friedrich Schiller, in his *Aesthetic Education of the Human Race*, seriously contended that the aesthetic training of man—to be sure, conceived very broadly—constituted the key to social and political progress, now that the French had evidently failed in their noble but misguided endeavors.[19]

The preoccupation with the "inner man"—at the expense of active-minded and public-spirited citizenship concerned with removing specific evils through specific action here and now—must also be viewed in the light of the political heritage of German Lutheranism. That heritage militated against the development of any kind of revolutionary outlook. It had provided one of the spiritual foundations of absolutism by its fetish of obedience to constituted authority; it had contributed to the disunity of Germany by investing every petty prince with the aura of divine right; and it had consecrated a social *status quo* in which hierarchical differentiation was viewed as an expression

---

[17] Ibid., p. 431, quoting from J. Droz, *La pensée politique et morale des Cisrhenans* (Paris, 1940), p. 39. On J. B. Gleich see J. Hashagen, *Das Rheinland und die französische Herrschaft* (Bonn, 1908), pp. 472-83.

[18] H. Schulz (ed.), *J. G. Fichte: Briefwechsel* (2 vols., Leipzig, 1925), I, 449. Friedrich Schlegel accepted Fichte at his own evaluation when he wrote in the *Athenäum* in 1798 (Fragment 216): "The French Revolution, Fichte's *Wissenschaftslehre*, and Goethe's *Wilhelm Meister* are the greatest developments (*Tendenzen*) of our age. Anyone who takes offence at considering these of comparable importance, or anyone who considers only noisy and material revolutions to be of importance, has not elevated himself to the point where he contemplates the history of mankind as a whole." Ernst Behler (ed.), *Friedrich Schlegel: Schriften und Fragmente* (Stuttgart, 1956), pp. 95-96.

[19] Friedrich Schiller, "Über die ästhetische Erziehung des Menschen in einer Reihe von Briefen," *Werke* (ed. L. Bellermann), x, 170-282.

of the will of God. Its explicitly formulated Erastian doctrine went far beyond what was permissible under Catholicism, even in its Febronian and Gallican forms; and Lutheranism produced nothing comparable to the doctrines of popular sovereignty and tyrannicide expressed by some Jesuit theorists. The Calvinism which existed in some parts of the empire had not led to the resistance doctrines of the French Huguenots; nor had it exercised a significant influence upon the development of institutions of self-government, as had been the case in the Scotland of Knox, the England of Hampden, and the New England of the Puritans.

The cumulative weight of all these objective factors, all deeply rooted in Germany's history, was soon reinforced by the revulsion felt by an increasing number of Germans as they watched the course of French developments. There was often a special note of bitterness as Germans turned against a revolution they had initially supported. Glowing hopes had been frustrated, and it was especially galling to find the French untrue to their own proclaimed principles. The men of 1789 had promised liberty and had established tyranny; had promised equality and had set up vexatious new discriminations; had promised fraternity, yet had turned Frenchmen against Frenchmen and France against most of Europe. They had solemnly renounced the very idea of aggressive war, only to resume a policy of annexation worthy of Louis XIV and other statesmen of a past which evidently could not be overcome. The unpolitical German, idealistic and innocent of the realities of political life, was surprised and disgusted as he encountered the dross which inevitably accompanies the most sincere resolve to translate noble principles into practical reality. He then easily jumped to the conclusion that the fault lay with the unworthy character of the French nation, not with the intrinsic difficulty of realizing Radical ambitions. From this it was but a step to the belief that the pure and uncorrupted German nation—which had already shown its mettle by the "revolution of the mind"—was destined to succeed where the French had failed. Germans would use education where the French had used violence; Kant's *Critique of Pure Reason* would replace the guillotine in mankind's struggle for a better society. It is unnecessary to add that this comforting and pharisaical belief did nothing to enhance the revolutionary potential of Germany in the 1790's.[20]

[20] The attitude of Germans toward the French—developing from admiration to contempt to burning hatred—is analyzed, although somewhat pedantically, by A. F. Raif, *Die Urteile der Deutschen über die französische Nationalität im*

Germany's Conservatives were wide off the mark in their fear of a German domestic upheaval, and their hysterical response does little credit to their judgment. Three things must, however, be said by way of explanation. The example of France—so recently the very pillar of the European *ancien régime*—suffering a cataclysmic transformation was bound to frighten all the beneficiaries of the *status quo* in neighboring lands, and make them confound the existence of reform demands with a clear and present threat of revolution. The Conservative fear of Radicalism was reinforced by patriotic indignation that some Germans could hope for the triumph of French principles—and arms—even after the outbreak of war. The most important reason for the Conservative hysteria lay, however, in the genuine external danger posed by the military situation after Valmy. The French invaders of the Rhineland encountered almost no resistance in the autumn of 1792, and the German population standing under French occupation generally acquiesced to alien rule or, in some cases, even rejoiced in the social "gains" introduced by revolutionary arms. The attitude of the German Rhinelanders toward French rule provides interesting side lights on the degree of the politicization of the lower classes and the extent to which an instinctive Conservatism was still prevalent in the 1790's.

THE ATTITUDE OF THE RHENISH POPULATION[21]

German Conservatives were naturally appalled as the Rhenish *ancien régime* collapsed like a house of cards upon the appearance of the first French soldier. The revolutionary army of Custine occupied Mainz in

---

Zeitalter der Revolution und der deutschen Erhebung (Berlin, 1911). A more limited study is P. Rudolf, *Frankreich im Urteil der Hamburger Zeitschriften 1789-1810* (Hamburg, 1933). An early partisan attack upon the French national character as the source of the crimes of the revolution is C. F. von Kruse, *Wahre Darstellung der grossen französischen Staatsrevolution in ihrer Entstehung, ihrem Fortgang und in deten Folgen* (2nd edn., Frankfurt, 1791). The author, *Konsistorialrath* in Oldenburg, first justified the validity of the concept of national character (pp. 1-16), then portrayed the character of the French in very unfavorable terms (pp. 16-35), and used the rest of his book to explain (or rather denounce) Revolutionary follies and crimes.

21 This section is based, unless other references are given, upon the classic work of J. Hashagen cited in n.17. Hashagen was the first author who overthrew the traditional view accepted by French historians with pride, by Germans with a sense of shame—that the Rhinelanders readily accepted French ways. The best survey of Rhenish conditions in 1789 is Max Braubach, *Das Rheinland am Vorabend der französischen Revolution* (Bonn, 1939). The main source collection is the above-cited Josef Hansen, *Quellen*. Hansen's results are discussed in two superb articles by H. Oncken, "Deutsche und rheinische

October 1792 without encountering significant resistance; the elector and his entourage fled under undignified circumstances; neither the population nor the garrison showed the slightest stomach for defense. A prominent officer of engineers named Eickemeyer was almost the only general officer who counseled resistance, and he was quickly overruled by his superiors. Eickemeyer was so disgusted by this conduct that he accepted Custine's offer to enter French service soon after the surrender of the city. This action should not be judged by nationalist criteria inapplicable in the 1790's; but it caused much comment at the time and became the basis of a Conservative conviction—widespread despite the absence of proof—that Mainz fell to the French because of the subversive conduct of German "traitors." The fact that Eickemeyer had been an *Illuminat* certainly encouraged this view, and he became a key exhibit for all those who believed in the existence of a dangerous German subversive party.[22]

Custine tried hard to win other prominent German collaborators to his side. He encouraged the founding of a *Society of the Friends of Liberty and Equality*, known generally as the local Jacobin club, to mobilize enthusiasm for the program of the revolution and support for the annexation of the Rhineland to France. The society won few members and some of its meetings required the protection of French bayonets; it was given, however, some respectability by the distinguished leadership of Georg Forster. Other attempts to drum up enthusiasm for the French cause proved equally unsuccessful. Of ninety-four merchants approached by the French, only thirteen declared themselves willing to cooperate. There was a mass boycott of the elections held in February 1793 to determine the question of future relations with France; only 345 voters out of approximately 10,000 eligibles gave their approval to annexation. The guilds submitted a declaration to the new municipal government (set up by the French) which protested the claim that liberty had been recently introduced in Mainz. The population had lived—so it was declared—"happily in its accustomed ways" under the old elector: "Our taxes were light, our economy flourished, and we could talk freely about all matters which

---

Probleme im Zeitalter der Französischen Revolution," *Sitzungsberichte der Pr. Akademie der Wissenschaften*, 1936, pp. 79-116, and 1937, pp. 65-104. See also Hansen's own summary, "Das linke Rheinufer und die französische Revolution 1789-1801," *Mitteilungen der Deutschen Akademie*, XII.

[22] On the case of Eickemeyer see the exhaustive discussion in K. T. Heigel, *Deutsche Geschichte*, II, 54ff.

concerned us. We fail to see how the French can possibly make us happier in any of these respects."[23]

There were, of course, several reasons for the lukewarm attitude taken by many Mainzers toward the French conqueror, quite apart from genuine attachment to the "good old ways." Many feared the early restoration of electoral rule if there were any reversal in military fortunes (as took place, indeed, in the spring of 1793) and it was certain that an electoral restoration would be accompanied by sharp reprisals against all collaborators. (There was the warning example of the punishment meted out to French collaborators by the victorious French armies in Longwy and Verdun, two cities which had been temporarily occupied by the Prussians in 1792.) Fear was reinforced by love in some Mainzers who expressed a simple patriotic loyalty to the Holy Roman Empire; a resolution passed by the guild of stonemasons exclaimed, "Woe to those subjects who cooperate with the enemies of their Fatherland."[24] Many Mainzers recognized the bad economic effects which must result from a disruption of normal trade relations with the Right bank of the Rhine. There was, above all, grave uncertainty about the future course of French internal developments. Wrote a farsighted anonymous pamphleteer, "Soon anarchy will breed a dictator who will impose despotic laws upon France; and perhaps generals at the head of armies will give orders to an impotent national Convent."[25] Was it not very risky to become mixed up with a country whose political future was shrouded in so much uncertainty?

Some Mainzers strove for a *via media* between the alternatives of restoration of the old regime and incorporation into Republican France. A prominent merchant named Daniel Dumont became the spokesman for a Conservative program of reform which sought to exploit the temporary French presence to modernize the old constitution while avoiding any sharp break in continuity. Dumont opposed the French notion of popular sovereignty (which Custine was attempting to use, albeit unsuccessfully, to build up a pro-French party) in the name of monarchical legitimacy and loyalty to the Holy Roman Empire; he insisted, however, that monarchical authority must be balanced by

[23] Quoted by Hashagen, op.cit., p. 55. E. Schmitt, *Das Mainzer Zunftwesen und die französische Herrschaft* (Frankfurt, 1929), documents the hostility of the guild masters to French rule. On the supporters of the French two old-fashioned works still have great value: J. Venedey, *Die deutschen Republikaner unter der französischen Republik* (Leipzig, 1870), and K. G. Bockenheimer, *Die Mainzer Klubisten der Jahre 1792 und 1793* (Mainz, 1896).

[24] Quoted in Hashagen, op.cit., p. 56.

[25] *Über di Verfassung von Mainz* (2nd edn., Deutschland, 1793), p. 26. Quoted in ibid., p. 57.

the election of powerful *Stände* under a franchise which included the burgher and artisan classes. (Dumont favored voting on an occupational basis.) He welcomed the French abolition of aristocratic and clerical privilege. His greatest fear was that an electoral restoration— which he obviously expected upon the conclusion of the war—would be accompanied by a complete counterrevolution; he desired a safeguard against this development by having a new Mainz constitution incorporated into any future peace treaty between France and Germany, thereby giving France a permanent "right of intervention." Dumont wanted to cooperate with the French on the principle that one must join what one cannot beat, but the French found him far too independent for their taste. They expelled him from Mainz after he refused to take the new oath of allegiance (April 1793), and confiscated his entire property. Dumont then worked for the elector as a liaison man with the Prussian army which was besieging Mainz, and vainly urged leniency in the treatment of Mainz collaborators after the recapture of the city in the summer of 1793. The failure of all his hopes is symptomatic of the difficulties encountered by Reform Conservatism in the Germany of the 1790's; its attempt to pursue a *via media* between Radicalism dependent upon France and Reaction which obstinately denied long-overdue reforms was doomed by the inevitable polarization of German political life.[26]

The French occupation of Mainz proved but an episode in 1792-93; the greater portion of the Rhineland fell under twenty years of French rule only in the autumn of 1794. The conquerors introduced, in the course of the next few years, most of the "achievements" of their "great revolution"—for example, the Civil Constitution of the clergy, the new type of municipal government, the abolition of guild privileges, and the elimination of feudal dues. Their policy won initial support from some of the most idealistic Rhinelanders—the publicist Joseph Görres is the best-known example—and some gratitude from the beneficiaries of social reform. There was also, however, a great deal of active antipathy to the French and all their works—antipathy which was naturally strongest among those victimized by French reforms. Officials of the *ancien régime* resented being replaced by "traitorous" collaborators. Guild masters bemoaned the fact that they were henceforth exposed to the cutting winds of free competition. Priests loathed an atheistic regime which not only deprived their Church of age-old privileges but also meddled with the internal life of Catholicism. The peasantry, while presumably appreciating certain

[26] On Dumont see ibid., pp. 385-90.

material gains, was outraged by the interference with its customary religious ritual.[27]

It cannot be stressed too strongly that the "cake of custom" was still virtually unbroken in the lower classes—in the Rhineland as in other parts of Germany—at this time; the prevalent attitude was a kind of phlegmatic attachment to the "good old ways" which constituted an important reservoir for Conservative sentiment, but which also tended to lead to acquiescence in any kind of *de facto* political authority. This phlegmatic attitude had been encouraged by centuries of absolutism. Admittedly this absolutism had been unusually mild in the Rhineland compared to other areas of Germany; it had nonetheless deadened whatever civic spirit had existed in earlier periods. Active collaboration with the French was practiced, as in the case of Mainz, by only a small part of the population. The predominant attitude was one of passive acquiescence; only a minority was actively hostile to the French—without, however, constituting any serious danger to the conqueror.

Opposition to the French took variegated forms. There were touching affirmations of loyalty to exiled rulers (especially Max Franz of Cologne), as hope was expressed for his early return. Requiem masses were held in several Rhenish churches for Louis XVI and Marie Antoinette on the anniversary of their executions—clearly a symbolic act of defiance against the new rulers. The Church proved, indeed, the focal point of resistance: monasteries refused to dissolve except at the point of the bayonet; religious processions were held in spite of French prohibitions; the Jacobin calendar was ignored as old holidays continued to be observed; the decrees ordering the removal of "superstitious" relics, statues, and crucifixes were quietly sabotaged; married priests were subjected to public ridicule; newly married couples refused to inscribe their names in the new civic registers; priests preached sermons extolling the surreptitious felling of liberty trees as an act pleasing to God. (The French government replied with draconic threats against "refractory priests"; many were exiled and some deported to Cayenne.)

There was a great deal of resistance to the externals of French rule, quite apart from cutting down liberty trees. Much of the public refused to participate in the elaborate festivals staged by the French in honor of liberty, or popular sovereignty, or the latest victory of revolutionary arms. Few "honest women" attended the revolutionary balls

[27] Hashagen, op.cit., pp. 197-206, analyzes the social composition of the opponents of French rule.

scheduled for the evening after such festivals. The wearing of revolutionary cockades was refused upon a variety of ingenious pretexts. The French prohibition of titles in the name of the egalitarian *citoyen* was systematically evaded; Germans continued to address one another as *Herr Doktor* or *Herr Geheimrat*. When an oath of allegiance was required of all officeholders, many refused to swear although this was courting dismissal. Some—for example, university professors—pleaded the formal reason that they were not really officials; others took refuge in international law by claiming that it prohibited oaths to any merely *de facto* authority (the empire did not formally cede the Rhineland to France until the Treaty of Lunéville in 1801); still others claimed that if they took the oath they would end their usefulness by losing all credit with the German population. The French did not dare carry out their program systematically in the face of all this Conservative obstruction.[28]

The threat of the introduction of a new municipal constitution evoked a spirited defense of the old in the imperial city of Cologne. The senate of Cologne addressed an elaborate memorandum to the French Convention on Jan. 26, 1795, which protested excessive contributions but which is interesting chiefly for an eloquent laudation of Cologne's glorious two thousand years of republican liberty.[29] Some citizens of Cologne considered this inflated claim rather ridiculous in view of the city's notorious record for oligarchic misgovernment and clerical intolerance; they were sharply reprimanded by several Conservative pamphleteers who viewed French liberty with the patronizing air of an aristocrat acknowledging the arrival of an upstart: "Cologne is grateful to Providence that it had already lived for cen-

---

[28] Many specific illustrations of the various forms of resistance can be found in Hashagen, op.cit., Ch. 1 covers *Anhänglichkeit an die deutsch-heimische Vergangenheit*; Ch. 2, *Widerstand gegen die französische Herrschaft*. Hashagen's work is supplemented by the excellent local study by W. Steffens, "Die linksrheinischen Provinzen Preussens unter französischer Herrschaft 1794-1802," *Rhein. Vjbll*, xix (1954), and the chronologically limited study by L. Klipffel, *Les debuts de l'occupation française sur la rive gauche du Rhin 1793-95* (Paris, 1933).

[29] The case of Cologne is covered by Hashagen, op.cit., pp. 9-53. The memorandum is summarized on pp. 13-15. It became the basis for an impassioned speech which the Cologne *Bürgermeister* J.M.N. Dumont delivered before the French Convent on Mar. 19, 1795 (pp. 19-21). The second imperial city under French rule was Aachen. See A. Pauls, "Beiträge zur Haltung der Aachener Bevölkerung während der Fremdherrschaft," *Zeitschr. f. Aachener Geschichte*, LXIII (1950).

turies without chains when the French nation was provoked at last . . . to break the chains of slavery."[30]

There was indignant protest when the French replaced the old city government by a new municipal ordinance (March 23, 1796); general rejoicing when General Hoche temporarily restored the old constitution a year later. Hoche's appreciation of Cologne's republican traditions was compared with Bonaparte's sparing of republican San Marino in the course of his Italian campaign. The restored Cologne city council soon quarreled, however, with the French commissar Rethel on the pressing problem of how to pay the contributions demanded for the support of the French army. Rethel, who was known for his rough ways with obstructionists even when they masqueraded in a republican garb, had the city fathers arbitrarily imprisoned (Aug. 22, 1797). When they continued to breathe defiance, he abolished the old city council for the second and last time; the city fathers replied with a sonorous proclamation which showed that their pride and sense of self-assertion remained unshaken. The masters (*Bannerherren*) of the various guilds, suspecting that their organizations were the next candidates for official suppression, petitioned the French to restore the old city council in Oct. 1797. This proved to be, however, a case of the dying pleading for the resurrection of the dead.

The defense of old institutions was accompanied by tenacious parochialism of an unmistakably Conservative character. The Free City of Cologne had engaged for centuries in a perennial feud with the archbishop-elector of Cologne, whose capital was in Bonn (though his metropolitan church was the cathedral in Cologne). To be placed under the administrative direction of Bonn was a terrible fate in the eyes of all true-hearted Cologners; yet the French had made Bonn the seat of their military administration for the entire Rhineland. The Cologne council (Jan. 2, 1795) protested this scandalous state of affairs in an official communication to Lamotte, an agent of the French Convention, arguing that "to place the free city of Cologne under an administration located in Bonn was like placing Calais under an administration located in Dover." It was outrageous to think of combining two utterly heterogeneous states, one the ancient seat of republican liberty, the other of ecclesiastical despotism—"two states with a long tradition of mutual hostility, with populations possessing incompatible temperaments (*zweien nie zusammen gestimmten Ge-*

[30] Quoted in Hashagen, op.cit., p. 13.

müthsvölkern), and with two completely incompatible forms of government."[31]

All the discontent which existed against Jacobin innovations was compounded by the ruthless requisitioning practices of the French armies. There is no reason to believe that these were any worse than those of other armies in the eighteenth century; what caused unusual resentment was the fact that the French talked like liberators while acting like conquerors. The best friends of France in the Rhineland—men like A. F. Rebmann and Joseph Görres—were driven to despair, although they long tried to bolster their faith by believing that French local agents were corrupting the pure intentions of a central government truly attached to liberty and justice. Many of them hoped for the creation of a Cis-Rhenish republic in 1797 which would combine revolutionary principles with the end of direct French domination. The Cis-Rhenish movement proved stillborn, however, as the French preferred direct annexation to the creation of a satellite republic, while the bulk of the Rhenish population remained indifferent, either through apathy or attachment to the "good old ways," to the Cis-Rhenians.[32]

It may be said, in conclusion, that German Conservatives had little objective reason to fear Radical subversion in advance of the arrival of French armies, and that acquiescence in French rule after conquest should not have been confused with sabotage of the German war effort behind the fighting armies. Acquiescence was but an example of the long-standing German habit of accepting any kind of *de facto* authority, and it found its limitation in the instinctive hostility of the Rhenish masses to any interference with their accustomed ways, even in the name of progress. These comforting facts were, unfortunately, not accepted at face value by most German Conservatives: they preferred to believe in the existence of a serious danger of internal subversion before the arrival of the French and mass collaboration thereafter. This belief influenced German Conservatism, both in its official and private forms, throughout the 1790's.

[31] Much fascinating material on the Cologne resentment against domination by Bonn is assembled in ibid., pp. 47-53. The quotation is from pp. 49-50.

[32] All earlier work on the Cis-Rhenish movement is superseded by the standard work of Jacques Droz cited in n.17, which is definitive on the ideas of the Cis-Rhenians. The social composition of the movement still awaits thorough analysis. The hostility provoked by French requisitioning practices in the Rhineland was, however, mild compared to the indignation provoked by French campaigning practices in South Germany. See J. M. Armbruster (ed.), *Sünden-Register der Franzozen während ihres Aufenthalts in Schwaben und Vorder-Oesterreich* (n.p., 1797).

The Official Response to the Revolution

THE PATTERN OF REPRESSION

The initial response of German princes and their ministers to the French events of 1789 ranged from the favorable to the indifferent. One could not expect in court circles the wild enthusiasm found among most German intellectuals, but there was much benevolent sympathy and very little initial feeling that the fall of French absolutism constituted a direct threat to the German political *status quo*. Among some statesmen—for example, Hertzberg in Berlin and Kaunitz in Vienna—there was satisfaction at the thought that the revolution had—so it was believed—impaired the external power of France. These observers were delighted that France was absorbed in internal affairs, instead of threatening Germany; was dismantling its army by forcing aristocratic officers into retirement; and was careening into total bankruptcy instead of putting her finances in order. This mood of complacency was to be rudely shaken when the French, far from being completely absorbed in their own affairs, began to export their revolutionary principles through propaganda; it received a ruder shock still when the fighting *élan* of the *Sansculotte* armies showed that the revolution, far from weakening France militarily, had in fact unleashed energies which multiplied her external power manifold.

The complacency of 1789 soon yielded to general panic which expressed itself in a witch hunt directed against real and imaginary revolutionary sympathizers in Germany. A rain of repressive edicts descended upon Germany, both for the empire as a whole—for example, the *Reichsgutachten* of February 25, 1793—and for most of the constituent states. It would be wearisome to enumerate them all; it is sufficient to remind the reader of what has been said above about the Saxon Decree Against Tumult and Insurrection (January 1791), the Austrian witch hunt of 1793 (Ch. 8), and the repression in Prussia in 1794 (Ch. 7). This was the period when Wöllner—of all people!—was accused by Frederick William of insufficient zeal in persecuting Radicals, and the king issued a stern reprimand against the (alleged) leniency of the censors. He called for renewed vigor in eliminating "the abuses which have crept into the censor's office to the point of paralyzing it," and explicitly linked religious with political subversion:

> The scandalous state of affairs, which has existed for some time, under which writings are published which attack the foundation

of all religion and make the most important religious verities suspect, contemptible, and ridiculous; or which make the Christian religion, the books of the Bible, and the historic and dogmatic truths contained therein, subjects of doubt or even ridicule among the common people [are denounced]. Such writings shake the foundations of practical religion, without which no civil society *(bürgerliche Ruhe und Ordnung)* can exist. It is equally necessary to crack down with vigor and persistence against all writings which attack the principles of the existing government and social structure; or describe the measures of the government from a misguided and spiteful point of view, or defend disobedience or refractoriness against either laws or legitimate authority; or encourage ordinary men to engage in useless meditation *(unnütze Grübeleien)* about topics which far transcend their understanding and judgment. We demand the ruthless punishment of all who have in any way offended against the existing rules of censorship.[33]

The intensification of the censorship was everywhere accompanied by new edicts against secret societies, student associations, and even ordinary reading clubs. Governments were increasingly suspicious of intellectuals, since this group of the population was most likely to succumb to irreligious and subversive ideas. There was a perceptible sharpening of the Conservative hostility to popular education. The Prussian monarchy, once the foremost champion of popular *Aufklärung* in Europe, gave official sanction to this Conservative hostility in an official school edict a few years later:

It suffices for the ordinary rustic of the countryside and the ordinary artisan of the cities—the two groups of people who compose the majority of Prussian subjects—that their education give them correct conceptions of religion and of their duties as subjects . . . and that it remove prejudices which might prove disadvantageous to the effective performance of their traditional occupation. Knowledge of "higher things" can only prove harmful to them by burdening their minds with conceptions which they are quite unable to understand anyway, and by giving them vague ideas concerning a "higher culture" which will make them discontented with the vocations to which society has called them.[34]

[33] Quoted in K. Eisner, *Das Ende des Reichs. Deutschland und Preussen im Zeitalter der grossen Revolution* (Berlin, 1907), p. 44. On Prussian policy at this time see the useful monograph by Kurt Heidrich, *Preussen im Kampfe gegen die französische Revolution bis zur zweiten Teilung Polens* (Berlin, 1908).
[34] *Neues Schulregiment für die Universität Breslau*, July 26, 1800. Quoted in

THEMES OF POPULAR COUNTERREVOLUTIONARY PROPAGANDA

A policy of repression was the major response of most German governments to the danger of subversion; there was, however, also a concerted effort to influence German public opinion in a Conservative direction. After 1790, when governments first became seriously alarmed, the country was flooded by a great number of Conservative pamphlets, brochures, printed sermons, songs, and fly sheets, some of private inspiration but many due to official encouragement and all approved by an increasingly vigilant censorship. A few themes appear again and again in all these materials.[35]

There was endless castigation of the French revolutionaries and their work. The Jacobins were attacked, often by the same author, for being at one and the same time bloodthirsty fanatics and opportunist racketeers. No description was too gory to cover the reign of terror, no tone too shrill to condemn the gap between the professed Liberal principles of the Jacobins and their tyrannical conduct. Much sympathy, calculated to evoke tears, was directed toward individual victims of the revolution, especially Marie Antoinette;[36] while many attacks were delivered against particular revolutionaries—the favorite targets being Mirabeau, Marat, Robespierre, and the Duke of Orleans —whose subsequent fate (in the last two cases) as victims of revolutionary "justice" provoked much ill-concealed *Schadenfreude*.[37]

Numerous pamphlets and even plays were devoted to ridiculing German Jacobins, especially after the Prussian army recaptured Mainz in 1793, and imprisoned many of these "traitors." The best known of these plays, the anonymous skit subtitled *The Devil is Loose*, brought the Mainz Jacobin Club on the stage. Its members

---

Eisner, op.cit., p. 177. The same point was expressed at great length in a *Schulverordnung* of Frederick William III concerning education in garrison schools (Aug. 31, 1799). Quoted in ibid., pp. 175-76.

[35] For a general survey see E. Sauer, *Französische Revolution*, pp. 16ff.

[36] See, for example, Johann Adolf Hermstädt, *Mörderische Hinrichtung Marien Antoinetten, Königin in Frankreich. Nebst noch etwas über den Tod ihres unglücklichen Königs* (Rothenburg an der Fulde, 1794). Hermstädt, a native of Gotha, owned a publishing house at Rothenburg. Most of the pamphlets mentioned in this section are available in a special collection at the Bonn University Library originally assembled by Clemens Perthes, author of the invaluable *Das deutsche Staatsleben vor der Revolution* (Hamburg, 1845) mentioned above.

[37] *Schadenfreude*, an untranslatable term for what some consider to be a distinctive German character trait, means roughly "malicious joy at another's misfortune." See, for example, Johann Adolf Hermstädt, *Reise des Herzogs von Orleans von Marseilles nach Paris ins Zuchthaus und endlich unter die Guillotine. Zur Warnung für Volksaufwiegler und Empörer* (Rothenburg, 1794).

were depicted as long-term, now-surfaced *Illuminati* conspirators, hated by the ordinary populace, concerned with advancing their careers when the French were winning, preoccupied with their personal safety when the French withdrew, and marked by low manners and morals, especially in sexual matters.[38]

The auxiliary bishop of Mainz, Dalberg (later to become Germany's most famous collaborator with Napoleon), offered a prize of one hundred thalers for "the best popular essay, instructing the German people in the advantages of the constitution of their own country and warning against the evils arising from exaggerated conceptions of unlimited freedom and utopian equality." The first prize was won by a rural clergyman who submitted an uncritical laudation of the constitution of the Holy Roman Empire and the principle of absolute monarchy by divine right.[39]

Many pamphlets contrasted the harmonious, patriarchal, and benevolent pattern of German government with the turbulence of revolutionary France. In Germany men had the inestimable advantage of living undisturbed in their accustomed ways; in France politics would not leave men alone. Germans were warned against the few demagogic voices of discontent who wanted to disturb this tranquillity. The existence of these voices could not be accepted as prima facie evidence that there was anything wrong with German conditions: "Even the best regent will always have discontented subjects; God Himself, the best and most perfect of all rulers, has the most."[40]

An anonymous pamphleteer threw a romantic sheen upon German conditions and warned those who had something—however little—to lose against encouraging the spirit of rebellion by their example: "Never has our government been more humane, moderate and considerate than today. Where can arbitrary power or exploitation be found? Is not justice everywhere administered in accordance with fixed law? Where is there any class in the state whose rights the government does not protect?" A natural harmony of interest existed between the rich and the poor: "If the rich are deprived of their income

[38] *Die Illuminaten in der Reichsvestung Mainz. Oder: Der Teufel ist los. Nebst Schilderung der Hauptklubisten* (3rd edn., Rothenburg an der Fulde, 1794).

[39] Anonymous, *Reden an Deutschlands Bürger über Staat, Rechte und Pflichten im Staat, deutsche Freiheit, und über Empörung* (Carlsruhe, 1794). The essay contest is described in the introduction.

[40] For example: Anonymous, *Zuruf an alle rechtschaffene Untertanen bey den gegenwärtigen Unruhen in Frankreich* (n.p., 1791). Another example, interesting in showing that antirevolutionary polemic became increasingly shrill after 1791, is the anonymous *Die rothe Freyheits Kappe. Zur Belehrung des deutschen Bürgers und Landmanns* (Chemnitz, 1793).

their dependent poor will inevitably suffer." The author, writing just after the Saxon revolt, also attempted to win over the landowning peasantry by pointing to the ultimate consequences of the spirit of rebellion. "What would happen if hired men and milk-maids began to demand wages sufficient to allow the purchase of a freehold? Would you peasants not consider this demand most unjust and inequitable?"[41]

Conservative pamphleteers frequently used dialogue forms as a device for propaganda. The dialogue is usually set in restaurants or beer halls and sometimes seems to be true to life, though the champion of the Conservative side invariably wins in the end. In one good example two peasants, symbolically named *Freyheitsträumer* (enthusiast for liberty) and *Hohenneiden* (envying the highborn), express their sympathy for the revolution and assert that a republic will mean the end of taxes, bureaucrats, and other evils. Their views are refuted by one *Klugmann* (intelligent man), a Conservative schoolteacher, who argues that taxes and bureaucrats are the inevitable corollary not of monarchy, but of government per se. He concludes with the following affirmation of monarchy after *Hohenneiden* has declared that all royalty is superfluous:

> I say emphatically "No." Men can no more dispense with regents than bees can with their queens. Moreover, regents must be sharply separated from their subjects through the awe of majesty. Their entire mode of life, and even their external appearance, must be distinctly superior to that of their subjects; for all respect would collapse if they were our equals.[42]

In another dialogue an ordinary citizen named Christian *Redlich* (integrity) shows the error of their ways to Hans *Taps* (folly), a pro-Jacobin peasant who thinks the French would abolish all corvées, and Willibald Naso, a village schoolmaster who (in sharp contrast to his above-mentioned professional colleague *Klugmann*) has all the social resentments of a petty bourgeois. They finally agree upon the desirability of a moderate freedom as opposed to Jacobin license, and expect such freedom to be secured by the amicable cooperation of prince and people.[43]

[41] Anonymous, *Der Friedensbote an den deutschen Bürger und Landmann* (n.p., n.d. [1791]). Quoted in Stulz-Opitz, *Volksbewegungen*, p. 102.

[42] Anonymous, *Der Freyheitsträumer nach dem Zuschnitte der Wahnsinnigen Jakobiner in Paris. In seiner Blösse dargestellt von Einen edeldenkenden und ruhigen Bürger in Deutschland* (Gotha und Rothenburg, 1794).

[43] Anonymous, *Freyheit und Gleichheit. Ein Wort zu seiner Zeit geredt. Allen Aristokraten und Demokraten in Deutschland gewidmet* (Erlangen, 1793).

A theme frequently expressed was that the right kind of reform could be achieved within the framework of existing German polities. Germany's princes were the most enlightened in Europe, and they were described as eager to meet the legitimate wishes of their subjects. They were firm guardians of the freedom of person and freedom of property, two freedoms abandoned by the French in their wild zeal for social reconstruction. The princes of Germany were working toward the gradual elimination of aristocratic and clerical privilege; was it not foolish to threaten this process through the quixotic pursuit of a totally utopian equality of condition? How great was the contrast between the steady reforms of enlightened absolutism and the wild paroxysms of the Jacobins?[44]

Many writers warned the population of Western Germany, directly threatened by French occupation, not to listen to the siren songs of Jacobin propaganda. One pamphlet compared French appeals to the invitation of a drunkard who urges sober men to join his stupor while oblivious to the hard awakening coming the next morning. Germans were warned that Jacobin talk about liberation from princely, aristocratic, and clerical oppression was only a cloak for the perennial aggressions of France, which were quite independent of the nature of France's internal regime. Germans must meet this challenge by mobilizing armies and invoking glories won on earlier battlefields: "Let us move against the French armies with German courage, and let them tell their countrymen, as they are forced into precipitate retreat, that Germans are still Germans, and that the Rhine will also have its Rossbach."[45]

Conservative pamphleteers frequently exposed the hypocritical character of France's pretended mission to extend the blessings of liberty to Germany—this at a time when liberty had been replaced in France by an unprecedented tyranny. The French had no intention of treating Germans as their equals, and the record of their military occupation in the Rhineland soon exposed a vast gap between their theatrical professions of liberty and equality and their odious record of requisition, plunder, rape, and extortion. (It need scarcely be repeated that this record was neither better nor worse than that of other

---

[44] C. G. Neuendorf, *Kurze Belehrung für Nachdenkende über bürgerliche Freiheit und Gleichheit* (Dessau, 1792).

[45] Anonymous, *Aufruf eines Deutschen an seine Landsleute am Rhein; sonderlich an den Nähr- und Wehrstand: im Jänner 1792* (n.p.), p. 16. The probable author was H. O. Reichard (see n.99). The subsidized character of the publication is indicated by the statement on the title page, "Ist überall umsonst zu haben." Rossbach was the scene of Frederick's great victory over the French in 1757.

military occupations during the eighteenth century, but that men did the French the honor of judging them by their own professions instead of customary canons of conduct.) The liberty which followed in the wake of a brutal military occupation was highly suspect in its origins.[46]

Even apart from these accompanying circumstances it was felt, especially in some of Germany's Free Cities, that Germany did not need the French type of liberty. These cities prided themselves on a tradition of republican liberty much older than the raw and recent French product. The proud citizens of the Hanseatic city of Hamburg expressed their sense of superiority in a "song of freedom" written in 1792 by Johann Friedrich Schink (1755-1816), director of the Hamburg theater and editor of the Conservative paper *Laune, Spott und Ernst*:

> Und *unsre* Freiheit drückt uns nicht
> Es fliesst durch sie kein Blut;
> Sie glänzt auf unserm Angesicht
> Nicht auf dem Band und Hut.
> So nehm' an unserer Freude teil,
> Wes Glaubens, Volks er sei—
> Und singe Heil dir, Hamburg, Heil,
> Denn du bist wirklich frei.[47]

The efforts of the patriotic poet were supplemented by the men of the cloth. The weekly Sunday sermon was still the single most important molder of German public opinion, and the governments used it purposefully to buttress the loyalty of the lower classes. The Saxon government ordered all ministers of the gospel—immediately after the suppression of the Saxon revolt in 1790—to "instruct and convince" their flock of "the obligation to lead a quiet and obedient life under

[46] Karl Fischer, *An den Herrn Philipp Adam Custine, Neufränkischen Bürger und General* (Germanien, 1793). The author was a prominent Württemberg publicist.

[47] Rough translation:

> "*Our* freedom does not oppress us
> She does not wallow in blood
> She shines radiantly on our faces
> Instead of being a matter of ribbons and
>   liberty caps
> You are welcome to participate in our joy
> Whatever your religion or nationality
> And sing 'Hail to thee' oh Hamburg
> For you are truly free."

Quoted by E. Sauer, *Französische Revolution*, p. 25.

465

the benevolent protection of constituted authority."[48] Many voices, both Catholic and Protestant, called for the union of throne and altar against the common revolutionary danger, and argued that a return to Christianity constituted the only effective defense against Jacobin ideas.[49]

Many published sermons and Conservative pamphlets illustrate how religion was enlisted to defend the social *status quo*. It was asserted that inequality, far from being a regrettable and remediable condition, was part of God's eternal plan for the universe. In this world some are weak, some strong; some foolish, some wise. Scripture tells us, "He made some rich and some poor, in accordance with His will and His wisdom." If this appeared unjust there was compensation in the fact that all wrongs would be righted in the life to come. "The Bible offers far greater future bliss to the poor than the rich."[50]

Another pamphleteer offered more secular comfort to those peasants who were impatient of future rewards. He claimed to be a former day laborer who had risen, much to his own regret, into the upper class (though there is no evidence that he sought to implement this regret by downward mobility to his former condition). He tried to convince those who had remained in a humble condition by the following soliloquy: "Would that I had remained what I was formerly! a position with fewer cares and fewer responsibilities, where I needed less, and where what little I had made me more happy and peaceful than I am now."[51] (This kind of argument has always proved more effective in salving the conscience of the rich than convincing the mind of the poor.)

It is impossible, of course, to measure the effect of Conservative pamphleteering upon German public opinion. What is significant, however, is that Conservative pamphleteers, often acting with governmental encouragement, now found it necessary and appropriate to

[48] Quoted in Stulz-Opitz, *Volksbewegungen*, Ch. 3, Sect. 1, "Repressivmassnahmen."

[49] For a Protestant example see the work of the Bremen pastor Gottfried Menken, *Über Glück und Sieg der Franzosen* (Bremen, 1795); a Catholic example, Karl von Eckartshausen, *Was trägt am meisten zu den Revolutionen jetztiger Zeiten bei?: Und welches wäre das sicherste Mittel, ihnen künftig vorzubeugen? Eine Schrift zur Beherzigung für Fürsten und Völker* (Munich, 1791). The latter pamphlet extended the ideas developed by the author before 1789. (See Ch. II above.)

[50] Anonymous, *Eines sächsischen Patrioten Gedanken über das Verhältniss der Unterthanen zu ihren Obrigkeiten* (n.p., 1790). Paraphrased in Stulz-Opitz, op.cit., p. 102.

[51] Gotthold Sachsenfreund [pseud.], *Sendschreiben an meine lieben Landsleute, die zu leiden glauben* (Leipzig, 1791). Quoted in ibid., p. 101.

descend into the arena of polemic to try to win over the lower classes. The above-mentioned Saxon Chancellor von Burgsdorff, to give only one example, commissioned H. O. Reichard, the Gotha librarian and well-known editor of the Conservative *Revolutionary Almanac* (described below), to counteract subversive writings by composing "in popular language a brief instruction on the evil consequences which flow necessarily from every kind of rebellion."[52] Loyalty could no longer be accepted as axiomatic or be produced by the simple threat of punishment; it was henceforth necessary to engage in exhortation and to combat Radicalism on the battleground of propaganda where Conservatism operated with the permanent disadvantage of a defensive position.

THE WAR AGAINST REVOLUTIONARY FRANCE

We have seen how Germany's princes sought to crush all expression of pro-Jacobin sympathy, and encouraged the development of a Conservative public opinion; but they realized that both policies could not be fully effective so long as the challenge of revolutionary France remained. The one certain way to restore tranquillity in Europe appeared to be to crush the French Revolution completely and to restore Bourbon absolutism and aristocratic and clerical privilege on its ruins. To achieve this objective was the maximum war aim of the Allied Powers when war began in 1792.

It would be incorrect to assume, however, that this Allied war objective constituted the main cause of the war. The problem of "war guilt" in connection with the war of 1792 is one of the most controversial questions of modern history; the desire of the "old Europe" to crush the "revolutionary hydra" was only one of several factors making for war.[53] Certainly the Emperor Leopold, the most influential statesman in Germany, had no intention of engaging in any counter-revolutionary crusade. His Liberal principles made him, on the contrary, sympathetic to most of the work of the Constituent Assembly; he rejoiced when Louis XVI accepted the new constitution of 1791.

[52] Reichard compiled a pamphlet which drew heavily upon Luther's condemnation of the Peasant Revolt of 1525: *Ein fein Gespräch zwischen zwei Nachbars- und Bauersleuten über Rebellion, Obrigkeit und jetzige Zeitläufte mit schönen Stellen aus D. Martin Luthers und andern frommen Männern Schriften andern zum Frommen und Nutzen herausgegeben und im Druck ergangen von einen Bürger und Bauernfreud* (n.p., 1791).

[53] Of the vast literature about the origins of the revolutionary wars see especially the admirable summary by K. T. Heigel, *Deutsche Geschichte*, Vol. i, Bk. ii, Chs. 3-4. The best account in English is still J. H. Clapham, *The Causes of the War of 1792* (Cambridge, 1899).

Leopold had little use for the French *émigrés*, whose Reactionary program appeared to him both undesirable and impracticable, and whose activity compromised the personal safety of the royal family. The emperor had, incidentally, no special sympathy for his sister Marie Antoinette, whom he had not seen for decades and whom he considered a foolish and frivolous woman. He advised against the "flight to Varennes" (June 1791) because it would embarrass him whether it succeeded or failed. In case of success the king would clamor to be restored to his throne by Austrian arms; in case of failure the king's domestic position would be undermined and the demand for Austrian intervention strengthened. One should add that Leopold had little fear of the revolution and was rather slow to grasp its universalist significance; he showed little of his customary perspicacity in viewing it for a long time as a purely French event.

The emperor also had several specific reasons for wishing to avoid a military showdown with France. He had recently pacified the Belgian rebels, and he feared that a French war would stir up new difficulties in that vulnerable province bordering on France. Moreover, Leopold knew that the outbreak of war in Western Europe would leave Poland open to the machinations of Catherine. Finally, he had reason to doubt that Prussia would give loyal and effective support to any invasion of France. An anti-Austrian faction at the Prussian court resented participation in a Western campaign because it might make Prussia a mere satellite of Austria, and distract attention from the Polish question which it considered paramount. This faction had been overruled when the king had decided upon the Reichenbach Convention; its power might, however, revive at any time.[54]

Leopold was quite right in his long-term assessment of policy, but in 1791 Frederick William II was far more desirous of crushing the French Revolution than Leopold himself. The Prussian king had a chivalrous sense of obligation toward Louis XVI as an insulted fellow monarch—a feeling far stronger than the emperor's sense of family loyalty to Marie Antoinette. Frederick William was imbued with the counterrevolutionary zeal of the Rosicrucian Order, whereas Leopold appreciated the value of the fundamental work of the revolution (however deplorable the excesses of the revolutionaries). There can be little question that the provocative Declaration of Pillnitz (August

---

[54] The standard treatment of Leopold's policy toward France has long been Adalbert Schultze, *Kaiser Leopold II und die französische Revolution* (Hannover, 1899), a solid dissertation directed by Max Lehmann; it is now largely superseded by the second volume of Wandruszka's biography of Leopold.

27, 1791), drawn up by Leopold and Frederick William after a conference at a Saxon hunting lodge, expressed the spirit of the Prussian king more than that of the Habsburg emperor. While intended to intimidate, it in fact only infuriated revolutionary France. The declaration spoke out in favor of concerted European action to restore legitimate government in Paris, though military intervention toward this end was contemplated only in case of unanimous support by all the European governments. Since it was common knowledge among diplomats that Great Britain would not agree to intervention at that time, the declaration was diplomatically stillborn; nevertheless, it inflamed the French Assembly and French public opinion, all the more since the Duke of Artois, leader of the *émigré* faction, had been permitted to attend the Austro-Prussian conference at which the document was drafted. Leopold's assent to this ill-considered declaration can be explained only in terms of the persistence of Frederick William, the incessant clamor of the *émigrés,* and, above all, the general excitement provoked by the virtual captivity of the French royal family after the return from Varennes. Leopold's hope of intimidating the French into more moderate conduct revealed a total misunderstanding of the psychology of the revolutionaries; and it set the pattern for the disastrous manifesto of the Duke of Brunswick the following year.

The Declaration of Pillnitz further embittered the already poisonous atmosphere which pervaded the discussion of several specific points of dispute between France and the Holy Roman Empire. French ecclesiastical legislation had unilaterally deprived several German bishops—most notably the bishops of Speyer, Mainz, Trier, and Cologne—of parts of their jurisdiction; the bishops appealed to the *Reichstag* for help in securing a return to the *status quo* of 1789. The *Reichstag* obliged them in a *Reichsgutachten* of Aug. 6, 1791, which instructed the emperor to support the episcopal claims in negotiations with France; the French, on the other hand, considered the entire question a purely domestic matter about which they consented to negotiate as a courtesy only. A similar problem arose over the demands for restoration, or at least compensation, made by several German princes whose remaining feudal rights in Alsace had been abolished by the Constituent Assembly in 1789. A further point of conflict, this time due to German rather than French action, was the friendly reception given by several Rhenish princes to the French *émigrés*. The latter were not only welcomed with open arms, but were permitted to train troops for an invasion of France in a manner incompatible with international law. French protests were at first answered with procrastination, and even after the empire acknowledged the validity of French complaints its remedial action was inadequate. Here was a clear case of German counterrevolutionary sympathies leading to conduct whose ultimate result could only be war.

Yet the responsibility was not exclusively German. It is best to see the outbreak of war in 1792 as a clash between two offensives on the part of belligerents both of whom were motivated by aggressive hopes and defensive fears—hopes and fears made especially explosive because they were accompanied by competing ideologies and material interests. There were several reasons why many Frenchmen wanted war, quite apart from their desire to export the blessings of liberty to neighboring lands. They saw that counterrevolutionary activities would persist at home so long as foreign intervention was planned abroad. Additional motives for war rose out of the deadlock which existed within France between the court and some Radical groups; both in fact desired war for special reasons. The king believed that he would benefit from war regardless of whether it led to victory or defeat. If the war were won he would return to Paris as head of a victorious army and with enhanced prestige; this would create a situation in which counterrevolution, or at least constitutional revision, would become feasible. If the war were lost the king would be called upon to mediate between France and the victorious Allied Powers under circumstances in which the latter would insist upon the restoration of absolutism. Certain Radicals in the Assembly wanted war for a very different reason: it would inevitably unmask the king's hypocrisy in accepting the new constitution of 1791, and drive him into an antipatriotic position or at least one in which his patriotism was bound to become suspect; thus the stage would be prepared for a "Second Revolution" leading to outright republicanism.

A further factor making for war in both France and Germany was a common failure to foresee the nature, length, and severity of the coming struggle. Many revolutionaries believed that the powers of "old Europe" would collapse immediately, once challenged by the armies of liberty. Most German Conservatives believed, on the other hand, that an invasion of France would be a military picnic. The *émigrés* had convinced them that most Frenchmen yearned for liberation from the Jacobin yoke, and that the French armies had become a worthless rabble after the dismissal of most of the old aristocratic officer corps. Alas for the impotence of human foresight!

SOME PROBLEMS OF THE WAR

German hopes of an easy French collapse were destroyed at Valmy, while French hopes of widespread German collaboration were equally disappointed in the autumn of 1792. The seat of war, originally in Northern France and Belgium, shifted definitely to Western Germany by 1794 and confronted the German powers with a formidable problem of defense. The war revealed the pitiful anachronisms upon which the military institutions of the empire were grounded: the *Reichsarmee* was mobilized in accordance with quotas established in 1681, and it was paid for by *Römermonate,* units of finance last established in 1521 when Charles V was planning an expedition to Rome! As Leopold had foreseen, Prussia became increasingly absorbed in the problems of Eastern Europe, while French statecraft concentrated upon driving a wedge between Austria and Prussia. French strategy prepared, meanwhile, for an invasion of South Germany in order to strike at Austria and dictate a victorious peace at Vienna.[55]

In order to defend Germany some voices called for arming the common people against the alien invader. Most Conservatives, however, were opposed to using such a revolutionary measure for even a Conservative end. Count Hardenberg, the Prussian minister in charge of administering the Franconian duchies, lent his voice to this opposition in a report to the king dated Jan. 10, 1794:

> While *we* need fear no deleterious consequences in Your Majesty's Franconian duchies from the arming of subjects, the same cannot be said of many neighboring territories in which there has been much discontent, quarrels with the prince, and public refractoriness. The arming of the people might perhaps be of some value in driving out the enemy, but the militiamen would make demands after their return—puffed up by a newly-acquired sense of power—which they would not dream of making now. This would lead to a dangerous situation in those states which do not maintain an adequate standing army [upon which the prince can rely]. Who, indeed, is in a position to calculate the consequences?[56]

[55] The conduct of the *Reichstag* in the years 1792-95 is treated definitively by Johannes Schick, *Der Reichstag zu Regensburg im Zeitalter des Baseler Friedens 1792-95* (Bonn, 1931), an excellent dissertation, directed by Max Braubach, based primarily upon the reports of the Cologne ambassador (now in the Düsseldorf archives).

[56] Quoted by Scheel, *Jakobiner,* p. 136. The fear that the arming of the populace would encourage domestic revolution while giving little help to the war effort was shared by the Habsburg Archduke Charles in 1800. H. Rössler,

When the arming of the people was discussed at the *Reichstag* in March of 1794 the Prussian delegate spoke up in opposition with two arguments: that a popular levy was militarily useless and politically dangerous. It was militarily useless against "an enemy invading Germany with big armies notable for their military skill, numerous artillery, and berserk fighting spirit (*rasende Wuth*)." It was politically dangerous, at the same time, "to take an ordinary man out of his customary domestic routine, and to give him arms, more especially against an enemy seeking to seduce his loyalty with tempting arguments."[57] This attitude was by no means peculiar to Prussia; it was used by the Austrian minister Colloredo three years later when Napoleon was advancing toward Vienna and arming the populace appeared the only way to save the capital: "I can satisfy the victorious enemy by the cession of a province—but to arm the people risks the overthrow of our throne."[58]

The war against France had never been popular among the masses of the German people, and even most governments began to weary of it by 1794. There was no longer hope of achieving a positive result: the guillotined Louis could not be restored to the throne; the social program of the revolution was evidently irreversible, since the *émigrés* were execrated by most Frenchmen as traitors allied with the enemies of France; the restoration in Alsace of the feudal rights of German princes and the ecclesiastical rights of German bishops had clearly become impossible. The problem had become, rather, one of defending the territorial integrity of the empire against France's ambition to secure the Rhine frontier, and of preventing the territorial reorganization which would become inevitable if Germany were forced to yield the Rhineland. With no military prospect of clearing the French armies out of Germany an increasing desire to end the war

---

Österreichs Kampf um Deutschlands Befreiung (2 vols., Hamburg, 1940), I, 120-21. The entire topic of arming the populace is discussed in the exhaustive monograph of Wilhelm Wendland, *Versuche einer allgemeinen Volksbewaffnung während der Jahre 1791 bis 1794* (Berlin, 1901). While many Conservatives opposed the arming of the lower classes as likely to do more harm than good, many Radicals opposed it out of sympathy for France. See the anonymous pamphlet, *Erklärung des vom Herrn Prinzen von Koburg den 30. Julius 1794 ergangenen Aufrufs, niedergeschrieben von einen rheinischen Bürger* (n.p., Aug. 1794), ridiculing the appeal of the Prince of Coburg, commander of the Imperial armies, for arming the common people.

[57] Quoted by Friedrich Foerster, *Deutschland und Preussen*, p. 392.

[58] Quoted by L. Häusser, *Deutsche Geschichte vom Tode Friedrichs des Grossen bis zur Gründung des Deutschen Bundes* (4 vols., Leipzig, 1854-57), II, 104.

by negotiation began to emerge—especially on the part of powers like Prussia, which had relatively little to lose. (It was certain that the French would be only too glad to encourage Prussian compensation in Central Germany for the loss of her small Left Rhenish provinces of Cleve and Guelders.) The elector-bishop of Mainz, fearing the loss of his capital city to the French, took the lead (in close consultation with Prussia) in introducing a motion at the *Reichstag* (Oct. 13, 1794) calling for the initiation of peace negotiations. The motion was bitterly opposed by a Conservative party headed by the imperial commissioner and the ambassador of Hannover (the latter representing the British crown). They argued that the motion was insulting to the emperor, who had not been consulted in advance; that it exposed the internal cleavages of the empire to the French enemy; that it paralyzed military preparations urgently needed for the campaign of 1794; that it was most inopportune after the recent French victories, since the empire would be negotiating from weakness rather than strength; that there was no recognized French government with which to negotiate; and that, most important of all, there was no basis for a negotiated peace since Germany could not renounce the Rhineland, which the French occupied at the moment and were obviously unwilling to surrender at the conference table.

The *Reichstag* settled for a feeble and meaningless compromise: Austria was asked to consult with Prussia about possible peace initiatives (which she obviously would not do with either vigor or sincerity), while all the princes were asked to strengthen Germany's negotiating position through an intensification of their military preparations (which obviously they were not prepared to do). Austria was as yet strong enough to prevent the empire from negotiating any peace of which it disapproved; it was not, however, strong enough to prevent Prussia from accepting the separate peace of Basel (April 5, 1795), which split the empire by taking all of Germany north of the so-called "line of demarcation" out of the war. The Prussian policy of withdrawal from the war was naturally condemned by numerous pamphleteers as "treason to the empire" and a betrayal of the Conservative cause upon whose victory depended the future welfare of Europe.[59]

[59] For a survey of some of these voices see O. Tschirch, *Geschichte der öffentlichen Meinung in Preussen vom Baseler Frieden bis zum Zusammenbruch des Staates 1795-1806* (2 vols., Weimar, 1933-34).

The Jacobin Conspiracy and Its Suppression

In the summer of 1794 the Austrian police discovered the one major attempt at something approaching conspiratorial subversion to occur in Germany in the 1790's. This so-called "Jacobin conspiracy" aroused enormous public interest; it confirmed the worst suspicions of all Conservative governments and became the favorite documentary exhibit of the advocates of the "conspiracy theory"—Starck, Hoffmann, and the writers of the *Eudämonia*—whose outlook will be examined in Ch. 10. The conspiracy deserves to be related in some detail for the light which it throws upon the social basis of Central European Jacobinism, the repressive techniques employed by the Austrian government, and the attitude of popular opinion. The historical importance of the episode is enhanced far beyond its immediate significance because of its far-reaching effects upon the young Emperor Francis II: it contributed to making the son of Leopold and nephew of Joseph an inflexible champion of the "Franciscan system," whose essence was a negative and purely repressive defense of an ever-more-anachronistic *status quo*.[60]

The rise of a nucleus of Jacobin conspirators in the Habsburg Monarchy after 1792 was a reaction against the abandonment of the Leopoldine reform policies by the Emperor Francis. Leopold had worked out far-reaching plans for modernizing the constitutional and economic structure of his realm, and he had patronized a group of secret collaborators who promoted those plans by means of pamphlets and the manipulation of petitions. Many "enlightened reformers" could believe until 1792 that the Habsburg Monarchy had taken up the torch of "enlightened" absolutism abandoned by Prussia, and that conspiratorial activity was not only hopeless but unnecessary as well. Their hopes were destroyed when Francis appeased the estates in

---

[60] The two best books on the Jacobin conspiracy, superseding all earlier studies, are Ernst Wangermann, *From Joseph II to the Jacobin Trials: Government Policy and Public Opinion in the Habsburg Dominions in the Period of the French Revolution* (Oxford, 1959), based upon extensive archival research though the materials are sometimes twisted into a procrustean Marxist framework; and Denis Silagi, *Jakobiner in der Habsburger Monarchie. Ein Beitrag zur Geschichte des aufgeklärten Absolutismus in Österreich* (Vienna, 1962), centered around the Hungarian conspirator Ignaz von Martinovics and arguing the convincing thesis that the conspiracy was "ein missgeleiteter Ausläufer der geheimen Reformpläne Kaiser Leopolds II." The thesis was first developed in the same author's *Ungarn und der geheime Mitarbeiterkreis Leopolds II* (Munich, 1961). Leo Stern "Zum Prozess gegen die österreichische 'Jakobiner Verschwörung,'" in W. Markow (ed.), *Maximilien Robespierre* (Berlin, 1958), pp. 473ff, is a recent Marxist account by an East German historian.

Hungary and several Austrian provinces by abandoning plans to increase burgher representation; purged or retired prominent Josephine officials like Kressel, whose Ecclesiastical Commission was dissolved; intensified newspaper censorship and reestablished a Central Police Ministry. Francis was eager to pursue the war against France until there was a full counterrevolutionary triumph, thereby infuriating those of his Progressive subjects who placed the "cause of humanity"—which they identified with Jacobin France—above conventional patriotic loyalties.

The Franciscan Reaction led a number of Habsburg subjects into conspiratorial activity, or at least talk, in both Austria and Hungary. Several of them had been collaborators of Leopold, most notably Ignaz von Martinovics (1755-95), the head of the Magyar Jacobins. This remarkable man was a secularized monk. His father, a Hungarian officer, had died young; his mother had sent him into a Franciscan monastery where he took his vows when he was eighteen, more or less under compulsion, and was ordained a priest a few years later. After teaching at a secondary school (*Gymnasium*) run by his Order he fled to the faraway Bukovina in 1781 to become a military chaplain. The publication of several works in the natural sciences brought him to the attention of Gottfried van Swieten, the head of Joseph's *Studienkommission,* who appointed him professor of physics at Lemberg University in Galicia in 1783. The accounts given of his character are generally unfavorable, though one must remember certain extenuating circumstances when looking at his personal weaknesses. Martinovics' opinions were vehemently atheistic after about 1780, yet he was indelibly in holy orders; the renunciation of ecclesiastical status was not permitted even in the Josephine state. Martinovics impressed men upon first meeting by his charm and conversational brilliance, but longer acquaintance usually led to a contemptuous dismissal of him as a shallow dilettante. His sociable nature and need for stimulating conversation made him suffer in the provincial isolation of Lemberg. The desperate desire to get to a metropolitan center such as Vienna or Budapest led him to engage in a good deal of deception—not to say outright lying—concerning his past career and accomplishments, and has provoked much ridicule from unsympathetic historians.[61]

This intense, frustrated, thoroughly "enlightened" man resigned his Lemberg professorship to join the "secret circle" of Leopold in July 1791. He wrote reports for the emperor on Hungarian affairs, com-

[61] On Martinovics' early life, see Silagi, *Jakobiner*, Bk. II, "Die Welt des Ignaz von Martinovics."

posed pamphlets, and organized the efforts of urban groups to submit petitions to the government which called for a broadening of the social composition of the *Reichstag* (where at present nobles and prelates were in unchallenged control). Leopold appointed several men recommended by Martinovics to Hungarian offices, perhaps to prepare for a future *coup d'état* in case the Magyar nobility remained intransigently hostile to reform. Martinovics did not confine his attention to Magyar affairs. He began to write to the emperor about Viennese Radicals in the winter of 1791-92 after claiming to join the *Illuminatenkirche* as a spy (Jan. 26, 1792); his reports consisted primarily of wild charges against alleged subversives which Leopold evidently failed to take seriously (as witnessed by the fact that he refused to move against the victims of Martinovics' denunciations). The problem of how and why Martinovics promoted Radicalism in Hungary while simultaneously denouncing Radicals (real and alleged) in Austria appears insoluble. The hypothesis of careerist opportunism is untenable, since Martinovics persisted in his Hungarian Radicalism after Francis made his peace with the Hungarian gentry in 1792. The hypothesis that he was an *agent provocateur* is not necessarily disproved by his execution as a traitor in 1795: it is possible that the government wanted to eliminate a man who "knew too much." It is made unlikely however, by the obvious sincerity of his Radical convictions before he came to Vienna, the tone of his pamphleteering in the years 1791-95, and the content of the Catechism of Faith which he penned while in jail in August 1794 (when it was certainly in his interest to express only moderate views). Whatever his motives and ultimate aims, he was sufficiently appreciated by Leopold to be appointed a Councilor at his old professorial salary of 500 florins in Oct. 1791, and to be given the post of court chemist (*Hofchemiker*), though without an additional salary, just before the emperor's death in February 1792.

The accession of Francis II changed Martinovics' position for the worse, for the new emperor showed no interest in his activities though he was retained on the imperial payroll. It is probable that Martinovics was bitter about the abandonment of the Leopoldine reform program and his loss of personal influence. At any rate he continued to advocate—now without imperial sanction—extensive Hungarian reforms. His pamphlets became ever more extreme, and he organized not one but two Hungarian secret societies in order to promote his ideas. The moderate Reform Society was nationalist in outlook and composed primarily of members of the lower Magyar

gentry; its avowed aims were a curious blend of the revival of anachronistic Magyar *Ständetum* and the advance to modern constitutionalism. The membership of this society remained completely ignorant
of the existence of a more Radical group, the Society for Freedom and
Equality, whose aims were republican and egalitarian. This second
group possessed between eighty and one hundred members and was
organized under a four-man directorate. It was evidently the hope of
Martinovics that the Reform Society would begin a revolution and
that the Society for Freedom and Equality would then exploit this
revolution as the Jacobins had built on the work of the Feuillants in
France. There can be little question about the sincerity of Martinovics'
Radical intentions, though he continued to report all his activities to
Franz Gotthardi, his old superior in Leopold's "secret circle." This
fact does not prove him an *agent provocateur*, for Gotthardi himself
half-sympathized with Radical views and was soon to be arrested and
sentenced along with the other conspirators.[62]

Franz Gotthardi (born 1750) was originally a German merchant
and coffeehouse owner in Budapest. His political interests are revealed by his early election as a city councilor *(Ratsmann)*; his principles, by his appointment by Joseph to the important post of Police
Director in the Hungarian capital in 1787. The collapse of the
Josephine system forced him to flee to Vienna, where Leopold made
him the head of his "secret circle" dealing with Magyar affairs. His
office was located in the *Hofburg* immediately under the imperial
apartments; his cover job was that of Councilor to the Theater Board
(*K. K. Rat bei der Theaterdirektion*) with a salary of 2100 florins.
Gotthardi established a broad network of agents who served both as
reporters and manipulators of public opinion. This organization was
inherited by Francis in 1792 and continued to operate although now
deprived of imperial guidance. It is certain that Gotthardi was privy
to the work of the Jacobin conspirators throughout the monarchy,
though he neither joined them nor denounced them to the regular
police.[63]

Franz von Hebenstreit, a first lieutenant in the Austrian army, was
the most Radical of the conspirators. He was born in 1748 in Prague,
the son of the director of the Philosophical Faculty of the university.
He joined the army in 1768 but deserted to the Prussians five years

[62] On Martinovics' conspiratorial work see Silagi, *Jakobiner*, Bk. III, "Martinovics in der französischen Zeit." Silagi prints his "Catechism of Faith," first
written in May 1794 and repeated while in jail in August 1794, in Appendix C.
[63] On Gotthardi see Silagi, *Ungarn*, Ch. 7, "Die Entstehung des leopoldinischen
geheimen Dienstes."

later. On the basis of a general pardon he returned to Austrian service in 1778. Hebenstreit was a man of broad interests and versatile talents. He composed revolutionary songs in German and political treatises in Latin verse. His principles were outright republican (*"Rex aliud non est quam non satiabile monstrum"*) and Communist (he criticized the French Jacobins for retaining the principle of private property), and he may be described as a kind of Austrian Babeuf. Hebenstreit also had technical interests and invented a new type of cannon which he sent by special emissary to the French government so that it could serve the cause of liberty. This conduct was certainly treasonable since Austria was at war with France at the time; the treason was compounded by the fact that Hebenstreit was an officer on active service.[64]

Another prominent figure among the Viennese Jacobins was Andreas Freiherr von Riedel, born in Vienna in 1744, the son of an officer. He was trained as an alchemist and was passionately interested in mesmerism and other attempts to explore the irrational. Riedel was professor of mathematics at the academy of Wiener Neustadt when Leopold, at that time Grand Duke of Tuscany, appointed him mathematics tutor to his oldest son Francis in the late 1770's. The relationship between teacher and pupil proved unsatisfactory. Francis hated the teacher of an unpleasant subject for which he had little aptitude; Riedel must have developed contempt for the monarchical system of government under which a dullard like Francis could exercise rule over his betters. Riedel offered his services to Leopold for confidential political work in the spring of 1790, but although Leopold conferred upon him an imperial knighthood his offer was refused. About the specific development of his political views nothing is known. We know only that after Francis' accession he distributed dozens of handwritten copies of a letter calling for a German revolution to start on November 1, 1792. Riedel specifically urged his (probably nonexistent) fellow conspirators to appear at 7:00 a.m. at the central squares of their respective towns, armed with knives and the tricolor cockade. This call for a popular rising may have been intended as a joke, but it certainly was a dangerous joke in questionable taste in the year 1792.[65]

[64] On Hebenstreit see Silagi, *Jakobiner*, pp. 161-62. A favorable view is presented by Franz Ernst Pipitz, *Der Jakobiner in Wien* (Zurich and Winterthur, 1842).

[65] The call to revolution is printed by Valjavec, *Entstehung*, pp. 505ff. On Riedel see Silagi, *Jakobiner*, pp. 162-63 and Appendix A, where Silagi prints the curious letter which Riedel wrote to Leopold in the spring of 1790 offering his services as political man Friday.

Some other conspirators in Vienna were Karl Traugott Held, a Lutheran minister from Saxony who carried the designs of Hebenstreit's cannon to Paris; Joseph Prandstätter, municipal counselor and a close personal friend of the assistant police chief Count Franz Joseph Saurau; Johann Gottlieb Wolstein, head of the Vienna veterinary school; and the seventeen-year-old Count Leopold von Hohenwart, nephew of the bishop of Pölten (who had been history tutor to Francis and was to succeed Migazzi as archbishop of Vienna).[66] The Hungarian conspirators included prominent figures like Joseph Hajnoczy, a lawyer and legal historian who was secretary of the royal *Kammer* in Ofen; Franz von Abaffy, a landowner, anticlerical and a long-standing foe of royal despotism; and the youthful aristocrat Franz von Szentmarjay, a key figure in the Magyar literary revival.[67] It is clear that the conspirators consisted of men of broad interests, high intelligence, and idealistic devotion to principle, though it was inevitable that adventurers should also be attracted to the group.

The conspirators—who numbered perhaps eighty in Vienna—were loosely organized in reading circles formed to discuss news from France and so-called subversive literature, which the police proved unable to repress. All members took the following oath in the course of colorful initiating ceremonies:

> I swear in the name of Nature, Reason, and Freedom to promote Virtue and to hate despotism and the hierarchy of the triple-crowned monster [i.e., the Catholic Church]. I will promote the Good to the utmost of my capacity, check fanaticism and other abuses, and love my brothers. To confirm this oath I place my finger upon this dagger and I drink this wine to the welfare of mankind; and we must embrace as brothers.[68]

Several conspirators participated in a festive ceremony where a liberty tree was planted and the notorious *Eipeldauerlied*—probably

[66] On the Vienna conspirators see W. C. Langsam, "Emperor Francis II and the Austrian 'Jacobins' 1792-96," *AHR*, L (1945), 471-90. Limitations of space preclude discussion of similar groups which existed in Graz and Innsbruck and perhaps other provincial centers as well.

[67] On the Hungarian conspirators see Paul Bödy, "The Hungarian Conspiracy of 1794-95," *JCEA*, XXII (1962), 3-26, and Heinrich Fodor, "Der Jakobinismus in Ungarn," *Archiv für Kulturgeschichte*, XXXVII (1955), 234ff. The background is sketched out in Peter F. Sugar, "The Influence of the Enlightenment and the French Revolution in Eighteenth Century Hungary," *JCEA*, XVII (1958), 331ff. A useful contribution to the very limited literature in English is R. R. Palmer and Peter Kenez, "Two Documents of the Hungarian Revolutionary Movement of 1794," *JCEA*, XX (1961), 423ff.

[68] Silagi, *Jakobiner*, p. 180.

composed by Hebenstreit—was sung. This song defended the execution of Louis XVI, ridiculed the "Child Emperor" Francis II, and called for the destruction of nobility and bureaucracy alike. It also called upon the masses in no uncertain terms to rise against their aristocratic exploiters:

> Drum schlagt's d'Hundsleut tot,
> Nit langsam, wie die Franzosen;
> Sonst machen's Enk no tausend Noth
> S'ist nimmer auf sie z'losen.[69]

The conspirators also sought to distribute subversive literature among the lower classes, though obviously with little success.

Did the conspirators have specific plans for overthrowing the government? And was there any genuine danger that they might succeed in their purpose? That some of the activities of the conspirators were questionable in the situation of 1794 few will deny; that they were dangerous few will affirm. It is understandable, however, that the Franciscan government became seriously alarmed about domestic subversion during a time of war when some of its subjects sympathized with a powerful external enemy. It is possible, of course—as argued by those historians who minimize the Jacobin conspiracy—that the government pounced upon the conspirators only to distract attention from its own failure to conduct the war efficiently;[70] but even if this theory is correct it must be admitted that the conspirators provided the government with a very convenient pretext. Hebenstreit sent his young friend Held to Paris in April 1794 not only with designs for the new cannon but also with general plans for a rising in the Austrian capital. The Austrian government learned about the mission as Held passed through Switzerland, and was henceforth on the trail of the conspirators. The Deputy Police Minister Count Saurau (1760-1832) instructed his star agent, the bookseller Joseph Vinzenz Degen (1763-1827), to contact Hebenstreit and act as an *agent provocateur*. Degen won Hebenstreit's confidence by pretending Radical sympathies. At a meeting on July 21, 1794, Hebenstreit became thoroughly

---

[69] Ibid., p. 180. A loose translation by W. C. Langsam, "Emperor Francis II," p. 479, runs as follows:

> "So kill the dogs with smashing blows
> Not like the Frenchmen, slowly;
> Else they'll cause you a thousand woes
> For naught to them is holy."

[70] This is one of the main themes of the otherwise excellent book by Wangermann, *From Joseph II to the Jacobin Trials*.

drunk and talked about a specific plan for a *coup d'état*, though it is probable that it had far greater specificity in his bibulous imagination than in reality. He bragged about the training of student agitators who would recruit some 2,500 determined characters among the most discontented of the lower classes—an easy task since, in Hebenstreit's words, "every artisan journeyman and day-laborer resented that the worker, throughout the Monarchy, possessed nothing and the idler much."[71] These 2,500 revolutionaries would seize Vienna on a dark night, arrest the garrison (most of whose members were expected to join the successful conspirators), seize the imperial family and three hundred aristocrats as hostages, and establish a provisional government. The emperor would be killed but only after trickery had induced him to sign a number of carte blanche documents. These would be used to summon a constituent assembly and to proclaim the abolition of all surviving feudal obligations. It is a sign of a certain realism on the part of the conspirators that they recognized that their project had no chance of success—in view of the unbroken Conservative loyalties of the broad mass of the Austrian population—without the appearance of imperial sanction; it is clear proof of the naïveté of the conspirators that they persisted in their plans despite their recognition of their isolation from the mass of the people.[72]

Emperor Francis II, when informed of Degen's report, ordered the immediate arrest of the leading conspirators. The first nine arrests were made in the late evening of July 23, and included Hebenstreit, Riedel, and Martinovics. A special commission *(Untersuchungs-Hof-kommission)* under Count Saurau was appointed to conduct the preliminary examination; its searching investigation soon led to thirty additional arrests in Austria (including Franz von Gotthardi). Martinovics proved a most cooperative prisoner, whether in a vain desire to

[71] Quoted by Silagi, *Jakobiner*, p. 181, as part of a paraphrase of Degen's report to Saurau concerning his July 21, 1794, conference with Hebenstreit.

[72] The plans of the conspirators (especially their recruiting methods and songs) can be studied in the anonymous, government-inspired pamphlet, *Geheime Geschichte des Verschwörungs-Systems der Jakobiner in den österreichischen Staaten. Für Wahrheitsfreunde* (London [Heilbronn], 1795), which deliberately sought to maximize the "ramifications" of the conspiracy. It may be noted that Degen was a rather unusual *agent provocateur*. He was a man of wide reading and well-articulated Conservative convictions developed under the influence of Burke and Hoffmann. The emperor rewarded Degen for his services by ennoblement and an annual pension of 600 florins (soon raised to 1000 florins) and by making him —somewhat later—director of the State Printing Office, *Hof und Staatsbuchdruckerei*). Silagi, *Jakobiner*, p. 179, and Appendix B, where Silagi prints extracts from a letter written by Degen to Count Saurau (July 8, 1794) justifying his actions as a secret government agent.

save his life or in the mistaken belief that the police already "knew everything anyway" is uncertain; in any case he betrayed the members of the two Hungarian societies which he had organized a few weeks previously. The first Hungarian conspirators were arrested on August 16, with further arrests (to the total number of fifty) following during the next three months.[73]

The investigative commission was composed of high officials of the Police Ministry, Judiciary, War Office, and Hungarian *Hofkanzlei*. The Police Ministry (meaning Saurau) wanted to simplify matters by giving the commission judicial power without further appeal— thus making it investigator and judge at the same time. The emperor decided against this short cut, however, when Freiherr von Martini, deputy president of the *Oberste Justizstelle* (the highest Austrian court) argued that this procedure would violate the principles of a civilized *Rechtsstaat*. A formal trial followed the completion of the preliminary investigation in October 1794. The court met *in camera* in order to avoid exciting the populace; the fact of secrecy cannot, however, be taken as proof that governmental officials had a bad conscience and believed that their conduct of the case could not stand the light of publicity. It was the normal way of conducting justice under the *ancien régime*.

Within these limitations it appears that the Austrians accused (the Hungarians were tried separately) got fair trials and, by the canons of the age, appropriate punishments. The indictment consisted of two counts: active accessory to intended treason and failure to report information concerning treasonable activity to the government. The evidence showed that the conspirators had taken illegal oaths in quasi-Masonic ceremonies, disseminated seditious books, pamphlets, and songs, and planned a specific *coup d'état* (at least if Degen's evidence was credible). Saurau was anxious to secure the death penalty for the conspirators, but this was made impossible—for Austrian civilians at least—by Joseph's abolition of capital punishment in 1784. Here the deputy president Martini refuted the hired opinion of an official named Paulsen, who had argued that the death penalty was permissible despite the 1784 prohibition. (Martini's role shows how deeply entrenched the principle of legality was in the Josephine bureaucracy.) The court sentenced the conspirators to long jail terms instead. Riedel received sixty years and remained imprisoned until liberated by French troops fourteen years later (in 1809); Gotthardi, thirty-five years, but he died in a Viennese jail in 1795. Ten other conspirators received terms ranging between twenty and thirty-five years.

[73] For this and the following paragraph see Silagi, *Jakobiner*, Ch. 4.

The emperor refused to issue any pardons until 1802, and even then he excluded his old mathematics tutor Riedel from the amnesty.

Hebenstreit, being a soldier on active service, was tried by a special military tribunal which sentenced him to death for the crimes of planning a *coup d'état* and maintaining treasonable contacts with the enemy. He was publicly hanged on January 8, 1795. Martinovics was tried along with the Hungarian conspirators in Budapest, though he had sought unsuccessfully to deny the court's jurisdiction on the plea that he was a regular resident of Vienna. (This was an important matter since Joseph's abolition of the death penalty did not apply to Hungary.) The court sentenced eighteen conspirators, including Martinovics and the four directors of the Society for Freedom and Equality, to death. Seven sentences were carried out on the "blood meadow" of Budapest on May 20 and June 3, 1795. The five directors, including Martinovics, were executed first; but the government insisted that at least two ordinary members of the secret society also be hanged, lest it be said that only directorship (not simple membership) of a subversive society constituted a capital crime. The remaining eleven capital sentences were commuted to life imprisonment. There can be no question that these sentences were ferociously severe and constitute a severe stain upon the reputation of the Franciscan government, though it must be remembered that "verbal treason" was punished severely in every European country at that time. It is certain that the conspirators had engaged in nothing but wild talk, and that they were far from constituting a "clear and present" danger in either Vienna or Budapest.

This is proved more than anything else by the popular impatience in Vienna to see the conspirators punished quickly and publicly. The open criticism directed against the tardiness of the investigation and the delay of the trial led the government to issue a fatherly admonition in the following terms:

> Instead of being impatient with the slow course of justice the Viennese should rejoice in living under an administration that not only protects innocence and property, but gives even the worst criminal time to build up his case and punish him according to the laws only after his guilt has been fully established.[74]

The execution of sentences always attracted a festive crowd in the Vienna of the *ancien régime*. The mob which turned out to see Hebenstreit hanged was composed of every social stratum from society lady on horseback to starving proletarian in rags. One of Hebenstreit's

[74] Quoted by Langsam, "Emperor Francis II," p. 482.

fellow conspirators—a soldier called Gilofsky—cheated the hangman by committing suicide in prison; when his body was hung nonetheless, the populace threw mud and stones at his corpse. Those who were sentenced to jail terms were pilloried by the populace as the judgment was read out. In the words of a contemporary newsletter:

At last the wish of the Viennese has come true. Yesterday, March 12, 1795, three members of the clubbist gang [including Gotthardi] were sentenced as accessories to the crime of treason. You just can't imagine the crush there was on the *Hohenmarkt* [the city square where the punishment was carried out]. The people were as thick as ants, and their heads waved back and forth so that the scene looked like a ripe wheatfield in the wind. Some people even clung to the housetops, and in the windows one head rose above the other. . . .[75]

The effect of the conspiracy upon Emperor Francis was to confirm his extemely narrow Conservative outlook. It appears that he panicked at the discovery of plans aiming at his own assassination and was deeply grateful to the high police officials who had saved his life. The censorship was now transferred to the Police Ministry (February 25, 1795), an infallible method for strangling Austrian intellectual life. The death penalty was formally restored (Jan. 2, 1795) to prevent future conspirators from cheating the noose; Francis evidently resented the fact that Riedel and others had been sentenced to jail terms only. The emperor's great suspicion of intellectuals was much enhanced, and the government now took positive steps to discourage elementary education and to increase clerical influence upon what schools survived. There was also a new determination to safeguard the social *status quo* in its entirety; Francis believed that the Josephine reform policies had unleashed forces of incalculable portent and must, therefore, be stopped. It is no exaggeration to say that what historians call the "Metternichean system" was developed in embryo by Francis during the mid-1790's. The triumph of this system was certainly promoted by the discovery of the Austrian Jacobin conspiracy of 1794, and the repressive ordinances which accompanied the punishment meted out by the Franciscan government set a pattern for the next fifty years of Habsburg history.[76]

[75] Ibid., p. 483, for the entire paragraph.
[76] The best summary of the effects of the conspiracy is to be found in Wangermann, op.cit. Ch. 6, "The Consequences of the Trials." Silagi calls the restoration of capital punishment and the censorship ordinance "the Magna Carta of the Franciscan system of Government." *Jakobiner*, p. 201. The specific effect of the conspiracy must, however, not be exaggerated, since there was already much

Prominent Opponents of the Revolution

SOME SELECTED INDIVIDUAL WRITERS

We have seen that the initial response of most Germans to the revolution was overwhelmingly favorable; there were, in fact, only very few prominent Germans who disapproved of the revolution from the very start. One opponent of the revolution was Johann Wolfgang von Goethe, whose views—though little known to the general public—were extensively discussed among his many literary friends. The poet deeply abhorred the revolution for bringing strife and contention into a previously tranquil world, and thereby making the quest for individual perfection—through the attainment of the Good, the True, and the Beautiful—immeasurably more difficult. Goethe's attitude paralleled that of Erasmus toward the Lutheran Reformation. Both men admitted that the violence which they disapproved had been provoked by genuine evils. But Erasmus and Goethe believed that the remedy was far worse than the disease; they believed that violence—which they too easily dismissed as "unnecessary"—had interrupted a slow but sure process of gradual reform of anachronistic abuses. Goethe's deeply Conservative outlook made him view the revolution as nothing less than the destruction of the "natural" order of society, under which he understood the rule of "legitimate" princes; the traditional pattern of social differentiation, under which everybody minded his own business and claimed liberty only within a restricted sphere; and governmental administration by bureaucratic professionals, with whose work mere amateurs ought not to meddle. Goethe believed that all attempts to overcome this "natural order" were based upon utopian dreams whose attempted implementation must inevitably lead to disastrous results. He feared and hated the revolution, whose far-reaching significance he immediately recognized, because he thought it had encouraged the masses to claim power they were unqualified to exercise and had given them a belief in the legitimacy of breaking up the legitimate order of society—two explosive forces from which Europe would suffer for a long time to come. Goethe did not possess any remedy for the evils he denounced, and he withdrew from the revolutionary challenge into the peaceful and parochial world of Weimar with the hope that this world would continue to give him the sheltered refuge needed for scientific and artistic work. Because he lacked the minimal sympathy which is

---

anti-Jacobin hysteria before its discovery. See Gustav Gugitz, "Die Jakobiner-furcht in Wien (1791-93)," in *Altwienerisches. Bilder und Gestalten* (ed. G. Gugitz and K. Blümml, Vienna, 1920), pp. 326-39.

necessary to do artistic justice to a disliked subject, his various attempts to treat revolutionary themes in his poetry are a failure (see especially his *Grosscophta* and *Bürgergeneral*).[77]

Johann Georg Zimmermann (1728-95) was another relentless foe of the revolution who never felt even momentary sympathy. A native of Switzerland and protégé of the great Albrecht von Haller, he became a celebrity in the two fields of medicine (he was Germany's leading society doctor) and literature. His famous work on national pride (*Über den Nationalstolz*, 1758) treated a problem of great interest to a cosmopolitan age; his still more famous work in praise of solitude (*Über die Einsamkeit*, 1756, expanded edition in four volumes, 1784) proved very attractive, by way of contrast, to an exceedingly gregarious age. Zimmermann had written these works while he was still a country doctor in Switzerland before he received a prestigious appointment as Hannoverian court physician in 1768; this post was a virtual sinecure since the elector (George III of Great Britain) resided in London. Zimmermann generally spent the summers in Bad Pyrmont, the leading spa of North Germany, where the fashionable world came to take the waters; the Duke of York and Justus Möser were among his prominent summer patients. His outstanding reputation led to his being summoned to Berlin in 1786 to attend Frederick the Great in his final illness. This visit led, however, to a series of unfortunate developments which made him a famous champion of German Conservatism but also embittered the remaining decade of his life.[78]

The trouble started when Zimmermann published a book in 1788

---

[77] The endless literature on Goethe's political views cannot be listed here. The best recent treatment of the whole subject is Wilhelm Mommsen, *Die politischen Anschauungen Goethes* (Stuttgart, 1948); of the poet's attitude toward the Revolution, E. Beutler, "Goethe und die französische Revolution," *Pr. Jahrb.*, ccxxxv (1934); an excellent brief summary can be found in Raumer, *Deutschland*, pp. 28-32. While Goethe was essentially a stubborn adherent of the *status quo*, there were also some "Reform Conservative" elements in his outlook; he viewed the French Revolution as a "natural event" in view of the decadent and unreformed character of the French *ancien régime*, and did not share the "conspiracy theory."

[78] On J. G. Zimmermann see the standard biographies by Rudolf Ischer, *J. G. Zimmermanns Leben und Werke* (Bern, 1893), and August Bouvier, *J. G. Zimmermann, un représentant suisse de cosmopolitisme littéraire au XVIIIᵉ siècle* (Geneva, 1925). The former is far better on his political views, which Bouvier only mentions briefly at the end of Ch. 3. Zimmermann's personality is portrayed brilliantly in the semifictional introduction of Ricarda Huch to her selections from his writings, *Zimmermanns "Friedrich des Grossen letzte Tage." Mit Zimmermanns tragischer Biographie* (Basel, 1920).

about his conversations with the dying king.[79] Many readers were offended by Zimmermann's turning a professional relationship to literary advantage; the offense was compounded by the fact that Zimmermann, who already possessed an unenviable reputation for vanity and self-exhibition, appeared to value his relation to Frederick as an opportunity more for advertising himself than helping his royal patient. (In his book the great Frederick appears as a mere foil for Zimmermann's brilliance.) For reasons which are now impossible to ascertain, Zimmermann also included a gratuitous attack upon the Berlin *Aufklärung*—an attack which was rather surprising because he had previously expressed support of Friedrich Nicolai's assaults upon monasticism and Catholicism and had hitherto always been considered an *Aufklärung* figure himself. His smug egotism provoked easy ridicule and his attack upon the *Aufklärung* made Zimmermann fair game for the Radicals.[80] A new spate of controversy broke out in 1790 when Zimmermann published a further book, *Fragmente über Friedrich den Grossen*, in which he renewed his attack upon what he called the *Aufklärungssynode* (roughly, a clique devoted to spreading *Aufklärung*).[81] This time he provoked specific replies from several prominent *Aufklärer*, including Friedrich Nicolai[82] and the inevitable Dr. Bahrdt.[83]

[79] J. G. Zimmermann, *Über Friedrich den Grossen und meine Unterredungen mit Ihm kurz vor seinem Tode* (Leipzig, 1788).

[80] Some examples: Anonymous [Friedrich Julius Knüppeln], *Widerlegung der Schrift des Ritters von Zimmermann über Friedrich den Grossen* (Germanien, 1788); and two witty pamphlets by men we have previously encountered in different contexts: the *Illuminat* Knigge and the Königsberg *Bürgermeister* Hippel. Anonymous [Adolf Freiherr von Knigge], *Über Friedrich Wilhelm den Liebreichen und meine Unterredungen mit Ihm; von J. C. Meywerk, Chur Hannoverscher Hosenmacher* (Frankfurt 1788), and Anonymous [Gottlieb Hippel], *Zimmermann I und Friedrich II, von Johann Friedrich Quitenbaum Bildschnitzer in Hannover* (London [?], 1790). For full paraphrases of these and several other attacks see Ischer, *Zimmermann*, pp. 349-65.

[81] J. G. Zimmermann, *Fragmente über Friedrich den Grossen zur Geschichte seines Lebens, seiner Regierung und seines Charakters* (3 vols., Leipzig, 1790).

[82] F. Nicolai, *Freimüthige Anmerkungen über Zimmermanns Fragmente über Friedrich den Grossen von einigen brandenburgischen Patrioten* (Berlin, 1791).

[83] The latter's sprightly but scurrilous attack upon Zimmermann's personality, medical skill, and literary work was written in his Magdeburg jail cell while he served his term for libeling Wöllner. He ridiculed Zimmermann's habit of advertising his academic and political connections, and the fact that Catherine the Great had sent him the order of St. Vladimir, third class, as a reward for his book *Über die Einsamkeit*, under the following title: *Mit dem Herrn Zimmermann, Ritter des St. Wladimirordens von der dritten Klasse, Königl. Leibarzt und Hofrath in Hannover . . . deutsch gesprochen von Dr. Karl Friedrich Bahrdt, auf keiner der deutschen Universitäten weder ordentlicher noch ausserordentlicher*

Zimmermann's reputation was damaged by the attack of his "enlightened" enemies; it was altogether ruined, however, by the imprudent zeal of one who considered himself Zimmermann's friend. The playwright Alexander von Kotzebue, wrote an anonymous attack upon Bahrdt in 1790 under the title *Dr. Bahrdt with his Iron Forehead.*[84] This vicious pamphlet portrayed Bahrdt as the keeper of a brothel who was visited by his various friends who all just happened to be Zimmermann's enemies—a theme so scurrilous that it succeeded in the almost impossible task of arousing popular sympathy for Dr. Bahrdt. Much of Germany's reading public was convinced that Zimmermann was the author even after he had denied under oath that he had had anything to do with the publication. His name stood under a heavy cloud until Kotzebue finally confessed his authorship in 1792.

By that time it was too late to retrieve Zimmermann's reputation, for he had passed from ordinary Conservative hostility to the *Aufklärung* to outright mania about the French Revolution and its German supporters. He called upon Emperor Leopold II to take strong measures against Masons and *Illuminati;*[85] when the emperor sent him a cordial reply and an expensive present (February 13, 1792), Zimmermann lost no time in parading this fact before the general public. He became convinced that Freiherr von Knigge—a bitter personal enemy since 1788, when Knigge had ridiculed Zimmermann's first book about Frederick with devastating effect—had never ceased to be an *Illuminat* and that, even as he masqueraded as a loyal servant of George III of England and Hannover, he continued to head a German Radical party. Zimmermann attempted to prove his case by collecting quotations from two pamphlets published by Knigge in 1792, one ridiculing German Reactionaries in the form of a "detailed report concerning the venerable order of dunces (*Pinsel Orden*)," the other warning Germany's princes that a revolution was inevitable unless they began the immediate reform of feudal abuses, clerical privilege, and absolutist patterns of government.[86] Zimmermann sought to expose

---

Professor, keines Hofes Rath, keines Ordens Ritter, weder von der ersten noch von der dritten Klasse, keiner Akademie der Wissenschaften, wie auch keiner einzigen Gelehrten noch ungelehrten Societät Mitgliede (Berlin, 1790).

[84] *Doctor Bahrdt mit der eisernen Stirn, oder Die deutsche Union gegen Zimmermann. Ein Schauspiel in vier Aufzügen von Freiherrn von Knigge* [sic!] (n.p., 1790).

[85] Anonymous [Knigge], *Des seligen Herrn Etatsraths Samuel Conrad von Schaafskopf hinterlassene Papiere; von seinen Erben herausgegeben* (Berlin, 1792).

[86] Knigge, *Joseph von Wurmbrand, kaiserlich abyssinischen Ex. Ministers jez-*

Knigge by publishing ex parte extracts from these pamphlets, accompanied by a salty commentary, in the Reactionary *Wiener Zeitschrift* (to be discussed in the next chapter).[87] The commentary pointed out, for example, that Knigge had praised Thomas Paine, a man proclaimed a dangerous subversive by the British ministers of the very King George whom Knigge was serving as a Hannoverian official! Knigge was convinced that Zimmermann—who was, after all, court physician to George III—was demanding nothing less than his own dismissal from office, and he decided to defend himself by suing for libel even as friends rushed to his defense with various pamphlets.[88] The prolonged lawsuit aroused much public interest as it dragged through the Hannoverian courts. It ended in 1795 with Knigge's complete vindication; the judges compelled Zimmermann to retract his charge that Knigge was a subversive conspirator. The entire case showed that Hannoverian justice had remained uncorrupted by the counterrevolutionary tide which was sweeping through Germany and that German Radicals could still go to court—at least in some German states—and secure legal protection against the Conservative smear technique of identifying all Radicalism with treason and subversion.

By the time that he lost his case Zimmermann had become a sad wreck of his earlier self. His personality had always been marked by insecurity and internal tensions. He loved solitude and wrote a famous work in its praise; yet he craved appreciation and strove desperately for fame. He complained about obscurity when he was a country doctor in Switzerland and about the burdens of fame after he had become a

---

zigen Notarii caesarii publici in der Reichsstadt Bopfingen politisches Glaubensbekenntniss, mit Hinsicht auf die französische Revolution und deren Folgen (Frankfurt and Leipzig, 1792). The standard monograph on Knigge and the French Revolution is Karl Spengler, *Die publizistische Tätigkeit des Freiherrn Adolf von Knigge während der französischen Revolution* (Bonn, 1931).

[87] Zimmermann, "Adolf Freiherr Knigge dargestellt als deutscher Revolutionsprediger und Demokrat," *Wiener Zeitschrift*, II (1792), 317-29, and "Politisches Glaubensbekenntniss des Kaiserlich-Abissinischen Exministers . . . Knigge, im Auszuge mitgeteilt," ibid., III (1792), 55-65. Knigge replied to Zimmermann's charges in *Auszug eines Briefes, die Illuminaten betreffend* (Leipzig, 1794).

[88] For example: Anonymous [H. C. Albrecht], *Rettung der Ehre Adolphs Freyherrn Knigge, welchen der Herr Hofrat und Ritter von Zimmermann in Hannover als deutschen Revolutionsprediger und Demokraten darzustellen versucht hat* (Hamburg, 1792). The book provoked a reply in the form of an open letter to Zimmermann written by the British scientist (also reader to Queen Caroline) De Luc, *De Luc in Windsor an Zimmermann in Hannover. Aus dem Französischen* (n.p., 1792). Many documents pertaining to the Knigge-Zimmermann lawsuit are printed in H. Klencke, *Aus einer alten Kiste. Originalbriefe, Handschriften und Dokumente aus dem Nachlasse eines bekannten Mannes* (Leipzig, 1853), pp. 234-92.

fashionable court doctor at Hannover and Pyrmont. He was both a proud Swiss democrat and a fervid supporter of German absolutism. He wielded a ferocious pen yet proved thin-skinned in the face of attacks for which he had given ample provocation. Throughout much of his life Zimmermann suffered from frequent bouts of disabling melancholy; this condition became chronic in the early 1790's as he despaired utterly of the world around him. He soon passed the boundary which separates the neurotic from the psychotic as he developed a morbid fear of poverty (which was ludicrous in the light of his earnings), revulsion against all food (for fear of being poisoned by the revolutionaries), and a belief that men shunned him because he suffered from a contagious disease (for which there was no warrant). Zimmermann was clearly a candidate for an institution before death released him from his torments, and freed German Conservatism from a grave embarrassment, in October 1795.

More representative than the cases of Goethe and Zimmermann are the writers who passed from initial approval of the revolution to sharp opposition. It would be idle to list, much less discuss, even the most distinguished here; their viewpoint may be studied in the attitude of Germany's most famous political writer, Professor Schlözer of Göttingen (1735-1809), editor of the *Staatsanzeigen* (1782-94). His enthusiasm for the revolution at the time of the convocation of the Estates General was certainly typical, but his disillusionment as early as the spring of 1790 showed that Schlözer was a leader rather a follower of public opinion. His "renegacy" was a much talked-about event, and aroused the indignation of German Radicals, who recalled that he had once before—at the time of the American Revolution—been on the side of royal tyranny (see Ch. 5).[89]

The importance of his defection must be assessed in the light of the commanding position held by the *Staatsanzeigen*. The paid circulation of 4,400—though large by the standards of the eighteenth century and sufficient to earn a fortune for Schlözer—gives a very inadequate measure of the journal's influence. It was read by all Germans who were seriously interested in politics, and it was a common saying among German princes, "We can't do this, because it would provoke adverse comment in the *Staatsanzeigen*." Schlözer was the first German publicist who sensed the power wielded by an enlightened public opinion bent upon removing abuses; and his journal did yeoman

[89] The general literature on Schlözer is listed in Ch. 11, n.2, in connection with a discussion of Schlözer's relationship to the Hannoverian School.

service in castigating the despotic practices of Germany's numerous petty tyrants.

A man of Schlözer's enlightened outlook was naturally delighted by the events of 1789. He exclaimed: "How wonderful that one of the greatest nations in the world, and unquestionably the most cultured, has thrown off the yoke of tyranny. God's angels in Heaven must, for a certainty, have sounded off a *Te Deum laudamus* in jubilation."[90] Schlözer defended the storming of the Bastille by giving credence to the story that Louis XVI had wanted to compete with Nero in setting his capital afire. While deploring all violence, Schlözer thought that the revolution had, when judged as a whole, achieved maximum results with minimal violence and that its violence had at least possessed a constructive purpose in contrast to the violence used by a despot like Louis XIV in pursuit of purely personal ends. The *Staatsanzeigen* at first even apologized for the events of October 1789 because Schlözer viewed them as a defensive move to thwart a new royal conspiracy.

Schlözer's attitude toward the revolution changed in the winter of 1789-90 when he saw that the Constituent Assembly experienced difficulty in repressing the popular passions it had unchained. He continued to deplore royal despotism, aristocratic privilege, and clerical intolerance, but thought that all these had ceased to be dangers in France: the real danger lay now in the rule of the mob (what Schlözer denounced as "ochlocracy"). His new fears changed his evaluation of the events of 1789 ex post facto in a significant way: he now denounced —on the basis of what he claimed was better, and previously unavailable, information—the storming of the Bastille, the march to Versailles, and the war against the chateaux as the work of criminals leagued with a Constituent Assembly whose conduct belied all its protestations of virtue. He was now convinced that the revolution could not lead to any constructive results, and he blamed France's earlier history for this tragic fact:

> The French go from one extreme to another. They turn their absolute King into an impotent Venetian doge, and when they can no longer be torn to pieces by a monarchical lion they allow themselves to be eaten by democratic vermin (*Ungeziefer*). It is a case of *habeant sibi*, and contemporaries and posterity join in saying: "The Cappadocian nation was unworthy in the sight of God, who would not allow so noble a revolution to succeed."[91]

[90] Quoted by K. T. Heigel, *Geschichte*, i, 295, as part of an excellent discussion of Schlözer's attitude toward the Revolution (pp. 295-97).

[91] Quoted by Raumer, *Deutschland um 1800*, p. 48. It may be added that

One of Germany's leading *Popularphilosophen,* the Halle professor Johann August Eberhard (1739-1809), took a similarly patronizing view toward the French in a widely read book on *The Constitution of States and Their Improvement.*[92] Eberhard's career is interesting for showing the opportunities which existed for gifted lower-class intellectuals if they won the right contacts and did not stray too far from the orthodoxy of Frederician Prussia. Born the son of a cantor in Halberstadt, he came to Berlin at the age of twenty-four to serve as tutor to the children of Freiherr von der Horst, a prominent bureaucrat who became a minister a few years later. Horst introduced him to the polished society of the Prussian capital, and he quickly became a member of the *Aufklärungssynode* centered around Friedrich Nicolai and Moses Mendelssohn. He won literary notoriety with an audacious attack upon the Christian doctrine of salvation in a book called *Neue Apologie des Sokrates* (1772); but he also won a reputation as a *Popularphilosoph* with his *Allgemeine Theorie des Denkens und Empfindens* (1776), which was crowned with a prize by the Berlin Academy. On the strength of this book Eberhard was appointed professor of philosophy at Halle in 1778, where his popular and lively lecturing style made him a favorite among students. He aroused the attention of the general reading public in 1788 with a sharp attack upon Kant's metaphysical obscurities in the name of common sense—an attack sufficiently damaging to induce the Königsberg philosopher to pen an elaborate reply in a rather heavy satirical style.[93]

A Radical in religion, Eberhard was in politics a faithful champion of "enlightened absolutism" and a sharp foe of the French Revolution. He acted as the outstanding spokesman of the view that the Germans had a national mission to promote true liberty and *Aufklärung* in place of the degenerate French, who had failed at their self-appointed task. Eberhard claimed that the Germans had in fact been superior to the French in true *Aufklärung* for several centuries:

> France may be superior to us in the arts of luxury and taste, and the works of poetry and eloquence, and may equal us in mathematics

---

Schlözer's hostility to the Revolution was considered inadequate by many German Conservatives, and that his continued criticism of tyrannical German princes led to the official suppression of the *Staatsanzeigen* in 1793.

[92] J. A. Eberhard, *Über Staatsverfassungen und ihre Verbesserungen* (2 vols., Berlin, 1793-94). On Eberhard's life see the two biographical articles by A. Richter, *ADB,* v (1877), 569-71, and L. Gabe, *NDB,* iv (1959), 240-41.

[93] Kant's work was entitled *Über eine Entdeckung nach der alle neue Kritik der reinen Vernunft durch eine ältere entbehrlich gemacht werden soll* (Berlin, 1790).

and physics; but it has always been far behind the Protestant part of Germany in philosophic penetration (*einer gründlicher Philosophie*) and enlightened jurisprudence and theology. When could France boast of an administration of justice as humane, lenient and simple as that of several large German states? What country took the lead in eliminating torture, the crime of witchcraft, and the punishment of heresy from its penal code? Where first arose a religion at once tolerant and conducive to the improvement (*Veredelung*) of the human race?

When the French nation—long notorious for its levity, frivolity, and rashness of spirit—[sought to gain liberty] there was an inevitable transition from superstition and practical immorality to atheism and theoretical immorality: a transition completely impossible in the Protestant part of Germany.[94]

Eberhard expanded this theme by eulogizing Protestant Germany with its religious toleration, absence of conflict between Church and state, enlightened and married clergy, and absence of lazy and superstitious monks—a situation conducive to the kind of pure religion and *Aufklärung* which inevitably promoted good government and human progress. The public spirit of France had, on the contrary, been cursed by an intolerant, ultramontane, monkish, celibate, and immoral clergy with a vested interest in opposing *Aufklärung* and progress—an evil combination whose unfortunate qualities had unhappily rubbed off on its worst enemy, the enlightened intellectuals of France who had made the French Revolution. Was it not preposterous that France, cursed by such a legacy, should arrogate to itself the mission of bringing progress to Germany, a country whose Protestant part was in a condition far superior to that of France herself? Was it not natural, rather, that Protestant Germany should serve as a model to mankind, influencing its development by example? Eberhard considered it axiomatic, incidentally, that Germany's pacific character—and the nature of "true *Aufklärung*"—precluded her from imitating France's conduct of seeking to export her principles to less favored lands by force of arms.

It may be said in conclusion that the high morale and complacent pharisaism of much of Germany's Protestant elite contributed to the country's immunity to revolutionary propaganda once the "true character" of the Jacobins had been exposed; and that national pride in the "enlightened" nature of German Protestant civilization proved an important factor in the development of German political nationalism

---

[94] Eberhard, *Über Staatsverfassungen*, I, 123-24.

side by side with the more frequently stressed romantic-organicist tradition.

SOME COUNTERREVOLUTIONARY PUBLICATIONS

The writings of individual opponents of the revolution were supplemented by several periodicals with a distinctly counterrevolutionary outlook. The most important of these, Schlözer's *Staatsanzeigen,* has already been mentioned; two others, the *Wiener Zeitschrift* and the *Eudämonia,* will be reserved for separate treatment in the next chapter. There were several additional journals which deserve at least a brief mention here.

The most widely read political magazine in Germany was the *Hamburger Politisches Journal,* published in Danish Altona from 1781 to 1804. It came nearer to providing a full coverage of news than any of its competitors, and was for that reason read by many who did not agree with its editorial opinions. It was comparatively nonpartisan in the years before 1789, when it established its reputation; its partisanship after 1789 was only rarely of a shrill or offensive character and probably did not alienate its established stock of readers. The *Hamburger Politisches Journal* made its editor, Gottlob Benedikt von Schirach (1743-1804), not only an influential citizen but a wealthy one as well.[95]

Another influential journal opposing the revolution was the biweekly *Politische Gespräche der Todten,* edited by Moritz Flavius Trenk von Tonder (1746-1810). It was published in the small Rhenish city of Neuwied but was read widely throughout the empire. Tonder, though the son of a Polish father and a Czech mother, was an ardent German patriot. He served for some years as an officer in the Habsburg army, but retired around 1780 and, after extensive travels through Europe, settled in Neuwied. He started the *Politische Gespräche der Todten* in 1786 and soon made newspaper history by combining the features of a political newspaper, a journal of instruction and entertainment (what was called a *Moralisches Wochenblatt*), and a special section providing political cartoons and satire. The usual issue consisted of sixteen pages; consecutive pagination through a half-year period encouraged readers to give permanence to their copies by binding them together. An advertising circular of 1789 shows that back issues could be bought in bound volumes for five gulden. The political part of the paper consisted of letters from Paris, Vienna, and other key cities where Tonder main-

[95] On Schirach see Carstens, "G. B. von Schirach," *ADB,* xxxi (1890), 307-08.

tained correspondents; biographies of newsworthy figures; book reviews; and frequent dialogues written by the editor himself. The dialogues proved an effective vehicle for conveying Tonder's political message: sharp condemnation of the French Revolution; hostility to Masons and *Illuminati* as actual or potential conspirators; ardent patriotic feeling which condemned German disunity and the national habit of imitating foreigners; a demand for Austro-Prussian cooperation to defend Germany against the French danger; and special attachment to the venerable imperial fabric and the House of Austria. The paper had its maximum influence in the early 1790's and earned its publisher 70,000 florins in the single year 1792 (despite losses caused by pirated editions in places as far from Neuwied as Pressburg and Prague). The French occupation of Neuwied forced Tonder to flee to Frankfurt in 1795, and, though he continued publication, the best days of the *Gespräche der Todten* were over.[96]

The *Revolutions-Almanach* of Heinrich Ottokar Reichard (1751-1828) was for several years a widely read publication (Göttingen, 1793-1801). The editor was librarian to Duke Ernst II of Saxe-Gotha, the "enlightened" protector of Adam Weishaupt and himself an ardent admirer of the French Revolution; this fact and the non-committal title gave several advance subscribers—including the Duchess of Gotha herself—the mistaken impression that Reichard's *Almanach* would be prorevolutionary in its outlook. It became in fact the most solid and effective of the antirevolutionary publications, and earned its editor fame, fortune, and many enemies. Reichard avoided all hysterical vituperation and was quite free of Reactionary sentiments; he frequently lauded the "true liberty" recently established in the United States in order to condemn French "false liberty" by way of contrast. One of his most effective articles was a printing of a list of all Frenchmen guillotined between March 1793 and July 1794 in order to show the indiscriminate character of revolutionary "justice." This was followed by a description of the fate of all presidents of the original Constituent As-

[96] The *Politische Gespräche der Todten* was rediscovered in the 1930's, unfortunately with excessive patriotic pathos, by Karl D'Ester, professor of *Zeitungswissenschaft* at the University of Munich. See the two exhaustive and profusely illustrated monographs, *Das politische Elysium oder Die Gespräche der Todten am Rhein. Ein Beitrag zur Geschichte der deutschen Presse und des deutschen Gedankens am Rhein* (Neuwied, 1936) and *Publizistische Wehr im Westen. Die Gespräche der Toten als Vorkämpfer des deutschen Gedankens von der französischen Revolution bis Bonaparte* (Neuwied, 1937). The former concentrates upon the journalistic, the latter upon the political significance of the journal. A good summary is the author's earlier *Der Neuwieder. Ein vergessener Vorkämpfer für die Freiheit des deutschen Rheines* (Neuwied, 1930).

sembly, most of whom had been subsequently executed or exiled. Reichard was also effective in ridiculing the ritualistic denunciation of German despots current among German Radicals: "I hear and read daily about despots; even novels are filled with endless descriptions of them. I have gone on a search for them around all of Europe, but find them nowhere except in France—seated on the Committee of Public Safety."[97]

The *Revolutions-Almanach* consisted primarily of factual descriptions of the course of the revolution and the discussion of historical parallels. Most of it makes uninteresting reading today because the author was too close to events to permit a balanced judgment; at the same time the secondhand character of his description lack the charm of eyewitness reports. The occasional bursts of satire are rather flat-footed, as may be seen by an example drawn from the article "Attempt at a Revolutionary Dictionary" in the *Almanach* for 1800. The following recipe, or definition, is given for a Jacobin:

> Take the seven moral sins; add the three scourges of pestilence, hunger, and war; mix all these together and dissolve the mixture in human blood and tears; cook it with the bone and brain of the worst scoundrels of history into a thick paste; and knead this paste into human shape. You will have a Jacobin.[98]

It is a sad commentary on the period that this kind of stuff found a wide circle of readers in the Germany of the 1790's and made Reichard one of the most admired (and hated) political writers of the country.[99]

The Feeble Stirrings of Reform Conservatism

The French Revolution did serious harm to the cause of gradual reform in Germany in several ways; it encouraged some German Radicals in the belief that only violence could achieve results; it threw most princes into a panic incompatible with Reform Conservatism; and it provided Reactionaries with the opportunity to tar all reformers with the Red brush. The Germany of the 1780's had seen much comparatively good-natured discussion of political and social reform. All this changed with the increasing polarization of political positions and

[97] *Revolutions-Almanach*, II (1794), 292.

[98] Quoted in Sauer, *Französische Revolution*, p. 77, as part of an excellent secondary account of the *Revolutions-Almanach*.

[99] On Reichard see, above all, his *Selbstbiographie*. (Abbr. and ed. H. Uhde, Stuttgart, 1877). The article by Schumann, "H.A.O. Reichard," *ADB*, XXVII (1888), 625-28, is better on his career as literary critic and theater director than his role as journalistic opponent of the French Revolution.

the ugly new climate of political controversy after 1790. The cause of Reform Conservatism was reduced to a few voices as antirevolutionary hysteria swept through Germany.

A small band of truly Conservative men continued to assert that repression promised at best only temporary success in opposing the far-reaching, irreversible historical tendencies expressed by the revolution. They took the view that Germany was threatened, perhaps not now but certainly in the long run, by an internal upheaval if existing governments did not embark upon immediate reforms to remedy genuine grievances. Their immediate objective was to end the fruitless war against France—a war which, it was now clear, could not lead to a victorious conclusion and whose continuation not only brought unnecessary suffering to the German people but also precluded the achievement of reforms "for the duration." Reform Conservatives wanted above all to end the war as a prelude to resuming reform; the purpose of reform was to provide Germany with immunity against otherwise inescapable revolutionary dangers, dangers all the greater because of the continued—inevitable—existence of a France eager to spread the revolutionary contagion.

An eloquent expression of this point of view is to be found in an anonymous pamphlet published on the occasion of the Mainz peace motion in 1794, *A Conversation between a German Prince and one of his Councilors (who is not an Illuminat)*.[100] The councilor argues in favor of offering France immediate peace. Germany has nothing to lose from making an offer: if it is accepted, a troublesome and useless war will end; if it is rejected, the rejection will help to improve the morale of Germany's soldiers by showing that they are fighting a just and defensive war. The prince is gradually won to the councilor's point of view, but remains worried on one point:

> *Prince*: Will the example of the republican government of France, formed after rebellion against constituted authority, and in opposition to the will of all the neighboring powers, not lead to revolutions in other countries?
>
> *Councilor*: I will give, my most gracious prince, an exceedingly frank answer to your question. It is Yes *and* No. The true answer lies in the hands of the princes themselves. . . .
>
> *Yes*—revolutions are to be feared in other states, *if* princes show

[100] *Unterredung zwischen einem deutschen Reichsfürsten und einem Seiner Räthe, der kein Illuminat ist; veranlasst durch den Churmainzischen Antrag wegen des zwischen dem deutschen Reiche und Frankreichs zu vermittelnden Friedens* (Deutschland, 1794). Copy in Bonn University library.

as little regard for the people, and the welfare of the vast majority of the citizens, as was the case in France before 1789; if princes and their ministers consider it beneath their dignity to concern themselves with public opinion, or to study the spirit of the age; if the resources of the state are wasted upon idle courtiers, superstition is preached in place of religion, subjects are surrendered to the tender mercies of selfish bureaucrats, freedom of thought is restricted, espionage is encouraged and any subject who speaks a single liberal word is treated as a rebel; when wars are waged for the sake of conquest and the sons of peasants and artisans are forced to become soldiers, perhaps even sold to fight in an alien land, without real necessity or the Fatherland's being in genuine danger; when a general fear of innovation prevents the reform of even those abuses which are admitted to be such.

No revolution is to be feared, on the other hand—especially in states inhabited by Germans—when a prince . . . has the desire to be the father rather than the master of his people, and practices the religion he professes through the strict performance of his duties; when he chooses his ministers in accordance with merit and their usefulness to the state rather than personal favor; when he modifies the rigors of the feudal system and prepares gradually for its total abolition, while also distributing the burden of taxes more equitably; when the government, remembering its true and noble vocation, is less interested in the *preservation* of its power than in its *use* for the welfare of its subjects; when it secures obedience through rational acceptance of its benevolent policies instead of requiring a stupid worship of all its decrees and orders; when it listens to the voices of the reasonable among its people under conditions of press freedom—irrespective of inevitable abuses—remedying *real* grievances previously overlooked, and instructing subjects whenever they voice purely *imaginary* grievances in the error of their ways; in brief, when the prince and his councilors find their greatest satisfaction in the happiness of the people and seek its confidence through wise government. *If* all this is done, *then* the example of France, where Revolution has led to the general disintegration of orderly society, can only strengthen the attachment of subjects to their ruler and constitution.

If governments follow these maxims in the future, as we can expect from the virtue and intelligence of our prince; *then* the terrible example of the French Revolution will have proved salutary to other nations by stirring the conscience of the privileged and discouraging rebellion among the lower classes. The French Revolution will then provide some compensation perhaps for all the evils which it has caused to the world.[101]

J. G. Schlosser, whom we have previously encountered as a foe of progressive education and critic of the Prussian *Allgemeines Landrecht,* urged a very specific reform program upon *Markgraf* Karl Friedrich of Baden in 1789. He called for a lowering of taxes and corvées, the restriction of hunting rights, new welfare measures to succor the poor, the relaxation of guild restrictions, the more rapid administration of justice, and a better selection of bureaucrats and closer supervision of their work. His program was typical for the omission of any proposals calculated to lead toward self-government.[102]

This indifference to any advance in the direction of democratic government was also characteristic of states where *Landstände* were still intact. The Hannoverian Rehberg (whose outlook will be analyzed in detail in Ch. 11) pleaded for a slight broadening of the social basis from which the *Stände* were recruited, but he did not press his proposal, despite its extraordinarily moderate character, with either vigor or confidence. The *Stände* of Cologne and Trier demanded a more equitable allocation of taxes in their respective electorates, but there was no attempt to give force to their demand by mobilizing the lower classes behind it.[103] The *Landtag* of Württemberg of 1796—famous for its quarrel with the duke and its attempt to enter into independent negotiations with France—paid no heed to various pamphlets urging a democratization of its composition. Among the flood of *Landtags-*

---

[101] Ibid., pp. 39-44. The theme of the dialogue is also expressed by August Friedrich Cranz, *Ein Wort zur Beherzigung, den Fürsten und Herren Deutschlands gewidmet* (2nd edn., Leipzig, 1791), a curious medley of superficial denunciation of the French *philosophes*, profound exhortation of Germany's princes to prevent further revolutions by a timely redress of grievances, and touching description of a reforming prince, made ludicrous, however, by being intended as a portrait of Frederick William II.

[102] Schlosser's proposals were publicized in *Neues Deutsches Museum,* II (1789), 584ff. Views similar to Schlosser's were advanced in two pamphlets by Johann Ludwig Ewald (1747-1822), court preacher and *Generalsuperintendent* at Detmold: *Ueber Revolutionen, ihre Quellen und die Mittel dagegen* (Berlin, 1792) and *Was sollte der Adel jetzt tun?* (Leipzig, 1793). Ewald's Reform Conservatism aroused so much antagonism that he found it advisable to leave Detmold for a post in the more Liberal atmosphere of Bremen. He was to end his career as a highly respected ecclesiastical official of the enlightened state of Baden. See Gass, *ADB,* VI (1877), 444-46.

[103] Liesenfels, *Klemens Wenzeslaus, der letzte Kurfürst von Trier, seine Landstände und die französische Revolution* (Trier, 1912), passim and W. Lüdtke, "Kurtrier und die Unruhen von 1789," *Trierer Zeitschrift,* V (1930).

schriften provoked by the Württemberg constitutional crisis, only a few called for a broadening of the representative basis through making the urban *Magistrate* (which appointed *Landtag* deputies) elective rather than cooptative; but such proposals threatened to destroy the very foundations of the Württemberg oligarchy.[104] Realistic German reformers conceded that reform could be advanced only through princely power, and that this fact made any demand for self-government inopportune because it threatened to compromise reforms which princes might be willing to enforce in the social and economic field. The dependence upon essentially unreliable princely support was, of course, the Achilles' heel of Reform Conservatism.

Among the few voices raised on behalf of extensive political reform in the 1790's is an anonymous *Memorial* (petition) to the princes of Western Germany published in 1793.[105] It purports to have been signed by 7,385 individuals, though only in code numbers in view of the danger of retaliation from Reactionary governments. The petition, while humble and respectful in tone, expresses the hope that princes will give a favorable hearing to the grievances of their loyal subjects; it explicitly repudiates the French method of securing changes through violence. The substance of the petition demanded far-reaching reforms: the introduction of written constitutions to secure a continuity in governing methods from reign to reign; the strengthening or (where they no longer existed) restoration of *Stände* bodies with far-reaching powers over taxation; the creation of uniform legal codes with provisions for public trials; and the abolition of arbitrary taxes, monopolies, corvées, conscription, and princely hunting rights. The petitioners asserted, in language which to princes must have sounded like a threat, that revolution was eventually inevitable unless the princes introduced the above-mentioned reforms soon. It is impossible to know, of course, whether the Conservative aim avowed by the petitioners constituted their true intention; but it suffices to note in our context that they used the *language* of Reform Conservatism at a time when there was little hope that the princes of Germany would accept their demands.

The Reform Conservatives of the 1790's were required to fight the usual two-front war against impatient Radicals and suspicious fellow

[104] The *Landtagsschriften* are surveyed in the excellent work of Erwin Hoelzle, *Das Alte Recht und die Revolution, eine politische Geschichte Württembergs in der Revolutionszeit* (Munich and Berlin, 1931), pp. 171-79.

[105] *Memorial der Einwohner der Fränkischen, Schwäbischen, Ober, Kur und Nieder-Rheinischen, dann Westphälischen Kreises an ihre Landesherrschaften. Die Darlegung ihrer Ehrfurcht, Liebe, Treue und Gehorsams, dann ihre ehrerbietige Bitten und Wünsche enthaltend* (n.p., 1793). A copy is in Bonn University library.

Conservatives. Radicals were certain that the Reform Conservatives deceived themselves about the possibility of achieving reforms peacefully and gradually from above; Reform Conservatives attempted to refute this contention by looking at the record. The *Deutsche Zeitung*, edited by Rudolf Zacharias Becker of Gotha, carried a regular column entitled *Proofs that Progress is taking place in Germany without Rebellion*.[106] This column brought together examples of forward-looking policies launched by benevolent princes. Another author assembled evidence to prove that the princes of Germany were becoming more enlightened all the time under the influence of better education, the inevitable spread of *Aufklärung*, and, last but not least, "fear of the honorable areopagus of our *Publizität*.[107] The basic contention was that the best days of "enlightened absolutism" were still to come, and that far more could be expected from enlightened monarchs than from mobs driven to madness by unscrupulous demagogues.

While Radicals questioned the effectiveness—and even the sincerity—of Reform Conservatives, Reactionaries inevitably accused them of conduct indistinguishable from that of Radicals, and certain to give aid and comfort to the latter. To give only one example: a delegation of the *Stände* of Lower Austria called upon Francis II on March 24, 1793, to complain about the conduct of two surviving Josephine *Hofräte* named Kees and Eger. Their "crime" had been to press, despite persistent aristocratic sabotage, for the amelioration of the condition of the peasantry, and they had added insult to injury by justifying their action in terms of their prince's obligation to *all* the people. The *Stände* accused them of being thinly disguised Jacobins. Francis, born autocrat that he was, refused, of course, to yield to outside pressure and fire Eger and Kees; the episode is significant, however, for illustrating the Reactionary attitude of the *Stände* and the complete dependence of Reform Conservatives upon the support of Germany's princes.[108]

Reform Conservatives insisted against the Reactionaries that there was good *Aufklärung*—their own—and bad *Aufklärung*—the Radicals'

[106] *Beweise, dass in Deutschland ohne Rebellion der Fortschritt zum Bessern vor sich gehe.* Cf. Wenck, *Deutschland vor 100 Jahren*, II, 163. Becker (1759-1822) was famous as editor, publisher, and author. He started the *Deutsche Zeitung* in 1784, the *Becker'sche Buchhandlung* (publishing house) in 1797. His numerous books include an edifying and thoroughly enlightened work, *Vorlesungen über die Rechte und Pflichten der Menschen* (2 vols., Gotha, 1791-92). See Kelchner, *ADB*, II (1875), 228.

[107] Karl Fischer, *An den Herrn Philipp Adam Custine*, p. 107.

[108] V. Bibl, "Die niederösterreichischen Stände und die französische Revolution," *Jbuch f. Landeskunde von Niederösterreich* (2nd edn., N.F., 1903), pp. 79-97.

—and that it was ignorant and unfair to refuse to accept the distinction. C. F. von Moser, whom we have previously met as a critic of absolutism and champion of the new *Nationalgeist,* wrote a whole article in January 1792 in support of this contention:

> One must understand the contrast between good and true *Aufklärung* on the one hand and evil and false *Aufklärung* on the other. The business of the former is the development and spread of light and truth so as to achieve harmony, order, tranquillity and peace for the entire human race. The business of the latter is deception rather than illumination, infatuation rather than instruction, destruction and discord rather than harmony, insolence rather than freedom, malicious confusion of heads and immoral seduction of hearts.[109]

Moser followed up this distinction with an attempt to establish his Conservative respectability by sharply denouncing complete freedom of speech as a demand of "false" *Aufklärung.* Vitriolic attack upon specific Radical demands came easily to him, as to many other Reform Conservatives of the period; their position required that they convince champions of the *status quo* that they must not be confounded with Radicals despite their occasional *ad hoc* cooperation. The utmost prudence appeared imperative to Reform Conservatives in view of the ever-more-hysterical tone of German political life in the 1790's. This decade saw the flourishing of the so-called "conspiracy theory," whose advocates denounced Reform Conservatives as innocent stooges at best, conscious instruments at worst, of an *Illuminati* conspiracy bent upon the total destruction of traditional European society. This theory is so interesting in itself, and was so important for much of future Conservative thought, that it deserves extended analysis in a separate chapter.

[109] C. F. von Moser, "Wahre und falsche politische Aufklärung," *Neues Politisches Archiv für Deutschland,* I (1792), 527-36.

CHAPTER 10

The Conspiracy Theory of the Revolution

Significance and Foreign Spokesmen

ONE OF the most notable Conservative phenomena of the 1790's was the widespread acceptance of the "conspiracy theory of the revolution" —a theory which sought to explain the outbreak of the revolution in France, and the spread of its ideas through Europe, in terms of the work of a small conspiratorial clique.[1] This type of theory has often proved very attractive to beneficiaries of a threatened *status quo* because of its optimistic implications: if the danger of revolution arises from the merely subjective will of a few conspirators—rather than the inexorable, objective development of social forces—then this danger can be removed simply by efficient police work, and there is no need for far-reaching reforms to remove genuine grievances. The conspiracy theory also has the attraction of satisfying the eternal—though thought-killing—human craving for a simple, all-embracing explanation of all troubles, preferably one which presents the Devil in a concrete form. Modern Conservatism has known several "secular demonologies" in recent centuries, such as the belief in all-pervasive Masonic, Communist, and—least plausible of all—Jewish world conspiracies.[2] All these theories suffer from certain generic flaws: they exaggerate the cohesiveness of conspiratorial forces in history; they tend to confuse the unorganized ambitions and endeavors of discontented groups with the deliberate manipulation of discontent for revolutionary ends; and men subscribing to these theories easily fall into the "idealistic" error of exaggerating the role played by ideas in history, forgetting that ideas exercise influence only in social situations prepared for them and that their spread is more often the consequence than the cause of political and social change.

The era of the French Revolution saw the development, on an international scale, of a highly articulated conspiracy theory which pro-

---

[1] There is no space here to take up the view of some historians that the conspiracy theory exercised an important role in the genesis of romanticism. See, for example, J. Droz, "La legende du complot illuministe et les origines du romantisme politique en Allemagne," *Revue historique*, ccxxvi (1961), 313-38. This chapter is concerned exclusively with the political significance of the conspiracy theory.

[2] It should be noted that the Left is no more free of the fear of the Devil than the Right, as witness at various times the fantastic beliefs in the existence of conspiracies of Jesuits or munitions manufacturers.

vided Conservatives with a facile explanation of the threat to the European *status quo*. Its three most distinguished champions were the French Jesuit Augustin Barruel, the Scottish scientist John Robison, and the German pastor Johann August Starck. All three exercised wide influence upon German Conservative circles. The works of Barruel and Robison were immediately translated into German, while Starck was one of the most widely read German political writers of his day. Though each of these writers was highly individual in personality, outlook, and approach, they all agreed on the fundamental fact of the existence of a powerful international conspiracy spearheaded by Masons and *Illuminati*.

Augustin Barruel (1741-1820), the son of a high French official, became a Jesuit novice at the age of fifteen. He was forced to flee from his native France when the Jesuits were expelled in 1765. After taking vows in Germany he returned to Paris in 1773 and won literary fame by publishing an *Ode sur le glorieus avènement de Louis Auguste*, which is said to have sold 12,000 copies. Barruel won for himself a considerable reputation—at a time when witty Conservative writers were a rarity—by conducting a vigorous polemic against the *philosophes* in a sprightly journal, the *Helviennes, ou lettres provinciales philosophiques* (1781-88): he fully appreciated the irony of a Jesuit patterning himself upon Pascal as he defended Catholic Orthodoxy against Jansenist and rationalist attack. The early years of the revolution found him the courageous editor of the *Journal ecclesiastique* (1788-92) until he was forced to flee to England to escape the September massacres. There he won the friendship of Burke and the patronage of Lord Clifford while composing his famous four-volume work, *Memoires pour servir à l'histoire du Jacobinisme* (London, 1797-98), one of the most widely read books in its day.[3]

Barruel described three successive phases of the world conspiracy that had culminated in the revolution: the *philosophes*, who attacked Christianity; the Masons, who attacked monarchy as well; and the *Illuminati*, who went still further in attacking all religion (not just Christianity), all government (not just monarchy), and the very principles underlying organized society (for example, private property). The Jacobin attack upon the Church, Louis XVI, and the French

[3] On Barruel see the dispassionate notice by M. Prevost in *Dictionnaire de Biographie Française*, v (1949), 627-28. It is interesting to note that Barruel showed a residual moderation by accepting the Napoleonic concordat of 1802 (thereby infuriating all ecclesiastical die-hards); but he paid for his unflinching loyalty to the Pope by suffering imprisonment in 1811.

social structure was in Barruel's view but the local French manifestation of this highly organized international conspiracy. He advanced this theory with eloquence, learning, and great satirical power, and his credibility was enhanced by the fact that his pre-1789 prophecies of world conspiracy—which had earned him much ridicule at the time— appeared to be vindicated by events.

The weakest part of Barruel's argument was his blanket attack upon Masonry. His florid imagination delighted in colorful descriptions of mystical observances, awe-inspiring initiation ceremonies, a variety of real and spurious Masonic degrees, and fanciful genealogies. He believed that Masonry was descended from the Manichean and Albigensian heresies, and accepted at face value the Strict Observance theory that Masonry was a revival of the Templar Order suppressed in 1307. The German pastor Starck, who sympathized with Barruel's over-all point of view, was sharply critical of this part of his work:

> Barruel has erred on many and important points, and his *a priori* convictions have led him into finding in Masonry elements which exist only in his imagination. He generalizes too easily on the basis of a few particulars, and has confused new, spurious, and recently invented Masonic degrees with those based upon old and authentic documents. His account contains many exaggerations which can only be ascribed to the ignorance of the author.[4]

Barruel's imaginative errors provoked easy ridicule from defenders of Masonry, but they added to the popular appeal of his work to credulous and Reactionary minds throughout Europe.[5]

The book of the Scottish scientist John Robison (1739-1805) was briefer and less fanciful than Barruel's encyclopedic work.[6] The author

[4] J. A. Starck, *Der Triumph der Philosophie im 18. Jahrhundert* (2 vols., Augsburg, 1803), ii, 172. Henceforth cited as Starck, *Philosophie.*

[5] The most effective reply to Barruel was written by Jean J. Mounier, an early president of the National Assembly of 1789 who had gone into voluntary exile in 1790 but returned to die as a Napoleonic prefect in 1806. Mounier's work was translated into German as *Ueber den vorgeblichen Einfluss der Philosophen, Freymaurer und Illuminaten auf die französische Revolution* (Tübingen, 1801). The excessive importance attached to authors by the "conspiracy theorists" was ridiculed, albeit in a rather pedestrian fashion, by the Göttingen professor Abraham Gotthelf Kästner, *Gedanken über das Unvermögen der Schriftsteller, Empörungen zu bewirken* (Göttingen, 1793). The vehement attack upon secret societies produced some vigorous replies, for example, I.Z.S.M. [probably G. F. Rebmann], *Apologie einer geheimen Gesellschaft edlerer Art gegen die Angriffe eines Ungenannten. Nebst einigen Bemerkungen über geheime Verbindungen überhaupt* (Frankfurt and Leipzig, 1792).

[6] *Proofs of a Conspiracy against all the Religions and Governments of Europe,*

was professor of natural philosophy at Edinburgh University (1773) and secretary of the Royal Society (1783). His researches on electricity had given him a European reputation; Sir James Mackintosh, himself a champion of the revolutionary cause, called him "one of the greatest mathematical philosophers of his age"; while James Watt, the inventor of the steam engine, said that "he was a man of the clearest head and the most science of anybody I have ever known." He is in fact an excellent illustration of the notorious fact that scientific eminence is not always accompanied by good political judgment. His sense for evidence—so acute in his scientific researches—abandoned him as he examined Masonry, Illuminism, the German Union, and the Jacobins in successive chapters of his book. Robison differed, however, from Barruel and Starck in his generally Liberal outlook. While detesting Radicalism, and especially conspiratorial Radicalism, he at the same time explicitly opposed the surviving relics of feudalism, absolute monarchy, and religious obscurantism. It is for this reason that J. J. Mounier, the ablest opponent of the conspiracy theory, spoke of him with a measure of grudging respect.[7]

J. A. Starck: *The German Philosopher of the Conspiracy Theory*

The life of Johann August Starck (1741-1816) is not marked by the forthrightness of Barruel and Robison. It deserves to be related in some detail, both because it possesses much intrinsic interest and because certain controversial aspects of it made Starck one of the most talked-about personalities in the Germany of his time. He was born the son of a Lutheran pastor in Mecklenburg, and was educated at Göttingen to follow in his father's footsteps. A Mason in 1761 at the age of twenty, he went to Russia shortly thereafter to accept a teaching appointment at the famous *Peterschule* in St. Petersburg. Here he established contact (according to his own account) with a Masonic lodge which claimed to be a survivor of the clerical branch of the Medieval Templarism suppressed by Philip the Fair in the fourteenth century. Starck asserted

---

carried on in the secret meetings of Free Masons, Illuminati and Reading Societies (London, 1797). A second edition (with a new postscript) appeared in Edinburgh in 1797, a third in Dublin in 1798, a fourth simultaneously in London and New York in 1798. The book is dedicated to William Wyndham, Secretary at War in Pitt's government.

[7] Mounier, op.cit., 6n. On Robison see George Stronach, "John Robison," *DNB*, XLIX (1897), 57-58, which stresses his scientific work while mentioning his anti-*Illuminati* campaign only in passing. Robison exercised some influence in the United States in the 1790's. See V. Stauffer, *New England and the Bavarian Illuminati* (New York, 1918).

that he was initiated into its secrets and rituals and, after his return to Germany in the late 1760's, he founded a chapter of the *Klerikat* at Königsberg, where he became a court preacher and professor. Negotiations with the *Heermeister* of the Strict Observance, Baron von Hund, led to mutual recognition of their respective orders, with Starck giving the impression that the *Klerikat* had chapters throughout Germany. He described himself at this time as *Frater Archidemides ab aquila fulva, cancellarius capituli generalis Cananicum VII^{ae} provinciae, Superior congregationis Regiomontanae.* In fact, there were never more than two chapters at most and the episode could be ignored if it did not throw a peculiar light upon Starck's judgment and honesty and the fantastic credulity of eighteenth-century Masonry. He was forced to break off ties with the Strict Observance in 1778 when his *Klerikat* secrets encountered well-justified skepticism at the Wolfenbüttel Convent.[8]

This break did not, however, mean the end of Starck's involvement with the *Klerikat,* for he succeeded in winning seven princes to the cause: Carl Wilhelm of Nassau; Frederick of Brunswick; Carl and Georg of Mecklenburg-Strelitz; and Ludwig Georg Carl, Georg Carl, and Ludwig of Hessen-Darmstadt. The last-named, after using his influence as crown prince to get Starck an appointment at Darmstadt as court preacher in 1781, gave him protection for the rest of his life. Starck's social gifts must have been considerable to have permitted him to live on terms of easy familiarity with the ordinarily exclusive princely aristocracy of Germany.[9]

Starck broke definitively with Masonry when he published in 1785 a much-discussed novel, *St. Nicaise,* which constituted a most effective exposure of the follies of eighteenth-century Masons.[10] Its hero, a French adventurer named St. Nicaise, has a series of hair-raising adventures which include being cheated by a London Mason who doubles as pawnbroker, being imprisoned by the Neapolitan inquisition, and being kidnapped by French initiates who hope to extort Masonic secrets from him under duress. The book includes a severe

[8] On Starck's life see Paul Konschel, *Hamanns Gegner, der Kryptokatholik Johann August Starck* (Königsberg, 1912); J. Blum, *Starck et la querelle du Crypto-Catholicisme en Allemagne* (Paris, 1912); Gustav Krüger, "Johann A. Starck der Kleriker. Ein Beitrag zur Geschichte der Theosophie im 18. Jahrhundert," *Festgabe Karl Müller* (Tübingen, 1922), pp. 244-66. The best account of the *Klerikat* is F. Runkel, *Freimaurerei,* i, 254-349.

[9] See G. Krüger, "Starck und der Bund der Sieben," *Festgabe für W. Diehl* (Darmstadt, 1931), pp. 237-57.

[10] *St. Nicaise, oder eine Sammlung merkwürdiger maurerischer Briefe, für Freymaurer und die es nicht sind* (Frankfurt, 1785).

indictment of the mystery-mongering and racketeering of the German Strict Observance and its *Heermeister* Hund. Starck's novel provoked innumerable replies; the controversy it aroused shows the enormous public interest in Masonry and Starck's central position in the discussion of its nature, value, and aims which raged in the 1780's.[11] It may be said in conclusion that Starck's relationship to Masonry appears to have been marked successively by credulity, imposture, and finally apostasy.

His professional career as a Lutheran pastor also stands under a cloud. He secretly went through the ceremony of conversion to Catholicism while visiting Paris in 1765, yet this did not prevent him from accepting a Lutheran rectorship in his native Mecklenburg in 1766 and a Königsberg professorship of theology a few years later. It is probable that he considered his conversion a youthful episode which he soon repented (it incidentally did not become publicly known until after his death). His extensive theological writing in the 1770's certainly contributed to the rationalist disintegration of Lutheran orthodoxy championed by figures like Semler and Bahrdt.[12] Starck appears to have turned simultaneously against Masonry and religious rationalism around 1780, and, being a man of extremes, he soon took the opposite position of seeking *rapprochement* with Catholicism on many points. Yet his "Crypto-Catholicism" did not preclude his acceptance of an attractive post as court preacher and *Konsistorialrath*

---

[11] The most notable replies were three pamphlets written by Christian Friedrich Kessler von Sprengseysen, who had been Hund's chief lieutenant and resented Starck's attacks upon his friend and master: *Anti-St. Nicaise. Ein Turnier im XVIII Jahrhundert* (Leipzig, 1786), *Archidemides, oder des Anti-St. Nicaise zweyter Theil* (Leipzig, 1786), and *Scala algebraica oeconomica, oder des Anti-St. Nicaise dritter und letzter Theil* (Leipzig, 1787). Starck replied with his *Über Kryptokatholicismus* (see n.13), which provoked Kessler's *Abgenöthigte Fortsetzung des Anti-St. Nicaise* (Leipzig, 1788), with Starck getting in the final word in his *Beleuchtung der letzten Anstrengung des Herrn Kessler von Sprengseysen* (Dessau und Leipzig, 1788). See also A. S. von Goué, *Bemerkungen über St. Nicaise und Anti St. Nicaise* (Leipzig, 1788). For a complete bibliography see Kloss, *Bibliographie der Freimaurerei* (Frankfurt, 1844), Nr. 3399-3432.

[12] Starck's *Hephästion* (Königsberg, 1775) sought to demonstrate, for example, that the main teachings of Christianity were derived from Egyptian mystery cults. Starck's anonymous *Freimütige Betrachtungen über das Christentum* (Berlin, 1780) marked his theological turn to the Right which was to lead him eventually to crypto-Catholicism, although he judged Bahrdt favorably as late as 1781. G. Krüger, "Die Eudämonisten," *HZ*, CXLIII (1931), 497, n.92. The theory that he was deliberately serving a Jesuit purpose when he promoted the rationalist disintegration of Lutheranism, for the ultimate benefit of Catholicism, appears farfetched and implausible.

in Darmstadt, and he enjoyed the prestige and emoluments of this high Lutheran office for the rest of his life.

In 1786 Starck's foes attacked him bitterly in the "enlightened" *Berliner Monatsschrift* as a "Crypto-Catholic," but they did not know the secret of his formal conversion twenty years earlier. If the secret had leaked out it certainly would have ruined him; Starck must have lived in constant fear of this possibility. A lawsuit against the editors of the *Berliner Monatsschrift* ended inconclusively while provoking a huge controversial literature.[13] His opponents viewed his continued receptive attitude toward Catholic interpretations of Christian dogma as proof of their worst suspicions, and they spread a tale (disproved at the time of his death in 1816) that his house contained a room for secretly reading mass. All that Starck sought, however, was to secure the solidarity of both Christian confessions against the "philosophic conspiracy" which had triumphed in France in 1789 and which threatened to triumph throughout Europe.

Starck gave expression to the "conspiracy theory" in various ephemeral publications throughout the 1790's, including a series of articles in the conservative journal *Eudämonia* (discussed below); but he first stated the theory at length, and with exhaustive documentation, in his magisterial *Triumph der Philosophie im 18. Jahrhundert* (2 vols. Germantown [Augsburg], 1803).[14] This work deserves paraphrase both because it constitutes the best statement of a theory once widely believed by German Conservatives, and because it exercised great influence upon several later Conservatives, most notably Karl Ludwig von Haller.

The core of Starck's argument was that the French Revolution did not result from such factors as feudal oppression, royal tyranny, and fiscal bankruptcy, but was, rather, the direct consequence of the pernicious doctrines of the "enlightened" philosophers and their conspiratorial followers. These doctrines possessed, unhappily, deep roots in European history, and Starck showed ingenious erudition as he traced the genealogy of evil back to Greek sophists and medieval heretics, Renaissance pantheists and Protestant rebels, German idealists and British empiricists. The indictment became increasingly detailed as Starck described the immediate forerunners of the revolution. Vol-

[13] J. Blum, op.cit., is a good account of the controversy. Starck undertook his defense in the form of a counterattack covering 1200(!) pages, *Über Kryptokatholicismus, Proselytenmacherey, Jesuitismus, geheime Gesellschaften* (2 vols., Frankfurt and Leipzig, 1787).

[14] A third edition was published as late as 1847.

taire's forthright attack upon the Church was animated by pathological hatred, but Rousseau's advocacy of a nonecclesiastical and sentimental Christianity was at least as subversive of traditional religion. The *Encyclopedia* was in intention a handbook for rebellion, though the cowardice and opportunism of its editors made it on the surface a curious mixture of Conservative and Radical doctrines. Rousseau's *Social Contract* set out a design for the democratic republic which was to replace every existing monarchy. The Physiocratic critique of the prevailing social and economic system threatened established customs and property rights. These vicious doctrines combined to make Frenchmen of all classes hostile to established religion, government, and morality.

The *philosophes* were by no means ivory-towered intellectuals preoccupied with the scholarly pursuit of truth; they were, rather, demagogic propagandists who deliberately sought mass support for their subversive ideas. They outwitted what censorship still existed by enlisting the support of royal ministers, such as Malesherbes, the chief censor of France, and of influential women like Mme. de Pompadour, the mistress of Louis XV. Their prestige was enhanced by the patronage of monarchs like Frederick II, Joseph II, and Catherine of Russia. A systematic literary dictatorship—based upon control of review organs, infiltration of the Academy, and the ruthless employment of ridicule—silenced the attempt of Catholic and royalist authors to answer their so-called "enlightened philosophy."

The *philosophes* themselves showed shrewd judgment in concentrating their fire upon abuses in clerical life, since the undermining of clerical prestige must always be the first step in the overthrow of the Church, the indispensable pillar of society. They attacked the worldliness of the secular clergy at the same time that they ridiculed the unworldliness (and hence the uselessness) of monasticism. The *philosophes* feared the Jesuits as their most dangerous adversaries, and their intrigue scored a great triumph when the order was expelled from France in 1764 and finally suppressed altogether by the weak and simoniacal Pope Clement XIV in 1773.

The exile of Jesuit schoolmasters left French youth defenseless against the advance of philosophic doctrine; Starck noted that the worst revolutionary horrors were later perpetrated by men whose education postdated the expulsion of the Jesuits. Voltaire's friend D'Alembert managed what amounted to an employment bureau for "enlightened tutors," with results which were fatally evident among the upper class from Naples to St. Petersburg. The focal point for all the forces of discontent in France was founded in 1773 as the Club Holbach. It subsidized the distribution of subversive tracts among the common people, and Starck attributed to it a significant role in the immediate genesis of the French Revolution.

The fuel which exploded in 1789 had been accumulating in France for several decades, but Starck believed that the spark was lighted in Germany. He spent nearly four hundred pages tracing the course of the *Aufklärung* which finally led to this tragic denouement. Authors such as Leibnitz, Thomasius, and Wolff had encouraged a rationalist revolt against Catholic and Protestant orthodoxy. The open adherence of Frederick the Great to "philosophic principles" gave them an unusual prestige throughout Germany. Berlin soon became the focal point of the *Aufklärung*, with Nicolai's *Neue Deutsche Bibliothek* performing a role comparable to that of the *Encyclopedia* in France. Its reviewers claimed that they wanted to purify Christianity from Jewish and Platonist survivals and Catholic superstitions, but though they talked only about eliminating abuses, they in fact aimed at the fundamentals of Christianity itself. Their attack was paralleled by figures like Lessing, Semler, and Bahrdt (Starck understandably enough failed to mention his own early contributions to "enlightened theology"). Voices of Lutheran orthodoxy, such as Goeze, became lost in the craze for *Aufklärung*, while Frederick silenced defenders of religion on the pretext that he must prevent sectarian strife. The advance of religious rationalism was undermining the vitals of German Catholicism in exactly the same way that Bahrdt was destroying traditional Lutheranism. The educational movement headed by Basedow contributed its part to undermining the established order, with boarding schools becoming seminaries of atheism, republicanism, loose thought, and looser morals; and the creed of the *Aufklärung* was promoted by many German monarchs eager to imitate Frederick the Great.

Starck emphasized the important role that Masonry played in German life in the second half of the eighteenth century; but, as we have seen, he refused to accept Barruel's blanket condemnation of the lodges. He was naturally contemptuous of the theory, advanced by his foes on the *Berliner Monatsschrift*, that the Strict Observance was a Jesuit plot to discredit Protestantism and *Aufklärung* for the ultimate benefit of Catholicism. Starck recognized that Masonry was not hostile either to religion or to government per se. He knew that belief in Christianity was a formal prerequisite for membership in most German lodges; while some forms of Masonry, such as his own *Klerikat*, had shown a distinctly Conservative tendency. Starck observed, however, that many lodges had shown deplorable weakness in resisting the danger of "philosophic infiltration." Orators had often used Masonic platforms to spread subversive principles. Some members of the Strict Observance had been driven into Radicalism by their belief that the present holders of former Templar properties were usurpers morally bound to return them to their rightful owner. His main charge was, however, that many lodges had allowed themselves to become "front organizations" for the *Illuminatenorden*.

Starck placed this order in the very center of his conspiracy theory. He suffered from fantastic illusions concerning the specificity of the *Illuminati's* subversive intent and the ramification of their influence. Their utopian belief in the eventual superfluousness of government (once mankind had become perfect) was mistaken for an anarchist plot. Their advocacy of "natural religion" made them appear eager to destroy all existing Churches. Starck also seriously misread the personal characters of the *Illuminati* leaders and the practices of their organization. He attacked Weishaupt's personal morals as utterly odious, and pounced gleefully upon the documented fact that Weishaupt had made his sister-in-law pregnant after the death of his wife.[15] Starck attached excessive importance to the invisible ink and poison found by the Bavarian authorities in the home of Weishaupt's trusted lieutenant Zwackh.[16] The internal practices of the order, including espionage, blind obedience, and the alleged grant of the *ius vitae et necis* aroused Starck's fascinated horror. He seized upon the immoral maxims occasionally proclaimed by Weishaupt in his confiscated correspondence, such as the justification of means by ends (by which Weishaupt had defended the theft of certain manuscripts required by the order), or the justifiability of abortion (when required to protect his own reputation in the affair with his sister-in-law), as typical of the order as a whole.[17]

Starck was convinced that the *Illuminati* had survived essentially intact the Bavarian government's persecution, and that Weishaupt continued to guide the order from his comfortable exile at Gotha. Knigge, whose claim to have broken with the order Starck frankly

[15] See Weishaupt's apology on this matter, as reprinted by Engel, *Illuminatenorden*, pp. 215-25, with commentary.

[16] On Zwackh see Richard Graf Du Moulin Eckart, "Aus den Papieren eines Illuminaten," *Forschungen zur Kultur- und Literaturgeschichte Bayerns*, III (1895), 186-239.

[17] On the justifiability of these charges see Engel, op.cit., passim. Weishaupt's notorious defense of stealing private papers is in a letter to Zwackh printed in *Originalschriften*, p. 330.

disbelieved, even held an influential post in the Hannoverian government. Starck maintained that Bahrdt's *Deutsche Union* was an attempt to spread *Illuminati* principles through the establishment of reading clubs. He was convinced that the campaign conducted against real and Crypto-Jesuits (*Jesuitenriecherei*), of which he had been a conspicuous target, was manipulated by an *Illuminati* clique. The main work achieved by the order was, however—in Starck's eyes—to ignite the spark which set off the French Revolution.

How did the remnants of a small persecuted order achieve such a prodigious feat? Through a mission undertaken to Paris in 1787 by two prominent *Illuminati*, Johann Bode and Freiherr von dem Bussche. Starck refused to accept the alleged purpose behind the journey, which was to explore animal magnetism and to combat the excesses of theosophy and spiritualism. The two Germans visited several Parisian Masonic lodges—the *Amis reunis, les neuf Soers,* and *de la Candeur*—whose members had shown an interest in these abstruse phenomena. Starck was absolutely convinced, as Barruel and Robison had been before him, that the two Germans had in fact taught their French pupils subversive *Illuminati* principles—the proof being that many revolutionary leaders had been members of the lodges they had visited. Starck explained that the leading French Masons did not join the *Illuminatenorden* itself, but that they formed secret committees (*comités secrets*) which possessed functions akin to those exercised by the secret superiors of the *Illuminati*. The head of the revolutionary network was identified as the Duke of Orleans, who supported subversion in the vain hope that disorders would pave his own way to the throne; he little suspected that the revolutionary conspirators looked upon him as a mere pawn in their ultimately republican designs. The *comités secrets* formed reading and discussion clubs which subsequently became centers for manipulating the Parisian mob. The most famous of these clubs was the Club Breton, which met initially in a room of the castle of St. Cloud belonging to the Duke of Orleans; it became the nucleus of the Jacobins.[18]

Starck was convinced that the French Revolution did not just *happen*: it was *made* by "the amalgamated philosophers and *Illumi-*

---

[18] Leopold Hoffmann (see below) devoted a whole pamphlet to the importance of the Bode-Bussche mission to Paris, *Fragmente zur Biographie des verstorbenen Geheimen Raths Bode in Weimar* (Rome [Vienna], 1795). The real story about the mission was uncovered only in 1942 by A. Rossberg, op.cit., pp. 80-84, on the basis of Bode's recently discovered diary. Rossberg, though hostile to the *Illuminati*, showed that Bode had not been engaged in instigating the revolution.

nati." He dismissed all other explanations advanced for the revolution. Exploitation of the people by the government? Pressure was much smaller under the benevolent Louis XVI than under his predecessors. Abuses in the clergy and aristocracy? Burke had shown that they were far less extensive than the revolutionaries charged. Moral revulsion against the extravagance and dissoluteness of court life? Both had declined since the time of Louis XV, while the leaders of the revolution, Mirabeau and Orleans, were hardly noted as models of puritanical decorum. The deficit in the national finances? This was the occasion, not the cause, of the revolution. The agitation of the *parlements* against the royal authority? This was indeed a contributory cause of the revolution, but it arose only because the *parlements* had been infiltrated by Jansenists and philosophers. The existence of "parliamentary opposition" only corroborated Starck's belief that the revolution had been planned and executed by a coterie of "revolutionary conspirators."

Their conduct after they had seized power was exactly what could have been expected: they threw France into irreligion and anarchy while promoting subversion in every other European country. Their first aim was to destroy Catholicism root and branch. They began with the Civil Constitution of the Clergy and the confiscation of clerical lands, and ended with the martyrdom of nonjuring priests, the celebration of sacrilegious orgies parodying the mass, and the transformation of the Pantheon into a "philosophic temple." The ensuing religious vacuum was filled by nothing better than an unseemly squabble between the atheism of Treilhard and the deism of La Reveillère-Lepeau.

The political system of the revolutionaries led from republican conspiracy before 1789 to an odious mixture of anarchy and tyranny after the early triumph of their cause. Starck was convinced that Necker had been used as a cat's-paw by the conspirators when he manufactured an artificial public opinion on behalf of the fatal "doubling of the third" in the elections for the Estates-General in 1789. He was probably co-responsible for the grain shortage which had been manipulated by the Duke of Orleans in the winter of 1788-89, in order to have famished mobs available for street demonstrations. The leading members of the constitutional committee of the National Assembly already favored a republic while they went through the motions of drafting a monarchical constitution. Lafayette had known in advance about Louis' plan to flee the country in 1791, but had treacherously permitted the escape in order to bring discredit to the throne. The collapse of the monarchy was followed by "an enormous depravity of manners, infamous conduct, and barbarous cruelty,"[19] with Starck anticipating Taine in assembling a catalogue of sadistic acts. Some two million Frenchmen, he asserted, had been killed in the terror[20]—a fantastic figure which showed that Starck was better at denunciation than arithmetic. Babeuf's hostility to property was a logical corollary of Jacobin principles; in fact, he simply advocated as a matter of general theory the very vandalism already put into practice against certain types of property, such as clerical lands and historic monuments. The complete collapse of the French educational system in the prevailing chaos made it certain that the next generation would lack morals and learning as well as sound religious and political principles. Starck, writing in 1803, expressed the view of many Conservatives when he praised Napoleon—however great his faults—for restoring at least a measure of religion, morals, and education to a France ruined by revolution.[21]

The final aim of the revolutionaries had been to subvert the established order in every European country. They set up a special center for propaganda which allegedly employed some 60,000 men to write and distribute pamphlets and broadsides among the discontented living in neighboring countries. The Strassbourg office, which was in charge of all German activities, was under the direction of the *Illuminat* Dietrich, who built up a propaganda network of fellow *Illuminati* throughout Central Europe. Peaceful penetration was soon supplemented by the invasion of Jacobin armies, whose work was facilitated by the treacherous collaboration of many Masons and most *Illuminati*. Starck believed that subversive elements had sabotaged the Allied war effort and had thereby allowed the French to conquer large sections of Germany.

Starck was gloomy about Germany's future as he surveyed her condition in 1803. It was far worse, indeed, than the condition of France had been on the eve of the revolution in 1789. He found altogether too much tolerance of subversive and irreligious writings; the educational system, from the village school to the university, was riddled with "enlightened" teachers; Protestantism had degenerated into a tepid, rationalistic deism, while the Catholic Church was reeling under the blow of the secularizations; and the secret society of the *Illuminati* continued to flourish despite feeble attempts at

---

[19] Starck, *Philosophie*, II, 405.

[20] Ibid., p. 412. He exaggerated a hundredfold. Modern historians place the figure at approximately 20,000. See the admirable studies by W. B. Kerr, *The Reign of Terror* (Toronto, 1927), and Donald Greer, *The Incidence of the Terror* (Cambridge, 1935).

[21] Starck, *Philosophie*, II, 428.

repression. The complacent belief of some princes that the example of the French Revolution would deter German revolutionaries unfortunately revealed a complete misunderstanding of the latter's mentality. The territorial division of Germany could not, of itself, provide a reliable barrier against revolution. The only hope lay in firm and farsighted policies undertaken by the princes. They must stop appeasing Radical intellectuals with mild government, and establish instead a rigid censorship against all subversive writings. They must go out of their way to protect and encourage revealed religion against its critics —"for no state can exist without revealed religion"[22]—even if this led to the charge of obscurantism. The educational system must be frankly grounded on the Biblical maxim that "the powers that be are ordained by God." They must, finally, ruthlessly repress dangerous secret societies and place innocent ones, like the Masons, under police supervision lest they be subverted for perverse ends. What little hope Starck felt about the future of Germany depended upon these measures being undertaken promptly and firmly by all her princes.

Starck's book was a brilliant and thorough statement of an intrinsically untenable thesis. It suffered from the general naïveté which characterizes all conspiracy theories and possessed in addition some special naïvetés of its own. The attempt to demonstrate a specific "philosophic conspiracy" behind the events of 1789 failed for lack of evidence, though Starck was no doubt correct in asserting the generally subversive influence of philosophy in the eighteenth century. Another weakness of the book lay in its failure to provide a precise definition of what was understood under the term "philosophy": Starck tended to use it as a miscellaneously stocked Pandora's box from which emerged all doctrines in any way contrary to orthodox Christianity, monarchy, and the traditional code of morality, even though these doctrines varied greatly among themselves. Starck habitually exaggerated the specificity with which a given philosopher desired to overthrow religion and government, mistaking the advocacy of a general principle for concrete revolutionary intent. His logical mind never appreciated the wide gap which exists in most men between their opinions and their conduct. The frequently reiterated view that irreligion must lead to widespread immorality was a case in point. It may be true, in terms of pure logic, that the denial of a revealed system of ethics, enforced by divine rewards and punishments, should lead to a great increase in immoral conduct; yet such is the role of tradition and habit in human nature that the imperatives of logic are frequently belied

[22] Ibid., p. 523.

by the facts. Starck looked back far too much to the religion-dominated medieval order of society, and underestimated the relatively orderly and stable world which remained possible even under secular conditions. His worst intellectual blunder was his obstinate refusal to see that the disintegration of Medievalism had been inevitable and was now irreversible, and that his program of police repression was grotesquely inadequate in the face of powerful political, social, and cultural forces making for modernity.

L. A. Hoffmann: The Conspiracy Theory on a Journalistic Level

Barruel, Robison, and Starck concentrated upon writing systematic treatises aimed at an educated audience. They neither sought nor gained influence upon the immediate course of events. In this they differed from the Viennese journalist Leopold Hoffmann, who agreed with their theory of a Jacobin world conspiracy but sought to combat the enemy on a more popular level and to achieve practical ends. In 1792 he founded the *Wiener Zeitschrift,* the first avowedly Conservative periodical in the history of Germany. Its vehement and indiscriminate hunt for subversives and its tendency to tar all reform proposals with a Red brush soon made Hoffmann a favorite bugbear of German Radicals.[23]

An instructive contrast may be drawn between the personalities and careers of Starck and Hoffmann. Starck was born into a humble but respectable Mecklenburg parsonage; a brilliant university record led him to a theology professorship by the time he was thirty-one; and he spent the last thirty-five years of his long life as a respected preacher and ducal favorite at the Darmstadt court. Hoffmann was born the youngest of nine children of an impoverished German-Bohemian tailor and was doomed to spend his life as a hack writer until he died in sickness, bitterness, and obscurity at the early age of forty-six. Starck was an erudite and polished man of letters whose talents won the grudging respect of even his adversaries; Hoffmann was an uncouth, rough-and-ready journalist whose vulgar language provoked only smiles from the world of rank and education even when it approved his political line. Both began as ardent champions and ended as bitter foes of *Aufklärung*

---

[23] All the biographical information about Hoffmann is taken, unless otherwise indicated, from Constantin von Wurzbach, "L. A. Hoffmann," *Biographisches Lexikon des Kaiserthums Österreich,* ix (1863), 161-64; Fritz Valjavec, "Die Anfänge des österreichischen Konservativismus: L. A. Hoffmann," *Festschrift Karl Eder* (Innsbruck, 1959), pp. 155-68; Marianne Lunzer-Lindhausen, "L. A. Hoffmann—Wiener Publizist im Schatten der Reaktion," *Wiener Geschichtsblätter,* xv (1960), 104-09; and the excellent recent study by D. Silagi, *Ungarn und der geheime Mitarbeiterkreis Kaiser Leopolds II* (Munich, 1961), Chs. 9-13.

but the circumstances accompanying their defections differ markedly. Starck's conduct was clouded by ambiguities throughout his life, while Hoffmann's was utterly straightforward. Where Starck was subtle, Hoffmann was essentially simple; in fact, he never lost the earthiness and self-confidence of a man of the people who believes the world to be much less complicated than it actually is. It is not surprising, in the light of these contrasts, that no personal love was lost between Starck and Hoffmann, though they were to cooperate on the journal *Eudämonia* in 1795.[24]

Hoffmann went to Prague when he was twenty and threw himself into writing. He made his debut as a champion of *Aufklärung* in various roles as literary drudge, editor of a stillborn journal, unsuccessful dramatist, teacher at a *Philanthropin*, and pamphleteer on behalf of Jewish emancipation. He soon tired of provincial Prague and moved to Vienna in 1782 in search of fame and fortune. His initial job in the capital was to coedit and largely write a religious journal of Josephine tendencies, the *Wöchentliche Wahrheiten für und über die Prediger in Wien*, whose columns specialized in "exposing" sermons delivered by "fanatical" priests; it was Hoffmann's task to go from church to church every Sunday and report on what was said by the priests—an obligation likely to confirm his anticlericalism through weariness and boredom. His articles caught the attention of Gottfried Freiherr von Swieten, the *Illuminat* who headed Joseph's Commission for Education and Censorship. Swieten transformed Hoffmann's fortunes by appointing him to a professorship for German language at the academy at Pest (in Hungary) in 1785—a remarkable appointment seeing that Hoffmann did not hold any doctoral degree, ordinarily a prerequisite for academic positions. The post had been created to promote the Josephine policy of Germanizing the Magyars, and its holder was bound to be disliked by the native population as a carpetbagger.[25]

Hoffmann had meanwhile become a Mason in 1783, though he was at that time two years under the minimum age for admission and was quite unable to pay the customary heavy initiation fees. His "enlightened" friends overlooked such minor irregularities in order to accommodate a man of such advanced principles. Hoffmann was at one

[24] Gustav Krüger, "Die Eudämonisten," *HZ*, CXLIII (1931), 487, 489.

[25] The tribulations of Hoffmann's early years as a writer provide the autobiographical background for his bitter and satirical remarks about the craft of authorship in his *Höchst wichtige Erinnerungen zur rechten Zeit* (2 vols., Vienna, 1795-96), I, 115-19. The best surviving specimen pamphlet of his Radical period is *Werden wir Katholiken noch im Jahre 1786 fasten?* (Vienna, 1786), a scurrilous attack upon Catholicism.

time on the verge of joining the *Illuminatenorden,* his pet phobia in later days, but he drew back at the last moment, because he was already horrified by the cult of secrecy practiced by the *Illuminati.*[26]

Hoffmann's political views shifted toward Conservatism in 1787 for reasons which are quite impossible to trace now. It has been suggested that he resented being sent to the Pest "hardship post" when a more attractive professorship was vacant at Prague, but there is no contemporary evidence for this charge. Hoffmann always claimed that his "conversion," which occurred when he was twenty-seven, was nothing more than a normal advance from political adolescence to maturity, and that his study of the *Illuminati* papers which had been confiscated and published by the Bavarian government at this time made him see the error of his earlier sympathies. His change of view, whatever its occasion, was one of principle rather than opportunism, for Conservatism became advantageous only five years later; it would do Hoffmann's foresight too much honor to think that he perceived the revolution and the Conservative reaction to come as early as 1787 and tailored his convictions to serve his future career at the expense of his present prospects.[27]

Hoffmann marked his conversion by publishing a number of pamphlets about Masonry demanding fundamental reforms in the lodges.[28] They should abandon secrecy in favor of open social-service activities, such as providing loans for the needy and scholarships for the able. They should end their rationalist campaign against Catholicism because it was undermining the very foundations of social order. Hoffmann was especially critical of the support given by Masons to Nicolai's campaign against "Crypto-Catholicism," a term whose vagueness possessed a fatal resemblance to some of Hoffmann's later categories of denunciation. He was pleased that these literary efforts brought him, in his own words,

> many interesting contacts with honorable Masons and also with well-informed *Illuminati,* who recognized that they had been deceived by their superiors, and repented of their former activities.

[26] Hoffmann told the story in detail to refute persistent accusations levied by his foes in ibid., II, LXXIII-CXX. A full account of his Masonic activities can be found in the very hostile article about Hoffmann in *Allgemeines Handbuch der Freimaurer,* I, 460.

[27] *Erinnerungen,* I, 30-32n.; II, LXIV-LXXIII. See also the various autobiographical remarks in Hoffmann's *Geschichte der Päpste von Petrus bis Pius VI* (Leipzig and Vienna, 1791).

[28] See especially Hoffmann's *Achtzehn Paragraphen über Katholizismus, Protestantismus, Jesuitismus, geheime Orden und moderne Aufklärung in Deutschland* (Vienna, 1787).

A group of us pledged ourselves to work for the overthrow of *Illuminatism,* and I was selected as spokesman for the group. My new acquaintances handed me secret papers whose content stimulated my zeal and indignation.[29]

The rest of his life was to be marked by a great deal of zeal and indignation in a never-ending campaign against the *Aufklärung* he had forsworn.

Hoffmann's years at Pest were unsuccessful and unhappy. His teaching efforts were uninteresting to himself and unappreciated by his students, while his attempt to found a journal, the *Pester Wochenblatt,* collapsed after a few issues. Indignity was added to failure when the Magyars expelled him in 1790 during their successful rising against Josephine officialdom. Hoffmann thereupon joined Martinovics and other malcontents in the "secret cabinet" of Emperor Leopold concentrating upon Hungarian affairs. His quick intelligence, indefatigable industry, and remarkable ability to write pamphlets on the basis of brief oral instructions made him a valuable "press jackal" for the emperor. Hoffmann's first commission was a biting pamphlet ridiculing Magyar pretensions, entitled *Babel.* The author identified himself with Josephine absolutism and contempt of the hoary cobwebs of Hungarian aristocratic constitutionalism; his brand of Conservatism defended the absolute monarchy of the present rather than the feudal *Ständestaat* of the past. He hated aristocratic *frondeurs* as much as Radical rebels, and in fact compared the Magyars with the contemporary French revolutionaries to the latter's slight advantage. This *faux pas* led to the condemnation of the entire pamphlet by head censor Swieten (Hoffmann's former patron), a condemnation soon overturned by the direct intervention of the emperor. (The entire episode is a bizarre example of how regular officialdom was kept uninformed about what Leopold's "secret cabinet" was doing.) Fifteen thousand copies of the pamphlet circulated in Hungary; each was accompanied by a model petition for Hungarian burghers, asking for increased city representation in the Diet to help break the power of the Reactionary anti-Josephine gentry.[30]

---

[29] *Erinnerungen,* I, 194-95.

[30] Full title of pamphlet: *Bebel. Fragmente über die jetzigen politischen Angelegenheiten in Ungarn* (Vienna, 1790). It was soon followed by *Ninive. Fortgesetzte Fragmente über die darmaligen politischen Angelegenheiten in Ungarn* (Vienna, 1790), a sharp attack upon the paralyzing "coronation diploma" presented by the Hungarian diet to Leopold. Hoffmann proposed again to mobilize burgher and even peasant representation to break the power of the Magyar

Hoffmann did not, however, confine his attention to Hungarian rebels. His earlier hostility to Masonry and his conversion to Conservative principles made him deeply suspicious of the activities of all Radicals. He agreed with Starck in viewing the French Revolution as part of the world conspiracy launched by the *Illuminati*, and soon made it his business to look into the conspiracy's local ramifications. When Hoffmann offered to the emperor—exactly as Martinovics did at the same time—to report on Viennese public opinion, Leopold apparently accepted with alacrity. He is supposed to have said, "Hoffmann is as stupid as a donkey, but he nonetheless performs valuable services for me as a spy."[31]

On the basis of his pre-1787 contacts with Left-wing circles Hoffmann drew up lists of Masonic and *Illuminati* suspects and urged Leopold to mark these men for reprimand, demotion, or dismissal. (To the emperor's credit, he refused to do this.) Hoffmann easily convinced himself that Vienna was haunted by a dangerous Radical party whose chiefs stood in close contact with the Parisian Jacobins. His worst suspicions appeared confirmed with the interception (in March 1791) of some French propaganda instructions addressed to seven Viennese Radicals (whose names were, unfortunately, written in a code which could not be deciphered).[32] It may be added that some of Hoffmann's suspicions proved justified in the light of the Jacobin conspiracy three years later; yet his own campaign of miscellaneous denunciation did not contribute one iota to the discovery of the Radical rationals. Hoffmann's bungling, shotgun approach suggests that the exposure of subversion is a task better left to police professionals than to demagogic amateurs.

Leopold appreciated Hoffmann's services sufficiently to appoint him professor of German language, official correspondence (*Geschäftsstil*), and practical eloquence at the University of Vienna in 1790, with the title of *K. K. Rath* (counselor and a salary of 2,000 guldens per annum. The emperor also commissioned him in the spring of 1791 to draw up plans for a Conservative secret society to combat the Jacobins on their own ground. Hoffmann quickly selected two faculty colleagues, Hein-

gentry. Hoffmann's relations with Leopold are examined by D. Silagi, op.cit., Ch. 9.

[31] F. X. Huber, *Beytrag zur Charakteristik und Regierungsgeschichte der Kaiser Joseph II, Leopold II, und Franz II* (Paris [?], 1800), p. 117. The quotation is doubted by D. Silagi, op.cit., p. 59, as intrinsically implausible, but Silagi is consistently biased in Hoffmann's favor and says far too little about the latter's discreditable qualities.

[32] *Erinnerungen*, I, 300-01.

rich Joseph Watteroth (later successor to the great Sonnenfels as professor of political science upon Hoffmann's recommendation in Dec. 1791) and Joseph Ernst Mayer (professor of philosophy) to help him draw plans for what he optimistically called "a work of all time and an unshakable foundation for all thrones."[33] The purpose of the secret society, called The Association, was, in Hoffmann's words:

> To counteract French propaganda, demagogic principles, the heady wine of philanthropic libertarianism, irreligion and false *Aufklärung* as well as all secret orders, factions, and societies devoted to these goals. Furthermore: to define and spread true principles which lead to the planting of correct religious concepts in men's minds, the establishment of a proper equilibrium between moderate monarchy and democracy, and the securing of unquestioned obedience to the laws of the state and the will of the prince.[34]

To achieve these purposes Hoffmann drew up elaborate statutes which reveal a remarkable resemblance to those of the *Illuminatenorden* he so much deplored. They provide for the secret recruiting of members, with preference to be given to men in influential positions and students likely to rise to such positions; secret superiors with undefined powers; classical names and a special cipher to assure the secrecy of communications; the duty to write regular reports about oneself and others; and elaborate initiation ceremonies with colorful ritual, a special oath, et cetera. Men were to be won by an appeal to "the three motives which are always to be found in any considerable enterprise: self-interest, ambition, and a properly directed enthusiasm (*Schwärmerei*)."[35] Self-interest was to be satisfied by promotion in public service, decorations, and cash; ambition, by assigning tasks which inflated men with a sense of their own importance; *Schwärmerei*, by the stipulation that "each new member should personally travel to the capital and there secure admission to the society with a proper ceremony arranged by the executive committee."[36] The specific goal of the Association, which Watteroth called the Society of the Friends of the Monarch and the People, was to work up "enthusiasm for the good

[33] Letter of Hoffmann to Leopold II, July 21, 1791, printed in Silagi, *Ungarn*, p. 121.

[34] Undated *Zweiter Entwurf eines Assoziationsplanes* (summer 1791), printed in ibid., p. 128. Additional purposes were to counteract aristocratic intrigues (meaning, presumably, Hungarian ambitions), to win the crown prince for the aims of The Association, and to seek to influence the policies of foreign powers.

[35] Undated *Erster Entwurf eines Assoziationsplanes* (summer 1791), printed in ibid., p. 126.

[36] Ibid., p. 126.

cause (*die gute Sache*), the regent, the state, the common welfare (*Gemeingeist*), and industriousness (*Arbeitsamkeit*); to establish newspapers, brochures, and journals, or to win over existing ones to promote the intentions of the regent and the purposes of this association";[37] to report on all subversive activities; and to provide examples of good citizenship.[38]

Leopold accepted these proposals in principle, and he asked Hoffmann to accompany him on his coronation journey to Prague (Sept. 1791) to talk over details. An unedifying rivalry between Hoffmann, Watteroth, and Mayer for leadership in the proposed society soon arose. The latter two challenged Hoffmann's claim to primacy, and forced through a triumviral arrangement under which Hoffmann headed a section for recruiting authors and journalists, Mayer for educators and clergymen, and Watteroth for public officials. Surviving documents reveal that Mayer asked Anton Spendou, canon of St. Stephen, to evaluate lists of Viennese priests, while Watteroth asked Joseph Anton von Riegger, *Gubernalrat* in Prague, to evaluate lists of Bohemian officials. The obvious intention was to assemble a list of eligibles for subsequent recruiting; this task was also facilitated when Watteroth received a blanket authorization of access to all official files (and hence officials) throughout the entire monarchy (Dec. 1791). This unusual authorization was plausibly justified, without arousing undue suspicions, by Watteroth's research needs in pursuance of his duties as professor of statistics and political science.[39]

Further elaboration of the Association was prevented by Leopold's sudden death on March 1, 1792, an irreparable loss to Hoffmann, since he was unable to establish a successful working relationship with Leopold's successor, Francis. This proved of major importance in determining the fate of the most significant enterprise launched by Hoffmann under Leopold—the founding and editing of the famous *Wiener Zeitschrift*. Hoffmann described his general literary relations with Leopold, and the specific origins of the *Wiener Zeitschrift*, a few years later in the following terms:

> The Emperor honored my talents as a writer with many proofs of his confidence. He gave me several specific assignments, and often insisted that I bring him manuscript drafts so that he could personally revise them. He frequently suggested improvements which I im-

[37] *Zweiter Entwurf*, ibid., p. 129.
[38] The best account of the entire Association Project is Silagi, *Ungarn*, Ch. 13.
[39] For the entire paragraph see the documentary appendices III-V in Silagi, *Ungarn*.

CHALLENGE OF FRENCH REVOLUTION AND NAPOLEON

mediately made in his own presence. He was so impressed by the success of several of my articles that he wanted to commission me to do additional work. I replied, however, with the consideration that too many small and isolated articles could not exercise any deep or lasting influence, or reach any considerable public; that it would be far preferable to start a general journal which could present the entire [Conservative] argument in a systematic and continuous form.[40]

Leopold, who was a notorious procrastinator, delayed in giving his final approval for about a year, but he urged Hoffmann to begin assembling a staff of contributors. Hoffmann had little success in this task, probably because his own reputation did not seem sufficient to sustain a major journal, though he himself claimed that his difficulties were due to the literary tyranny which *Illuminism* exercised over Germany. The advertisement for the *Wiener Zeitschrift* brought only thirteen advance subscriptions, but the first issue, appearing in January 1792, was remarkably successful in selling five hundred copies. Circulation rose after the first few numbers to a maximum of about two thousand, but declined, before the journal expired in September 1793, to about one thousand. These figures are, of course, an insufficient index of the journal's importance, for it was patronized by both Leopold II, who regularly sent it official documents for publication, and by the Prussian King Frederick William II, who honored Hoffmann with a warm letter of approval.[41]

Hoffmann set the theme of the *Wiener Zeitschrift* in a characteristic Prologue worth giving in full both for its content and its intemperate language:

[40] *Erinnerungen*, I, 300-01.

[41] The best account of the *Wiener Zeitschrift* is the excellent monograph by Friedrich Sommer, *Die Wiener Zeitschrift 1792-93. De Geschichte eines anti-revolutionären Journals* (Leipzig, 1932). A brief and rather hostile treatment can be found in Adalbert Fäulhammer, "Politische Meinungen und Stimmungen in Wien in den Jahren 1793 und 1794," *Programm des Staatsgymnasiums in Salzburg 1893* (Salzburg, 1893), pp. 16-18. Hoffmann printed the two letters he received from the Prussian King in *Wiener Zeitschrift*, I (1792), 273-77. He claimed, in his *Erinnerungen*, I, p. 310, that he did this only after the specific urging of Leopold. The financing of the journal was made possible by 10,000 florins donated by Leopold, if a letter from Wöllner to Frederick William II (Dec. 26, 1791) may be trusted. See Schultz, *Der erste Kulturkampf*, p. 234. Some indications of the circulation of the W. Z. in North Germany are given in Eberhard Crucius, "Konservative Kräfte in Oldenburg am Ende des 18. Jahrhunderts," *Niedersächsisches Jahrbuch für Landesgeschichte*, XXXIV (1962), 224-53. Court Doctor Heinrich Marcard (1747-1817) propagandized vigorously on behalf of the W. Z.

The intoxication with liberty which is presently sweeping over Europe, the revolts of several traditionally loyal nations against their sovereigns, the general atmosphere of political fermentation, and the prevalent irreligion are all the fruits of an unbridled *Aufklärung*, a fanatical "philosophy," and the writings of a horde of cosmopolitan and "philanthropic" authors who take Mirabeau as their model.

These authors throw out their poison daily in every European country. . . . Public opinion is completely in their hands. Their famous or rather infamous names, their brazen and unbridled loquaciousness, their flair for intrigue and manipulation, all combined with the terrifying omnipotence of secret societies, succeed in giving their disastrous principles prestige, influence and tragic effectiveness everywhere.

It is high time that public opinion be turned in a different direction and that the voices of subversion be muzzled: for otherwise every throne stands in danger of being buried under its own debris, and every European government will be driven by democratic license into the most horrible anarchy as the natural result of philosophic *Aufklärung*.

[Conservative] Authors must, therefore, take up combat against [subversive] authors. . . . Nations must be instructed about their true interests, demagogues must be unmasked, and subversive political assassins (*Mordbrenner*) must be exposed in the public arena with implacable determination. This work should be the common task of all honest and wise friends of humanity in Germany; it is probably already the wish of most, but the voices of such men have so far not been heard with the required volume and resonance.

To mobilize these latent voices is the primary purpose of the *Wiener Zeitschrift*. It refuses to be intimidated by the rage of the prevalent "enlightened barbarism" (*Aufklärungsbarbarei*) and its false apostles. It will have the courage to expose without mercy the sly wickedness of treasonable demagogues, wherever they may be found. It will call upon the German nation, which is now narcotized in so many of its parts, to stop listening to the tricks and insinuations of a certain class of philosophers who preach the happiness of man but in fact promote only his misfortune.[42]

The *Wiener Zeitschrift* remained true to this announcement with monotonous determination. It did not pretend to possess a positive program, other than to praise the Leopoldine government, but special-

[42] *Wiener Zeitschrift*, I (1792), 2-6.

ized, rather, in denouncing the *Aufklärung*, secret societies, the French Revolution, and, above all, its German sympathizers. A brief survey of a single issue will give a better indication of the content and tendency of Hoffmann's magazine than an elaborate analysis of the whole. The first number (January 1792) contained twelve items other than the Prologue, beginning with a defense of Leopold's Censorship Edict of Aug. 10, 1790. Hoffmann praised Leopold for prohibiting at long last the subversive and irreligious writings which Joseph had so unwisely legalized by his patent of 1781. Next came a feature which was repeated until the emperor's death—"contributions to a chronicle of Leopold's legislation"—in this case the text of three recently issued imperial decrees dealing with prison reform, the abolition of a newspaper tax, and the promise to consider anonymous as well as signed petitions—all decrees which made the emperor appear in a benevolent light. The third item was an open letter sent by Hoffmann to the author J. H. Campe. It attacked the latter's influential *Letters from Paris*, written in the early days of the revolution, for their subversive tendency. The fourth item printed a declaration drafted by the white settlers of a French West Indian colony, in which they accused the Jacobin-sponsored *Friends of the Negro People* of encouraging rebellion, rape, and murder on the part of former Negro slaves. Next came a recurring column, entitled "Follies of *Aufklärung*" (*Aufklärungs-Scottisen*), in which Hoffmann collected revealing tidbits calculated to throw unfavorable light upon Radical figures—in this case Campe, Bahrdt, and Eulogius Schneider. The column also denounced the tyrannical censorship exercised by "enlightened" public opinion over the stage, as witnessed by the forced cancellation in Leipzig of performances of two anti-Jacobin plays, Kotzebue's *Club of Female Jacobins* and Iffland's *Cockades*. The sixth item praised a new Viennese police regulation (Nov. 11, 1791) which provided free medical care for those too poor to pay the regular fees of doctors, surgeons, and midwives. Next came a defense (composed by Hoffmann) of the right claimed by governments to open the private correspondence of persons suspected of subversion—a current practice which had been criticized recently by Wieland's *Deutscher Merkur*. The right of the government to inform itself was paralleled by a duty to protect the mail of loyal individuals against tampering by agents of subversive societies. (Hoffmann was convinced that the all-pervasive *Illuminati* were spying upon his private correspondence.) There followed a passionate appeal (probably written by Hoffmann) calling upon the rulers of Europe to beware of the plans of the *Illuminati*.

The ninth item printed the protest issued by the exiled Bourbon princes against the acceptance of the new French constitution by Louis XVI—an acceptance considered null and void because Louis obviously signed only under duress. Item ten printed a cabinet order of Leopold (Dec. 1, 1791) which reprimanded certain tax officials who had harassed a Galician Jew because he had dared to denounce their extortionate irregularities—again an example of the benevolent rule of Leopold, who was depicted as solicitous to protect his subjects against mistreatment by his own officials. The two remaining items were a rather vapid poem, *The Tower and the Rock*, and a digest of academic news. The poem was a Conservative allegory showing the interdependence of the aristocracy (described as a tower) and the peasantry (described as a rock on which the tower is built), the point being that the collapse of the tower would crush the rock foundation underlying its structure. The academic news included as its most important item the announcement that Professor Hoffmann's lecture course on business style and practical eloquence "had just been made, by virtue of a personal decision of H. I. Majesty, a required subject for all students enrolled in the fourth division of law";[43] the grades in the subject were to appear henceforth on job applications. The clear inference was that the editor of the *Wiener Zeitschrift* was an important university personage enjoying the special favor of the emperor.

The subsequent issues of the *Wiener Zeitschrift* all followed a similar pattern. It is not surprising that the public, even that section which agreed with Hoffmann's principles, soon tired of such a monotonous diet. On the whole Hoffmann was unsuccessful in soliciting articles from well-known outside contributors; only J. G. Zimmermann, the Hannoverian doctor; H. O. Reichard, the Gotha librarian; Ernst von Göchhausen, the early foe of the *Illuminati*; and K. L. von Haller, the future "restorer of political science," proved occasional exceptions. What variety the journal possessed was due to the fact that Hoffmann constantly found new Radicals to attack; he understood that a successful campaign of exposure can be maintained only by the continuous discovery of new victims. Hoffmann's suspiciousness could be relied upon to find a regular supply of the innocent as well as the guilty. It is understandable that he attacked, to mention only prominent figures, Forster, the head of the Mainz Jacobins; Mauvillon, Mirabeau's friend; Campe, the Brunswick writer; Knigge, the former *Illuminati* leader; and the various German writers, including Schiller and Klopstock, who accepted honorary French citizenship from the National

---

[43] Ibid., p. 128.

Assembly. It is more surprising that he castigated August Ludwig von Schlözer as a dangerous Jacobin because his *Staatsanzeigen* continued to demand German reforms even after Schlözer had turned sharply against the French Revolution. Hoffmann struck back furiously when the *Jenaische Allgemeine Litteratur Zeitung,* the most respected review journal in Germany, dared to criticize the *Wiener Zeitschrift* for levying unfounded accusations against innocent individuals. The denunciation of the *J.A.L.Z.* as a subversive organ was especially ludicrous at the very time when its pages were graced by Rehberg's brilliant antirevolutionary book reviews (see Ch. 11). It must be said that Hoffmann lacked both judgment and scruple in his indiscriminate campaign of denunciation, though it is probable that he believed everything that he wrote. His mind was distorted by his sincere belief in the conspiracy theory.[44]

One example of Hoffmann's character assassination will illustrate his method. Hoffmann disbelieved Freiherr von Knigge's account that he had left the *Illuminatenorden* in 1785;[45] he dismissed Knigge's warning against secret societies—which had an obvious ring of sincerity, coming from a man who had burnt his fingers—as an attempt to throw sand into the eyes of princes.[46] Hoffmann looked upon Knigge as the indirect instigator of the French Revolution, since it was he who had initially recruited Mauvillon for the Order (who had, in turn, won Mirabeau), and since he was a personal friend of the Bode who had made the famous journey to Paris in 1787. Hoffmann presented his accusations in the following bill of particulars:

I accuse you (Knigge) personally, and those auxiliaries whom you have hired, organized, and directed, of having been the most effective promoters of the French Revolution. You have been the guiding spirit behind the German revolutionary and democratic movement, and continue to act in this role to this very day. I shall prove this to you without fear and without being deterred by the fact that you have won, by your superior connections and customary flair for intrigue, your lawsuit against Zimmermann when he levelled this same charge. I shall prove that you have been the instigator of Masonry, of the recently destroyed Strict Observance, of the com-

[44] A good survey of the victims of the *Wiener Zeitschrift* is provided by Sommer, op.cit., Ch. 4.
[45] See Knigge's *Philo's endliche Erklärung und Antwort auf verschiedene Anforderungen und Fragen* (Hannover, 1788).
[46] Hoffmann, *Erinnerungen,* I, Ch. 6, ridiculing Knigge's remarks in his *Umgang mit Menschen,* Pt. II, Ch. 8.

pletely corrupted Rosicrucian movement [!] and that you have been, in consequence, one of the chief promoters of the French Revolution, and, finally, the main author of the infamous *Deutsche Union*.[47]

It is unnecessary to add that Hoffmann was quite unable to support any of these charges.

Hoffmann's advice to the princes of Germany on how to curb the revolutionary danger was similar to Starck's call for censorship, suppression of secret societies, and encouragement of religion. Hoffmann added a specific note by urging that men like Knigge be prosecuted as traitors; princes must never forget that the Jacobins in France did not allow men with known counterrevolutionary principles to remain at large.[48] He further urged the princes to impose a special anti-*Illuminati* oath upon certain categories of the population—an example of the recurring fallacy that a compulsory oath can be an effective method of ferreting out disloyalty.[49]

Hoffmann combined these proposals for repression with frank advocacy of some obscurantist principles which are more frequently believed in private than asserted in public. He declared that freedom of speech and freedom of writing were both absurd and fraught with dangerous consequences. The government licensed every conceivable craft and profession from cobbling to medicine and law. Why should literature be alone exempt from governmental regulation? Did books and newspapers not affect the public interest to an unusual degree? Hoffmann proposed rather naïvely that the government create "a tribunal composed of a few men of known integrity, religious convictions, and solid learning . . . with the duty of examining all candidates for the craft of literature before they would be permitted to enter the guild of authors."[50] He exposed his own grievances as a literary hack without status when he claimed that such licensing was in the best interest of authors themselves since it would give them a secure social position—such as that which doctors secured by being officially differentiated from medical quacks. Hoffmann wanted the government to give loyal authors not only status but income as well. At present they could scarcely make a living since the *Illuminati* possessed a

[47] Hoffmann, *Aktenmässige Darstellung der Deutschen Union* (Vienna, 1796), pp. 175-76.

[48] Hoffmann, *Erinnerungen*, i, Ch. 5. This is a good example of how Conservative Cassandras often show a sneaking admiration for the ruthlessness of their revolutionary foes.

[49] *Erinnerungen*, i, Ch. 7.   [50] Ibid., p. 110.

stranglehold on the German reading public. Princes must be taught the importance of creating a Conservative public opinion. A policy of suppressing subversive authors was indispensable, but it must be supplemented by the subsidization of loyal authors. These proposals reflect the fact that Hoffmann frequently felt neglected, spiritually and materially, by the society and government which he was trying to defend against subversion.[51]

Hoffmann ridiculed writers who resented the kind of governmental regulation he proposed, and confronted them with what one might describe a general "philosophy of compulsion":

These obstructive, refractory ranters (*Schreier*) who resent any kind of compulsion (*Zwang*) by authority must learn that all states, indeed any kind of society, is based upon compulsion, upon the sacrifice of natural freedom, and upon voluntary acceptance of the need of such sacrifice. . . . If they would only use their eyes they would see that the world everywhere requires the principle of compulsion as both necessary and useful: compulsion leads the peasant to tend the plough, though he would prefer to be an aristocrat; compulsion forces men to pay every kind of tax; compulsion rules in every business enterprise and government office; in every council chamber, court, ministry and cabinet; it constrains every day laborer, artisan, domestic servant, and above all every soldier. [The ranters] obviously lack the knowledge of human nature to recognize that most men will do what is good and necessary even for themselves only under compulsion. One must repeat again and again the golden words: "What cannot be, cannot be (*Was nicht sein kann, dass kann nicht sein*); one must never demand the impossible. It is sweet and pleasant to be allowed to do what one pleases; but it is wiser and more reasonable to do what requires to be done for the general welfare."[52]

Hoffmann wanted to control not only the quality but also the quantity of newspapers, books, and pamphlets. He was convinced that the basic truths of religion, philosophy, and ethics had long been known and set forth in excellent books, and hence did not require to be stated anew—an argument akin to that allegedly used by the Arabs to justify their destruction of the Alexandrian library. Only in science, history, and some other fields did new discoveries warrant new publications.[53] More important, however, was Hoffmann's second

[51] Ibid., pp. 235-38; ii, 97-121. [52] Ibid., i, 105-06.
[53] Ibid., p. 142.

argument: the imperative need of preventing the development of a half-educated reading public. His hatred of the half-educated was sharpened, perhaps, by his uncomfortable knowledge that he belonged to the upper brackets of this unfortunate group himself. The development of a vulgar reading public forced authors—under the pressure of profit-hungry publishers—to debase their literary currency. Hoffmann sometimes wished that Europe could return to a condition where books were published in Latin only, and he was a vitriolic critic of popular education because it promoted only "freshness, obtrusiveness, wild manners, insolence and dictatorial loquaciousness."[54]

Hoffmann had correctly predicted, at the time his journal was first launched, that the expression of these views would goad his "enlightened foes" into fury. Several pamphlets were written specifically against him. The Vienna poet J. B. von Alxinger examined the early numbers of the *Wiener Zeitschrift* piece by piece, denouncing the unwarranted denunciations and ridiculing the crudeness of Hoffmann's literary style—a matter of some embarrassment since Hoffmann was after all a university professor of practical eloquence. Alxinger proposed to introduce a new word, *Hoffmannismus*, into the German language with the following dictionary definition: "The habit of depicting only the worst side of a matter, combined with the shameless malice of scolding meritorious men as if they were schoolboys."[55] Knigge replied to Hoffmann's attacks by a witty satire, *The Papers of the recently deceased Samuel Conrad von Schaafskopf*, in which Hoffmann was depicted as the leader of a newly founded Order of Dunces.[56] The most effective ridicule of Hoffmann was penned by the radical G. F. Rebmann in a satire on *The Guardians of Zion*. An excerpt will give the flavor of the attack:

> The obscurantists [headed by Hoffmann] do not see in the French Revolution the consequence of easily traceable causes . . . but rather the work of a secret society headed by a very few men. One is asked to believe by this party [the obscurantists] that two truly super-

[54] Ibid., p. 73.
[55] Johann von Alxinger, *Anti-Hoffmann* (2 parts, Vienna, 1702-93), Pt. I, 42. On Alxinger see E. Probst, "Johann Baptist von Alxinger," *Jahrbuch der Grillparzer-Gesellschaft*, VII (1897), 171-202.
[56] Knigge, *Des seligen Herrn Etatsraths Samuel Conrad von Schaafskopf hinterlassene Papiere; von seinen Erben herausgegeben* (Breslau, 1792). Some of Knigge's attacks upon Hoffmann were less good-natured. He once compared, for example, the content of the *Wiener Zeitschrift* with Hoffmann's liquid excrement emerging after he had eaten the wrong kind of (intellectual) food. *Reise nach Braunschweig* (Hannover, 1792), p. 37.

human individuals Philo [Knigge] and Spartakus [Weishaupt], of whom the former has been an invalid for years and spends most of his time in bed, while the latter lives a quiet life whose tranquillity is only occasionally disturbed by the publication of an obscure philosophical work—that these two, truly superhuman men have in fact worked for the last decade upon the implementation of a plan which the tongues of men and of angels dare not utter, and the minds of men cannot comprehend. The most heterogeneous men, things, and events are all seen as machines in the hands of those two beings: the *Allgemeine teutsche Bibliothek*; the *Litteraturzeitung* in Jena; a few hundred scholars who in fact frequently do not know one another; a few hundred court marshals, ambassadors, yes even princes; the *Magic Flute* [by Mozart], the armies in the Champagne; the generals of the coalition; the dysentery which caused the Prussians so much trouble [on the retreat from Valmy]; the Duke of Orléans; the Temple of Reason in Paris; the *Marseillaise*; the bookseller Vollmer at Erfurt; Mirabeau, Sieyes, Robespierre, Cagliostro, etc.[57]

The most damaging attack upon Hoffmann came from the pen of Franz X. Huber (1750-1809), a moderate liberal journalist. He was a protégé of Sonnenfels, the leader of the Viennese *Aufklärung*, one of the primary targets of the *Wiener Zeitschrift*,[58] and possessed, as did Hoffmann himself, regular access to the emperor. Huber apparently convinced Leopold that Hoffmann's advertising of the *Wiener Zeitschrift* as a semiofficial organ did grave injury to the reputation of the government, and he proposed to Leopold that the claim to official status be deflated by the publication (with censorship approval) of an anti-Hoffmann pamphlet written by himself. The emperor gave his approval to this plan in accordance with his principle of "divide and rule," though it is said that he considered the actual language of Huber's denunciation too sharp.[59] The struggle between Hoffmann and Huber

[57] G. F. Rebmann, *Die Wächter der Burg Zion. Nachricht von einem geheimen Bunde gegen Regenten und Völkerglück; und Enthüllung der einzigen wahren Propaganda in Deutschland* (Hamburg, 1796), pp. 8-10.

[58] Watteroth, "Fragmente für die künftigen Biographen des Herrn Hofraths von Sonnenfels," *Wiener Zeitschrift*, i (1792), 56-70, 371-87. Hoffmann's bitter hostility to Sonnenfels and his feeling of social inferiority toward him come out poignantly in *Erinnerungen*, i, 6-7.

[59] Franz Xaver Huber, *Kann ein Schriftsteller wie Herr Professor Hoffmann Einfluss auf die Stimmung der deutschen Völker und auf die Denkart ihrer Fürsten Haben?* (Vienna, 1792). The rivalry between Huber and Hoffmann is described in [Pipitz, Franz Ernst], *Der Jakobiner in Wien* (Zurich, 1842), Ch. 4. The position of Hoffmann, Huber, and Alxinger is dissected with impartial dis-

for the emperor's favor had not been brought to an issue when Leopold died suddenly on March 1, 1792.

The loss of his benevolent—if somewhat wavering—protector constituted the beginning of the end for Hoffmann's *Wiener Zeitschrift.* Francis II was not much interested in using Hoffmann to build up a Conservative public opinion, though he had subscribed to the *Wiener Zeitschrift* while he was crown prince and really agreed with its principles far more than did his father, Leopold. A special memorandum submitted to the emperor on June 26, 1793, though tailored to meet Francis' obscurantist principles, was unable to win Hoffmann a secure place in the emperor's favor.[60] Leopold's commission to found a secret Conservative society was quietly withdrawn and Hoffmann's amateurish espionage activities were made superfluous by Francis' reorganization of the secret police. The loss of his professorship soon followed. Hoffmann had never been successful in divorcing his academic work from his politics, and he unwisely used his university platform to denounce his enemies Huber and Alxinger. This questionable conduct provoked some noisy student demonstrations. The faculty, which had been hostile to him from the beginning because Leopold had imposed him as an outsider, took the unusual step of petitioning the government for Hoffmann's immediate retirement; Francis was willing to oblige. Hoffmann thus found himself a retired professor on half pay at the age of thirty-three. His difficulties were soon complicated by ill health brought on by overwork, as he strove desperately to keep the *Wiener Zeitschrift* alive without official favor. It finally collapsed in September 1793 after eighteen issues.

Hoffmann withdrew to Wiener Neustadt, a village some fifty miles south of the capital, in the hope of regaining his health in semiretirement. He did not, however, propose to give up the Conservative struggle. A two-volume work, entitled *Most Important Memoirs,* was advertised as a continuation of the *Wiener Zeitschrift,* and is valuable because it contains much autobiographical information.[61] It was followed by a special pamphlet attacking the recently deceased J. C.

---

gust against all parties in a vigorously written anonymous pamphlet, *An und Ueber Hoffmann, Alxinger und Huber. Eine wohlverdiente Rüge des Litterarischen Unfugs dieses philosophisch-patriotischen Triumvirats* (Vienna, 1792).

[60] "An seine K.K. Majestät Franz II. Privat-Promemoria über die zweckmässigsten Mittel, die sämmtlichen geheimen Orden für jeden Staat unschädlich zu machen," printed in S. Brunner, *Die Mysterien der Aufklärung in Österreich 1770-1800* (Mainz, 1869), pp. 516-22.

[61] *Höchst wichtige Erinnerungen zur richtigen Zeit* (2 vols., Vienna, 1795-96), frequently cited above.

Bode as the instigator of the French Revolution during his Parisian journey of 1787.[62] Hoffmann's next book was a detailed exposure of K. F. Bahrdt and his *Deutsche Union*.[63] When tiring of denunciations he took time out in 1797 to write a textbook on *Christian enlightened Wisdom for the Conduct of Life for all Classes*.[64] A further publication gravely warned Napoleon, then first consul of France, to beware of *Illuminati* activity in the French-occupied Rhineland; it included a sharp attack upon Hoffmann's old enemy G. F. Rebmann, then holding a high judicial post at Mainz.[65] These ceaseless publications did little to maintain Hoffmann in the public eye. He was almost forgotten by the time he died in 1806.

At the height of his notoriety—one can scarcely say reputation—in 1792 he was one of the three or four most talked-about publicists in Germany. He proudly accepted the Radical charge that he stood at the head of a Conservative "party," and worked vigorously to turn a militant and alert minority into the dominant current of German public opinion. He did not see the need, or possess the capacity, to elaborate any comprehensive program of political and religious Conservatism which would anticipate the "systems" of Burke or Maistre or Haller; it sufficed for him to affirm the value of the Leopoldine *status quo* in state and Church. He took up the defense of political absolutism rather than feudal constitutionalism, and his Catholicism was sufficiently diluted with Josephine elements to give little comfort to the orthodox Catholic party.[66] These two facts help to explain why he did not exercise any long-range influence upon German Conservatives. Hoffmann was repudiated—when he was not ignored—by the rising group of neomedievalist romantics whose theory called for the revival of the Christian *Ständestaat*.

Hoffmann has no importance as a Conservative theorist, but he possesses a paradigmatic significance as one kind of practical champion of Conservatism. His combative temperament was never satisfied with defending the established order against attack; it compelled him to engage in incessant counterattack. He never calmly analyzed the

---

[62] *Fragmente zur Biographie des verstorbenen Geheimen Raths Bode* (Vienna, 1795).

[63] *Actenmässige Darstellung der Deutschen Union* (Vienna, 1796).

[64] *Lehrbuch einer christlich-aufgeklärten Lebensweisheit für alle Stände* (Vienna, 1797).

[65] *Schreiben an den Oberconsul Frankreichs, Bonaparte* (Deutschland [Vienna?], 1800).

[66] See the observations in Sommer, op.cit., p. 18. Hoffmann even satirized monasticism in *Wiener Zeitschrift*, VI (1793), 220ff.

general historical forces which were making much of the *status quo* obsolete; he never tried to draw the poisonous fangs from Radicalism by meeting its more reasonable demands and working toward a synthesis of old and new. He believed, instead, that Radical demands existed only because of the malice of perennial troublemakers, and found his lifework in exposing and crushing their nefarious efforts. His specialty was personal denunciation, and his denunciations were too often unsubstantiated, being based upon an a priori belief in conspiracy rather than specific evidence. They brought undeserved obloquy to hundreds of people, and helped poison the general atmosphere of public discussion in Germany. Hoffmann forgot that responsible Conservatism requires not only the defense of an established order, but the scrupulous maintenance of certain traditional ethical values as well. The observance of fair play, even in political controversy, and the adherence to truth, even while denouncing Radical foes, are two essential elements of a civilized moral code, and Hoffmann erred grievously in offending against both. It is not necessary to assume that he was a deliberate liar, or an unprincipled opportunist, as has frequently been charged; but his character can be vindicated only at the expense of his judgment. He was a polemical rather than a rational man, an unbalanced fanatic who was haunted by revolutionary specters. The actual effect of his work was disastrous, and cannot be excused by his subjective sincerity of purpose.

The spirit he represented was dominant long after he ceased to exercise any personal influence. Much of it remained, indeed, the prevalent outlook of official Austria in the Franciscan and Metternichean period.

The Eudämonia: The Journalistic Rally of Conservatism

We have now outlined the antirevolutionary writings of several Conservative publicists during the 1790's: Möser, Zimmermann, Schlözer, Eberhard, Tonder, and Reichard; and we have analyzed in detail the outlook of J. A. Starck, the philosopher of the "conspiracy theory," and Leopold Hoffmann, its most vigorous journalistic spokesman. All these men worked in comparative isolation, and even when they published journals—as in the case of Schlözer, Schirach, Tonder, and Hoffmann—these tended to be essentially one-man affairs. What German Conservatism needed to rally and spread its influence was a distinctive journal which would draw together scattered talents. This function was to be fulfilled, at least to a degree, by the *Eudämonia. A*

Journal for the Friends of Truth and Justice, which appeared for three years between 1795 and 1798.[67]

The *Eudämonia,* though famous in its day, was virtually forgotten for over a hundred years until the Bonn historian Max Braubach published an article about it in 1927.[68] Braubach was somewhat handicapped in his analysis by the anonymity of the editors and most contributors. He made, however, intelligent guesses on both scores, as was shown when Gustav Krüger's happy archival discovery in Darmstadt in 1931 uncovered some correspondence between Grolman (the main editor) and Zimmermann (a prospective contributor).[69] We know today about the *Eudämonia* all that we are ever likely to know, and a great deal more than is known about most eighteenth-century journals; though unfortunately we lack information on many matters of primary importance, such as details about the financing, profit, circulation, and readership of the journal.

The founding of the *Eudämonia* in the winter of 1794-95 shows an interesting combination of private initiative and governmental encouragement. The *spiritus rector* of the enterprise was Ludwig Adolf Christian von Grolman (1741-1809), a high Hessian official of bourgeois origin who had been ennobled for his services to the government in 1786. He was *Regierungsdirektor* of the university city of Giessen in the 1790's, and had recently served as legal adviser to his friend J. A. Starck during the latter's unsuccessful libel suit against the editors of the *Berlinische Monatsschrift* (who had, it will be recalled, accused him of "Crypto-Catholicism"). His friendship with Starck was cemented by their common repudiation of an active Masonic past. Grolman had not only served as master of a lodge established at Giessen, but had even entered the junior grades of the *Illuminatenorden* and been a personal friend of Knigge's. In the latter connection he had secured possession of the instructions drawn up by Weishaupt and Knigge for the *Illuminati* ranks of priest and regent, and he caused a

---

[67] *Eudämonia oder Deutsches Volksglück. Ein Journal für Freunde von Wahrheit und Recht.* A complete set is in the Bonn University library.

[68] M. Braubach, "Die *Eudämonia* (1795-98). Ein Beitrag zur deutschen Publizistik im Zeitalter der Aufklärung und der Revolution," *Historisches Jahrbuch der Görres-Gesellschaft,* XLVII (1927), 309-39. All the information in this section not otherwise acknowledged is taken from this definitive article.

[69] Gustav Krüger, "Die Eudämonisten. Ein Beitrag zur Publizistik des ausgehenden 18. Jahrhunderts." *H.Z.,* CXLIII (1931), 467-500. The article is based upon the correspondence between Ludwig von Grolman, Hessian *Regierungsdirektor* (see below) and Johann Zimmermann, the Hannoverian doctor, in October 1794, and quotes all key passages verbatim.

literary sensation by publishing these in 1794.[70] Grolman clearly had the personality of a renegade fanatic, and he was all too prone to believe anything nefarious concerning his former confreres. It so happened that he and Starck were "taking the waters" together in 1789 at the resort town of Schwalbach when they received word of the storming of the Bastille. Grolman remembered that they looked at one another knowingly and exclaimed in unison: "*That* is the work of the *Illuminati.*"[71]

The two friends became increasingly alarmed about the ramification of the *Illuminati* conspiracy in Germany and what they believed to be its "terroristic stranglehold" over German public opinion. Grolman repeatedly pleaded with his ruler, *Landgraf* Ludwig X of Hessen-Kassel, to take energetic steps to protect his throne against subversive action and opinion; but he was thwarted because the *Landgraf* stood under the influence of Wilhelm von dem Bussche, the notorious *Illuminat* who had accompanied Bode on his much-discussed Parisian journey in 1787. Ludwig remained unmoved by the hysterical warnings about conspiracy; and what Grolman considered to be his inexcusable apathy communicated itself to most of his ministers. Grolman resolved to found a society which would defend Conservative principles—if necessary in spite of the princes who ignored both their duty and their interest—by publishing a journal devoted to the exposure of the machinations of the *Illuminati*. In Grolman's words:

> One thing alone remains possible for us: that honest, informed and courageous men should unite themselves and shout so loudly that princes are compelled to listen (*so lange schreien, bis die Fürsten hören*). We must speak up on behalf of the good cause with the same boldness with which the opposite party has called for its destruction. We must instruct the people through a journal which must achieve, cost what it may, prestige, permanence, and a large readership. Such a journal must use the power of truth to expose the intrigues spun by the enemy; scourge the inciters of discontent; and avenge the treatment handed out to Conservative authors [by

[70] *Die neuesten Arbeiten des Spartacus und Philo in dem Illuminatenorden; jetzt zum erstenmal gedruckt, und zur Beherzigung bey gegenwärtigen Zeitläuften herausgegeben* (Munich, 1794). Grolman's implication that these writings were of recent origin is, of course, false, though it is probable that he believed it himself. When his former *Illuminati* friends condemned his breach of confidence, he claimed that he had never taken the oath which pledged *Illuminati* to absolute secrecy in case they should leave the order. Krüger, *Eudämonisten*, p. 471.

[71] All the biographical information is from ibid., pp. 470ff., which follows Grolman's own autobiographical account written in 1794.

Radical review organs]. It must exploit all the opportunities afforded by the freedom of the press and use the same techniques of intrigue . . . as the enemy. We must recognize that we are embarked upon a life and death struggle—yet we can take comfort in the thought that even in defeat we would lose no more than would be lost by maintaining silence.[72]

The first task of Grolman and Starck was to assemble a staff of contributors. They contacted Ernst August von Göchhausen, the *Kammerrat* in Eisenach whom we have already encountered as the anonymous author of the first sensational exposé of the *Illuminati*.[73] Göchhausen drew up a memorandum, outlining the plan for a Conservative journal, for submission to any prince who might be interested.[74] Starck and Göchhausen were joined at a conference in Frankfurt in early September 1794 by Johann Karl Philipp Riese, a *Legationsrat* from Sachsen-Gotha who had published several antirevolutionary pamphlets[75] and was to take a prominent part in the editing of the *Eudämonia*. Grolman also won the support of a fellow townsman of Giessen, Heinrich Köster, the professor of history who was editor of the antirationalist *Neueste Religionsbegebenheiten*. H. O. Reichard, the editor of the *Revolutions-Almanach*, was also approached. Johann Zimmermann declared his sympathy with the *Eudämonia* in several letters to Grolman, but his death in October 1795 prevented his active participation. Leopold Hoffmann, who was disliked by some of the other contributors as an uncouth parvenu, was belatedly approached after the journal was a going concern, and he contributed only a single article. The statement sometimes made, that the *Eudämonia* was a continuation of the *Wiener Zeitschrift*, is clearly false.[76]

After a staff of contributors had been assembled, the next problem was one of raising sufficient money. Grolman wanted to rely upon private subscription alone, but his collaborators saw the need of securing government patronage. The prospects for this appeared favor-

[72] Quoted in ibid., p. 479.

[73] *Enthüllung des Systems der Weltbürger-Republik* (Leipzig, 1786). See Ch. 1 above.

[74] It is probably identical with the "Fragment eines Memoires eines deutschen Anti-Illuminaten an einen deutschen Fürsten," printed by L. A. Hoffmann in his *Höchst wichtige Erinnerungen* (2 vols., Vienna, 1795), ii, 98-116.

[75] Including the widely read *Geschichte und Anecdoten der Französischen Revolution von der Thronbesteigung Ludwigs des Sechzehnten an bis zu seinem Tod* (2 vols., Frankfurt and Leipzig, 1794).

[76] For the entire paragraph see Krüger, *Eudämonisten*, passim. To this list of contributors should be added Count Friedrich Leopold zu Stolberg and Matthias Claudius, two poets who played a significant role in the German religious revival.

able in the autumn of 1794, for the princes of Southwest Germany were at last becoming seriously alarmed about the French danger. The Austrian armies had withdrawn from the Netherlands; the Prussian armies were concentrated in the east to crush the Polish revolt of Kosziusko. The *Sansculottes* stood poised on the Rhine for an invasion of Germany, and there were widespread fears that they would find sympathizers and even collaborators in their path.

Markgraf Karl Friedrich of Baden, the most enlightened of the enlightened despots, feared for the throne he had filled with such distinction for half a century. He hoped to supplement the obviously inadequate military efforts of the empire by the creation of a special league of princes, modeled in some ways upon the *Fürstenbund* but directed against France rather than Austria. Karl Friedrich issued invitations in the late summer of 1794 for a preliminary conference of interested princes "to consult confidentially concerning all matters which are likely to encourage and spread the dangerous spirit of revolution, and to coordinate governmental measures to check this spirit." The meeting was held at Wilhelmsbad from September 29 to October 2, 1794, despite a disappointing attendance. The Duke of Württemberg, who had promised to come, was prevented at the last moment by an accident; the *Landgraf* of Hessen-Darmstadt received his invitation too late; while the influential Karl August of Weimar failed to come for reasons unknown. The conference became in fact a meeting between Karl Friedrich of Baden and Ludwig X of Hessen-Cassel.

All plans for the establishment of a new *Fürstenbund* were quickly abandoned, but consultation about ways of meeting the revolutionary danger resulted in the decision to give support to an antirevolutionary journal. The Rosicrucian Fleckenbühl, the one minister at Cassel who had given some previous encouragement to Grolman, had invited Johann Riese to the conference to submit and explain the memorandum drawn up by Göchhausen at the Frankfurt meeting. The princes gave Riese a very sympathetic hearing and decided to support his plan after he had shown that his collaborators were "men of the world" (*Gesellschaftsmänner*) rather than "enlightened garret philosophers" (*Stubenphilosophen-Aufklärer*). Karl Friedrich and Ludwig formally approved the establishment of a "society of patriotic scholars" (*Gesellschaft patriotischer Gelehrter*) which would publish a Conservative journal and distribute Conservative writings. The two princes offered to subscribe to one hundred copies apiece for distribution to their friends and entourage, and a younger son of the *Landgraf* of Hessen secured his father's permission to become "financial angel" to the *Eudämonia*.[77]

Grolman had been hesitant about approaching the princes and would have preferred to go ahead and await their patronage ex post facto. He expressed his hopes and his conception of the function of the *Eudämonia* in the following words:

> Our journal will primarily serve to expose the knavish tricks (*Schurkereien*) [of the Illuminati conspiracy], to unmask their infamous books and intentions, to praise good books and to write replies (*Antirezensionen*) when good books are unfairly criticized and dangerous books receive excessive praise. If we do this with resolution for only a year the opposite party will become more cautious and there will be an end to the present situation where every guttersnipe feels free to throw dung at every monarch and every altar. Miserable scribblers will keep more of their rubbish to themselves. Discouraged Conservative writers will regain confidence as their books will secure wide circulation once the Radical control of the reading market is broken. . . . For this task we do not need princes, we do not need patronage. The thing will run of itself if only we can raise enough capital to pay the printers for the first issues and to establish an adequate circulation network. . . . The protection of princes will come in due course as soon as we have demonstrated our usefulness . . . through the effective proclamation of sound principles.[78]

Grolman was, however, willing enough to accept princely money and protection when it was offered after Wilhelmsbad, and the *Eudämonia* was launched as a monthly in Leipzig at the *Chursächsische Zeitungsexpedition* (a firm licensed by the Saxon elector which specialized in the printing and circulation of newspapers) in the spring of 1795. The publication was shifted to Frankfurt in 1796 *bei der K. Reichs-Ober-Postamts-Zeitungs-Expedition und in Commission in der Hermann'schen Buchhandlung*. The increasing influence exercised by the French throughout West Germany forced its transfer to Nürnberg *in Commission der Raw'schen Buchhandlung* in 1798. Each number had about eighty pages; six numbers were bound together into a hard-

---

[77] On the Wilhelmsbad conference see the old documentary publication edited by B. Erdmannsdörfer, *Politische Korrespondenz Karl Friedrichs von Baden 1783-1806* (Heidelberg, 1892), II, 155-308. Its relevance to the founding of the *Eudämonia* is discussed by Krüger, *Eudämonisten*, pp. 481-83, and Schnee, *Jakobiner*, pp. 57-58.

[78] Quoted in Krüger, *Eudämonisten*, p. 484.

cover volume and sold as a unit; there were thirty-six monthly issues (six volumes of six issues each) altogether before the *Eudämonia* expired in 1798.

The title of every issue carried the following motto: "Hold together, you men of virtue, whether you know one another or not! Defend one another! Do not be ashamed of one another! The wicked also hold together, but not as firmly as you." The outlook of the journal and the principles of its editors were forcefully expressed in the introductory article of the first number (dated March 1795). The editors bemoaned the sad condition of Germany and deplored the incomprehensible negligence shown by Germany's princes in the face of atheism, blasphemy, and calls for revolution. They stated that they had resolved—fearful of future reproaches if they failed to act—to stem imminent catastrophe by founding the *Eudämonia* journal to serve as a rallying point for the "well-intentioned" (*Gutgesinnten*). Its sole aim was "to preserve Germany's happy religious and political constitution"—or rather, what was still left of it in 1795.

The proposed contents of the new journal were described in the following terms: essays defending "the blessed constitutional structure" of the Holy Roman Empire; "historical reports about humble subjects who gratefully recognize the good fortune they enjoy by living under the protection of legitimate authority; to be contrasted with essays describing the dangers inherent in, and the damage usually wrought by, rebelliousness"; also "reports concerning the noxious designs, enterprises, societies, etc. which aim at the destruction of the Christian religion and of the legitimate constitution of the various states," and "denunciation and reprimand of the various 'revolutionary sins' (*Revolutions-Sünden*) perpetrated by contemporary journalists, whether scholarly or popular."

The *Eudämonia's* introductory article also announced a specific political program which was faithfully maintained throughout the three years of the journal's life. The avowed aim was to promote the "public happiness" of the people, what the Greeks had called *eudaemonia*: hence the name of the journal. *Eudaemonia* could be promoted in two ways: by encouraging the people of Germany to be contented with their traditional ways, and by exposing the harmful and alien character of the agitation which sought to undermine their happiness. The former could be achieved by describing "the civic happiness enjoyed by the members of all German states, without exception, through the prevalence of conditions of personal security, protection of all legitimately acquired property, and the tranquillity which arises from the acceptance of long-established authority." The editors made no claim that Germany's existing order was in any way perfect; they argued, on the contrary, the important Conservative theme that men must learn to understand that all human conditions must inevitably remain imperfect everywhere and at all times. Genuine improvements could come only through cautious and piecemeal reforms sought within the framework of the existing polity. The tragic course of the French Revolution had shown that "rash, hasty, and violent methods" were—however sincerely pursued—self-defeating and tended to make political and social conditions worse. It was far better "to live quietly in an old building than to tear it down before a new one could be constructed." Was this not exactly what the Jacobins had done in France, and what their agents and followers now sought to do in Germany?

The content of the *Eudämonia* was dominated by the "conspiracy theory" previously outlined in the works of two of its contributors, J. A. Starck and L. A. Hoffmann. There was much personal polemic against such German "Jacobins" as Knigge, Fichte, Mauvillon, and Rebmann, all of whom were denounced as dedicated members of an operating *Illuminati* network. They were permitted to spread their poison because of the prevalence of dangerous conceptions of freedom—more especially, "unlimited freedom of the press, . . . license enjoyed by teachers and professors to teach whatever they think, by means of which the growing generation is impregnated with poisonous ideas; . . . and the continued existence of secret societies and more especially the *Illuminati*.

The *Eudämonia* advocated the following forthright remedy:

> . . . the prudent but strict curtailment of the freedom of the press; the minute police supervision of all teachers and professors; and the ferreting out of Illuminism in its most secret recesses. . . . The result will be that henceforth no one will be able to corrupt the opinion of the people, . . . and that the real happiness of the people will no longer be threatened by the destruction of religion and the subversion of society.[79]

The editors of the *Eudämonia* attached the greatest importance to governmental supervision of the press. They chronicled with approval the restrictive edicts issued by several German states, and collected evidence to prove the need of imperial legislation in this field.[80]

[79] *Eudämonia*, ii, 106. Quoted by Braubach, *Eudämonia*, p. 328.
[80] "Materialien zu einem neuen Reichsgesetz gegen das schriftstellerische Unwesen," *Eudämonia*, iv, 168-77, and continued in several subsequent issues.

The editors singled out for attack all champions of the freedom of the press; Friedrich Gentz, who advocated such freedom in his congratulatory address to Frederick William III in 1797, earned a special rebuke which makes comic reading in the light of his later position as the most prominent exponent of the Metternichean system.[81]

The articles in the *Eudämonia* frequently distinguished between "true" and "false" *Aufklärung*, as C. F. Moser had done in the passage quoted above. A writer accused the latter of doctrinaire fanaticism on behalf of truth (irrespective of concrete circumstances) and countered it with a frankly utilitarian standard of judgment:

> Although it may be said generally that knowledge of the truth is preferable to either ignorance or error, yet one frequently encounters circumstances where truth can be harmful to certain individuals or even to the broad mass of the people because of the conditions of their life. Sometimes the truth lies simply outside of the people's range of experience; they do not need it and may be distracted by it from more important concerns; they may be induced by it to waste much time in pondering and brooding (*Nachdenken und Grübeln*) without really getting to understand problems. . . . They also may draw false corollaries and go on to dangerous actions based upon those corollaries. The end result will be that truth has not made them wiser, happier, or more perfect; has, indeed, thrown them, and perhaps others as well, into misery.[82]

The *Eudämonia's* outspoken advocacy of Conservative principles, its practice of ferreting out so-called "Radicals" with little regard for the evidence, and its generally vituperative tone made numerous enemies. The publicist Joseph Görres launched his literary career by a sharp satire, in the first issue of his *Rothes Blatt* in 1797, against "the fathers and foster-fathers of the *Eudämonia,* the whole gang of aristocrats, bigots, and obscurantists."[83] The philosopher Johann Fichte made a vigorous reply in the *Jenaische Allgemeine Litteraturzeitung* to its accusation of atheism and subversion.[84] The latter journal made several attacks against the *Eudämonia,* and finally took the unprecedented step of closing its advertising columns to the *Eudämonia.* The *J.A.L.Z.* tried to justify this unusual measure by asserting that the editors of the

---

[81] "Über des Kriegsrats Gentz Anpreisung der Pressfreiheit in der dem Könige bei der Thronbesteigung überreichten Schrift," ibid., vi, 239-55.

[82] From an article, "Heutige Aufklärungsmethode," in ibid., vi, 337-51. Quoted by Braubach, *Eudämonia,* p. 318, 23n.

[83] Quoted by ibid., pp. 309-10.

[84] *J.A.L.Z.,* April 16, 1796, columns 409-13.

Eudämonia lacked personal integrity as proved by the fact that the attack upon Fichte contained obvious inaccuracies. "This must lead to suspicion concerning all other articles in the *Eudämonia*";[85] the *J.A.L.Z.* must protect its readers against dishonest goods. The attacked editors replied that the advertising boycott itself was good advertising and led to an increase in both contributors and readers, but they found that this was at best only a short-term effect.[86]

The sharpest attack of all against the *Eudämonia* was delivered by the Radical publicist G. F. Rebmann in his *Obscurantenalmanach* for the year 1799, just after the journal's decease:

> When the partisan struggles of our era have been long forgotten it is probable that the *Eudämonia* will still be remembered in the way that Herostrat is. We have seen many journals notable for one-sidedness and filled with the most repulsive partisan spirit, but none can stand comparison with its violent intolerance, calumny, and mayhem (*Scharfrichterei*) directed against all who have different beliefs, and its spirit of exaggeration and incendiarism (*übertriebene mordbrennerische Art*).[87]

Rebmann probably instigated the threats against the *Eudämonia* which resulted in its withdrawal from Frankfurt to Nürnberg in the spring of 1798 and its eventual collapse. The French had reoccupied Mainz in December 1797 after an interval of four and a half years. Rebmann, as a refugee from Germany, accepted a high judicial appointment in Mainz from the French government and became the leading figure in the reopened Jacobin Club. He also edited the *Mainzer Zeitung,* and was responsible for an article critical of the Frankfurt *Magistrat* because it tolerated a publication like the *Eudämonia* (March 14, 1798); this article was soon followed by another, critical of the bookseller Hermann, publisher of the *Eudämonia*. These were no idle threats since the French armies stood only thirty miles from Frankfurt and had repeatedly violated armistice lines in the past; Hermann in fact refused to continue as publisher and the Frankfurt *Magistrat* prohibited the sale of the *Eudämonia* within the city limits.

[85] *J.A.L.Z. Intelligenzblatt* (i.e., advertising supplement), March 5, 1796, column 233.

[86] "Über das Bemühen der Jenaischen Allgemeinen Litteraturzeitung, das Journal Eudämonia ausser Curs zu bringen," *Eudämonia,* pp. 505-32.

[87] G. F. Rebmann, "Geist der Eudämonia," *Obscurantenalmanach* (1799), p. 90. The article contains a large number of *horrenda* extracted from the pages of the *Eudämonia*.

The editor's attempt to set up shop in Nürnberg could only postpone, not prevent, the collapse of the journal.[88]

The *Eudämonia* had the misfortune that the zeal of its enemies was not matched by similar zeal on the part of its natural friends. There is no evidence that the two original protectors, Karl Friedrich von Baden and Ludwig of Hessen-Kassel, lifted a finger in its defense; on the contrary, by 1798 they were preoccupied with securing French support in the territorial scramble unleashed by the Franco-Austrian Peace of Campoformio. All the Southwest German states had embarked upon the policy which was to make them outright French satellites in the Confederation of the Rhine a few years later. The center of gravity of German Conservatism had moved east to Berlin and Vienna, two places where the *Eudämonia* could not expect a favorable reception: Prussia had begun to abandon the excesses of Wöllnerite obscurantism after the accession of Frederick William III in 1797, while the Habsburg Empire remained so obscurantist that its rulers did not even see the need for the public championing of obscurantism. (Hoffmann's fall from favor in 1793 was merely a straw in the wind.) The *Eudämonia* had, in a characteristic error resulting from excess of zeal, denounced Retzer (1754-1824), the chief Viennese censor, as an *Illuminat* in 1795. It is not surprising that several of its issues were thereupon prohibited by the censor even before an imperial decree of Dec. 21, 1797 issued a total prohibition of the *Eudämonia* and similar journals. The decree stated that:

> Although they contain much that is good and useful, yet they do not effectively refute the dangerous and false principles which they attack. They do not attain their avowed purpose and serve indeed to give publicity to many errors and thereby do more harm than good to the good cause.[89]

The Franciscan government was opposed to any political thinking regardless of whether it was Conservative or Radical in content; it believed that the unreflective acceptance of the *status quo* provided the only basis for a truly Conservative society.

The main interest of the *Eudämonia* to the historian lies in the fact that it gives faithful expression to the hysterical quality of much of the

[88] The harassment of the *Eudämonia* is chronicled with some bitterness in the concluding article of the final issue, dated Hamburg, May 10, 1798: "Ein Sermon über die Schicksale des Journals Eudämonia sogut als eine Parentation mit Personalien," *Eudämonia*, vi, 533-51.

[89] The *Eudämonia* printed this with pained embarrassment in "Auszug eines wichtigen Briefes von Wien vom 24. Feb. 1798," vi, 281-87.

German Conservatism of the 1790's. Its champions found a comforting explanation for the evils of the age in the conspiracy theory, and inevitably advocated police repression and censorship as remedies. They were more concerned with attack than defense—the *Eudämonia's* pages are filled with columns devoted to denunciation and character assassination, whereas there is remarkably little of that explicit defense of the German *status quo* which the editors had promised in their introductory prospectus. It displayed a willful disregard of the rules of evidence (not to mention elementary decency) in much of its polemic, and a tone of fanatical self-righteousness which even some of its supporters—such as H. O. Reichard—found hard to take. Its worst blemish was, however, the typical fault of *all* Status Quo Conservatism—the failure to understand the simple fact that the vast historical forces set loose by economic developments and the *Aufklärung* could not be dammed up by any purely repressive policy. The Hannoverian statesman and publicist August Rehberg, discussed in the following chapter, was one of the few prominent Germans who combined hostility to the Jacobins with advocacy of a specific program of reforms; for all of his limitations and essentially parochial significance, he deserves to be analyzed as the best spokesman of that Reform Conservatism whose weakness we have already noted above.[90]

[90] The *Eudämonia* stated specifically (vi, 77) that Rehberg was not among its contributors—a fact not surprising in view of the very different character of his brand of Conservatism.

CHAPTER 11

Rehberg and the Hannoverian School

The Hannoverian Milieu and
the Hannoverian School

THE ELECTORATE of Hannover, covering most of the broad plains of Northwest Germany, possessed a distinct political individuality influenced by its dynastic union with Great Britain since 1714. The absence of the sovereign, except for occasional visits from London, precluded the development of the personal absolutism so characteristic of eighteenth-century Germany. The *Ständestaat* remained virtually intact, the old estates retained much power in legislation and taxation, while the aristocracy practically monopolized public life. The connection with England tended at one and the same time to freeze the preabsolutist polity while enlarging Hannoverian horizons through contact with the very different world of the British parliamentary state. Both elements had a decisive influence in shaping a distinctive school of Conservatism: Hannoverians were proud of their preabsolutist *Ständetum*, while looking toward its possible evolution in the direction of the British constitution. They disliked the predominant German pattern of absolutism, especially the militarist despotism of neighboring Prussia; yet they were equally hostile to the doctrine of popular sovereignty propagated by revolutionary France. They viewed the English governmental system of historically rooted representative institutions as a healthy *via media* between opposite and equally undesirable extremes of monarchical despotism and popular democracy.

The intellectual center of Hannoverian Conservatism was the University of Göttingen, first opened in 1737.[1] It fully realized the designs of its founder Münchhausen in becoming a new type of German university. The theology faculty was dethroned from its traditional eminence, and priority was given to the study of law and the social sciences (*Staatswissenschaften*). Münchhausen wanted to train statesmen and administrators more than schoolmasters and village pastors, and he deliberately aimed at attracting a predominantly aristocratic student clientele. A remarkable degree of academic freedom made for intellectual liveliness; close contacts were maintained with English and Dutch universities; the library quickly became the best in Germany

---

[1] The standard history of Göttingen, Götz von Selle, *Die Georg-August Universität zu Göttingen 1737-1937* (Göttingen, 1937), is especially good on the eighteenth century.

(especially for all studies connected with England); while the Göttingen Academy of Science and its journal, the *Göttingen Gelehrten Anzeigen*, spread the fame of the university throughout the learned world. Of even greater importance was its able faculty in the social sciences; the best-known member was August Ludwig von Schlözer, the editor of the influential *Staatsanzeigen*.[2]

Schlözer was a forerunner rather than a member of the Hannoverian Conservative school described in this chapter. His political ideas lacked precision, partly because he was a worldly journalist rather than an academic thinker, partly because he was essentially a man of the pre-1789 world before consistent political positions were clearly differentiated. Schlözer's eclecticism embraced admiration for "enlightened despots" like Frederick and condemnation of the ordinary run of German princes; he admired the English constitution while believing that its principles defied imitation in less fortunate countries; and he valued surviving German *Stände* institutions as barriers against despotism while being unable to envisage for them any dominant role in Germany's political future. His ideal of German government never went beyond the harmonious collaboration between reforming princes and cooperative *Stände*.

We have seen already that Schlözer became a resolute foe of the French Revolution and of all ideas of popular sovereignty. He was convinced that the masses of the people were now, and must ever remain, unfit for self-government. Sovereignty can belong to the people, he said in a memorable phrase, only "the way an entailed estate belongs to a newly born baby whose mother and father have just died."[3] The people required a competent guardian, and Schlözer readily identified this guardian with the prince and the traditional upper classes of Germany. His sharp distrust of the people was shared by all Hannoverian Conservatives and limited their influence upon an increasingly democratic age.

Schlözer's cosmopolitan range of interests prevented his giving more than cursory attention to the distinctive problems of Hannover. These problems were the constant preoccupation of two distinguished Hannoverian writers, Ernst Brandes and August Rehberg. Brandes (1758-

---

[2] On A. L. von Schlözer see the essay by F. Frensdorff, *ADB*, xxxi (1890), 567-600, which is excellent on his life but weak on his thought. His political ideas are discussed in Arnold Berney, "A. L. von Schlözers Staatsauffassung," *HZ*, cxxxii (1925), 43-67, and Friederike Fürst, *August Ludwig von Schlözer, ein deutscher Aufklärer im 18. Jahrhundert* (Heidelberg, 1928), Ch. 3. We have already discussed his hostility to the French Revolution in Ch. 9.

[3] *Staatsanzeigen*, xiv, 155n., cited in A. Berney, op.cit., p. 59.

1810), whom we have previously encountered as a foe of Prussian absolutism, the emancipation of women, and progressive education, had an influential career as curator of Göttingen University after 1790, a post in which he succeeded his father in accordance with the quasi-hereditary pattern characteristic of the Hannoverian civil service. He showed his enlightened Conservatism by maintaining academic freedom at Göttingen in the midst of the anti-Jacobin panic which swept Germany after 1792. Brandes was an especially thorough student of English conditions and visited that country in 1784. His journey resulted in a close friendship with Edmund Burke, who henceforth valued Brandes as an encyclopedic source on Hannoverian affairs. In 1785 Brandes wrote an excellent essay on *The Public Spirit of England*;[4] its content will be analyzed below because it provides the best statement of the Anglophile outlook of the Hannoverian school. The rest of his life was spent in a combination of administrative work and Conservative pamphleteering. His numerous writings are more notable for their negative criticism of existing evils than for their suggestion of Conservative alternatives. His views parallel, however, those of his more distinguished friend Rehberg, and hence it is unnecessary to discuss them separately.[5]

Rehberg is an important figure in several respects. He was one of the leading administrators of Hannover for an entire generation. He was also the closest personal friend of the Prussian reformer Stein in their common formative years, and exercised much influence upon the development of Stein's political conceptions. He became, next to Friedrich Gentz, the ablest literary opponent of the French Revolution in Germany. His criticism of the doctrine of natural law, and of the Code Napoleon which claimed to be based upon it, made him an important forerunner of the "historical school of law." Rehberg was, finally, the most articulate spokesman of Hannoverian Conservatism, far outdistancing Brandes in his philosophical depth, breadth of interest, and

[4] Ernst Brandes, "Ueber den politischen Geist Englands," *Berlinische Monatsschrift*, vii (1786), 101-26, 217-41, 293-323.

[5] There is remarkably little secondary literature on Brandes. The main facts of his life are stated in Erich Botzenhart, "Ernst Brandes," *NDB*, ii (1955), 518-19. The article on him by Spehr in the *ADB*, iii (1876), 241-42, is very brief and does not even mention his writings against the French Revolution. His relationship to Burke is discussed in the valuable article by Stephan Skalweit, "Edmund Burke, Ernst Brandes, und Hannover," *Niedersächsisches Jahrbuch für Landesgeschichte*, xxviii (1956), 15-72; while much light is thrown on his personality and political opinions in his last years in Carl Haase, "Ernst Brandes in den Jahren 1805 und 1806. Fünf Briefe an den Grafen Münster," ibid., xxxiv (1962), 194-223.

ability to combine criticism of other views with a constructive program of reform.

Rehberg's thought can be understood only in the light of his specific Hannoverian milieu and the facts of his rather checkered biography.[6] His personality shows many qualities often attributed to the people of Lower Saxony: tenacious attachment to local custom with a tendency toward parochialism; shrewd business sense and aptitude for practical work; little imagination and a dry distrust of the brilliant and the unusual; devotion to calculable and attainable goals; imperturbability which more volatile people easily mistook for coldness and obstinacy; and an almost English attachment to common sense which made him feel uncomfortable in the presence of mysticism and any kind of intellectual fuzziness. There was nothing of the rebel or "outsider" in Rehberg's outlook, and his close identification with his native milieu gave strength and self-confidence to his opinions.

His political principles were as much attuned to Hannover as his personality. Rehberg always viewed the Hannoverian *Ständestaat* as the norm for Germany, absolutism as an—unhappily widely prevalent —exception. He accepted the hierarchic social structure of Hannover as the "natural order" of society; his reform proposals aimed at modernizing rather than overthrowing the *ancien régime*. Hannover was still predominantly agrarian in character and Rehberg's theories never assigned an adequate place to the middle classes which were rapidly advancing to ascendancy in the more important countries of Europe. Hannover remained a loose agglomeration of seven duchies with separate *Stände* and separate customs. Its executive government was composed of three different bodies—the *Geheime Ratskollegium* for general administration, the *Kammerkollegium* for finance, and the *Kriegskanzlei* for military affairs. Each was a collegial body long on deliberation but short on decision, and over-all coordination of the administration was virtually unknown. Rehberg's love of local variety,

---

[6] There is no adequate biography of Rehberg. The best account of his life and writings is still F. Frensdorff, "A. W. Rehberg," in *ADB*, xxvii (1883), 571-83, a remarkably detailed survey. Ernst von Meier, *Hannoversche Verfassungs- und Verwaltungsgeschichte 1680-1866* (2 vols., Leipzig, 1898-99), ii, 229-32, and passim, includes an ill-tempered attack upon Rehberg both as a man and writer. Karl Mollenhauer, *A. W. Rehberg, ein hannoverischer Staatsmann im Zeitalter der Restauration* (2 pts., Blankenburg am Harz, 1904-05), is a well-informed rehabilitation. The best analyses of his thought are provided by authors primarily interested in his influence upon Stein: Erich Weniger, "Stein und Rehberg," *Niedersächsisches Jahrbuch*, ii (1925), 1-124; Erich Botzenhart, *Die Staats-und Reformideen des Freiherrn vom Stein* (Tübingen, 1927), pp. 106-62; and Gerhard Ritter, *Stein: Eine politische Biographie* (2 vols., Berlin, 1931), i, 143-83.

hostility to any kind of unitarian centralization, and preference for collegial administrative bodies was a faithful reflection of his Hannoverian experience.[7]

The sympathies governing his political outlook were obviously based upon the institutions of his native country; the same can be said of the antipathies which guided his reform program. Hannoverian life was controlled by a narrow and selfish nobility which monopolized social and political power. Its bureaucracy was dominated by a small number of aristocratic families assisted by a few quasi-hereditary bourgeois assistants who filled the lower posts. Rehberg had the misfortune to be born only into the latter group, and his ambition naturally chafed against a system marked by obstacles to his own ascent. He took pride, on the other hand, in the fact that his real influence belied his title of mere cabinet secretary, and he was evidently of two minds about the merits of the Hannoverian governmental system as a whole. Rehberg sometimes criticized aristocratic exclusiveness and legal privilege in sharp terms and obviously resented the fact that aristocrats with talents inferior to his own were always his superiors. Yet at other times both he and his friend Brandes praised government by a hereditary caste as superior to government by parvenus, and engaged in almost extravagant eulogy of the Hannoverian system and its ruling class.[8] It is hard to say whether this praise was due to opportunism, a psychological need to "overidentify" with a group which never fully accepted him, parochial patriotism, or simple inability to envision any fundamental alterations in his country's government. It is certain, at any rate, that observation of the governmental conditions of Hannover was the starting point of Rehberg's political theory.

His conceptions of foreign policy were equally determined by his Hannoverian background. The Hannoverian ruling class had no

[7] Good accounts of Hannoverian social and governmental conditions can be found in H. von Treitschke, *Deutsche Geschichte* (5 vols., Leipzig, 1879-94), III, 534-57, a picturesque description; Otto von Heinemann, *Geschichte von Braunschweig und Hannover* (3 vols., Gotha, 1892), III, 379-402, strong on political and constitutional, weak on economic conditions; Ernst von Meier, *Hannoversche Verfassungs und Verwaltungsgeschichte 1680-1866* (2 vols., Leipzig, 1898-99), passim, the standard work despite its pro-Prussian, anti-Hannoverian bias; and, above all, the classic description by Friedrich Thimme, *Die inneren Zustände des Kurfürstentum Hannover unter der französisch-westfälischen Herrschaft* (2 vols., Hannover and Leipzig, 1893-95), I, 1-34. The best contemporary description is to be found in a long letter from Brandes to Burke, dated Oct. 29, 1796, printed in the valuable article by Skalweit cited in n. 5.

[8] See, for example, Ernst Brandes, "Ist es den deutschen Staaten vorteilhaft, dass der Adel die ersten Staatsbedienungen besitzt?", *Berliner Monatsschrift*, X (1787), 395-439. The answer is stridently affirmative.

ambition to see their country play the arduous role of a Great Power; the army was kept small and the outlook of the aristocracy was not molded by military values. Hostility to neighboring Prussia was the dominant political feeling, for the monarchy of Frederick the Great was in every way the antipode of the Hannoverian *Ständestaat*. The fundamental spirit of the Prussian polity—with its sacrifice of individual happiness to the greatness of the state—was as alien to Rehberg as it was to most of his fellow Hannoverians. It should also be noted that sympathy for the venerable structure of the Holy Roman Empire played little role in the particularist atmosphere of North Germany, so Rehberg lacked—compared, for example, with his friend Stein—this potential source of a broad national outlook. He was content to spend his life in improving the domestic condition of his small Hannoverian fatherland and he looked upon "foreign" complications—whether due to Prussian occupation, French conquest, or the threat of German nationalism—as extraneous and incalculable factors which need not be taken into account by political theory. His Hannoverian parochialism was perhaps the major factor in limiting his influence among contemporaries and giving him a bad reputation with later historians.

Rehberg's Life[9]

August Rehberg was born in 1757 into a home marked by cultured tastes and moderate affluence. His father was employed as a secretary by the *Stände* of Calenberg, one of the duchies of which Hannover was composed, and young Rehberg early absorbed a point of view sympathetic to *Ständetum*. His first intellectual interests were directed toward philosophy and literature rather than politics; he showed remarkable precocity by learning to read Greek, Latin, Italian, Spanish, French, and English authors in their original tongues before he was fifteen. His boyhood qualities, like those of his mature years, were exactly what one would expect of a scion of the cultured, Protestant middle class of North Germany: a strong appetite for knowledge, persevering industry, ascetic puritanical values, plain living, and high thinking.

The family's conventional Lutheranism could not long stand the test of Rehberg's precocious intellect. When Rehberg was only fourteen a tutor made the mistake of presenting Christianity to him in the form of a subtle but dry system of metaphysical dogmas. The pupil's faith

---

[9] All the biographical facts are taken from either F. Frensdorff, op.cit., or the autobiographical sections of Rehberg's *Sämmtliche Schriften* (3 vols., Hannover, 1828-31), unless another source is given.

was shaken when he could think up rational objections to every dogma; he was soon convinced of the unconvincing character of every Christian metaphysic. His rationalism led him to a completely skeptical position in religion; while the prosaic nature of his personality precluded any kind of spiritual experience which might have served as a counterweight. He remained for the rest of his life an unbeliever, though this fact did not prevent him from praising Christianity on pragmatic grounds as the bulwark of European society.

His preoccupation in early manhood was metaphysics; his first ambition, to become a professor of philosophy. This phase of his life was to leave a permanent imprint upon the nature of his subsequent Conservative outlook. A lucid style and a passion for precision—the hallmarks of a trained thinker—characterize his work; they set him apart in an age when romantic fantasies and obscure aphorisms were increasingly esteemed as evidences of profundity. The emotional and irrational side of human experience was alien to him—a lacuna of which he was poignantly aware. He himself related as an old man (in 1828) that he had been on the verge of tears for several weeks after reading Goethe's *Werther* at seventeen, *not* in pity for Werther's fate, but rather in masochistic despair because his own desiccated nature would not allow him to become a Werther-like lover.[10] His despair proved short-lived, and like most healthy personalities he learned to live with his own limitations. His early sense of inadequacy was soon replaced by a quizzical wonder at a world which included so many people dominated by irrational motives and incapable of his own kind of prudence and self-discipline.

Rehberg found little intellectual stimulation at Göttingen, which he attended from 1774-77, for its leading philosophers did not go beyond the superficial "popular philosophy" of the German *Aufklärung*. He decided, in the absence of external guidance, to study on his own the great metaphysical systems, especially those of Leibnitz and Spinoza, only to discover that all contained logical flaws and depended ultimately upon some arbitrary premises. Rehberg presented these skeptical conclusions in an essay submitted in a competition organized by the Berlin Academy in 1779 on the topic *The Nature and the Limitations of Human Faculties*. The judges expected an answer in accordance with the system of Leibnitz, the Academy's original patron —a consideration which forced Rehberg to present his anti-Leibnitzean views in a somewhat indirect manner. He analyzed the Spinozist

[10] Rehberg is quoted in F. Frensdorff, "G. Brandes," *Zeitschrift des historischen Vereins für Niedersachsen*, LXXVI (1911), 42-43.

philosophy as both the supreme achievement of metaphysics and the parent of skepticism (since even it was ultimately unconvincing), and then presented the Leibnitzean system as the best possible defense against Spinozism and skepticism alike. The best, but—so ran the implication of Rehberg's argument—by no means an *adequate* defense. The judges of the contest understood his meaning all too well, for they gave the prize to an obscure orthodox Leibnitzean while they consoled Rehberg with an honorable mention only. Merian, the secretary of the Academy, was, however, deeply impressed by the essay, and tried to persuade Frederick the Great to appoint the twenty-four-year-old philosopher to a teaching vacancy which occurred shortly afterward at the Berlin *Ritterakademie*. Merian found the king as prejudiced against German philosophy as Möser found him against German literature; he was told it was royal practice to hire philosophers in Switzerland and only cooks in Hannover.[11] One need not regret Frederick's decision, for Rehberg lacked the speculative originality to become a great philosopher. His talents were far better fitted for the career of publicist and administrator to which he reluctantly turned after the frustration of his academic ambitions.

Rehberg's further philosophical labors can be briefly summarized. He was one of the first to recognize the importance of Kant's *Critique of Pure Reason* for launching a fundamental reconstruction of philosophy, and he spent some years as a popularizer of Kant, though he was critical of the latter's specific views on religious, political, and ethical questions. Rehberg viewed these as relapses into the very dogmatism pulverized by the *Critique*. He specifically condemned Kant's confident belief in natural law and his political system based upon freedom and equality as mere subjective fantasies without rational warrant. Rehberg here took a position on purely philosophical grounds which in many ways anticipated his later repudiation of these Liberal dogmas on historical and practical grounds.[12] The result of all his philosophical inquiries was a total skepticism without flinching or escapism—a position similar to that which had served Hume thirty years earlier as the epistemological foundation of a Conservatism which accepted the *status quo* because no alternative social order could be declared preferable by the test of rational analysis. Rehberg's skepticism was also reinforced by a profound anticipation of the conclusions of the contemporary "sociology of knowledge." He delivered the following dictum as a young man of twenty-three:

[11] Rehberg tells this story himself in *Sämmtliche Schriften*, I, 9.
[12] See his articles on "Recht der Natur" and "Natürliches Staatsrecht" in ibid., I, 95-122.

It seems to me that since philosophers shape their systems primarily in the light of their own experience it is not the duty of philosophy to teach men *what* to think, but rather to explain *how* different philosophical systems have been produced by different personal and social conditions.[13]

Rehberg never allowed his perception of historical relativism to paralyze either his judgment or his practical conduct. He is a good example of the paradoxical fact that an intelligent man will often combine religious disbelief and metaphysical skepticism with a pharisaical dogmatism in the field of ethics. Rehberg's most striking trait is an inflexible adherence to the puritanical moral code which was hammered into him from childhood. When his faith in divinely revealed Christian ethics collapsed, he replaced it with a strait-laced Stoicism which prided itself on seeking virtue for its own sake rather than in expectation of future heavenly reward.[14] Rehberg hated idleness, frivolity, sensuality, and every kind of egoism. His puritanism colored his judgment on the most diverse subjects. Thus he never allowed himself to do full justice to Goethe's writings because he disliked the immorality of the poet's sexual conduct.[15] Rehberg's admiration for Charles James Fox was cooled by Fox's gambling habits and propensity for bad company.[16] Rehberg disliked the Hannoverian fiscal system because it relied too exclusively upon a popular vice—the drinking of heavily taxed brandy—to fill the state treasury.[17] He was a resolute opponent of the new penology which sought to explain crime in terms of the environment of the criminal rather than his innate wickedness; he believed that the theory must destroy personal responsibility and cause men to excuse when they ought to condemn.[18] The advance of progressive education was his special bête noire; he complained that Rousseau's *Emile* was "only concerned with removing obstacles to the free development of human nature, instead of controlling that development through laws, regulations, and positive instructions."[19]

[13] Rehberg, *Cato* (Basel, 1780), vii.

[14] See his dialogue, *Cato*, mentioned in the previous footnote. It is set in Africa just before the younger Cato commits suicide to avoid falling into the hands of Caesar. The Stoic Cato refutes the Platonist position on virtue and immortality, and supports the sincerity of his argument by taking his own life.

[15] Rehberg, "Goethe und sein Jahrhundert," *Brans Minerva*, IV (August 1835).

[16] Rehberg, *Sämmtliche Schriften*, IV, 59.

[17] Rehberg, *Constitutionelle Phantasien* (Hamburg, 1832), pp. 70-71.

[18] Rehberg, "Criminal Psychologie," *Sämmtliche Schriften*, I, 406-15, and his remarks in *Zur Geschichte des Königsreichs Hannover* (Göttingen, 1826), pp. 211-19.

[19] *Sämmtliche Schriften*, I, 375. The quotation is from his "Prüfung der

These examples could be multiplied a hundredfold. They reveal Rehberg's confident assurance in the binding character of his moral principles and his contempt for men and theories which did not live up to his stringent standards.

Rehberg's zeal to make morality prevail was one factor which made the choice of an administrative career natural for him, once he had wearied of philosophy. His personal contacts with public-spirited men in his Göttingen years pointed in the same direction. Schlözer had been his most inspiring teacher; Karl vom Stein, his most intimate contemporary, although their interests were quite divergent during their student years. Stein, deeply religious and indifferent to metaphysics, was absorbed in the study of law and history, while Rehberg was preoccupied with the search for a metaphysical surrogate for his vanished faith. Yet the two friends were closely united by common traits of character. Both possessed a native idealism which always chafed against the commonplace world, an energy which never relaxed, and an unfailing diligence in the pursuit of knowledge. Their common aspirations permitted them to transcend the barriers of class, status, and intellectual interests. Stein and Rehberg got into the habit of sharing a daily walk on the walls of Göttingen, and the imperial knight even brought his bourgeois friend to the Nassau family castle for a holiday.[20]

Ernst Brandes, whom Rehberg had known as a playmate since childhood, was second only to Stein in Rehberg's affections. He was already known for his encyclopedic knowledge of English conditions, and he urged young Rehberg to balance his reading of abstruse philosophers with a study of English pamphlets and parliamentary debates. The young metaphysician was at first surprised that Fox's East India Bill could be as fascinating as Kant's categorical imperative. He threw himself into his new interest with all his customary application, and exploited the formidable resources of the Göttingen library to the full; while frequent walks with Brandes (after Stein had left Göttingen) further ripened his opinions. What drew both men to English affairs was the broad canvas of English politics compared with the

---

Erziehungskunst," originally published in 1792, reprinted in ibid., I, 305-80. As late as 1827 Rehberg deplored that this treatise, "the best in thought, narrative and expression which I have ever written" (p. 380), had fallen completely flat. His hatred of progressive education was also based upon his belief that the classical languages must remain the backbone of any sound education. "Alte Sprachen," originally published in 1788, reprinted in ibid., I, 261-304.

[20] I have paraphrased the classic account of the friendship given by G. H. Pertz, who knew both men well, in his *Das Leben des Ministers Freiherrn vom Stein* (6 vols., Berlin, 1849-55), I, 12-15.

narrowness characteristic of Hannover. For the rest of their lives they strove to infuse the institutions of Hannover with some measure of the generous civic spirit they so much admired in the English model.

Rehberg experienced serious difficulty in gaining a suitable first position in public service after graduating from Göttingen in 1779. The death of his father in 1770 placed the family in straitened circumstances and deprived Rehberg of the social contacts required to enter the charmed circle of the Hannoverian bureaucracy. He encountered much prejudice because his obvious intellectual attainments promised to make him an uncomfortable subordinate,[21] and was finally forced to eke out a living as a German tutor to the Englishmen whom his mother took in as boarders. Four years of frustration and humiliation came to an end only in 1783 when he became secretary to the Duke of York, then bishop of Osnabrück under the curious arrangement described in Ch. 6.

The secretary's primary duty was to conduct the official correspondence with the Osnabrück ministry, a correspondence necessitated by the fact that the bishop preferred residence in comparatively lively Hannover to his intolerably provincial see. Rehberg's first assignment was to go to Osnabrück for a five-month apprenticeship of rummaging through the city archives. This period proved of great importance in his intellectual development, for it brought him into almost daily contact with Justus Möser, the leading citizen of Osnabrück, who quickly became his "fatherly friend." He urged Rehberg to forget about both Kantian metaphysics and the far-away English constitution and to concentrate instead upon mastering the intricacies of Germany's own political and social life. Rehberg followed this advice and always venerated Möser as his great teacher:

> He taught me the basic principles of [German] civil society as they prevailed before the French Revolution, and corrected the faulty perspectives I derived from my study of English parliamentary proceedings.[22]

In those months Rehberg absorbed a good deal of Möser's outlook, such as the stress laid upon individuality, the correlation which must exist between political institutions and social forces, and the desira-

---

[21] The attempt made by the poet Boie to secure Rehberg's appointment to the military secretaryship he was vacating failed for this reason. See Karl Weinhold, *Heinrich Christian Boie. Ein Beitrag zur Geschichte der deutschen Literatur im 18. Jahrhundert* (Halle, 1868), which includes a good description of the Hannoverian circle in which Rehberg moved (pp. 77-82).

[22] *Sämmtliche Schriften*, ii, 24.

bility of basing political rights upon property ownership rather than abstract "natural rights." Rehberg never became, however, an uncritical pupil: he rejected, for example, Möser's analogy between the state and a joint-stock company as too mechanical, and considered Möser's idealization of the early Middle Ages, and more especially its crude peasantry, as rather grotesque.[23]

The Duke of York valued Rehberg as a capable subordinate and found him a new job as a secretary of the Hannoverian *Geheime Ratskollegium* (one of the three central institutions) when he returned to England in 1786. The *Ratskollegium* was a dilettantish body to which counselors were appointed through aristocratic nepotism; its effective work was done by bourgeois secretaries who participated in a nonvoting capacity. Rehberg was put in charge of the correspondence with the *Stände* of Calenberg (the very body which had employed his father). This new activity gave him an intimate knowledge of the Hannoverian *Stände*, a knowledge which made him increasingly pessimistic about the prospects of enlarging German constitutional life in the foreseeable future: "I soon learned in my new position how little one could apply English principles to the governing of German countries"[24]—Rehberg's practical experience clearly corroborated Möser's earlier advice. Yet his desire to have Germany evolve on the English or, as he preferred to call it, "old Germanic" pattern remained undiminished; and when the French Revolution broke out a few years later he opposed it in the belief that the English method of gradual evolution within the framework of the existing constitution was far better suited to Germany than the French method of violence.

The outbreak of the French Revolution, when Rehberg was thirty-one, proved the great turning point in his life. He had already abandoned his ambition to become a philosopher and had made a satisfactory start in his governmental career; yet the future promised him nothing more exciting than gradual advancement, with little prospect of influencing the general course of even Hannoverian events.

---

[23] Rehberg's relationship to Möser comes out best in ibid., II, 20-24, and in Rehberg's *Untersuchungen über die französische Revolution* (2 vols., Hannover, 1793), I, 50-51. The independence of Rehberg toward his master already became clearly defined in 1787, when he challenged Möser in a controversy on religious toleration in the columns of the *Berliner Monatsschrift*. Rehberg argued in favor of absolute freedom of religion and printing (but not speech) in the spirit of Kantian natural law, a position which he abandoned after the outbreak of the French Revolution. Reprinted in *Sämmtliche Schriften*, I, 172-224. Rehberg later felt that Möser's Laodicean personality was an anachronism in the "fighting age" which began in 1789. Ibid., II, 24.

[24] Ibid., p. 25.

His political principles had developed under the guidance of Brandes and Möser, but as yet fell far short of a general system attracting general interest. French affairs presented him with a challenge and an opportunity. He must test his raw principles against the very different tenets of revolutionary France, and work out a program to build up German defenses against the French doctrines he abhorred. Rehberg welcomed an invitation extended to him in 1789 by the editor of the *Jenaische Allgemeine Litteratur-Zeitung* to review the flood of books which were appearing on French affairs; he could thereby refine his own point of view while educating German public opinion.

It is one measure of the interest aroused by the revolution that a series of *ad hoc* review articles, written in hours snatched from his laborious employment, quickly established for Rehberg a national reputation. He was even confronted with the threat of a pirated collection of his articles, a threat he forestalled by turning out an official collection himself in 1792.[25] Men were impressed by Rehberg's combination of implacable hostility to the revolution with his avoidance of vituperation; his remarkable confidence in the validity of his antirevolutionary principles at a time when prorevolutionary sentiment was sweeping Germany in the first years after 1789; and his early prediction that France must drift toward violence and anarchy despite the apparent stability achieved in 1790.

His outlook was similar to that of Edmund Burke, though he cannot be described as Burke's disciple since he arrived at his conclusions well before the latter published the famous *Reflections* in November 1790.[26] Rehberg's *point d'appui* was, moreover, very different from Burke's. The latter wrote for a united nation with great institutions which evoke general pride; only a small minority of his countrymen

---

[25] *Untersuchungen über die französische Revolution* (2 vols., Hannover, 1793). The book is a valuable collection of Rehberg's views, though the reader must be prepared to put up with poor organization, hasty composition, and an irritating failure on the author's part to develop many profound ideas thrown out only as hints. The scholar interested in the development of Rehberg's views must use the book with some caution, since Rehberg rewrote some of his articles from the period 1789-90 to make them conform to his attitude of 1792. Most of the changes are, however, quite minor; checking the latter against the earlier version is facilitated by Rehberg's listing of all his review articles in *Sämmtliche Schriften*, II, 74-82. On the *Jenaische Allgemeine Litteraturzeitung* see L. Salomon, *Geschichte des Deutschen Zeitungswesens* (2nd edn., 2 vols., 1906), I, 196ff.

[26] *Untersuchungen*, II, 383-84. Rehberg incidentally dissociated himself from Burke's intemperate attack upon Rousseau, excessive whitewashing of the *ancien régime*, and faulty belief that France had possessed a workable constitution in 1789.

was attracted by alien Jacobin doctrines. Rehberg was in a less fortunate situation, and expressed himself poignantly as follows:

> The collection of states into which Germany is divided possesses nothing in common but their language, culture, and certain traits of character. There are no national institutions for Germans to cherish in common, while few of the institutions of the individual states deserve to be defended.[27]

It was only natural under these circumstances that German public opinion should favor the revolution and hope that its blessings would spread to Germany. Rehberg ascribed the political immaturity which hailed the French Revolution in terms of Germany's lack of self-government; the widespread vulnerability to Jacobin propaganda was the nemesis of the princely absolutism which had kept Germans in their political nonage.[28]

It was natural, therefore, for Rehberg to advocate the development of a revived *Ständetum* as the best antidote to the revolutionary disease; and he argued that such a revival required an antecedent reform of the aristocracy. His reformist outlook inevitably placed him in an uncomfortable middle position between the parties contending for the public opinion of Germany. Aristocratic defenders of the *ancien régime* looked upon him as a stalking horse for the Jacobin party, and denounced Rehberg's avowed intention of saving the German aristocracy through timely reforms as either hypocritical or stupid. Rehberg struck back at his aristocratic critics in harsh words:

> Why does the nobility consider its nonaristocratic defenders to be false friends? Why does it refuse to believe that any one can honestly and humbly respect rights in which he does not participate? The aristocrats have doubts about the sincerity of their defenders because they recognize in their hearts that aristocratic privileges are excessive, aristocratic demands unfounded, and aristocratic exploitation of the lower classes unjust.[29]

While German Reactionaries denounced Rehberg as a Radical, he was condemned by the genuine German Radicals as the hired lackey of Reaction. The fact that he was a civil servant made him vulnerable to

---

[27] *Sämmtliche Schriften*, ii, 30. The passage technically refers to Möser but Rehberg is obviously thinking of himself.

[28] Rehberg discusses the immature German reaction to the revolution in *Untersuchungen*, ii, 405-08.

[29] Rehberg, *Über den deutschen Adel* (Göttingen, 1803), p. 192. Henceforth cited as *Adel*.

the charge that he wrote to curry favor with the Hannoverian government and aristocracy, though the accusation was in fact ridiculous in view of aristocratic protests provoked by his reform proposals. He was in danger of being prosecuted as a Jacobin subversive[30] at the very time that German friends of the revolution feared him as their most trenchant antagonist.[31]

Rehberg was naturally most concerned about the opposition from the Right; he replied to it by stating the Conservative case for reform, and for meeting argument with argument, in unforgettable language. The timorous Reactionaries who feared all intellectual activity—even that advanced on behalf of the Conservative cause—because they considered intellectual activity to be subversive per se aroused his special anger. He denounced them as

arrogant men of wealth or lineage, who think only of the loss which social change brings to themselves; panic mongers who believe in the existence of revolutionary spectres wherever there is any serious discussion of controversial problems. . . . They consider it treasonable to attempt to evaluate one constitutional system against another. They claim that to justify and defend an existing constitution shows a want of proper respect toward it, for this respect is violated by acknowledging the possibility that there might be critical argu-

[30] Anonymous, "Erinnerung an den verstorbenen Geheimen Cabinetsrath Rehberg," *Civilistisches Magazin vom Geheimen Justizrath Ritter Hugo*, VI, (Berlin, 1837), 416.

[31] For a Liberal attack on Rehberg see J. G. Fichte's *Beiträge zur Berichtigung der Urteile des Publikums über die französiche Revolution* (2 vols., n.p., 1793). Certain portions of the book are directed against Rehberg (especially I, 66ff.). The Left-wing accusations against Rehberg were given some plausibility when he wrote a pamphlet to defend the rather arbitrary dismissal, by the Hannoverian ministry, of Freiherr von Berlepsch from a judicial post because he had opposed the foreign policy of the government in the Calenberg *Ritterschaft*. An immense literature exists about the once-famous Berlepsch case (1794-97). Good summaries of the main facts are William von Hassel, *Das Kurfürstentum Hannover vom Baseler Frieden bis zur preussischen Okkupation im Jahre 1806* (Hannover, 1894), pp. 110-22 (hostile to Berlepsch), and E. von Meier, op.cit., I, 317-20 (favorable). The conduct of the Hannoverian government was attacked by the Liberal publicist Carl F. Häberlin, *Über die Rechtssache des Herrn Hofrichters auch Land- und Schatzraths von Berlepsch* (Berlin, 1797). Rehberg's reply was entitled *Actenmässige Darstellung der Sache des Herrn von Berlepsch, zur Berichtigung des Herrn Hofrat Häberlin, Über die Dienstentlassung* [sic] *des Herrn Hofrichters, auch Land- und Schatzraths von Berlepsch* (Hannover, 1797). On Häberlin, a worthy antagonist of Rehberg's, see the definitive dissertation by Ernst Fischer, *Carl F. Häberlin, ein braunschweigischer Staatsrechtslehrer und Publizist* (Göttingen, 1914). The issue of Hannoverian neutrality is discussed exhaustively in G. S. Ford, *Hannover and Prussia 1795-1803: A Study in Neutrality* (New York, 1903).

ments worthy of being refuted. They endorse the maxim of the old Venetian Republic, that praising the *principe* is as sacrilegious as criticizing him. They claim that every part of the existing constitution must be held equally inviolate, even those accidental accretions whose removal would not cause the slightest injury to the whole.[32]

Rehberg then ridiculed those Conservatives who argued that reform was dangerous under all circumstances:

In tranquil periods they think it a crime to awaken sleeping dogs. In stormy periods they say it is dangerous to enflame partisan passions further. . . . When tranquillity has returned through general exhaustion—though none of the causes of the revolutionary upheaval have been removed, nor justified complaints remedied—those who have retained possession of their privileges treat reformers with a mixture of indifference, anger and ridicule.[33]

Rehberg was profoundly conscious that the questions opened by the French Revolution would inevitably continue to agitate men for years to come:

It is impossible to remove from public discussion political, constitutional, and social problems once they have become the subject of general curiosity, serious examination, and impertinent criticism. It is vain to yearn for a return to that earlier state of instinctive reverence when people accepted their customary institutions as eternal and necessary. . . . Vain fools may succumb to the happy illusion that rulers who control armies and policemen can ignore what they contemptuously label the idle chatter of discontented Radicals. Both attitudes are, however, completely ineffective in coping with a dynamic world where a new generation had emerged from its revolutionary experience with a new outlook. The habits and opinions of the old generation, with their roots in a completely different life experience, have inevitably become meaningless to the new.[34]

Rehberg next asked, How can the new generation be taught a Conservative outlook?

The existing structure of society must be buttressed by new pillars as the old pillars of custom and prejudice become ineffective. When critical discussion can no longer be prevented it is essential to replace the voice of authority, as it ceases to command automatic obedience, by arguments addressed to reason. It becomes impossi-

[32] *Adel*, pp. 5-6.   [33] Ibid., pp. 6-7.   [34] Ibid., pp. 7-8.

ble, moreover, to preserve institutions which have become unjust or even harmful, on the mere ground that they have existed for a long time. . . . Even the demonstration that what is now considered evil possessed once a legitimate origin has little value as a defense, for what was formerly just, equitable, and useful is not necessarily so today; even as much that appears unjust and harmful today was not necessarily so in former times. All social institutions (*bürgerliche Verhältnisse*) have arisen out of the circumstances of earlier periods and can be explained only in terms of the needs, modes of thought, and customs of their periods of origin. It is foolish and unjust to hold them in contempt because they have arisen from human contrivance rather than the dictates of a self-evident, universally valid Reason. It is just as wrong, however, to claim for these children of a specific age the privilege of immortality and immutability. Even the basic principles of social organization, upon which all moral ties are founded, and the eternal laws of justice and benevolence, by which all societies must abide, are as variable in their application as are the needs of different ages and societies. Happy the state, whose constitution provides for a steady adaptation to changed circumstances and thereby forestalls sudden revolutionary shocks! But I fear it is impossible to weave such a principle of regenerative change into the texture of the laws. . . . Reforms must be left to the wisdom and resolution of the men who rule over nations in every successive generation. A state is fortunate, indeed, when it possesses a ruler who prevents violent convulsions by continuous, but almost invisible concessions as they are required by a new age, and whose upper classes possess the wisdom . . . to guide or at least to support the benevolent measures of such a ruler.[35]

No opportunity was given to Rehberg to translate his conception of Conservative reform into practical legislation before 1814. His lowly birth precluded the attainment of a position commensurate with his abilities, and indigenous reform was made, in any case, impossible when first France (1803) and soon Prussia (1806) occupied Hannover. Rehberg's unhappy experience as a temporary Prussian subject intensified his long-standing hostility to the state of Frederick the Great. Rehberg saw no value in a Great Power status achieved at the expense of *Stände* rights, local custom, and private happiness.[36] His Prusso-

[35] Ibid., pp. 8-10.
[36] Rehberg always thought in terms of the *Wohlfahrtsstaat* (maximizing human welfare), never the *Machtstaat* (maximizing power). When translating Machiavelli's *Prince* he characteristically insisted that the book was a rhetorical exercise,

phobia exploded in a book published immediately after Napoleon had replaced Prussian rule in Hannover by a second French occupation following the Battle of Jena.[37] Rehberg wrote:

> One frequently encounters in the writings of profound theorists (for example, Montesquieu and Möser) the observation that despotism will not tolerate variety. It seeks to destroy private rights, lawful traditions, and local customs by the imposition of general laws. . . . Those monarchs who find their personal vocation on the parade ground show a special aptitude for these evil practices. . . . It is, to be sure, easy to conduct a government when a single will from above controls all the strings of administration and secures automatic obedience to its edicts. But will the mechanical uniformity of a homogeneous system of administration secure the best conduct of public business? Is there not an advantage if subjects cooperate willingly with their government? Does strength of character in subjects not presuppose an individuality with claims to be respected? If men are reduced to machines they are easily controlled in ordinary times: but they will prove incapable of coping with any problem lying outside the range of their customary experience.[38]

Rehberg made these remarks with reference to the sheepish helplessness shown by the Prussian population after the debacle of 1806. He could scarcely conceal his *Schadenfreude* when viewing the nemesis of Frederician despotism—an attitude which contributed to the saddest

---

not a serious treatise on politics. He could not envisage a dualistic universe where secular and moral values were sometimes incompatible. He rejected the basic contention of *Staatsräson* that states can sometimes be preserved only by the employment of immoral means. He thought that Machiavelli's admission that a prince required the reputation for virtue—as opposed to its reality—damaging to the system, since a reputation could not, in the long run, be maintained contrary to the facts. Rehberg forgot that history is often decided in the short run, and that men forget very easily what they do not want to remember. Rehberg, *Das Buch vom Fürsten von Machiavelli, aus dem Italienischen übersetzt und mit Einleitung und Anmerkungen versehen* (Hannover, 1810), Ch. 8.

[37] *Über die Staatsverwaltung deutscher Länder und die Dienerschaft des Regenten* (Hannover, 1807). Henceforth cited as *Staatsverwaltung.* Two notable Prussian replies are Friedrich von Bülow, *Bemerkungen, veranlasst durch des Herrn Hofraths Rehberg Beurteilung der Königl. Preussischen Staatsverwaltung und Staatsdienerschaft* (Frankfurt, 1808), defending the Prussian judicial system, and H. W. Heerwagen, *Anleitung zur richtigen Kenntniss der preussischen Staatswirthschaft* (Berlin, 1809), defending Prussian economic policies against Rehberg's attack.

[38] *Staatsverwaltung*, pp. 28-30.

experience of Rehberg's life, namely, the breakup of the friendship with Stein which had lasted more than a quarter of a century. The spirit of their intimacy had been expressed by Stein in a letter to another friend written in 1792:

> Among all human beings there are only three with whom I feel a perfect agreement in ideas and sentiments, in whose company I feel completely at ease, whose opinions, actions and behavior accord completely with my own, and to whom giving in is an easy duty [in the rare case of disagreement]. I make it a point to share all my thoughts with them. These three are Rehberg, my sister Marianne, and you.[39]

Rehberg and Stein had collaborated in working out a common set of political principles. They were in perfect agreement on such fundamental points as admiration for England, hostility to the French Revolution, and the desirability of reviving *Ständetum* in Germany. Their intellectual companionship had been intensified by frequent personal meetings when Stein became Prussian *Oberpräsident* at Minden (within easy traveling distance of Hannover) in 1796. Stein made repeated attempts to draw Rehberg into Prussian service, but this project was predestined to fail in view of Rehberg's parochial attachment to his native Hannover.

Several developments placed a certain strain on their friendship even before their respective loyalties to Hannover and Prussia came into open conflict. Rehberg's reform proposals placed him at loggerheads with the high Hannoverian nobility, an exclusive group with which Stein associated after the Nassau knight married the daughter of the Hannoverian General Wallmoden in 1793.[40] Rehberg probably resented, however subconsciously, the fact that Stein's career was far more brilliant than his own. He must have reflected that if only he had been born in similar circumstances—an Imperial Knight with an adequate fortune—there would have been no natural ceiling to his political ambition. He would have been superhuman not to feel some bitterness as his friend—in many ways a pupil and certainly not his intellectual equal—became a Prussian minister while he remained a mere Hannoverian cabinet secretary. The main cause of their break was, however, their conflicting political loyalties. Both Stein and Rehberg

[39] Stein to Mrs. von Berg, Sept. 9, 1792. First printed in G. H. Pertz, *Das Leben des Ministers Freiherr vom Stein* (6 vols., Berlin, 1849-55), I, 114-15.

[40] Wallmoden, who was a natural son of George II, rose to become commander-in-chief of the Hannoverian army.

were so passionately absorbed in their public work that each could scarcely maintain civil relations, much less intimate friendship, with a political opponent. Rehberg condemned Stein as an accomplice of Prussia's immoral annexationism; Stein, his old friend as a stubborn Hannoverian particularist. They ceased to meet after the Prussian occupation of Hannover in 1806, and the breach became final when Stein resented Rehberg's post-Jena, anti-Prussian book as an unchivalrous assault upon a fallen foe.[41]

Rehberg secured little satisfaction from the collapse of Prussian rule since Hannover was immediately incorporated into the French satellite kingdom of Westphalia (1807-13). His loyalty to native traditions—rather than the national outlook which became dominant in Stein's politics after 1807—made him bitterly hostile to the new regime and placed him in a sad personal position. Family obligations made emigration unthinkable; principle forbade acceptance of any important post under King Jerome. He reluctantly entered the ranks of what we today call "collaborators" by accepting appointment as chief revenue collector for one of the departments into which the kingdom was divided.

Rehberg employed on literary work the involuntary leisure resulting from his undemanding job; he wrote a manuscript which denounced the introduction of the Napoleonic Code into Germany and could be published only after the fall of Napoleon.[42] It contained a vehement condemnation of the code as an instrument of French imperialism and called upon other princes to follow the example of the Duke of Dessau in revoking the alien law the moment that the departure of the French armies made them free agents again. Rehberg challenged the claim of the code to embody an abstract universal rule of reason in law; he developed the contrary "historical doctrine" that law must result from the cumulative traditions of a people rather than the deliberate work of specialized lawmakers or, worse still, the dictates of conquerors. The book won the praise of Savigny and placed Rehberg among the foremost legal writers of his day.[43]

The restoration of 1814 brought Rehberg back into an influential though still not a leading executive position. As *Geheimer Kabinettsrath* he worked directly under Count Münster, now the dominant figure

---

[41] The best account of the breach between Stein and Rehberg is in Weniger, op.cit., pp. 15-31.

[42] *Ueber den Code Napoleon und dessen Einführung in Deutschland* (Hannover, 1814).

[43] Friedrich Carl von Savigny, *Vom Beruf unserer Zeit für Gesetzgebung und Rechtswissenschaft* (Berlin, 1814), pp. 44, 55, 112.

in the Hannoverian government. Rehberg showed his capacity for constructive statesmanship by arranging and managing the *Ständever-sammlung* of 1814, whose legislation belatedly realized some of his long-cherished ideals. The renewed absorption in administrative work ended his career as a Conservative writer. The books and articles he composed after his retirement in 1825 are of little value and met with no popular response. His fruitful years as a publicist span the quarter century from 1789 to 1814, during which his works form a remarkably consistent and well-integrated whole which we shall now examine under the three headings of Rehberg's admiration for England, his criticism of the French Revolution, and his reform program for Germany.

Admiration for England

The deep admiration which Schlözer, Brandes, and Rehberg expressed for England must be viewed in the context of the so-called "Anglo-mania" (*Anglomanie*) which swept through Germany in the years after 1760. At about that time the prestige of French culture and institutions, predominant in Germany for more than a century after the Peace of Westphalia, began to fade. The limitations of political absolutism became apparent in the domestic misgovernment of Louis XV, economic stagnation, and his military defeat in the Seven Years' War. The literature of the *Sturm und Drang* rejected the classical models of France in the name of an indigenous German *Volksgeist*. Yet Germans were in fact not yet ready to proclaim Germany's cultural self-sufficiency; they still required a surrogate to occupy the pedestal left empty by the fall of French idols. The institutions and culture of England were ideally suited to fill the position vacated by France. Germany's resurgent national pride took comfort in the thought that England was a "fellow-Germanic community" whose institutions had originally emerged from the forests of Tacitean Germany. England was admired for its Liberal constitution, viewed as an adaptation of Germanic *Ständetum* to modern conditions. The "moderate" character of the British enlightenment contrasted favorably with the anticlerical fanaticism of Voltaire and the democratic fantasies of Rousseau. English culture exercised a powerful attraction, whether it was represented by the common-sense empiricism of Locke, the lachrymose sentimentality of Richardson, or the primitive strains of Ossian. The prestige of England was naturally enhanced by her commercial supremacy, her world-wide colonial empire, and the triumphant war management of Chatham—although there was some disillusionment (as noted previously) at the time of the American

Revolution, and France was easily restored to the position of favorite by the great events of 1789.

The German reading public became flooded by a great number of travel books about England in the 1780's, of which Karl Philipp Moritz' *Reisen eines Deutschen in England im Jahre 1782* was the most famous. The fact that a potboiling collection of travel letters by an impoverished Berlin schoolteacher could become a national best seller is an indication of strong interest in English affairs.[44] This interest is also attested to by the wide circulation of several systematic treatises devoted to explaining the workings of the English constitution.[45] The sixth book of Montesquieu's *Spirit of the Laws* (1749), analyzing English institutions in terms of the separation of powers, shaped the thought of a whole generation of Europeans on problems of government. De Lolme's *Constitution of England*, first published in French in 1771 and translated into German five years later, exercised an almost comparable influence.[46] It paralleled Montesquieu in finding the secret of English liberty in the principle of equilibrium, and pleased many readers by its explicit polemic against Rousseauesque democracy to balance Montesquieu's detestation of monarchical absolutism. Both Montesquieu and De Lolme admired the aristocratic and oligarchic structure of English life, and hailed the English constitution as in many ways a suitable model for imitation.

Brandes and Rehberg described themselves as pupils of Montesquieu and De Lolme in their English studies, but they were equally influenced by several other authors. Brandes, in his articles on *The Public Spirit of England*, specifically mentioned Blackstone's *Commentaries*, Hume's *Essays*, and Macpherson's *History of England* among secondary treatments,[47] and he owed still more to the writings and personal conversation of Edmund Burke. Brandes and Rehberg also drew much information from the *Parliamentary Register* (much of which was written by Burke during these years) and the endless stream of politi-

[44] For a discussion of Moritz' book and other travel literature see R. Elsasser, *Über die politischen Bildungsreisen der Deutschen nach England vom 18. Jahrh. bis 1815* (Heidelberg, 1917), pp. 40-59.

[45] For a survey of eighteenth-century works dealing with the British constitution see H. Christern, *Deutscher Ständestaat und englischer Parlamentarismus* (Munich, 1939), Ch. 2.

[46] I have used the English edition. Jean Louis De Lolme, *The Constitution of England* (London, 1790). The first German edition appeared in Leipzig in 1776. On De Lolme see Edith Ruff, *De Lolme und sein Werk über die Verfassung Englands* (Berlin, 1934).

[47] Brandes, *Über den politischen Geist*, pp. 108-14.

cal pamphlets provoked by the constitutional struggles of the reign of George III.

The two Hannoverian publicists showed their political realism and independence of judgment by downgrading the emphasis placed by Montesquieu and De Lolme upon the separation of powers as the dominating principle of English political life. They recognized that the legislative and the executive powers were in fact closely interwoven in English constitutional practice. The House of Commons possessed decisive influence upon the composition of the cabinet, since ministers could not govern without a parliamentary majority; the king—whose actual power Rehberg and Brandes exaggerated, being deceived by the large role played by King George in the 1770's—possessed an absolute veto power over legislation. The working of the constitution required the harmonious cooperation of four different factors: the king, the ministers, parliament, and public opinion. How could this cooperation be established in view of the absence of any clear-cut locus of sovereignty? Brandes, who can be assumed to speak for Rehberg as well, answered the question by pointing to the nature of English party life, and he became perhaps the first continental author who developed, presumably under the influence of Burke, a positive theory of political parties.

The successful functioning of English parliamentary life required the existence of parties, i.e., groups of men dedicated to common principles for ruling the country. Vigor and unity of governmental action were assured when a party possessing a majority in the House of Commons could compel the king to appoint its leaders to the executive cabinet; solidarity was achieved through personal friendships, agreement on governmental measures, and fear of being replaced by the opposition. Parliamentary support was won in part by corruption —an evil, but a necessary one in the opinion of Brandes—but primarily by providing good government in accordance with the wishes of the governed. An alert opposition saw to it that no government could ever rest on its laurels, and Brandes believed that even the much-decried habit of opposition for opposition's sake prevented the far greater evil of complacency. The regular debate of great public issues in parliament, pamphlets, and periodicals provided Englishmen with a continuing education in public affairs. The system worked all the better because talented men from the *bourgeoisie* were able to make their careers in England without encountering insuperable barriers. The aristocracy did not monopolize the top posts, even apart from the fact that entry into the aristocracy was comparatively easy. The leading positions in the government, in the Church, and on the bench were in fact frequently held by commoners. How different was this English political life from the small, somnambulant, privilege-ridden world of Hannover! Brandes' observations concerning England were rarely free from a certain touch of nostalgic envy.[48]

Brandes found the English constitution as admirable in detail as in general structure. He praised the composition of the House of Lords for combining the claims of heredity with those of talent. Its independence allowed it to screen a courageous king who defied unreasonable mob opinion, while at other times it could protect the people against royal tyranny. It poised a perfect counterweight against hasty action by the House of Commons. Brandes admired the variegated franchise by which members of the Commons were elected. The chaotic lack of system was based upon historical evolution rather than theoretical principle, and it worked well. How absurd to desire its supersession by a democratic system justified by nothing except abstract theory! Brandes was opposed to parliamentary reform, an attitude which Rehberg abandoned only late in life.[49] English freedom was protected by the traditions of constitutional government, the existence of an enlightened public spirit, the liberty of the press, and the jury system.

Brandes made a notable attack upon those continental critics who refused to believe in English freedom because they approached the problem of freedom with a priori notions. Rousseau had attacked the parliamentary system on the grounds that it allowed real freedom only once every seven years at election time; he confused freedom with the continuous exercise of democratic sovereignty. His pupils confused freedom with equality, and were disturbed by England's oligarchic franchise and hierarchic social structure—a structure which in fact constituted the best guarantee against royal and democratic tyranny alike. Some economists equated freedom with the absence of heavy taxation, and criticized the fact that English taxes yielded higher returns than those of any continental state. They forgot that high revenues were natural in the most prosperous country in Europe, and that they were easy to bear since the aristocracy was not exempted from paying its share. Many German Radicals identified freedom

[48] For Brandes' notable defense of party spirit and recognition of the inextricable connection between parliamentary government and the party system see ibid., pp. 293-320.

[49] Rehberg, *Lord Porchester's Aufenthalt in Spanien während der Revolution des Jahres 1820* (Brunswick, 1834), pp. 106-40. The section approves of the Reform Bill of 1832.

with the license to do what one pleased, and were surprised by the English habit of obedience to law. They saw no necessary connection between freedom and law in a self-governing country.[50]

The modern reader is startled by the extent to which Hannoverian Conservatives idealized the England of George III. Many pieces are obviously missing from a "true" historical picture: the prolonged rule of a servile opportunist like Lord North, whose mismanagement led to the loss of the American colonies; the gross methods employed to make the parliamentary system work; the arrogant ministerial defiance of public opinion even when it expressed a genuine grievance, as in the Wilkes case; the malevolent pettiness of George III in his role as party manager of the "King's Friends"; the violence and irresponsibility of party factions; the violation of the freedom of the individual by the press gang; and, finally, the utter helplessness of society and government in the face of the problems raised by the industrial revolution. It required a good deal of Anglomania to idealize the English constitution in the face of these obvious evils; but these Hannoverian Conservatives either ignored them or believed them outweighed by the vigor of a political life whose attractions were magnified by distance and comparison with their own parochial milieu.[51]

The constitutional practice of England served Rehberg and Brandes as a norm when they proposed political reform in Germany. Their usual Conservative opposition to borrowing the institutions of another country was modified in this case by the fact that they viewed England as a "fellow-German community" in which the "old German constitution" had survived intact during the seventeenth century when French-inspired absolutism destroyed that constitution in most of the states of Germany.[52] Rehberg's political program came to center around the revival of the surviving residues of Germany's preabsolutist constitutions. He hoped to make the *Stände* again what they had been in their origins—bodies roughly comparable to the medieval English parliament; the inflated power of most German monarchs must be diminished by powerful *Stände*, a large measure of press freedom, and an enlightened public opinion. Rehberg's program was one of

[50] Brandes, op.cit., pp. 115-26.

[51] I hold to this unfavorable view of Georgian England despite the work of Sir Lewis Namier and Herbert Butterfield's attempted rehabilitation in *George III and the Historians* (London, 1957).

[52] This process is well described in the two important works by F. L. Carsten, *The Origins of Prussia* (Oxford, 1954), and *Princes and Parliaments in Germany from the Fifteenth to the Eighteenth Century* (Oxford, 1959), though Carsten exaggerates the constructive possibilities inherent in *Ständetum* and does not do justice to the "objective" factors making for the triumph of absolutism.

constitutional advance under the disguise of antiquarian claims. In this respect he can be compared with the English Whigs of the seventeenth century.

Rehberg's moderate program, oriented toward the English example, inevitably made him hostile to the program of the French revolutionaries of 1789. A very brief initial period of sympathy with French developments was based upon his belief that the French were trying to model their constitution upon England's. His antagonism became unmistakable as soon as he understood the full democratic implications of the work of the Estates-General; the sharp criticism directed thereafter against the French revolutionaries carried as a foil a continuous laudation of English ways.[53]

Rehberg's Hostility to the French Revolution[54]

THE CRITICISM OF REVOLUTIONARY ACTION

Rehberg was fully aware that France required extensive social and political changes in 1789: the monarchy was weak; taxation of the poor was arbitrary and heavy; unjustified aristocratic privilege abounded; and religious toleration was far from complete.[55] Rehberg condemned the few royalist writers who demanded a return to absolutism and dissociated himself explicitly from Burke's whitewashing of the *ancien régime*.[56] The moderate Anglophile French reformers who dominated the early months of the National Assembly possessed Rehberg's sympathy, while he ridiculed the theory that the entire revolution was the result of an organized Masonic conspiracy.[57] He did not, of course, desire any mechanical imitation of the English constitution by the French, for "to transplant that constitution successfully to another country presupposes that not only its social structure, but also its history, be essentially similar to that of the English

---

[53] Rehberg's views about England come out most clearly in his *Untersuchungen über die französische Revolution* (2 vols., Hannover, 1793), i, 100-76; ii, 369-77. A good secondary summary can be found in Annelise Mayer, *England als politisches Vorbild und sein Einfluss auf die politische Entwicklung in Deutschland bis 1830* (Endingen, 1931), pp. 34-35.

[54] On this entire topic see the useful book by Kurt Lessing, *Rehberg und die Französische Revolution. Ein Beitrag zur Geschichte des literarischen Kampfes gegen die revolutionären Ideen in Deutschland* (Freiburg, 1910).

[55] Rehberg condemned the *ancien régime* most forcefully in his *Sämmtliche Schriften*, ii, 32-39, written in 1828 when his attitude had become more "Liberal" than it had been in 1789.

[56] *Untersuchungen*, i, 16-18; ii, 377-84.

[57] Rehberg often attacked the Masons and *Illuminati*, but he did not fear them as an organized power. *Sämmtliche Schriften*, ii, 15-16.

people."[58] The divergence between English and French society was obviously great, yet not so great as to preclude some cautious French evolution toward the English pattern of government. Rehberg hoped that the Estates-General might be organized to play a role comparable to that of the British parliament, that the social gap which existed in France between nobility and *bourgeoisie* might be narrowed to allow political cooperation on the English model, and that the absolutism of Louis XVI might be reduced to the level of power exercised by George III.

The moderate character of Rehberg's hopes contrasted notably with the vast expectation of a new heaven and a new earth which swept through Germany in 1789. He abandoned even these small hopes as soon as the revolution became radicalized in the autumn of that first year. Rehberg shuddered with horror as the Constituent Assembly broke with all the traditions of France in order to implement abstract theories, and the country fell into a strange mixture of anarchy, violence, and despotism. He became positively alarmed when the revolutionaries, not satisfied with merely ruining France, sought to extend their doctrines to Germany by missionary propaganda and military conquests. Two questions dominated all his subsequent thinking about French affairs: (1) why had the generous—and, in its origin, justifiable—reform movement of 1789 led to such a catastrophic denouement? and (2) what measures were required to protect Germany against a similar catastrophe?

Rehberg provided a very acute analysis of the mistakes made by the rulers of France—first those of Louis XVI, then those of the Constituent Assembly—which allowed a desirable reform movement to degenerate into an uncontrolled revolution. The king failed to provide leadership in the fiscal crisis which led to the convocation of the Estates-General, or the controverted question of the composition of that body. The Constituent Assembly drafted an unworkable constitution based upon the complete separation of powers. It needlessly enflamed tempers by abolishing, rather than reforming, the French aristocracy, and by interfering with the internal life of the Catholic Church through the Civil Constitution of the clergy. These policies inevitably provoked a powerful counterrevolutionary movement which led to open civil war and the use of terror—terror which belied the original idealistic and humanitarian aspirations of the revolutionaries.[59]

[58] *Untersuchungen*, I, 56.
[59] Rehberg's criticism of the king can be found in ibid., II, 66-104; of the

Why did the Constituent Assembly engage in such disastrous constitutional, social, and religious policies? The explanation could not be simple incompetence, for the Assembly contained many able men. Rehberg never accepted Burke's view that the revolutionaries were pettifogging lawyers prompted by sordid motives. With greater charity as well as accuracy he explained their follies in terms of their honest adherence to misguided principles. Rehberg viewed the French revolutionaries as zealous fanatics dominated by certain dogmas about men and society. He set himself the task of refuting these dogmas in a spirit of fair-minded polemic. His philosophical training in fact made him especially well qualified to subject to thorough criticism all the cardinal doctrines advocated by the revolutionaries—Rousseau's general will, the sovereignty of the people, equality, the rights of men, and the contempt for historical development. The strength of Rehberg's attack upon the revolution was due to the fact that he was equally at home in pragmatic criticism of revolutionary action and theoretical refutation of revolutionary doctrine. Burke had embarked upon a similar double purpose, but his prejudice in favor of the *ancien régime* and his reliance upon rhetoric rather than argument causes his famous critique to fall considerably short of that of the obscure Rehberg.

THE REFUTATION OF REVOLUTIONARY DOCTRINE

Rehberg stated that Rousseau had based his entire political theory upon the "contrast between the abstract rational general will (*volonté générale*) and the concrete, immediate will of all (*volonté de tous*)."[60] The insistence that the general will should triumph over the will of all was essentially an affirmation that society should be governed in accordance with an objective ethical norm rather than the subjective will of its members—even if this will should be held unanimously or by a large majority. Rousseau had also insisted in a famous paradox that a man's subjection to the general will left his personal freedom unimpaired, because it only subordinated his "lower will" to his "real will," or what he *ought* to want.

Rehberg was always contemptuous of individual hedonistic caprice, and the impersonal, objective, and severely ethical character of Rousseau's general will was obviously attractive to his austere personality. He nonetheless rejected the entire concept because it provided no practical help in solving concrete political problems. Rehberg's philo-

---

separation of powers, ibid., pp. 100-16; of the antiaristocratic policy of the revolutionaries, i, 224-54; and of the anticlerical policy, ibid., pp. 177-224.

[60] *Sämmtliche Schriften*, iv, 268.

sophical skepticism made him question the "existence" of the general will; besides, even if the concept should be metaphysically valid there would be endless controversy about its application in any particular situation. What fiscal, foreign, or judicial policy would the general will dictate on any specific occasion? And even assuming that it would possess any specific content, who was authorized to determine that content? Assuming further that such a person could be found, through what institutional mechanism could he secure the consent of the people to what he proclaimed to be the dictate of the general will? Rousseau had failed even to raise, much less to answer, any of these questions—a clear proof that the conception of the general will was the fruit of idle speculation rather than a contribution to the art of government. The very imprecision of the concept allowed its exploitation by Jacobin fanatics who justified their tyrannical rule by proclaiming themselves custodians of the general will.[61]

The French revolutionaries rather illogically combined the theory of an "objective" general will with the dogma of the "subjective" sovereignty of the people. Rehberg was irritated by the vagueness of such terms as "people" and "sovereignty." Who were the "people" in political life? Everybody acting with unanimity? Or a majority speaking for the whole? Or even an enlightened minority expressing what everybody "really" wanted? "Sovereignty" presumably meant that the people, however defined, had the legal right to do whatever they wanted to do—a concept completely at variance with that of the "objective" general will. The fuzziness of these notions showed itself in the social-contract theory of the origin of government through the voluntary action of the "people." Rehberg considered this theory to be both unhistorical and intrinsically self-contradictory. He anticipated nearly all the objections subsequently elaborated by Haller and a legion of later critics. How could presocial men living in the state of nature be capable of the social act of forming society? How could they be induced, presumably with unanimity, to agree to abide by the rule of the majority? And how could men speak for future generations when they established a form of government which it would be difficult for their posterity to alter?[62]

A once-for-all social contract as the permanent expression of popular sovereignty was logically untenable: the latter dogma clearly required the *continuous* expression of the will of the "people." This was obviously

---

[61] *Untersuchungen*, I, 6-21.
[62] Rehberg criticizes the social contract theory in ibid., I, 43-99, passim, especially 51.

difficult to achieve, especially as many of the disciples of Rousseau shared the master's distrust of representative institutions. The Jacobins asserted, instead, the right of revolution, i.e., the right of the "people" to alter its established framework of government whenever it found itself dissatisfied. Rehberg was adamantly opposed to this so-called right. It raised all the problems of unanimity, majority, and minority already mentioned with reference to the original social contract. Rehberg's main objection rested, however, upon practical and moral rather than logical grounds. He recognized the fact that revolutions are usually made by determined minorities, and that the claim of the Jacobins to speak for the "French people"—many of whom were cowed by terror—was mere verbal chaff. He thought that a violent program of revolution must always provoke counterviolence and leave revolutionaries with no recourse but to unleash mob passions. Yet how could constructive results possibly emerge from this kind of situation?[63]

Rehberg did not condemn revolution upon empirical grounds alone, but also proclaimed a fundamental moral objection. Modern revolutions were made in the name of equality and frankly aimed at the destruction of the existing hierarchical structure of society. Rehberg condemned this objective on the ground that men were morally bound to honor the obligations of their customary social status. They had no right to repudiate those obligations merely because they were freshly fired by a new social vision which identified justice with equality.[64]

Rehberg believed that the dogma of equality was a pernicious metaphysical abstraction contradicted by all the facts of historical experience. He followed Möser in asserting that the basic unit of political society is not man as such—a category which included criminals, lunatics, and infants—but rather the citizen whose rights were proportionate to his ownership of property:

When discussing political conditions one must distinguish clearly between men and citizens. There exists, indeed, a general community where all men are equal in their rights, and none may place himself above another: the Christian Church. All men are equal before God, but only in their relationship to Him as their Creator. They are

---

[63] Rehberg criticizes the right of revolution in ibid., pp. 77-83. He was too good a Whig to oppose the "right of resistance" to tyranny in the same unconditional manner, while being perplexed about the problem of who should possess the right of determining at what moment resistance was justified. He was willing to grant it to the Catholic Church in Catholic countries. *Das Buch vom Fürsten*, p. 153.

[64] *Untersuchungen*, I, 81-83.

not equal among themselves. The fact of citizenship and the rights attached to it, do not flow from the general qualities of human nature: they are rather the result of human contrivance.[65]

This contrivance is, of course, not arbitrary but rooted in a historical development over which man has little control. Rehberg criticized Möser's comparison between the state and a joint-stock company for failing to give adequate expression to the dynamic and the involuntary character of social status and political rights.[66] He recognized that both were in continuous flux, and we shall see later that Rehberg not only accepted, but even desired, a limited form of individual social mobility; but it was always mobility within a hierarchical structure of society, not the replacement of the principle of social differentiation by the novel concept of human equality.

This concept was closely connected with the general concept of the "rights of man" which played such a large role in revolutionary theory. Rehberg believed that these so-called rights were incompatible with the existence of any kind of organized society. He attacked the famous declaration of 1789 for being vague and abstract to the point of meaninglessness. It gave people expectations which could not be realized, and the consequent frustration was bound to perpetuate revolutionary unrest.[67] Any society, including the Jacobin society of France, was forced to repress many individual rights for the sake of social self-preservation. Rehberg argued, for example, that the right to a free press could never be absolute:

> The laws of every country provide for the punishment of any man who induces individual soldiers to desert. Should it, then, be permitted, to tell all the soldiers of the world by means of the printing press: you are miserable slaves hired by a despot, for the purpose of murdering your wives and brothers at his whim—in short to defame an honorable estate [with the inevitable consequence of encouraging desertion]. Is a crime to go unpunished simply because it is accomplished by the use of the same instrument [i.e., the printing press] through which salutary instruction is often spread among the people? The best refutation of the curious theory of the inviolability of the scribbling craft is provided by the example of Marat. . . . When he was reproached for having printed a placard advising the people to let five or six hundred heads roll, he replied in justification: *c'est*

[65] Ibid., pp. 49-50.
[66] Rehberg criticizes Möser in ibid., pp. 50-51.
[67] Ibid., pp. 116-30.

mon opinion à moi. Shall we follow him on this road? Anyone who retains any feeling for the value of civil society shudders at the very thought. It is essential that the products of the printing press be subjected to the authority of the state, and regulated by law, in the same way as any other method of inciting to disorder and subversion.[68]

The use of the freedom of the press to subvert society must obviously be restrained by specifically prohibiting certain kinds of utterances —as was done, in fact, in all existing communities. Rehberg wished, however, to go farther. He feared the generally evil effects wrought by too much political discussion, by means of the popular press, in such immature communities as the France and Germany of 1789. Such discussion bred an artificial dissatisfaction with the *status quo.* It stirred up the masses by giving them half-baked political knowledge and debasing the level of public controversy. These evils must be checked by governmental censorship, though Rehberg saw that this remedy could, like most other good things, be abused in its turn. He favored a situation in which serious political controversy between educated men remained unrestrained, while popular newspapers and pamphlets were prevented through censorship from damaging the public welfare. We have already seen how he ridiculed obscurantist Conservatives for opposing all intellectual discussion per se, and how he praised English political life because it was based upon frank debate of great public issues. There is no contradiction in these statements despite differences of emphasis. Rehberg always opposed the idea that freedom of the press was a "natural right," and he made the specific extent of permissible freedom—which must everywhere be curbed to some extent—dependent upon the specific circumstances of the country and the age. The stable England of the 1790's could obviously have greater freedom than a Germany threatened by military invasion and internal subversion.[69]

Rehberg believed that all the revolutionary follies he condemned— the general will, the social contract, the sovereignty of the people, equality, and natural rights—originated from a common source—the "metapolitical" way of looking at social problems which had come to prevail as part of the *Aufklärung* of the eighteenth century. This method postulated the existence of a universally valid natural law which could explain society in the same rational and deductive manner as Newton had explained the physical universe. Rehberg believed

[68] Ibid., II, 409-10.   [69] Ibid., pp. 408-13.

that its devotees showed an intolerable arrogance in their lack of reverence toward historical development and in their contemptuous dismissal of whatever facts failed to fit their preconceived ideas. They were, in short, doctrinaires who refused to see the world as it actually was, and were easily tempted to violence in a futile desire to make it conform to their a priori conceptions.[70]

Rehberg's Reform Proposals

It was characteristic of Rehberg's criticism of the doctrine of the revolutionaries that he should seek to present a constructive alternative on every point. He opposed the general will by the historical theory of the state, popular sovereignty by the cooperation of prince and *Stände*, equality by a hierarchic order of society adapted to modern needs, and the *rights* of man by their *duties*. On all these points he wrote as a German primarily for Germans, and his constant concern was to prevent French doctrines from winning acceptance in Germany. It is not surprising, therefore, that his counterdoctrines, and the reform program which he based upon these doctrines, were very much rooted in his German milieu and therefore appear parochial when contrasted with the universal significance of the criticized doctrines. This limitation—inherent in any Conservative theory—is balanced, however, by the concreteness and relevance of Rehberg's proposals to the contemporary German situation.

THE HISTORICAL VIEW OF THE STATE

We have already seen how Rehberg attacked Rousseau's theory of the general will as a metaphysical abstraction which provided no help in governing specific societies. It postulated that a single norm, based upon reason rather than experience, was valid at all times and in all places. Rehberg followed his master Möser in confronting this abstract universalism with the claims of individuality and history. He stressed the fact that mankind is differentiated into various nations, and that each of these has laws and institutions peculiar to itself. The individual character of every nation is shaped by a distinctive spirit (the *Volksgeist*) which pervades every manifestation of its life. Rehberg insisted that a nation was more than a collection of individuals now living: it was, rather, a superpersonal, organic entity persisting over the sequence of generations. The individual belonged to it by the

---

[70] Rehberg gives the best statement of his "historical" criticism of "metapolitical" reasoning in his *Untersuchungen*, I, 51-55, 162-65.

fact of birth, not by the personal, rational decision postulated by social-contract theorists.[71]

What factors made the national spirit of one nation differ from another? Rehberg followed Montesquieu in recognizing the role played by climate and soil.[72] The major determinant was, however, the traditions built up in the course of historical development. Rehberg never developed precise views on what were the generative causes of historical evolution, but he warned against any oversimple explanation in terms of a single factor. Where Adam Müller—and later Hegel—erred in attaching too great importance to ideas, and Karl Ludwig von Haller in overstressing the role of physical power, Rehberg was empirical, eclectic, and vague on the question. He was in fact more concerned about respecting the results of history than explaining their cause; the former was a matter of imperative moral conduct, the latter a mere matter for inconclusive speculation.[73]

His stress upon national individuality, as developed by history, inevitably made him a foe of the doctrine of natural law as developed by the thinkers of the *Aufklärung*. His hostility was, however, neither absolute nor unconditional, and he did not accept the purely positivist counterdoctrine most conspicuously championed by the Göttingen professor Gustav Hugo—that law was simply the will of the sovereign. Who, asked Rehberg, is the legitimate sovereign, and by what right does he secure the right to decide on all laws? Rehberg sought to escape from the completely arbitrary and relativistic conclusions of Hugo's "positive theory of law" by falling back upon the fundamental proposition underlying the theory of natural law—that objective reason dictates certain universally valid norms for human conduct. He thought, for example, that the institution of marriage was necessary everywhere and at all times to provide for the objective needs of growing children; or, to give another example, that the institution of private property was required by human nature to provide incentives under any kind of economic system. The specific form of marriage and property differed, of course, in accordance with the *Volksgeist* of different nations. Rehberg's residual retention of natural law, and his new emphasis upon the role of the *Volksgeist* in shaping law, provided him with a

[71] Rehberg gives his theory of the state most explicitly in *Code Napoleon*, pp. 7-10.

[72] *Sämmtliche Schriften*, IV, 117-18.

[73] The best secondary account of Rehberg's view of history is Gunner Rexius, "Studien zur Staatslehre der historischen Schule," *HZ*, CVII (1911), 513-26. Rehberg never stated his views systematically. They must be pieced together primarily from his essays on Müller and Haller in *Sämmtliche Schriften*, IV, 121-62, 240-77.

firm *point d'appui* for criticizing arbitrary despotism in both its monarchical and democratic forms.[74]

The best example of the gradual, continuous unfolding of national institutions in accordance with the *Volksgeist* was provided by English constitutional development. A warning example of what happened when men tried to substitute reason for the *Volksgeist* was provided revolutionary France. The revolutionaries inevitably encountered resistance as men clung to what was customary and familiar—a resistance which the revolutionaries sought to crush by the use of terror. It was soon evident that the old traditions of France revenged themselves upon their would-be extirpators: the alleged dictates of reason—liberty, equality, and fraternity—all remained unattained. In fact, there was in many ways a change for the worse. The revolutionaries would have achieved far more if they had forgotten all about their high-sounding general dogmas and concentrated upon correcting specific French abuses in a manner compatible with the *Volksgeist*. They should have taken the pattern of gradual English development as their model. Its end result, the British constitution, possessed a coherence and practical utility far superior to what the revolutionaries were able to patch together by their doctrinaire and deliberate contrivance.[75]

The French revolutionaries were equally contemptuous of the *Volksgeist* as they sought to impose their principles upon conquered Germany. We have already seen that Rehberg was indignantly opposed to the introduction of the Code Napoleon in several German states. Its German champions claimed, to be sure, that its alien origin could not diminish its value since it expressed principles of natural law equally valid in Germany and in France. Rehberg attacked this universalist claim by demonstrating that the code was in fact the implementation of certain French revolutionary aspirations incongruently mixed with some of the practices of the French *ancien régime*. He was willing to admit that the code constituted an achievement for France; but this made it all the more unsuitable to a Germany whose historical traditions and social conditions were very different. The

[74] Rehberg wrote an elaborate criticism of Hugo's *Lehrbuch des Naturrechts* (3rd edn., Göttingen, 1809) in *Sämmtliche Schriften*, IV, 103-21. On Hugo see the valuable monograph by Heinrich Weber, *Gustav Hugo. Vom Naturrecht zur historischen Schule* (Göttingen, 1935). He in fact did not differ from Rehberg's views as much as the latter believed. Rehberg's own diluted natural law doctrine is similar to the "eternal Conservatism" developed in the Introduction of this book.

[75] See Rehberg's praise of the Anglophil reformers and regret that they were displaced by the doctrinaire Jacobins. *Untersuchungen*, II, 19-65. On the Revolutionaries not achieving what they intended see ibid., I, 77-83.

France of 1804 was "a society totally disintegrated into its primary elements: that is, isolated individuals legally independent one from another and united only by general laws applicable to every inhabitant of France."[76] Social relations in Germany were, on the other hand, still governed by various kinds of communal law and custom: territorial, urban, feudal, ecclesiastical, guild, and family. The introduction of the Napoleonic Code required the abolition of all these laws consecrated by the *Volksgeist*. This must be resisted not only by every Conservative but by every patriot: "A nation which abandons its inherited conditions, laws, customs, and language stands forever humiliated."[77]

Any deliberate reconstruction of society, whether in the name of reason—as in France—or in accordance with an alien dictate—as in Napoleonic Germany—was a crime against the principle of historical development. Rehberg's "historical view" did not, however, lead him into any political quietism, fatalism, or passive attendance upon historical development. He accepted as inevitable many developments which he intrinsically distrusted—for example, the rise of the *bourgeoisie*, the emancipation of the peasantry, and the collapse of a stable society based upon the general and instinctive acceptance of the *status quo*. The assimilation of these new developments into the framework of existing society could not possibly be either painless or automatic. What was necessary was that cautious men who knew and loved traditional society take the lead in achieving reforms in conformity with the *Volksgeist* before the postponement of reforms led to revolution.[78]

THE COOPERATION BETWEEN PRINCE AND STÄNDE

Rehberg thought that a legitimate monarch was more likely to achieve reforms in the proper historical spirit than a parvenu and doctrinaire Jacobin; he also believed that monarchies, where kings often transcended class interest, could generally be reformed more easily than republics with their tendency toward selfish oligarchy.[79] His hopes for

---

[76] *Code Napoleon*, p. 24. Law tends to reflect, even under an arbitrary despotism like Napoleon's, the social condition of society—a point Rehberg brought out forcefully in his criticism of the loose Napoleonic provisions on marriage and divorce, which were intelligible only in terms of the lax sexual standards prevailing in postrevolutionary Paris. *Code*, pp. 120-43.

[77] Ibid., x. This is the main theme of the entire book.

[78] Rehberg's reformism, stated explicitly in *Adel*, pp. 4-10 (quoted above), will be documented throughout this entire section.

[79] Republican oligarchies were hard to reform, but their excesses were likely to be restrained by the criticism maintained by opposition members of their de-

achieving reforms in the Germany of his lifetime were based upon confidence in the harmonious cooperation between monarch and *Landstände*. Such cooperation could not be expected, however, without considerable changes in the existing outlook of both political partners. The monarch required the assistance of officials far more open-minded and capable than those prevailing in German bureaucracies; the *Landstände* had to be freed from their present domination by selfish aristocratic cliques. Rehberg made detailed proposals for reforming both the *Stände* and the bureaucracy. He considered these to be not only imperative in themselves, but also the prerequisites for achieving all subsequent reforms through regular constitutional channels.

Rehberg saw the special importance of an enlightened bureaucracy in a Germany where political leaders could not arise outside the administrative apparatus. The English parliamentary system tended to produce large-minded, public-spirited men like Walpole, Burke, and Pitt in every generation; Germany lacked a similar reservoir for leaders, since the *Stände* bodies were too limited in their functions to attract men of outstanding abilities. It was all the more urgent, therefore, that Germany should organize her bureaucracy in such a way that the talents of her potential statesmen did not atrophy in the pedantic routine of subordinate office.

Rehberg had very specific ideas about how to achieve a better bureaucracy, ideas which obviously owed much to his own experience. The preparation of young men for public service should include a prolonged period of general education at a university. (Rehberg never regretted the years he had devoted to philosophical studies.) There was no other way to acquire a broad outlook in a country with a public spirit as anemic as Germany's. A specialized and professionalized mind tended to succumb readily to becoming an instrument of despotism; a cultivated mind possessed the secret of eternal youth and never surrendered its internal independence.[80] Able men must, moreover, be encouraged by a system of promotion geared more to merit than seniority.[81] (Rehberg suffered for years from doing only routine, subordinate work.) The existing Hannoverian system of reserving top posts to born aristocrats was incompatible with the public interest. (Rehberg could never hope to become a minister while it prevailed.)

---

liberate assemblies. Rehberg always stressed that open criticism makes for good administration. *Adel*, pp. 243-45.

[80] *Staatsverwaltung*, pp. 89-98. [81] Ibid., pp. 98-103.

The system encouraged laziness in aristocrats untroubled by competition, while bourgeois officials became consumed with anger, frustration, and jealousy.[82] To avoid the one-sidedness inevitable in any homogeneous group, Rehberg also desired the recruitment of bureaucrats from broad and variegated social strata. He desired, however, some preference for the sons of bureaucrats since the ethos of public service (a quality not easily tested in competitive examinations) was best stimulated by paternal example (as in Rehberg's own case).[83] He also insisted that good salaries were necessary to attract able men to the service and to assure their honesty after their appointment. Montesquieu's preference for unpaid officials who took their rewards in honor represented a hopeless anachronism in a world emerging from feudalism.[84] (Rehberg felt harassed for much of his life, raising a large family on an inadequate salary.) He departed from modern civil-service ideals on only one point: his insistence that bureaucrats must be dismissable at the discretion of their superiors. Absolute security of tenure bred complacency and inefficiency; but he thought that any dismissed official should be given a pension proportionate to his age and service, and the additional burden placed upon state finances by the support of prematurely retired officials would make unjustified dismissals extremely rare.[85] Rehberg incidentally showed his incorrigible puritanism in defending the dismissal of officials not only for incompetence but also for leading "immoral" private lives.[86] An administrative system based upon the traditional collegial bodies, which Rehberg wanted to retain despite their ungainly inflexibility, required a kind of mutual trust and *esprit de corps* incompatible with private immorality.[87]

Rehberg saw clearly that there were limits to the number of statesmen that could be drawn from a bureaucracy even after his proposed reforms had been implemented. While he believed that there was no real substitute for parliamentary bodies in training statesmen, he hoped that the surviving *Stände* might indirectly play a similar role in Germany. These bodies could not be expected to produce great leaders from their midst in the foreseeable future; but they might serve as a spur for whatever greatness lay latent among upper-level bureaucrats. Rehberg expected that princes forced to cooperate with *Stände* bodies would select as their ministers nonbureaucratic bureaucrats—that is,

[82] *Adel*, pp. 223-40.
[84] Ibid., 152n.
[86] Ibid., pp. 177-90.

[83] *Staatsverwaltung*, pp. 150-62.
[85] Ibid., pp. 162-77.
[87] Ibid., pp. 135-50.

men with broad and flexible outlook, able to hold their own in deliberative assemblies. His argument ran as follows:

> Employment in a bureaucracy is dependent upon the will of the prince. Aspiring bureaucrats . . . are trained to conduct business, and to think, in a spirit of routine and obedience. Membership in a *Stände* assembly depends, on the other hand, upon either hereditary right or election by one's fellow citizens. *Stände* deliberations and decisions know nothing of routine or servility toward superiors. Public questions are judged in a spirit of freedom, and men carry weight in proportion to their skill at persuasion rather than their position in the table of organization. A royal minister compelled to deal with *Stände* will develop qualities which must atrophy in a statesman who only executes the will of his absolute sovereign.[88]

Rehberg gave as examples: initiative, the art of compromise, and deference to public opinion.

This utilitarian argument for the revival of *Stände* life was reinforced in Rehberg's mind by veneration for the role played by *Stände* in Germany's historical tradition. He recognized, of course—indeed, reiterated repeatedly—that the German *Stände* had never been, and could not in the foreseeable future become, bodies comparable to the British House of Parliament. They had never won full control over either the budget or the administration. Why this difference? Rehberg pointed to the fundamental social differences between Germany and England. Germany lacked the two social groups which dominated English parliamentary life: an open aristocracy standing in an easy relationship with the rest of the nation, and a politically conscious and public-spirited *bourgeoisie*. Where German *Stände* survived, they were dominated by selfish aristocrats and spineless city oligarchs. Their usual preoccupation was wrangling with the prince in defense of narrow privileges instead of cooperating in pursuit of the general welfare.[89]

Rehberg made detailed proposals about how the *Stände* could be revived to play a larger role in German political life. He demanded, in the first place, that they change their mode of procedure and their attitude toward their own work. Rehberg believed that deliberation according to separate estates, and the cumbersome traditional methods of communication between different estates and the prince, were

---

[88] Ibid., pp. 224-25.
[89] Rehberg drew a sharp contrast between German *Landstände* and the British parliament in ibid., pp. 197-207.

hopelessly anachronistic. The *Stände* must frankly recognize the fact that the constitutional position of German princes had advanced during the last two centuries. They must abandon their claim to control some of the executive functions of government—such as the separate collection and administration of certain taxes by *Stände* committees—which they had possessed earlier in defiance of all rational principles of administration. They must demonstrate their value by exercising what functions remained to them, especially in the fields of taxation and legislation, with moderation and a willingness to meet the genuine needs of the modern state. Rehberg believed that princes would recognize the value of such *Stände* and benefit from their periodic assembly.

Regular meetings were the best way denaturing the revolutionary potential inherent in any legislative body; the French Estates-General of 1789 proved so explosive primarily because it was confronted with reform demands accumulated over 175 years.[90] All his life Rehberg had an Arcadian vision of harmonious cooperation between wise princes and public-spirited *Stände* bodies. He never understood the political dynamics of the modern constitutional state, in which legislative bodies inevitably seek to become the dominant factor in political life by controlling the executive and where such control can be avoided only if a hereditary monarch (possessing real power) is replaced by a presidency based upon direct election.

Rehberg demanded, in the second place, that the *Stände* alter their composition. He followed Möser in wishing to base participation upon the traditional basis of land ownership, for he foresaw that the direct representation of people—rather than property—must lead by inevitable stages to universal franchise. His own reform proposals were confined to the abolition of existing restrictions which prevented some categories of landowners from possessing *Landstandschaft* (i.e., the right to take part in *Stände* work). This right was tied to particular estates but could be exercised only if the owners were personally of noble status. If a noble sold his estate to a fellow noble, the purchaser automatically acquired *Landstandschaft* along with the land; if he sold to a commoner, the purchaser did not. Rehberg favored the dilution of the aristocratic *Stände* by giving *Landstandschaft* to all bourgeois purchasers of "noble" property. He proposed at the same time to broaden the existing character of city representation by discouraging the prevailing practice of selecting delegates only from the narrow

[90] Ibid., pp. 221-23.

circle of magistrates. Rehberg favored the continuance of clerical representation because it gave special political weight to men of culture and he thought clergymen especially well suited to mediate conflicts between the aristocracy and the *bourgeoisie*.[91]

Rehberg shocked many German Conservatives by envisioning the eventual participation of the peasantry in *Stände* life, once serfs had become independent proprietors:

> When the former serfs have become assimilated [to the previously privileged class] in respect to wealth, mode of life, and other conditions they will no longer tolerate a striking inferiority in their political rights. When the peasant approaches the nobleman in all these respects he becomes capable of playing a role in *Stände* life— at that time, but no earlier, he will desire and achieve active political participation.

Rehberg hastened to assure his readers that he foresaw such a development only in the very remote future:

> I am not speaking of something that is likely to happen in the course of the nineteenth century, but only of the ultimate goal of a journey upon which our age has embarked [when it began to abolish serfdom]. No one can foretell the length of the journey. One can be certain only that eventually a new class of citizens will be formed and demand recognition as an estate within the realm. Inevitable developments can be delayed for a long time by reasons either good or bad. . . . But neither insight, nor obstinacy, nor folly can permanently forestall what is dictated by the course of historical development, whose pattern is determined by higher powers than the will of man.[92]

Rehberg's proposals for the reform of *Stände* life are thoroughly characteristic of the man in their combination of profound theoretical insight and extremely cautious practical application. He was willing to submit to the principle of historical development, while deluding himself very much on the pace at which Germany would develop. His abhorrence of democracy and popular sovereignty led him to oppose adamantly the modern representative principle. His reform proposals were limited to what could be achieved within the Procrustean bed of *Landstandschaft* tied to land ownership. He saw the absurdity of aristocratic exclusiveness, but advocated no more far-reaching remedy

---

[91] Ibid., pp. 228-36.   [92] *Adel*, pp. 92-93.

than slightly enlarging the charmed circle by the infusion of bourgeois purchasers of land previously owned by nobles. He looked upon the aristocratic domination of society as an axiomatic fact, and wished to strengthen the governing aristocracy by loosening its exclusive character.

Rehberg's desire to abolish many aristocratic privileges was prompted by the same motive. He followed Möser in admiring the English practice of primogeniture, with its tendency to break down barriers between noble and commoner; while the distinction between nobility and gentry restricted the privileged nobility to a manageable number and spared the English the German plague of impoverished but pretentious aristocrats. These English practices were unfortunately so contrary to the pattern of German development that their introduction would constitute an undesirable revolutionary innovation.[93] Rehberg limited his proposals to urging the princes to pursue a policy of outlawing all customs which tended to insulate the nobility from the rest of the nation—for example, the prohibition of marriage between nobles and commoners and the statutory requirement of many foundations that only individuals possessing sixteen blue-blooded ancestors could hold their benefices. Princes should encourage the principle of an open aristocracy by frequent ennoblement, and they should counteract aristocratic arrogance by enlarging the body of men receivable at court (possessing *Hoffähigkeit*). The present exclusion of all burghers from participation in court activities was intolerable: "It arouses resentment in even very wise and humble men, which only those can ridicule who do not know the mainsprings of human nature, or are completely indifferent to them."[94] Rehberg did not fear any overcrowding of the "best society," for only men who combined wealth with breeding and culture could feel comfortable in it and wish admission. In this he probably underestimated the aggressiveness of thick-skinned parvenus.[95]

Rehberg was, of course, far from approving any promiscuous intermixture of classes:

The separation between the aristocracy and its nonaristocratic fellow-citizens is rooted, as are most long-established customs, in a sound instinct for what is proper and necessary. Differences in vocation and occupation bring about class differences in every country under every kind of constitution. . . . Social connections are established not upon the basis of wealth alone but rather upon

[93] Ibid., pp. 192-97.   [94] Ibid., p. 222.   [95] Ibid., pp. 210-14.

similarity in customs and conditions of life. . . . Differentiation is not only natural, but also necessary for the protection of good customs. . . . Frequent contact between men differing sharply in birth, education, culture and vocation generally produces demoralization. The vices of every class are readily transferable, the virtues stand in indissoluble connection with its particular circumstances: their attempted imitation tends only to provide material for satirists.[96]

Rehberg thought specifically of aristocrats who became speculators, plutocrats who sought to conceal their *arriviste* status by aping the aristocracy, and bureaucrats who were corrupted by social contacts with wealthy men whose affairs fell within their official jurisdiction.

Rehberg's goal was the modernization rather than the abolition of social differentiation. His reformist demands appealed to history, morality, and utility but never to the rationalist egalitarianism of the French revolutionaries. Aristocratic privileges had developed historically as a *quid pro quo* for the performance of knight service in Medieval armies. Knight service had long been replaced by standing armies; yet the privileges had not been terminated *pari passu*. Serfdom, originally justified as necessary to provide the aristocracy with the material basis for performing its military and political functions, had now become a crying injustice. Patrimonial courts, originally a corollary of serfdom, should have been abolished as soon as serfdom was ended. The exemption from taxation had been understandable when aristocrats performed numerous unpaid services to the community; it became unjustified as soon as the modern state began to perform these functions through its own officials. Rehberg insisted, however, upon the necessity of paying compensation whenever long-established practices, such as the labor obligations of the serfs, were terminated. He emphasized that reform and compensation must be a gradual process if economic chaos was to be averted; the essential point was, however, to take the first steps in the right direction now. This was the only way of preventing the otherwise inevitable polarization of German society between revolutionaries and Reactionaries.[97]

Rehberg was convinced that an inegalitarian structure of society could be maintained for the indefinite future, provided the traditional hierarchy were adapted to the requirements posed by new histori-

[96] Ibid., pp. 160-61.
[97] Ibid., pp. 19-41. Rehberg drew a sharp line between his own proposals, designed to reform the aristocracy to bring it abreast of the new age, and those of Friedrich Buchholz in his *Untersuchungen über den Geburtsadel* (1808), who wanted to abolish it *in toto* as an anachronism. *Sämmtliche Schriften*, IV, 209-16.

cal developments. This confidence rested upon the belief that a hierarchical structure of society accorded with the "very nature of things." Man did not possess any abstract "natural rights" incompatible with hierarchy: he was morally bound by the concrete nexus of established duties which was indelibly attached to every social status. Liberty, properly understood, meant freedom from interference in one's traditional status, and above all security against its violation by a despotic government. The liberty of an aristocrat differed from that of a peasant in degree rather than kind. Every social class constituted an honorable estate with a duty to promote the common good in its own distinctive way. The happiness and self-fulfillment of every individual was best served if he took pride in the observance of his specific social duties; it could never be attained by the utopian pursuit of an equality which only bred discontent with one's customary condition without replacing it by a satisfactory new status.[98]

Rehberg was not opposed to all social mobility by individuals or families, but he wanted mobility to remain the exception rather than become the rule. He was well aware that some mobility was a safety valve against discontent, and that the best way to strengthen the position of the upper classes was to permit it to absorb talent from below. His unit for mobility was the family rather than the individual. It was neither necessary nor desirable that anybody should be able to attain any social status within the brief span of a single lifetime. It was sufficient if he could make some advance on the social ladder and leave the rest to his children and grandchildren. Too rapid advance tended to demoralize the individual climber and disturb the stability of society. Rehberg saw the key to social advance in the acquisition of property, and wanted political advance to occur as the corollary of newly acquired property ownership. The capstone of nobility should be conferred on all who possessed the means, and the willingness, to lead an aristocratic mode of life—by which Rehberg meant the ownership of a large estate combined with an attitude of *noblesse oblige* toward the lower classes.[99]

Conclusion—Rehberg's
Historical Position and Reputation

Rehberg is a good example of the Reform Conservative. He yielded to none in his hostility to the violent changes undertaken by the French

[98] Rehberg's view that society must be based upon hierarchic stratification as determined by history is stated most clearly in *Untersuchungen*, i, 43-55.
[99] Ibid., pp. 59-67.

Revolution and the unhistorical spirit which animated its work. Yet his hatred of the Jacobins never led him to whitewash the French *ancien régime*; nor did his fear of Jacobin progress in Germany make him a blind supporter of the *status quo*. He wanted to meet the revolutionary danger with a broad reform program looking toward an improved bureaucracy, modernized *Stände*, and an aristocracy shorn of anachronistic privileges. His proposals, while insufficient when compared to the real needs of Germany, sounded audacious coming from a high official of the noble-dominated Hannoverian government. He advanced them in a series of books notable for their seriousness, persuasiveness, and expert knowledge of German problems.

His historical position is best defined by comparison with his teacher, Justus Möser. Möser lived a serene and happy life in the stable world of Osnabrück without becoming too deeply alarmed about the future of Germany. He regretted the gradual passing of accustomed ways, but expected his familiar world to last for a long time yet. The French Revolution came too late in his life to alter his complacent tranquillity: he deplored its attack upon the *ancien régime* in France but never understood that it constituted the great turning point in the history of modern Europe. His Conservative function was limited to praising the old and condemning the new, without engaging in passionate controversy about either. He was essentially a self-effacing observer rather than an active combatant, and made little effort to become a leader of German public opinion.

Rehberg was clearly a man of the next generation. The French Revolution, occurring when he was thirty-two, was the decisive event of his life. He saw clearly that powerful historical forces were inevitably destroying the entire world of the *ancien régime*, and that European society could *never* regain its old stability once the Jacobins had questioned every established institution. This new situation required Conservatives to enter active battle against the forces of subversion, and made Möser's complacency a dangerous anachronism. In Rehberg's own words:

> The new age which emerged toward the end of Möser's life required qualities far different from his. Respect toward old forms was disappearing: this made Möser's desire to avoid all offense a prescription for ineffectiveness. When it became necessary to take risks, and expose oneself to achieve great results, Möser refused to play the role required of him. Under the new conditions it was no longer a recommendation to have no enemies; it was far better, *to fear none.*

In the general chaos of ideas, principles, and desires, where right and wrong stood inextricably mixed together on all sides, and customary rules of conduct could no longer suffice, it became difficult to avoid mistakes; impossible to leave the combat unscarred.[100]

Rehberg did not hesitate to enter the combat arena of a Germany in fermentation. His impact upon his contemporaries of the 1790's was very great, though the *ad hoc* character of his writings made it necessarily temporary. He was forgotten long before his death in 1836. There are several other reasons why he did not attain a lasting reputation commensurate with his talents. His influence as a statesman was restricted to the narrow horizons of his native Hannover, quite apart from the barrier of aristocratic privilege which prevented him from securing a leading position even there. His influence as a writer was restricted by his deliberate decision to write only for a select audience of princes, aristocrats, bureaucrats, and professors. Rehberg was a self-conscious elitist in his hostility to any popular—and, in his view, necessarily demagogic—discussion of political affairs, and he rigidly bound himself to his self-denying creed.[101] His books were written in a ponderous style which scorned rhetorical ornament and made no concessions to lazy or inattentive readers. Composed in leisure stolen from heavy administrative duties, they frequently showed the marks of part-time authorship by their chaotic want of organization. They all dealt with specific current problems. He never attempted to present his ideas in systematic form or to develop points to their logical conclusions. These flaws were reflections not only of Rehberg's external circumstances, but also of certain intrinsic limitations of Rehberg's mind. He possessed an intellect which, for all its richness, was critical and receptive rather than creative. Even where he was comparatively original, as in his historical view of the state, he buried his discovery in the midst of discussions concerned with matters of less importance but more immediate concern.

Rehberg's intellectual limitations were partly the cause and partly the consequence of an undeniable parochialism of spirit. This fact is brought out forcibly when one compares his career with that of his contemporary, Friedrich von Gentz (1764-1832). Both men came from the same social milieu; the fathers were aspiring bureaucrats in Hannover and Prussia, with career prospects circumscribed by their bourgeois origins. Rehberg and Gentz drank the heady wine of philosophy in their university years at Göttingen and Königsberg respectively,

---

[100] *Sämmtliche Schriften*, II, 20.   [101] *Adel*, pp. 10-11.

with Rehberg—ever the man to pursue any subject systematically—becoming a far better metaphysician but acquiring a heaviness and pedantry which never embarrassed the brilliant pen of Gentz. Both men entered the bureaucracy and suffered under the routine work of junior appointments. At this point their careers, hitherto similar, diverge sharply. Rehberg became an exemplary bureaucrat determined to climb the official ladder the regular way; he forswore literature except as a hobby outside of office hours. Gentz entered the social whirl of Berlin as a fish takes to water, refused to take his bureaucratic obligations seriously, and threw his heart and soul into his writing. He was in no way confined by loyalty to his native Prussia, but was only too eager to enter the larger world of the Habsburg Monarchy when opportunity beckoned. He was determined to "crash" the narrow circle of the aristocracy by the force of his brilliance and personal charm, and he was unburdened by middle-class scruples in such matters as money and sex. His ability made him the greatest German political pamphleteer of his age; his connections allowed him to become the "secretary of Europe" at the time of the Congress of Vienna. Rehberg, meanwhile, lived a plain and blameless life on the narrow Hannoverian stage, neither seeking nor finding contact with the larger world of European affairs. He exemplified in a copybook fashion all the puritan virtues, and no doubt became the most valuable Hannoverian public servant of his age. But he remained an incorrigibly parochial figure comparatively little noted by contemporaries and ignored by posterity.

Rehberg's reputation in later life was compromised, moreover, by his hostility to romanticism and nationalism—forces which played an increasingly important role among his fellow Germans. The romantic mentality was alien to a man steeped in common sense and rational argument.[102] His ascetic personality instinctively rejected the romantic deification of emotion at the expense of traditional moral restraints. He valued religion as a social cement rather than a mystical experience, and never lost a Protestant dislike of theocratic medieval society. Rehberg's cult of objectivity could not appeal to an increasingly subjectivist age.[103] It may be said, in fact, that the qualities of his mind—in contrast to the substantive conclusions of his thought—were thoroughly characteristic of the *Aufklärung* of the eighteenth century, and helped to make him an anachronism long before his death.

His hostility to German nationalism—which more than any other

---

[102] The best statement of Rehberg's hostility to romantic thought can be found in his essays on Adam Müller and Fichte. *Sämmtliche Schriften*, IV, 240-85.
[103] His view of religion is best expressed in *Code*, pp. 110-20.

factor led to his low reputation with later historians—resulted from a compound of cultural cosmopolitanism, Hannoverian particularism, and hatred of Prussia's use of nationalism as a tool in her ambition to become a Great Power. His primary loyalty was to his native Hannover; his greatest fear that she might become a prey to Prussian despotism. The appeal to national pride—that a Germany consolidated under Prussia could play a larger role in the European international system—left him completely cold: he hated Great Powers with their constant preoccupation with aggrandizement and their sacrifice of the individual to the state.

His genius for placing himself between various stools was a final reason why his reputation remained well below his talents. He prided himself on his precocious and thorough hostility to the French Revolution; yet many of his antirevolutionary colleagues deplored his want of total commitment to the cause of the *ancien régime*. Aristocrats resented his demand that they reform themselves; clericals, his purely utilitarian defense of Christianity. The friends of the revolution, on the other hand, hated him as their resolute foe. They refused to believe in his intellectual honesty since he remained a servant of the Hannoverian government. His reform proposals appeared half-hearted, inadequate, and impracticable. They ridiculed his basic Conservative beliefs that society must be based upon hierarchical stratification and that the majority of men could never play a constructive role in political life. His desire to tinker with the obsolete *Stände* system, instead of accepting the introduction of modern representative institutions, made them understandably impatient. They were incapable of appreciating his insistence that necessary changes should be achieved only gradually and in a reverent spirit, and his conviction that only institutions rooted in the past could grow in the future.

CHAPTER 12

The Napoleonic Revolution in Germany: The End of the Ecclesiastical States and the Imperial Knights

The Ascendancy of France[1]

WE HAVE seen that there was very little danger of internal subversion in Germany during the age of the French Revolution. It should be added that attachment to the *status quo* had been strengthened throughout the 1790's by disillusionment with the course of the French Revolution and by the sufferings accompanying a war caused, or at least prolonged by, the imperialist ambitions of France; while loyalty to Germany's traditional institutions had been promoted by the propaganda work of German Conservatives.

Any confident attitude toward Germany's political future was precluded, however, by the sorry record made by the empire during the revolutionary wars. The cumbersome procedure of the *Reichstag*, the military feebleness of the *Reichsarmee*, the outdated methods of imperial finance, and the constant bickering between emperor and *Reichstag* and between different *Stände*—all showed that the empire was no longer able to play any effective role on the European stage. Many of its members—especially the ecclesiastical states in the Rhineland—completely lacked the ability to defend themselves, the acid test of viability in a competitive world. It should be noted, however, that these conditions had been chronic for over a hundred and fifty years since the Peace of Westphalia without leading to the formal dissolution of the empire. The question confronting the historian is not, Why did the empire collapse during the Napoleonic Revolution? but rather, What had permitted the Holy Roman Empire to survive all these years in spite of the paralysis of all its institutions?

The fact of survival must be explained partly in terms of the power which tradition and custom exercised over men's minds. Most Germans found it very difficult to conceive of a Central European order without their thousand-year-old empire, which went back to Charlemagne and Otto the Great. It must be remembered also that the "holy" character of that empire suggested associations and evoked loyalties which as

[1] This section and the following are based upon the previously cited standard works of L. Häusser, K. T. Heigel, M. Braubach, and E. R. Huber.

yet transcended any merely secular and utilitarian frame of reference. The empire symbolized man's eternal aspiration toward the universal sway of law and justice—an ideal whose appeal could only be strengthened by its contrast with the brutal eighteenth-century reality of parochial statecraft guided by the precepts of Machiavelli.

These intangible factors played a significant role in buttressing the empire; still more important was, however, the operation of the principle of political equilibrium both within Germany and in Europe as a whole. The major component members of the empire—Prussia, Austria, and half a dozen middle states mortally afraid of both—jealously neutralized one another's ambitions. There were no major territorial changes in the course of the eighteenth century, with the notable exception of Prussia's seizure of Silesia in 1740; and this required three wars before Prussia could feel secure in her new conquest. When Joseph II attempted a similar coup against neighboring Bavaria, he was checked by Frederick in the "Potato War" of 1778 and by the negotiations of the *Fürstenbund* in 1785. The maintenance of the German equilibrium was closely connected with the European equilibrium, especially since the two major German powers, Hohenzollern Prussia and Habsburg Austria, were also members of the so-called European Pentarchy of Great Powers. Europe would not easily permit the aggrandizement of either Prussia or Austria in Germany—witness the European coalition against Frederick the Great during the Seven Years' War (1756-63) and the support which Russia and France gave to Prussia's opposition to the Bavarian designs of Joseph II (Peace of Teschen, 1779). It was the common belief of statesmen that the interests of Europe required a weak, decentralized, and pluralistic political structure in Central Europe—one strong and cohesive enough to prevent outside domination (for centuries threatened by France), yet so paralyzed internally as to pose no threat to its neighbors. The empire survived for centuries because it was a German habit and a European necessity.

The revolution in France and the triumphant successes of revolutionary armies in the mid-1790's undermined many of the factors which had hitherto buttressed the imperial structure. The power of tradition and habit was weakened throughout Europe when France, its premier power, abolished its aristocracy, persecuted its Church, executed its king, and sought to reconstruct its polity in accordance with the dictates of Reason. Were Germany's feudal princes more secure than the French nobility, Germany's bishops more inviolate than their

French colleagues, Germany's emperor more sacred than Louis XVI, an anointed king by divine right? These questions were all the more pertinent now that frontiers were losing much of their meaning (and their stability) as an "international civil war" was added to the conventional war between France and the various states of Europe. The result of the War of the First Coalition (1792-97) was a strong France which aspired toward European hegemony and was in a position to preside over the reconstruction of Germany in violation of the general principle of the European equilibrium. It succeeded in exploiting the traditional friction between Austria and Prussia for its own advantage and the disadvantage of the empire; and it encouraged the long-repressed rapaciousness of Germany's middle states, who could now hope to aggrandize themselves at the expense of their weak neighbors, provided they were willing to become clients of France.

The result of this situation—first created during the period of the Directory but exploited most successfully by Napoleon after he became First Consul in 1799—was the so-called "Napoleonic Revolution" in Germany. This complex phenomenon consisted of the humiliation of Austria through a series of military defeats which left her no choice but to acquiesce in the French-directed reorganization of Germany; the swallowing up of numerous political units—ecclesiastical states, Free Cities, knightly territories, and small states generally—by several middle states as a reward for their servility toward Napoleon; and, finally, the abdication of Francis II, the last Holy Roman Emperor, and the formal dissolution of the empire, as a result of a Napoleonic ultimatum in August 1806. The French domination of Germany was to be completed by the disastrous defeat of Prussia in October 1806, after Prussia, following a decade of withdrawal from the larger politics of Europe, had belatedly challenged Napoleon under hopeless circumstances. These events ended an entire era of German history and set the stage for completely new problems.

The impact of France upon Germany altered the relative power of Radicalism and Conservatism, to the great advantage of the former. It will be recalled that Radicalism was already losing its strongest ally —enlightened despotism—before the outbreak of the revolution, a trend which was strengthened when most princes yielded to counter-revolutionary panic after 1792; at that time Radicalism became a despised and persecuted political sect. The victorious arms of revolutionary France reversed this entire situation. Radicalism—in the sense of "forward-looking reforms"—received official patronage wherever territory fell under French occupation, most notably in the Rhineland, where French institutions were introduced directly; while the princes of the middle states began to curry favor with their French masters by imitating their policies. Yet it should not be thought that they were merely implementing the wishes of France; they were often also revitalizing the domestic tradition of enlightened absolutism which had been briefly interrupted by the triumph of Conservatism during the revolutionary era. Their Radicalism was inevitably confined to administrative, social, and religious questions, as was characteristic of all "Radicalism from above"; the princes could not be expected to cut into their own prerogatives by political reforms looking toward eventual self-government.

The encouragement given to Radicalism was by no means limited to the satellite states organized into Napoleon's Confederation of the Rhine in 1806. It was equally important, though very different in form, in Austria and Prussia—two states with proud traditions which were unwilling to become satellites of Napoleon though they were frequently forced to behave like satellites after the debacles of 1805-07. To be sure, both countries retained the essential structure of the *ancien régime* with its monarchical absolutism, aristocratic domination, and close alliance of throne and altar. They were forced, however, by the sheer exigencies of survival in Napoleonic Europe, to make concessions to many Radical demands. After 1806 two great Reform Conservatives, Stadion in Austria and Stein in Prussia, embarked upon a policy of "defensive modernization" because they saw that some of the demands of Radicalism—for example, the change from the *Obrigkeitsstaat* to a state in which citizens concerned themselves with public affairs—were imperative to enhance the external power of the state. Some of their advanced followers went much farther on the Radical road: their burning hatred of the French led them to a passionate nationalism with revolutionary implications for internal policy.[2]

The new opposition of some Radicals to France went hand in hand with the survival of much Conservative hostility to the country of revolution. Many German pamphleteers continued their work of the nineties by attacking France and warning their fellow countrymen against the seduction of the revolutionary spirit; their work differed, however, from their predecessors in that they could no longer expect official encouragement since Germany's princes were now competing for

---

[2] E. R. Huber, *Verfassungsgeschichte*, i, 13-15, provides an especially penetrating analysis of the revolutionary democratic nationalism of Arndt and Fichte.

Napoleon's favor. As there were no new themes to develop, we can be brief in characterizing this type of literature; though it should be emphasized that lack of novelty does not imply diminished significance.

Many pamphleteers called for the continuation, indeed intensification, of the counterrevolutionary crusade. They stressed with wearisome repetition that the export of the revolution had caused destruction, confusion, and unhappiness; that its so-called blessings had nowhere won spontaneous assent; that French domination was completely incompatible with Christianity; and that Germany's princes must recognize that no reliance could be placed upon the word of the unscrupulous French.[3] Another set of pamphleteers—following the main theme of the now-defunct *Eudämonia*—criticized Germany's princes for their lack of vigor in the important business of crushing the subversive spirit in their realms. They demanded more stringent censorship and police surveillance of Radicals, and they felt called upon to act as vigilantes, filling a vacuum left by the alleged lethargy of Germany's governments.[4] Still other pamphleteers felt that the repression of Radical thought dealt only with symptoms when a far-reaching attack upon causes was imperative; they called for the development of a loyal, contented citizenry through a system of education explicitly devoted to inculcating the spirit of counterrevolution.[5]

The most interesting development in Conservative pamphleteering—though one as yet quantitatively unimportant whether reckoned by the number of pamphlets or their influence upon public opinion—was the appearance of authors advocating what later generations would call a "Conservative Revolutionary" program. These authors used a Conservative vocabulary and wanted Germany to return to the pre-1789 *status quo*. They argued, however, that this aim could not be achieved through reliance upon Germany's governments, which had "gone over" to the Radical enemy; it could be achieved only by "true Conservatives" banding together and taking all steps necessary—no matter how vio-

[3] See, for example, the anonymous pamphlet *Darstellung des Betragens der Neufranken gegen mehrere Staaten im Jahre 1798 und 1799; mit einer Schilderung der wichtigsten Ereignisse bis zum Ausgang des letzten Jahrs* (Germanien, 1799).

[4] See, for example, the anonymous pamphlet *Ein Wink an Deutschlands Regenten über die schädlichen Missbräuche der deutschen Pressfreiheit in Beziehung auf den Staat und dessen Verfassung, mit Zurückweisung auf die hierüber bestehenden älteren und neueren Reichsgesetze* (Germanien, 1800).

[5] See, for example, an article by J. G. Rhode, "Wie kann man dem, unser Zeitalter charakterisirenden, in so vieler Hinsicht verderblichen Revolutionsgeist, am sichersten entgegenwirken?" *Berlinisches Archiv der Zeit*, II (1799), 193-205.

lent, extreme, and distasteful to established governments—to achieve their goals. The Conservative Revolutionaries were imbued with an intensely nationalist outlook and castigated Germany's princes for their betrayal of the national spirit. Their immediate aim was the overthrow of the Napoleonic hegemony in Germany, and they believed that this could be achieved through mass risings which would either force princes into cooperation or sweep them away as obstacles to the nation's regeneration. There were calls for the massacre of every Frenchman stationed in Germany on the prearranged day of national wrath; better still would be the assassination of Napoleon by a determined patriot.[6] These views were, of course, advocated only by isolated writers and were in no danger of being implemented. They are of interest primarily because they anticipate the "Revolutionary" type of Conservative which became so influential in Germany a hundred and twenty years later.[7]

The Road to the Reichsdeputationshauptschluss

The ascendancy of France in Germany was registered by the following diplomatic events: the Peace of Basel (April 5, 1795), which led to Prussia's withdrawal from the First Coalition; the Peace of Campoformio (Oct. 17, 1797), which did the same for Austria and amounted to an abandonment of the empire by the emperor; the Congress of Rastatt (November 1797-April 1799), where the territorial reorganization of Germany was discussed upon the basis of the secularization of the ecclesiastical states; the Peace of Lunéville (Feb. 9, 1801), terminating the stay of execution granted to the imperial structure by the War of the Second Coalition, and, finally, the appointment of a special *Reichstag* committee (the *Reichsdeputation*) which resumed the task of reorganization begun at Rastatt. The committee, working under strong Franco-Russian pressure, completed its work on February 25, 1803; the *Reichstag* accepted its final report—though it was certainly the most far-reaching proposal ever submitted at Regensburg—after only perfunctory discussion; and the emperor quickly added his ratification on April 27, 1803. The *Reichsdeputationshauptschluss* was in fact a revolution though it was achieved through the use of traditional constitutional forms; it was accomplished, moreover, under

[6] See two pamphlets by an author writing under the pseudonym Hans Deutschmann, *Der Moloch unserer Tage und sein Hohenpriester in Deutschland* (n.p., 1804) and *Patriotenspiegel für die Deutschen in Deutschland. Ein Angebinde für Buonaparte bei seiner Kaiserkrönung* (Teutoburg [Berlin], n.d. [1804]).

[7] See Introduction, 7n.

alien dictation which exploited German avarice and ambition.

The French were successful in playing off Prussia against Austria throughout the entire period from 1795 to 1803. They disrupted the First Coalition when Prussia accepted the separate Peace of Basel, under whose terms not only Prussia, but all of Germany north of a "line of demarcation," withdrew from the war in obvious disregard of obligations to the empire. The treaty created a grotesque situation in which the empire remained at war against France while nearly half of its members entered into friendly treaty relations with the Republic. Prussia's statesmen considered Reason of State, not support of the empire, their first loyalty. Prussian Reason of State dictated a policy of aggrandizement in North Germany: such aggrandizement could be attained far more easily in cooperation with France—the traditional foe of the empire—than with Austria, whose ruler wore the Imperial Crown and could not approve of Prussia's forming a cohesive North German *imperium in imperio*. Additional considerations which governed Prussian policy were financial exhaustion, preoccupation with Polish affairs, and disgust at Austria's ineffective conduct of military operations. These were all understandable reasons for withdrawal from the war; it should be reiterated, however, that Prussia showed a total lack of loyalty to the empire and thereby contributed to the early extinction of that venerable institution.

It should not be thought, however, that Austria showed any more disinterested loyalty to the empire than her North German rival. When making peace with France at Campoformio (1797), Francis II was governed by Austrian Reason of State exactly as Frederick William II had been by Prussian Reason of State at Basel two and a half years earlier. In return for consolidating her Italian position Austria agreed to French annexation of much of the Rhineland, thereby abandoning all Left Rhenish *Stände* to the tender mercies of revolutionary France, and to the principle of compensatory secularization, thereby agreeing to the extinction of many (if not all) ecclesiastical states, hitherto the most loyal pillars of imperial authority. The resulting territorial reorganization inevitably involved a total revolution in the imperial constitution; and the emperor agreed to this in principle without consulting the *Stände*, although in his coronation oath he had sworn to protect the latter's interests.

The precise terms of territorial reorganization were to be worked out at a congress at the city of Rastatt, which was officially composed of three French commissioners and the envoys of ten German states selected by the *Reichstag* in 1795 (shortly after the Peace Motion of

Mainz mentioned earlier). Because Prussia had left the war in 1795 its government did not formally participate in the congress, although in fact Prussian observers were regularly consulted. The German delegation at first hoped to engage in give-and-take negotiations with the French, but the secret commitments of Austria and the thinly veiled military pressure of near-by French armies gave an unreal character to the negotiating process. The congress followed the terms of Campoformio in accepting the cession of the Left Rhine bank and the principle of secularizing ecclesiastical states to provide compensation for princes dispossessed by this decision. The implementation was delayed, however, by the outbreak of the War of the Second Coalition (1799-1801); there was a flicker of hope that France might be driven back to the frontiers of 1792, the German *status quo ante bellum* restored, and the planned territorial revolution avoided altogether.

The military victories of France allowed Napoleon to impose the Treaty of Lunéville (February 9, 1801) upon a humbled Austria, a treaty which confirmed the provisions of Campoformio as already confirmed by the Congress of Rastatt before its interruption. Quick ratification by the *Reichstag* (March 7, 1801) was a foregone conclusion because Napoleon had made the evacuation of his troops from Germany conditional upon the formal promulgation of the treaty. The *Reichstag* then elected (Nov. 7, 1801) an eight-state committee (*Reichsdeputation*) to work out the territorial details of the reorganization of Germany. It included two ecclesiastical states (Mainz and *Hoch und Deutschmeister*, the latter headed by a Habsburg prince), a fact which indicated that hope remained for saving some ecclesiastical states since the two on the committee could not be expected to agree to their own extinction. Its six secular members were Bohemia (a part of the domain of Francis II), Brandenburg (no longer excluded, since it was now recognized that its consent was certainly necessary for any stable new order in Germany), Saxony, Bavaria, Hessen, and Würzburg. (The latter state, formerly a bishopric, had already been secularized for the benefit of a Habsburg prince who needed compensation for losses suffered in Italy.) The important North German state of Hannover was excluded because its ruler, the English King George III, was still at war with Napoleon. The imperial cities were excluded because it was generally agreed that most of them would join the bishoprics on the list of victims of the process of compensation.

The committee proved, in fact, a rubber stamp for Napoleon, who dictated its terms not only in general principles but in many minutiae as well. The governments of France and Russia had decided upon a compensation plan on June 3, 1802, which the committee agreed to make the basis of its work at the opening session on August 24. The Franco-Russian plan in turn incorporated the terms of treaties negotiated earlier between France and the destined beneficiaries of the compensation principle: Prussia, Bavaria, and Württemberg. The term "compensation," in its conventional meaning of "gain equivalent to losses suffered," does not adequately describe the arrangements made; other considerations—such as dynastic connections, French Reason of State, and even the amount of cold cash paid to Talleyrand and his assistants—also played a role. Napoleon was far more interested in achieving certain political ends than in compensating injured princes in the name of justice (even the dubious type of justice under which victims are "compensated" by the robbery of innocent third parties). France was eager to build up Prussia as a counterweight to Austria, and to create a small number of satellite "middle states" strong enough to become valuable allies, tied to France by their need for support while digesting ill-gotten loot, yet too weak to pursue independent policies. These various considerations explain—to give only two examples—why Prussia gained four and a half times what it lost (558,000 people against losses of 127,000); while Baden—whose ruler Karl Friedrich had the good fortune to be the father-in-law of Tsar Alexander—gained nine and a half times what it lost (237,000 people against losses of 25,000).

The main terms of the *Reichsdeputationshauptschluss* were as follows:[8] All ecclesiastical states (including nineteen bishoprics) were secularized, with the exception of the territories of the *Hoch-und Deutschmeister* (as we have seen, a member of the committee and a Habsburg prince) and the Grand Prior of the Order of Malta (in which Tsar Alexander took a personal interest). A new archbishopric was created in Regensburg for the Archbishop-Elector of Mainz, Count Dalberg, presumably because he had been a committee member. His see had traditionally been combined with the position of Imperial Chancellor, and he promised to become a faithful executor of Napoleon's German policy. Five middle states soon destined to become members of the Confederation of the Rhine—Bavaria, Württemberg, Baden, Hessen-Darmstadt, and Nassau—received generous compensation far beyond their actual losses; their future loyalty was

[8] The text of the *Reichsdeputationshauptschluss* is conveniently available in E. R. Huber, *Dokumente zur deutschen Verfassungsgeschichte* (2 vols., Stuttgart, 1961-64), I, 1-26. The best modern commentary is E. R. Huber, *Verfassungsgeschichte*, I, 42-60.

henceforth certain to gravitate toward Paris rather than Vienna or Regensburg. All Free Imperial Cities except six (the three Hanseatic cities and Frankfurt, Nürnberg, and Augsburg) were mediatized through incorporation in neighboring territorial states. Nothing was decided about the future of the Free Imperial Knights, but it was certain that they would soon suffer the fate of the ecclesiastical states and the Free Cities to satisfy the voracious appetite of Germany's territorial princes.

The *Reichsdeputationshauptschluss* caused important changes in the structure of the *Reichstag* at Regensburg. The *curia* of the Free Cities, reduced from fifty-one to six members, henceforth played an even less significant role than previously. The *curia* of electors was changed through both subtractions and additions. Two ecclesiastical electors, Trier and Cologne, were eliminated as the result of the secularizations; while the third—Mainz—survived through transferal to Regensburg. The five secular electors (Bohemia, Brandenburg, Bavaria, Saxony, Hannover) received four additions to their ranks: Württemberg, Baden, Hessen, and Salzburg (the latter a former ecclesiastical state now secularized, like Würzburg, for the benefit of a dispossessed Habsburg prince from Italy). The enlargement of the electoral college never acquired any practical significance, since the early dissolution of the empire meant that no more imperial elections were held; it shows, however, that a competition for rank and title—long one of the more ludicrous features of German politics—persisted to the bitter end of the empire and that many Germans expected the renovated structure of 1803 to last long enough to make jockeying for position within it worth while.

The *Reichsfürstenrat* (curia of princes) also experienced considerable changes. The votes of the secularized ecclesiastical states were assumed by their new rulers in accordance with the long-standing practice of adding votes when territory was transferred; under the new arrangement Prussian voting power, to give only one example, advanced from eight to fifteen. The total number of *Reichstag* votes was increased by thirty-one despite the elimination of 22 Left Rhenish princes, for 53 new votes were created for the benefit of "compensated princes" and previously unrepresented princes. The enlargement of *Reichsfürstenrat* membership from 100 to 131 appeared less important, however, than the change in the confessional ratio which resulted from the Protestant annexation of secularized bishoprics. The Protestants, previously in a minority of 43 as against 57 Catholics, now secured a majority of 77 to 54. It indicates the significant survival of confessional antagonisms that the emperor refused his sanction to this provision—and only this provision—in his ratification decree of April 27, 1803. This placed the entire matter in constitutional suspense, which was ended only by the formal dissolution of the empire three years later.

The religious passions aroused by the *Reichsdeputationsschluss* were fanned further by the fact that it provided not only for the secularization of "immediate" bishoprics and abbeys, but also gave express authorization to territorial princes to expropriate ecclesiastical property within their states. Such expropriation was, of course, not unprecedented; it had been undertaken on a large scale at the time of the Reformation and on a lesser scale by several "enlightened despots" during the eighteenth century, most notably Joseph II. What was unprecedented was the *national* authorization given to all princes, the frankly *political* motivation, and the enactment of some specific safeguards for the protection of the dispossessed. The expropriating princes were required, under Article 35 of the *Hauptschluss,* "to provide adequate and permanent support for all cathedral churches and pensions for the dispossessed canons." It was understood at the time that "adequate and permanent support" could best be achieved through landed endowment, although in fact annual government payments became the customary practice for supporting the German Church. It was further stipulated that expropriated monastic property should be used "to support religion, education, and charity (*andere gemeinnützige Anstalten*) as well as for general revenue." This flexible provision made it illegal for princes to use monastic revenues exclusively for general state purposes, though it left the precise allocation of these revenues between different purposes to the discretion of the princes. Article 35 was in fact to lead to a century of legal controversy between Church and State in Germany. The Catholic Church interpreted it as constituting a warrant for far-reaching compensatory claims, to be implemented by lawsuits if necessary; the various governments asserted that it constituted no more than a moral obligation to be discharged at their own discretion.

The Secularizations[9]

THE DEMAND FOR SECULARIZATION

It is time to take a closer look at the single most important part of the Napoleonic Revolution in Germany: the suppression of all ecclesi-

---

[9] There is no definitive work about the secularizations, and most of the literature is necessarily partisan. Two useful little works, from opposite points

astical states (save three, temporarily) and the greatest expropriation of ecclesiastical property since the Reformation. The mediatization of the ecclesiastical states in 1803 was, of course, neither a sudden nor an unexpected event. It will be recalled that these anachronistic political units had been on the defensive since the mid-1780's, and that their suppression had been accepted in principle by the Congress of Rastatt. Numerous pamphleteers now argued the desirability of their suppression—from a religious as well as a political point of view—in the following terms. The abandonment of the Left bank of the Rhine to France was necessary in order to secure peace for Germany. This abandonment meant the total or partial dispossession of several German secular princes. Equity required that they be compensated in Right Rhenish territories, since it would be most unfair to make them bear all the losses incurred in a war fought by the empire as a whole. The ecclesiastical states constituted the only available source for compensations, and their special status made it both inevitable and just that they be used for compensatory purposes. The lands and regalian rights of bishops had been conferred upon them conditionally by the emperor, and were subject to revocation. Such revocation was indicated by three developments since the original enfeoffment of the bishops in the Middle Ages: the forward march of *Aufklärung*, which had overthrown the superstitions upon which theocracy was formerly based; the development of a purer religion, meaning that the incompatibility between religious and governmental responsibilities was now clearly understood; and the increasing impatience of public opinion with the notorious misgovernment of ecclesiastical states. It was also argued that the ecclesiastical states bore an unusual degree of responsibility for the war, because they had given irresponsible encouragement to *émigré* activity on their soil; they had made an inadequate contribution to the war they had so rashly provoked; and they had revealed a total inability to defend themselves.[10]

---

of view, are Karl Kästner, *Die grosse Säkularisation in Deutschland* (Paderborn, 1926), a collection of documents with a sprightly pro-Catholic connecting commentary, and Arthur Kleinschmidt, *Die Säkularisation von 1803* (Berlin, 1878), a brilliant but prejudiced Protestant pamphlet written at the height of the *Kulturkampf*. J. P. Harl, *Deutschlands neueste Staats-und Kirchenveränderungen, politisch und kirchenrechtlich entwickelt* (Berlin, 1804), is one of the best contemporary accounts approving the secularizations; Karl Moriz Fabritius, *Über den Werth und die Vorzüge geistlicher Staaten und Regierungen in Teutschland* (2 vols., Frankfurt and Leipzig, 1797-99), one of the best hostile accounts.

[10] Of the numerous pamphlets on behalf of secularization I have found most lucid: Anonymous, *Über die Pacification und Indemnisation, oder Plan zur*

The case for the expropriation of ecclesiastical property was also argued in terms of economic expediency. The unprecedented burdens of the French war had driven every German government treasury to the verge of bankruptcy, and there was an imperative necessity to siphon off the excess wealth of a bloated clergy to meet pressing public needs. The increasing scope of the welfare activities of the modern state made some forms of church charity superfluous and thereby justified a transfer of revenues. To invigorate Germany's stagnant economy also required mobilizing the landed property of the Church, at present paralyzed by the principle of the "dead hand."

Most important of all, however—at least among the publicly stated reasons for confiscation—was the need to remove all obstacles to *Aufklärung*. Count Montgelas, the great Bavarian reform minister, stated in an official communication (Jan. 25, 1802) that the welfare of society required "the moral education of the people," and that government had the obligation to remove all obstacles standing in the way of moral education:

> One of the most powerful obstacles is to be found in the present condition of the Bavarian monasteries, and more especially of the mendicant monks. They recognize themselves that the new spirit of the age has led to a change in public attitude toward them; but this has only led them to redouble their efforts to work for their own preservation. They have encouraged the perpetuation of superstition and of the most baneful errors; they have built up obstacles against the spread of enlightened principles; and they have sown suspicion against every institution working for true moral education. . . .[11]

Entschädigung der Reichsstände, deren Länder und Besitzung zu Erlangung des Friedens vom Reiche zum Opfer gebracht werden. Von einem Deutschen (Germanien, 1798). A Leipzig professor of law, Christian Weisse, made an influential defense of the often disputed *right* of the empire to sacrifice its constituent members when this was demanded by the common welfare: *Ueber die Säkularisationen deutscher geistlicher Reichsländer* (n.p., 1798).

[11] Quoted in Kästner, *Die grosse Säkularisation*, p. 24. The most exhaustive treatment of the secularizations in Bavaria is the encyclopedic, strongly pro-Catholic work by A. M. Schleglmann, *Geschichte der Säkularisation im rechts-rheinischen Bayern* (3 vols., Regensburg, 1903-08). The situation in neighboring Württemberg is covered in the brilliant work of a youthful amateur historian named Matthias Erzberger, written on the eve of his meteoric rise to statesmanship: *Die Säkularisation in Württemberg von 1802-1810* (Stuttgart, 1902). The actual condition of the monasteries (i.e., whether there was objective justification for their suppression) is shrouded in controversy. The contemporary antimonastic literature is surveyed by Bonifaz Wöhrmüller, "Literarische Sturmzeichen vor der Säkularisation," *Studien und Mitteilungen zur Geschichte des Benediktinerordens*, XLV (1927), 12-41.

Many arguments in defense of the ecclesiastical states were originally stated, it will be recalled, during the 1780's in response to the threat of secularization spearheaded by Carl Friedrich von Moser. The various advantages of elective monarchy under which the public welfare could be pursued free of dynastic consideration; of a dualistic polity free from militarist despotism; of small states uncursed with Great Power ambitions; and of the harmonious union of Church and State—all these themes continued to be reiterated by numerous writers. There was special stress now, however, upon themes which had appeared academic in the stable pre-1789 world, but which assumed a burning immediacy in 1798: the suppression of the ecclesiastical states would set an evil precedent for the suppression of the Free Cities, the knights, and defenseless *Stände* generally; the fate of the empire was inextricably tied to the fate of the ecclesiastical states; and the suppression of the ecclesiastical states would mean the triumph in Germany of the law of the jungle, by which the strong could swallow the weak regardless of considerations of justice.

The prolonged agony of the ecclesiastical states, stretching over the five years from the capital sentence pronounced at Rastatt (1798) to its execution in the *Reichsdeputationshauptschluss* (1803), saw the reiteration of all these old points and the development of several new ones. Our analysis will concentrate upon pamphlets designed to refute the specific case for secularization advanced at the time of the Rastatt Congress. It is impossible to weigh the influence which these pamphlets exercised over public opinion—certainly not enough to affect the course of events. Most of the pamphleteers remained anonymous; if one judges from internal evidence, they were either priests or canon lawyers. It may be added that the defenders of the ecclesiastical states were Conservatives in the sense that they supported threatened institutions (deeply rooted in German history) against attack; the foes of the ecclesiastical states were, however, only in few cases genuine Radicals. They were, rather, rapacious princes who at best hired Radical pamphleteers to provide them with a properly "enlightened" rationalization for aggrandizement. The debate on the survival of the ecclesiastical states throws an interesting light, nonetheless, on the state of political opinion at the turn of the century.

The opponents of secularization advanced the following case:

1. They denied the premise of the secularizers that the abandonment of the Left bank—the source of the claim to compensation which

lay behind the demand for secularization—was either a necessary or a sufficient price to pay for peace with France. They asserted, on the contrary, that peace with France was in any case intrinsically unattainable because of the unstable and insatiable nature of the revolutionary regime. The French rulers could not and would not be satisfied with the Rhine frontier:

> Could one really expect as much from cowardly and treacherous tyrants, who can find personal security only in a general orgy of chaos and destruction; who advance their despicable cause with fire and sword, plunder and destruction, high treason and bribery; who do not respect any kind of law, whether divine, human, natural or international; who do not hesitate to break the most sacred treaties and to overthrow the happiest and most legitimate constitutions, in order to deprive their subjects—the slaves of freedom and equality—of any opportunity to make comparisons to the disadvantage of their miserable interim republic.[12]

To seek to appease such men by sacrificing the Rhineland was an utterly fatuous policy. Men must accept the stark fact that war would and must continue until revolutionary France suffered total defeat; then there would be no cession of the Rhineland and consequently no need for secularization.

2. If one assumed, however, the inevitability of the loss of the Rhineland, the question must still be asked: Why compensate the dispossessed secular princes? International law did not provide for the compensation of the victims of territorial transfers at the expense of innocent third parties; the traditional rule was that such victims were simply out of luck. Why should this rule be breached in the present case? It was true that the French had demanded compensation for their victims, presumably to create vested interests in support of the newly established *status quo*. But should Germany revolutionize her territorial and constitutional structure just to satisfy her hereditary enemy?[13]

3. Even if the compensation principle were accepted, it was most unjust to turn it against the ecclesiastical states and make them bear the sole brunt of Germany's losses. The arguments advanced in behalf of such a course were either fallacious, or hypocritical, or both. The bishops were not responsible for the war, however incautious their attitude to the *émigrés* before 1792; was it not notorious that the

[12] Fabritius, *Über den Werth*, II, 17-18.
[13] Ibid., pp. 23-30.

war had been a Jacobin war of aggression?[14] The bishops had faithfully voted supplies for the war at the Regensburg *Reichstag,* whereas some of their present spoliators (most notably Prussia) had shamefully neglected their duties to the empire.[15] The notion that the ecclesiastical states were centers of obscurantism ignored the progress which true *Aufklärung*—not, of course, *Aufklärung* of the Radical and subversive type—had made in most of these states during the last generation. The argument that the combination of priestly and worldly power was obsolete "because we are no longer, like the men of the Middle Ages, barbarians,"[16] was fallacious; the Jacobins and their German supporters were in fact the worst barbarians known in the history of Europe.

4. Least convincing of all was the argument that the title of the ecclesiastical states rested upon less secure foundations than that of the secular princes. Their feudal ties to the emperor were not different in character from those of secular princes, while their performance of their vassalic duties compared very favorably with that of their secular rivals. The much-cited new spirit of *Aufklärung,* with its stress upon the idea that government must express the will of the people rather than the whims of the ruler, was far more damaging to hereditary monarchs than to elective bishops. Had not the thinkers of the *Aufklärung* exposed the absurd character of divine-right hereditary monarchy as a blasphemy against God and a system which left good government to the vagaries of biological accident? The champions of the ecclesiastical states asserted that the sovereignty of the people was better approximated under the mitre than under the crown, since the people in the ecclesiastical states could be said to have delegated their elective power to the cathedral chapters—to be sure, a legal fiction, but at least one more convincing than the contention of the champions of monarchical government that acquiescence in established monarchy was tantamount to approval by the people.[17]

5. The defenders of the ecclesiastical states complained bitterly that all secularization proposals bartered away the population of these states in total disregard of human dignity:

Are the people of Würzburg, Bamberg, Fulda, and Münster less free and independent than the people of Hessen, Hannover, or

[14] Ibid., Ch. 5.   [15] Ibid., Ch. 4.
[16] Ibid., p. 65.
[17] Ibid., pp. 45-64. On this entire topic see the anonymous pamphlet *Ueber die geistlichen Staaten in Deutschland und die vorgebliche Notwendigkeit ihrer Säkularisation* (Deutschland, 1798).

Brunswick? . . . Are they simply a herd of cattle? Are the ecclesiastical states nothing more than pieces of landed property (*Meyerhöfe*) of which one may dispose at pleasure, by exchange, sale, or division, when, as, and to whom one pleases?[18]

6. Opponents of secularization pointed out that its strongest advocate was the revolutionary government of France—a fact which should serve as a warning to all patriotic Germans. Why was France so interested in secularization? Partly to turn German against German and further weaken the tottering political structure of the Holy Roman Empire. No single measure was more calculated to arouse suspicion, envy, and distrust throughout the country. A second reason was that France had deliberately chosen to ally itself with all disreputable elements in Germany: rapacious princes eager for aggrandizement; Protestants delighted at the prospect of eliminating long-standing Catholic rivals; lapsed Catholics "who continue to profess Jesus with their tongues, but have repudiated Him in their hearts"; and the group of "propagandists, Jacobins, and Illuminati notable for their energy, audacity, and wickedness."[19] The patriarchal *Kleinstaaterei* exemplified by the ecclesiastical states stood in the way of the malevolent designs of all these groups:

Each of these people [standing under ecclesiastical rule], however small (*Völker und Völckchen*), has its own government, its own capital, its own courts; each has its own pride, its Catholic religion, and its traditional pattern of society. Its citizens, living within their narrowly circumscribed customary sphere, are far happier than the millions of subjects of a big monarchy; a type of government where even the most conscientious of monarchs, armed with the best intentions in the world, is scarcely able to view the whole, much less to examine specific problems, to track down all abuses to their source, and to alleviate misery no matter how far removed from public attention. It is not surprising that the Jacobins are bent upon the destruction of this beautiful group of small, quiet, contented and happy peoples.[20]

7. Many pamphleteers also warned the princes that their reputation would suffer severe damage if they expanded at the expense of their weaker ecclesiastical neighbors. The criticism directed against divine-right monarchy had already placed princes upon the defensive:

[18] Fabritius, *Über den Werth*, II, 109-10.
[19] Ibid., pp. xv-xvi.   [20] Ibid., p. xi.

Participation in the process of secularization will give a final blow to their reputation. Will it not demonstrate that *nothing* is sacred to Germany's princes: neither the rights of their fellow-*Stände,* nor their defenselessness, nor the fact that the property of these states is devoted to God and applied primarily to works of charity.[21]

The felony of the princes was compounded by the fact that many of them had specifically promised to uphold the ecclesiastical states in the past, and were now piling perjury on top of piracy. Emperor Francis II had sworn in his electoral capitulation of 1792 to give his protection to "the Church, the Empire, the *Stände* and all their legitimate rights." This general pledge had been made specific in paragraph 2 of Article I: "We make a special promise to protect archbishops and bishops in the boundaries of their existing dioceses, as well as all their metropolitan and diocesan rights."[22] Another highly placed offender, King Frederick William II of Prussia, had emphatically repudiated the idea of secularization as recently as Feb. 22, 1794, in a communication to the Franconian *Kreisversammlung:*

> His Majesty has never contemplated securing for himself any kind of compensation at the expense of the Empire, whose constitution he holds sacred (*heilig*) and for whose preservation, as is well known, he has made frequent sacrifices in the past. His Majesty will remain faithful to these sentiments in the future and will do his utmost to preserve the integrity of the Imperial constitution and territory, and the rights and property of each of the *Stände,* whether ecclesiastical or secular.[23]

It was hypocritical, to say the least, for the king, shortly after making this declaration, to enter into negotiations with the French with a view to acquiring ecclesiastical booty for himself.

8. There were many laments about the catastrophic consequences which must inevitably attend the secularization process. The predictions included the decline of religion through the princely refusal to give the Church adequate revenues; the collapse of education through the closing of Catholic schools and universities; the dissipation of artistic treasure when philistine bureaucrats alienated monastic property with a view to purely fiscal considerations; and the impairment of morality as common thieves followed the example of their

[21] Ibid., p. 141.
[22] Quoted in Kästner, *Grosse Säkularisation,* p. 8.
[23] Ibid., p. 9.

governments by seizing what did not belong to them.[24] More accurate was the prediction of specific political disasters in the near future. The empire would not long survive the elimination of its most loyal *Stände*; other weak members of the empire—especially Free Cities and Imperial Knights—would inevitably accompany or follow the ecclesiastical states to the grave; Austria would be further humiliated, and the emperor forced to abdicate; and Germany would come to be dominated by a small number of militarist, despotic states allied to France.[25]

We have hitherto considered the objections levied against the secularization of the ecclesiastical states; a word remains to be said about the protests directed against the other feature of the secularization process, the expropriation of church lands within the individual territorial states. It would serve little purpose to quote here the endless complaints about sacrilege, robbery, et cetera, made in a manner familiar since the Reformation and heard again recently with special virulence in Josephine Austria. More interesting—though not, of course, more important at the time—were protests against the expropriations on constitutional grounds. An example is the statement made on May 31, 1800, by Baron von Kern, a prominent Bavarian aristocrat, at a meeting of the *Landschaftsverordnete* (the permanent committee of the *Landschaft*, which had survived long after the *Landtag* had ceased to play a significant role). Kern complained that the suppression of the monasteries, including as it did the cancellation of their *Landstandschaft,* involved the destruction of the traditional Bavarian constitution. It was significant, he noted, that this suppression was undertaken by an "alien" minister, Count Montgelas, and a group of "alien advisers" who lacked a solid stake in the country:

Our old constitution is to be replaced by an arbitrary despotism—a system which destroys but cannot construct, a system which is not represented by native officials but by birds of passage and parvenu unpropertied spinners of projects (*Projektenmacher*). Our immediate objective must be the confirmation by the prince of the old *ständische* liberties as part of the traditional ceremony of homage (*Erbhuldigung*). This is not a matter of going back to old forms—under which incidentally, prince, *Stände* and subjects were far happier, united and prosperous than they are likely to be under any

[24] Anonymous, *Wie wird es im säkularisierten Teutschland gehen?* (n.p., 1803).
[25] Anonymous, *Die Folgen der Säcularisation. Cuique suum* (Germanien, 1801).

new dispensation—but rather a matter of maintaining an existing constitution of acknowledged excellence.[26]

Kern believed that the survival of the traditional constitution in Bavaria required the survival of the monasteries, even as it was argued by others on the national level that the ecclesiastical states and the imperial constitution stood and fell together. Both arguments were confirmed by events, but neither was able to save the anachronistic constitution—whether of Bavaria or the Holy Roman Empire—that it was designed to defend.

These, then, were the arguments advanced by the last-ditch defenders of the ecclesiastical states upon the eve of their secularization. A few Catholic pamphleteers, recognizing the impossibility of preventing secularization per se, strove for the lesser objective of minimizing the scope of the secularizations. A prominent spokesman for this moderate position was Josef von Ullheimer, a pamphleteer writing in 1798 under the pen name of Riphelius von Solemel.[27] While denouncing secularization as unjust in principle and avaricious in motive, Solemel nonetheless worked out a specific plan under which the three ecclesiastical electorates would be preserved in a somewhat diminished form, and the compensation principle applied honestly instead of serving as a cloak for sheer aggrandizement.

Solemel's flexible approach to the secularization question and his specific plans for distributing an inevitable burden aroused the anger of both rapacious princes bent upon maximum aggrandizement and of defenders of the ecclesiastical states still convinced that the *status quo* could be saved. The latter group accused Solemel of having whetted the princely appetites by his proposals in the first place, and of being a bad Catholic because he was willing to contemplate *some* secularization. Solemel replied that his entire position was maliciously misunderstood by his critics. He had reluctantly developed his moderate secularization project only after the *Reichsfriedensdeputation*

[26] Anton Freiherr von Ow, "Streiflichter zur Geschichte der Säkularisation in Bayern," *Zeitschr. f. bayerische Landesgeschichte*, IV (1931), 187-206. The quotation is from pp. 189-90.

[27] Riphelius von Solemel, *Auch Ein Entschädigungsplan an den Friedens-Kongress zu Rastadt* (n.p., 1798). Ullheimer (1747-1810) was a prominent professor of law (in his native Bamberg) 1772, *Regierungsrath* 1776, and judge at the *Reichskammergericht* at Wetzlar 1789 (as nominee of the Franconian Kreis). His position obviously required the maintenance of anonymity. See *ADB*, XXXIX (1895), 189. A plan similar to Ullheimer's was presented several years later by a high official of the Würzburg government, von Seyffert: *Versuch einer doctrinellen Auslegung des 7. Friedensartikels von Lunéville* (Germanien, 1801).

at Rastatt had accepted the principle that secular princes should be compensated with ecclesiastical lands (April 5, 1798); his purpose was to preserve as many ecclesiastical states as possible, and to minimize any major alteration in Germany's constitution. The charge that he was a bad Catholic was beneath contempt, for several Popes themselves had bowed to historical necessity and acquiesced in secularizations which they could not prevent. He could not be expected to be more Catholic than the Pope, and Catholics would act in a suicidal manner if they made no attempt to prevent the catastrophic suppression of *all* ecclesiastical states by the timely—albeit reluctant—abandonment of *some*.[28]

THE EFFECT OF THE SECULARIZATIONS

The dire lamentations of clerical pamphleteers that the *Reichsdeputationshauptschluss* would prove disastrous to German Catholicism was completely belied by subsequent events. The secularizations proved in fact a singular and generally unexpected blessing to the religious life of Germany, for they broke the aristocratic stranglehold which had paralyzed German Catholicism for centuries. Every German see had been filled by a blue-blooded aristocrat in 1803, and most bishops had been attracted by the temporal prestige rather than the spiritual obligations of their office. Cathedral chapters had for centuries been a form of outdoor relief for the younger sons of the Catholic aristocracy; nunneries, a respectable refuge for unmarriageable daughters. We have seen that the mode of life of bishop-princes did not differ significantly from that of their secular neighbors, always excepting the formal maintenance of celibacy. Many bishops had striven to secure a reputation for *Aufklärung* even if this meant conflict with their obscurantist (or merely faithful Catholic) clergy.

This situation changed entirely after 1803. It is said that not a single Catholic nobleman took holy orders in the decade 1803-13, and the consequent democratization of the higher Catholic clergy was to prove an enormous source of strength to the Church throughout the tribulations of the next generations. The class struggle within the Church which had bedeviled its life before 1803—especially when questions of class became intertwined with questions of ideology, as "superstitious" rural priests of peasant origin confronted "enlightened" urban canons from aristocratic families—became largely a matter of the past. Bishops were no longer distracted from religious concerns by governmental ob-

[28] Solemel replied to his critics in a thirteen-page appendix to the second edition of his book.

ligations; cathedral canons henceforth became an ecclesiastical elite instead of a nobiliar club. These beneficent changes did not, of course, all come at once, for the secularizations did not remove existing ecclesiastical personnel; but they were all implicit in the Napoleonic Revolution of 1803.

While the long-run effects of this revolution were certainly beneficial to Catholicism, some of its short-run effects proved as serious as had been predicted by the defenders of the ecclesiastical states. The mild, patriarchal government of traditionalist bishops was replaced by the harsh and despotic government of absolute princes bent upon power and modernization. The result was heavy taxes, rational administration, universal conscription, and other characteristic, but frequently unpopular, aspects of modernity. A systematic pattern of Erastianism was imposed upon the Church, not necessarily an improvement over the miscellaneous vested interests—ranging from the local nobility to the distant Pope—which had dominated ecclesiastical appointments in the past. The new secular rulers were usually downright stingy in the performance of their legal duty of financing maintenance of cathedrals, diocesan seminaries, and church-conducted schools and charities. The confiscation of monastic property inevitably led to much injustice to individuals; anticlerical fanaticism, to the vandalism of priceless treasures of art. Most accurate of all was the prediction that the elimination of bishops and abbots would set a precedent for the destruction of all other weak members of the German polity.

The Mediatization of the Imperial Knights

THE CONDITION OF THE REICHSRITTERSCHAFT

BEFORE THE STORM[29]

The sheltered world of the Holy Roman Empire had permitted the survival into the nineteenth century of the picturesque but anachronistic order of Free Imperial Knights. The order consisted of approximately 350 families, who exercised authority over some 1,500 minute

[29] The best surveys of the condition of the *Reichsritterschaft* in the late eighteenth century are J. J. Moser, *Neueste Geschichte der unmittelbaren Reichsritterschaft unter den Kaysern Matthias, Ferdinand II, Ferdinand III, Leopold, Joseph I und Joseph II* (1776), an encyclopedic contemporary account; Karl Freiherr Roth von Schreckenstein, *Geschichte der ehemaligen Reichsritterschaft in Schwaben, Franken und am Rheinstrome* (2 vols., Tübingen, 1859-71), a moderate and thorough attempt at rehabilitation; Peter Schnapp, "Die Reichsritterschaft," *Deutsche Geschichtsblätter*, xiv (1913), 157-94, 215-25, a popular account; Heinrich Müller, *Der letzte Kampf der Reichsritterschaft um ihre Selbstständigkeit 1790-1815* (Berlin, 1910), Ch. 1, an admirably balanced sur-

territories (often but single villages) with a total population of about 350,000 subjects. The knights were frequently indistinguishable from ordinary landlords in their general mode of life, but they differed in their specific attribute of being immediate to the emperor, i.e., they were not subordinated to any territorial prince. In legal status they were technically the equal of princes, except for the important fact that they were not represented, either individually or collectively, at the Regensburg *Reichstag*. They did, however, possess the usual "sovereign rights" of princes in such matters as appointing officials, levying taxes, conscripting troops, decreeing capital punishment in their courts, and regulating economic life. Imperial Knights could marry into princely families because they possessed *Ebenbürtigkeit*; their judicial disputes could not be settled on a level lower than that of the Imperial Courts; and they naturally possessed immunity from military service as well as complete freedom as regards education and choice of career (if they decided to leave the family estate). In these respects they differed sharply from much of Germany's territorial nobility; the Prussian Junkers, to give only one example, were rigidly held to military service and their education was closely regulated by the government.

The knightly order was a strictly regional phenomenon limited to Southern and Western Germany—a fact which contributed to this region's territorial parcellation, but also to its still strong "imperial consciousness" (*Reichsbewusstsein*). The knights possessed an elaborate organizational structure divided into three "circles" (*Kreise*)— Swabia, Franconia, and the Rhineland—which were in turn subdivided into fourteen cantons. Each canton was headed by a *Direktorium* (governing body) consisting of a *Ritterhauptmann* (elected for life) and several *Ritterräte* (elected for fixed terms); the actual administrative work was performed by a number of *Konsulenten* (legal experts) who were not usually themselves knights but naturally identified themselves with their employers. The knightly organization culminated in a *Generaldirektorium* which watched vigilantly over the

---

vey; and the superb summary of Hanns Hubert Hofmann, *Adelige Herrschaft und souveräner Staat. Studien über Staat und Gesellschaft in Franken und Bayern im 18. und 19. Jahrhundert* (Munich, 1962), pp. 95-107. Three samples of many local accounts (often apologetic in character) are J. G. Weiss, "Die Reichsritterschaft am Ende des alten Reiches," *Zeitschr. für die Geschichte des Oberrheins* N.F., VIII (1893), 289-311; Eberhard Freiherr von Wächter, "Die letzten Jahre der deutschen Reichsritterschaft," *Württ. Vjh. für Landesgeschichte*, XL (1935), 243-89; and Karl Siegfried Bader, "Zur Lage und Haltung des schwäbischen Adels am Ende des alten Reichs," *Ztschr. für württ. Landesgeschichte*, V (1941), 335-89.

interests of the order as a whole. To prevent any alienation of estates it could exercise the *jus retractus*, i.e., the right to repurchase within three years, at the original price, any knightly estate sold to a nonknight. To prevent the loss of revenue it regularly exercised the *jus collectandi*, i.e., the right to collect the taxes owed by knights to their order, even from alienated knightly estates. Its main function was, however, to prevent—by protest, propaganda, or lawsuit—any impairment of the status of immediacy which was the order's special pride and glory.

The demand of the thinkers of the *Aufklärung* for equality, self-government, and rational units of administration inevitably placed the knights on the defensive in eighteenth-century Germany. The behavior of many knights made matters easy for their critics. Too often their life of idleness and comparative luxury was unaccompanied by any constructive function. The knights' desire to maintain their relative socio-economic position in a Germany gradually becoming more prosperous necessitated fleecing subjects through heavy taxes (the so-called *Rittersteuer*), exploiting manorial rights (corvées, banalities, and dues) and imposing unusually severe judicial fines. There were, of course, many knights who dispensed a benevolent patriarchal rule, but cases of exploitation—often combined with neglect of education and welfare and the appointment of tyrannical and servile police officials—received far more publicity. It must be added that the knightly territories, being rural, inevitably remained backward, and in any case they were far too small for their economies to be stimulated effectively by mercantilist policies.[30]

Finally, the knights were indelibly linked with the Holy Roman Empire, which was not only responsible for their survival but was in turn buttressed by their special loyalty. The emperor and the knights were natural allies against the princes, whose thirst for full sovereignty required the incorporation of knightly territories and the emancipation from what little survived of imperial authority. The knightly territories were the favorite recruiting ground of the Habsburg armies. Many knights entered imperial service as diplomats, soldiers, or bureaucrats. The clerical sons of Catholic knights constituted a significant part of the ruling group of the ecclesiastical states, and

---

[30] The validity of many of the charges against the *Reichsritterschaft* is admitted by its ablest apologist, Christoph Ludwig Pfeiffer, himself a *Konsulent* and close friend of Carl August Freiherr von Gemmingen, *Direktor* of the canton Odenwald. See Pfeiffer's *Der Reichscavalier auf seinem Reichsohnmittelbaren Gebiet; nach beider Prärogativen, Gerechtsamen, Freiheiten und Obliegenheiten summarisch abgebildet* (Nürnberg and Altdorf, 1787).

reinforced the "imperial loyalty" which differentiated the ecclesiastical states from most of their secular neighbors. These considerations show that there was the closest affinity of interest between the empire, the ecclesiastical states, and the imperial knights; it is not surprising that they all collapsed together in the course of the Napoleonic Revolution in Germany.

THE CONFLICT BETWEEN THE REICHSRITTER AND THE PRUSSIAN-FRANCONIAN GOVERNMENT

The war of 1792 brought severe difficulties to the *Reichsritterschaft*, whose territories were located in that part of Germany easily penetrated by the French armies. While the knights of the Rhineland and Swabia suffered the requisitions of war, a still worse fate befell the Franconian knights who lived in the vicinity of the Prussian duchies of Bayreuth-Ansbach. After 1795 they had the advantage, to be sure, of enjoying neutrality because they lay north of the "demarcation line" which Prussia had negotiated at Basel; but they only exchanged the occasional hardships of war for the systematic attempt of the Prussian government, already begun in 1792, to degrade them from a position of imperial immediacy to one of subjection to the Prussian crown. This process of mediatization in the late 1790's anticipated the fate of all imperial knights in the years 1802 to 1806, and many contemporary observers understood the importance of the precedent which was being created. The action of the Prussian government, and the feeble defensive measures undertaken by the knights, provoked much public interest and occasioned a good deal of *Publizistik* on behalf of the threatened order.[31]

The duchies of Ansbach and Bayreuth, long ruled by a collateral line of the House of Hohenzollern, passed to the Brandenburg line in 1791. The political structure of these two South German areas had not advanced to the stage of centralized absolutism achieved by Branden-

[31] The most valuable contemporary source is the anonymous *Neue Vertheidigung der reichsritterschaftlichen Freyheit und Unmittelbarkeit gegen die neuesten Angriffe der Königlichen Regierung zu Ansbach und Bayreuth* (Nürnberg, 1803). Henceforth cited as *Neue Vertheidigung*. It prints all key documents, including the official Prussian 220-page *Öffentliche Erklärung wegen der Brandenburgischen Insassen in den Fränkischen Fürstenthümern, die sich zur Reichsritterschaft halten*, originally published in July 1796. The most valuable secondary literature is Fritz Hartung, *Hardenberg und die preussische Verwaltung in Ansbach-Bayreuth* (Tübingen, 1906); Karl Süssheim, *Preussens Politik in Ansbach-Bayreuth 1791-1806* (Leipzig, 1802); Hans Haussherr, *Hardenberg. Eine politische Biographie 1750-1800* (Cologne, 1963), Chs. 6-8; and, above all, H. H. Hofmann, *Adelige Herrschaft und souveräner Staat*, pp. 161-209 and the full bibliographical discussion on pp. 18-23.

burg under her great kings; the consequent disparity made it inevitable that the Berlin government should seek to impose its "superior" type of administration upon its "backward," chaotic, and still "feudal" South German acquisitions. King Frederick William II found a capable instrument for this work in the person of Count Karl Hardenberg (1750-1822), the later reformer of the Prussian state. Hardenberg was an ardent champion of "enlightened absolutism." An aristocrat himself, he was certainly not opposed to the principle of aristocracy; he accepted in fact the traditional system under which the aristocracy performed many governmental functions, but he insisted that such functions must be conceived as delegated, not inherent, and that they must be supervised by the government. Hardenberg believed in the centralized state with clear-cut frontiers in which the king alone was sovereign; he was irreconcilably opposed to any surviving *imperium in imperio*.

These principles were bound to lead to a sharp conflict between the Prussian territories; the complicated web of Franconian legal relation- the estates of the *Reichsritter* were frequently enclaves within Prussian territories; the complicated web of Franconian legal relationships was in fact incompatible with the imperatives of modern administration. Jurisdiction in one and the same village was frequently divided between the Prussian government and some imperial knight; many knights stood in a position of feudal vassalage toward the Prussian king—a position which certainly complicated their relationship as legal equals in their common condition of imperial immediacy. The precise meaning of legal vassalage was a lawyers' nightmare; the Prussian government was certainly not averse to stretching it to the point of claiming that it involved a measure of political subordination. It pursued its program of aggression against the Franconian knights on the plea that it was but "revindicating" (*Revindikation*) rights which the weakness of preceding rulers had permitted to fall into desuetude.

The campaign against the knights began when Prussian troops nailed copies of Frederick William's *Regierungsantrittspatent* (proclamation of accession) of Jan. 5, 1792, to public buildings not only in Bayreuth-Ansbach proper, but in several neighboring knightly territories as well—territories where Prussia's authority was uncertain at best, and in fact had not been actively exercised for centuries. The troops entered these territories accompanied by the loud beating of drums and, needless to say, without permission of the imperial knights involved. Many of these proclamations were torn down by enraged villagers soon after the departure of the Prussians, but this invariably led to the immediate return of the troops. They not only nailed up the proclamation anew, but also arrested the guilty parties for the crime of *lèse majesté*, hauled them off to Prussian jails, imposed severe fines, and finally released them with a stern warning that a new offense would be punished more severely, perhaps even with death for rebellion (*Leibes-und Lebensstrafe*). The knights were stunned by this unexpected invasion and naturally protested to the king and the assembly of the Franconian *Kreis*. They won a temporary success in securing a quasi apology from Frederick William in a manifesto dated March 17, 1792. Prussia then stood on the verge of the war of 1792, and its government did not want to complicate its relationship with its new Austrian ally by attacking the knights. The knights were lulled into a quite unjustified sense of security by the Prussian concession, and believed—what they obviously wanted to believe—that the Prussian action had been the work of hotheaded, uninstructed junior officials. They were further reassured by the gracious words which the king addressed to various knightly delegations during his visit to the duchies in the summer of 1792.

After the king's departure, however, his ministers resumed the policy of harassment against the knightly territories. They applied the much-hated Prussian conscription system in some disputed territories; imposed the duty to pursue Prussian deserters upon all neighboring knights (even though the deserters were often men illegally conscripted who only sought refuge with their friends and neighbors); forced artisans living in knightly territories to join Prussian guilds after payment of heavy initiation fees; and applied some Prussian taxes even as they prohibited customary dues to the cantonal organizations of the knights. The Prussian government insisted that all disputes on these points must be tried in Prussian courts, and the knights had reason to compare these with the notorious Chambers of Reunion of Louis XIV. The Prussian government contended sanctimoniously that it was only "revindicating" its legal rights in a perfectly legal manner; the mask was finally thrown off, however, when open aggression replaced piecemeal encroachment with a declaration of Oct. 1, 1795. This stated that all Franconian knightly estates would henceforth be deemed *landsässig* in the duchies, i.e., their owners would be treated as subjects of the king of Prussia despite their contrary claim to imperial immediacy. This declaration stood in flat contradiction to the above-mentioned manifesto of March 17, 1792, issued on the eve of war; Prussia had meanwhile made peace with France and no longer needed to defer to Austria.

The knights vigorously protested against the new policy to Hardenberg, and they threatened to appeal directly to the emperor if their just grievances remained unredressed. Such an appeal, they argued in rather pathetic language, would be "a necessity imposed upon us by the simple duty of self-preservation. It is also required by our unshakable loyalty to the German Imperial constitution; as faithful Germans we would rather be buried under its ruins than be disloyal to it"[32] by accepting the loss of the status of immediacy. Hardenberg did not deign to honor this protest with a reply. Instead he commissioned a professor of law at Jena, Theodor Kretschmann, to write a detailed defense of Prussian claims, which was published in July of 1796.[33] The imposition of Prussian conscription, taxation, and justice upon the territories of the defenseless knights was intensified, and they and their subjects were finally compelled to swear an oath of fidelity to the Prussian king. Nonjurors were punished by imprisonment, confiscation, and the quartering of troops. Most knights, when subjected to this pressure, forgot their rhetoric about dying under the ruins of the empire and acquiesced sullenly in their new status as Prussian subjects. Hardenberg had, incidentally, no desire to carry matters to extremes; he permitted the knights to swear a conditional oath of allegiance with the reservation that "this enforced oath cannot and will not alter our relationship to Emperor, Empire, and the corporation of the *Ritterschaft*, or deprive us of any of our rights as immediate princes"[34]—a reservation which negated the substance of the oath but did not alter its humiliating character.

Hardenberg could not prevent the knights from appealing, meanwhile, to everybody willing to listen to their grievances: the emperor, the Arch-Chancellor, and the Franconian *Kreis*. All offered sympathy and condemned the illegal actions of the Prussians, sometimes in strong language; none, however, was able to provide a remedy. The fundamental issue was expressed in a *Kreisschluss* (resolution) of the Franconian *Kreis* in very trenchant language on February 27, 1797:

> The Franconian *Kreis* is deeply concerned about the disintegrative consequences which must result from the utterly unprecedented conduct of the Prussian government. If the powerful can arrogate to themselves the right of being both party and judge in their con-

---

[32] *Neue Vertheidigung*, p. 158.
[33] This is the *Öffentliche Erklärung* already cited in footnote 31.
[34] *Neue Vertheidigung*, p. 170.

troversies with the weak; if they can break through the hitherto inviolable barriers created by the basic laws of the Empire, by peace treaties purchased at the price of torrents of blood, and by sacred contractual obligations voluntarily assumed; if they can turn their back upon the courts established by our constitution, and arbitrarily use their superior strength to deprive their neighbors of age-old rights: if all this goes unpunished, then Germany will no longer be governed in accordance with law and justice; then all social ties (*staatsgesellschaftliche Bande*) will be dissolved all at once; then the entire Imperial constitution will not only be shaken but indeed destroyed in its very foundations.[35]

With protests unavailing, with calls for support evoking only expressions of platonic sympathy, the knights resorted to the obsolete court machinery of the empire. The *Ritterkreisdirektorium* of Franconia brought suit against the Prussian government in the Viennese *Reichshofrath* in the autumn of 1796. The supporting brief argued that Prussia's conduct was contrary to natural law, which protected property against violence; that it violated such basic imperial laws as the *Landfriede* of 1548 and the *Exekutionsordnung* of 1555; the Peace of Westphalia, safeguarding all princes in their possessions; Article 21 of the Imperial Electoral Capitulation of 1792, requiring the emperor to protect the existing rights of all *Stände*; and innumerable specific laws and precedents supporting the rights of the *Ritterschaft*, such as a decree of Emperor Ferdinand I of 1559. The *Ritterkreisdirektorium* reinforced these positive contentions by effective ridicule of the claims advanced by the hired Professor Theodor Kretschmann in his official brief for the Prussian government.[36]

A statement of the detailed legal contentions advanced and refuted is not necessary in order to understand the pathetic position of the Imperial Knights. Their enemy advanced with the sword while they were forced to rely upon the less-than-mighty pen; their legal and Conservative arguments—however impressive and even irrefutable— did not exert the slightest influence upon the course of events. The *Direktorium* observed that Kretschmann supported the Prussian case by precedents drawn from the reign of Albert Achilles (1469-76), as if the intervening three hundred years were not sufficient to establish prescriptive rights; but, quite apart from this fact, Kretschmann got

[35] Ibid., p. 166.
[36] Ibid., Ch. 10, "Eröffnung der gerichtlichen Verhandlung an beiden höchsten Reichsgerichten."

much of his history wrong or lacked the skill (or good will) to interpret historical precedents properly.[37]

As was to be expected, the *Reichshofrath* decided in favor of the knights against the Prussian government. The emperor thereupon issued a *Höchstrichterliches Mandat* (decree implementing a judicial decision) on May 22, 1797, ordering the king of Prussia to cease and desist from his illegal course, and threatening stern but unspecified punishment in case of defiance. The Prussian agent attached to the *Reichshofrath* significantly refused to accept a copy of this *Mandat* because it was insulting to his master, and it thereupon had to be delivered by mail. King Frederick William II had, of course, no intention of abiding by the decision of the *Reichshofrath*; he openly defied it in a royal patent issued on June 12, 1797, which warned all affected persons against obeying its terms. The total paralysis of imperial institutions could not have been demonstrated more clearly: the refusal of the Prussian government to accept the decision of the *Reichshofrath*, and the inability of the emperor and the *Reichstag* to enforce it, showed that there was no judicial remedy in the empire when the weak were harassed by the strong.

The Franconian *Ritterschaft* had no choice but to acquiesce under protest to Prussian rule. Its members soon found that their new status was not without its advantages, as Prussia was able, for example, to maintain the neutrality of Franconia in the War of the Second Coalition. They also appreciated the fact that the Prussian king was entirely willing to give them a highly privileged status within his monarchy, once the burning question of sovereignty had been settled in his favor. A *Publikandum* (declaration) of July 12, 1796—issued at the time when Prussian troops were occupying all knightly territories—made far-reaching promises to all knights willing to take the new oath of allegiance. They were encouraged to free themselves from all residual duties of vassalage by petitioning for the "alodification" of their estates through the payment of a small fee. The Crown offered to round out their estates and terminate overlapping jurisdictions by exchanging parcels of land. They were encouraged to continue to exercise all their governmental functions—holding courts, appointing police officials, collecting taxes, and recruiting soldiers—as delegates of the Prussian king, and it was understood that the former knightly territories would serve as separate units of Prussian local administration. They were promised *Landstandschaft* in the *Stände* bodies of the

[37] Ibid., Pt. II: "Widerlegung der Kgl. Preuss. Staatsschrift," 74-95.

duchies, though the foreseeable impotence of the *Stände* made this an honor rather than a source of political power. They were, finally, promised the establishment of a credit institute which would provide needy knights with loans at low rates of interest by making the *Ritterschaft* collectively responsible for repayment—a type of financing which had proved very advantageous to the Junkers of the East.[38]

Clearly the Prussian monarchy offered the knights a very tolerable existence if only they would be willing to swallow their pride and their hankering after the obsolete status of imperial immediacy. Some champions of the knights insisted, however, that their order lost not only honor but cold cash through their degradation from Free Knight to Prussian subject. They argued with some substance, but also much exaggeration, that the loss of immediate status led to a catastrophic fall in the value of knightly estates. The value of the latter had usually been capitalized at 2 1/2% or 3%, whereas ordinary aristocratic estates (*landsässige Güter*) were capitalized at 4 to 7%.

> The knightly estate which cost 600,000 florins in the condition of immediacy is reduced in value—the moment it becomes *landsässig*—to 200,000 or at the most 300,000 florins. The knightly family which had acquired the estate through purchase, exchange, or inheritance at the former value did so in the confidence that the law and the constitution of the Empire would remain intact; the moment it is forced to accept the *Landsassiat* it loses not only the honorable, but also lucrative, prerogatives of its sovereignty (*Landesherrlichkeit*) but also half, or perhaps even two-thirds, of the value of its inheritance, which is usually the primary (and in many cases the sole) source of its livelihood.[39]

This kind of injustice required an urgent remedy; the remedy suggested, in the words of a knightly pamphleteer in 1803, was a return to "a condition in which the sanctity of property was again held in honor; in which the small were again protected against the great; thus restoring to our Fatherland its blessed former prosperity, happiness, contentment, and the tranquillity of which it has been too long deprived."[40] The pamphleteer did not, unfortunately, specify how Germany *could* return to its earlier condition. On the contrary, the subjection of the Franconian knights by Prussia established a precedent

---

[38] For the *Publikandum* of July 12, 1796, addressed to "allen ritterschaftlichen Insassen, die ihren Huldigungseid ablegen" see H. H. Hofmann, *Adelige Herrschaft*, pp. 181ff. and 189ff.

[39] *Neue Vertheidigung*, pp. XXXII-III.

[40] Ibid., p. XXXIV.

for the complete mediatization of the order which other states—especially Bavaria—were only too eager to follow. However, these states were unlike Prussia, too weak to embark upon a program of spoliation on their own; they required and received the permission of Napoleon before they could round out their territories at the expense of the Imperial Knights.

THE DEMISE OF THE IMPERIAL KNIGHTS

The future position of the *Ritterschaft,* thrown into question by Prussia's ruthless mediatizations in 1796, became a subject for general discussion at the Congress of Rastatt. This congress agreed, it will be recalled, to the secularization of the ecclesiastical states and the cession of the Left bank of the Rhine to France. Both decisions had very adverse effects upon the *Ritterschaft.* Knightly families were heavily represented among the cathedral canons now to be suppressed, and there was no blinking the fact that the cavalier elimination of an entire category of "sovereign" states boded ill for the survival of the *Reichs-ritterschaft,* whose position was weaker than that of the ecclesiastical states because it was unrepresented at the Regensburg *Reichstag.* The cession of the Rhineland left many knightly territories within the borders of the newly enlarged France, and raised the issue whether the affected knights were entitled—like other dispossessed Left Rhenish secular princes—to compensation on the Right bank. This issue involved very fundamental questions concerning the nature of the *Ritterschaft* and inevitably led to bitter divisions within that body. Many Left Rhenish knights despaired of ever receiving compensation for their losses, or did not wish to claim compensation from their dispossessed ecclesiastical brethren (the only possible source); they therefore favored a policy of accommodating the French and renouncing all claims to sovereignty, in the hope that the French would respect their economic position as landlords if they renounced all political pretensions. Others, vigorously supported by many Right Rhenish knights who feared the precedent of the renunciation of sovereignty, were resolved to defy the French at whatever economic sacrifice, and placed all their hopes upon Right Rhenish compensation. The members of the German peace delegation at Rastatt favored the former view because compensation for dispossessed knights would inevitably decrease compensation available for others; the French were also willing to accept the "nonsovereignty" solution, provided the affected knights agreed to become ordinary French citizens and to accept the abolition of all feudal rights without compensation. The

Reichsritter were understandably unhappy about these terms, which the peace delegation advised them to accept as the best attainable. Most knights were delighted when the congress was disrupted by the War of the Second Coalition before it could finish its business, and they hoped that the defeat of France would permit a return to the *status quo* of 1792.[41]

The question raised at Rastatt concerning the sovereign status of the knights showed that the survival of the order was in doubt; yet most of its members refused to read the handwriting on the wall. Several factors contributed to this blindness. The knights felt that they could rely upon the support of Emperor Francis II, who gave a gracious interview to the leader of the *Ritterschaft*, Karl Freiherr von Gemmingen, on April 22, 1801. They secured expressions of sympathy from several electors, including the increasingly influential Arch-Chancellor of the Empire, Dalberg (himself a Free Knight by birth). They took confidence in the fact that knights held prominent positions in the ministerial councils and diplomatic services of many German princes (for example, Stein in Prussia) and believed that their influence was strong enough to prevent their princes from attacking their order. (The knights blithely ignored the fact that Hardenberg was a Free Knight, and that Stein had remained silent in the crisis of 1796.) They were reassured by the fact that two prominent statesmen (Schulenburg-Kehnert of Prussia and Buol von Schauenstein of Austria) chose this time to apply for membership in the knightly order following the acquisition of knightly estates. Many knights also developed a touching faith in Napoleon, whose military outlook was supposed to make him especially appreciative of the historical ideals of the German knights; they seriously believed that the just-established Legion of Honor was modeled upon the German knighthood.[42]

The more realistic leaders, headed by Gemmingen, recognized, of course, that the *Ritterschaft* was endangered by the developing alliance between France and the South German states, states which since 1796 had longed to imitate Prussia's conduct toward the Franconian knights. They saw the urgent necessity of securing the constitutional

[41] Müller, *Der letzte Kampf*, Ch. 4. This entire section is based upon Müller's excellent archival study which exploits the records of the Regensburg *Sub-delegationskommission* of 1804-05 and the reports of the Austrian envoys Stadion and Hügel (both in Vienna); the reports of Thürheim, Bavarian *Generalkommissar* in Franconia, and Zentner, Bavarian *Referent* for *Reichsritter* affairs (both in Munich); the reports of the Ansbach-Bayreuth administration to Berlin; and the surviving archives of the *Ritterschaft*.

[42] Ibid., Ch. 5.

position of the knights through the introduction of a safeguarding clause (*salvatorische Klausel*) into the *Hauptschluss* being hammered out at Regensburg. Such a clause was opposed by Prussia as a reproach to its past conduct and by Bavaria as an obstacle to its future ambitions. Gemmingen had no illusions concerning the nature of the Regensburg proceedings. He emptied what was left of the knightly treasury and sent the money to his representative in Paris, a Danish *Kammerherr* by the name of von Wächter. The latter took the money to the foreign ministry and paid heavy bribes to Durand and St. Foy, Talleyrand's two principal advisers on German affairs. The knights got their money's worth when instructions were sent to Laforest, the French representative at Regensburg, that he should press for the inclusion of the safeguarding clause; the French wish had, of course, the force of law. The knights had some reason to rejoice at this diplomatic victory, the emptiness of which was not immediately apparent.[43]

Their joy was much diminished, however, by the simultaneous implementation of the principle of secularization, which deprived hundreds of knightly cathedral canons of their accustomed livelihood. It also raised complicated problems concerning feudal ties, which had already caused trouble at the time of the Franconian mediatizations in 1796. Many knights owed some kind of feudal obligation to the Franconian bishoprics now acquired by Bavaria, and Bavaria was certain to follow the Prussian example of squeezing every ounce of political advantage out of these obsolete feudal ties. This was made clear on Nov. 22, 1802 (three months before the formal enactment of the *Hauptschluss*) when Bavaria "jumped the gun" in occupying her ecclesiastical loot, and for good measure occupied knightly enclaves and adjoining territories as well. The Bavarian aggression was thinly disguised—exactly as had been the parallel Prussian aggression six and a half years earlier—by the plea that it constituted no more than the enforcement of vassalic obligations.[44]

The knights were stunned by the unexpected Bavarian action and bitterly divided on how to respond. A few decided upon voluntary submission in the hope of negotiating favorable terms for themselves. This step was first taken by a disreputable character, the former

[43] Ibid., pp. 100ff. A vivid account of the lobbying undertaken by the *Ritterschaft* at Regensburg is to be found in A. von Brauer, "Tagebuchaufzeichnungen eines Reichsritters zur Zeit des Reichsdeputationshauptschlusses," *Deutsche Revue*, XXXII (1907), 360-87, based upon the diary of Philipp Reinhard von Berstett, president of the Ortenau *Ritterschaft*.

[44] H. H. Hofmann, *Adelige Herrschaft*, pp. 219ff.

Weimar *Kammerpräsident* August von Kalb, whom his successor, Goethe, characterized as "a mediocre bureaucrat, a worse statesman, and a man abominable in his private conduct." Kalb and his brother had married into a Franconian knightly family and they hoped to remedy their bankrupt condition through a lawsuit against a brother-in-law concerning the control of several estates. They needed Bavarian support in their family disputes, and Bavaria did not scruple to offer this support in return for the Kalbs' agreeing to become Bavarian subjects. The discredited bankrupts thereupon informed the *Direktorium* of the *Ritterkanton* Steigenwald that they had withdrawn from the *Reichsritterschaft*.[45]

Their announcement was received with indignation by the canton, which immediately fired off a heated protest to the emperor (March 25, 1803), arguing that the Kalbs had no right to renounce their obligations unilaterally. Their action was "without precedent in the history of Germany, and must be punished not only by the well deserved contempt of public opinion, but by the operation of the law as well." The emperor submitted the question to the *Reichshofrath*, which hastened to declare the action of the Kalbs null and void because incompatible with their knightly obligations (May 16, 1803). The emperor followed up this decision with a patent addressed to all members of the Franconian knighthood:

> In view of the most dangerous consequences which the imitation of the conduct of the Kalb brothers would involve for our Imperial prerogatives and the entire constitution of the *Reichsritterschaft*, it is incumbent upon me to warn you, the members of our Franconian *Reichsritterschaft*, explicitly and *reichsväterlich*, against such conduct as contrary to all principles of honor and duty, and incompatible with the rights of the knightly order, the Imperial *privilegus*, and indeed our Imperial and knightly *juribus*. I command you, upon pain of our Imperial displeasure and the certainty of severe punishment, to scrupulously observe and fulfill all obligations owed to the knightly order and to Ourselves as your immediate sovereign (*Oberhaupt*).[46]

This imperial mandate, however cheering to the members of the

[45] On the Kalb case see pp. 223-24, which also contains the quotation from Goethe.

[46] Quoted in Freiherr L. von Stetten-Buchenbach, "Vom Ende der Reichsritterschaft," *Preussische Jahrbücher*, cxiii (1903), 482. The entire article gives a vivid account, based upon the family papers of the mediatized Stetten family, of how mediatization proceeded in a particular case.

Franconian *Direktorium*, proved but empty rhetoric. The Kalb brothers and the Bavarian government defied the decision of the *Reichshofrath*; the Bavarian ambassador to Vienna, Freiherr von Gravenreuth (himself a knight), observed coolly, "We must deprive the *Reichshofrath* of the desire to exhibit its own impotence."[47]

The Bavarian government placed Count Friedrich of Thürheim, an exceptionally able official, in charge of securing the submission of the Franconian knights by means of a policy which combined harassment with inducements. He invited sixteen prominent knights to meet with him at Bamberg on Nov. 15, 1803, and made it clear to them that refusal to appear would be punished by quartering expensive *Executionskommandos* (troops enforcing allegiance) on the estates of the recalcitrants. The assembled knights at first talked loudly about their duties to the emperor and the importance of their continued immediacy; but they soon yielded to Thürheim's pressure and accepted a statute for a new corporation, the *pfalzbayerische Ritterschaft in Franken*, whose members must withdraw from the old. The participants of the Bamberg meeting followed Thürheim's suggestion that they constitute themselves the provisional *Direktorium* of the new corporation. The specific rights which Bavaria guaranteed to the members of the new *Ritterschaft* followed closely those offered by Hardenberg to the knights of Prussian Franconia in 1796. These terms were so favorable, and the consequences of defiance in terms of Bavarian military occupation so terrible, that 76 out of 176 affected knights agreed to participate in the new corporation; 61 refused and 39 procrastinated.[48]

The question, "To submit or not to submit?" inevitably caused much soul-searching and even more recrimination among the knights. To submit meant open defiance of the specific injunctions of the emperor, and the abandonment of the immediate status which had for centuries formed the particular glory of the knighthood; to refuse submission, while required by every consideration of pride and honor, must immediately result in economic ruin and perhaps imprisonment. Many knights also had the feeling that submission was sooner or later inevitable, and they doubted that the Bavarian government would ever again offer terms as favorable. On the other hand, was it certain that Bavaria was strong enough to resist the anticipated imperial protest against her lawless conduct? Or might not Austria use the existing imperial machinery to force Bavaria to cease and desist, and restore

---

[47] Quoted by H. H. Hofmann, *Adelige Herrschaft*, p. 224.
[48] Ibid., pp. 225-30.

matters to the *status quo* of 1802? The knights who submitted now would look awfully foolish if there should be a restoration of the knightly order to its old immediacy.

The signs of the times were ambiguous concerning the probable future course of developments. It boded ill for the knighthood that the Bavarian action was imitated by several other governments—most notably Württemberg, Hessen, and Nassau—in the autumn of 1803. They pleaded that the Bavarian precedent left them no choice if they were to protect their interests in the anticipated general expropriation of the *Ritterschaft*, since possession was likely to prove nine points of the law. The course of events was remarkably similar in all knightly territories. Invading troops nailed placards advertising the new order to all prominent buildings; knightly officials were confirmed in their jobs but told to look to their new rulers for instructions; communications with members of the suppressed *Direktoria* of the various cantons were declared punishable. The knights invariably protested their victimization but acquiesced in what they could not prevent.[49]

The most famous protest was issued by a Free Knight serving as a Prussian *Kammerpräsident* in Münster, the future reformer Stein, whose ancestral estates were occupied by the Duke of Nassau in Dec. 1803. Stein protested in an open letter against the loss of a family property "demonstrably seven hundred years old." He said he would henceforth "refuse to visit a place where he would be surrounded by objects evoking bitter memories, and where everything would constantly remind him of the loss of his old independence and the clanking of his new chains." What made the loss especially galling was that "the sacrifice exacted was not serving any great, honorable purpose required by the common weal" but only the despotic rapacity of a petty Nassau duke. Stein realized that the suppression of the knightly territories had become inevitable, but he wished that their suppression should at least serve the interests of the German Fatherland rather than those of a contemptible duke:

> The cause of German independence and national defense will gain little from the incorporation of the knightly estates into the small principalities which have hitherto surrounded them. If these great and useful national purposes are to be attained, it is necessary indeed to unite these very principalities with the two great monarchies [Austria and Prussia] upon whose continued existence

[49] For the entire paragraph see ibid., pp. 235-37.

depends the survival of the German name. May Providence permit me to live to see this blessed event.

Stein took obvious pleasure in warning the Duke of Nassau, who was now mediatizing Stein's estates, that he himself stood in serious danger of mediatization. The concluding sentence of the letter reminded the duke of the fact that "there exists a conscience which judges, and a God who punishes."[50]

While the knights suffered deprivation, an unexpectedly vigorous and temporarily successful action of the Austrian government revived their hopes for an early restoration. In early December the emperor sent a sharp protest to the Bavarian government concerning the suppression of knightly rights; he supported his protest by the mobilization of his troops on the Bavarian frontier. The government in Munich suddenly found itself diplomatically isolated and militarily defenseless. Alone, its army was no match for Austria's, and its French protector was preoccupied with planning the invasion of Britain. Prussia, the most powerful fellow spoliator of knights, was resolved to maintain the policy of neutrality begun in 1795. Russia declared her sympathy with the knights and was prepared to give at least diplomatic support to Austria. The emperor was also able to use the still-surviving imperial machinery to apply legal and moral pressure against Bavaria. The *Reichshofrath* issued a decree (Jan. 23, 1804), the so-called *Konservatorium*, which ordered Bavaria to restore knightly rights to the *status quo* of 1802. To enforce the judgment of the *Reichshofrath* a *Subdelegationskommission* was appointed at Regensburg from the ranks of princes who had refused to participate in the spoliation: the Arch-Chancellor Dalberg, the dukes of Baden and Saxony, and the emperor in his role of Duke of Austria.[51]

This very last case of a *Reichsexecution* in the history of the Holy Roman Empire proved in fact one of the most effective. The Bavarian government capitulated on February 17, 1804, in notes addressed to the emperor, the *Reichstag*, and the members of the *Subdelegations-*

---

[50] Stein's open letter, dated Jan. 10, 1804, has often been printed; for example, *Freiherr vom Stein. Ausgewählte Politische Briefe und Denkschriften*. (ed. E. Botzenhart and G. Ipsen, Stuttgart, 1955), pp. 39-41. Stein did not live up to his pledge that he would never visit his estates again, but at least he never swore submission to the Duke.

[51] The situation leading to the *Konservatorium* is vividly described in the anonymous pamphlet (often attributed to the Austrian diplomat Hügel), *Reskript und Information für den . . . schen Gesandten am Reichstag zu Regensburg am 14. Feb. 1804 gegen die gewaltsame Drängung der im reichsritterschaftlichen Verbande stehenden Glieder in Franken durch den Kurfürsten von Pfalz-Bayern* (Regensburg, 1804).

kommission. The princes who had followed the Bavarian example in spoliation now had no choice but to follow in capitulation as well. Knightly territories were everywhere restored by the withdrawal of the military occupation. Stein, to give only one example, was once again master of his ancestral Nassau estates. Count Thürheim, only recently the tyrant who bullied Franconian knights into submission, now talked a very different language. The captive provisional *Direktorium* set up at Bamberg just three months earlier was dissolved "out of respect for the intervention of His Imperial Majesty and in order to promote public tranquillity and unity in the German Empire."[52] Thürheim returned the documents of submission he had extorted from 76 knights. The 61 nonjurors and the 39 procrastinators felt fully vindicated by events and assumed a highly pharisaical attitude toward their weaker brethren. A well-attended assembly of knights (*Ritterkonvent*) held at Nürnberg on March 21, 1804, censured the knights who had submitted to Bavaria and the Bavarian government found itself flooded with imperious demands for restitution, reparations, and satisfaction. The knights demanded, for example, that Bavarian troops must themselves, before evacuating a territory, tear down the placards proclaiming Bavarian sovereignty—a humiliation which the Bavarian government could not possibly accept. It cannot be said that the knights showed either moderation in victory or understanding of the conditions which were likely to make their victory ephemeral. Duke Max Joseph of Bavaria had reason to complain that the knights were "seeking to enhance the measure of their triumph through the degradation of our prestige."[53]

While the knights were crowing in triumph, Austria advertised a great diplomatic victory. It was said that the successful *Reichsexecution* had put a final stop to the process of imperial disintegration. This kind of pride was bound to come to a fall, for the last thing that Napoleon wanted was a new consolidation of the empire under Austrian leadership. He was firmly wedded to the policy of alliance with the middle states headed by Bavaria, and these states had postponed rather than abandoned their ambition to mediatize the knights. The French ambassador at Regensburg hinted to the members of the *Subdelegationskommission* that too much zeal in enforcing the *Konservatorium* was contrary to Napoleon's wishes. The initial Bavarian willingness to grant full restitution plus some reparation cooled noticeably. Soldiers illegally recruited from knightly territories were

[52] Quoted in H. H. Hofmann, *Adelige Herrschaft*, p. 239.
[53] Quoted in ibid., p. 243.

not released from the Bavarian colors; Bavarian negotiators proved evasive in settling financial claims stemming from the attempted mediatizations; there was renewed stress upon the feudal rights possessed by the duke over knightly vassals, and the issuance of quite preposterous financial demands based upon those rights. A deliberate policy of making the knights "stew in their juice" of sovereign immediacy was also launched. Knightly territories were treated systematically as "foreign countries" so far as economic regulations were concerned. Their artisans could not sell their goods in neighboring Bavarian villages; their residents could not draw Bavarian pensions—a pressing matter for many canons who had returned to their knightly families after being dispossessed by the secularizations (Bavaria was obligated by the terms of the 1803 *Hauptschluss* to pay pensions to the canons she had dispossessed); Bavarians who wanted to move into knightly territories were subjected to heavy fines as "emigrants."[54]

The complaints directed by the knights to the *Subdelegationskommission* against this kind of chicanery proved ineffective in view of French opposition; the knights thereupon appealed directly from the *Kommission* to its instructing body, the *Reichshofrath*. The latter sided with the plaintiffs and expressed its dissatisfaction with the *Kommission* in an *Exzitatorium* of March 26, 1805, which ordered full compliance with the *Konservatorium* within two months. This order proved singularly ineffective, and it was flatly countermanded by a letter written by Napoleon to the *Kommission* on July 2, 1805, ordering it not to enforce the *Konservatorium*. A word from Napoleon proved stronger than an order from the *Reichshofrath*: Bavaria was able to continue its policy of pinpricks with impunity.[55]

A few knights saw the importance of using the reprieve of 1804 for reform purposes in order to increase their chances of survival in the unfavorable political climate of Napoleonic Germany. Some proposed that the knights consolidate their scattered territories, through a vast exchange of lands, in order to form an integrated state which could claim a seat at the *Reichstag* on the grounds of area and population. (It would be governed as a knightly oligarchy like the glorious Teutonic order of the thirteenth century.) Others eschewed such utopian dreams and frankly recognized that the knights had become anachronisms whose life expectancy was at most a very few years. Was

[54] Ibid., pp. 239-44.
[55] For the entire paragraph see H. Müller, op.cit., Ch. 8.

it not prudent, then, to negotiate with Germany's princes, from the present position of strength, a general agreement abandoning immediacy and settling on *Landsasserei* with favorable terms, including the continuation of the collective life of the knighthood in some form? The knights could not, however, agree upon any definite policy; the reprieve of 1804 remained unused; and the order became one of the first casualties of the War of the Third Coalition.[56]

Napoleon's South German allies, especially Bavaria and Württemberg, used the defeat of the Austrian armies in the autumn of 1805 to reoccupy the knightly territories which they had been forced to evacuate under the terms of the *Konservatorium* a year and a half previously. The Duke of Bavaria frankly proclaimed that his earlier withdrawal had been necessitated by external pressure and accompanied by the resolve to resume his policy upon the first opportunity: "We were moved . . . to postpone the pursuit of our just cause until its attainment would no longer be hindered by the powerful intervention of external obstacles." The "just cause" was the elimination "of a condition, which violates every principle of a sound constitutional and political order—namely, the existence of parcels of land which are not under the jurisdiction of the prince as enclaves in the middle of his territories." Max Joseph announced that it was his firm will:

> that all vassals and knights who resided in our Franconian duchies completely renounce their disloyal connection (*pflichtwidrige Verbindung*) with an independent corporation standing outside of our sovereign laws and decrees for both themselves and their dependent peasantry (*Hintersassen*).

To those knights who refused submission he threatened dire penalties, whereas those who submitted were promised ducal protection of their property and of all their traditional rights, "insofar as these are compatible with our sovereign authority."[57]

The knights, deprived of any chance of future support by the defeat of their Austrian protector at Austerlitz, had no choice but to submit and make the best of a very bad situation. Count Thürheim, resuming the policy he had been forced to abandon by the Bavarian capitulation to the *Konservatorium*, again applied ruthless pressure upon the knights of Franconia. There was an exact repetition of the events of 1803; Bavarian placards were nailed upon conspicuous buildings; an oath of allegiance was imposed upon the knights and all

[56] Ibid., pp. 189-92.
[57] All quotations are from H. H. Hofmann, *Adelige Herrschaft*, p. 246.

their officials; correspondence with the surviving organization of the old *Ritterschaft* was prohibited. Resistance was punished immediately by sequestrating estates and quartering, at the knight's expense, Bavarian troops. Bavarian taxes and Bavarian conscription were introduced as visible evidence of the restored Bavarian sovereignty. It may be added that the sad fate of the *Ritterschaft* was shared by numerous other small princes at the time—though not, contrary to Stein's prediction, by the Duke of Nassau, whose mediatization by Prussia was to be postponed until 1866.[58]

The knights placed their last hopes upon Napoleon, although the French emperor had no reason to restrain the acquisitiveness of his princely allies. He gave a cold shoulder to a delegation of knights which called upon him in Munich on Jan. 12, 1806; thereafter the knights decided that they must submit to their princely conquerors, a decision soon facilitated when Emperor Francis II, renouncing the imperial throne, freed all his vassals from their oath of allegiance. The governments of Bavaria, Württemberg, and Baden agreed upon the precise division of knightly spoils, while the Act of Confederation between sixteen Napoleonic satellites, signed on June 12, 1806, confirmed the sovereignty of each confederation member over the knights within its territory. The precise terms of submission were dictated by the several states to their knights in declarations issued in 1806-07. They were everywhere allowed to keep their lands, exercise powers of administration, police, and justice, and enjoy certain privileges such as immunity from conscription and exemption from certain taxes— privileges which were later incorporated in the various constitutions after 1815. The knights lost their collective political role but frequently became influential individual members of the states which had mediatized them.[59]

The loss of the knights' semisovereign position caused few regrets among those not directly affected. The order had constituted a classic case of the survival of privilege after the termination of its original accompanying function. The elimination of the knights' position was an essential step on the road toward rational administration, legal equality, and democratic self-government. Yet it should not be for-

[58] Ibid., pp. 247-48.

[59] Müller, op.cit., Ch. 8. The terms granted by Bavaria to the knights (along with other mediatized rulers) in March 1807, "Bestimmung der künftigen Verhältnisse der der Kgl. Souveränitat unterworfenen Fürsten, Grafen und Herren zu den verschiedenen Zweigen der Staatsgewalt," are printed in Guide von Meyer, *Staatsakten für Geschichte und öffentliches Recht des Deutschen Bundes* (3 vols., Frankfurt, 1858-69), I, 16ff.

gotten that suppression brought loss as well as gain, as remote bureaucratic government replaced—in some cases, at least—benevolent patriarchal administration, and men were wrenched from customary ways of life with which they were still well-content. The utterly lawless manner of their suppression—made more odious by the legalistic abuse of a shadowy feudal suzerainty to enforce concrete sovereignty—remains a blot on the record of Germany's princes; but it must be remembered that the princes had no alternative if they wished to create modern states in which they could exercise sovereign political authority within clearly defined frontiers.

CHAPTER 13

The Napoleonic Revolution in Germany: The End of the Imperial Cities and the Final Agony of the Empire

The End of the Imperial Cities

WE HAVE seen above that the fifty-three Free Imperial Cities of the Holy Roman Empire had become anachronisms by the end of the eighteenth century. They were unable, with the exception of a few Hanseatic cities, to adapt themselves to modern economic conditions; their internal power structure, with its pattern of patrician-oligarchic domination, was increasingly challenged by commercial and lower-class elements; and they obviously would be unable to defend themselves once the appetites of their neighbors had been unleashed by the breakdown of imperial restraints. Their suppression in the course of the Napoleonic Revolution may be considered inevitable. The cities located left of the Rhine, most notable Cologne, were directly annexed by France; those to the right were thrown with the ecclesiastical states into the vast "compensation mass" (*Entschädigungsmasse*) available for princes who had suffered losses by the cession of the Rhineland to France. The imperial structure, which had hitherto afforded protection to its weak members, was disintegrating; the creation of viable political and economic units, transcending the confines of parochial municipalities, was the order of the day, and the middle and lower classes, while not yet capable of self-government, were eager to accept the benefits of an "enlightened absolutism" which would sweep away the cobwebs of the past.

The vast majority of the Imperial Cities were too weak even to attempt to perpetuate their independent existence. They yielded meekly to annexation and were incorporated with remarkable smoothness into the realms of their new masters. Only six imperial cities—Augsburg, Nürnberg, Frankfurt, Hamburg, Bremen, and Lübeck—survived the *Reichsdeputationshauptschluss* with their immediacy intact; yet even these were to be annexed by neighboring states within the next seven years (though the three Hanseatic cities regained their independence in 1814). A close look at two of these cities—Augsburg and Nürnberg, selected because they made great though ultimately unsuccessful efforts to preserve their independence—will convey an impression of the forces, foreign and domestic, at work in determining the Free Cities' ultimate fate.

THE CASE OF AUGSBURG[1]

The city of Augsburg had been a great commercial center in late medieval and early modern times; in the age of the Fuggers it had briefly become the financial capital of the European world. In the late eighteenth century, however, travelers could find few reminders of its earlier glories, and they noted that it was beset with serious political, administrative, religious, and economic problems which it could not master.[2] The municipal government was conducted in accordance with a charter conferred by Charles V in 1548. This charter was based upon a stratified society. The lower classes were denied any political recognition; the upper and middle classes were divided into three categories: patricians, merchants (*Kaufmannschaft*), and commoners (*Gemeine*, also called *Bürgerschaft*). Each separately elected deputies to the 45-man municipal council (*Innerer Rat*). The patricians elected thirty-five, the merchants three, the commoners seven. The *Innerer Rat* in turn elected the seven-man executive council (*Geheimer Rat*) which supervised the general administration of the city and was in exclusive charge of foreign policy. It stood at the apex of an incredibly cumbersome administrative apparatus consisting of 600 (!) offices which had developed, without any rational allocation of functions, over the past six centuries; vested interests always prevented the abolition of any office, however obsolete. The spirit of the administration was characterized by that combination of caution, lethargy, and pompousness often found in institutions living on borrowed time. Observers ridiculed Augsburg's stiff adherence to old forms and pointed out the

---

[1] This section is based upon the standard monograph by Karl Haupt, *Die Vereinigung der Reichsstadt Augsburg mit Bayern* (Munich and Freising, 1923), which incorporates, but goes beyond, the materials of two earlier standard works: the second volume of Franz Freiherr von Seida's *Augsburgs Geschichte von Erbauung der Stadt bis zum Tode Maximilian Josephs* (2 vols., Augsburg, 1826), especially important because Seida, an Augsburg patrician, personally participated in the events described; and two detailed articles by city archivist Adolf Buff, "Des reichsstädtischen Augsburgs Ende," in *Sammler*, 1882 and 1885, important for using all the materials in the city archives. Haupt's primary contribution lies in placing the parochial events chronicled by his parochial predecessors in the general historical framework of the Napoleonic Revolution.

[2] The best-known travel descriptions are by C.F.D. Schubart, *Lebenserinnerungen* (2 vols., Stuttgart, 1793), II, 10ff.; [L.W. Wekhrlin], *Anselmus Rabiosus, Reise durch Oberdeutschland* (Nordlingen, 1778), I; and F. Nicolai, *Beschreibung einer Reise durch Teutschland und die Schweiz* (Berlin and Stettin, 1786-87), VII and VIII.

grotesque gap between the pretense and reality of a city which treated its far-more-powerful neighbors (for example, the elector of Bavaria, Augsburg's predestined heir) with the spirit of an aristocrat magnanimously deigning to notice a parvenu.

The city's unsolved problems were numerous. A rational administration of judicial and financial affairs was made impossible not only by the city's hoary bureaucratic apparatus but also by the survival of several ecclesiastical immunities within city walls. The citizens of Augsburg had won municipal autonomy from the bishop of Augsburg in the Middle Ages, but the latter continued to rule from his capital of Dillingen on the Danube as prince-bishop over an ecclesiastical state which surrounded the city. The bishop of Augsburg possessed, however, full judicial and financial autonomy over his palace located within the city; and he did not hesitate to abuse his autonomy by turning a wing of his palace into a tavern where tax-exempt liquor was sold to the thirsty citizens of Augsburg to the detriment of the municipal exchequer! Several monasteries in the city also enjoyed far-reaching autonomies, although they at least provided a *quid pro quo* by supporting the city's six Catholic parishes with revenues derived from estates located outside.

There was a good deal of religious friction in Augsburg. Two thirds of the population was Catholic and stood under the strong influence of the ex-Jesuits, the most outspoken foes of the *Aufklärung* in Germany. The Protestant third of the city, on the other hand, was strongly permeated with the spirit of *Aufklärung*; moreover, it had much of the militancy of a diaspora. It clung with special tenacity to a pattern of confessional parity in public appointments—a pattern which had been established in the sixteenth century to safeguard minority rights but which was now maintained at the cost of much duplication, inefficiency, and sectarian squabbling. In the words of the satirist Christian Schubart,

> Whatever repulses the stranger in his first view of Augsburg as crooked, hateful, musty, stiff, and disagreeable is the result of confessional parity: this is a double-headed monster which barks out of two jaws (*Rachen*), breathes poisonous suspicions into men's minds out of two gullets (*Schlünde*), and makes them entirely incapable of unconstrained, harmonious happiness.[3]

Serious financial and social problems confronted Augsburg. Its finances had been ruined in the 1770's when high grain prices forced

---

[3] Quoted by Haupt, op.cit., p. 6.

the city fathers to import grain at municipal expense to distribute to the poor—an example of patriarchal conduct which, however, no longer earned the gratitude it would have won in an earlier age. The *Innerer Rat* proved incapable of raising adequate new revenues and its members clung to the multiplicity of useless offices by which their families had lived off the city for centuries. In 1795 the merchants, following the example set by the neighboring Free City of Ulm in 1782, forced the appointment of a *Bürgerausschuss* to investigate the chronic mismanagement of city finances; they also insisted that it become a regular part of the constitution (*konstitutionsmässiges Organ*) —a demand which made the established patrician racketeers shudder. Their appeal to the *Reichshofrath* led to the suppression of the *Bürgerausschuss* (Jan. 27, 1797) with nothing accomplished and tempers inflamed. In 1794 a riot of weavers, fired by news of the French Revolution, had also remained without immediate consequence but it was a warning signal of lower-class unrest.

The shape of future events had been revealed as early as the winter of 1788-89 when friction over the mistreatment of Bavarian merchants led to a Bavarian embargo of grain and wood against Augsburg. The embargo had caused intense suffering to the population and demonstrated the city's utter economic dependence upon its powerful neighbor. The people's anger, initially directed against Bavaria, was soon channeled against the *Innerer Rat* whose incompetence had allowed matters to come to such a disastrous impasse. There was even some discussion about giving up the city's unprofitable immediacy in order to enjoy the economic advantages of being part of a larger territorial unit. Such discussion naturally diminished, however, after the immediate crisis had been resolved through the intercession of the bishop of Augsburg and by the city's promise to treat Bavarian merchants more kindly in the future.

The patrician ruling class was well aware that the compensation provisions of the Treaty of Lunéville constituted a mortal threat to the future of the city as an independent political body. Even if Augsburg's own immediacy should be spared, it was seriously affected by the plans for secularizing ecclesiastical territory; the ecclesiastical immunities within the city limits, relatively innocuous when enjoyed by weak clerical bodies, would become dangerous if they passed into the hands—as expected—of the powerful elector of Bavaria, who was certain to exploit them in a manner harmful to the city's independence. The object of Augsburg policy became the buttressing of municipal independence through the purchasing of all the "sovereign" rights of ecclesiastical bodies within its walls, and, if possible, the outlying possessions of the monasteries which had hitherto financed Catholic religious life within the city. To achieve this goal the city sent envoys to Paris, the bourse of German territorial transfers, and to Regensburg, where specific terms were hammered out by the *Reichsdeputation* under French dictation. The envoys were authorized to spend whatever was necessary to achieve their goal; their problem was one of deciding how much money should be offered to whom, at what time and with what kind of security, in return for what specific gains.

It would be tedious to recount all the steps taken by Augsburg envoys to secure by the combination of cold cash and warm argument the survival of Augsburg. The key to the situation was the policy of France; the key to French policy, the desire of French officials, from Talleyrand on down, to receive bribes. The delicacy of such transactions required secrecy and the employment of somewhat dubious intermediaries. Relations with the Habsburg Monarchy—the other Great Power most concerned with the territorial reorganization of Germany—were less problematical, for the emperor eagerly desired the survival of Augsburg in order to permit the maintenance of the municipal *curia* at Regensburg. His diplomats gave the envoys of Augsburg precise advice when the discussion of the territorial settlement reached its crisis in the middle of September 1802. The envoys sent the city fathers the following report of a nocturnal visit paid them by *Geheimer Rat* von Weckbecker, the first assistant of the Imperial *Konkommissar* Freiherr von Hügel. Weckbecker was breathless from haste and excitement as he conveyed the following news:

Regensburg and Wetzlar [two imperial cities whose survival had been expected because they were the seats of the *Reichstag* and *Kammergericht*] are lost, and if Augsburg is lost also *everything* will be lost, for then the *collegium civitatense* [the municipal *curia*] will disappear; its survival is, however, urgently desired by the Emperor, for otherwise his *Reichstag* influence will be reduced to zero and Prussia will dictate *en chef*. What can still be done? . . . Who can help? *Only* the French, for the French set all the terms here, they give and take away, not once but repeatedly, in short their wishes are law. . . . Do you know what you should do? You should go tomorrow morning, early, to Matthieu [the French ambassador]. He is the principal actor in this tragedy. Offer him, on the spot, for the continued existence of your city and everything that is *intra moenia*—forget about possessions *in alieno*, which make everybody indignant and would only cause you trouble if you got them—2, 3 or 400 thousand gulden, perhaps half a million, perhaps even more. I have said enough. See that it gets done, no matter what the price, there is no alternative. The Emperor urgently desires it; the *collegium civitatense* must not collapse. The problem of raising the money will come up only later; there is a possibility that the sum will be scaled down, time will help in the solution of this problem. But you must act quickly *now*.[4]

The city fathers got the message and they authorized the offer of 600,000 florins, provided that Augsburg received satisfaction on the ecclesiastical immunities within its walls. The French, reinforced by the Austrians, then pressed successfully for the inclusion of Augsburg on the short list of cities spared by the *Hauptschluss*. Money apart, they desired the survival of some German cities which would be dependent upon France; and Napoleon probably wanted to retain some bait to hook the South German states who were now becoming his satellites.

Initially most Augsburgers rejoiced at the escape of their city as an independent political body; but they were far less enthusiastic when they began to understand the financial burden which they had assumed as the price of this independence. No one knew how the 600,000 florins could be raised in a city more than 3 million florins in debt; and the long-sought-after secularizations proved a burden rather than a gain. Austria insisted that the venerable bishop Klemens Wenceslas (a pluralist already exiled from his electoral see of Trier) must not be disturbed in his immunities during his lifetime. The confiscated monastic buildings were economically useless and filled with monks who, under the terms of the *Hauptschluss*, must be paid pensions; the outlying properties of the monasteries, which had previously supported the urban establishments, had passed to Bavaria rather than Augsburg. Bavaria refused to maintain the Catholic services financed by these outlying estates, and it procrastinated in negotiating the allocation of monastic debts. The Bavarian government insisted that it was the general heir to the rights, immunities, and properties of the bishop of Augsburg and the affected monasteries, and that Augsburg, being a partial heir, must negotiate with the general heir in order to secure its share of the succession.

The next two years (1803-05) were filled with far-from-amicable negotiations between the Bavarian government and Augsburg on the precise disposition of the ecclesiastical properties and immunities. The

[4] Report of Stetten-Steinkühl, Augsburg ambassador, to *Geheimer Rat*, Sept. 13, 1802. Quoted in ibid., p. 34.

Augsburgers found that the secularizations had raised its revenues by only 14,000 florins, whereas its additional obligations in pensions to monks, support of the church services, and payment on monastic debts amounted annually to 37,000 florins. In view of this unexpected situation and the emptiness of the city treasury, the city fathers decided that they were entitled to delay payment on their obligations to France since the *quid pro quo* for their 600,000 florins—independence *plus* a satisfactory settlement of the ecclesiastical problem—had not been met. The Augsburg sense of honor differentiated with some delicacy between obligations owed to persons and obligations owed to France; the former were honored in cash, the latter were postponed on the pretext that the precise mode of payment must still be settled through further negotiations. Talleyrand received a gift of 22,000 florins; Durand, his main assistant on German affairs, 11,000; Laforest and Matthieu, French ambassadors at Regensburg, 5,500 apiece; Bacher and Maraudet, their assistants, 2,200 apiece. To disguise the character of these bribes the imperial *Konkommissar* Hügel was also prevailed upon to accept a gift of 5,500 florins. (The scale of these rewards was obviously proportionate to services rendered.) It is possible, though not provable, that these timely bribes were reciprocated by a pledge not to press Augsburg too hard in the negotiations concerning the payment of the 600,000 florins; the Frenchmen must also have known of Augsburg's actual inability to raise the large sum.

How did public opinion in Augsburg respond to the proceedings of the years 1801 to 1805? The diplomatic negotiations proceeded, by necessity as well as tradition, in secrecy, and the inevitable result of this secrecy was endless rumor and speculation. When news leaked out that the *Geheimer Rat* planned to pay heavily for the continuation of imperial immediacy, two kinds of objections were raised: some argued—and they were soon sustained by events—that the loss of independence was inevitable anyway, and that it was foolish to make financial sacrifices to prolong briefly a doomed existence; others argued—as soon became apparent to all—that the specific financial terms demanded by France exceeded Augsburg's ability to pay, and that independence was worthless if accompanied by bankruptcy. The able *Ratskonsulent* Johann Melchior Hoscher took this position in a memorandum submitted to the *Innerer Rat* on Jan. 22, 1804; he pointed to the city's bankruptcy and came to the conclusion that incorporation into the Bavarian state was the only solution to Augsburg's difficulties.[5]

[5] Hoscher, when he could not prevail upon the city fathers, took the somewhat

This was the prevalent view in the merchant community, which expected great economic advantages from incorporation and shunned the sacrifices which independence involved. The city government, after attempts to borrow money at Kassel and at Frankfurt proved unsuccessful, turned to its own merchant community but received a flat refusal. The frustrated *Geheimer Rat* then turned to the local Jews to meet its most pressing needs. Under existing Augsburg law these Jews were not permitted to live in the city itself, but had long resided in neighboring villages and commuted daily to their business establishments. The *Rat* now offered them residential privileges in return for an adequate loan at a low rate of interest, a policy which infuriated the largely anti-Semitic citizenry of Augsburg. Further domestic dissatisfaction was stirred by the ex-Jesuits, who fanned popular agitation against the "godless secularizations" perpetrated by the government. Catholics found themselves, however, in an embarrassing position: they disliked the government, yet very much approved its objective of maintaining the independence of Augsburg, since the alternative was rule by the even more anticlerical government of Bavaria under Count Montgelas.

The days of Augsburg's independence were clearly numbered when Napoleon needed Bavarian help in the War of the Third Coalition. This became evident when Napoleon visited the city on Oct. 22, 1805, and gave a forty-five-minute audience to a *Rat* delegation. The delegation complained of the burden of requisitions, the obligations brought by the secularization process, and the heavy indebtedness of the city. Napoleon, his pride reinforced by his recent victory at Ulm, showed little sympathy: he said the requisitions imposed upon Augsburg were smaller than those upon Munich and Ulm, the two chief cities of his Bavarian ally, and had been poorly paid at that; the problem of supporting dispossessed monks was common to dozens of German states; and Augsburg's indebtedness he ascribed to financial mismanagement and to the fact that the city was too small to be a viable economic unit. The delegation's complaint about Augsburg's lack of a hinterland—and consequent weak economy—led to a terse interruption by the emperor: "Voulez-vous être de la Bavière?" He left no doubt that he would do nothing to help Augsburg prolong its independence.

unusual step of sending the essence of his memorandum to the Bavarian Premier Montgelas under the title *Über die Verhältnisse der R. St. Augsburg, nach welchen es bei der jetzigen Lage der Dinge gedachter R. St. unmöglich fällt, ihre Selbstständigkeit andauernd zu behaupten.* Hoscher evidently wanted to prod the Bavarian government into annexation and to curry favor with the predestined future ruler. Ibid., p. 82.

The rulers of Augsburg saw realistically that their city's fate was now completely out of their hands, and that they could do nothing to influence the course of events. Their attitude was expressed by *Rats-konsulent* Schmid in November 1805 in the following words:

> If it suits the policy of the French Emperor to retain an Imperial body in some corporate form, I do not doubt that the remaining Imperial Free Cities will survive. If, on the other hand, the Empire is dissolved into separate sovereign units, the Free Cities cannot expect any better fate than the Imperial knighthood, whose grave has already been dug and whose funeral bell is tolling now.[6]

Napoleon offered Augsburg to Bavaria shortly after the Battle of Austerlitz, and Bavarian troops occupied the city on Dec. 20, 1805. The *Innerer Rat* thereupon sent a letter to the elector of Bavaria in which it offered its humble submission and expressed hopes for a prosperous future under his benevolent rule. Dignity was maintained—and the irreconcilable patricians temporarily satisfied—by the declaration,

> It is not possible for us to renounce our immediate tie to His Imperial Majesty and the Empire, until we are freed by the highest authority of the Empire of the duties owed under our oath of fealty; until this is done we must view the military occupation ordered by Your Highness as a measure which we can neither recognize nor prevent.[7]

The majority of the merchant community was, on the other hand, unabashedly happy about an event it had long desired; and almost all Augsburg citizens were relieved that the uncertainty which had troubled them for the last four years was ended at last.

The new Bavarian administration, headed by Freiherr von Widnmann, achieved many of the reforms which, though long overdue, could not have been secured so long as the cumbersome old constitution remained intact. Hundreds of superfluous offices, however old and venerable, were abolished by a stroke of the pen. The principle of confessional parity in the bureaucracy was abolished. The *Geheimer Rat* was enlarged and its members now specialized on the model of ministers of a modern cabinet; whereas previously they had exercised a rather vague supervisory role, they were now given specific administrative responsibilities. The patrician monopoly of the *Rat* was broken

---

[6] Quoted in ibid., p. 94.

[7] Letter of Augsburg Rat to the Elector of Bavaria, Dec. 22, 1805. Quoted in ibid., p. 97.

in favor of a gifted merchant. A rational pattern of police and judicial administration, now no longer encumbered by ecclesiastical privileges, was established. The debt was met by imposing new taxes, better collecting of old taxes, rationalizing the administration which led to economies, and establishing a sinking fund which paid off the outstanding debt of 3,113,383 florins within twenty years. The main force behind this achievement was the impetus given to the long-lagging Augsburg economy by its inclusion in a large thriving state.

A most interesting report, written by the Bavarian Commissioner von Widnmann, describes how the population of Augsburg responded to the new and vigorous Bavarian administration:

> Public opinion is deeply divided on the basis of religion. The Protestants are delighted to pass under the rule of a prince under whose wise government trade and art flourish and harmful prejudices long nourished in darkness, are eliminated by the torch of *Aufklärung*. The Catholics are . . . , on the other hand, openly discontented because they fear that the new government will dissolve the remaining monasteries, turn churches into barracks of theatres, prohibit litanies, rosaries, and brotherhoods, and compel the ex-Jesuits to emigrate to Russia: they fear the city will lose both divine favor and earthly happiness. Both confessions are agreed upon one thing, that the old municipal constitution had become useless and could no longer survive; and they share the apprehension that their sons may be drafted into the Bavarian army.

Widnmann found the members of the old *Innerer Rat* divided in their attitude:

> The majority takes the end of Augsburg's immediacy deeply to heart but recognizes its inevitability in the light of the geographical position of the city and its financial bankruptcy; and it congratulates itself on having fallen into the hands of so wise and enlightened a monarch. A minority is inconsolable, especially since it has learnt that *Ratsherren* are expected *to work* under Bavarian rule and cannot simply murmur their customary assent to the memoranda drafted by the *Ratskonsulenten*. This minority party includes a number of Catholic zealots who have been indignant ever since the *Reichsdeputationsschluss* about the use of secularized ecclesiastical properties for profane purposes; they now expect total defeat and bemoan their future weakness.

Widnmann concluded by noting that the Catholic clergy, both high and low, secular and regular, was fanning popular discontent, and that it was having some success with the class of "bankrupts, intellectuals (*Raisonneurs*), servants, and lazybirds (*arbeitsscheue Leute*), all groups which should be placed under regular police supervision." The merchants, guild masters, and Protestant pastors, on the other hand, were pillars of the pro-Bavarian party.[8]

It should be noted, finally, that the inconsolables did not remain irreconcilable for long. The Bavarian government kept most of the old Augsburg officials on the city payroll; the prosperity resulting from membership in a large state quickly disarmed much hostility; and the obvious permanence of Bavarian rule made the irreconcilables appear increasingly quixotic. Augsburg soon became a loyal Bavarian city which refused to pine for an immediacy which had lost its attractions long before the Bavarian annexation.

THE CASE OF NÜRNBERG[9]

The fate of Nürnberg resembled that of Augsburg in many ways. Nürnberg could also look back upon medieval glories quite remote from the prosaic realities of its eighteenth-century situation. Its economy began losing ground about 1600, when tax revenue stood at 3 million florins; by 1790 this sum had declined by more than two thirds, to 900,000. The external debt stood at 9,450,000 florins, triple what was considered an unbearable burden at Augsburg. Many Nürnbergers now despaired of the future of the city, and were willing to be incorporated into the adjoining Prussian territory of Ansbach-Bayreuth. In 1796 the municipal government went so far as to accept a treaty of submission suggested by Hardenberg; but King Frederick William II refused to ratify the document because he feared the wrath of Austria and the heavy burden of Nürnberg's debts. The emperor made the next attempt to bring some order into the city's finances by appointing a *Subdelegationskommission* under *Regierungsrat* Philipp Ernst Gemming in 1797, but its efforts had no success because it could not eliminate the oligarchic privileges for which the city was notorious.

---

[8] Widnmann's report to the K. B. *Generallandeskommissariat* Ulm, dated Sept. 23, 1806, is summarized with many quotations in ibid., pp. 99-100.

[9] This section is primarily based upon the excellent monograph by Georg Schrötter, "Die letzten Jahre der Reichsstadt Nürnberg und ihr Übergang an Bayern," *Mitt. des Vereins für die Geschichte der Stadt Nürnberg*, XVII (1906), 1-177. Many key documents are printed, with a connecting narrative, by Jos. Baader, *Streiflichter auf die Zeit der tiefsten Erniedrigung, oder Die Reichsstadt Nürnberg in den Jahren 1801-1806* (Nürnberg, 1878).

Effective political power was wielded by a seven-man all-patrician council which was drawn from the narrow ranks of some twenty families, long accustomed to feeding at the city trough and hence unwilling to launch basic reforms.

Nürnberg had survived the *Reichsdeputationshauptschluss* by paying cash into the same French palms that had been greased by the envoys of Augsburg. In the drastic words of a report from Nürnberg's mission to Paris (Feb. 9, 1803): "How could we survive if we could no longer rely upon the French government? Our Imperial immediacy would be what beautiful red color is to a consumptive: a most delusive sign of health."[10]

The second reason for Nürnberg's continued survival lay in the jealousy of its two most powerful neighbors, Prussia and Bavaria. Hardenberg hoped to consolidate Prussia's position in South Germany by annexing Nürnberg, which now formed a wedge between Bayreuth and Ansbach; Bavaria hoped eventually to expand into Prussian Franconia and therefore feared any such consolidation. Neither could permit the other to mediatize Nürnberg; both cultivated good relations with Napoleon, the ultimate arbiter of German affairs. The French emperor's refusal to decide between the two rivals temporarily prolonged Nürnberg's independent life, but both Bavaria and Prussia were allowed to nibble at Nürnberg's territorial integrity by occupying several disputed outlying areas in 1792 and 1796, respectively.[11]

Nürnberg did everything in its power to curry French favor to buttress the independence retained in 1803. It expelled an *émigré* colony which had settled there since 1793, curtailed the printing of all political works lest some should prove offensive to Napoleon, and hastened to offer congratulations when the latter assumed his imperial title. Napoleon, gracious reply (Jan. 16, 1805) was immediately leaked to the *Hamburger Korrespondenz* to scotch all rumors that the French emperor was indifferent to the fate of the Imperial Free City.

The outbreak of the War of the Third Coalition sealed Nürnberg's doom as certainly as Augsburg's, although the death throes of the

[10] Quoted by Schrötter, op.cit., p. 12. The attitude of the French toward Nürnberg is documented in detail in Pt. I of Baader's documentation, "Nürnberg's erste Deputation nach Paris im Jahre 1801," *Streiflichter*, pp. 3-52.

[11] Prussia and Bavaria agreed to coordinate their policies toward Nürnberg in a *Generallandesvergleich* of June 30, 1803, which left Nürnberg isolated; its attempts to enter into negotiations with Prussia are documented in the excellent "Berichte des Legationsrathes Woltmann an Nürnberg aus den Jahren 1803-1806," Pt. II of Baader's *Streiflichter*, pp. 54-153. Karl Ludwig Woltmann (1770-1817), Nürnberg envoy to Berlin, was a man of broad culture who subsequently became professor of history at Jena.

former were somewhat more prolonged. When Napoleon forced Prussia to hand Ansbach over to Bavaria in February 1806, in return for compensation in North Germany, it meant the collapse of the Prusso-Bavarian balance of power in Franconia; Bavaria was certain to seize the city the moment French troops were withdrawn.

Count Thürheim, the Bavarian commissioner in Franconia whom we have already encountered as the scourge of the Imperial Knights, developed a plan for winning Nürnberg's voluntary submission in June 1806—such a submission would obviously be preferable to forcible annexation. He hoped to win over the Council of Seven by "promising personal advantages in accordance with the needs and desires of the Councillors in the form of jobs for their children and monetary rewards for themselves." Thürheim wanted to supplement their personal bribes by offering generous political terms to the city: no conscription (a concession which was no sacrifice because "commercial and factory towns breed only cripples anyway"); no quartering of troops, since Nürnberg's plentiful barracks made this unnecessary; the preservation of the existing city government with only a minimum of Bavarian supervision; the retention of all city officials in their present jobs; the incorporation of the five-hundred-man Nürnberg army into the Bavarian army at every soldier's present rank; and the guarantee of the heavy municipal debt.

Thürheim believed that the merchants of the city would welcome Bavarian rule because of the advantage of entering a larger economic unit. The imperial *Subdelegat* would readily submit his resignation upon "a promise of amnesty concerning his administration [there had been talk of irregularities] and a pension of a few thousand gulden." The French army in Nürnberg—whose acquiescence was needed if the scheme were to work out smoothly—would cooperate after the distribution of judicious gifts to Marshal Bernadotte, the commanding officer, and his subordinates. Thürheim's main hopes were set, however, upon the Council of Seven: "Its members will be motivated, *as patriots*, by the prospect of serving the common good; while as *individuals* and *fathers of families* they will be unable to resist the personal advantages offered."[12] The Bavarian government approved Thürheim's plan on July 8, 1806, but told him to proceed cautiously in implementation:

"Our plan must be to secure the submission of Nürnberg to our sovereignty in as *constitutional* a manner as possible; it is most im-

[12] Thürheim's memorandum of June 21, 1806, is printed verbatim in Schrotter, op.cit., pp. 105-11.

portant to avoid the method of revolution, whether it be through the tumultuous cooperation of the military or a mob suborned for our cause."[13] The Bavarian government wanted to achieve a revolutionary aim while forswearing the use of revolutionary means.

The Council of Seven discussed Thürheim's proposals in almost daily sessions after July 15, 1806. There was general recognition that the independence of Nürnberg could no longer be maintained, but there was still hope of avoiding the hated Bavarian rule by the desperate expedient of submitting to direct French annexation. The council showed its misunderstanding of Nürnberg's true position by offering to submit to France in return for a guarantee of all traditional privileges (July 18, 1806). Apart from freedom from conscription and quartering, preservation of the existing city government, retention of all officials including the soldiers, and guarantee of the municipal debt— the same terms offered by Thürheim—the Nürnbergers also demanded that all members of the "patriciate secure all the personal and material rights enjoyed by any aristocrat anywhere in the realm; and that all patrician foundations, fiefs, entails, and family laws governing successions be confirmed." The maintenance of patrimonial courts must also be guaranteed. Nürnbergers must become eligible for employment everywhere in France, although in many respects Nürnberg would not become an integral part of France. What the city demanded was all the rights of Frenchmen while shirking the accompanying duties.[14]

This fantastic proposal never had a chance, quite apart from the fact that it was made too late; for Napoleon had promised Nürnberg to Bavaria when the Confederation of the Rhine had been formed the previous week (July 12, 1806). When the Nürnberg *Rat* learned the bad news it decided to send a delegation to Munich with instructions to offer Max Joseph (now king of Bavaria) terms of submission similar to those just offered to France. The Nürnbergers even hoped that Max Joseph would agree to a loose personal union under which he would become *Burggraf von und zu Nürnberg* in addition to his Bavarian royal title, but the two administrations would remain completely distinct. The delegation received a chilly reception upon its arrival in Munich. Assurances were given on the guarantee of the municipal debt and the retention of civil servants at their present salaries, but nothing else; the delegates were wryly told that they would have gotten much

[13] Quoted in ibid., pp. 115-16.
[14] The Bavarian proposal to France is paraphrased in ibid., pp. 119-21.

better terms if only they had agreed to a voluntary submission a month earlier.

Count Thürheim was suspicious of what the Nürnberg *Rat* might do in the remaining days before the official Bavarian takeover; he sent a trusted subordinate, *Landesdirektionsrat* Freiherr von Lochner, to the city on Aug. 8 to keep a close watch on the situation. His suspicions were fully justified, for the *Rat* had responded to the coming end with carnival-style irresponsibility. It sold numerous municipal buildings at bargain prices to the friends and relatives of *Ratsherren*, and it decreed many salary increases to officials in the expectation that these would be honored by the new government. Lochner brought a quick stop to this kind of monkey business as he worked at preparations for Sept. 15, 1806, the day the French garrison was scheduled to leave and Bavarian troops would enter the city.

The formal passing of Nürnberg's independence began with a parade of the departing French troops before the *Rathaus* at 9:00 a.m. This was followed by the reading of the royal proclamation of annexation (*Besitzergreifungspatent*) at several public places; then a band of trumpeteers brought the "good news" to all parts of the city. The existing *Rat* swore allegiance to the new master in a solemn ceremony and was temporarily confirmed in office. The Bavarian king decreed special church services for the following Sunday, Sept. 21: "The sermon should comment on a suitable text referring to the change in government, and it should be followed by the singing of a solemn *Te Deum laudamus.*"[15] All city officials were required to attend in black dress.

Nürnberg followed the example of Augsburg in becoming a loyal city of the Bavarian monarchy. Its loyalty was rewarded by administrative rationalization, prosperity, and financial solvency. All hopes of a restoration of Free City status were dashed by the general recognition that the Imperial Free Cities were part and parcel of the fabric of the Holy Roman Empire and could not survive its collapse. It was no coincidence that the summer of 1806, which saw the end of Nürnberg's independence, also brought the final dissolution of the empire.

Last Proposals for Imperial Reform

The venerable structure of the Holy Roman Empire had been transformed but not destroyed by the *Reichsdeputationshauptschluss* of 1803. The western boundary had shifted to the Rhine, the ecclesiastical states and most Free Cities had been mediatized, and the Imperial Knights were marked for early elimination. The emperor remained,

[15] Quoted in ibid., p. 175.

however, with his traditional prerogatives intact; the *Reichstag* continued to meet at Regensburg; the imperial courts still sat at Wetzlar and Vienna; and there seemed no necessary reason why the empire, which had survived many shocks in a thousand years of history, should not survive the shock of the Napoleonic Revolution. Historians have tended to view the events of 1803 as but the prelude to the inevitable finale of the empire; this was not, however, the view of most contemporaries. There was a rash of pamphlets devoted to describing the transformed constitution of the empire, and many proposals to buttress it against further shocks were made. It will be useful to describe a few of these, for they were often animated by a Conservative spirit, whether in the form of exhortations to maintain the new *status quo* or proposals to reform and adapt the imperial structure still further to the new constellation of Germany's political forces.[16]

Several pamphleteers saw the key to strengthening the empire—as Moser had suggested in 1765 in his *Essay on the National Spirit*—in the revival of imperial patriotism. The emperor must give precedence to the interests of the empire over those of his Austrian realm; the electors must support the imperial power instead of whittling it down in successive electoral capitulations; and the princes must learn to act as imperial *Stände* rather than sovereign rulers. The passage of the *Reichsdeputationshauptschluss* had shown that the *Reichstag* was capable of far-reaching legislation: let it bestir itself to reform the military system, to codify German law, to enlarge the executive powers of the emperor, and to prepare a religious settlement with the Papacy patterned upon the Napoleonic concordat of 1802. The strengthening of the empire also required the more effective functioning of the institutions of the *Kreise* by giving greater powers to the *Kreisdirektoren*. In all these ways the empire could again be made a living political reality; long dormant institutions could be revived without any formal breach in continuity; and the specter of future revolutionary violence could be banished by creating a national political structure adequate to Germany's needs at the beginning of the nineteenth century.[17]

[16] I have followed the definitive dissertation by Hermann Schulz, *Vorschläge zur Reichsreform in der Publizistik von 1800-1806* (Giessen, 1926). Of the contemporary literature the frequently cited anonymous book [by Johann F. Reitemeier?], *Die deutsche Reichsverfassung seit dem Lunéviller Frieden, in Hinsicht auf ihre Form und ihre Natur betrachtet. Mit Vorschlägen zur Verbesserung ihrer Gebrechen* (Deutschland, 1803), is a great disappointment.

[17] See, for example: Anonymous, *Deutschlands höchst-notwendige politisch-publizistische Regeneration. Allen Freunden des gemeinsamen Vaterlandes ge-*

A second school of pamphleteers blamed the selfishness of the two Great Powers of Germany—Austria and Prussia—for the past and present weakness of the empire. It viewed this selfishness as incorrigible and wanted to concentrate, therefore, upon the consolidation of the "third Germany"—the territories lying between Austria and Prussia—into a cohesive confederation utilizing established imperial institutions (most notably, the *Reichstag* and the *Kammergericht*) but breathing new life into them. An effectively organized "third Germany" could easily raise an army of 200,000 men, command the respect of all the Great Powers of Europe, and perhaps mediate their existing conflicts; it might even prove strong enough to recover the territories on the Left bank ceded to France by the Treaty of Lunéville. The "third Germany" would earn the loyalty of all of Germany's princes by guaranteeing their independence against the perennial danger of Austrian and Prussian aggrandizement. Leadership in the crucial fields of military and foreign policy would be placed in a four-power *Generalkriegsrat* composed of two permanent members (Bavaria and Saxony) and four alternating members (Brunswick, Hessen, Württemberg, Baden). This utopian project—utopian because neither Austria nor Prussia could be expected to acquiesce in its establishment—was soon to be caricatured under French auspices in the Confederation of the Rhine.[18]

A third school welcomed the consolidation of the "third Germany" as part of a larger plan of creating a genuine tripartite German federation. It frankly accepted the fact that Great Powers like Prussia and Austria must be given a special position in any German-imperial constitution. Since they would always enjoy such a position *de facto*, it appeared best to give it to them *de jure* as well. The "third Germany" must, however, consolidate itself to provide a counterweight to the two giants; this plan was similar to that proposed by the second school except that it stressed the importance—and possibility—of close ties among the three Germanies. The Prussian statesman Hardenberg proposed, in the spring of 1806, that Germany be rearranged into six *Kreise* with effective *Kreisdirektoren*, military contingents, and courts with final appellate jurisdiction. These *Kreise* would be dominated by

---

widmet (n.p., 1803); Braun, "Allgemeine Grundzüge zum weiteren Nachdenken von dem Geheimen Hofrat Braun," *Häberlins Staatsarchiv*, vii (1804), 325ff. Both summarized in Schulz, op.cit., pp. 20-24.

[18] Anonymous [Heinrich Gottlob Heinse], *Der deutsche Fürstenbund nach den Forderungen des 19. Jahrhunderts von Hieronimus à Lapide dem Jüngeren. Ein Mittel zur Erhaltung Deutschlands und vielleicht des Gleichgewichts von Europa* (Leipzig and Gera, 1804). Summarized by Schulz, op.cit., pp. 36-38.

Austria, Prussia, Bavaria, Saxony, Hessen, and Württemberg; lesser princes would be bound to obedience while otherwise retaining their princely prerogatives. The six *Kreise* would in turn be merged into three larger federations: North Germany, composed of Prussia, Saxony, and Hessen under the leadership of Prussia; South Germany, composed of Bavaria, Württemberg, and Baden under the leadership of Bavaria; and the existing federation of the Habsburg Monarchy. The *Reichstag* would be reorganized into three *curiae*: namely, the three leaders of federations (Austria, Prussia, Bavaria); the major states (Austria, Prussia, Bavaria, Württemberg, Hannover, Hessen, with the possible addition of Holstein and Mecklenburg); and all other surviving princes. The best that could be said of this plan is that it was based upon a realistic assessment of the political forces of Germany in 1806, though it certainly did not provide the outlines of a workable polity. There is a suspicion, indeed, that Hardenberg was primarily interested in the Prussian domination of Northern Germany through Berlin's securing control over Saxony and Hessen, and that the proposal for imperial reform was but a fig leaf for covering the naked aggrandizement of the House of Hohenzollern. Yet even if this suspicion were true, the plan is nevertheless a tribute to the strength which the imperial idea still exercised over the public mind of Germany.[19]

A fourth school of thought saw the key to a stronger Germany in the harmonious cooperation of Austria and Prussia within the existing imperial structure. The famous publicist Friedrich von Gentz, at that time in the process of shifting his base of operations from Berlin to Vienna, was an eloquent spokesman for this point of view. Germany's future would be secured if Austria and Prussia could only abandon the rivalry which had marred their relations since the First Silesian War of 1740. Their cooperation would inevitably lubricate the rusty legis-

[19] Hardenberg's plan, dated Feb. 5, 1806, is printed in Leopold von Ranke, *Hardenberg und die Geschichte des preussischen Staates* (5 vols., Leipzig, 1877), III, 352. Summarized by Schulz, op.cit., pp. 41-46. A somewhat similar plan, though arbitrarily excluding Austria, was advanced by a Bavarian author (probably Georg Heinrich Kayser), *Von den höchsten Interessen des deutschen Reiches mit besonderer Rücksicht auf den Einfluss, welchen Bayern gegenwärtig auf jene behauptet* (Heilbronn, 1806). He pleaded in effect for a Prussian-Bavarian dualism. It should be remembered that at the time Bavaria was closely and Prussia loosely allied with France, and that Napoleon might be expected to support such an anti-Austrian project. It is unnecessary in this context to discuss the numerous pamphlets which explicitly aimed at the aggrandizement of Prussia in Northern Germany, since these did not pretend to aim at conserving the imperial constitution as shaped by the events of 1803, though they frequently asserted that the interests of Prussia and Germany were identical. See the discussion in Schulz, op.cit., pp. 65-76.

lative machinery of Regensburg and permit the raising of a powerful imperial army (which the sanguine Gentz even estimated at half a million men). His conception was favored by Stadion in Austria and Stein in Prussia, though neither man was able to put his personal imprint upon the policy of his respective state before the collapse of the empire in 1806; Gentz's plan in many ways anticipated the post-1815 pattern of Austro-Prussian cooperation, which proved successful in safeguarding the German internal and external *status quo* for an entire generation.[20]

The latter-day observer is struck by the futility of all of these proposals for buttressing the tottering imperial structure. There was no apparent reason why imperial patriotism, a sentiment virtually moribund for centuries, should suddenly revive in the constituent members of the empire. The "third Germany" obviously lacked the power and solidarity to play an independent role in either German or European affairs, and when it finally was organized under Napoleonic auspices it did not buttress the empire but signalized, instead, its formal dissolution. The plans to reorganize the German constitution on a tripartite or a dualistic basis were usually cloaks for the aggrandizement of one or more of the leading members; when they were meant sincerely, they optimistically assumed that the Great Powers could transcend traditional antagonisms and recognize the need for cooperation against the common French foe. The falsity of all these assumptions is indicated by the fact that no reform plan passed beyond purely literary advocacy in the years after 1803; the utter hollowness of the empire was to be demonstrated by its unlamented end in 1806.

The End of the Empire[21]

THE AUSTRIAN IMPERIAL CROWN OF 1804

The imperial prerogatives of Francis II had been left technically intact by the Napoleonic Revolution, but there could be no question that his

[20] The most succinct statement of Gentz's views is his memorandum of Sept. 6, 1804, printed in G. Schlesier, *Schriften von F. Gentz* (Mannheim, 1840), IV, 23-34. Summarized in Schulz, op.cit., pp. 24-26.

[21] This section is based, unless otherwise indicated, upon the standard monograph by Heinrich Ritter von Srbik, *Das Österreichische Kaisertum und das Ende des Heiligen Römischen Reiches 1804-1806* (Berlin, 1927). Hellmuth Rössler, *Napoleons Griff nach der Karlskrone. Das Ende des alten Reiches 1806* (Munich, 1957), is a sprightly account which popularizes many of the conclusions of the author's magisterial *Österreichs Kampf um Deutschlands Befreiung. Die deutsche Politik der nationalen Führer Österreichs 1805-1815* (2 vols., Hamburg, 1940), Bk. II, Ch. 1, "Das Ende des Ersten Reichs. Der Rückzug der deutschen Politik in die Idee."

influence as emperor had been reduced to the vanishing point. He had been unable to check the intervention of France and Russia in German affairs, or to prevent the elimination of those *Stände*—especially the ecclesiastical states and the Free Cities—hitherto most loyal to the House of Habsburg. The South German states were becoming satellites of France at the same time that most of Northern Germany was falling under Prussian domination. The political power of the emperor was confined more than ever to his hereditary Habsburg provinces, and there was considerable apprehension that he might soon lose the shadow along with the substance of his power. Would the new electoral college established in 1803 pick a Habsburg prince at the next imperial vacancy? The loss of the Imperial Crown would certainly be a calamitous blow to the prestige of the House of Habsburg.

The advisers of Francis were pondering this problem when a new factor was introduced by Napoleon's assumption of a French Imperial Crown on May 18, 1804. Would the Habsburg dynasty be able to maintain parity of status with the Bonapartist dynasty in the future? Some doubted that the German elective crown would be considered the equal of the French hereditary crown, aside from the doubt whether the elective crown would always remain with the House of Habsburg. The simplest way to protect Habsburg interests would have been to make the German Imperial Crown hereditary in the descendants of Francis II. This simple solution was unfortunately impossible from both the standpoint of law and politics. The emperor had, as had all of his predecessors, pledged in his electoral capitulation that he would not seek to make his dignity hereditary. None of the states of Germany had any reason to give a sympathetic consideration to a request by Francis for hereditary status. Prussia and the South German states, egged on by Napoleon, were especially hostile to the consolidation of the empire implied in a hereditary crown; while those states which had recently gone to some trouble to achieve the status of electors—such as Württemberg, Baden, and Hessen—had an extra reason to dislike the introduction of the hereditary principle. The potential supporters of a hereditary dignity—bishops, Free Cities, and Imperial Knights— had been politically eliminated in 1803 or were about to be eliminated.

It was clear, therefore, that a hereditary Habsburg crown could not be established in connection with the Holy Roman crown; it could be established—if at all—only on the territorial basis of the hereditary provinces of the House of Austria. There was much to be said in favor of the latter solution. The Habsburg lands were certainly extensive and powerful enough to warrant an imperial title which would not appear inferior to those of Napoleon and Alexander I. Such a title, providing a new cement between historically very heterogeneous lands, would provide a desirable reinforcement of the Pragmatic Sanction of 1713. There was little practical danger, moreover, of conflict between the old German Imperial Crown and a new Habsburg crown: so long as Francis held both, any friction would be resolved within his own breast; if they should ever be separated, the occasion for friction would be minimized by the long-existing *de facto* exemption of the Habsburg provinces from imperial jurisdiction in such matters as justice, army recuitment, and finance.

The legal situation, however, was quite different from the factual one. It was an unwritten law of the Holy Roman Empire that there would be only *one* emperor within its territory; henceforth that part of the Habsburg Monarchy which belonged to the empire (Bohemia, the Austrian duchies, et cetera) would stand under *two* Imperial Crowns. The new crown would be a clear violation of the imperial constitution, and Francis would violate his coronation oath if he became the accomplice (or, worse still, the instigator) of the creation of the new crown. The difficulty could have been avoided if the new Austrian crown could have been based only upon those Habsburg territories— Hungary, Venetia, and Galicia—which stood outside the empire and in which Francis was a sovereign prince by dynastic right. This solution would have prevented, however, the achievement of that new measure of unity for all the Habsburg territories which was, apart from fear of loss of the German crown, the primary motive behind the establishment of the new dignity.[22]

Francis proclaimed his new Austrian imperial title on Aug. 10, 1804, after he had secured Napoleon's advance approval in a diplomatic bargain which provided for the reciprocal recognition of the new French and Austrian crowns. He had little difficulty in securing general European recognition for the new title, though Prussia and England were obviously reluctant and Russia delayed its acceptance until it negotiated a secret Austro-Russian alliance (the core of the Third Coalition) on Nov. 6, 1804. The *Reichstag* was informed rather than consulted about the new dignity, though it was the party most directly affected. Its members acquiesced in what they could not prevent;

[22] All the problems connected with the Austrian imperial title are exhaustively discussed in two standard monographs: F. Tezner, *Der österreichische Kaisertitel* (Vienna, 1899), and J. M. Berger, *Der grosse Titel des Kaisers von Österreich und sein historischer Aufbau* (Vienna, 1907).

there was general agreement that it would be unsporting to embarrass Austria by public discussion of the unconstitutionality of its action. The only state that refused to abide by this "gentlemen's agreement" and insisted upon speaking out on behalf of the violated German constitution was Sweden, whose hothead legitimist King Gustavus IV was also Duke of Hither Pommerania. His ambassador introduced a motion on Aug. 26, 1804, that the *Reichstag* should debate the Austrian action in order "to give each of its members the opportunity of expressing his views upon the constitutional issue"; for Francis' action inevitably impinged upon "the general problem of the composition of the German Empire."[23] The Regensburg assembly was visibly embarrassed by the Swedish motion and decided upon a heroic step to avoid debate: it adjourned until Nov. 12 to give its hard-working members a well-earned—though until Aug. 27 unscheduled—extra vacation.

Apart from the action of Sweden, there was no official protest to the Austrian assumption of the new title and to the further disintegration of the empire which it signaled. There was, however, a good deal of private criticism directed against a step which broke imperial law and amounted to a public confession by Francis that he despaired about maintaining his old imperial title much longer. Friedrich von Gentz, though anxious to make his way in the Austrian service, wrote an indignant letter to his friend Count Metternich, then Habsburg ambassador to the court of Dresden, on Aug. 22, 1804:

> What do you have to say about the unspeakable meanness (*namenlose Erbärmlichkeit*) of the new Austrian Imperial title? . . . An Emperor of Austria is in and of itself a true political solecism, for Austria is a province subordinated to the Empire by feudal ties; one could just as well speak of an Emperor of Salzburg, of Frankfurt, or of Passau. If the German Imperial dignity remains with the House of Habsburg—and how stupid to admit publicly now, when no immediate danger presses, that one fears to lose it!—the new dignity will prove quite useless; if we lose the true Crown the *false* imitation will never allow us to maintain equality of rank: for an Austrian Emperor will always—and inevitably—stand in subordination to a German Emperor, and cannot be the equal of either the latter or the French Emperor. And to find this nonsensical title [of Francis] grafted upon the most hateful of all usurpations [Napoleon's]! A counterpart to the Empire of Bonaparte! To justify [by our parallel action] the most insolent elevation of this

[23] The Swedish motion is quoted by Srbik, op.cit., p. 34.

murderous theatrical King! which every decent mind, if it does not wish to sink into despair, must view as a purely temporary phenomenon! What an entanglement of insipidity, wretchedness, and vileness.[24]

Gentz's *cri de coeur* is a good example of how easily indignation can lead able minds to faulty conclusions. His prediction that an Austrian crown must always be subordinate to a German crown was quite mistaken, and his argument ignored the strong possibility that the German Imperial Crown would soon disappear altogether. It was but elementary prudence for Francis to establish a fallback position in advance of a new crisis, and to secure French recognition at a time when Napoleon was willing to extend a *quid pro quo*. The additional advantage of consummating the union of all Habsburg lands was fully achieved. The alternative policy of clinging to the German crown and defying Napoleon—even to the point of refusing to recognize *his* new title, also advocated by Gentz[25]—was obviously beyond Austria's strength. Francis' conduct appears justified in the light of subsequent developments, although it cannot be denied that it put an additional nail in the coffin of the much-battered empire. It revealed in advance that Austria was not prepared to fight to maintain its German position, and that the Holy Roman Emperor would do nothing to prop up the dying Holy Roman Empire in its final agony.

THE WAR OF THE THIRD COALITION

A prolonged period of peace in Germany might have seen the consolidation of the constitutional structure of 1803; but prolonged peace proved impossible in Napoleonic Europe. England and France resumed warfare in 1803, and the Conservative Powers of the Continent—especially Austria and Russia—were far from reconciled to French hegemony in Western Europe. Gentz's outburst signaled the fact that many European Conservatives were irreconcilably opposed to Napoleon because they saw him as the heir of the hated French Revolution. Their view was reinforced when a French platoon, under Napoleon's

---

[24] *Briefe von und an Friedrich von Gentz* (ed. F. C. Wittichen and Ernst Salzer), III (1), 28ff.

[25] See Gentz's memorandum addressed to Count Cobenzl, the Austrian foreign minister, on June 6, 1804: *Memoire sur la nécessité de ne pas reconnaître le titre imperial de Bonaparte*, printed in Gustav Schlesior, *Memoires et lettres inedites du chevalier de Gentz* (Stuttgart, 1841). Gentz's opposition to the French imperial title is the subject of a special monograph: Max Pflüger, *Friedrich von Gentz als Widersacher Napoleons I. Ein Beitrag zu der Geschichte des 18. Mai 1804* (Reichenbach, 1904).

orders, invaded Baden and kidnaped the duke of Enghien; his judicial murder quickly followed (March 21, 1804). The *Reichstag* at Regensburg exposed its utter impotence by its mute acquiescence in this outrageous violation of German territory in time of peace.

The prospect of renewed war between France and Conservative Europe quickly produced many additional signs of imperial disintegration. The South German states, checked briefly in their campaign against the Imperial Knights by the *Konservatorium* of Jan. 23, 1804, were preparing to resume their policy of spoliation. They recognized that their ambitious desire for "sovereignty" required the support of France, and when Napoleon prepared to attack Austria in the autumn of 1805 he could count upon their willing alliance. Times had changed since 1795, when Prussia's neutrality in a war between the emperor and France had aroused a good deal of moral indignation; few were surprised ten years later when Bavaria, Baden, and Württemberg took the further step of active alliance with France in flat disregard of their obligations to the empire. Their support proved important in defeating Austria in the Austerlitz campaign—a military catastrophe which forced Francis to accept the humiliating Treaty of Pressburg (Dec. 26, 1805).[26]

Pressburg marked a further stage in the prolonged agony of the empire. The loss of its Adriatic territories and of the German provinces of Vorarlberg and Tyrol weakened Austria and thereby added to its difficulties in playing an effective role in German affairs. Even more important was Bavaria and Württemberg's elevation to "sovereign kingdoms" within the *Confédération Germanique* (a significant new term used in Article VII of the treaty for what had previously been called the *Empire Germanique* in diplomatic documents). A "sovereign kingdom" totally within the empire was a constitutional novelty, for the royal title of the Hohenzollerns had been based upon that part of Prussia lying outside of the imperial boundaries. Napoleon immediately permitted his "sovereign" satellites to gobble up all the small principalities in their neighborhood; the winter of 1805-06 saw the

---

[26] The indispensable book on South German developments during this period is Theodor Bitterauf, *Die Gründung des Rheinbundes und der Untergang des alten Reiches* (Munich, 1905), which caused a "historiographical revolution" when first published because it broke with the practice of the "National Liberal" historians who condemned the conduct of the South German states by the application of anachronistic national standards. The public opinion of the period is surveyed in the admirable dissertation by Siegmund Satz, *Die Politik der deutschen Staaten vom Herbst 1805 bis zum Herbst 1806 im Lichte der gleichzeitigen deutschen Publizistik* (Berlin, 1908). Henceforth cited as Satz, *Die Politik.*

final mediatization of the Imperial Knights. These events showed that the empire had become an empty shell; it had been so insignificant—and divided—during the recent hostilities that it had failed to declare war against the French invader.

How did Prussia, the second Great Power of the empire, conduct its policy while the future of Germany was being shaped by French arms? In the same spirit of irresolution and vacillation which had characterized Prussian policy since the Treaty of Basel in 1795. Prussia desired to win a hegemonial position in Northern Germany—a goal which must be opposed by Austria (as incompatible with its traditional pre-eminence in Germany) and England (as threatening the independence of Hannover); a goal which in fact could be achieved only by taking bold, resolute steps in close cooperation with France. Cooperation with France involved the danger of satellite status; bold and resolute steps could easily lead to war. Frederick William III and his incapable entourage were desperately anxious to avoid both. The result was that their policy was often inactive when strong measures were imperative and—on the rare occasions when they roused themselves into activity—unsteady to the point of arousing universal distrust. Prussia exposed her covetous desires without quite daring to grab; she cooperated with France without quite daring to break openly with France's enemies—Russia, Austria, and England. King Frederick William III placed himself between all stools; Prussia soon became a *quantité negligéable* on the European scene.

At the beginning of the Austerlitz campaign Napoleon showed his contempt for Prussia by marching his troops through the Prussian territory of Ansbach. Frederick William responded by allowing himself to be pressured into an alliance with Austria and Russia in the Treaty of Potsdam (Nov. 3, 1805), a treaty sealed by a sentimental scene at the grave of Frederick the Great. A resolute Prussia could now have made itself the master of Europe by striking with overwhelming force against the overextended lines of communication of the French army standing in distant Bohemia; but the irresolute Frederick William agreed only to sending an ultimatum to Napoleon, warning that Prussia would enter the war on December 15, 1805, unless France should by that date accept what were obviously unacceptable terms. The incapable Haugwitz was selected to carry this ultimatum to Napoleon, but Austerlitz had transformed the entire situation before he could complete his mission. Haugwitz, evidently following oral instructions from the king, thereupon reversed the objective of his mission and agreed to an alliance with France (Treaty of Schönbrunn, Dec. 15, 1805). Under this treaty Prussia received Hannover at the hands of Napoleon—a transaction which was, in the classic phrase of the English minister Fox, "a compound of everything that is contemptible in servility with everything that is odious in rapacity."[27] At Schönbrunn Prussia gave its advance approval to the as-yet-unspecified terms of the Treaty of Pressburg, terms which were certain to strengthen the ascendancy of France in Germany. The Prussian occupation of Hannover led inevitably to an English declaration of war which inflicted ruinous losses upon Prussia's merchant marine (June 1806). Yet even though France and Prussia were then at war against a common enemy, there could be no cordial or lasting friendship between them. Napoleon refused to treat Prussia as an equal and Prussia was not yet prepared to become a satellite; it was, however, willing to acquiesce in the French policy which in the summer of 1806 struck the final blow against the Holy Roman Empire.[28]

THE IMPERIAL ABDICATION

After the Treaty of Pressburg the leading statesmen of Austria were deeply divided on the foreign policy their country should pursue. The group headed by Archduke Charles, a prince whose legendary reputation as a soldier far exceeded his merits, favored a full alliance with France and was deeply suspicious of Austria's recent ally, Russia. He was willing to abandon what was left of the Habsburg position in Germany, favoring the early abdication of the Roman crown as the best way of winning Napoleon's friendship. A group headed by Count Philipp Stadion, who had been appointed foreign minister at the time of Pressburg, favored the opposite policy of cultivating close relations with Russia and England and wooing Prussia for the resumption of an anti-Napoleonic policy. He was deeply anti-French and antirevolutionary in his outlook and devoted to the Holy Roman Empire. Both parties were agreed, however, on one basic point: Austria, crushed by the Austerlitz campaign, must avoid any renewal of war in the foreseeable future.

The French emperor, realizing this, set out to create a series of *faits*

[27] Quoted in J. A. Marriott and C. Robertson, *The Evolution of Prussia* (Oxford, 1917), pp. 210-11.

[28] For a devastating contemporary indictment of the conduct of Prussian policy see the anonymous *Das gepriesene Preussen oder Beleuchtung der gegenwärtigen Regierung, Parallelen, Anekdoten und Erzählungen. Alles Aktenmässige Wahrheiten. Unächtes Metall scheint nur in grosser Entfernung wie Gold* (n.p., 1805). The well-informed author was probably a high Prussian official.

accomplis to achieve the complete domination of Germany. The major South German states, his most faithful allies in the recent campaign, were encouraged to swallow up their weaker neighbors. Servility toward Napoleon had its disadvantages, however, for the South German princes were forced to contribute to the respectability of the Bonapartist crown by a series of dynastic marriages to Napoleonic relatives. Further steps aggrandizing the Bonapartist dynasty were the creation of the new Duchy of Berg for the benefit of Napoleon's brother-in-law Murat (March 1806) and the appointment of Napoleon's uncle, Cardinal Joseph Fesch, as Coadjutor to Arch-Chancellor Dalberg (May 1806). The latter step was of great potential importance, since it might give a relative of Napoleon the key position in a future imperial election. There was little doubt that most of Germany was becoming a Napoleonic province—a situation which became clear to all when on July 12, 1806, sixteen South and West German states formed a new Confederation of the Rhine—under Napoleon's protection—and formally pledged themselves to secede from the Holy Roman Empire. This act was clearly unconstitutional, since the empire was a perpetual body without any recognized right of secession; the surviving imperial authorities were confronted with the alternatives of war or abandoning the pretense that the empire still retained vitality. It was certain that Francis II would eventually choose the latter course and abdicate his empty title; he was quickly *forced* to do so, however, when he was confronted by Napoleon's ultimatum in late July. The formal act of abdication was promulgated on August 6, 1806.

This step had been pondered since early spring, when Napoleon's aim of dominating Germany became unmistakable. Philipp Stadion had received (in May 1806) advisory memoranda from two exceptionally well-qualified Austrian diplomats stationed at Regensburg—his own brother Friedrich Stadion, the Bohemian ambassador, and Johann Alois Freiherr von Hügel, the imperial commissioner (*Konkommissar*). Both ambassadors saw the inevitability of the abdication and refused to become sentimental about the loss of the old Imperial Crown. What concerned them was the possibility that Francis would be forced to abdicate without the simultaneous end of the empire; the ensuing vacancy might be filled by Napoleon himself or one of his creatures; then there might be a revival of imperial prerogatives to the detriment of the House of Austria (since many of its provinces would then fall under the sovereignty—however diluted in practice—of an "alien" ruler). Both Hügel and Stadion counseled that an abdication must be accompanied by strict safeguards against such undesirable consequences. In the words of Hügel:

> We must keep in mind as a basic principle that the Imperial Crown should be laid down as soon as this step can be taken without the mentioned disadvantages to the Austrian Monarchy, and provided we can maintain all the privileges and exemptions from Imperial burdens we now enjoy; and we must of course seek any additional advantages which may be attainable by way of compensation. Our willingness to renounce the Crown, subject to the above conditions and the achievement of compensatory advantages, need not be kept secret; it should, in fact, be bruited in general terms to the public and announced confidentially through diplomatic channels.[29]

Friedrich Stadion argued in favor of abdication, since the basis of imperial power had disappeared since the Treaty of Pressburg. Before 1805 the emperor had carried some political weight in Germany because he held a strong position in the Swabian *Kreis* with his Breisgau territory, could count upon the loyal support of the Imperial Knights and other groups now mediatized, and exercised the widely recognized function of protecting the German empire against the interference of France. All these conditions for the effective performance of imperial duties had now vanished; it was dangerous for the prestige of the emperor to retain a function after he had been deprived of the means for its adequate performance. Retention of the Imperial Crown now would only perpetuate unnecessary friction with France.[30]

The memoranda of Hügel and Stadion have been criticized by some modern historians for their lack of reverence for the venerable institution of the thousand-year-old empire;[31] both ambassadors viewed the question of the pros and cons of an abdication exclusively from the point of view of the interests of the House of Austria. This is but further proof that the final hour of the long-lingering empire was at hand: it had long ago lost its physical strength; it now proved increasingly incapable of inspiring even sentimental loyalty. A more pertinent criticism is that neither Hügel nor Stadion saw the urgency of the abdication question. They did not foresee the pace at which Na-

---

[29] Hügel's *Gutachten* of May 17, 1806: *Ob das österreichische Kaiserhaus nach den eingetretenen Folgen des Pressburger Friedens die römisch-deutsche Kaiserwürde forttragen solle?* Quoted in H. Rössler, *Österreichs Kampf*, I, 211.

[30] Stadion's memorandum, dated May 24, 1806, is paraphrased by Srbik, op.cit., pp. 46-47.

[31] Srbik gives passionate expression to this view. Ibid., pp. 43ff.

poleon would press his German policy, and they believed that the French emperor would agree to favorable conditions in the course of leisurely negotiations. At any rate, no attempt was made to initiate negotiations while a *quid pro quo* might still be won in return for a timely voluntary abdication. Count Philipp Stadion shared the procrastinating outlook of his advisers and apparently hoped that the empire might survive the present crisis.[32] He and his imperial master were to be rudely surprised by the creation of the Confederation of the Rhine.

Yet the establishment of the new confederation proved a blessing in disguise because it ended the possibility—which had given so much worry to Hügel and Stadion—that the empire might continue under a new emperor after the abdication of Francis. The secession of sixteen states was a revolutionary act which the empire could not survive. The note by which the new Confederate States announced their secession at Regensburg (Aug. 1, 1806) was notable for its servility toward Napoleon, "that monarch whose intentions have always shown themselves to be in complete conformity with the true interests of Germany"; it was entirely accurate, however, in its description of the conditions which had led to secession:

> The events of the last three wars, which have troubled Germany almost without interruption, and the political changes which have resulted from those wars, have placed in a glaring light the sad truth, that the ties which have hitherto united the various members of the German political body, are no longer adequate for achieving that purpose. In truth this body has long been in total dissolution as every true German heart knows only too well. Depressing as the experience of the last few years has been, it has but revealed the decrepitude of a constitution venerable in its origins but become inadequate through the changeableness which adheres to all human institutions. . . . [This decrepitude] became unmistakably clear in 1795 [when the Treaty of Basel] led to the separation of North from South Germany. From that moment on, all ideas of a common Fatherland with common interests necessarily disappeared: such words as *Reichskrieg* and *Reichsfrieden* (Imperial war and peace) became empty words without substance; one looked in vain for Germany in the midst of the Imperial body. The princes with lands located near France, lacking protection and exposed to the horrors

[32] This is the plausible surmise of the greatest authority, H. Rössler. *Österreichs Kampf*, I, 219.

of war which could not be terminated through the existing constitutional machinery, were forced to separate themselves from the Empire through individual peace treaties. The Peace of Lunéville, and even more the *Reichsschluss* of 1803, appeared at first to breathe new life into the old Imperial constitution through the elimination of the weak parts of the system and the strengthening of the main pillars. The events which have transpired during the last ten months have destroyed, however, this last hope and have shown beyond the slightest shadow of doubt the total inadequacy of the existing constitution.[33]

The declaration of secession was accompanied by a provocative French note which withdrew diplomatic recognition from the empire (*Sa Majesté l'Empereur est donc oblige de declarer, qu'Il ne reconnait plus l'existence de constitution germanique*). The reason given for this unprecedented insult was the weakness of the empire, whose *Reichstag* lacked a will of its own, whose imperial courts were unable to enforce their judgments, and which was generally incapable of coherent action. The French declaration dryly noted the Prussian annexation of Hannover and the rise of the South German states to sovereignty as symptoms of imperial decay—an accurate-enough observation, though it came with some gall from the main instigator of these events.[34]

The French declaration at Regensburg had been preceded by an ultimatum to Austria demanding the abdication of the crown by August 10, 1806. The Emperor Francis hastened to comply, since resistance would have meant an undesired war at an undesirable time; there is, incidentally, no evidence that the pedestrian Francis was in any way concerned with the historic significance of a renunciation which brought a thousand-year-old institution to an official close. Philipp Stadion, though he was only too poignantly aware of the historic glory of the empire, reluctantly counseled abdication. He drafted the official document which avoided all reference to the real reason for abdication (the French ultimatum) but mentioned a good reason instead:

We owe it to our principles and our dignity to renounce the Crown the moment we are convinced of the impossibility of our continuing to fulfill the duties of our Imperial office. This Crown had value in

[33] *Austrittserklärung der Rheinbundstaaten*, Aug. 1, 1806. Printed in E. R. Huber, *Dokumente zur deutschen Verfassungsgeschichte* (2 vols., Stuttgart, 1961-64), I, 32-33.
[34] *Erklärung des französischen Gesandten am Reichstag zu Regensburg*, Aug. 1, 1806. Printed in ibid., pp. 34-35.

our eyes only as long as we were able to justify the confidence which the Electors, princes and other members of the Empire placed in us, and we were convinced that we were able to perform all our obligations in a satisfactory manner.

As he renounced the Roman crown Francis explicitly freed all the *Stände* and all the officials of the empire—and, more specifically, the judges of the imperial courts and all imperial civil servants—"from all obligations which they owed to us as the legal head of the Empire under the constitution"; and he generously promised in a separate declaration that all imperial salaries would be paid by the Austrian exchequer for the lifetime of the present incumbents. Francis concluded his act of renunciation by safeguarding the interests of his House against the contingency—however remote—that the empire should survive, or be restored, under some non-Habsburg ruler; he followed the precedent set by the Confederate States of formally withdrawing his Austrian provinces from the empire's jurisdiction.[35]

While there is no question that Francis was personally entitled to abdicate a crown he was no longer willing to wear, he certainly had no constitutional power to dissolve the fabric of imperial obligation per se. The empire, like all sovereign states, was intended to be perpetual and the emperor had sworn to maintain it to the best of his ability. He broke his coronation oath when he declared it dissolved, and he failed to consult the *Stände* assembled at Regensburg about his highly irregular procedure. One can argue, therefore, that the imperial death warrant was technically *ultra vires* and therefore null and void, and that the empire "legally" continued to exist after 1806. The question was not, however, one of constitutional law but one of politics and public opinion. All European states, both German and non-German, acquiesced in the dissolution and refused to lift a finger in defense of the empire. It is true, of course, that the end of the empire in 1806 was more the result of French intervention than an expression of the will of German "domestic" political forces, but it is also significant that no serious attempt was made to restore the imperial structure when Germans were again masters in their own house after the collapse of French power in 1813.[36]

---

[35] *Niederlegung der Kaiserkrone durch Kaiser Franz II.* Printed in ibid., pp. 35-36.

[36] For a brilliant discussion of the legal issues connected with the dissolution of the empire see E. R. Huber, *Verfassungsgeschichte*, I, 72-74.

It is extremely difficult to secure a balanced impression of how German public opinion reacted to the end of the empire, although certainly there was no widespread indignation. The oft-quoted remark made by Goethe (August 7, 1806) when, traveling home from Karlsbad in a public carriage, he learned about the secession of the Confederate States—"Quarrel between coachman and a servant on the coach-box, which agitated us more than the split of the Roman Empire"—is certainly indicative of the indifference of many Germans; it must be set, however, against the letter which Goethe's mother wrote from Frankfurt when hearing of the empire's dissolution:

> I feel the way I feel when an old friend is very ill and the doctors have abandoned all hope. One knows that he will die, yet despite this certainty one is nonetheless shaken when the death notice finally arrives in the mail. This is my mood and that of the entire city. Yesterday the prayer for Emperor and Empire was omitted for the first time from the Church service.[37]

Certainly many politically interested people treated the dissolution with remarkable indifference. Professor C. D. Voss of Halle, editor of the journal *Die Zeiten*, wrote on Aug. 26, 1806:

> The dissolution of the German Empire cannot arouse much indignation from those of us who were free of illusions concerning its vitality; indeed it scarcely arouses any deep interest. The only surprising fact is that this dissolution did not occur half a century, or even two or three centuries, earlier.[38]

Other voices, however, expressed deep sorrow and sharp indignation. An anonymous poet wrote in September 1806 in an obscure journal, *Der Zeitstrom*:

> "Alle klagen wir nun
> Denn geraubet wird uns ein Heiliges, das wir seit früher
> Jugend geheget mit frommen Sinn."[39]

Schirach's *Politisches Journal*, which we have encountered as a sharp foe of revolutionary France, included an article, "Todtenopfer am

---

[37] Both quotations are cited by Raumer, *Deutschland um 1800*, pp. 172-73.
[38] Quoted in S. Satz, *Die Politik*, p. 71.
[39] Ibid., p. 70. "All of us are complaining about the forcible deprivation of something holy which we have cherished since early youth in a spirit of reverence."

Sarkophage des heiligen Römischen Reiches Deutscher Nation," in its issue of September 1806:

> The beautiful thousand year old tie, which united 24 million Germans . . . has been torn asunder. Public spirit (*Gemeingeist*) which had survived in a few individuals at least, has now vanished altogether; no German heart will henceforth beat faster at the mention of Hermann's name.[40]

There is abundant evidence that the community of envoys at Regensburg was deeply moved by the secession of the Confederate States and the news of the imperial abdication.[41] For example, Count Goertz, the ambassador of Prussia (a state not noted for its imperial loyalty), wrote to his chief, Foreign Minister Haugwitz, on Aug. 1, 1806:

> So the Empire which is the oldest and by its rank the foremost of the Empires of Europe has come to an end! My pen is unable to give adequate expression to the feelings of pain, lamentation, and despair which this great event has aroused among all people here. History will consider it a very important revolution—perhaps it will even become, what God may prevent, a prelude to a still more general revolution.[42]

Goertz's worst apprehensions were to be exceeded less than three months later when the end of the moribund empire was followed by the collapse of the supposedly vigorous and dynamic monarchy of Frederick William III. Prussia capped the folly of a decade's weak and cowardly foreign policy by an utterly rash challenge of Napoleon. It had failed to join the European coalition when victory beckoned in 1805; it now singlehandedly took on the entire French army. This kind of *hubris* found its nemesis in the disastrous Battle of Jena (Oct. 14, 1806); the pitiful record of both the government and the army in the aftermath of that battle showed that much was rotten in a state long the showcase of "enlightened absolutism."

Germans might well despair as the fateful year 1806 drew to a close. A thousand and six years of empire, going back to Charlemagne's coronation in Rome, had come to an inglorious close; the Habsburg Monarchy, thrice defeated in war and now deprived of the German

---

[40] Ibid. Hermann, alias Arminius, had maintained German liberty against Roman imperialism in the battle of the Teutoburg Forest in A.D. 9.

[41] Srbik assembles a large collection of voices in *Das Österreichische Kaisertum*, pp. 65-66.

[42] Quoted in K. T. Heigel, *Deutsche Geschichte*, ii, 667.

Imperial Crown, had withdrawn from German affairs; the Prussian Monarchy, long the terror and envy of much of Germany, was occupied by the French conqueror except for a small corner east of the Vistula; Napoleonic France had annexed the Rhineland and dominated two thirds of Germany through the satellite Confederation of the Rhine. German opinion, insofar as it took an interest in public affairs, was shocked and numbed; the few isolated protests, like that of the Nürnberg bookseller Palm, were silenced by French execution squads. There was much to be ashamed of in the recent past; the present filled all patriotic Germans with despair; and they had little reason to expect a better future soon.

CHAPTER 14

Conclusion and Prospectus

THE GERMANY of 1806 was very different from that of 1770. How could it be otherwise? In 1770 the structure of the empire stood intact; Prussia and Austria were proud and independent powers in the European pentarchy; the map of Germany was littered with unviable units left over from the Middle Ages: "enlightened absolutism" had only begun its alliance with an embryonic Radicalism. Apart from a few intellectuals there was little overt discontent. For the broad mass of the population, whether in country or town, the "cake of custom" was still unbroken. Most Germans could as yet scarcely conceive of society as other than it was.

By 1806 this Germany, marked by traditionalism in *Weltanschauung* and obsolescence in political institutions, was gone. Prussia and Austria had suffered humiliating defeats and stood in danger of becoming French satellites; hundreds of small states—ecclesiastical, municipal, and knightly—had fallen victim to rapacious neighbors; "enlightened absolutism" now flourished in the middle states which had consolidated their territories under the benevolent, though not disinterested, patronage of Napoleon; the old Holy Roman Empire had been replaced by the brand-new Confederation of the Rhine. The "cake of custom" *had* been broken; now Germans increasingly wanted and expected change, and the age-old pattern of relative stability was irretrievably gone.

These changes were only to a small extent the work of indigenous Radical forces. The ideas of the *Aufklärung* had, to be sure, undermined much spiritual allegiance to the *ancien régime*; but Germany's social development was as yet too backward to permit these ideas to become the weapon of a Radical *bourgeoisie* bent upon overthrowing the *status quo*. The groups in Germany that benefited from the existing situation were easily able, and only too willing, to suppress the feeble forces of Radicalism, especially after Conservatives had become aroused by the challenge of the French Revolution.

The situation was transformed, however, after France began to interfere directly in German affairs in the late 1790's. This intervention ended the precarious equilibrium which had supported Germany's political structure; France was able to ally itself with several medium-sized states whose ambitions had hitherto been curbed by the surviving imperial fabric. They now not only aggrandized themselves at the expense of their weaker neighbors, but launched thoroughly Radical policies in the fields of administration, economics, and religious affairs. The "enlightened despots" of the medium states were intent upon crushing all obstacles to state omnipotence while simultaneously pleasing their French master. The Napoleonic Revolution proved a victory for and a stimulant to German Radicalism.

Germany's social structure was changed far less than the political in the years 1770 to 1806. The prevailing policy of mercantilism was only slightly diluted by laissez-faire, and then only in a few states such as Prussia and Baden. The hierarchic structure of society remained essentially intact. Guild restrictions were somewhat relaxed; Jews (especially in Austria) experienced some improvement in their status; the lot of the peasantry was ameliorated in some places, although the main work of emancipation (especially in Prussia) came only in the years after 1806. The legally privileged position of the aristocracy, however, survived everywhere except in the territories directly annexed by revolutionary France. More than a vigorous reform absolutism was necessary for the effective destruction of aristocratic privilege; it would have required a strong and self-confident *bourgeoisie* and an aroused peasantry—two groups as yet conspicuous by their absence in Germany at the beginning of the nineteenth century.

There were great religious changes during this period, though their full impact was felt only in the years after 1806. The principle of toleration, still challenged in the 1770's, won general acceptance. Protestantism remained internally deadlocked between an increasingly assertative neology, which denied more and more traditional tenets of the sixteenth-century reformers, and an orthodoxy which had launched a counterattack in Wöllnerite Prussia and showed surprising vitality. An important revival of pietistic Protestantism appeared in circles like Emkendorf in Schleswig-Holstein,[1] a revival which contributed to the reconstruction of theology begun by Friedrich Schleiermacher in his epochal *On Religion; Speeches to its Cultured Despisers*.[2] This Reform Conservatism in the theological sphere—consisting, as it did, of the abandonment of obsolete dogmas and the restatement of Protestantism as a living message to the nineteenth century—was as yet confined, however, to a small cultured elite.

---

[1] The standard work is O. Brandt, *Geistesleben und Politik in Schleswig-Holstein um die Wende des 18. Jahrhunderts* (Stuttgart, 1925).

[2] *Ueber die Religion. Reden an die Gebildeten unter ihren Verächtern* (1799), often reprinted (English trans. John Oman, London, 1893).

In the course of the Napoleonic Revolution the Catholic Church was deprived of its secular jurisdiction and much of its property. This cataclysmic event provoked many jeremiads but proved in fact a blessing in disguise. The association of the Church with the *ancien régime*, and, above all, the monopoly of leading ecclesiastical positions enjoyed by the aristocracy, was broken by the principle of "careers open to talent" and a genuine religious revival. Deadening state control over the Church, while temporarily strengthened by the Josephine program and the secularizations of 1803, proved incompatible with Catholicism's new vitality. Ultramontane loyalties were inevitably enhanced as a result of the persecutions and expropriations of the revolutionary and Napoleonic eras. At the same time the movement loosely labeled "romanticism" was restoring the prestige of Catholicism in the intellectual community. The period saw the development of Catholic circles like the *Sacra Familia* in Münster under Princess Gallitzin[3] and the group around St. Klemens Hofbauer in Vienna;[4] while the century-old cultural supremacy of Protestant Germany was challenged by figures like Count Leopold Stolberg, Friedrich Schlegel, and Adam Müller (all three, significantly, converts to Catholicism.[5]

How stood the prospects of German Conservatism in 1806? There was some reason for optimistic confidence even at that seeming nadir of Conservative fortunes. The *Weltanschauung* of the *Aufklärung* had been discredited, at least in part, by the excesses of the revolution and by the tyranny of Napoleon, often called "the last of the enlightened despots." The Romantic movement—appealing to the eternal human craving for miracle, mystery, and authority—had begun to put the *Aufklärung* on the defensive in German cultural life. Political Romanticism, with its built-in Conservative tendency,[6] was only beginning to influence public opinion; but it had already found an inspired voice in the radiant figure of Friedrich Hardenberg, author of the essay

[3] The standard works are the brilliant P. Brachin, *Le Cercle de Münster (1779-1806) et la Pensée Religieuse de F. L. Stolberg* (Paris, 1952), and the pedestrian Ewald Reinhard, *Die münsterische "Familia Sacra"* (Münster, 1953).

[4] The standard work is R. Till, *Hofbauer und sein Kreis* (Vienna, 1951).

[5] The standard works are: on Stolberg, Johannes Jannsen, *Friedrich Leopold Graf zu Stolberg* (2 vols., Freiburg, 1877); on F. Schlegel there is no standard work, though R. Volpers, *F. Schlegel als politischer Denker und deutscher Patriot* (Berlin, 1917), is a useful study; on Müller, J. Baxa, *Adam Müller, ein Lebensbild aus den Befreiungskriegen und der deutschen Restauration* (Jena, 1930), and L. Sauzin, *Adam Heinrich Müller. Sa vie et son oevre* (Paris, 1937).

[6] I hold to this traditional contention despite the brilliant thesis of Carl Schmitt in his *Politische Romantik* (1919) that Romanticism is "subjective occasionalism" without definable objective content.

674

Christendom or Europe.[7] Romantic scholarship was to give powerful support to the Conservative cause through the work of figures such as F. C. von Savigny, the champion of the "historical theory of law";[8] Romantic philosophy, a distinguished advocate in Adam Müller, author of the path-breaking *Elements of Politics.*[9] Two other major German intellectual figures, though far from being romantics themselves, co-operated with romanticists by lending their powerful voices to the Conservative cause: Karl Ludwig von Haller, the self-proclaimed "restorer of political science,"[10] and Friedrich von Gentz, the journalistic mouthpiece of Prince Metternich.

The articulation of Conservative thought by this galaxy of thinkers changed not only the entire tone of German intellectual life, but also contributed to political developments which resulted in the overthrow of the Napoleonic hegemony seven years later. A strong feeling of nationalism, though primarily provoked by resentment against French domination, was stimulated by the work of the romanticists. The Prussian reform movement under Freiherr Karl vom Stein was imbued with the nationalist spirit; romanticism was one of the sources —side by side with Kantian philosophy and the continued vitality of "enlightened absolutism"—of that movement. The Austria of Count Philipp Stadion drew many romantic intellectuals into its service as the Habsburg government fostered a patriotic revival by means of official propaganda. Though nationalism and political romanticism suffered serious setbacks with Stein's fall from power—at the behest of Napoleon—in 1808 and the defeat of Austria in the premature war of 1809, both movements were to contribute to the liberation of Germany in 1813.

Prince Klemens Metternich—the main architect of Napoleon's overthrow who succeeded Stadion in the Austrian foreign ministry in 1809 —was still serving his political apprenticeship as Austrian ambassador to Napoleon's court in 1806. This able defender of the *Status Quo* was very distrustful of nationalist and Romantic forces; he preferred to achieve the liberation of Germany through an old-fashioned "cabinet War" rather than a popular uprising; and he so conducted the war of

---

[7] *Die Christenheit oder Europa* (1799), often reprinted.

[8] His best-known work is *Vom Beruf unserer Zeit für Gesetzgebung und Rechtswissenschaft* (Heidelberg, 1814).

[9] *Die Elemente der Staatskunst* (1809). Reprinted in a critical edition by J. Baxa (Jena, 1922).

[10] See his book *Restauration der Staatswissenschaft* (6 vols., Winterthur, 1816-34). Its main themes were first stated in Haller's *Handbuch der allgemeinen Staatenkunde* (Winterthur, 1808).

675

1813 that nationalist demands could be ignored in the peace settlement. To secure the expulsion of the French and the restoration of Conservative ascendancy he readily accepted Russian intervention in German affairs. In fact, Russia did for the lagging cause of German Conservatism in 1813 what France had done for lagging Radicalism in 1803.

The Vienna settlement of German affairs incorporated the results of the Napoleonic Revolution; Metternich rejected the Reactionaries' program for reviving the Holy Roman Empire and its component anachronisms (ecclesiastical states, Free Cities, and Imperial Knights) although he insisted upon restoring Austria's traditional pre-eminence in German affairs. The new Confederation of 1815 proved so well-attuned to the parallelogram of forces in Central Europe that it survived for half a century—no small achievement in turbulent nineteenth-century Europe. The Radical challenges of the *Burschenschaften* (1817-19), the July Revolution of 1830, and even the events of 1848 could not topple the "Metternichean System"; this was achieved only by the skillful and ruthless policy pursued by Bismarck in 1866. The strength of that durable system—whether one looks at the institutions of the German Confederation or at the measures employed in its defense—owed much to its emergence from the fiery crucible of half a century of Conservative struggle against, and accommodation to, the *Aufklärung*, the revolution, and Napoleon.

Bibliographical Essay

RATHER THAN list all the books, pamphlets, newspapers, and articles consulted in the preparation of this study, it appeared more useful to add a selective bibliography in the form of an essay characterizing major primary sources and secondary works, with special emphasis upon books containing bibliographies useful for further study. The essay will be divided into three parts dealing with general works, German Conservatism before the French Revolution, and Conservatism in the period 1790-1806. A certain amount of overlapping is inevitable, but each title will be mentioned only once.

PART I:

General Works

There are no works specifically devoted to the genesis of German Conservatism, but the subject is raised, albeit incidentally, in the following standard books dealing with Germany in the second half of the eighteenth century: Clemens Theodor Perthes, *Das deutsche Staatsleben vor der Revolution. Eine Vorarbeit zum deutschen Staatsrecht* (Hamburg and Gotha, 1845), a brilliant, too often neglected study written from a moderate Conservative point of view which antagonized Legitimists and Liberals alike; Karl Biedermann, *Deutschland im 18. Jahrhundert* (2 vols., with Vol. II in three separate sections, Leipzig, 1854-80), a vividly written pioneering study by a National Liberal publicist; Ludwig Häusser, *Deutsche Geschichte vom Tode Friedrichs des Grossen bis zur Gründung des Deutschen Bundes* (4 vols., Leipzig, 1854-57), an influential work which too often degenerates into a political and military chronicle; Woldemar Wenck, *Deutschland vor hundert Jahren* (2 vols., Leipzig, 1887-90), a useful collection of information drawn from scattered and not readily accessible magazine sources; Karl Theodor Heigel, *Deutsche Geschichte vom Tode Friedrichs des Grossen bis zur Auflösung des alten Reiches 1786-1806* (2 vols., Stuttgart 1899-1911), primarily a diplomatic history of Austro-Prussian relations but including also a valuable survey of public opinion; Max von Boehm, *Deutschland im 18. Jahrhundert* (2 vols., Berlin, 1921-22), a picturesque, beautifully illustrated, but superficial and undocumented popular work; and W. H. Bruford, *Germany in the Eighteenth Century* (Cambridge, England, 1935), a judicious introduction in English. All these works are destined to be superseded by the magisterial, as yet unpublished *Habilitationsschrift* of Rudolf Vierhaus, *Deutschland vor der Französischen Revolution* (Munster, 1962). Fritz Valjavec, *Die*

677

Entstehung der politischen Strömungen in Deutschland 1770-1815
(Munich, 1951) is of capital importance for its theme of the precocious
crystallization of German Liberal and Conservative thought before
1789, its use of little accessible pamphlet material, and its comparison
between German conditions and those of the Habsburg Monarchy.

The social history of eighteenth-century Germany—so essential for
understanding the rise of Conservatism—is still largely a virgin field
of scholarship. Some outstanding recent studies are the following:
Hans Gerth, *Die sozialgeschichtliche Lage der bürgerlichen Intelligenz
um die Wende des 18. Jahrhunderts* (Frankfurt, 1935), acute in its
sociological analysis; Hans Rosenberg, *Bureaucracy, Aristocracy and
Autocracy. The Prussian Experience 1660-1815* (Cambridge, Mass.,
1958), an effective indictment of the seamy side of Prussia too long
neglected by authors working in the framework of the "Borussian
legend"; and Otto Busch, *Militärsystem und Sozialleben im alten
Preussen 1713-1807: Die Anfänge der sozialen Militarisierung der
preussisch-deutschen Gesellschaft* (Berlin, 1962), a pioneering analysis.

Of the many works on the Enlightenment one of the best is still the
remarkable article of Ernst Troeltsch, "Aufklärung," in *Realencyclopädie für protestantische Theologie und Kirche* (3rd edn., 1897), II,
225-41. Ernst Cassirer, *Die Philosophie der Aufklärung* (Tübingen,
1932) is a great work of intellectual history though it is Germanocen-
tric, traces everything back to Leibnitz and forward to Kant, and is
virtually indifferent to the sociological background. The posthumous
work of Fritz Valjavec, *Geschichte der abendländischen Aufklärung*
(Vienna and Munich, 1961), is exceptionally broad in its range and
lucid in the exposition of detail. A profound analysis of the rise of the
Enlightenment is Reinhart Koselleck, *Kritik und Krise. Ein Beitrag zur
Pathogenese der bürgerlichen Welt* (Freiburg and Munich, 1959)
though it is bitterly hostile to the Enlightenment.

PART II:

German Conservatism before the French Revolution

The rise of self-conscious Conservatism is the theme of an important
article by Karl Mannheim, "Das konservative Denken. Soziologische
Beiträge zum Werden des politisch-historischen Denkens in Deutschland," *Archiv für Sozialwissenschaft*, LVII (1927), 68-142, 470-95. Early
examples of self-conscious Conservative writing are Karl von Eckartshausen, *Über Religion, Freydenkerei und Aufklärung. Eine Schrift zu
den Schriften unserer Zeiten, der Jugend geweiht* (Augsburg, 1789),
arguing against irreligion, as does J. A. Weissenbach, in *Die Vorbothen*

des neuen Heidenthums und die Anstalten, die dazu vorgekehrt wor-
den sind . . . zum Gebrauch derjenigen, denen daran liegt, die Welt zu
kennen (2 vols., n.p. [Basel], 1779), by a prominent Jesuit; and anonymous [Göchhausen], *Enthüllung des Systems der Weltbürger-Repub-*
lik. In Briefen aus der Verlassenschaft eines Freymaurers (Rome
[Leipzig], 1786), the first systematic "exposure" of the alleged *Illumi-*
nati conspiracy.

Thorough accounts of the suppression of the *Illuminati* can be found
in the two standard works, both including full bibliographies; Leopold
Engel, *Geschichte des Illuminatenordens* (Berlin, 1906), an apologia
by a writer who wanted to revive the order, and R. Le Forestier, *Les*
Illuminés de Bavière et la Francmaçonnerie allemande (Paris, 1914),
an impartial and encyclopedic book. Ludwig Wolfram, "Die Illuminaten in Bayern und ihre Verfolgung," *Programm des kgl. humanistischen*
Gymnasiums in Erlangen (2 parts, Erlangen, 1899-1900) is a valuable
though pedestrian chronicle. The Rosicrucians of the 1780's are discussed exhaustively by Arnold Marx, *Die Gold-und Rosenkreuzer*
(Berlin, 1929), briefly by Gustav Krüger, *Die Rosenkreuzer. Ein Über-*
blick (Berlin, 1932); Rosicrucian practices are described in Bernhard
Beyer, *Das Lehrsystem des Ordens der Gold-und Rosenkreutzer* (Leipzig, 1925), a work of piety as well as scholarship; while the practical
influence of Rosicrucianism is examined voluminously by Paul
Schwartz, *Der erste Kulturkampf in Preussen um Kirche und Schule*
(Berlin, 1925). A glaring lacuna in the literature is a monograph on
the decline, fall, and disappearance of the Order.

The best introduction to religious controversies in German Protestantism during the second half of the eighteenth century is Karl Aner,
Die Theologie der Lessingzeit (Halle, 1929), though it substantially
identifies itself with neology. The struggle for religious toleration in
the Rhineland can be followed in J. Hansen, *Quellen zur Geschichte*
des Rheinlandes im Zeitalter der französischen Revolution (4 vols.,
Bonn, 1931-38). The best account of the Goeze-Lessing controversy
is still Georg Reinhard Röpe, *J. M. Goeze, eine Rettung* (Hamburg,
1860), although it is a rehabilitation of Goeze. Goeze's philippics
against Lessing were collected by Erich Schmidt in *Streitschriften*
gegen Lessing (Stuttgart, 1893). The intractable problem of the "true
character" of Lessing's religion has been recently reexamined by Helmut Thielicke, *Offenbarung, Vernunft und Existenz. Studien zur Re-*
ligionsphilosophie Lessings (3rd edn., Gütersloh, 1957). An exhaustive
examination of the contemporary literature dealing with Wöllner's
Edict of Religion is H. P. C. Henke, *Beurtheilung aller Schriften,*

*welche durch das Religions-Edikt und andere damit zusammenhäng-
ende Verfügungen veranlasst sind* (Hamburg, 1793). The controversial
problem of the Catholic *Aufklärung* is covered from opposite points
of view by Heinrich Brück, *Die rationalistischen Bestrebungen im
katholischen Deutschland, besonders in den drei rheinischen Erzbistümern in der 2. Hälfte des 18. Jahrhunderts* (Mainz, 1865), sharply
hostile to the Catholic *Aufklärung,* and Sebastian Merkle, *Die katholische Beurteilung des Aufklärungszeitaltes* (Berlin, 1909), an influential rehabilitation. The most important works on Josephinism are
Eduard Winter, *Der Josephinismus und seine Geschichte. Beiträge
zur Geistesgeschichte Österreichs 1740-1848* (Brünn, 1943), by an un-
frocked priest who views Josephinism as a positive form of "Reform
Catholicism" stupidly opposed by the Curia; Fritz Valjavec, *Der
Josephinismus. Zur geistigen Entwicklung Österreichs im 18. und 19.
Jahrhundert* (2nd edn., Munich, 1945), a brilliant survey with a very
broad conception of "Josephinism" going far beyond the conventional
religious sphere, and including an especially valuable bibliographical
introduction; and Ferdinand Maass, *Der Josephinismus. Quellen zu
seiner Geschichte in Österreich* (4 vols., Vienna, 1951-59), a monumental source collection with exhaustive introductions written from
an Orthodox Catholic point of view. The standard biography of Cardinal Migazzi, written by the Benedictine Cölestin Wolfsgruber,
Christoph Anton Kardinal Migazzi, Fürsterzbischof von Wien (Ravensburg, 1897), Vol. 2, is a general indictment of Josephinism, as is
Sebastian Brunner, *Die Mysterien der Aufklärung in Österreich 1770-
1800* (Mainz, 1869). The standard biography of Joseph, by the Russian
historian Paul von Mitrofanov, *Joseph II. Seine politische und kulturelle Tätigkeit* (Vienna, 1910), is favorable to the Emperor's religious policies.

There are few modern studies analyzing the social controversies of
Germany in the last decades of the eighteenth century. Two exceptions
are Johanna Schultze, *Die Auseinandersetzung zwischen Adel und Bürgertum in den deutschen Zeitschriften der letzten drei Jahrzehnte des
18. Jahrhunderts* (Berlin, 1925), a valuable content analysis though
written in an intolerable jargon, and Fritz Martiny, *Die Adelsfrage in
Preussen vor 1806 als politisches und soziales Problem* (Berlin, 1938),
providing indispensable sociological background for the controversies
dealing with the Prussian Junkers. Examples of contemporary Conservative defense of the principle of aristocracy in general, and aristocratic privilege in particular, are August von Kotzebue, *Vom Adel.
Bruchstück eines grösseren historisch-philosophischen Werkes über*

Ehre und Schande, Ruhm und Nachruhm, aller Völker, aller Jahr-hunderte (Leipzig, 1792), a sprightly written account by the popular playwright; Carl F. Häberlin, "Worauf beruhet die Steuerfreiheit des Adels, und ist sie ungerecht?", *Braunschweigisches Magazin* (February 1793), pp. 82-91, a defense of aristocratic tax exemptions by a well-known professor of public law; Ernst Brandes, "Ist es in den deutschen Staaten vorteilhaft, dass der Adel die ersten Staatsbedienungen besitzt?", *Berliner Monatsschrift*, x (1787), 395-439, a defense of privileged aristocratic access to public office by a prominent Hanno-verian bureaucrat (himself a commoner); Friedrich Wilhelm von Ramdohr, "Über das Verhältniss des anerkannten Geburtsadels deutscher monarchischer Staaten zu den übrigen Klassen ihrer Bürger in Hinsicht auf die ersten Staatsbedienungen," *Berliner Monatsschrift*, xvii (1791), 124-74, 250-83, a more moderate statement of the same position by an aristocratic Hannoverian judge, which includes a polemic against Brandes' extreme position; and J. G. Schlosser, "Von dem Adel" (1789), in *Kleine Schriften* (Basel, 1793), Vol. vi, a defense of aristocracy as a valuable "intermediary power" between prince and people, by a prominent Badenese civil servant. The best contemporary introduction to the controversies posed by the survival of serfdom is Christian Garve, "Über den Charakter der Bauern und ihr Verhältniss gegen die Gutsherren und gegen die Regierung," in *Vermischte Aufsätze* (Breslau, 1796), i, 1-128. Conservative pamphlets in favor of the abolition of serfdom, in view of its inefficiency, are C. F. G. West-feld, *Über die Abstellung des Herrendienstes* (Lemgo, 1773) and P. A. F. von Münchhausen, *Über Lehnsherrn und Dienstmann* (Leip-zig, 1793). The former won a prize from the Göttingen Academy, the latter aroused much attention because its author was a prominent Hannoverian nobleman. The controversy posed by the survival of gilds was exhaustively examined by J. H. Firnhaber, *Historisch-politische Betrachtung der Innungen und deren zweckmässige Einrichtung* (Hannover, 1782), a lucid work by a moderate Conservative. The debate concerning Jewish emancipation is examined, with a full bibliography, by Franz Reuss, *C. W. Dohms Schrift "Über die bürgerliche Verbes-serung der Juden" und deren Einwirkung auf die gebildeten Stände Deutschlands. Eine kultur-und literaturgeschichtliche Studie* (Kaisers-lautern, 1891); the author is critical of the (allegedly undue) conces-sions which Dohm made to his Conservative critics. Dohm's own work, *Über die bürgerliche Verbesserung der Juden* (2 vols., Berlin, 1781-83), is still worth reading; the second volume contains Dohm's replies to his various critics. Two of these were especially prominent: Anonymous [Hissmann, a Göttingen professor], *Anmerkungen über Dohms bürgerliche Verbesserung der Juden* (Vienna, 1782), originally a review article in the *Göttinger Gelehrten Anzeigen*; and Friedrich T. Hartmann, *Untersuchung, ob die bürgerliche Freyheit den Juden zu gestatten sey* (Berlin, 1783), a statement of the thesis that anti-Semitism is a justifiable response to indelible Jewish wickedness. The emancipation of women, anonymously championed by Theodor Gottlieb von Hippel, *Über die bürgerliche Verbesserung der Weiber* (Berlin, 1792), was bitterly attacked by an anonymous polemicist in "Über die politische Würde der Weiber. Gegenstück zu Hippels Versuch über die bürgerliche Verbesserung der Weiber," *Berlinisches Archiv der Zeit*, ɪ (1799), 403-12, 502-10 and ɪɪ (1799), 56-66.

Turning to political controversies, there are two valuable monographs on the attitude of eighteenth-century Germans toward the Empire: E. R. Huber, "Reich, Volk und Staat in der Reichsrechtswissenschaft des 17. und 18. Jahrhunderts," *Zeitschrift für die gesamte Staatswissenschaft*, ɪɪ (1942), good on the attitude of the legal profession, and Wolfgang Zorn, *Reichs-und Freiheitsgedanken in der Publizistik des ausgehenden 18. Jahrhunderts (1763-1792)*, especially good in assessing "public opinion." Two contemporary defenses of the Imperial structure against "enlightened" attack are Nicolaus Vogt, *Ueber die europäische Republik* (5 vols., Frankfurt, 1787-92), by a professor at Mainz who became a close collaborator of Dalberg and was befriended in old age by Metternich, and Anonymous [Julius Freiherr von Soden], *Deutschland muss einen Kaiser haben* (n.p. [Vienna], 1788), by a prominent publicist writing with the support of the Habsburg court. The advantages of *Kleinstaaterei* were lauded (though not without awareness of the disadvantages) by W. A. F. Danz, "Deutschland, wie es war, wie es ist, und wie es vielleicht werden wird. Eine ungedruckte Vorlesung, gehalten am 11. February. 1792, am Geburtstage des regierenden Herrn Herzogs Karl zu Würtemberg," *Neues Patriotisches Archiv für Deutschland*, ɪɪ (1794), 133-66; and by many other authors paraphrased by Eduard Sieber in a useful monograph, *Die Idee des Kleinstaats bei den Denkern des 18. Jahrhunderts in Frankreich und Deutschland* (Basel, 1920). The Conservative character of the Prussian-organized *Fürstenbund*, as defense of the existing Imperial structure against Josephine aggression, is stressed by C. W. Dohm's semi-official pamphlet, *Über den deutschen Fürstenbund* (Berlin, 1785). The most recent treatment of the *Fürstenbund* is to be found in the introduction of H. Tümmler, *Politischer Briefwechsel des Herzogs und Grossherzogs Carl August von Weimar* (2 vols.,

Stuttgart, 1954), Vol. 2. Excellent introductions to the problems of "enlightened absolutism" are F. Hartung, "Der aufgeklärte Absolutismus," *HZ*, CLXXX (1955), 15-42, W. Mommsen, "Zur Beurteilung des Absolutismus," *HZ*, CLVIII (1938), 52-76, and E. Walder, *Zwei Studien über den aufgeklärten Absolutismus (Schweizer Beiträge zur allgemeinen Geschichte*, XV [1957]). The problem of continuity between late Medieval *Ständetum* and modern self-government is examined by F. L. Carsten, *Princes and Parliaments in Germany from the Fifteenth to the Eighteenth Century* (Oxford, 1959) and H. Christern, *Deutscher Ständestaat und englischer Parliamentarismus am Ende des 18. Jahrhunderts* (Munich, 1939). The best modern treatment of the long-lasting constitutional struggle in Württemberg is the introductory section of Erwin Hoelzle's *Das alte Recht und die Revolution. Eine politische Geschichte Württembergs in der Revolutionszeit 1789 bis 1805* (Munich and Berlin, 1931). The blatant "absolutist catechism" of Bishop Limburg-Stirum is printed, with a salty commentary, as "Probe eines Deutschen politischen Volcks-Catechismus: 'Pflichten der Untertanen gegen ihren Landesherrn. Zum Gebrauch der Trivialschulen im Hochstift Speyer. Auf gnädigsten Befehl, Bruchsal, 1785.' Nebst einem Prolog und Anhang," in C. F. Moser's *Neues Politisches Archiv für Deutschland*, I (1792), 309-402. A popular and influential contemporary defense of "enlightened absolutism" is J. A. Eberhard, *Über Staatsverfassungen und ihre Verbesserungen* (2 vols., Berlin, 1793-94).

The best introduction to the problems of the anachronistic ecclesiastical states is C. F. Moser, *Über die Regierung der geistlichen Staaten in Deutschland* (Frankfurt and Leipzig, 1787), though it argues in favor of their replacement by elective monarchies. A. J. Schnaubert, *Über des Freiherrn von Moser's Vorschläge zur Verbesserung der geistlichen Staaten in Deutschland* (Jena, 1788), approved of Moser's proposal but considered it impracticable. P. A. Frank, *Etwas über die Wahlkapitulationen in den geistlichen Wahlstaaten* (Frankfurt, 1788), argued that reform was the only alternative to destruction. The thesis that "nothing was fundamentally wrong" with the ecclesiastical states was argued by Josef Edler von Sartori, *Gekrönte Preisschrift. Eine statistische Abhandlung über die Mängel in den geistlichen Wahlstaaten und von den Mitteln, solchen abzuhelfen* (n.p., 1787). The response of German public opinion to the American Revolution is covered in two solid but pedestrian monographs, containing full bibliographies, Herbert P. Gallinger, *Die Haltung der deutschen Publizistik zum amerikanischen Unabhängigkeitskrieg 1775 bis 1783* (Leipzig, 1900) and Henry S. King, "Echoes of the American Revolution in

German Literature," *University of California Publications in Modern Philology*, XIV (1929), 23-193.

The standard works on Justus Möser, all including full bibliographies, are L. Rupprecht, *Justus Mösers soziale und volkswirtschaftliche Anschauungen* (Stuttgart, 1892), which exaggerates the contrast between Möser's "Medievalism" and the views of his contemporaries; Otto Hatzig, *Justus Möser als Staatsmann und Publizist (Quellen und Darstellungen zur Geschichte Niedersachsens*, XXVII [Hannover and Leipzig, 1909]), a pioneering study, unfortunately limited to the years 1764-83, which first showed, on the basis of archival studies, the intimate connection between Möser's administrative and publicistic work; Heinz Zimmermann, *Staat, Recht und Wirtschaft bei Möser* (Jena, 1933), both a solid monograph and an uncritical eulogy devoted to the mistaken theme that Möser's thought could help Germany out of the "great depression" of the early 1930's; Ulrike Brünauer, *Justus Möser* (Berlin, 1933), a brilliant study concerned, under obvious Mannheimian influences, with not only *what* Möser thought, but *why* he thought as he did; and Peter Klassen, *Justus Möser* (Frankfurt, 1936), a work concentrating upon Möser's "rejuvenation" of the German spirit and his contributions to historiography. The following significant monographs have appeared since the publication of these standard studies: Paul Göttsching, *J. Mösers Entwicklung zum Publizisten* (Frankfurt, 1935), an exhaustive analysis of the writings of the period 1757-66; Wolfgang Hollmann, *Justus Mösers Zeitungsidee und ihre Verwirklichung* (Munich, 1937), an indispensable book with a bibliography of 987 items (including a chronological list of all of Möser's articles) marred, however, by Nazi sympathies and an arrogant contempt for all earlier Möser scholars; Wilhelm Spael, *Common sense, oder Gesunder Menschenverstand und sein Ausdruck bei Justus Möser* (Essen, 1947), a useful analysis of a specialized topic; and Ludwig Bäte, *Justus Möser: Advocatus Patriae* (Frankfurt, 1961), a popular work which sometimes degenerates into a local chronicle and is weak on intellectual history. In a category of its own is Friedrich Meinecke's discussion of Möser in *Die Entstehung des Historismus* (1936; new edition with an introduction by Carl Hinrichs, Munich, 1959), pp. 303-54. Meinecke hails Möser as a pioneer of "historicism" while admitting his parochialism, mediocrity at critical scholarship, and lack of creative passion. Although he gives a vivid picture of Möser's personality and the genesis of his thought, Meinecke has very little to say about Möser's Conservatism; he gives no evidence to support his inaccurate designation of Möser as a "reforming Conservative" (p. 353).

The following editions of Möser's writings should be noted. *Sämmtliche Werke*, ed. B. R. Abeken (10 vols., Berlin, 1842-43), was long the standard edition, though in many ways unsatisfactory; see the sharp attack upon Abeken's editorial methods in Erich Haarmann, "Über Mösers Art zu schaffen, mit einer Bemerkung über B. R. Abekens editorische Tätigkeit," *HZ*, CXL (1929), 87-99. A definitive edition is now in preparation: *Justus Mösers sämtliche Werke, Historisch-kritische Ausgabe* (ed. Werner Kohlschmidt, Ludwig Schirmener, *et al.*) (7 vols. to date, Oldenburg and Berlin, 1943-58). Two excellent anthologies, printing everything of importance, are Karl Brandi, *Justus Möser. Gesellschaft und Staat* (Munich, 1921) and Curt Loehning, *Advocatus Patriae. Justus Möser. Schriften* (Berlin, 1948). An important edition of Möser's *Briefe* was edited by E. Beins and W. Pleister (Hannover, 1939).

PART III:

German Conservatism in the Period 1790-1806

The standard works on the impact of the French Revolution upon Germany are: G. P. Gooch, *Germany and the French Revolution* (London, 1920), which is catalogic and superficial; A. Stern, *Der Einfluss der französischen Revolution auf das deutsche Geistesleben* (Stuttgart and Berlin, 1928), which is too exclusively concerned with "great thinkers"; J. Droz, *L'Allemagne et la Révolution française* (Paris, 1949), excellent though it shows a certain patronizing contempt towards Germany and Germans; and Kurt von Raumer, *Deutschland um 1800* (Konstanz, 1962), 24-119, an exhaustive textbook treatment. The path-breaking work of R. R. Palmer, *The Age of the Democratic Revolution:* Volume 2, *The Struggle* (Princeton, 1964), Ch. 14, examines the German reaction to the Revolution in the general European context. Eberhard Sauer, *Die französische Revolution von 1789 in zeitgenössischen Flugschriften und Dichtungen* (Weimar, 1913) has many valuable references but its general theme—that German public opinion was comparatively little aroused—is unconvincing.

The character of the Prussian state of the *ancien régime* was the subject of a famous and furious controversy between Max Lehmann, who delighted in exploding "Borussian legends," and Ernst von Meier, as an administrative historian of strong Conservative tendencies: Lehmann, *Freiherr vom Stein* (3 vols., Leipzig, 1902-05), esp. II, 11-65, and Meier, *Französische Einflüsse auf die Staats-und Rechtsentwicklung Preussens im 19. Jahrhundert* (2 vols., Leipzig, 1907-08), esp. Vol. I, Sect. I. Two contemporary eulogies of the Prussian state are

J.T.F., "Über das Eigenthümliche der Preussischen Monarchie," *Berlinisches Jahrbuch für Aufklärung*, II (1789), 54-75, III (1789), 148-61, IV (1789), 43-49; and Brunn, "Der preussische Staat, der glücklichste unter allen in Europa," *Berlinisches Jahrbuch für Aufklärung*, V (1789), 104-61. The standard work on the reign of Frederick William II was written by Martin Philippson, *Geschichte des preussischen Staatswesens vom Tode Friedrichs des Grossen bis zu den Freiheitskriegen* (2 vols., Leipzig, 1880-82), though it actually ends with 1797. It was the first work which explored the archives for the period, and retains its value despite a dated outlook composed of National Liberalism, a belief in Prussia's German mission, and an excessive fear of Wöllnerite "obscurantism." Friedrich Paulig, *Friedrich Wilhelm II, König von Preussen* (Frankfurt/Oder, 1895), is an attempt to "rehabilitate" the King, written from a Christian-legitimist point of view, not to say one of outright superstition (the author affirms, for example, the authenticity of Frederick William's contacts with ghostly media). An admirable treatment of the latter topic is Paul Schwartz, "Der Geisterspuk um Friedrich Wilhelm II," *Mitteilungen des Vereins für die Geschichte Berlins* (1930), 45-60, based upon the protocols of the Commission which investigated the conduct of the King's mistress, the Countess Lichtenau, in 1798, and the King's correspondence with her.

The first scholarly treatment of J. C. Wöllner, the famous author the Edict of Religion, was J. D. E. Preuss, "Zur Beurtheilung des Staatsministers von Woellner," *Zeitschrift für preussische Geschichte und Landeskunde*, II (1865), 577-604, 746-74, III (1866), 65-95, who attacked Wöllner for "betraying" the Frederician legacy of religious freedom. Paul Bailleu, "Woellner," *ADB*, XLIV (1898), 148-58, is better balanced and so detailed as to make a specialized biography almost unnecessary. Wöllner's assistant, Hermes, is covered in a definitive, though one-sidedly contemptuous, monograph written by Georg Hoffmann, *Herrmann Daniel Hermes, der Günstling Wöllners* (Breslau, 1914). Johannes Schultze, "Hans Rudolf von Bischoffwerder," *Mitteldeutsche Lebensbilder*, II (Magdeburg, 1928), 134-55, describes Bischoffwerder as an honest fanatic with a deep Rosicrucian sense of mission. The same author's "Die Rosenkreuzer und Friedrich Wilhelm II," *Mitteilungen des Vereins für die Geschichte Berlins* (1929), 41-51, based upon Bischoffwerder's reports to his Rosicrucian superior Wöllner, is very hostile to Rosicrucianism while also minimizing its influence. A remarkable modern defense of Wöllner's Edict is Fritz Valjavec, "Das Woellner'sche Religious Edict und seine geschichtliche Bedeutung," *Hist. Jahrbuch der Görres-Gesellschaft*, LXXII (1953), 386-

400. The implementation (or, rather, nonimplementation) of the Edict on the local level is examined by Colmar Grünhagen, "Der Kampf gegen die Aufklärung unter Friedrich Wilhelm II mit besonderer Rücksicht auf Schlesien," *Zeitschrift des Vereins für Geschichte und Altertümer Schlesiens*, xxvii (1893), 1-27.

The best book on the codification of the *Allgemeines Landrecht* is the Marxist work by Uwe Jens Heuer, *Allgemeines Landrecht und Klassenkampf. Die Auseinandersetzung um die Prinzipien des Allgemeinen Landrechts Ende des 18. Jahrhunderts als Ausdruck der Krise des Feudalsystems in Preussen* (East Berlin, 1960). Hermann Conrad, *Die Geistigen Grundlagen des Allgemeinen Landrechts für die preussischen Staaten von 1794* (Cologne, 1958), places the codification in the context of the times and praises the remarkably Liberal objectives of its authors. The main author, Svarez, is treated in the excellent though old-fashioned biography by Adolf Stölzel, *C. G. Svarez. Ein Zeitbild aus der 2. Hälfte des 18. Jahrhunderts* (Berlin, 1885). Svarez' important *Vorträge über Recht und Staat*, delivered to the Prussian Crown in 1791-92 (at the time of the codification) have recently been published by Hermann Conrad and Gerd Kleinheyer (Cologne-Oplanden, 1960); they are a source of capital importance for the understanding of the Prussian *Aufklärung*. An excellent secondary introduction is the dissertation of Gerd Kleinheyer, *Staat und Bürger im Recht. Die Vorträge des Carl Gottlieb Svarez vor dem preussischen Kronprinzen* (Bonn, 1959). C. G. Svarez and C. Gossler, *Unterricht über die Gesetze für die Einwohner der Preussischen Staaten, von zwei preussischen Rechtsgelehrten* (Berlin, 1793), is a brilliant contemporary introduction to the ALR, written at a time when its opponents had forced its (temporary) suspension on the alleged ground that it was still insufficiently known. The journal *Annalen für Gesetzgebung und Rechtsgelehrsamkeit in den preussischen Staaten* (Berlin, 1788ff.), ed. E. F. Klein, was an additional attempt to educate public opinion on behalf of the codification.

The Conservative opposition to the reforms of the Emperor Joseph II is covered exhaustively in the monumental work of Paul von Mitrofanov, *Joseph II. Seine politische und kulturelle Tätigkeit* (Vienna and Leipzig, 1910). The essentially Conservative purpose of Joseph is argued by F. Valjavec, "Die Josephinischen Wurzeln des österreichischen Konservativismus," *Südost-Forschungen*, xiv (1955), 166-75. All earlier studies of Leopold are superseded by the great work of Adam Wandruszka, *Leopold II. Erzherzog von Österreich, Grossherzog von Toskana, König von Ungarn und Böhmen, Römischer Kaiser* (2 vols.,

687

Vienna, 1963-64). The Conservative aspirations of the Bohemian Diet of 1790-92 are treated definitively by Robert J. Kerner, *Bohemia in the Eighteenth Century, a study in political, economic and social history with special reference to the reign of Leopold II* (New York, 1932). The early life of the Emperor Francis is examined in the exhaustive tome of Cölestin Wolfsgruber, *Franz I. Kaiser von Österreich* (2 vols., Vienna and Leipzig, 1899) and the sprightly study of W. C. Langsam, *Francis the Good. The Education of an Emperor 1768-92* (New York, 1949). The best biography of Francis is V. Bibl, *Kaiser Franz, der letzte römisch-deutsche Kaiser* (Leipzig, 1937), despite its passionate hostility.

Two pedestrian studies which nonetheless throw valuable light on the "Radical danger" in the Germany of the 1790's are Sidney Biro, *The German Policy of Revolutionary France. A Study in French Diplomacy during the War of the First Coalition* (2 vols., Cambridge, Mass., 1957) and Heinrich Scheel, *Süddeutsche Jakobiner. Klassenkämpfe und republikanische Bestrebungen im deutschen Süden Ende des 18. Jahrhunderts* (East Berlin, 1962). The latter work is marred by much Marxist jargon and the tendency (usual among East German treatments of our period) to exaggerate the importance of Radical currents. The same criticism must be leveled against the nonetheless indispensable, pioneering studies of Percy Stulz and Alfred Opitz, *Volksbewegungen in Kursachsen zur Zeit der Französischen Revolution* (East Berlin, 1956) and Hedwig Voegt, *Die deutsche Jakobinische Literatur und Publizistik* (East Berlin), which is centered around the figure of G. E. F. Rebmann. J. Droz, *La penśee politique et morale des Cisrhenans* (Paris, 1940) is a definitive study. The best book on French rule in the Rhineland is still J. Hashagen, *Das Rheinland und die Französische Herrschaft* (Bonn, 1908). The opposition of the Mainz artisans to the French is chronicled in E. Schmitt, *Das Mainzer Zunftwesen und die französische Herrschaft* (Frankfurt, 1929). The beginnings of militant gallophobia are covered in A. F. Raif, *Die Urteile der Deutschen über die französische Nationalität im Zeitalter der Revolution und der deutschen Erhebung* (Berlin, 1911). A vivid contemporary attack upon French misconduct is J. M. Armbruster (ed.), *Sünden-Register der Franzosen während ihres Aufenthalts in Schwaben und Vorderösterreich* (n.p., 1797).

All earlier books on the "Jacobin conspiracy" in Vienna in 1794 are superseded by two recent studies, both with exhaustive bibliographies: Ernst Wangermann, *From Joseph II to the Jacobin Trials: Government Policy and Public Opinion in the Habsburg Dominions in the Period of the French Revolution* (Oxford, 1959), a sophisticated Marxist treatment based upon extensive archival research, and Denis Silagi, *Jakobiner in der Habsburger Monarchie. Ein Beitrag zur Geschichte des aufgeklärten Absolutismus in Österreich* (Vienna, 1962), advancing the convincing thesis that the conspiracy constituted a radicalization of the Leopoldine reform plans abandoned by Francis. An anonymous contemporary account, inspired by the government and intended to maximize the conspiracy's ramifications, is *Geheime Geschichte des Verschwörungs—Systems der Jakobiner in den österreichischen Staaten. Für Wahrheitsfreunde* (London [Heilbronn], 1795).

Important studies of individual opponents of the revolution include Wilhelm Mommsen, *Die politischen Anschauungen Goethes* (Stuttgart, 1948); Rudolf Ischer, *J. G. Zimmermanns Leben und Werke* (Bern, 1893); and Karl D'Ester, *Der Neuwieder, ein vergessener Vorkämpfer für die Freiheit des deutschen Rheines*, analyzing the life of Trenck von Tonder. Burke's influence upon several German foes of the Revolution is treated in Frida Braune, *Burke in Deutschland. Ein Beitrag zur Geschichte des historisch-politischen Denkens* (Heidelberg, 1917). Several political theorists are covered in the valuable work of Reinhold Aris, *History of Political Thought in Germany from 1789 to 1815* (London, 1936).

There is no adequate monograph dealing with the conspiracy theory of the revolution. For an annotated bibliography concerning J. A. Starck and L. A. Hoffmann, two of its most prominent German champions, see Appendix A to this bibliographical essay. For the journal *Eudämonia*, see the two important articles by Max Braubach, "Die *Eudämonia* (1795-98). Ein Beitrag zur deutschen Publizistik im Zeitalter der Aufklärung und der Revolution," *Historisches Jahrbuch der Görres-Gesellschaft*, XLVII (1927), 309-39, and Gustav Krüger, "Die Eudämonisten. Ein Beitrag zur Publizistik des ausgehenden 18. Jahrhunderts," *H.Z.*, CXLIII (1931), 467-500.

An annotated bibliography concerning Rehberg and the Hannoverian School is provided in Appendix B to this bibliographical essay.

There is no definitive modern work on the secularization of Germany's ecclesiastical states consummated in 1803. Two excellent contemporary accounts are J. P. Harl, *Deutschlands neueste Staats-und Kirchenveränderungen, politisch und kirchenrechtlich entwickelt* (Berlin, 1804), voicing approval, and K. M. Fabritius, *Über den Werth und die Vorzüge geistlicher Staaten und Regierungen in Teutschland* (2 vols., Frankfurt and Leipzig, 1797-99), criticizing secularization proposals. Two excellent modern regional studies, strongly pro-Catholic in their points of view, are M. Erzberger, *Die Säkularisation in Württemberg von 1802-1810* (Stuttgart, 1902), and A. M. Schleglmann, *Geschichte der Säkularisation im rechtsrheinischen Bayern* (3 vols., Regensburg, 1903-08).

The mediatization of the Imperial knights is discussed in two excellent modern works: Heinrich Müller, *Der letzte Kampf der Reichsritterschaft um ihre Selbstständigkeit 1790-1815* (Berlin, 1910) and Hanns Hubert Hofmann, *Adelige Herrschaft und souveräner Staat. Studien über Staat und Gesellschaft in Franken und Bayern im 18. und 19. Jahrhundert* (Munich, 1962). A large number of documents illustrating the struggle between the Imperial knights and the Prussian government is printed in the anonymous *Neue Vertheidigung der reichsritterschaftlichen Freyheit und Unmittelbarkeit gegen die neuesten Angriffe der Königlichen Regierung zu Ansbach und Bayreuth* (Nürnberg, 1803), though it is an *ex parte* selection on behalf of the knightly cause.

Two standard monographs on the mediatization of individual Free Imperial Cities are Karl Haupt, *Die Vereinigung der Reichsstadt Augsburg mit Bayern* (Munich and Freising, 1923) and Georg Schrötter, "Die letzten Jahre der Reichsstadt Nürnberg und ihr Übergang an Bayern," *Mitteilungen des Vereins für die Geschichte der Stadt Nürnberg*, xvii (1900), 1-177.

Proposals for Imperial reform in the last years of the Empire are discussed in the useful monograph of Hermann Schulz, *Vorschläge zur Reichsreform in der Publizistik von 1800-1806* (Giessen, 1926). Two standard studies dealing with the final dissolution of the Empire are Heinrich Ritter von Srbik, *Das Österreichische Kaisertum und das Ende des Heiligen Römischen Reiches 1804-1806* (Berlin, 1927), based primarily upon the reports of the Austrian commissioners in Regensburg, and Hellmuth Roessler, *Napoleons Griff nach der Kaiserkrone* (Munich, 1957), a lively, popular narrative unhappily marred by many questionable generalizations. The founding of the Confederation of the Rhine is covered in the classic work of Theodor Bitterauf, *Die Gründung des Rheinbundes und der Untergang des alten Reiches* (Munich, 1905), which first broke with anachronistic nationalist value judgments in its treatment, and Siegmund Satz, *Die Politik der deutschen Staaten vom Herbst 1805 bis zum Herbst 1806 im Lichte der gleichzeitigen deutschen Publizistik* (Berlin, 1908), using virtually inaccessible contemporary newspaper and periodical sources.

690

APPENDIX A

Critical Bibliography for Chapter XI, "The Conspiracy Theory of the Revolution."

I.

Johann August Starck

1. STARCK'S WRITINGS

Hephästion (Königsberg, 1775). A sensational piece of theological writing in which Starck sought to demonstrate that the main teachings of Christianity were derived from Egyptian mystery cults. The book is written in the rationalist spirit which he assailed in his later works. It was condemned by the Königsberg consistory and evoked several counter-pamphlets.

Apologie des Ordens der Freimaurer. Neue, ganz umgearbeitete und einzig authentische Ausgabe (Berlin, 1778). Seeks to show that the Eleusian mysteries, Christianity, and Masonry are all based upon the same principles, an argument which ignores the specifically revealed character of Christianity. The last of Starck's "enlightened" theological writings.

Freimütige Betrachtungen über das Christentum (Berlin, 1780). Reveals Starck's theological development to the Right, with Starck abandoning the rationalism of the *Hephästion* in favor of a *Vermittlungstheologie* (theology of mediation) which is tolerant not only of Lutheran, but also of Catholic orthodoxy (including even transsubstantiation).

Saint Nicaise, oder eine Sammlung merkwürdiger maurerischer Briefe, für Freymaurer und die es nicht sind. Aus dem Französischen übersetzt (n.p. [Frankfurt], 1785). A famous novel of exposure directed against Strict Observance Masonry, which evoked furious controversy upon its appearance. Written in the form of letters which the editor claimed to have found among the papers of a deceased acquaintance whom he met while going from Hamburg to Paris in 1783. The bulk of the work (29-304) is the autobiographical narrative of one St. Nicaise, written after his retirement to a French monastery, in which he relates his harassing experiences with Masonry (including contact with a swindler in London, imprisonment by the Neapolitan inquisition, abduction to extort his Masonic secrets etc.). The author castigates the Strict Observance for mystery-mongering, pretension, and racketeering.

Über Krypto-Katholicismus, Proselytenmacherey, Jesuitismus, geheime Gesellschaften, und besonders die ihm selbst von den Verfassern der

Berliner Monatsschrift gemachte Beschuldigungen, mit Acten-Stücken belegt (2 vols., Frankfurt and Leipzig, 1787). An incredibly long and thorough defense against the charge that Starck was not only a "crypto-Catholic," but even a member of the fourth class of Jesuits. Starck combines defense with counterattack through a minute examination of the entire campaign waged by the *Berliner Monatsschrift* against Catholic (and more especially Jesuit) plots. Starck finds the anti-Jesuit charges nothing but a malicious product of the diseased imagination of the leaders of the Berlin *Aufklärung*.

Volume I describes the provocation which forced Starck to bring suit against the *B. M.* (1-74) and then systematically examines the campaign of the *B. M.* against all those accused of "Crypto-Catholicism": (1) chronology of their campaign (74-148); (2) *Geheime Proselytenmacherey, und dazu angeblich dienende Mittel* (148-375); (3) *Von Jesuiten, ihren wirklichen und angeblichen Machinationen zum Nachtheil der Protestanten* (376-525); (4) *Religionsvereinigung als Mittel zur Beförderung der geheimen Proselytenmacherey* (525-76), followed by documents pertaining to Starck's petition to the Prussian King for trial (579-608).

Volume II was printed in different places to speed publication and is divided into four different, separately paged parts. The first part continues the exposure of the shameless campaign of the *B.M.*, with its accusations: (1) *Von den geheimen Gesellschaften, als Mitteln zur Verbreitung des Katholicismus* (3-272). (2) *Von den Personen, die von den Berliner Monatschriftstellern als Krypto-Katholiken, Jesuiten und Jesuitenwerkzeuge verläumdet werden* (Dreykorn, Lavater etc.), 273-404. Next section, newly paged, covers *Die dem Dr. Starck gemachte Beschuldigungen und seine Rechtfertigung* (1-384), a step-by-step defense against the personal accusations of the *B. M.* Next section, newly paged, denounces *Moralität der neuen Kezzer-Jagd. Folgen derselben und Absichten, die man erreichen wollen* (1-54), with Starck calling upon the King to suppress the *B. M.* as a defamatory journal. Final section (1-154) brings many miscellaneous documents, especially those pertaining to Starck's lawsuit against *B. M.*

Beleuchtung der letzten Anstrengung des Herrn Kessler von Sprengseysen (Dessau und Leipzig, 1788). Starck's biting reply to Kessler's *Abgenöthigte Fortsetzung*.

Apologismos an das bessere Publikum (Leipzig, 1789). Starck's apology against charge that he was a crypto-Catholic. It includes a sharp attack upon natural religion. A much abbreviated version of his long *Über Krypto-Katholicismus*. Provoked a reply, partly written by Bahrdt, *Beleuchtung des Starck'schen Apologismos* (Leipzig, 1790).

Der Triumph der Philosophie im 18. Jahrhundert (2 vols., Germantown [Augsburg], 1803). Starck's *magnum opus* of his "reactionary" period. Follows Barruel in tracing the conspiracy which allegedly prepared the revolution. First volume goes back to Greece but centers upon France, second volume concentrates upon German *Illuminati*. Clearly and attractively written, with appearance of objectivity aided by occasional sharp criticism directed against Barruel and Robison. Accusation is mainly against *Illuminati*, with insistence upon the importance of the Bode mission to Paris 1787.

Theoduls Gastmahl, oder über die Vereinigung der verschiedenen Christlichen Religionssocietäten (Frankfurt, 1809). Pleads in effect for the Protestant return to Catholicism, on the ground that Protestantism has degenerated into a rationalist naturalism. Starck obviously identifies himself with the Catholic Abbot Odilo, who defends Catholic doctrine and assails the Reformation in conversations with three Protestants: Theodul himself and his friends Eduard and Huldreich von Setten. The book is irrefutable proof that Starck sympathized with Catholicism in his later years even though he retained his job as Protestant *Oberhofprediger* at Darmstadt.

2. CONTEMPORARY WRITINGS ABOUT STARCK

Goué, A. S. von. *Bemerkungen über St. Nicaise* (Leipzig, 1788). Shows interest which was aroused by the Starck-Kessler controversy.

Anonymous [Christian Friedrich Kessler von Sprengseysen]. *Anti-St-Nicaise. Ein Turnier im XVIII Jahrhundert gehalten von zwey T(empel) H(erren) als etwas für Freymaurer und die es nicht sind* (Leipzig, 1786). Defense of Strict Observance against the attack of J. A. Starck. The author was a faithful follower of Hund, who is defended against Starck's accusations. The book takes up point by point all statements in the *St Nicaise* which are critical of the Strict Observance. Kessler obviously knows that Starck is his antagonist despite the anonymity of the *St. Nicaise*. He especially seeks to refute Starck's charge that the Strict Observance was hostile to either state or Church.

Anonymous [Christian Friedrich Kessler von Sprengseysen]. *Archidemides, oder des Anti-St-Nicaise zweyter Theil mit der Silhouette des Verfassers* (Leipzig, 1786). A reply to a hostile review of Kessler's previous book, probably written by Starck, in the *Allgemeine Litteraturzeitung*, Nr. 48, but also a supplement to the *Anti-St-Nicaise*.

Valuable for printing correspondence between Hund and Starck which makes the latter appear in an odious light.

Anonymous [Christian Friedrich Kessler von Sprengseysen]. *Scala algebraica oeconomica, oder des Anti-St-Nicaise dritter und letzter Theil* (Leipzig, 1787). Defends the just-deceased Schubart, Hund's closest associate, against Starck's attack. Also prints *Oeconomischer Plan* worked out in 1766 and Starck's counterplan of 1767.

Kessler von Sprengseysen, Christian Friedrich. *Abgenöthigte Fortsetzung des Anti-Saint-Nicaise, als eine Beleuchtung des von dem Herrn Oberhofprediger Starck herausgegebenen Krypto-Katholicismus* (Leipzig, 1788). Kessler's reply to Starck's *Über Krypto-Katholicismus.* Kessler was a friend of Biester's, the editor of the *B.M.*, whom Starck had attacked in the feud over *St Nicaise.*

Prozess über den Verdacht des heimlichen Katholizismus zwischen dem Darmstädtischen Oberhofprediger D. Starck als Kläger und den Herausgebern der Berlinischen Monatsschrift, Oberkonsistorialrat Gedicke und Bibliothekar Dr. Biester, als Beklagte, vollständig nebst der Sentenz; aus den Akten herausgegeben von den los gesprochenen Beklagten (Berlin, 1787). Trial record of Starck libel suit, published by Biester and Gedicke.

Textor, L. *Charakteristik der jetzt lebenden bekanntesten Hessen-Darmstädtischen Theologen und Prediger* (Giessen und Darmstadt, 1801). Includes favorable section on Starck (pp. 90ff.).

3. MODERN SECONDARY WORKS ABOUT STARCK

Blum, Jean. *Starck et la querelle du Crypto-Catholicisme en Allemagne* (Paris, 1912). Standard French account, with a larger perspective than Konschel but not based upon archival research.

Konschel, Paul. *Hamanns Gegner der Kryptokatholik D. Johann August Starck, Oberhofprediger und Generalsuperintendent von Ostpreussen Ein Beitrag zur Geschichte der Aufklärungszeit* [Schriften der Synodalkommission für ostpreussische Kirchengeschichte. Heft 13 (Königsberg, 1912)]. A superficial study written by a Lutheran pastor in Königsberg. Succumbs to the *genius loci* by concentrating disproportionately upon Starck's Königsberg years (1770-77) and his conflicts with Hamann (the author's special hero). Very weak as intellectual history; it contributes little about Starck's relationship to Masonry or his founding of the *Klerikat.* Author interprets Starck as a subjectively honest person who successively yielded to two dominant currents of his age, "enlightened" theology and reactionary, Catholic mysticism. The book is valuable for explaining Starck's rapid Königsberg career on the basis of local archival sources, but it peters out on the more important Darmstadt period.

Krüger, Gustav. "Johann A. Starck der Kleriker. Ein Beitrag zur Geschichte der Theosophie im 18. Jahrhundert," *Festgabe von Fachgenossen und Freunden Karl Müller zum 70. Geburtstag dargebracht* (Tübingen, 1922), 244-66. Learned article which supplements the works of Konschel and Blum, with very full bibliography.

Krüger, Gustav. "Starck und der Bund der Sieben," *Festgabe für W. Diehl* (Darmstadt, 1931), 237-59. Important article on Starck's relationship to his seven princely friends. The next section in the book, "Starck im Licht der Briefe Petersens" (pp. 260-70), also throws valuable light on his personality.

II.

Leopold A. Hoffmann

1. HOFFMANN'S WRITINGS

Wöchentliche Wahrheiten für und über die Prediger in Wien (9 vols., Vienna and Prague, 1782ff.). A Josephine journal edited by Hoffmann which specialized in criticizing clerical fanaticism. Important for documenting the intensity of Hoffmann's "enlightened" views before 1786. Hoffmann's journal made him known to the influential Gottfried van Swieten.

Werden wir Katholiken noch im Jahre 1786 fasten? (Vienna, 1786). Scurrilous attack upon the priesthood and Catholic practices, written before Hoffmann's shift to Conservatism.

Uber den wahren Endzweck der Freimaurerei (n.p. [Vienna], 1786). Speech delivered by Hoffmann upon the opening of the Pest lodge *Zur Grossmut* on April 5, 1786. Criticizes Masonic penchant for mystical ritualism and urges instead civic-humanitarian conduct aiming at practical improvement. Hoffmann evidently still hoped at this time to reform Masonry from the inside.

Kaiser Josephs Reformation der Freymaurer. Eine Denkschrift fürs achtzehnte Jahrhundert. Von E. . . (2 parts, Deutschland [Vienna], 1786). Written by Hoffmann in the role of a candid friend of Masonry, urging the brethren to reform their ways in accordance with Josef's benevolent regulation. They should abandon secrecy-mongering and become a "friendly society" providing loans to the needy, scholarships for the able, etc.

Briefe eines Biedermannes an einen Biedermann über die Freymauerer in Wien (Munich, 1786). Attack upon Viennese Masonry, in the

695

literary form of six letters ostensibly written from Vienna to Munich. The avowed aim is to purify Masonry by drastic reforms.

Achtzehn Paragraphen über Katholizismus, Protestantismus, Jesuitismus, geheime Orden und moderne Aufklärung in Deutschland. Eine Denkschrift an deutsche Regenten und das deutsche Publikum (Vienna, 1787). Warns Masons against the danger of *Illuminati* infiltration, while considering Masonry per se to be ludicrous rather than dangerous. The first of Hoffmann's sharply anti-Masonic publications, and as such signaling his "turn to the right." It was also hostile to the Berlin *Aufklärung* and its campaign against Jesuits and Crypto-Catholics. Hoffmann acknowledged his authorship in *Erinnerungen*, I, 194.

Babel. Fragmente über die jetzigen politischen Angelegenheiten in Ungarn (n.p. [Salzburg], 1790). Vigorous attack upon the aristocratic revolution in Hungary. Notable for its excoriation of aristocratic misrule, ridicule of the idea of freedom, and favorable judgment upon Joseph and his attempt to reform historic abuses by virtue of his *absolute* royal rights (which are deemed better founded than Hungarian constitutional *traditions*). Includes comparison between the Magyar and the French Revolutions, much to the disadvantage of the former, with Hoffmann making remarkably tolerant judgments about the intentions of the French National Assembly (although not its works). Hoffmann is especially indignant about Prussian contacts with Magyar rebels. Fifteen thousand copies of the book and its successor were printed, and its circulation was facilitated by special order of Leopold after the Censorship Board had attempted to prohibit it.

Ninive. Fortgesetzte Fragmente über die dermaligen politischen Angelegenheiten in Ungarn (n.p. [Salzburg], 1790). Written by Hoffmann, although author claims in preface it is an independent supplement to *Babel*. Prints objectionable Hungarian *Krönungsdiplom* to which Hoffmann had made critical allusions in *Babel* (pp. 94-149). Fragmentary preliminary observations attack the Magyar nobility for disreputable *Landtag* proceedings, treasonable opposition to Turkish war, persecution of Germans, and brutal suppression of burghers and peasants. Predicts that a new *Landtag* with burgher and peasant representation, and acting under royal leadership, will end the aristocratic misrule now prevailing in Hungary.

Vorlesungen über die Philosophie des Lebens (Vienna, 1791). Lectures which Hoffmann delivered at Pest in 1789. Includes valuable confrontation between "true" and "false" *Aufklärung*.

Geschichte der Päpste von Petrus bis Pius VI (Leipzig and Vienna, 1791). Includes important preface with valuable autobiographical information.

Wiener Zeitschrift (6 vols., Vienna, 1792-93). Hoffmann's famous journal which appeared in six quarterly volumes between January 1792 and September 1793. Most of the articles were written by himself, and the whole bears the imprint of his personality.

Endliche Beurlaubung von dem Herrn Joh. von Alxinger, berühmtem Verfasser des Anti-Hoffmann (Vienna, 1793). Hoffmann's counterattack against Alxinger's criticism, written in a deliberately calm tone which avoided personal invective in order to create the appearance of moral superiority.

Höchst wichtige Erinnerungen zur rechten Zeit, über einige der allerernsthaftesten Angelegenheiten dieses Zeitalters. Als erster (und zweiter) Nachtrag der W. Zeitschrift, den Lesern und Gegnern derselben gewidmet (2 vols., Vienna, 1795-96). A continuation of the *Wiener Zeitschrift*, written after Hoffmann withdrew to Wiener Neustadt. Includes very important autobiographical information especially on his relations with Leopold and the flat denial that he had ever been an *Illuminat*. The main theme of the miscellaneous work is that revolutions are caused by subversive writers, and that governments must license writers in sheer self-defense. A constant undercurrent of complaint shows that Hoffmann resented his neglect by the Austrian government he was trying to defend against its adversaries.

Fragmente zur Biographie des verstorbenen Geheimen Raths Bode in Weimar. Mit zuverlässigen Urkunden (Rome [Vienna], 1795). Develops thesis that the French Revolution was promoted by the journey to Paris of the German *Illuminat* Bode in 1788. Successful in showing that Bode did in fact travel to Paris, but proof that he influenced the revolution is confined to the assertion that Jacobin and *Illuminati* principles were identical. Also ridicules Bode's anti-Catholicism and the theory that the Jesuits had infiltrated Masonry.

Aktenmässige Darstellung der Deutschen Union, und ihrer Verbindung mit dem Illuminaten—Freimaurer—und Rosenkreutzer Orden. Ein nöthiger Anhang zu den höchst wichtigen Erinnerungen zur rechten Zeit (Vienna, 1796). A detailed exposure of Bahrdt's *Deutsche Union* on the basis of its official documents. Hoffmann received some of these when he pretended to be interested in membership; how he received the others is not made clear, but there is no question of their authenticity. The book primarily prints documents, with Hoffmann's contribution being limited to long salty footnotes. He develops the questionable thesis that the *Deutsche Union* was founded by the *Illuminati* as part of their plan of world conquest. He wisely says very little about the specific influence of the *Deutsche Union* itself (which in fact proved stillborn).

Die zwo Schwestern P(rag) und W(ien) oder neu entdecktes Freimaurer—und Revolutionssystem. Ganz Deutschland, besonders aber Österreich aus Originalfreymaurerschriften vorgelegt (n.p. [Vienna], 1796). A vehement attack upon the conduct of the Masons during the last century. Often ascribed to Hoffmann; but his authorship is far from certain in view of its anonymity (at a time when Hoffmann usually signed his works) and its blanket attack upon Masonry as a whole (whereas Hoffmann usually singled out the *Illuminati*). See Sommer, *Wiener Zeitschrift*, p. 117. The book is a series of reviews of articles contained in the Viennese *Journal für Freymaurer* (1784), with author printing extracts and biting commentary.

Lehrbuch einer christlich-aufgeklärten Lebensweisheit für alle Stände (Vienna, 1797). A platitudinous work outlining Hoffmann's *Weltanschauung*.

Schreiben an den Oberconsul Frankreichs, Bonaparte (Deutschland [Vienna?], 1800). Warns Napoleon concerning the danger of the German *Illuminati* and Jacobins, with advice that he keep them out of the French controlled Rhineland. Includes a furious denunciation of Hoffmann's personal enemy Rebmann, then a judge in Mainz.

2. CONTEMPORARY WRITINGS ABOUT HOFFMANN

Alxinger, Johann von. *Anti-Hoffmann* (2 parts, Vienna, 1792-93). Sharp attack on Hoffmann by the prominent Viennese poet. Examines the early issues of the *Wiener Zeitschrift* piece by piece and is especially critical of Hoffmann's literary style.

[Anonymous]. *An und Ueber Hoffmann, Alxinger und Huber. Eine wohlverdiente Rüge des litterarischen Unfugs dieses philosphisch-patriotischen Triumvirats* (Vienna, 1792). A pamphlet putting a "plague on all your houses" in its criticism of the low polemical tone of the three contestants. Author successively attacks Huber, Alxinger, and Hoffmann. Huber and Hoffmann are accused of being motivated by personal hatred based upon the rivalry of their newspapers, *Bürger-Kronik* and *Politisches Sieb*. Alxinger does not even have this excuse, and his personal polemics are deemed unworthy of a man of his literary reputation.

Huber, Franz Xaver. *Kann ein Schriftsteller, wie Herr Professor Hoff-*

mann Einfluss auf die Stimmung der deutschen Völker, und auf die Denkart ihrer Fürsten haben? An Herrn La Veaux, Verfasser des Strasburger französischen Couriers (Vienna, 1792). Vigorous attack upon Hoffmann's demagogy, poor literary style, etc., supposedly written with Leopold's approval before the emperor's death. Includes a very unflattering description of Hoffmann's life before 1792.

Anonymous [Huber, Franz Xaver]. *Beytrag zur Charakteristik und Regierungsgeschichte des Kaiser Josephs II, Leopold II und Franz II* (Paris, 1800). A very important contemporary account, written by the liberal publicist Huber who competed with Hoffmann for Leopold's favor. It is the contemporary source upon which most modern anti-Hoffmann writing is based.

Rebmann, G. F. *Die Wächter der Burg Zion* (Hamburg, 1796). A witty satire directed against Hoffmann and the *Wiener Zeitschrift*.

3. MODERN SECONDARY WORKS ABOUT HOFFMANN

Brabbée, Gustav. "L. A. Hoffmann, der freimaurerische Judas, der Erzschelm. Skizze als Beitrag zur Geschichte der Reaktion und der Unterdrückung des Freimaurerordens in Österreich in den neunziger Jahren," *Latomia. Freimaurerische Vierteljahresschrift*, XXIII (1864), 206ff. Sharp attack upon Hoffmann as a Masonic apostate who changed his views for opportunistic reasons.

Brunner, Sebastian. *Die Mysterien der Aufklärung in Österreich* (Mainz, 1869). A famous polemical Catholic treatment of the subject. Includes Hoffmann's *Privat-Promemoria über die zweckmässigsten Mittel, die sämtlichen geheimen Orden für jeden Staat unschädlich zu machen*, written for Emperor Francis II (dated July 4, 1793), pp. 516-22.

Fäulhammer, Adalbert. "Politische Meinungen und Stimmungen in Wien in den Jahren 1793 und 1794," *Programm des Staatsgymnasiums in Salzburg 1893* (Salzburg, 1893), pp. 3-32. Useful summary of the following Viennese journals: *Eipeldauer, Wiener Zeitschrift, Magazin der Kunst und Literatur*, and *Österreichische Monatschrift*, with author sympathizing with the latter and especially its brilliant editor, Schreyvogel.

Lunzer-Lindhausen, Marianne. "Leopold Alois Hoffmann—Wiener Publizist im Schatten der Reaktion," *Wiener Geschichtsblätter*, XV (1960), 104-109. A useful biographical summary, hostile to Hoffmann and declaring him to have been a man of mediocre talents.

Anonymous [Pipitz, Franz Ernst]. *Der Jakobiner in Wien. Österreichische Memoiren aus dem letzten Decennium des 18. Jahrhunderts*

(Zurich und Winterthur, 1842). Superb account of the Viennese atmosphere in the years 1790-97, from the death of Joseph II to the Treaty of Campo Formio. Partly descriptive, partly a novel with a thin plot. Extremely hostile to the prevalent police repression, with false view that the Jacobin plot was purely a police invention. Ch. 4 is a well-informed account of Hoffmann's activities as a police spy for Leopold II, which is drawn primarily from Huber's *Beytrag* (1800).

Probst, E. "Johann Baptist von Alxinger," *Jahrbuch der Grillparzergesellschaft*, vii (1897), 171-202. Standard account of Hoffmann's leading foe.

Silagi, Denis. *Ungarn und der geheime Mitarbeiterkreis Kaiser Leopolds II* (Munich, 1961), Chs. 4-12 and Appendices iii & iv. Very favorable portrait of Hoffmann by the greatest living authority. Attests Hoffmann's intelligence, journalistic skill, and integrity while deploring his mania for conspiracy.

Sommer, Friedrich. *Die Wiener Zeitschrift (1792-93). Die Geschichte eines antirevolutionären Journals* (Zeulenroda-Leipzig, 1932). Excellent monograph, originally a Bonn dissertation directed by Max Braubach. Provides full biographical information about Hoffmann, including his relations with Emperor Leopold; content analysis of W.Z.; and description of the hostile echo it found among contemporaries. Sommer believes in Hoffmann's honesty of purpose but considers him a man of mediocre talent who too easily succumbed to a pathological fear of the *Illuminati* and Jacobin danger.

Valjavec, Fritz. "Die Anfänge des österreichischen Konservativismus: Leopold Alois Hoffmann," *Festschrift Karl Eder* (Innsbruck, 1959), pp. 155-68. A brief and superficial survey of Hoffmann's writings from 1786-93. Valjavec hails him as the first influential Conservative political publicist in Germany. He emphasizes his subjective honesty of conviction (proved by his becoming a Conservative before 1789) and his close relationship with Leopold.

Wurzbach, Constantin von. "Leopold Alois Hoffmann," *Biographisches Lexicon des Kaiserthums Oesterreich*, ix (1863), 161-64. Important biographical sketch of Hoffmann, hostile and contemptuous in tone. Wurzbach denounces Hoffmann as a mere spy and witch hunter, and scarcely mentions his close relationship with Leopold. Includes a full but by no means complete bibliography.

Zenker, E.V. *Geschichte der Wiener Journalistik von den Anfängen bis zum Jahre 1848* (Vienna, 1892). Includes brief, superficial and hostile account of *Wiener Zeitschrift*. Very unfair toward Hoffmann.

APPENDIX B

Critical Bibliography for Chapter XII, "Rehberg and the
Hannoverian School."

1. REHBERG'S WRITINGS

Cato (Basel, 1780). A youthful first book, dedicated to Stein. It is in
the form of a dialogue between the younger Cato, who is just preparing to commit suicide, and a Platonist called Demetrius. They
discuss whether there is a future life, which the Stoic Cato denies,
Demetrius affirms, and the moral consequences of either belief. Cato
argues that the denial of immortality leads men to concentrate upon
living worthily in this—the only—life, and that emphasis upon immortality leads, on the contrary, to a relaxation of effort. Cato is
ready to show by his own contemplated suicide that a denial of immortality facilitates a refusal to live a life of dishonor. It is uncertain
to what extent Rehberg, who obviously admires Cato, identifies himself with all his arguments.

Philosophische Gespräche über das Vergnügen (Nürnberg, 1785).
Dialogue between Arist (who seeks happiness in the conduct of
practical affairs benefitting his fellow citizens) and Eleanth (a
moderate Epicurean who seeks happiness through satisfying his
senses), where Rehberg obviously identifies himself with the former.
Interesting for many expressions of Conservative views, including
the belief that the individual pursuit of personal happiness must
undermine society. Introduction notes that Rehberg is writing a
supplement to his *Cato*, and that he refuses to introduce a complete
skeptic as a character, for such a man "is so unhappy and dangerous,
that I would deny all my principles if I were to bring him before the
public" (p. xii).

Ueber das Verhältniss der Metaphysik zu der Religion (Berlin, 1787).
Rehberg's main philosophical work, written under the strong influence of Kant. Seeks to demonstrate that metaphysics, although not
incompatible with religion and morality, cannot assert anything con-
clusive about either. Rehberg draws no specific political consequences, and the book is of little importance for understanding
Rehberg's Conservatism.

Untersuchungen über die Französische Revolution, nebst kritischen
Nachrichten von den merkwürdigsten Schriften, welche darüber in
Frankreich erschienen sind (2 vols., Hannover and Osnabrück, 1793).
A systematic summary of Rehberg's views on the French Revolution,
incorporating (often in a revised form) many review articles orig-

inally published in the *Jenaische Allgemeine Literaturzeitung* from 1790-1792. Volume I is an examination of the principles of the Constitution of 1791: Rehberg's negative verdict antedates the collapse of that constitution, as the preface was written September 4, 1792. The whole volume provides the best discussion of Rehberg's political views. Volume II discusses the historical course of the revolution, with Rehberg suggesting what steps undertaken at what time could have led to happier results. The character of the book, as a paste-and-scissors collection of earlier review articles, makes it hard to read. Rehberg frequently throws out profound suggestions, as when he opposes his own historical view of the state to the Jacobin "rationalist" view, but does not adequately develop his ideas. The appendix includes a notable defense of censorship of books and newspapers.

Actenmässige Darstellung der Sache des Herrn von Berlepsch, zur Berichtigung der Schrift des Herrn Häberlin, über die Dienstentlassung des Herrn Hofrichters, auch Land und Schatzraths von Berlepsch (Hannover, 1797). A point-by-point refutation of Häberlin's pamphlet, written with the purpose of preventing the Calenberg *Stände* from proclaiming their solidarity with Berlepsch. It attacks not only Berlepsch's proposal that Calenberg remain neutral in the war between England and France but seeks to widen the issue by castigating Berlepsch's fiscal policy in his three roles as *Hofrichter*, *Schatzrath*, and member of the *Ritterschaft*. The pamphlet of 88 pages was successful in its immediate purpose, but it earned Rehberg an odious reputation for being a hired publicist of the Hannoverian court. The accusation was unjust, for in fact Rehberg only applied his earlier stated Conservative principles to a specific case.

Ueber den deutschen Adel (Göttingen, 1803). The most important of Rehberg's writings as a "Reform Conservative." Urges a drastic reform of aristocratic privilege with the abolition of serfdom, patrimonial jurisdictions, tax exemption, and privileged access to bureaucratic posts. He wants nobles to retain a large role in political and social life, but a role in which they must compete with other strata and open their ranks to newcomers. Rehberg writes as the candid friend of the aristocracy and claims that his consistent opposition to Jacobin revolution gives him a special right and obligation to press for reform.

Ueber die Staatsverwaltung deutscher Länder und die Dienerschaft des Regenten (Hannover, 1807). A collection of sensible observations, often suggested by Rehberg's practical experience, on the best way of organizing a bureaucracy in a German state. Includes an important introduction which castigates Prussian administrative practices, which Rehberg encountered during the Prussian occupation of Hannover the year the book was written. There is also an important appendix on German *Landstände* which emphasizes the need to reform their composition. Rehberg insists, however, that the *Stände* have developed in Germany under such circumstances as to preclude the full imitation of the British parliament.

Das Buch vom Fürsten von Machiavelli, aus dem Italienischen übersetzt und mit Einleitung und Anmerkungen versehen (Hannover, 1810). Rehberg's translation of Machiavelli's *Prince*, with an excellent historical introduction. Rehberg comments on the individual chapters often reveal his own position on specific problems, though he shows his caution by making few contemporary allusions. Perceptive readers could, however, find between the lines some observations attacking the Napoleonic tyranny. Rehberg has no understanding of the ideal of the power state and believes rather complacently that virtue and success will always coincide in the long run. He treats Machiavelli's book as a "rationalistic speculation" which ignored the role emotion, morals, and sentiment play in real political life.

Ueber den Code Napoleon und dessen Einführung in Deutschland (Hannover, 1814). An important treatise revealing Rehberg as a forerunner of Savigny (who praised the book) and the historical school of law. Main theme is call for the repeal of the Code Napoleon wherever it has been introduced in Germany, because it is an instrument of social revolution and French imperialism. The book is hard to read because it is poorly organized and lacks chapter headings, while the detailed discussion of the Code Napoleon has little permanent interest.

Zur Geschichte des Königreichs Hannover in den ersten Jahren nach der Befreiung von der westphälischen und französischen Herrschaft (Göttingen, 1826). Gives, in effect, an account of Rehberg's stewardship, for he was (despite his formally subordinate position) the soul of the Hannoverian administration from 1814 to 1816. It is severely impersonal in tone and rarely mentions Rehberg directly. Gives nothing but the truth, but certainly not the whole truth. There is no discussion of the political differences within the Hannoverian government. The account lacks over-all organization and frequently bogs down in unreadable detail, but the description of the summoning of the *Ständeversammlung* of 1814-16, and especially of the precautionary measures taken to assure the assembling of a responsible body, is very valuable (pp. 99-139).

Sämmtliche Schriften, Vols., I, II, and IV (Hannover, 1828, 1831, 1829). Rehberg planned a four-volume collected edition of his works after his retirement, in which he proposed to include everything he considered of permanent value. He did not hesitate to abbreviate and alter, in order to make his works more readable and to bring his earlier views into concordance with his outlook in the late 1820's. The changes he made provide an interesting record of his comparative "liberalism" after 1814. The edition did not realize Rehberg's hopes of lifting him out of the obscurity into which he had fallen. Only three volumes appeared at irregular intervals (1828, 1829, 1831) and not in the order originally planned, and the publisher withdrew from the money-losing enterprise before Volume III could be issued. Rehberg connected his works by a valuable autobiographical commentary which constitutes the main source for his life.

Volume I (1828) contains abstracts of all his major philosophical writings, and is especially valuable for his critique of Kant. Also includes his controversy with Justus Möser on religious toleration and his writings on education and penology.

Volume II (1831) is of the greatest importance for understanding Rehberg's political development. Some newly written pages (pp. 16-32) explain his relationship to Möser and the French Revolution. The bulk of the volume contains a much abbreviated version of his *Untersuchungen* (1793) and *Ueber den deutschen Adel* (1803). The equally important *Staatsverwaltung* (1807) and *Code Napoleon* (1814) were presumably saved for the third volume, which never appeared.

Volume IV (1829), subtitled *Politisch-historische kleine Schriften*, contains unimportant reviews of books on English affairs (Part I), very important analyses of the works of Hugo, Haller, Joh. Müller, Buchholz, Adam Müller, Fichte, and Arndt (Parts II and III), significant judgments on several economic writers (Part IV), and interesting memoirs about his friends Brandes and Heyne (Part V).

Constitutionelle Phantasien eines alten Steuermanns im Sturme des Jahres 1832 (Hamburg, 1832). A revised version of articles originally published in the *Hannoverische Zeitung*. Contains Rehberg's reform proposals on all current questions, presented, however, with irritating tentativeness and vagueness. Indispensable for Rehberg's views after his retirement.

Lord Porchester's Aufenthalt in Spanien während der Revolution des Jahres 1820. Aus dem Englischen übersetzt, mit Bemerkungen über die neuesten Ereignisse in England (Braunschweig, 1834). Primarily a translation of Porchester's book dealing with the problems of the Spanish Revolution of 1820. Rehberg obviously shared Porchester's sympathy with the Liberal cause while deploring many of the doctrinaire follies committed by the Liberals. His specific criticisms often parallel the criticisms he had levied against the French Revolution of 1789, but his basically pro-revolutionary attitude mirrors the "liberal evolution" of his political views in later life. The book is especially valuable for a long appendix (pp. 106-40) in which Rehberg expresses his approval of the English Reform Bill of 1832, though he had disapproved of parliamentary reform in the 1790's.

Die Erwartungen der Deutschen von dem Bunde ihrer Fürsten (Jena, 1835). A brief and unimportant work that belies the large expectations aroused by the title. Includes a survey of the nature of German *Stände* and the need for university reforms, but bogs down in an uninspired discussion of detail. The whole shows Rehberg's continued blindness to the national idea.

2. SECONDARY WORKS ABOUT REHBERG

Anonymous [G. H. Pertz?]. "Errinerung an den verstorbenen Geheimen CabinetsRath Rehberg," *Civilistisches Magazin von Geheimen JustizRath Ritter Hugo VI* (Berlin, 1837), pp. 393-419. A well-informed obituary article first published in the *Hamburger Correspondenten* of December 9, 1836. Hugo's introduction briefly relates his own (quite unimportant) personal relations with Rehberg. The obituary is the ultimate source of much of our biographical information about Rehberg.

Botzenhart, Erich. *Die Staats-und Reformideen des Freiherrn vom Stein* (Tübingen, 1927), pp. 106-62. Definitive monograph on Rehberg's attitude toward the French Revolution, superseding Lessing and occasionally correcting the competing work of Weniger.

Braune, Frida. *Burke in Deutschland* (Heidelberg, 1917), Ch. 4. Shows how Rehberg and Burke fundamentally agreed on French Revolution. A routine analysis devoid of original insights.

Bülow, Friedrich von. *Bemerkungen, veranlasst durch des Herrn Hofraths Rehberg Beurteilung der Königl. Preussischen Staatsverwaltung und Staatsdienerschaft* (Frankfurt u. Leipzig, 1808). Ostensibly a reply to Rehberg's anti-Prussian pamphlet, although Bülow made things easy for himself by limiting himself to comparing the

Prussian with the Hannoverian administration of justice (a topic scarcely mentioned by Rehberg) instead of replying to Rehberg's criticism of the general spirit of Prussian administration. Bülow, who had been a high Hannoverian judge before entering Prussian service, had little difficulty demonstrating that justice was administered more efficiently in his newly adopted state; he did not reply to Rehberg's point that efficiency can be purchased at too great a price. Bülow had served on the Prussian commission which organized the incorporation of Hannover into Prussia in 1806, and is contemptuous of the motives of those Hannoverians—like Rehberg—who opposed the new Prussian rule (esp. pp. 254-60).

Fichte, Johann Gottlieb. *Beitrag zur Berichtigung der Urteile des Publikums über die französische Revolution* (2 vols., n.p., 1793). Includes sharp criticism of Rehberg's *Untersuchungen* (especially Vol. I, pp. 66ff.) from the point of view of natural law and implies that Rehberg's antirevolutionary opinions were influenced by the fact that he was employed by the reactionary Hannoverian government.

Frensdorff, F. "A. W. Rehberg," *ADB*, xxvii (1888), pp. 571-83. Brilliant, very detailed, laudatory yet not uncritical account, making a detailed biography almost unnecessary.

Heerwagen, H. W. *Anleitung zur richtigen Kenntniss der Preussischen Staatswirthschaft. Veranlasst durch die Schrift des Herrn Hofraths Rehberg zu Hannover; über die Staatsverwaltung deutscher Länder und die Dienerschaft des Regenten* (Berlin u. Stettin, 1808). A reply to Rehberg's anti-Prussian pamphlet written to defend the Prussian administrative record in the fields of commerce, factories, mining and statistics. The author held the post of *Kriegsrath und Assessor bei dem Manufaktur und Kommerz-Kollegium* and was an expert on the subjects covered. He writes to supplement the defense of the Prussian judicial administration undertaken by Bülow. Heerwagen fails to answer Rehberg's general attack upon the militarist and absolutist spirit of Prussia but throws suspicion upon Rehberg's motives by noting that his book was written at the moment when Prussia was reforming long-standing Hannoverian abuses of which Rehberg was a beneficiary. Heerwagen urges Rehberg to bring out a new edition purged of error and prejudice.

Kestner-Köchlin, Hermann. *Briefwechsel zwischen August Kestner und seiner Schwester Charlotte* (Strassburg, 1904). Includes some description of Rehberg's serenity and cheerfulness after his retirement (esp. pp. 167-211)—valuable because of the absence of other testimony.

Lessing, Kurt. *Rehberg und die französische Revolution. Ein Beitrag zur Geschichte des literarischen Kampfes gegen die revolutionären Ideen in Deutschland* (Freiburg, 1910). The first scholarly monograph on Rehberg, now largely superseded by the work of Botzenhart and Weniger. Mostly a detailed and rather pedantic examination of Rehberg's *Untersuchungen*. Hails Rehberg as the earliest influential German opponent of the revolution and champion of the historical view of the state; deplores the journalistic character of his work which precluded the systematic development of his ideas. Lessing studies only Rehberg's attitude toward the revolution in the years 1789-93, ignoring the more liberal attitude he adopted in later life.

Mollenhauer, Karl. *A. W. Rehberg, ein hannoverscher Staatsmann im Zeitalter der Restauration* (2 parts, Blankenburg am Harz, 1904-05). An excellent survey of Rehberg's life and writings, worth reading despite its obscure publication as two successive installments of the *Jahresbericht über das Herzogliche Gymnasium zu Blankenburg am Harz*. Mollenhauer gives a sympathetic account of Rehberg's personality and good summaries of his major philosophical, pedagogic, and political writings. Rehberg's career as a statesman is somewhat slighted despite the title.

Niebuhr, B. G. *Lebensnachrichten über B. G. Niebuhr aus Briefen desselben und aus Erinnerungen einiger seiner nächsten Freunde.* (2 vols., Hamburg, 1838-39). Includes remarkable eulogy of Rehberg in a letter to his wife (June 6, 1828) in which Niebuhr contrasts his own nature with Rehberg's and praises the plan of Rehberg's *Sämtliche Schriften* (III, 214-15).

Pertz, G. H. *Das Leben des Ministers Freiherrn vom Stein* (6 vols., Berlin, 1849-55). Valuable on Rehberg's friendship with Stein since Pertz knew both men and corresponded with Rehberg while preparing the biography. Volume I brings important information on their common Göttingen years (pp. 12-15) and the breach in their friendship (pp. 158-62).

Rexius, Gunner. "Studien zur Staatslehre der historischen Schule," *HZ*, CVII (1911), 513-26. Pioneering analysis of Rehberg as a pupil of Möser and Burke and a forerunner of the "Historical School." Includes a valuable discussion of Rehberg's criticism of Müller, Haller, and the *Code Napoleon*.

Richter, Ludwig Aemilius. "A. W. Rehberg," *Konversationslexikon der neusten Zeit und Literatur*, III (Leipzig, 1833), 711-16. Very full account of Rehberg's life, written by a personal friend with materials provided by himself and published in his lifetime. It expresses in concise form how Rehberg wished to be remembered by posterity.

Ritter, Gerhard. *Stein. Eine politische Biographie* (2 vols., Berlin, 1931), I, 143-83. Excellent monograph on Rehberg, who is discussed as an important force influencing Stein's personal development.

Roscher, Wilhelm. *Geschichte der National-Oekonomik in Deutschland* (Munich, 1874), pp. 744-47. Respectful survey of Rehberg's economic views, stressing his two-fronted war against Smith and Müller, and his recognition of the role played by ethical and institutional factors in economic life. Roscher smiles at Rehberg's Hannoverian particularism.

Weinhold, Karl. *Heinrich Christian Boie. Beitrag zur Geschichte der deutschen Literatur im 18. Jahrhundert* (Halle, 1868). Includes a good account of Hannoverian social life in the late 1770's when Boie held a post there as military secretary and wanted to make Rehberg his successor. Boie was a close friend of the Rehberg family and knew all the same people (pp. 77-82).

Weniger, Erich. "Stein and Rehberg," *Niedersächsisches Jahrbuch*, II (1925), 1-124. Pioneering study which first established the importance of the close intellectual relationship between Stein and Rehberg. Weniger portrayed Rehberg as the intellectual superior who gave more than he received in the friendship. Rehberg is praised as the main spokesman of the "Anglo-Hannoverian" school and precursor of Savigny.

3. ERNST BRANDES' WRITINGS

"Über den politischen Geist Englands," *Berlinische Monatsschrift*, VII (1786), 101-26, 217-41, 293-323. Best statement of the Anglophile position of the Hannoverian Conservatives.

"Ist es den deutschen Staaten vorteilhaft, dass der Adel die ersten Staatsbedienungen besitzt?", *Berlinische Monatsschrift*, X (1787), 395-439. Remarkable defense of the privileged access to public office possessed by Hannoverian aristocrats.

Ueber die Weiber (Leipzig, 1787). Early attack upon female emancipation, calling upon all husbands to keep their wives in their place.

Politische Betrachtungen über die französische Revolution (Jena, 1790). Documents Brandes' initially favorable attitude toward the revolution, with justification of violence as necessitated by danger of counterrevolution.

Über einige bisherige Folgen der französischen Revolution mit Rücksicht auf Deutschland (Hannover, 1793). Reverses earlier defense of French violence by the claim that there is no evidence for the existence of counterrevolutionary plans. Brandes remains calm, however, and denies that there is any revolutionary danger in Germany.

Betrachtungen über das Weiblichel Geschlecht und dessen Ausbildung in dem geselligen Leben (3 vols., Hannover, 1802). Lengthy blast against the emancipation of women, arguing the importance of physical and moral differences between men and women and the consequent desirability of concentrating female education upon developing good wives and mothers.

Über das Du und Du zwischen Eltern und Kindern (Hannover, 1809). Criticizes modern trend of excessive familiarity between parents and children.

Betrachtungen über den Zeitgeist in Deutschland in den letzten Decennien des vorigen Jahrhunderts (Hannover, 1808). A bitter book written at the moment of Germany's deepest humiliation tracing the causes of its decline to such variegated factors as the obsolescence of the Imperial Constitution, the advance of irreligion and progressive education, Prussian absolutism, Josephine reforms, Kantian philosophy, the frozen caste structure, etc.

Ueber den Einfluss und die Wirkungen des Zeitgeistes auf die höheren Stände Deutschlandes; als Fortsetzung der Betrachtungen über den Zeitgeist in Deutschland (2 vols., Hannover, 1810). A diffuse work of miscellaneous declamation. Volume I is a vague, moralistic attack upon the *Zeitgeist* in general; Volume II attacks eight specific groups: princes, nobles, officers, bureaucrats, pastors, authors, merchants, and upper-class women, for having succumbed to the *Zeitgeist* through their sensuality, frivolity, and egotism.

4. SECONDARY WORKS ON BRANDES

Preliminary Note: There is no adequate monograph on Brandes. Summaries of his thought can be found in the above-mentioned works of Botzenhart (pp. 69-105) and Ritter (I, 143-83). He is generally treated, as I have treated him, as an appanage to his more famous friend Rehberg. Valuable information on Brandes can be found in the following works.

Braune, Frida. *Burke in Deutschland* (Heidelberg, 1917), pp. 74-113. Shows large measure of agreement between Burke and Brandes on the French Revolution.

Eigen, Paula. *Ernst Brandes im Kampfe mit der Revolution in der Erziehung* (Weinheim, 1954). Analyzes Brandes' attack against progressive education.

Haase, Carl. "Ernst Brandes in den Jahren 1805 und 1806. Fünf Briefe an den Grafen Münster," *Niedersächsisches Jahrbuch für Landes-geschichte*, xxxiv (1962), 194-223. Throws valuable light on Brandes' personality and politics.

Rehberg, A. W. "Ernst Brandes," *Sämtliche Schriften* (Vol. iv, 1829), 407-26. Obituary article written when Brandes died in 1810. Basic source on Brandes' life though Rehberg's temperamental reticence prevented a full discussion of their friendship.

Skalweit, Stephan. "Edmund Burke, Ernst Brandes, und Hannover," *Niedersächsisches Jahrbuch für Landesgeschichte*, xxviii (1956), 15-72. Prints, with valuable commentary, salient portions, in the original English, of a long letter written by Brandes to Burke explaining Hannoverian conditions (October 29, 1796).

Index

PREFATORY NOTE

This index omits key terms such as Conservatism (and each of its subspecies—Traditionalism, Defender of the *Status Quo*, Reform Conservative, and Reactionary), Radicalism, and Progressivism, as well as key events (such as the French Revolution and the Seven Years' War) which are referred to constantly.